Perfect
Plant

Perfect
Place

Perfect Plant Perfect Place

ROY LANCASTER

DORLING KINDERSLEY
London • New York • Sydney • Moscow

A DORLING KINDERSLEY BOOK

EDITORS Anna Cheifetz, Clare Double, Lesley Malkin, Simon Maughan
ART EDITORS Martin Hendry, Stuart Perry, Helen Robson, Colin Walton
MANAGING EDITORS Mary-Clare Jerram, Anna Kruger, Jonathan Metcalf
MANAGING ART EDITORS Peter Cross, Lee Griffiths, Steve Knowlden, Amanda Lunn
PRODUCTION MANAGERS Meryl Silbert, Michelle Thomas
DTP DESIGNERS Mark Bracey, Robert Campbell, Louise Waller

First published in Great Britain in 2001 by
Dorling Kindersley Limited, 80 Strand, London WC2R 0RL
A Penguin Company

A CIP catalogue record for this book is available from the British Library
ISBN-13: 978-0-7513-3592-7
ISBN-10: 0–7513–3592–4

Reproduced by Colourscan, Singapore; GRB Editrice, Italy and
Scanner Services, Italy.
Printed and bound by Star Standard Industries, Singapore.

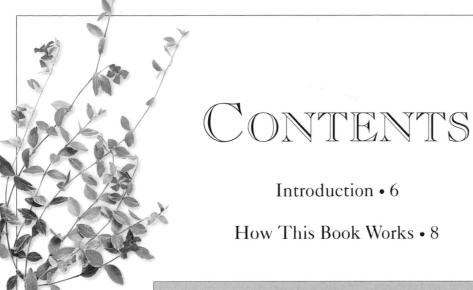

CONTENTS

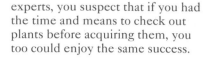

INTRODUCTION

THE DIVERSITY OF PLANTS available to gardeners today is such that we need never again suffer the disappointment of watching a recently acquired plant struggling and even dying because it was planted in the wrong place, or it was not a good plant for the job.

△ GARDEN CENTRE TEMPTATIONS
It is tempting to buy a plant for the initial impact of its flowers, fruit, or foliage, instead of its suitability for your garden.

A great many people acquire plants for their garden on impulse. You see a plant that takes your fancy, or a fellow gardener offers you an offset or cutting, and with little regard for its suitability, you take it home and lose no time in planting it, usually wherever a space beckons.

Sometimes the site proves just right and your plant thrives. More often than not, though, the site is vacant for a very good reason; too wet or too dry perhaps, too shady, too shallow, or filled with the roots of other plants. When a plant fails for one of these reasons, you may shrug it off and keep trying or, your confidence knocked, give up and switch your attentions elsewhere.

Don't you ever ask yourself how the lovely gardens you see down your street, on television, and in magazines are achieved? Of course you do, and although it is easy to dismiss them as the gardens of experts, you suspect that if you had the time and means to check out plants before acquiring them, you too could enjoy the same success.

GARDENERS' QUESTIONS

I worked for a major British nursery for many years, advising customers on the choice of plants for their gardens. I dealt with a variety of people; some were professionals, or gardening enthusiasts, who already had a good idea of the plants likely to grow in their gardens, but who were seeking something new or special. Most people, however, were first-time gardeners, with little knowledge or experience of plants and their uses, but who were eager to learn and anxious to make the best choice for their money.

On the whole, my enquirers belonged to one of two categories: those who had seen a plant they liked and wanted to know if it would grow in their garden; or those who had no specific idea of what they wanted but knew what purpose they wanted it for. This confirmed my belief that most

△ AUTHOR'S GARDEN Hosta *'Halcyon'* *at the base of an armillary sundial is just one example in my garden of the use of foliage to provide a striking feature. The bloomy blue leaves match the sundial.*

◁ ORIGIN OF A SPECIAL PLANT
I grow a wide variety of plants from seed collected in the wild, such as this bottlebrush Callistemon viridiflorus from Tasmania.

people seeking help simply want to know either what plants will grow in a given situation, taking factors such as soil, aspect, and exposure into account; or what plants will create a desired effect, such as seasonal features, colour, fragrance, and ultimate size or shape.

GARDENERS' ANSWERS

Many years of visiting gardens and interviewing people for television programmes about gardening have convinced me that poor or adverse conditions can often be improved. If this is not practical, some choice usually exists for most sites and situations as they stand, thanks to the wealth of garden plants that is currently available.

Perfect Plant, Perfect Place is a guide to selecting the best plants for given conditions and ornamental effects. It will assist beginners in finding plants suited to their gardens, and hopefully remind more seasoned gardeners of excellent contenders they may have overlooked. Never before have so many ornamental plants been available to gardeners. Among those in this book are a host of tried and tested representatives. Success with these should inspire you to try more challenging plants. Let *Perfect Plant, Perfect Place* be your guide.

For many people, choosing the best plants for indoors is almost as important as selecting those for outdoors. It is a curious fact that growing plants successfully in the relatively protected, if not cosseted, environment of your own home can provide a greater challenge than growing hardy plants in your garden. The pricinpal reasons for this are all to do with climatic conditions and light levels – not surprising considering that many of our houseplants come from warm or tropical regions of the world. Yet, despite the difficulties, we rightly accept houseplants as an essential ingredient in our lives to the extent that no home seems complete without them. Apart from their ornamental qualities, houseplants can improve the air we breathe indoors, helping to create conditions conducive to healthy living. The indoor plants section of this book sets out to familiarize you with the rich variety of plants available as well as the growing conditions needed to help them flourish.

△ SPECIAL EFFECTS IN SUMMER
This is an excellent example of what can be achieved with perennials of varied height, and foliage and flower effect, to create an appealing summer border.

▽ A VITAL COMPONENT
Container plants are a valuable addition to the garden if carefully placed. They can provide a welcome feature or be used to fill gaps where earlier displays have finished.

How This Book Works

IN THIS BOOK, my aim is to help you choose the most suitable plants for a given garden or indoor situation, taking account of the growing conditions, plant characteristics, and any special ornamental effects. The outdoor plants chapter is divided into five sections by plant type: Perennials, Climbers, Shrubs, Conifers, and Trees. All woody plants listed, with the exception of conifers, are deciduous unless specified evergreen. Perennials are herbaceous unless described as evergreen. The indoor plants chapter is also divided into five sections: Floral Effect, Foliage Effect, Locations, Specific Uses, and Specialist Plants.

PLANT NAMES

Currently accepted botanical names are used throughout. Well-known synonyms appear in the index and are cross-referenced. Common names in general use are given, and where none exists, the generic name is repeated, or else an English name common to the whole genus is given. In the case of specialist groups such as roses, the category is specified.

KEY TO pH ACIDITY SYMBOL

The majority of plants will grow in most soils. Those that require lime-free soil are highlighted with this symbol *(see p.12).*

PH ▾	*Requires lime-free soil*

KEY TO HARDINESS SYMBOLS

Hardiness is a measure of a plant's ability to withstand winter cold. It can vary depending on available shelter, favourable localized conditions, and natural variations in a plant's cold-tolerance. Frost-hardiness indicates a plant's ability to withstand winter frost. Many more plants are susceptible to late spring frosts once new growth has begun. The symbols are given as a guide to a plant's cold-tolerance and err on the side of caution.

❄❄❄	*Fully hardy – will survive winter outside in temperate climates.*
❄❄	*Semi-hardy – may require winter protection outside in temperate climates.*
❄	*Tender – may require winter protection outside, even in mild areas. Suitable for growing under glass.*

BOTANICAL AND COMMON PLANT NAMES •
Below each plant's botanical name is the common name or, if none exists, the generic name.

SYMBOLS FOR LIGHT LEVEL, HARDINESS, AND ACIDITY •
Light level and hardiness are given for all plants. The pH symbol appears only if a plant requires lime-free soil (see boxes).

Shrubs Tolerant of Shade

YOU MAY BE SURPRISED at the range of shrubs suitable for growing in shade. Many are woodlanders in the wild, preferring to grow where they are not directly exposed to the sun's rays. This does not mean they can survive without any light – all green-leaved plants need light to photosynthesize. Some, however, are more tolerant of lower light levels than others, and it is these that are most successful when planted in the shade of deciduous trees, or that cast by buildings.

Euonymus fortunei 'Sunshine'
EVERGREEN EUONYMUS ☼ ☀ ❄❄❄ ‡ 60cm (24in) ↔ 1.5m (5ft)

A low-growing, dense evergreen shrub crowded with leathery, gold-margined leaves, looking bright gold from afar. Ideal as ground cover or as a specimen shrub.

Euonymus fortunei var. *vegetus*
EVERGREEN EUONYMUS ☼ ☀ ❄❄❄ ‡ 30cm (12in) ↔ 2m (6ft)

The presence of both creeping and erect stems enable this tough, bushy evergreen to form extensive patches. Its green leaves and pinkish seed capsules are numerous.

Crinodendron hookerianum
LANTERN TREE ☼ ☀ ❄❄❄ ▾ ‡ 3m (10ft) ↔ 2m (6ft)

From late spring through to early summer, the branches of this handsome evergreen are strung with beautiful red flowers that resemble lanterns. Dislikes dry soils.

OTHER DECIDUOUS SHRUBS TOLERANT OF SHADE

Cornus canadensis, see p.184
Euonymus obovatus
Hydrangea macrophylla
   'Générale Vicomtesse de Vibraye'
Hypericum androsaemum
Kerria japonica
Rhodotypos scandens, see p.203
Rubus odoratus
Rubus spectabilis 'Olympic Double'
Symphoricarpos × chenaultii 'Hancock'

Daphne laureola subsp. *philippi*
SPURGE LAUREL ☼ ☀ ❄❄❄ ‡ 30cm (12in) ↔ 60cm (2ft)

A dwarf variety of a woodland evergreen, this is just as effective when grown in full sun. Crowded light green flower clusters emerge in late winter and early spring.

Hydrangea macrophylla 'Veitchii'
LACE-CAP HYDRANGEA ☼ ☀ ❄❄❄ ‡ 1.5m (5ft) ↔ 2.5m (8ft)

Broader than it is high, this bold-foliaged bush carries heads of tiny flowers, each surrounded by a ring of larger florets, from mid- to late summer. Dislikes dry soils.

200

SHRUBS

• **PLANT DESCRIPTION**
Gives features of interest such as flowering time(s), distinctive traits, preferred site(s) or condition(s), and specifies when plant is evergreen.

KEY TO LIGHT LEVEL SYMBOLS

Light preferences are given with symbols. More than one symbol indicates plant's preferred range.

☼	*Full sun – prefers, or even requires, as much sun as is available.*
☀	*Partial-shade – tolerant of (some even prefer) limited or indirect sunlight.*
☀	*Shade – will grow in a site receiving low light, such as under a tree canopy.*

PLANT DIMENSIONS

Plant dimensions vary depending on growing conditions. Sizes are a guide to mature size in average conditions. The height includes flowering stems in perennials.

↕	*Average height*
↔	*Average spread*
↕↔	*Average height and spread*

PLANTS WITH A SEAL OF APPROVAL

The Royal Horticultural Society gives an Award of Garden Merit to plants whose decorative effect, good constitution, and availability is excellent. It identifies the best species and cultivars available. The AGM symbol is displayed on plants in garden centres.

♔	*Award of Garden Merit*

THE THUMB MARKERS

The different sections of this book are identified by colour thumb markers on the left- and right-hand-sides of each page. Perennials are split into five sub-sections, each identified by their individual thumb markers: Soil and Aspect, Specific Uses, Floral Effect, Foliage Effect, and Specialist Plants.

SHRUBS TOLERANT OF SHADE

Hydrangea serrata 'Bluebird'
LACE-CAP HYDRANGEA
☀ ❄ ✽✽✽   ↕1.2m (4ft) ↔1.5m (5ft)

The pointed leaves of this dense, bushy shrub often colour well in autumn. Violet-blue, lace-cap flowers in summer have pale marginal florets. Dislikes dry soils. ♔

Pachysandra terminalis
JAPANESE SPURGE
☀ ❄ ✽✽✽   ↕10cm (4in) ↔20cm (8in)

This evergreen, suckering shrublet likes moist soils, and makes a superb ground cover for shade. Its dark green leaves back little white flower spikes in spring. ♔

Skimmia japonica 'Wakehurst White'
SKIMMIA
↕75cm (30in) ↔75cm (30in)

If you plant a male variety of this dense, low evergreen nearby to effect pollination, this spring-flowering skimmia cultivar will produce an abundance of white berries.

• HEIGHT AND SPREAD
Gives the average ultimate size of the plant, in metric and imperial.

Lonicera pileata
SHRUBBY HONEYSUCKLE
☀ ❄ ✽✽✽   ↕60cm (24in) ↔2m (6ft)

Its low and wide-spreading habit makes this an excellent evergreen ground cover. Tiny, inconspicuous late spring flowers are occasionally followed by violet berries.

Prunus laurocerasus 'Otto Luyken'
CHERRY LAUREL
☀ ❄ ✽✽✽   ↕75cm (30in) ↔1.2m (4ft)

The branches of this low evergreen shrub are clothed with narrow, glossy, leathery leaves. Erect spikes of white flowers in late spring are followed by black fruits. ♔

OTHER EVERGREEN SHRUBS TOLERANT OF SHADE
Aucuba japonica 'Rozannie', see p.214
Buxus sempervirens 'Latifolia Maculata'
Daphne pontica
x *Fatshedera lizei*, see p.212
Fatsia japonica, see p.216
Osmanthus heterophyllus
Rubus tricolor
Ruscus hypoglossum
Sarcococca confusa
Viburnum davidii, see p.185

• THUMB MARKER
Identifies each of the different sections in the book (see above).

SHRUBS

Mahonia nervosa
CASCADES MAHONIA
☀ ❄ ✽✽✽✽   ↕60cm (24in) ↔1m (3ft)

This evergreen, suckering shrub produces short, erect stems with handsome leaves that turn red or purplish in winter. Spikes of yellow flowers appear in early summer.

Vinca major 'Variegata'
VARIEGATED LARGE PERIWINKLE
☀ ❄ ✽✽✽   ↕30cm (12in) ↔1.5m (5ft)

Striking, variegated leaves are margined creamy white, and form a superb ground cover that is rampant if unchecked. Blue flowers last from spring to autumn. ♔

201

• AGM ♔
Shows the plant has achieved the RHS Award of Garden Merit.

OTHER PLANTS •
Lists more plants suitable for the site or effect, with page references given for those illustrated elsewhere in other parts of the book.

HOW THE TREES CHAPTER WORKS

Prunus serotina
RUM, OR BLACK, CHERRY
☀ ❄ ✽✽✽   Moderate growth   ↕15m (50ft) ↔15m (45ft)

A free-growing tree with an oval crown of pendulous or arching branches, its deep green, glossy leaves are deciduous, becoming yellow or red in autumn. Small white spring flowers are carried in drooping tassels, and give way to shining black fruits.

281

TREES

• TREE ARTWORK
Shows typical shape of mature tree; bare branches indicate tree is deciduous, full leaf that it is evergreen.

• GROWTH RATE
This is given as either vigorous, moderate, or slow.

INDOOR PLANTS – USING THE CULTIVATION NOTES

SPECIFIC

Lytocaryum weddellianum
DWARF COCONUT PALM
↕2m (6ft) ↔1.5m (5ft)

One of the most beautiful palms for the home and tolerant of low light. Handle the fragile roots with care when repotting. Formerly sold as *Microcoelum* or *Cocos*.

Schefflera elegantissima 'Castor'
FALSE ARALIA, FINGER ARALIA
↕2m (6ft) ↔90cm (3ft)

This plant produces an elegant, lacy outline. The dark coppery-green leaves have long, narrow leaflets that widen with age. Also known as *Aralia* or *Dizygotheca*.

395

• CULTIVATION NOTES

Concise notes on the most important care factors are introduced by the following five symbols. See also pages 14–21.

☀ *Light*
Light needs are divided into three categories – Bright, Moderate, and Shady. "Shady" does not mean devoid of light. "Summer sun" means scorching midday sun.

🌡 *Temperature and humidity*
Temperatures are given as Low (4–9°C/39–48°F), Moderate (10–15°C/50–59°F), or Warm (16–21°C/61–70°F). Humidity is Low, Moderate, or High.

💧 *Feeding*
Feed at the specified intervals, when a plant is in active growth (usually spring to autumn). Unless stated in the entry, feed with any general houseplant fertilizer.

💧 *Watering*
References such as "when dry" relate to the compost surface. Water when the stated conditions apply. "Sparingly" means just enough to avoid desiccation.

▨ *Propagation*
The most common and reliable ways of increasing your plants are given in each individual entry. See pages 20–21 for a more detailed explanation of each method.

OUTDOOR PLANTS

A greater number and variety of plants are available to gardeners than ever before. The following is a selection of the very best. Whether your garden is large or miniscule, there is something here to give it that magic touch.

△ AUTUMN JEWEL Anemone x hydrida *'September Charm'* *is a reliable and free-flowering perennial for autumn effect.*

◁ MIDSUMMER MORNING *Bold plantings of ornamental alliums front this summer border of hardy perennials.*

Plant Finder

I F YOU HAVE a specific site, condition, or decorative effect in mind, refer to the condensed index below. The page numbers alongside each entry take you to visual lists of plants that thrive there, or the author recommends to achieve the desired effect. The colour-coded bands match the section markers.

	PERENNIALS	CLIMBERS	SHRUBS	CONIFERS	TREES
SIZE AND SHAPE					
Bold form, foliage			216		266, 285
Large-sized			178, 188	244	266
Medium-sized			180	250	268
Small-sized			182, 186	258	270
Tall or columnar				248	304
Weeping or wide-spreading				246	288
SEASONAL FEATURES					
Autumn interest	102, 140		226		296, 298
Evergreen	120	170	214		286
Spring interest	96				
Summer interest	98				
Winter interest	76, 104		236		298
continued	141		238		300
Long flowering season	106				
COLOUR					
Cool or pale flowers	112, 114				
Golden or yellow leaves	134		220	262	292
Hot flowers	110				
Purple, red or bronze leaves	138		224		295
Silver or blue-grey leaves	136		222	263	294
Variegated leaves	130, 132		218	261	290
OTHER PLANT FEATURES					
Berries for birds			232		298
Butterflies, flowers attractive to	78		234		
Cut flowers and foliage	73, 74				
Fragrance	116, 127	172	228, 230		
Hedging and screening			208	256	281
Herbs	54				
Multi-purpose					302
Ornamental fruits			231		298
Pest-proof	88–93		240		
Specimen plants			178, 188		266
Thorns			239		
Low allergen types	86				

Soil Guide

THE SIZE and proportion of clay, sand, or silt particles present in your garden soil influence its chemical and physical nature. They make it either heavy (wet and poorly drained), or light (dry and free-draining), and thus determine what plants will thrive on it. Its chemical nature, or pH value, is measured on a scale of 1 to 14. Below neutral (7), soils are progressively acid (or lime-free); above neutral they are progressively alkaline (limy). You can establish what type of soil you have by looking at the colour, feeling the texture, and observing what kind of plants will grow on it or, if you prefer, by doing a soil test.

AVERAGE ideal for *Forsythia*
Different cultivation requirements and variable local conditions make average soil hard to define. Usually, it is moist but well-drained, with a reasonable humus content, neutral to slightly acid pH, and suits the widest range of plants.

HEAVY CLAY ideal for *Berberis*
Minute clay particles stick together, making clay soils slow-draining after rain, sticky, and likely to bake hard in dry sun. Often highly fertile, they can be improved by draining, or by adding grit or coarse organic matter.

SANDY ideal for *Potentilla*
Sand particles are much larger than clay particles, making sandy soils light, free-draining, and quick to warm up in spring. Some plants may need frequent irrigation and feeding, though fertility can be improved by adding organic matter.

LIME-FREE ideal for *Rhododendron*
Peaty or lime-free soils are generally dark, and rich in organic matter. Acid in nature and moisture-retentive, they are favoured by plants intolerant of alkaline soils. Can be made more free-draining by adding coarse sand.

ALKALINE ideal for *Kolkwitzia*
Limy or alkaline soils, including chalk, are usually pale, shallow, and stony. Free-draining, they warm up quickly in spring, and are moderately fertile. Like sandy soils, they benefit from the addition of organic matter.

Aspect Guide

Plants need sunlight, either directly or indirectly, to photosynthesize, so aspect is crucial to plant growth and health. Many are flexible in their light needs, preferring one aspect, but tolerating another. Most thrive as long as they are in a position open to the sky.

• *THE SUN'S POSITION*
The position of the sun varies during the year. In midwinter, the sun is lower and the shadows much larger. In the height of summer, the sun is high and the shadows are small.

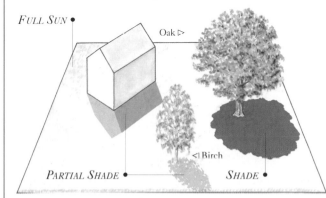

☼ FULL SUN

Open to the sun for the greater part of the day, full sun sites are not subject to shade cast by trees or buildings. Numerous garden plants grown for their flowering display, including many perennials, annuals, and shrubs (*see above*), prefer sunny sites – sun and warmth ripens woody growth, so encouraging flowering and fruiting. Many plants at their best in full sun will also tolerate a degree of shade, like that found near buildings (at certain times of day) and on the edge of woodland.

☼ PARTIAL SHADE

Sites in partial shade are subject to reduced light. They are found near buildings that block direct sunlight, but do not hide the sky above. Partial shade is also found in the lee of, if not directly beneath, trees such as birch *(Betula)*, which cast a light, dappled shade. If the soil is moist, these conditions suit many plants, some of which may also be tolerant of full sun or even heavier shade. Numerous foliage perennials, and those found naturally in woodland sites (*see above*) thrive best here.

☀ SHADE

This defines sites subject to permanent shade, or shade during the main growing season (summer). Such sites may be closely surrounded by tall buildings or, more usually, beneath or in the lee of dense-canopied trees. Even here, the degree of shade varies. If combined with dry or compacted soil, such as that often found beneath large conifers or similar evergreen trees, the choice of suitable underplanting is limited to the few shade-tolerant plants growing in such sites in the wild.

PERENNIALS

IF TREES AND SHRUBS form the bones of a garden, then perennials provide its flesh, forming the bulk of border plants and ground cover. No other plant group offers such great variety of form, flower, and foliage, from tiny rock plants through to large bamboos. This section includes bulbs (with tubers and corms), and annual or biennial plants.

△ *Oenothera speciosa* 'Rosea'

△ SUN LOVING *The bold flowerheads of a superb spurge,* Euphorbia characias subsp. wulfenii, *enjoy a place in the sun.*

THE BEAUTY OF PERENNIALS

- Provide massed effects in borders.
- Bold single specimens or groups can create special effects in lawns.
- Ideal for carpeting rock gardens and screes, or draping retaining walls.
- Provide mass impact as spring bulbs.
- Ideal as ground cover beneath trees.
- Perfect for planting in containers for terraces, patios, or courtyards.
- Annuals or biennials give fast results.
- Offer striking waterside or bog plants.

Some perennials have evergreen foliage, which gives year-round effect, but most are herbaceous, and die to below ground level, usually in winter. Unless otherwise stated, all plants in this section are herbaceous. The pleasurable anticipation associated with their annual re-emergence is something of which we never tire, and makes them all the more exciting and valuable in the garden.

PLANTS FOR EFFECT
For many gardeners, no finer sight exists than that of a perennial bed at its best in summer. Whether we are inspired by Gertrude Jekyll's plant associations, or prefer a more haphazard mix of colour, perennials to suit every taste abound. When

planting borders, foliage effect is just as important as floral display, and it is worth remembering the beautiful, nostalgic effects that are possible in winter when certain dead seed heads are spared.

PLANTS FOR ALL PLACES
Warm, sunny sites in the garden are ideal for growing those perennials that enjoy hot, dry conditions in the wild. The abundance of plants thriving in such situations are best planted in raised beds or beneath sunny walls in cooler areas. To take advantage of shady places, consider plants native of woodland. Ferns, spring-flowering perennials, and bulbous plants such as trilliums and miniature cyclamen tolerate shade and form attractive ground cover.

△ SHADE CARPET *Miniature cyclamen* (Cyclamen repandum) *form a lovely spring carpet in a beech tree's shade.*

◁ WINTER BEAUTY *The elegance of dead seed heads and leaves in winter is further enhanced when they are coated with frost.*

▷ EARLY SUMMER SPECTACLE *This cottage garden border boasts a glorious mix of perennials, annuals, and biennials.*

Perennials through the Seasons

PERENNIALS THAT GIVE A LONG-
LASTING DISPLAY

Acanthus mollis 'Hollard's Gold'
Ajuga reptans 'Jungle Beauty', see p.52
Bergenia 'Bressingham Ruby'
Cyclamen hederifolium, see p.102
Darmera peltata, see p.66
Dryopteris erythrosora, see p.148
Hakonechloa macra 'Aureola', see p.130
Helleborus argutifolius, see p.120
Lamium galeobdolon 'Hermann's Pride',
    see p.41
Paeonia mlokosewitschii, see p.157
Phlomis russeliana
Rodgersia podophylla, see p.139

EACH SEASON has its own particular character and brings new features to the garden landscape. Perennials mirror this seasonal passage by offering continual changes in growth, foliage, and flowers. While spring and summer are often considered to be the high points of the gardening calendar, with careful thought and positive planting perennials can provide year-round interest and colourful or dramatic effects, with one plant taking over as another is on the wane.

Seasonal changes in the garden are reflected most clearly in flowering and foliage displays. While some perennials flower for only a comparatively brief period, their spectacular blooms may be long remembered and eagerly looked forward to in subsequent years. Other perennials with extended flowering, often spanning several months, provide strong links between the seasons, and their contribution can be relied upon year after year. This is particularly important in smaller gardens, where each plant must justify its place in the planting scheme. Perennials with attractive foliage will provide an even longer season of interest, and can be invaluable where space is limited. While herbaceous plants often have richly tinted leaves in autumn, it is worth planting some of the many perennials that have evergreen, brightly coloured, or variegated foliage for longer-lasting colour and texture in the garden.

SPRING

The re-emergence of herbaceous perennials in spring is, for many gardeners, one of the most exciting events in the year. Rootstocks that have lain below ground all through winter now send out strong, and sometimes brightly coloured, new shoots. As many trees and shrubs are slower to produce new growth in spring, perennials provide much of the first garden colour of the new year. Bulbs will bring welcome early blooms and are excellent for planting in groups, naturalizing in large drifts, or underplanting beneath trees or shrubs. Tulips,

△ SPRING CONTAINER *Bulbs, like these* Narcissus, *are ideal for naturalizing or for tubs. They are a useful source of early colour in the garden, providing a rich variety of spring flower effects.*

▷ SUMMER BORDER *Perennials can bring a blaze of colour to the garden during the summer months. In this border, the bright blooms of delphiniums, lupins,* Anthemis, Oenothera, *and* Geranium psilostemon *compete with a multitude of other plants for our attention.*

△ EARLY WINTER *After flowering, many perennials produce decorative seed heads. These can provide enchanting effects when gilded with hoar frost, a bonus that tidy-minded gardeners often forfeit.*

◁ AUTUMN COLOUR *The richly tinted foliage of* Geranium macrorrhizum *is a striking backdrop for colchicums in autumn. The leaf colour will continue to develop after these flowers have faded.*

daffodils, and many other bulbs can also provide some of the first cut flowers of the year, and will thrive in containers on a patio.

SUMMER

After the initial rush of spring flowers, the garden settles down to a more leisurely pace. Many of our most popular border perennials, such as *Achillea*, *Heliopsis*, *Inula*, and other members of the huge daisy family are at their best now. Long-flowering perennials, like *Oenothera*, will bloom throughout summer and even on into autumn. Summer is also the time when perennials with a stately habit or bold foliage attain their ultimate size, stamping their presence on the garden scene. In areas where summers are dry, it is worth growing perennials such as eryngiums and yuccas, which will tolerate hot sun and little water.

AUTUMN

Perennials with late flowers, fruits, or richly tinted foliage can make autumn one of the most colourful seasons, despite its place at the end of the growing year. Autumn bulbs, such as colchicums and dwarf cyclamen, flower alongside golden rod (*Solidago*) and michaelmas daisies (*Aster*). Foliage can also make an important contribution – the dying leaves of herbaceous perennials such as *Geranium wlassovianum* providing brilliant tints of purple, yellow, and red to accompany the bright seed heads, often good for cutting, borne by many other plants. Wise gardeners will also use ornamental grasses, like the striking pampas grass (*Cortaderia selloana*), to add interest to borders or containers. In addition to their bold form and foliage, many of these grasses have striking flowers or long-lasting seed heads.

WINTER

The winter months are often least liked by gardeners, but this does not have to be a featureless time

▷ MID-WINTER *Use perennials to bring warmth and colour to the winter garden. Here,* Bergenia *'Bressingham Ruby' provides a lovely foil for some snowdrops.*

when the garden is either ignored or avoided. Numerous perennials, including bamboos, have attractive overwintering or evergreen foliage, some of it brightly coloured. These foliage plants, invaluable in their own right, will also provide a setting for mid- to late-winter-flowering pulmonarias and hellebores, as well as for snowdrops and other similar miniature bulbs that signal the oncoming spring. Perennials whose dried superstructures or seed heads survive through autumn into winter will provide further beauty and dramatic interest in the garden.

SOIL AND ASPECT

THE TYPE OF SOIL found in your garden and how much sun or shade it enjoys are two of the most critical factors to consider when selecting plants for your plot. While many perennials are flexible in their needs, tolerating a range of garden situations, they can be used to better effect if you are aware of their preferences.

Anemonopsis macrophylla
for moist soil in shade

Soils vary considerably in their physical and chemical nature, and while most perennials thrive on what is commonly called average or "moist but well-drained" soil, which retains enough moisture to satisfy a plant's needs without becoming waterlogged, some have more specific requirements. Look at the colour and texture of your soil and use the soil guide on p.14 to establish which type of soil you have.

All plants require some sunlight to survive, but while some demand full sun for top performance, others tolerate, or even prefer, varying degrees of shade. Many perennials thrive in the partial shade cast by buildings, walls, or light-canopied deciduous trees, like birch. A more careful choice of plants is needed, however, for sites in the heavy shade found beneath dense, and especially evergreen, tree canopies.

Perennials in this section are grouped according to their soil and lighting needs to provide planting solutions for a range of garden sites.

△ REACHING FOR THE SUN Verbascum bombyciferum *is a biennial that makes a striking, white-woolly feature in a sunny summer border. It also has a handsome rosette of overwintering leaves.*

△ SHADY BORDER *Many perennials, like these hostas and irises, enjoy a partially shady site, especially if the soil is moist.*

◁ SUNNY CORNER *Make use of warm, sheltered sites and corners to grow sun-loving, tender, or more exotic perennials.*

▷ DRY GARDEN *These striking sedums, eryngiums, and ornamental grasses will thrive in full sun and a well-drained soil.*

Low to Medium Perennials for Heavy Clay Soil

HEAVY CLAY SOILS can be wet and sticky in winter, but hard and lumpy in dry summers. They can also be, when well worked and mulched, fertile and amenable to the cultivation of a wide range of perennials. None of the following will grow much above 90cm (36in), and are suited to small gardens, or the front of larger borders and beds.

OTHER LOW TO MEDIUM GROWERS FOR HEAVY CLAY SOIL

Astilbe 'Rheinland'
Astrantia major 'Shaggy', see p.106
Brunnera macrophylla, see p.84
Polemonium 'Lambrook Mauve', see p.85
Pulmonaria 'Mawson's Blue', see p.97
Solidago 'Golden Fleece'
Stachys macrantha, see p.99
Thermopsis rhombifolia, see p.85
Veronica gentianoides

Ajuga reptans 'Multicolor'
COMMON BUGLE

☼ ❄❄❄   ↕ 15cm (6in) ↔ 90cm (36in)

This bugle forms a dense, evergreen mat of creeping stems and bronze-green leaves splashed pink and cream. Short spikes of deep blue flowers open in early summer.

Aster × frikartii 'Mönch'
ASTER

☼ ❄❄❄   ↕ 70cm (28in) ↔ 40cm (16in)

Well worth growing for its reliable display of big, long-lasting, lavender-blue daisies, borne on strong stems in late summer and autumn. It may require support. ♔

Campanula takesimana
BELLFLOWER

☼ ☼ ❄❄❄   ↕ 50cm (20in) ↔ 1m (3ft)

Reliable on clay soils, this suckering plant has erect stems and heart-shaped leaves. Nodding white bell-flowers, pink-flushed and spotted within, are borne in summer.

Aquilegia vulgaris 'Nora Barlow'
GRANNY'S BONNET

☼ ☼ ❄❄❄   ↕ 90cm (36in) ↔ 45cm (18in)

During spring and early summer, tall, erect stems produce showers of nodding, pale green and red pompon flowers above a mound of prettily divided leaves. ♔

Bergenia crassifolia
ELEPHANT'S EAR

☼ ☼ ❄❄❄   ↕ ↔ 45cm (18in)

A tough perennial, developing a mound of bold, leathery, evergreen leaves. Reddish stems carry dark pink flowers above the foliage during late winter and early spring.

Hemerocallis 'Stella de Oro'
DAYLILY

☼ ❄❄❄   ↕ 30cm (12in) ↔ 45cm (18in)

During early summer, clusters of bright yellow flowers open in succession above the dense, low clump of strap-shaped, semi-evergreen leaves. It is very reliable.

Hosta 'June'
PLANTAIN LILY
☀ ☀ ❄❄❄   ↕ 40cm (16in) ↔ 70cm (28in)

This beautiful foliage plant is a sport of
the lovely *H.* 'Halcyon'. It has fleshy,
long-pointed, yellow-splashed leaves and
bears lavender-grey flowers in summer.

Lamium orvala
DEAD NETTLE
☀ ☀ ❄❄❄   ↕ ↔ 50cm (20in)

The softly-hairy, nettle-shaped leaves
form a bold, non-invasive clump. Whorls
of two-lipped, pinkish purple flowers are
produced from late spring into summer.

Paeonia lactiflora 'Laura Dessert'
PEONY
☀ ❄❄❄   . ↕ 75cm (30in) ↔ 60cm (24in)

In early summer, large, fragrant, double,
creamy yellow blooms, with pink-flushed
outer petals, are borne above a bold clump
of deeply divided, light green leaves. ♈

Ranunculus aconitifolius 'Flore Pleno'
FAIR MAIDS OF KENT
☀ ☀ ❄❄❄   ↕ 60cm (24in) ↔ 45cm (18in)

Old-fashioned and very popular, this has
beautiful, deeply lobed leaves and bears
branched stems of double white button
flowers in spring and early summer. ♈

Prunella grandiflora 'Loveliness'
SELF-HEAL
☀ ❄❄❄   ↕ 15cm (6in) ↔ 30cm (12in)

A mat-forming, semi-evergreen perennial
with erect stems bearing whorled heads of
two-lipped, soft pink flowers in summer.
It will provide good ground cover. ♈

Rudbeckia fulgida var. *sullivantii*
'Goldsturm'
☀ ☀ ❄❄❄   ↕ 60cm (24in) ↔ 45cm (18in)

As long as it is kept moist in summer, this
colourful perennial is reliable. Its large,
dark-centred, golden yellow daisy-heads
open from late summer into autumn. ♈

Medium to Tall Perennials for Heavy Clay Soil

MANY OF THE MORE ROBUST perennials are tolerant of heavy clay soils. Some have densely fibrous rootstocks, others are deep-rooted, allowing them to survive so long as their site is not waterlogged. The following perennials, all 1–2m (3–6ft) tall, will do even better in these conditions if drainage can be improved by adding coarse grit and compost.

Delphinium 'Emily Hawkins'
DELPHINIUM
☼ ❄❄❄ ↕ 1.7m (5½ft) ↔ 60cm (24in)

No perennial border on clay soil should be without a delphinium. This one produces neat, semi-double, light violet flowers, with fawn-coloured eyes, in summer. ♆

Aconitum x cammarum 'Bicolor'
MONKSHOOD
☼ ◐ ❄❄❄ ↕ 1.2m (4ft) ↔ 60cm (24in)

This stout perennial has deeply divided, sharply toothed, dark green leaves and bears branched heads of helmet-shaped, blue and white flowers during summer. ♆

Centaurea macrocephala
CENTAUREA
☼ ❄❄❄ ↕ 1.5m (5ft) ↔ 90cm (36in)

Throughout summer, large, chunky heads of golden yellow cornflowers, with shiny brown bracts, top the erect, leafy stems of this striking, clump-forming perennial.

Eupatorium purpureum
'Atropurpureum'
☼ ❄❄❄ ↕ 2.2m (7ft) ↔ 1.2m (4ft)

The domed heads of pink-purple flowers, loved by butterflies and bees, are borne by stout, erect clumps of purplish, tall, leafy stems in summer and autumn. ♆

Aruncus dioicus
GOATSBEARD
☼ ◐ ❄❄❄ ↕ 2m (6ft) ↔ 1.2m (4ft)

An impressive perennial forming a bold clump of large, much-divided, fern-like leaves, with equally attractive plumes of frothy, creamy white summer flowers. ♆

Actaea simplex 'Scimitar'
BUGBANE
☼ ◐ ❄❄❄ ↕ 2m (6ft) ↔ 60cm (24in)

A handsome perennial with tall, branched spikes of tiny white flowers that rise over the large, bold clumps of deeply divided, fern-like leaves during autumn.

Helianthus 'Capenoch Star'
PERENNIAL SUNFLOWER
☼ ☀ ❄❄❄   ↕ 1.5m (5ft) ↔ 90cm (36in)

The sharply toothed leaves of this bold, clump-forming plant are joined in summer and autumn by branched heads of large, lemon-yellow, dark-centred daisies.

Heliopsis helianthoides var. *scabra*
'Light of Loddon'
☼ ☀ ❄❄❄   ↕ 1.1m (3½ft) ↔ 90cm (36in)

During summer and autumn, the erect, stout, stiff-branching, leafy stems produce a regular display of semi-double, bright yellow flowerheads with domed centres.

OTHER MEDIUM TO TALL PERENNIALS FOR CLAY SOIL

Campanula lactiflora 'Loddon Anna', see p.34
Helianthus 'Monarch'
Helianthus salicifolius
Inula helenium
Ligularia 'Gregynog Gold'
Ligularia 'The Rocket', see p.109
Macleaya cordata 'Flamingo'
Rheum palmatum
Sanguisorba canadensis

Persicaria amplexicaulis 'Firetail'
PERSICARIA
☼ ☀ ❄❄❄   ↕ 1.2m (4ft) ↔ 90cm (36in)

A striking and reliable border perennial, with dense clumps of leafy stems bearing long, arching, slender spikes of bright red flowers from summer into autumn.

Rodgersia aesculifolia
RODGERSIA
☼ ☀ ❄❄❄   ↕ 1.7m (5½ft) ↔ 90cm (36in)

This lovely rodgersia produces a clump of long-stalked, toothed, horse-chestnut-like leaves, topped by bold plumes of creamy white flowers during summer.

Silphium terebinthinaceum
PRAIRIE DOCK
☼ ☀ ❄❄❄   ↕ 2.5m (8ft) ↔ 1m (3ft)

Branched heads of yellow daisy-flowers adorn this statuesque plant in summer and autumn. The stalks of the coarse-toothed upper leaves are fused, forming cups.

Low to Medium Perennials for Sandy/Free-draining Soil

THERE ARE NUMEROUS PERENNIALS less than 1m (3ft) in height that are suitable for well-drained soils, especially those benefiting from full sun. These small plants have a multitude of uses, particularly at the front of borders, in raised beds, or on the tops of walls. Some are also excellent for growing in containers on patios or paved areas.

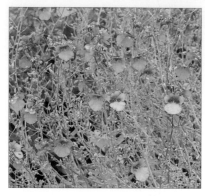

Diascia 'Joyce's Choice'
DIASCIA
☼ ❄❄ ↕ 25cm (10in) ↔ 50cm (20in)

A free-flowering diascia, forming a mat or carpet of trailing stems and small leaves, topped throughout summer and autumn by loose sprays of apricot flowers. ♔

Acanthus hirsutus
ACANTHUS
☼◐ ❄❄❄ ↕↔ 30cm (12in)

This low, suckering perennial forms a clump or patch of deep-cut, weakly spiny leaves. In summer, erect, greenish white flower spikes emerge from prickly bracts.

Artemisia 'Powis Castle'
ARTEMISIA
☼ ❄❄ ↕ 60cm (24in) ↔ 90cm (36in)

The filigree, silvery grey foliage of this plant is hard to beat. It forms a low, neat mound, eventually becoming woody and untidy, when it should be replaced. ♔

Eriophyllum lanatum
WOOLLY SUNFLOWER
☼ ❄❄❄ ↕↔ 50cm (20in)

This vigorous clump-former has woolly, silvery grey leaves and bears a succession of bright yellow daisy-flowers from late spring into summer. It is drought-tolerant.

Agapanthus 'Midnight Blue'
SOUTH AFRICAN LILY
☼ ❄❄❄ ↕ 45cm (18in) ↔ 30cm (12in)

In summer, fleshy stems rise from the clump of strap-shaped, dark green leaves to carry loose heads of dark blue trumpet-flowers. It is very reliable in most gardens.

Borago pygmaea
BORAGO
☼ ❄❄❄ ↕↔ 60cm (24in)

A short-lived plant, with loosely branched stems rising from rosettes of leaves. Pale blue, nodding bell-flowers emerge over a long period from early summer to autumn.

Eryngium bourgatii
ERYNGIUM
☼ ❄❄❄ ↕ 45cm (18in) ↔ 30cm (12in)

Small blue flowerheads, with collars of spine-tipped bracts, open in summer on branching stems. The spiny, silver-veined, deeply divided leaves form rosettes. ♔

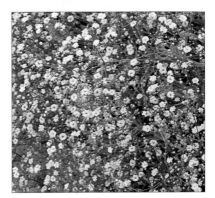

Gypsophila 'Rosenschleier'
GYPSOPHILA
☼ ❄❄❄   ↕ 40cm (16in) ↔ 1m (3ft)

The pretty carpet of bluish green leaves is peppered in summer with tiny, double white flowers, which later turn pale pink. It is also known as *G.* 'Rosy Veil'. ▽

Limonium platyphyllum 'Violetta'
SEA LAVENDER
☼ ❄❄❄   ↕ 60cm (24in) ↔ 45cm (18in)

This sea lavender forms a bold rosette of large, dark green leaves. Branched heads of tiny, deep bluish violet, late-summer flowers are good for cutting and drying.

Linum narbonense
LINUM
☼ ❄❄❄   ↕ 50cm (20in) ↔ 45cm (18in)

In summer, clumps of slender, wiry stems, clothed in narrow, blue-green leaves, bear a mass of short-lived, white-eyed blue flowers. A relative of the flax or linseed.

Oenothera speciosa 'Rosea'
OENOTHERA
☼ ❄❄❄   ↕ ↔ 30cm (12in)

From early summer to autumn, saucer-shaped, pale pink blooms, with yellow and white centres, decorate the hummock of narrow leaves. Free-flowering but invasive.

OTHER LOW TO MEDIUM GROWERS FOR SANDY/FREE-DRAINING SOIL

Acanthus dioscoridis, see p.32
Agastache 'Firebird'
Allium cristophii, see p.32
Anagallis monellii
Ballota 'All Hallows Green'
Centranthus ruber, see p.92
Delphinium tatsienense, see p.32
Dianthus deltoides, see p.106
Dictamnus albus, see p.114
Euphorbia nicaeensis, see p.82
Euphorbia rigida
Geranium 'Brookside', see p.33
Geranium malviflorum
Hordeum jubatum, see p.145
Iris innominata
Lychnis coronaria
Pulsatilla vulgaris 'Alba', see p.33
Tanacetum parthenium

Origanum laevigatum 'Herrenhausen'
OREGANO
☼ ❄❄❄   ↕ 50cm (20in) ↔ 45cm (18in)

Bees and butterflies love this plant. The stiffly erect stems, crowded with aromatic leaves, are topped by dense heads of rich pink flowers in summer and autumn. ▽

Medium to Tall Perennials for Sandy/Free-draining Soil

THOSE OF YOU WHO HAVE ADMIRED the huge mound of a *Crambe cordifolia* in bloom, or the lavender-blue spires of a *Perovskia*, may already know how well these two, and other similar perennials, thrive in well-drained soil, especially in sunny sites. The following, mostly 1–2m (3–6ft) tall, also enjoy such conditions, and will bring presence to a border or bed.

Asphodeline lutea
KING'S SPEAR
☼ ❄❄❄   ↕ 1.5m (5ft) ↔ 30cm (12in)

Well named, as the slender spikes of starry yellow flowers, borne above the clumps of grassy, blue-grey leaves in summer, really do have the appearance of golden spears.

Crambe cordifolia
CRAMBE
☼ ◐ ❄❄❄   ↕ 2.5m (8ft) ↔ 1.5m (5ft)

Truly imposing when in full bloom, the tiny, pure white flowers are borne in huge, branching heads above mounds of bold, dark green foliage in early summer. ▽

Echinops bannaticus 'Taplow Blue'
GLOBE THISTLE
☼ ◐ ❄❄❄   ↕ 1.2m (4ft) ↔ 60cm (24in)

The prickly balls of bright blue flowers in mid- to late summer make this a favourite with both children and butterflies. It has handsome, deep-cut, spiny leaves. ▽

Cortaderia selloana 'Rendatleri'
PINK PAMPAS GRASS
☼ ❄❄❄   ↕ 2.5m (8ft) ↔ 2m (6ft)

A favourite pampas grass, with a huge pile of narrow, saw-toothed, evergreen leaves, and tall stems flaunting bold plumes of rosy lilac spikelets during late summer.

Dierama pulcherrimum
WANDFLOWER
☼ ❄❄❄   ↕ 1.5m (5ft) ↔ 1.2m (4ft)

Known also as angel's fishing rod, because of its graceful, arching stems hung with magenta-pink or purple bell-flowers in summer. Its seed heads are attractive too.

Eryngium eburneum
ERYNGIUM
☼ ❄❄   ↕ 4m (12ft) ↔ 2m (6ft)

This statuesque plant bears tall-stemmed, branching heads of white-green flowers in summer, above bold clumps of rapier-like, spine-toothed, evergreen leaves.

Kniphofia 'Prince Igor'
TORCH LILY
☼ ☼ ❄❄❄   ↕ 1.8m (6ft) ↔ 90cm (36in)

This is an outstanding kniphofia, bearing narrow, rich green leaves, and numerous sturdy stems with large, dense pokers of deep orange-red flowers during autumn.

Linaria dalmatica
TOADFLAX
☼ ❄❄❄   ↕ ↔ 90cm (36in)

Bushy with a creeping rootstock, this toad-flax has erect stems crowded with bloomy, blue-green leaves. Long spikes of yellow snapdragon flowers open during summer.

HERBACEOUS, MEDIUM TO TALL GROWERS FOR SANDY SOIL

Achillea filipendulina, see p.76
Echinops ritro 'Veitch's Blue', see p.76
Echinops sphaerocephalus
Eremurus robustus, see p.34
Eremurus stenophyllus, see p.39
Eryngium pandanifolium
Lilium regale, see p.116
Malva alcea var. *fastigiata*, see p.99
Salvia involucrata 'Bethellii'
Verbascum chaixii 'Album', see p.109

Romneya coulteri
MATILIJA
☼ ❄❄   ↕ ↔ 2m (6ft)

A suckering, woody-based perennial or subshrub, in time forming patches of sea-green, bloomy, leafy stems. In summer, it bears large white poppy flowers. ♓

Salvia cacaliifolia
ORNAMENTAL SAGE
☼ ❄❄❄   ↕ 1.2m (4ft) ↔ 90cm (36in)

A robust, branching, hairy perennial with triangular leaves, and slender sprays of deep blue flowers from midsummer to autumn. It needs a warm, sunny site. ♓

Lavatera x *clementii* 'Kew Rose'
TREE MALLOW
☼ ❄❄❄   ↕ ↔ 2m (6ft)

Deservedly popular, this mallow produces branching, woody-based stems of semi-evergreen leaves, and a succession of pink flowers in summer. Likes a sheltered spot.

Perovskia 'Blue Spire'
RUSSIAN SAGE
☼ ❄❄❄   ↕ 1.2m (4ft) ↔ 90cm (36in)

This drought-tolerant, aromatic, woody-based sage has erect, downy stems, and branched spires of flowers in summer and autumn. Herbaceous in cold winters. ♓

Verbascum 'Gainsborough'
MULLEIN
☼ ❄❄❄   ↕ 1.2m (4ft) ↔ 30cm (12in)

Beautiful but short-lived, this mullein has downy, wrinkled leaves in attractive, over-wintering rosettes. Branched spires of soft yellow flowers appear in summer. ♓

Low-growing Perennials for Lime-free Soil

WHILE THE NUMBER OF PLANTS that demand lime-free conditions for successful cultivation is small compared with those that do not, the category includes some of the loveliest and most desirable of perennials. The perennials below will not grow much above 30cm (12in), making them suitable for rock gardens or for small peat gardens and beds.

OTHER LOW-GROWING
PERENNIALS FOR LIME-FREE SOIL

Cautleya spicata 'Robusta'
Dodecatheon hendersonii
Gentiana × *macaulayi* 'Edinburgh'
Gentiana sino-ornata, see p.61
Iris Californian Hybrids
Iris innominata
Lithodora diffusa 'Heavenly Blue'
Phlox × *procumbens* 'Millstream'
Shortia galacifolia
Viola pedata

Celmisia walkeri
NEW ZEALAND DAISY
☼ ☼ ✺✺✺ ↕ ↔ 30cm (12in)

This mat-forming, evergreen perennial or subshrub has rosettes of leathery, greyish leaves, and white, yellow-centred daisies borne on sticky stems in early summer.

Dodecatheon meadia f. *album*
SHOOTING STAR
☼ ☼ ✺✺✺ ↕ 40cm (16in) ↔ 25cm (10in)

In spring, this exquisite plant bears loose umbels of nodding, pure white flowers, with yellow beaks of stamens, on slender stems above a basal rosette of leaves. ♔

Iris 'Arnold Sunrise'
PACIFIC COAST IRIS
☼ ☼ ✺✺✺ ↕ 25cm (10in) ↔ 30cm (12in)

A tough, clump-forming plant, forming patches of long, narrow, evergreen leaves. Erect stems bear yellow-stained white flowers in spring. Will tolerate dry soil. ♔

Gentiana × *macualayi* 'Kingfisher'
GENTIAN
☼ ☼ ✺✺✺ ↕ 5cm (2in) ↔ 30cm (12in)

In autumn, beautiful trumpet-shaped blue flowers, with white and darker blue sripes on the outside, are borne among the semi-evergreen mats of rosetted, narrow leaves.

Lithodora diffusa 'Grace Ward'
LITHODORA
☼ ✺✺✺ ↕ 15cm (6in) ↔ 90cm (36in)

Deep azure-blue flowers top the prostrate, leafy stems of this dense, carpeting, evergreen perennial or subshrub in late spring and summer. Ideal for rock gardens. ♔

Medium to Tall Perennials for Lime-free Soil

THE FOLLOWING PERENNIALS all perform best in lime-free, preferably acid conditions. Many are natives of woodland and mountain sites and require some moisture in spring and summer (but not waterlogged soil) in order to thrive. They will grow to around 1m (3ft) tall, and provide superb displays of foliage and flowers for a bed or garden with peaty soil.

Meconopsis chelidoniifolia
MECONOPSIS
☼ ❄❄❄ ↕ 1m (3ft) ↔ 60cm (24in)

Elegant yet informal, this plant develops clumps of leafy, slender, semi-scandent, branching stems. Nodding, saucer-shaped, pale yellow flowers are borne in summer.

Blechnum chilense
BLECHNUM
☼ ☼ ❄❄❄ ↕ 1m (3ft) ↔ 1.2m (4ft)

This large, evergreen fern forms a bold clump of laddered, leathery, sterile fronds. Stiff, fertile fronds crowded with brown spore clusters rise from the centre. 🏆

Thalictrum rochebruneanum
MEADOW RUE
☼ ❄❄❄ ↕ 1.2m (4ft) ↔ 30cm (12in)

A stately, upright perennial with clumps of large, much-divided, fern-like leaves and tall stems. Fluffy, white or lavender-pink flower clusters are borne in summer.

Iris ensata 'Variegata'
JAPANESE IRIS
☼ ❄❄❄ ↕ 1m (3ft) ↔ 45cm (18in)

In summer, this clump-forming iris bears dark red-purple flowers on erect stems above its upright, sword-shaped, white-striped green leaves. Enjoys moist soils. 🏆

Lilium auratum
GOLDEN-RAYED LILY
☼ ☼ ❄❄❄ ↕ 1.5 (5ft) ↔ 30cm (12in)

Tall stems, crowded with lance-shaped leaves, each bear up to 12 large white blooms, speckled crimson and striped gold, in late summer and early autumn.

> **OTHER MEDIUM TO TALL PERENNIALS FOR LIME-FREE SOIL**
>
> *Cardiocrinum giganteum* var. *yunnanense*, see p.44
> *Iris ensata*
> *Meconopsis betonicifolia*
> *Meconopsis grandis*
> *Meconopsis* x *sheldonii* 'Slieve Donard'
> *Nomocharis pardanthina*
> *Osmunda regalis*, see p.67
> *Thalictrum chelidonii*
> *Thalictrum diffusiflorum*

Low to Medium Perennials for Alkaline Soil

CONTRARY TO THE BELIEF of some gardeners that many of the choicest garden plants demand lime-free soil, more perennials in fact thrive on, rather than dislike, alkaline conditions. None of the following will grow to more than 1m (3ft) high and are therefore suitable for the front of borders, as well as for raised beds and rock gardens.

Bergenia 'Beethoven'
ELEPHANT'S EAR
☼ ☀ ✳✳✳   ↕45cm (18in) ↔60cm (24in)

This fine hybrid of German origin forms a low clump of bold, leathery leaves, above which loose heads of white flowers with reddish calyces are borne in spring.

Campanula punctata
BELLFLOWER
☼ ☀ ✳✳✳   ↕ ↔40cm (16in)

In early summer, this rewarding, reliable perennial produces erect stems hung with large, tubular-bell-shaped, white to dusky pink flowers, heavily spotted within.

Acanthus dioscoridis
ACANTHUS
☼ ✳✳✳   ↕40cm (16in) ↔60cm (24in)

A striking relative of *A. mollis*, forming clumps of lance-shaped, hairy leaves, and bearing dense spikes of rich pink flowers with green bracts in spring and summer.

OTHER LOW TO MEDIUM PERENNIALS FOR ALKALINE SOIL

Anthericum liliago, see p.36
Campanula glomerata 'Superba'
Centranthus ruber, see p.92
Erodium manescaui
Euphorbia rigida
Geranium sanguineum 'Max Frei', see p.76
Platycodon grandiflorus, see p.83
Scabiosa caucasica 'Clive Greaves', see p.99

Allium cristophii
ORNAMENTAL ONION
☼ ✳✳✳   ↕60cm (24in) ↔15cm (6in)

One of the most spectacular and reliable alliums, its large, globular heads of starry, pink-purple flowers in early summer are followed by ornamental seed heads. 🏆

Delphinium tatsienense
DELPHINIUM
☼ ✳✳✳   ↕60cm (24in) ↔30cm (12in)

A refreshing change from the tall, spiked hybrids, this delightful species produces slender, branching stems of long-spurred, bright cornflower-blue flowers in summer.

Geranium 'Brookside'
CRANESBILL
☼ ◐ ✻✻✻ ‡ 50cm (20in) ↔ 75cm (30in)

The finely cut leaves of this vigorous plant form a low mound, which is covered in summer with showers of saucer-shaped, deep clear blue, white-eyed flowers.

Milium effusum 'Aureum'
BOWLES' GOLDEN GRASS
☼ ✻✻✻ ‡ ↔ 60cm (24in)

Delicate in habit and golden in effect, this is one of the brightest and most reliable of ornamental grasses. It will seed freely and comes true. Excellent with *Myosotis*. ♛

Dianthus 'Mrs. Sinkins'
OLD-FASHIONED PINK
☼ ✻✻✻ ‡ 40cm (16in) ↔ 30cm (12in)

Richly fragrant of cloves, this popular cottage-garden plant has abundant double, fringed, white blossoms in early summer, above evergreen, greyish green leaves.

Helleborus x *ericsmithii*
HELLEBORE
☼ ◐ ✻✻✻✻ ‡ 30cm (12in) ↔ 45cm (18in)

This bold hybrid has attractively marbled, bristle-toothed leaves, and large, saucer-shaped, white or pink-tinted flowers in winter. Previously known as *H.* x *nigristern*.

Pulsatilla vulgaris 'Alba'
PASQUE FLOWER
☼ ✻✻✻ ‡ ↔ 20cm (8in)

A beautiful white form of a popular plant, forming a clump of finely divided, silky-hairy leaves. Silky seed heads follow the white spring flowers. ♛

Francoa sonchifolia
BRIDAL WREATH
☼ ◐ ✻✻ ‡ 90cm (36in) ↔ 60cm (24in)

Clumps of evergreen, deeply lobed, hairy leaves are topped in summer by slender pink flower sprays, marked in darker pink. The flowers are excellent for cutting.

Lathyrus vernus
SPRING VETCHLING
☼ ◐ ✻✻✻✻ ‡ 30cm (12in) ↔ 45cm (18in)

The loose racemes of purplish blue pea-flowers in spring make this a reliable and easily grown favourite. Its deeply divided, glossy green leaves are attractive too. ♛

Viola cornuta
Alba Group
HORNED VIOLET
☼ ◐ ✻✻✻ ‡ 15cm (6in) ↔ 30cm (12in)

This violet's long flowering time makes it invaluable. A continuous supply of white flowers tops the mat of toothy, evergreen leaves throughout spring and summer. ♛

Medium to Tall Perennials for Alkaline Soil

NOT ALL THE PERENNIALS recommended here for alkaline soils actually prefer them to lime-free or neutral soils, but they have proved amenable to these conditions and can be relied on to do well. The following selection, around 1–3m (3–10ft) in height, represents some of the most impressive plants for these limy or chalky sites.

Cortaderia selloana 'Pumila'
PAMPAS GRASS
☼ ❄❄❄   ↕ 1.5m (5ft) ↔ 1.2m (4ft)

Although smaller than most other pampas grasses, this is an impressive specimen for a lawn. In late summer, it has crowded plumes of silvery cream spikelets. ♛

Euphorbia sikkimensis
SPURGE
☼ ☼ ❄❄❄   ↕ 1.2m (4ft) ↔ 60cm (24in)

The upright stems of this tough, reliable spurge bear narrow, willow-like leaves, and yellow flower clusters during summer. Bright pink new shoots appear in spring. ♛

Artemisia lactiflora
WHITE MUGWORT
☼ ❄❄❄   ↕ 1.5m (5ft) ↔ 90cm (36in)

This vigorous plant has dense clumps of erect stems clothed in divided, jaggedly cut leaves. Branched heads of tiny cream flowers open in summer and autumn. ♛

Campanula lactiflora 'Loddon Anna'
BELLFLOWER
☼ ☼ ❄❄❄   ↕ 1.5m (5ft) ↔ 90cm (36in)

Reliable and easily grown, this bellflower's conical, branched heads of soft lilac-pink blooms top clumps of downy, leafy stems during summer. May need support. ♛

Eremurus robustus
DESERT CANDLE, FOXTAIL LILY
☼ ❄❄❄   ↕ 3m (10ft) ↔ 1.2m (4ft)

Magnificent, long-stemmed racemes of starry, pale pink flowers rise in summer above clumps of strap-shaped, blue-green leaves, which wither after flowering. ♛

Lavatera × *clementii* 'Barnsley'
TREE MALLOW
☼ ❄❄   ↕ ↔ 2m (6ft)

A summer-long succession of white, red-eyed flowers, and semi-evergreen, greyish green leaves, make this one of the most satisfying of all large perennials. ♛

Thalictrum flavum subsp. *glaucum*
YELLOW MEADOW RUE
☼ ❅❅❅ ↕ 1.5m (5ft) ↔ 60cm (24in)

The deeply divided, blue-green, bloomy
leaves of this stately plant are invaluable
for contrast with greens or purples. Fluffy
yellow flowerheads appear in summer. ♈

Oenothera stricta 'Sulphurea'
EVENING PRIMROSE
☼ ❅❅❅ ↕ 90cm (36in) ↔ 15cm (6in)

Over many weeks in summer, this choice
perennial bears big, fragrant, pale yellow
flowers, which open in the evening on
slender, erect stems. It will seed around.

Veronicastrum virginicum f. *album*
VERONICASTRUM
☼ ☼ ❅❅❅ ↕ 2m (6ft) ↔ 60cm (24in)

Distinctive clumps of slender, stiff, erect
stems, clothed in whorls of narrow, toothy
leaves, carry dense, tapering spikes of
white flowers from summer to autumn.

Phytolacca polyandra
POKEWEED
☼ ☼ ❅❅❅ ↕ 1.2m (4ft) ↔ 60cm (24in)

A striking plant in every way. In autumn,
the fleshy stems turn crimson, the leaves
yellow, and dense, erect spikes of bold but
poisonous, glistening black fruits appear.

Polygonatum verticillatum
WHORLED SOLOMON'S SEAL
☼ ☼ ❅❅❅ ↕ 90cm (36in) ↔ 30cm (12in)

In late spring and summer, clusters of
tubular, greenish white flowers, then red
berries, hang from the erect, slender stems
clothed in long, narrow, willow-like leaves.

**OTHER MEDIUM TO TALL
PERENNIALS FOR ALKALINE SOIL**

Anchusa azurea 'Loddon Royalist',
  see p.112
Anemone x *hybrida* 'Königin Charlotte',
  see p.56
Campanula latifolia var. *macrantha*
Centaurea macrocephala, see p.24
Cephalaria gigantea, see p.78
Lavatera x *clementii* 'Rosea', see p.101
Phygelius x *rectus* 'African Queen',
  see p.107

Perennials for Dry Soil in Sun

W ITH THE INCREASING occurrence of droughts or water shortages in many cool-temperate regions, perennials that will tolerate dry, sunny conditions are at a premium. Fortunately, a number of plants can survive without rain or watering for long periods. Many of these have long tap-roots, or densely hairy or waxy leaf-surfaces to reduce water loss.

OTHER HERBACEOUS PERENNIALS FOR DRY SOIL IN SUN

Acanthus hirsutus, see p.26
Baptisia australis, see p.98
Cynara cardunculus, see p.136
Echinops ritro 'Veitch's Blue', see p.79
Iris 'Jane Phillips'
Linaria purpurea 'Canon Went'
Linum narbonense, see p.27
Oenothera stricta 'Sulphurea', see p.35
Pennisetum setaceum
Sedum spectabile 'Carmen'

Anthericum liliago
ST. BERNARD'S LILY
☼ ✳✳✳   ‡ 90cm (36in) ↔ 60cm (24in)

Popular in cottage gardens, this perennial produces elegant racemes of small, lily-like white flowers above clumps of grassy leaves in late spring and early summer.

Asteriscus maritimus
ASTERICUS
☼ ✳✳   ‡ 25cm (10in) ↔ 90cm (36in)

A woody-based perennial forming a dense carpet or low mound of small, rough-hairy leaves, studded with daisy-like yellow flowerheads from late spring to summer.

Artemisia alba
ARTEMISIA
☼ ✳✳✳   ‡ 45cm (18in) ↔ 30cm (12in)

The slender, upright, grey-white stems of this dense, woody-based perennial are clothed in aromatic, filigree, silvery grey foliage, giving a plumose or frothy effect.

Catananche caerulea 'Bicolor'
BLUE CUPIDONE
☼ ✳✳✳   ‡ 50cm (20in) ↔ 30cm (12in)

This short-lived perennial forms clumps of grassy leaves. Its slender, erect stems each carry a single white, purple-centred cornflower from midsummer to autumn.

Crepis incana
PINK DANDELION
☼ ✳✳✳   ‡ ↔ 30cm (12in)

During late summer, beautiful, clear pink flowerheads, on slender-branched stems, rise over the dense grey-hairy leaf rosettes of this lovely dandelion relative. ♔

Eryngium x *tripartitum*
ERYNGIUM
☼ ✳✳✳   ↕ 60cm (24in) ↔ 50cm (20in)

Stiff, wiry, many-branched stems produce long stalked leaves and, from summer to autumn, small heads of violet-blue flowers with prickly grey-blue bracts. 🏆

Phlomis purpurea
PHLOMIS
☼ ✳✳   ↕ ↔ 60cm (24in)

A woody-based perennial or subshrub with woolly shoots and softly-hairy, grey-green leaves. In summer, clusters of pink to purple, two-lipped flowers appear.

Yucca gloriosa
SPANISH DAGGER
☼ ✳✳✳   ↕ 2m (6ft) ↔ 1m (3ft)

Evergreen, sword-shaped, spine-toothed, blue-green leaves crown the short, stout, woody stem. In late summer or autumn, a huge panicle of ivory flowers emerges. 🏆

OTHER EVERGREEN PERENNIALS FOR DRY SOIL IN SUN

Cortaderia selloana 'Pumila', see p.34
Delosperma cooperi
Euphorbia nicaeensis, see p.82
Iris innominata
Iris unguicularis 'Walter Butt'
Marrubium libanoticum
Phlomis russeliana
Santolina pinnata subsp. *neapolitana*
Santolina rosmarinifolia 'Primrose Gem'
Stachys byzantina 'Big Ears'

Papaver orientale 'Perry's White'
ORIENTAL POPPY
☼ ✳✳✳   ↕ ↔ 90cm (36in)

The deep-rooted clumps of stout, bristly-hairy stems, with deep-cut, rough-haired leaves, bear large, solitary white flowers with maroon-purple centres in summer.

Tropaeolum polyphyllum
TROPAEOLUM
☼ ✳✳   ↕ 10cm (4in) ↔ 1m (3ft)

Long-spurred, orange- or deep yellow blooms crowd the shoots of this vigorous, trailing plant in summer. Its lobed leaves and fleshy stems are bloomy blue-green.

Zauschneria californica subsp. *cana* 'Dublin'
☼ ✳✳   ↕ 30cm (12in) ↔ 50cm (20in)

One of the best perennials for a dry site, with its low, bushy habit, narrow, downy, grey-green foliage, and tubular, bright red flowers in late summer and autumn. 🏆

Bulbs for Dry Soil in Sun

Agreat number of our garden bulbs, including many tulip species, foxtail lilies, and ornamental onions, come from the Mediterranean region and similar warm, sunny, dry-summer areas of the world, including western and central Asia. None of the following bulbs enjoy shade, preferring the brightness and warmth of full sun and a site in well-drained soil. Many of these bulbs will require some protection during the winter months in cold, frost-prone regions.

Arum creticum
Arum
☼ ❄❄ ‡ 50cm (20in) ↔ 30cm (12in)

This showy plant forms healthy clumps of rich green, broadly arrow-shaped leaves. In spring, the foliage is accompanied by hooded flowers with projecting tongues.

Amaryllis belladonna 'Hathor'
Belladonna Lily
☼ ❄❄ ‡ 60cm (24in) ↔ 10cm (4in)

In time, this lily forms patches of erect, fleshy stems. These bear umbels of pure white, trumpet-shaped flowers in autumn, before the strap-shaped leaves appear.

Anomatheca laxa
Anomatheca
☼ ❄❄ ‡ 20cm (8in) ↔ 8cm (3in)

A charming little plant, free-seeding when established, especially in light or sandy soils. It has small, iris-like leaves, and bears sprays of red flowers in summer. ♉

Anemone x *fulgens*
Anemone
☼ ❄❄❄ ‡ 25cm (10in) ↔ 15cm (6in)

A splendid tuberous perennial, especially when planted in groups or drifts. Brilliant red flowers with darker eyes are borne in spring. It needs protection in colder areas.

Other Bulbs for Dry Soil in Sun

Allium cristophii, see p.32
Allium schubertii
Anemone pavonina, see p.58
Anomatheca laxa var. *alba*
Eucomis zambesiaca
Ixiolirion tataricum
Lilium candidum
Lilium regale, see p.116
Lilium x *testaceum*
Muscari macrocarpum
Nerine bowdenii 'Mark Fenwick', see p.102
Ornithogalum arabicum
Oxalis adenophylla, see p.61
Pancratium illyricum
Ranunculus asiaticus
Triteleia laxa
Tulipa saxatilis

Dracunculus vulgaris
Dragon Arum
☼ ❄❄ ‡ 90cm (36in) ↔ 60cm (24in)

The darkly mottled stems of this strange and striking perennial bear long-stalked, deeply divided leaves, and large, velvety, deep maroon-purple flowers in summer.

Hermodactylus tuberosus
WIDOW IRIS
☀ ✳✳✳ ↕ 30cm (12in) ↔ 10cm (4in)

This sombre but charming iris relative has narrow, grassy leaves, which are joined by green or greenish yellow flowers in spring. The outer petals have blackish brown tips.

Tulipa clusiana
LADY TULIP
☀ ✳✳✳ ↕ 30cm (12in) ↔ 10cm (4in)

A beautiful tulip of slender, elegant poise. It produces narrow grey leaves and white spring flowers with dark crimson eyes and pinkish crimson backs to the outer petals.

Eremurus stenophyllus
FOXTAIL LILY
☀ ✳✳✳ ↕ 1m (3ft) ↔ 60cm (24in)

Although not strictly a bulb, this perennial has a divided, fleshy crown that produces a cluster of strap-like leaves, and tall spires of starry yellow flowers in summer. ♔

Scilla peruviana
SCILLA
☀ ✳✳ ↕ 30cm (12in) ↔ 15cm (6in)

The basal rosettes of broad, strap-shaped, fleshy green leaves are topped, during late spring, by striking, large, conical heads of small, star-shaped blue flowers.

Gladiolus communis subsp. *byzantinus*
WHISTLING JACKS
☀ ✳✳✳ ↕ 1m (3ft) ↔ 25cm (10in)

Reliable and easy to grow, this robust plant quickly forms a clump, then a patch, of leafy stems that sport bold spikes of vivid magenta flowers during summer. ♔

Triteleia hyacinthina
TRITELIA
☀ ✳✳ ↕ 70cm (28in) ↔ 5cm (2in)

Like a white-flowered ornamental onion without the smell, this very attractive and reliable bulb produces umbels of starry flowers on slender stems in early summer.

Tulipa tarda
TULIP
☀ ✳✳✳ ↕ 15cm (6in) ↔ 10cm (4in)

One of the most reliable and lovely small tulip species, producing a rosette of glossy, narrow leaves, and bearing star-shaped yellow, white-tipped flowers in spring. ♔

Perennials for Dry Soil in Shade

DRY, SHADY SITES, often found under trees and shrubs, are one of the most difficult garden situations to deal with successfully. One solution is to cultivate the perennials listed here, which will tolerate such conditions. If tree roots are a serious problem, the ground can also be covered with a proprietary landscaping fabric and a fresh layer of soil.

OTHER EVERGREEN PERENNIALS FOR DRY SOIL IN SHADE

Acanthus mollis Latifolius Group
Alchemilla mollis, see p.90
Euphorbia amygdaloides 'Purpurea'
Geranium macrorrhizum, see p.89
Helleborus foetidus
Ophiopogon japonicus
Pachyphragma macrophyllum
Reineckia carnea
Vinca major subsp. *hirsuta*, see p.57
Waldsteinia ternata

Buglossoides purpurocaerulea
PURPLE GROMWELL
☼ ◐ ❅❅❅ ↕ 60cm (24in) ↔ 90cm (36in)

This low-growing or scrambling perennial sends out long shoots that root at the tips. Erect stems bear purple flowers, turning deep blue, from late spring to summer.

Epimedium perralderianum
EPIMEDIUM
☼ ◐ ❅❅❅ ↕ 30cm (12in) ↔ 60cm (24in)

In spring, racemes of bright yellow flowers rise above the clumps of evergreen, glossy, dark green leaves, which each have three leaflets, and are bronze-red when young.

OTHER HERBACEOUS PERENNIALS FOR DRY SOIL IN SHADE

Cyclamen hederifolium, see p.102
Dicentra eximia
Dicentra formosa
Geranium × *monacense* 'Muldoon'
Geranium nodosum
Geranium × *oxonianum* 'Claridge Druce'
Geranium phaeum 'Joan Baker'
Lunaria rediviva
Symphytum ibericum
Symphytum orientale, see p.57

Claytonia sibirica
PINK PURSLANE
☼ ◐ ❅❅❅ ↕ 20cm (8in) ↔ 15cm (6in)

Short-lived but free-seeding, this plant develops tufts of fleshy green leaves and freely bears loose heads of small, pink or white flowers from late spring to summer.

Euphorbia amygdaloides var. *robbiae*
MRS. ROBB'S BONNET
☼ ◐ ❅❅❅ ↕ 75cm (30in) ↔ 60cm (24in)

A vigorous, creeping evergreen with erect stems bearing leathery, dark green leaves, and crowded racemes of greenish yellow flowers from spring to early summer. ♕

Geranium phaeum 'Album'
MOURNING WIDOW
☼ ☼ ❄❄❄ ↕80cm (32in) ↔ 45cm (18in)

One of the loveliest geraniums, bearing showers of pendent white, yellow-beaked flowers above clumps of shallowly lobed, soft green leaves from summer to autumn.

Iris foetidissima var. *citrina*
GLADWYN
☼ ☼ ❄❄❄ ↕75cm (30in) ◄►60cm (24in)

A useful and adaptable evergreen, with clumps of strong-smelling, strap-shaped, shiny leaves, and yellow summer flowers. In winter, it bears orange seed capsules.

Lamium galeobdolon 'Hermann's Pride'
☼ ☼ ❄❄❄ ↕60cm (24in) ↔ 1.2m (4ft)

During summer, dense mounds of erect stems bear clusters of two-lipped yellow flowers from the axils of coarsely toothed, silver-marbled, evergreen leaves.

Saxifraga stolonifera
MOTHER OF THOUSANDS
☼ ☼ ❄❄❄ ↕30cm (12in) ↔ 20cm (8in)

Red runners, forming new plantlets at their tips, grow from the rosettes of long-stalked, pale veined leaves. Erect stems bear showers of white flowers in summer. ♈

Symphytum 'Hidcote Pink'
COMFREY
☼ ☼ ❄❄❄ ↕↔45cm (18in)

Excellent for ground cover, this creeping perennial forms low patches of erect, leafy stems. Pendent clusters of funnel-shaped, pink and white flowers emerge in spring.

Tolmiea menziesii
PICK-A-BACK PLANT
☼ ☼ ❄❄❄ ↕↔60cm (24in)

A creeping perennial with loose clumps of hairy leaves that bear new plants at their bases. In spring and summer, airy panicles of tiny, brownish green flowers appear.

Trachystemon orientalis
ABRAHAM-ISAAC-JACOB
☼ ☼ ❄❄❄ ↕30cm (12in) ↔ indefinite

In time, this creeping plant forms large, dense patches of long-stalked, rough-hairy leaves. Its bristly stems bear blue flowers with "beaks" of stamens during spring.

Perennials for Moist Soil in Shade

SOME OF THE MOST EXQUISITE and desirable perennials are native to deciduous woodland, where the harshness of the summer sun is filtered and weakened by branches and leaves. These woodland plants are excellent for beds on the shady side of the house and similar cool sites in the garden, where plenty of moisture is guaranteed during the growing season.

Actaea rubra
RED BANEBERRY
☼ ❄❄❄ ↕ 45cm (18in) ↔ 30cm (12in)

A poisonous plant, but well worth growing for its clump of deeply divided leaves, and dense, terminal clusters of shining red berries in late summer and autumn.

Convallaria majalis var. *rosea*
LILY-OF-THE-VALLEY
☼ ☀ ❄❄❄ ↕ 20cm (8in) ↔ 30cm (12in)

A pretty variant of a familiar and much-loved perennial, forming a carpet of paired leaves. It bears loose racemes of nodding, mauve-pink bell-flowers during spring.

Dactylorhiza foliosa
TERRESTRIAL ORCHID
☼ ❄❄❄ ↕ 60cm (24in) ↔ 15cm (6in)

In time, this spectacular orchid forms a clump of stout, lush, leafy stems. These sport bold, dense spikes of bright purple flowers in late spring or early summer.

Anemonopsis macrophylla
ANEMONOPSIS
☼ ❄❄❄❄ᴾᴴ ↕ 75cm (30in) ↔ 45cm (18in)

This aristocrat of the woodland forms a clump of ferny leaves and bears delicate sprays of cup-shaped, nodding, waxy, lilac and violet flowers during late summer.

Corydalis flexuosa
CORYDALIS
☼ ❄❄❄ ↕↔ 30cm (12in)

During spring and early summer, startling showers of blue flowers rise above the ferny, blue-green foliage, which emerges in autumn and dies down in summer.

Deinanthe caerulea
DEINANTHE
☼ ❄❄❄ ↕↔ 30cm (12in)

The attractive, crinkly leaves of this choice, creeping perennial will eventually form a clump. Loose panicles of nodding, fleshy blue flowers open in summer.

Trillium cernuum
TRILLIUM
☼ ☼ ❄❄❄ PH ↕ 50cm (20in) ↔ 30cm (12in)

Impressive when planted in groups, this
charming perennial has clumps of broad,
wavy-edged leaves, and small, nodding,
white to pale pink or red flowers in spring.

Glaucidium palmatum
GLAUCIDIUM
☼ ☼ ❄❄❄ ↕ ↔ 45cm (18in)

This lovely woodlander produces a clump
of large, attractively lobed and toothed
leaves. In late spring and early summer, it
has poppy-like, mauve or lilac flowers. ♈

Trillium sessile
TOAD-SHADE
☼ ☼ ❄❄❄ PH ↕ ↔ 30cm (12in)

Quite unlike *Trillium cernuum*, and a good
contrast, this has broad, often beautifully
marbled leaves in threes, and stemless,
erect, red or maroon flowers during spring.

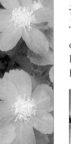

Hacquetia epipactis
HACQUETIA
☼ ❄❄❄ ↕ 15cm (6in) ↔ 30cm (12in)

One of the earliest woodlanders to appear
in spring, bearing curious collared, yellow-
green flowerheads, followed by emerald-
green leaves. Both useful and reliable. ♈

Sanguinaria canadensis 'Plena'
BLOODROOT
☼ ☼ ❄❄❄ ↕ 15cm (6in) ↔ 30cm (12in)

Exquisite, double white blooms open in
spring as leaves appear. The lobed, grey-
green leaves are loosely rolled around the
stems on emergence, and then unfurl. ♈

Uvularia grandiflora
LARGE MERRYBELLS
☼ ☼ ❄❄❄ ↕ 75cm (30in) ↔ 30cm (12in)

This favourite woodland plant forms a
clump of erect, slender, leafy shoots with
nodding tips. It bears pendent, tubular to
bell-shaped yellow flowers in spring. ♈

Bulbs for Moist Soil in Shade

MANY OF OUR MOST POPULAR and best-loved bulbs are found growing in the cool, moist soils and partial shade of deciduous woodlands. They include numerous snowdrops, bluebells, and erythroniums, some of which will eventually establish large colonies where space and conditions permit. Most are easy to grow in any shady, moist site.

Cardiocrinum giganteum var. *yunnanense*
GIANT LILY
☀ ❄❄❄ ‡ 2.5m (8ft) ↔ 45cm (18in)

Magnificent and monumental in flower, this perennial bears long heads of fragrant, pendent, creamy white summer blooms on tall dark stems. It dies after flowering.

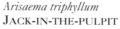

Allium moly
GOLDEN GARLIC
☀ ☀ ❄❄❄ ‡ 25cm (10in) ↔ 10cm (4in)

Quick to form substantial clumps of broad, strap-shaped grey leaves, this bulb bears umbels of starry, bright yellow flowers in early summer. Will tolerate some sun. ♔

Arisaema triphyllum
JACK-IN-THE-PULPIT
☀ ☀ ❄❄❄ ‡ 60cm (24in) ↔ 15cm (6in)

A woodland plant that will also tolerate sun. Its long-stalked green leaves, divided into threes, are accompanied in spring by hooded green, sometimes striped, flowers.

Arisaema sikokianum
ARISAEMA
☀ ❄❄❄ ‡ 40cm (16in) ↔ 15cm (6in)

A really striking perennial, with its leaves often beautifully marked and divided into threes. The dark flowers have contrasting white throats. Excellent grown in groups.

Brimeura amethystina
BRIMEURA
☀ ☀ ❄❄❄ ‡ 20cm (8in) ↔ 8cm (3in)

Resembling a small, slender bluebell, this bulb bears one-sided racemes of tubular, bright blue flowers in late spring or early summer. Will spread freely in a good site.

Erythronium 'Pagoda'
TROUT LILY
☀ ❄❄❄ ‡ 35cm (14in) ↔ 10cm (4in)

In spring, dark stems bear pendent yellow flowers, with upswept petals, above lush rosettes of mottled green leaves. This is a vigorous bulb which seeds freely. ♔

Erythronium revolutum
TROUT LILY

☼ ❄❄❄ ↕ 30cm (12in) ↔ 10cm (4in)

One of the best erythroniums for general
cultivation, with beautifully mottled
leaves, and elegant pink, yellow-centred
flowers in spring. It can seed freely. ♆

Leucojum aestivum 'Gravetye Giant'
SUMMER SNOWFLAKE

☼-☼ ❄❄❄ ↕ 90cm (36in) ↔ 10cm (4in)

Erect clumps of green leaves are quickly
formed by this robust, easily grown bulb.
The umbels of nodding white, green-
tipped flowers emerge in late spring. ♆

Galanthus elwesii
GIANT SNOWDROP

☼ ❄❄❄ ↕ 22cm (9in) ↔ 8cm (3in)

Easy to grow and reliable, this variable
bulb usually has narrow, grey-green leaves,
and white flowers in late winter, the inner
segments marked green at both ends. ♆

Galanthus plicatus
SNOWDROP

☼ ❄❄❄ ↕ 20cm (8in) ↔ 8cm (3in)

In time, this vigorous snowdrop will form
colonies. Its blue-green leaves have edges
folded under, and its late winter flowers
have green-tipped inner segments. ♆

Narcissus pseudonarcissus
LENT LILY

☼-☼ ❄❄❄ ↕ 35cm (14in) ↔ 10cm (4in)

A charming woodland species, and parent
of many hybrids. Its pale yellow spring
flowers have deep yellow trumpets, flared
at the mouths. Excellent for naturalizing.

Perennials for Warm, Sheltered Sites

FOR THOSE FORTUNATE ENOUGH to garden in mild areas, there are many exciting, often exotic-looking perennials that can be grown with little effort. Some of these will also survive in colder areas in a warm, sheltered site, especially in cities where favourable microclimates often occur. They can also be grown in containers and moved indoors for winter.

Erythrina crista-galli
COCK'S COMB
☼ ❄❄   ↕ 2m (6ft) ↔ 1.2m (4ft)

Herbaceous or woody-based in cold areas, this perennial forms a shrub or small tree in frost-free regions. Strong, thorny stems bear red pea-flowers in late summer. ♔

Begonia sutherlandii
TUBEROUS BEGONIA
☼ ❄   ↕↔ 45cm (18in)

In summer, low hummocks of fleshy red stems, with long-pointed, toothed leaves, freely bear drooping clusters of orange, red-stalked flowers. ♔

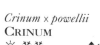

Bletilla striata 'Albostriata'
BLETILLA
☼ ☼ ❄   ↕↔ 60cm (24in)

A beautiful ground orchid, eventually forming patches of strongly veined, white-margined, bamboo-like leaves. Magenta flowers open in spring and early summer.

Crinum x *powellii*
CRINUM
☼ ❄❄❄   ↕ 1.2m (4ft) ↔ 60cm (24in)

Stout, fleshy stems carry loose umbels of fragrant, lily-like pink blooms above the bold clumps of long, arching, strap-shaped leaves from late summer to autumn. ♔

Eucomis comosa
PINEAPPLE FLOWER
☼ ❄❄❄   ↕ 60cm (24in) ↔ 30cm (12in)

Dense racemes of greenish white flowers, with leafy tufts at the top, rise on fleshy stems during late summer, above rosettes of strap-shaped, shiny green leaves.

Fascicularia bicolor
FASCICULARIA
☀ ❄   ↕ ↔ 60cm (24in)

A striking relative of the pineapple, with narrow, spine-toothed, evergreen leaves in bold rosettes. In summer, the inner leaves turn red when powdery blue flowers open.

OTHER HERBACEOUS PERENNIALS FOR WARM, SHELTERED SITES

Begonia grandis subsp. *evansiana*
Canna iridiflora
Commelina tuberosa Coelestis Group
Eucomis bicolor, see p.70
Gladiolus callianthus
Gladiolus cardinalis
Impatiens tinctoria
Leonotis ocymifolia
Lobelia tupa
Musa basjoo

Hedychium gardnerianum
GINGER LILY
☀ ❄❄❄   ↕ 2m (6ft) ↔ 1m (3ft)

This vigorous perennial forms a clump of erect, leafy stems that bear large heads of fragrant, pale yellow flowers, with long, red stamens; during late summer. ♔

Lobelia laxiflora var. *angustifolia*
LOBELIA
☀ ❄❄❄   ↕ 60cm (24in) ↔ 1m (3ft)

The erect, woody-based stems of this fast-spreading lobelia bear narrow, willow-like leaves, and lax, tubular, red and yellow flowers in late spring and early summer.

Melianthus major
HONEY BUSH
☀ ❄   ↕ 2m (6ft) ↔ 1m (3ft)

A spectacular foliage plant with a clump of hollow stems, large, lush, sharp-toothed and deeply divided, blue-grey leaves, and spikes of red-brown summer flowers. ♔

Ostrowskia magnifica
GIANT BELLFLOWER
☀ ❄❄❄❄   ↕ 1.2–1.5m (4–5ft) ↔ 45cm (18in)

The erect stems bear whorls of blue-green leaves and masses of big, outward-facing, white to pale blue bellflowers in summer. Requires a warm, well-drained site.

Puya alpestris
PUYA
☀ ❄❄❄   ↕ 1.5m (5ft) ↔ 1.4m (4½ft)

After several years, the evergreen rosette of narrow, spine-toothed leaves produces an erect stem topped by a striking, dense spike of waxy, blue-green summer blooms.

OTHER EVERGREEN PERENNIALS FOR WARM, SHELTERED SITES

Agapanthus praecox subsp. *orientalis*
Astelia chathamica
Beschorneria yuccoides
Dicksonia antarctica, see p.128
Eryngium proteiflorum
Geranium maderense
Ochagavia carnea
Puya chilensis, see p.126
Wachendorfia thyrsiflora
Watsonia beatricis

Senecio pulcher
SENECIO
☀ ❄❄❄   ↕ 60cm (24in) ↔ 50cm (20in)

The basal clumps of semi-evergreen, long, scalloped leaves are woolly when young. Attractive, large, carmine-purple, yellow-centred flowerheads emerge in summer.

SPECIFIC USES

WHETHER YOU WANT plants to fill a difficult site, to provide cut flowers or foliage, or to attract bees and butterflies to your garden, perennials have the variety and versatility to answer your needs. A good choice of plants is usually available to solve even the most specific garden problems.

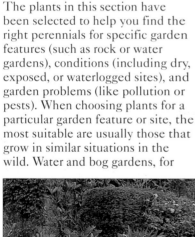

Houttuynia cordata 'Chameleon' for water gardens

△ LOVED BY BUTTERFLIES *The flowers of perennials like* Inula hookeri *attract bees, butterflies, and other welcome insects.*

The plants in this section have been selected to help you find the right perennials for specific garden features (such as rock or water gardens), conditions (including dry, exposed, or waterlogged sites), and garden problems (like pollution or pests). When choosing plants for a particular garden feature or site, the most suitable are usually those that grow in similar situations in the wild. Water and bog gardens, for instance, require plants that are naturally tolerant of wet soils. At the other extreme, rock gardens and screes are suited to perennials that thrive, if not depend, on sharp drainage. Similarly, coastal gardens in exposed sites require robust perennials like eryngiums that are adapted to the harsh conditions. Toughness and persistence are also needed by plants naturalized in grass, hedge bottoms, or other wild areas, where the ability to withstand competition is vital for survival.

PROBLEM SOLVERS

Perennials offer more than just a wide range of options for specific sites; they can also help us address some of the problems that often plague our gardens. Pests, such as snails, deer, and rabbits, may be thwarted by a surprising number of unpalatable plants. The garden can also be stocked with many low-allergen (mostly insect-pollinated) perennials, useful for gardeners who suffer from allergies that are aggravated or induced by plants.

DECORATIVE USES

The wide-ranging ornamental value of perennials is not always fully appreciated. Many are ideal for containers on a shady or sunny patio or paved area, or for specimen plants. Others have foliage and flowers good for cutting, extending their garden value into the home. During quiet periods in the garden, dried seed heads can provide the material for arrangements.

△ NATURAL EFFECT *Many perennials, especially bulbs like these fritillaries, are excellent for naturalizing in grassy sites.*

◁ ROCK GARDEN *Perennials from well-drained, rocky habitats in the wild will thrive in a rock garden, wall, or scree bed.*

▷ WATERSIDE *A pond planted with lush marginal and aquatic perennials makes a bold feature and a good wildlife habitat.*

Perennials for Ground Cover in Sun

GROUND COVER PLANTS, while ornamental, also perform one of the most useful and valuable jobs in the garden by clothing bare ground. They are usually fast-growing, and the following, given a sunny site, will repay your confidence in them by providing a superb display of foliage and flowers. For even faster results, plant these perennials in groups.

Helianthemum lunulatum
ROCK ROSE, SUN ROSE
☼ ❄❄❄   ↕ 15cm (6in) ↔ 30cm (12in)

A carpeting, woody-based perennial with evergreen, hairy, greyish green leaves, and clusters of yellow flowers with orange-yellow stamens in late spring and summer.

> **OTHER EVERGREEN PERENNIALS FOR GROUND COVER IN SUN**
>
> *Acaena saccaticupula* 'Blue Haze'
> *Arabis* x *arendsii* 'Rosabella'
> *Aubrieta* 'Joy'
> *Cerastium tomentosum*, see p.136
> *Geranium sanguineum* var. *striatum*
> *Erigeron glaucus*
> *Helianthemum* 'Rhodanthe Carneum'
> *Lamium maculatum* 'Album'
> *Persicaria affinis* 'Donald Lowndes'
> *Veronica umbrosa* 'Georgia Blue'

Ceratostigma plumbaginoides
HARDY PLUMBAGO
☼ ❄❄❄   ↕ 30cm (12in) ↔ 45cm (18in)

This creeping perennial eventually forms a dense patch of leafy reddish stems that turn red-orange in autumn. Clusters of rich blue flowers open in late summer. ♇

Diascia 'Salmon Supreme'
DIASCIA
☼ ❄❄❄   ↕ 15cm (6in) ↔ 50cm (20in)

Free-flowering over a long period during summer and autumn, the slender racemes of pale flowers rise above semi-evergreen mats of small, heart-shaped leaves.

Geranium 'Ann Folkard'
CRANESBILL
☼ ☼ ❄❄❄   ↕ 60cm (24in) ↔ 1.5m (5ft)

Few cranesbills will flower or scramble as freely as this one, with its dense blanket of deeply lobed, yellow-green leaves, and magenta flowers in summer and autumn. ♇

Persicaria vacciniifolia
PERSICARIA
☼ ☼ ❄❄❄   ↕ 15cm (6in) ↔ 30cm (12in)

This fast-creeping plant forms a carpet of small, glossy leaves that colour richly in autumn. Its erect, deep pink flower spikes open from late summer into autumn. ♇

OTHER HERBACEOUS PERENNIALS FOR GROUND COVER IN SUN

Alchemilla conjuncta, see p.84
Geranium malviflorum
Hippocrepis comosa
Hypsela reniformis
Oenothera macrocarpa, see p.107
Phuopsis stylosa
Potentilla aurea
Saponaria ocymoides
Scutellaria orientalis
Tropaeolum polyphyllum, see p.37

SPECIFIC USES

Phyla nodiflora
CAPEWEED, MATGRASS
☼ ✶✶✶ ↕ 5cm (2in) ↔ indefinite

Sometimes sold as *Lippia*, this perennial soons forms carpets of slender stems and small leaves. Its long-stalked clusters of tiny flowers open in summer and autumn.

Silene schafta
CAMPION
☼ ☼ ✶✶✶ ↕ 25cm (10in) ↔ 30cm (12in)

Slender stems and semi-evergreen, bright green leaves form a low mound, good for edging. Long-tubed, red-pink flowers are borne freely from summer to autumn. ♔

Rhodanthemum hosmariense
RHODANTHEMUM
☼ ✶✶ ↕↔ 30cm (12in)

A low and spreading, woody-based plant with dense, finely divided, silvery downy leaves. The large daisy-flowers are borne freely from early spring to autumn. ♔

Sedum spurium 'Schorbuser Blut'
STONECROP
☼ ✶✶✶ ↕ 10cm (4in) ↔ 60cm (24in)

Popular as a vigorous carpeter, this stonecrop has glossy, evergreen leaves that are purple-tinted when mature. Starry, deep pink flowers open in late summer. ♔

Stachys byzantina
LAMB'S EARS
☼ ✶✶✶ ↕ 38cm (15in) ↔ 60cm (24in)

The white-woolly leaves and prostrate stems provide effective, evergreen ground cover. White-woolly, pink-purple flower spikes rise above the foliage in summer.

Perennials for Ground Cover in Shade

SHADY AREAS CAN SUPPORT a wealth of plants, as long as the soil remains sufficiently moist. A number of shade-loving perennials are naturally creeping or otherwise spreading and low-growing, and are useful and attractive as ground cover beneath shrubs or trees. Many are also evergreen, and will brighten shady spots with their year-round carpets of foliage.

Cyclamen repandum subsp.
peloponnesiacum
☼ ☀ ❈❈❈   ↕ 10cm (4in) ↔ 15cm (6in)

A tuberous perennial that forms patches of scalloped, heart-shaped, silver-speckled leaves. In spring, it bears fragrant, pale pink flowers with dark mouths. ⚱

Ajuga reptans 'Jungle Beauty'
BUGLE
☼ ☼ ☀ ❈❈❈   ↕ 15cm (6in) ↔ 1m (3ft)

Grown here with *Lysimachia nummularia* 'Aurea', this semi-evergreen, far-creeping carpeter has shiny, bronze-green leaves, and rich blue flower spikes in late spring.

OTHER EVERGREEN PERENNIALS FOR GROUND COVER IN SHADE

Euphorbia amygdaloides var. *robbiae*,
  see p.40
Saxifraga 'Dentata'
Saxifraga rotundifolia
Saxifraga spathularis
Symphytum ibericum
Tiarella wherryi
Veronica umbrosa 'Georgia Blue'
Viola labradorica 'Purpurea'
Waldsteinia ternata

Duchesnea indica
INDIAN STRAWBERRY
☼ ☼ ☀ ❈❈❈   ↕ 10cm (4in) ↔ 1.2m (4ft)

The dense, fast-growing, evergreen carpet of strawberry-like leaves is peppered with yellow flowers in summer. The fruits resemble strawberries but are unpalatable.

Chrysogonum virginianum
CHRYSOGONUM   ☼ ☼ ☀
❈❈❈   ↕ 25cm (10in) ↔ 60cm (24in)

This fast-growing woodland plant forms dense carpets of small, semi-evergreen leaves. Bright and cheerful yellow flowers are produced during spring and summer.

Epimedium pinnatum subsp. *colchicum*
EPIMEDIUM
☼ ☼ ☀ ❈❈❈   ↕ ↔ 40cm (16in)

One of the most reliable epimediums, with clumps of evergreen, softly prickle-margined leaves, topped by loose spires of four-petalled yellow flowers in spring. ⚱

Tiarella cordifolia
FOAM FLOWER
☼ ☀ ❄❄❄ ↕ 25cm (10in) ↔ 30cm (12in)

A reliable old favourite, especially pretty
in late spring, when foamy spires of white
flowers rise above the evergreen foliage.
The leaves are often tinted in autumn. ♛

Geranium macrorrhizum 'Czakor'
CRANESBILL
☼ ☀ ❄❄❄ ↕ 30cm (12in) ↔ 60cm (24in)

A first rate carpeter, with prettily lobed,
aromatic, evergreen leaves, which become
purple-tinted in autumn. It bears profuse,
small magenta flowers in early summer.

Lamium galeobdolon 'Florentinum'
YELLOW ARCHANGEL
☼ ☀ ❄❄❄ ↕ 60cm (24in) ↔ 2m (6ft)

One of the most striking, but invasive,
ground-cover perennials. It has evergreen,
silver-zoned leaves, and spires of two-lipped
yellow flowers in summer. Keep it confined.

**OTHER HERBACEOUS PERENNIALS
FOR GROUND COVER IN SHADE**

Adiantum pedatum, see p.125
Aegopodium podagraria 'Variegatum'
Anemone nemorosa 'Flore Pleno'
Anemone nemorosa 'Robinsoniana'
Arisarum proboscideum
Convallaria majalis 'Fortin's Giant'
Cyclamen hederifolium, see p.102
Galium odoratum
Maianthemum bifolium
Trachystemon orientalis, see p.41

Gymnocarpium dryopteris
OAK FERN
☼ ☀ ❄❄❄❄^{PH} ↕ 20cm (8in) ↔ 30cm (12in)

Delicate looking but hardy, this little fern
forms a low patch of triangular, prettily
divided fronds on slender, wiry stems.
The fronds turn rich green with age. ♛

Meehania urticifolia
MEEHANIA
☼ ☀ ❄❄❄ ↕ 30cm (12in) ↔ 2m (6ft)

In time, this vigorous perennial forms
clumps of heart-shaped leaves. One-sided
spikes of two-lipped, deep violet flowers
are borne in late spring and early summer.

Vinca minor 'Gertrude Jekyll'
LESSER PERIWINKLE
☼ ☀ ❄❄❄ ↕ 15cm (6in) ↔ indefinite

Strictly a creeping shrub, but excellent
ground cover for use with perennials. The
pure white flowers in spring and summer
contrast with the dark green leaves. ♛

Perennial Herbs for Borders

PERENNIALS VALUED FOR either their culinary or medicinal attributes are frequently cultivated together in herb or kitchen gardens, or borders and beds. This certainly makes it much more convenient for picking or harvesting, but does not always make the best use of these plants' varied growth habits, or their often ornamental foliage and flowers. In fact, they can be grown just as easily, and more effectively, with other perennials in mixed plantings in the garden.

Achillea ptarmica 'Boule de Neige'
SNEEZEWORT
☼ ✳✳✳ ↕ 60cm (24in) ↔ 45cm (18in)

During summer, the clump of erect stems, with narrow, toothed, dark green leaves, is smothered in small, double white flower-heads. All parts have medicinal uses.

Allium schoenoprasum 'Forescate'
CHIVES
☼ ✳✳✳ ↕ 60cm (24in) ↔ 12.5cm (5in)

An attractive, vigorous form of a kitchen-garden favourite, with clumps of edible, hollow leaves, and dense heads of bright purplish pink flowers in summer.

Aristolochia clematitis
BIRTHWORT
☼ ☼ ✳✳✳ ↕ 90cm (36in) ↔ 60cm (24in)

Curious, slender-tubed yellow flowers emerge from the axils of the heart-shaped leaves in summer. The creeping rootstock forms clumps and patches of erect stems.

Agastache foeniculum
ANISE HYSSOP
☼ ✳✳✳ ↕ 90cm (36in) ↔ 45cm (18in)

Spikes of blue flowers with violet bracts top the four-angled stems in summer. The softly-downy, aniseed-scented leaves are used as a fragrant tea and in pot-pourri.

Althaea officinalis
MARSH MALLOW
☼ ☼ ✳✳✳ ↕ 2m (6ft) ↔ 1.5m (5ft)

Loose clumps of downy stems bear three-lobed, velvety, greyish leaves, and white or pale pink late-summer flowers. Its root sugars were once used for marshmallow.

OTHER PERENNIAL HERBS FOR BORDERS

Armoracia rusticana 'Variegata', see p.132
Cichorium intybus 'Roseum', see p.82
Foeniculum vulgare 'Purpureum', see p.125
Melittis melissophyllum, see p.79
Mentha suaveolens 'Variegata'
Meum athamanticum, see p.125
Monarda fistulosa
Origanum vulgare 'Gold Tip'
Persicaria bistorta
Pulmonaria officinalis
Salvia officinalis 'Icterina', see p.127
Saponaria officinalis 'Rosea Plena'
Scutellaria baicalensis
Symphytum peregrinum 'Rubrum'
Tanacetum balsamita subsp. *balsamitoides*

Melissa officinalis 'Aurea'
LEMON BALM

☀ ❄❄❄   ↕ 60cm (24in) ↔ 45cm (18in)

The hairy green, yellow-splashed leaves of this vigorous, bushy plant are lemon-scented when bruised. The tiny flowers, loved by bees, are borne in summer.

Myrrhis odorata
SWEET CICELY, WILD ANISEED

☀ ◐ ❄❄❄   ↕ 90cm (36in) ↔ 1.5m (5ft)

All parts of this plant are aniseed-scented. It has bold clumps of hollow stems, large, ferny leaves, and flattened heads of white summer flowers, followed by brown fruits.

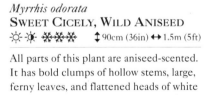

Rumex scutatus 'Silver Shield'
FRENCH SORREL

☀ ❄❄❄   ↕ 50cm (20in) ↔ 30cm (12in)

This small, woody-based perennial has prostrate and upright stems with broadly arrow-shaped, silver-green-topped leaves. Spires of green flowers open in summer.

Levisticum officinale
LOVAGE

☀ ❄❄❄   ↕ 2m (6ft) ↔ 1m (3ft)

Much-divided, dark green leaves clothe the bold, erect clumps of smooth, hollow stems. These are topped by umbels of greenish yellow flowers during summer.

Origanum vulgare 'Aureum'
GOLDEN WILD MARJORAM

☀ ❄❄❄   ↕ 45cm (18in) ↔ 30cm (12in)

The dense clumps of four-angled stems, crowded with rounded, aromatic golden leaves, bear dense clusters of pink flowers from summer into autumn. ♈

Salvia officinalis 'Tricolor'
COMMON SAGE

☀ ❄❄❄   ↕ 80cm (32in) ↔ 1m (3ft)

A woody-based, evergreen perennial or bushy subshrub, bearing aromatic, woolly, greyish leaves with cream, purple, and pink zones. It has blue flowers in summer. ♈

Perennials for Hedge Bottoms and Wild Margins

MANY OF THE LOVELIEST WILD FLOWERS are frequently found thriving beside roads or at the bases of hedges. They provide some of the most colourful displays in rural areas, and there is no reason why similar effects should not be created within our gardens, making use of perennials that can tolerate competition from other plants in the same way.

Heliopsis helianthoides var. *scabra* 'Sommersonne'

☼ ❄❄❄ ↕ 90cm (36in) ↔ 60cm (24in)

The bold clumps of leafy, branched stems carry large, single to semi-double, golden yellow daisy-heads, with brownish yellow centres, from late summer to autumn.

Anemone x *hybrida* 'Königin Charlotte'
JAPANESE ANEMONE

☼ ☼ ❄❄❄ ↕ 1.5m (5ft) ↔ indefinite

A vigorous perennial forming colonies of branched stems with handsome, grey-green leaves. Big, semi-double pink flowers open in late summer and autumn. ▽

Carex pendula
PENDULOUS SEDGE

☼ ☼ ❄❄❄ ↕ 1.2m (4ft) ↔ 1.5m (5ft)

Arching, three-cornered stems and dark green leaves form large clumps, topped in late spring and summer by long, pendent green flower spikes. Prefers moist shade.

Lathyrus latifolius
PERENNIAL PEA

☼ ❄❄❄ ↕ ↔ 2m (6ft)

From summer to autumn, this vigorous, herbaceous climber produces long-stalked racemes of pink or purple pea-flowers on long, scrambling, winged stems. ▽

Campanula latifolia
GIANT BELLFLOWER

☼ ☼ ❄❄❄ ↕ 1.5m (5ft) ↔ 60cm (24in)

In summer, the stout clumps of vigorous, erect, leafy stems produce large, tubular, pale to deep violet or white bell-flowers from the axils of the uppermost leaves.

Helianthus x *multiflorus*
PERENNIAL SUNFLOWER

☼ ❄❄❄ ↕ 2m (6ft) ↔ 90cm (36in)

Dark green leaves clothe the tall clumps of branching stems, which produce yellow, dark-centred daisy-heads in late summer and autumn. It prefers a moist site.

OTHER EVERGREEN PERENNIALS FOR WILD AREAS

Epimedium x *perralchicum*
Epimedium pinnatum subsp. *colchicum*, see p.52
Euphorbia amygdaloides var. *robbiae*, see p.40
Iris foetidissima var. *citrina*, see p.41
Luzula sylvatica
Polystichum setiferum, see p.148
Vinca major
Vinca major 'Variegata', see p.133

Lysimachia punctata
LOOSESTRIFE
☼ ☀ ❋❋❋   ↕ 1m (3ft) ↔ 60cm (24in)

A reliable, robust perennial with clumps of leafy, erect stems. In summer, the leaf axils are crowded with cup-shaped yellow flowers. Too invasive for beds or borders.

OTHER HERBACEOUS PERENNIALS FOR WILD AREAS

Campanula rapunculoides
Campanula trachelium
Cicerbita plumieri
Dryopteris filix-mas
Leucanthemum × superbum
Myrrhis odorata, see p.55
Pentaglottis sempervirens, see p.81
Persicaria amplexicaulis
Salvia glutinosa
Symphytum caucasicum

Saponaria officinalis 'Rubra Plena'
SOAPWORT
☼ ❋❋❋   ↕ ↔ 90cm (36in)

The creeping rootstock of this reliable, easily grown plant forms patches of leafy stems, crowned in summer with clusters of fragrant, double, rose-pink flowers.

Rumex sanguineus
BLOODY DOCK
☼ ❋❋❋   ↕ 90cm (36in) ↔ 30cm (12in)

This tap-rooted dock is valued mainly for its rosetted, red- or purple-veined leaves. In autumn, erect stems first bear clusters of tiny green flowers, then brown fruits.

Symphytum orientale
WHITE COMFREY   ☼ ☼ ☀
❋❋❋   ↕ 70cm (28in) ↔ 45cm (18in)

Nodding clusters of funnel-shaped white flowers open on the erect, little-branched stems of this hairy plant in late spring and early summer. It tolerates dry shade. ♛

Vinca major subsp. *hirsuta*
GREATER PERIWINKLE
☼ ☼ ❋❋❋   ↕ 45cm (18in) ↔ indefinite

This vigorous, scrambling or creeping, evergreen perennial or subshrub produces narrow-lobed violet flowers as new shoots emerge in spring, and into summer.

Bulbs for Naturalizing

T HERE ARE FEW SIGHTS in the plant world more inspiring than a meadow, woodland floor, or alpine pasture studded with wild flowers, creating a carpet of colour as far as the eye can see. Bulbs especially lend themselves to such displays and, where space permits in the garden, there is a multitude of species and varieties that can be used for this purpose. For a natural effect, plant bulbs in scattered groups, with space between to allow for expansion or self-seeding.

Anemone pavonina
ANEMONE
☼ ❄❄❄   ↕ 25cm (10in) ↔ 15cm (6in)

This feathery-leaved anemone is ideal for sunny, well-drained sites in short grass or borders. Glowing red flowers with a white ring and dark eye are spectacular in spring.

Crocus vernus 'Jeanne d'Arc'
DUTCH CROCUS
☼ ❄❄❄   ↕ 12cm (5in) ↔ 5cm (2in)

Attractive and reliable, this large-flowered crocus soon forms clumps or patches in short grass or borders. White flowers with orange stigmas are produced in spring.

Erythronium dens-canis
DOG'S-TOOTH VIOLET
☼ ☼ ❄❄❄   ↕ 15cm (6in) ↔ 10cm (4in)

The exquisite, pinkish purple flowers are poised above rosettes of fleshy, beautifully mottled leaves in spring. Excellent for use in short grass and in woodland. ♗

Fritillaria meleagris
SNAKE'S HEAD FRITILLARY
☼ ☼ ❄❄❄   ↕ 30cm (12in) ↔ 8cm (3in)

A uniquely charming bulb, with narrow, greyish leaves, and nodding, chequered bell-flowers on slender stems in spring. It thrives in moist grass or beneath shrubs. ♗

Camassia leichtlinii
CAMASSIA
☼ ☼ ❄❄   ↕ 1.3m (4½ft) ↔ 10cm (4in)

An easily grown bulb, suitable for moist meadows or grassy sites. Long spires of star-shaped, blue or cream flowers rise in summer above the slender leaves. ♗

OTHER BULBS OR TUBERS FOR NATURALIZING IN SHADE

Anemone nemorosa 'Atrocaerulea'
Arisarum proboscideum
Arum italicum 'Marmoratum', see p.141
Colchicum speciosum
Crocus kotschyanus
Crocus tommasinianus, see p.104
Cyclamen coum
Cyclamen hederifolium, see p.102
Cyclamen repandum
Eranthis hyemalis, see p.104
Erythronium oregonum
Galanthus elwesii, see p.45
Hyacinthoides non-scripta
Lilium pyrenaicum
Narcissus 'Golden Harvest'
Narcissus 'Mount Hood', see p.91
Ornithogalum nutans
Scilla bithynica

Galanthus nivalis
COMMON SNOWDROP
☼ ❄❄❄   ↕ ↔ 10cm (4in)

Large drifts of this familiar woodland snowdrop are spectacular in early spring. It naturalizes readily by seed and division, and will tolerate sun if the soil is moist. ♗

Nectaroscordum siculum
NECTAROSCORDUM
☼ ☼ ❋❋❋   ↕ 1.2m (4ft) ↔ 10cm (4in)

In summer, tall, strong stems sport loose
umbels of drooping green bell-flowers,
flushed with purple. The straw-coloured
seed capsules are equally ornamental.

Tulipa sylvestris
TULIP
☼ ❋❋❋   ↕ 45cm (18in) ↔ 10cm (4in)

This tulip is easily established in grass-
land or in open woodland, where it forms
patches. Star-shaped yellow flowers open
in spring, but are not always freely borne.

Hyacinthoides hispanica
SPANISH BLUEBELL
☼ ☼ ❋❋❋   ↕ 40cm (16in) ↔ 10cm (4in)

This robust bulb forms large patches of
shiny green leaves, with nodding blue
flowers borne on strong stems in spring.
It may be too vigorous for a small garden.

Lilium martagon
MARTAGON LILY
☼ ☼ ❋❋❋   ↕ 2m (6ft) ↔ 25cm (10in)

An old and reliable lily for naturalizing in
grass or in a border. The tall stems bear
whorled leaves, and panicles of nodding
flowers in a variety of colours in summer.

Narcissus bulbocodium
HOOP-PETTICOAT DAFFODIL
☼ ❋❋❋   ↕ 15cm (6in) ↔ 8cm (3in)

A real charmer with its narrow, thread-like
leaves, and striking, funnel-shaped, pale
yellow spring flowers. It will thrive and seed
itself on a moist, grassy, sloping site. ♔

**OTHER BULBS OR TUBERS FOR
NATURALIZING IN SUN**

Allium flavum
Allium unifolium
Anemone coronaria
Camassia quamash
Chionodoxa luciliae, see p.96
Colchicum autumnale
Gladiolus communis subsp. *byzantinus*,
  see p.39
Gladiolus papilio
Lilium duchartrei
Lilium hansonii
Lilium pardalinum
Narcissus obvallaris
Nectaroscordum siculum subsp.
  bulgaricum
Tulipa kaufmanniana
Zantedeschia aethiopica 'Crowborough',
  see p.67

Perennials for Rock Gardens and Screes

S OME OF THE LOVELIEST and most satisfying flowering perennials are those suitable for growing on rock gardens and screes. Many of these plants have a carpeting habit and will provide excellent ground cover in the garden. Others form small clumps or low hummocks, and associate well with miniature bulbs, such as chionodoxas, crocuses, and scillas.

Dianthus 'Pike's Pink'
ALPINE PINK
☼ ❄❄❄   ↕15cm (6in) ↔ 20cm (8in)

The low, evergreen cushion of narrow, blue-grey leaves is topped in summer by double pale pink flowers, darker zoned in cerise, and with a delicious clove scent. ♛

OTHER PERENNIALS FOR ROCK
GARDENS AND SCREES

Anthemis marschalliana
Armeria juniperifolia
Euphorbia myrsinites
Gentiana acaulis
Geranium argenteum
Hypericum olympicum 'Sulphureum'
Iris pumila
Linaria alpina
Phlox subulata 'Amazing Grace'
Potentilla nitida

Aethionema 'Warley Rose'
STONE CRESS
☼ ❄❄❄   ↕↔20cm (8in)

A long-established favourite, forming an evergreen hummock of slender stems with narrow, blue-grey leaves. Its pink flowers open in late spring and early summer. ♛

Anthyllis montana
ANTHYLLIS
☼ ❄❄❄   ↕30cm (12in) ↔ 60cm (24in)

In summer, the dense carpet of deeply divided, silky, grey-green leaves is covered with rounded, clover-like heads of pink to purple, white-tipped flowers.

Anemone sylvestris
SNOWDROP ANEMONE
☼ ◐ ❄❄❄   ↕↔30cm (12in)

This low-grower forms patches of deeply cut, ferny leaves. Pure white flowers with gold stamens appear in spring and early summer, followed by silky seed heads.

Campanula carpatica 'Chewton Joy'
BELLFLOWER
☼ ◐ ❄❄❄❄   ↕30cm (12in) ↔ 50cm (20in)

The low, trailing stems are clothed with toothed, heart-shaped leaves, and bear upturned blue bell-flowers with paler centres over several months in summer.

Diascia barberae 'Blackthorn Apricot'
DIASCIA
☼ ❄❄   ↕25cm (10in) ↔ 50cm (20in)

This is a gem among the numerous diascias. In summer, it bears abundant, slender racemes of apricot flowers above the mat of trailing green stems. ♛

OTHER PERENNIALS FOR ROCK
GARDENS WITH LIME-FREE SOIL

Celmisia spectabilis
Dodecatheon meadia f. *album*, see p.30
Houstonia michauxii
Lewisia cotyledon hybrids, see p.65
Lithodora diffusa 'Heavenly Blue'
Oxalis enneaphylla
Phlox adsurgens 'Wagon Wheel'
Phlox x *procumbens* 'Millstream'
Potentilla aurea
Tanakaea radicans

Gentiana sino-ornata
AUTUMN GENTIAN
☼ ☀ ❄❄❄❄**PH**❄ ↕ 7cm (3in) ↔ 30cm (12in)

One of the most famous and spectacular
autumn-flowering gentians, with an overwintering mat of trailing, leafy stems and
upturned, deep blue trumpet flowers. ♈

Gypsophila repens 'Rosa Schönheit'
ALPINE GYPSOPHILA
☼ ❄❄❄ ↕ 20cm (8in) ↔ 50cm (20in)

Also known as 'Pink Beauty', as the semi-
evergreen mat of slender, bluish green
stems and leaves is smothered for many
weeks in summer by tiny pink flowers.

Geranium cinereum 'Ballerina'
CRANESBILL
☼ ☀ ❄❄❄ ↕ 15cm (6in) ↔ 30cm (12in)

A neat little perennial, producing a loose
hummock of small, grey-green leaves, and
purplish red flowers with dark veins and
eyes over a long period in summer. ♈

Oxalis adenophylla
ALPINE OXALIS
☼ ❄❄❄ ↕ 10cm (4in) ↔ 15cm (6in)

The tuft of deeply divided, greyish green
leaves is accompanied during spring by
funnel-shaped, purplish pink flowers with
pale centres and dark throats. ♈

Roscoea cautleoides 'Kew Beauty'
ROSCOEA
☼ ☀ ❄❄❄ ↕ 40cm (16in) ↔ 15cm (6in)

Appearing in late spring, this gorgeous
perennial produces a small clump of erect,
leafy stems, which bear loose spikes of
large, pale yellow, orchid-like flowers. ♈

Bulbs for Rock Gardens and Screes

ROCK GARDENS, RAISED BEDS, AND SCREES are ideal sites for cultivating the many miniature bulbs available for the garden, as well as for larger bulbous plants, such as *Eucomis*, which like well-drained, gritty soil and full sun. Most of the following are hardy, and should be planted in groups or drifts for best effect. They are also suitable for containers.

Eucomis autumnalis
EUCOMIS
☼ ✻✻✻ ↕ 30cm (12in) ↔ 20cm (8in)

Fleshy stems bear crowded, green-white flower spikes in late summer and autumn, above bold clumps of broad, wavy-edged leaves. It likes a sheltered site. ♔

Allium insubricum
ORNAMENTAL ONION
☼ ✻✻✻ ↕ 30cm (12in) ↔ 5cm (2in)

This choice species forms a small clump of grass-like, grey-green leaves. Clusters of nodding, red-purple or pale pink bell-flowers open on upright stems in summer.

Colchicum agrippinum
AUTUMN CROCUS
☼ ✻✻✻ ↕ 12cm (5in) ↔ 10cm (4in)

A vigorous and unusual crocus producing its strap-shaped, glossy green leaves in spring. The deep purple-pink, heavily tessellated flowers appear in autumn. ♔

Fritillaria pallidiflora
FRITILLARIA
☼ ✻✻✻ ↕ 40cm (16in) ↔ 7.5cm (3in)

During late spring and early summer, this handsome bulb bears nodding, creamy yellow bell-flowers from the axils of long, narrow, bloomy grey-green leaves. ♔

Chionodoxa forbesii
SNOW GLORY
☼ ✻✻✻ ↕ 20cm (8in) ↔ 10cm (4in)

A free-flowering, reliable bulb, forming small tufts of narrow green leaves. In early spring, it produces loose clusters of lovely star-shaped blue flowers with white eyes.

Crocus cartwrightianus 'E.A. Bowles'
CROCUS
☼ ✻✻✻ ↕ 7cm (3in) ↔ 5cm (2in)

This popular, spring-flowering crocus has slender green leaves, and lemon-yellow flowers, each with a bronze-green base and purple feathering on the outside. ♔

OTHER BULBS FOR SCREES AND ROCK GARDENS

Arum creticum, see p.38
Crocus corsicus
Eucomis bicolor, see p.70
Iris bucharica
Iris magnifica
Ornithogalum arabicum
Scilla peruviana, see p.39
Tulipa kaufmanniana
Tulipa humilis Violacea Group
Urginea maritima

OTHER MINIATURE BULBS FOR
SCREES AND ROCK GARDENS

Allium mairei
Allium oreophilum
Anomatheca laxa, see p.38
Crocus biflorus
Crocus cartwrightianus 'Zwanenburg
   Bronze'
Iris 'Joyce'
Iris 'Katharine Hodgkin'
Muscari comosum
Narcissus triandrus

SPECIFIC USES

Iris danfordiae
MINIATURE IRIS

☼ ❄❄❄   ↕ 10cm (4in) ↔ 5cm (2in)

One of the most beautiful early bulbs, this
miniature iris has slim, four-angled leaves
and bears yellow flowers marked with
greenish yellow in late winter and spring.

Scilla bifolia
SCILLA

☼ ❄❄❄   ↕ 15cm (6in) ↔ 5cm (2in)

An easily grown bulb, which will increase
rapidly. It bears two narrow green leaves,
and loose sprays of star-shaped, blue to
purple-blue flowers in early spring. ♛

Narcissus minor
MINIATURE DAFFODIL

☼ ❄❄❄   ↕ 12.5cm (5in) ↔ 7.5cm (3in)

This little daffodil forms tufts or patches
of narrow, grey-green leaves. Its prettily
inclined, small yellow trumpet-flowers are
borne above the foliage in early spring. ♛

Puschkinia scilloides
PUSCHKINIA

☼ ❄❄❄   ↕ 15cm (6in) ↔ 7.5cm (3in)

Cheerful and reliable, this perennial soon
forms a small clump of slender leaves,
accompanied in spring by clusters of very
pale blue flowers with darker blue stripes.

Tulipa aucheriana
TULIP

☼ ❄❄❄   ↕ 25cm (10in) ↔ 15cm (6in)

Starry pink flowers, with yellow centres
and stamens, are borne singly or in twos or
threes during spring. The narrow, bloomy
green leaves are also attractive. ♛

Perennials for Wall or Rock Crevices and Paving

Rock CREVICES, especially in mountain areas, are the favoured habitat of a range of attractive perennials, which often have trailing or carpeting stems, or form small rosettes or hummocks. In the garden, these plants can be grown in the cracks of a dry stone wall, or between paving slabs, where they will get the good drainage they need.

Asarina procumbens
ASARINA
☼ ☼ ❈❈   ↕ 5cm (2in) ↔ 60cm (24in)

This free-growing evergreen has trailing, hairy stems. In summer, it produces pale yellow, snapdragon flowers from the axils of its kidney-shaped, grey-green leaves.

Aurinia saxatilis 'Dudley Nevill'
GOLD DUST
☼ ❈❈❈   ↕ 20cm (8in) ↔ 30cm (12in)

A popular, clump-forming, woody-based plant with evergreen, grey-green leaves, and clusters of tiny, soft yellow-buff flowers from late spring to early summer.

Convolvulus sabatius
CONVOLVULUS
☼ ❈❈   ↕ 15cm (6in) ↔ 60cm (24in)

The trailing, leafy stems of this carpeting, fast-growing perennial are studded with pale to deep lavender-blue flowers over many weeks in summer and autumn. ♔

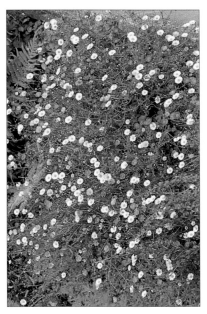

Erigeron karvinskianus
MEXICAN FLEABANE
☼ ❈❈❈   ↕ 30cm (12in) ↔ 1m (3ft)

In summer, a succession of little white daisies, which fade to pink then purple, smother this charming plant's loose, airy clump of slender, branching stems. ♔

Aubrieta 'J.S. Baker'
AUBRETIA
☼ ❈❈❈   ↕ 5cm (2in) ↔ 60cm (24in)

Aubretias are among the most colourful and reliable evergreen perennials for walls or rock-work. This one is smothered with purple, white-eyed flowers during spring.

Campanula carpatica 'Jewel'
BELLFLOWER
☼ ☼ ❈❈❈   ↕ 10cm (4in) ↔ 45cm (18in)

The small, dense, heart-shaped leaves of this popular and attractive, compact bell-flower are almost hidden by its upturned, bright purple-blue blooms in summer.

OTHER HERBACEOUS PERENNIALS FOR CREVICES AND PAVING

Anthemis marschalliana
Erinus alpinus
Erodium chrysanthum
Hypericum cerastioides
Incarvillea arguta
Origanum rotundifolium
Persicaria vacciniifolia, see p.50
Saponaria 'Bressingham'
Zauschneria californica susbp. *nana* 'Dublin', see p.37

Gypsophila repens 'Dorothy Teacher'
GYPSOPHILA
☼ ❋❋❋ ‡ 5cm (2in) ↔ 40cm (16in)

Slender, crowded stems carpet the ground
with small, narrow, semi-evergreen blue-
green leaves. The tiny, pale pink flowers,
borne in summer, darken with age. ♔

> **OTHER EVERGREEN PERENNIALS**
> **FOR CREVICES AND PAVING**
>
> *Arabis* x *arendsii* 'Rosabella'
> *Corydalis lutea*, see p.88
> *Dianthus gratianopolitanus*
> *Erigeron glaucus*
> *Euphorbia myrsinites*
> *Lithodora diffusa* 'Heavenly Blue'
> *Onosma alborosea*
> *Phlox subulata*
> *Ramonda myconi*
> *Sempervivum* 'Othello'

Helianthemum 'Wisley White'
ROCK ROSE
☼ ❋❋❋ ‡ 25cm (10in) ↔ 45cm (18in)

This woody-based, evergreen perennial,
or wide-spreading shrublet, bears creamy
white, yellow-centred flowers over a long
period from late spring into midsummer.

Saxifraga 'Southside Seedling'
SAXIFRAGE
☼ ☼ ❋❋❋ ‡ 30cm (12in) ↔ 20cm (8in)

The bold, arching sprays of red spotted
white flowers are a fine sight in late spring
and early summer above the rosette of
evergreen leaves. Also good in a trough. ♔

Haberlea rhodopensis 'Virginalis'
HABERLEA ☼ ☼
❋❋❋❋ PH ‡ 15cm (6in) ↔ 25cm (10in)

Loose umbels of funnel-shaped white
flowers top the dense, evergreen clump of
hairy, coarse-toothed leaves in late spring
and summer. Charming for a shady wall.

Lewisia cotyledon hybrids
LEWISIA ☼ ☼
❋❋❋❋ PH ‡ 25cm (10in) ↔ 30cm (12in)

In late spring and early summer, loose
heads of magenta-pink, yellow, or orange
flowers rise above the rosette or clump of
thick, wavy-margined, evergreen leaves.

Verbascum dumulosum
MULLEIN
☼ ❋❋❋ ‡ 25cm (10in) ↔ 40cm (16in)

An evergreen, woody-based perennial, or
low subshrub, with downy, grey-green
stems and leaves. Its rich yellow flowers
are borne in late spring and summer. ♔

Perennials for Bog Gardens and Waterside Areas

A WEALTH OF ORNAMENTAL PERENNIALS are available for those fortunate enough to have water in their garden, even if it is only a wet, muddy depression. These plants rely on a constant supply of moisture for top performance, and include perennials with large or colourful flowers, as well as those with bold or even spectacular foliage.

Iris laevigata
IRIS

☼ ☀ ❄❄❄   ↕ 80cm (32in) ↔ 20cm (8in)

This famous iris from Japan has erect, grey-green leaves and single purple, blue, or white flowers borne in summer. It will grow in shallow water. ♔

OTHER FOLIAGE PERENNIALS FOR BOG & WATERSIDE GARDENS

Astilbe rivularis
Carex elata 'Aurea', see p.134
Gunnera manicata
Hosta 'Big Daddy', see p.129
Hosta 'Frances Williams'
Houttuynia cordata 'Chameleon', see p.68
Iris pseudacorus 'Variegata', see p.122
Matteuccia struthiopteris, see p.71
Petasites japonicus var. *giganteus*
Rodgersia podophylla

Astilbe chinensis 'Purpurlanze'
ASTILBE

☼ ☀ ❄❄❄   ↕ 1.2m (4ft) ↔ 90cm (36in)

The English name 'Purple Lance' aptly describes the stiff, purple-pink flower panicles of this late-flowering astilbe. Its deeply divided leaves form bold clumps.

Filipendula palmata 'Rubra'
FILIPENDULA

☼ ❄❄❄   ↕ 1.2m (4ft) ↔ 60cm (24in)

Sometimes confused with *F. rubra*, this stately, clump-forming perennial produces boldly lobed or divided leaves and dense plumes of tiny, rose-red summer flowers.

Darmera peltata
UMBRELLA PLANT

☼ ☀ ❄❄❄   ↕ 1.1m (3½ft) ↔ 75cm (30in)

This handsome perennial has creeping rhizomes that form a large patch of long-stalked leaves, colouring richly in autumn. Pink flowerheads are borne in spring. ♔

Hosta 'Zounds'
PLANTAIN LILY

☼ ☀ ❄❄❄   ↕ 55cm (22in) ↔ 1m (3ft)

Striking and relatively slug-proof, this hosta forms a big clump of boldly veined and dimpled, rounded leaves. In summer, the greenish yellow foliage ages to yellow.

Lysichiton americanus
YELLOW SKUNK CABBAGE

☼ ☀ ❄❄❄   ↕ 1m (3ft) ↔ 1.2m (4ft)

This has to be one of the most spectacular and easily recognized plants. It bears large yellow flowers in spring, followed by huge clumps of paddle-shaped leaves. ♔

Oenanthe javanica 'Flamingo'
WATER DROPWORT
☼ ☀ ✳✳✳   ↕ 40cm (16in) ↔ 90cm (36in)

The deeply cut, green and white leaves of this creeping, fleshy-stemmed perennial become pink flushed in autumn. Small white flowerheads emerge in late summer.

Osmunda regalis
ROYAL FERN
☼ ☀ ✳✳✳   ↕ 1.5m (5ft) ↔ 1.2m (4ft)

An impressive fern, forming a bold clump of deeply divided fronds that often colour richly in autumn before dying. It produces spikes of red-brown spores in summer. ♈

Primula prolifera
CANDELABRA PRIMULA
☼ ☀ ✳✳✳   ↕ 60cm (24in) ↔ 15cm (6in)

In early summer, slender, erect stems with many whorls of yellow flowers rise above the basal rosettes of deep green leaves. It is excellent for planting in drifts. ♈

Rheum palmatum 'Bowles' Crimson'
ORNAMENTAL RHUBARB
☼ ☀ ✳✳✳   ↕ 2.5m (8ft) ↔ 1.8m (6ft)

The big, jaggedly lobed leaves of this spectacular perennial emerge crimson and form a giant clump. Statuesque panicles of red flowers are produced in early summer.

Rodgersia pinnata
RODGERSIA
☼ ☀ ✳✳✳   ↕ 1.2m (4ft) ↔ 75cm (30in)

Superb for both foliage and flowers, with its deeply divided, veined leaves, tinted red in autumn and spring, and its frothy white flower plumes borne in summer.

OTHER FLOWERING PERENNIALS FOR BOG & WATERSIDE GARDENS
Eupatorium purpureum 'Atropurpureum', see p.24
Euphorbia palustris
Filipendula purpurea, see p.128
Iris ensata
Ligularia japonica
Lysichiton camtschatcensis
Lythrum salicaria 'Blush'
Mimulus cardinalis
Primula pulverulenta

Zantedeschia aethiopica 'Crowborough'
EASTER LILY
☼ ☀ ✳✳✳   ↕ 90cm (36in) ↔ 60cm (24in)

Also called Lily of the Nile, this handsome perennial has large, arrow-shaped leaves, and beautiful, long-stalked white flowers in summer. It will grow in shallow water. ♈

Aquatic Perennials

THERE ARE VERY FEW RICHER, or more ornamental, wildlife habitats in the garden than in and around a well-planted pond or pool. Aquatic perennials will attract a varied fauna, and although large ponds offer the most scope for planting, water can be introduced into even the smallest backyard or town garden using containers. The planting depths below indicate the depth of water required; plant heights are from water level.

Nymphaea 'Fire Crest'
WATER LILY
☀ ❋❋❋   ↕ 7.5cm (3in) ↔ 1.2m (4ft)

This water lily's rounded, floating leaves are purple when young. Its fragrant pink flowers open in summer. Ideal for a small pond. Plant 15–45cm (6–18in) deep.

Aponogeton distachyos
WATER HAWTHORN
☀ ◐ ❋❋❋   ↕ 7.5cm (3in) ↔ 1.2m (4ft)

In spring and autumn, deliciously vanilla-scented white flower spikes rise above the floating, semi-evergreen, oblong leaves. Plant in water 30–60cm (12–24in) deep.

Houttuynia cordata 'Chameleon'
HOUTTUYNIA
☀ ◐ ❋❋❋   ↕ 30cm (12in) ↔ indefinite

A low-spreading, marginal aquatic plant for water to 10cm (4in) deep, or moist soil. The orange-peel-scented leaves have pale yellow, green, and red variegation.

Nymphaea 'Gladstoneana'
WATER LILY
☀ ❋❋❋   ↕ 7.5cm (3in) ↔ 2.4m (8ft)

This popular, vigorous water lily has starry white flowers in summer, and rounded, wavy-edged, floating leaves, bronze when young. Plant 45–90cm (18–36in) deep. ♧

Butomus umbellatus
FLOWERING RUSH
☀ ❋❋❋   ↕ 1.2m (4ft) ↔ 45cm (18in)

A robust plant for pond margins, forming a patch of long, three-cornered leaves. Tall stems bear umbels of rose-pink flowers in summer. Plant 7–13cm (3–5in) deep. ♧

Nymphaea 'Marliacea Chromatella'
WATER LILY
☀ ❋❋❋   ↕ 7.5cm (3in) ↔ 1.5m (5ft)

Free-flowering and vigorous, this reliable plant has beautiful, canary-yellow flowers in summer, and bronze-splashed floating leaves. Plant 45–90cm (18–36in) deep. ♧

Nymphoides peltata
WATER FRINGE
☀ ❋❋❋   ↕ 7.5cm (3in) ↔ indefinite

Ideal for a large pond, this fast-spreader has rounded, floating leaves, and golden, funnel-shaped, fringe-petalled flowers in summer. Plant 30–60cm (12–24in) deep.

Orontium aquaticum
GOLDEN CLUB
☼ ✻✻✻　↕ 30cm (12in) ↔ 60cm (24in)

A vigorous marginal aquatic with oblong, blue-green leaves, and curved white stalks bearing yellow flower spikes from summer to autumn. Plant 30–40cm (12–16in) deep.

Pontederia cordata
PICKEREL WEED
☼ ✻✻　↕ 75cm (30in) ↔ 60cm (24in)

During late summer, dense spikes of blue flowers poke through the clumps of erect, glossy leaves. Plant this vigorous marginal aquatic 7–13cm (3–5in) deep. ⚱

Sagittaria latifolia
DUCK POTATO
☼ ✻✻✻　↕↔ 90cm (36in)

A tuberous marginal aquatic with slender, triangular stems and arrow-shaped, long-stalked leaves. In summer, whorls of white flowers open. Plant 7–13cm (3–5in) deep.

Stratiotes aloides
WATER SOLDIER
☼ ✻✻✻　↕ 15cm (6in) ↔ 20cm (8in)

Pineapple-like rosettes of saw-toothed leaves rise to the water surface in summer, as the erect, three-petalled white flowers are borne. Plant 30–90cm (12–36in) deep.

OTHER AQUATIC PERENNIALS

Acorus gramineus
Alisma plantago-aquatica
Calla palustris
Cyperus eragrostis
Hottonia palustris
Hydrocharis morsus-ranae
Iris laevigata, see p.66
Menyanthes trifoliata
Mimulus ringens
Myriophyllum verticillatum
Nuphar lutea
Nymphaea 'Escarboucle'
Nymphaea 'Gonnère'
Nymphaea 'James Brydon'
Peltandra sagittifolia
Ranunculus aquatilis
Utricularia vulgaris
Zantedeschia aethiopica 'Crowborough', see p.67

Typha minima
SMALL REEDMACE
☼ ✻✻✻　↕ 75cm (30in) ↔ 45cm (18in)

A rush-like marginal aquatic with slender leaves. The stems of brown flowerheads in summer turn into fluffy seed heads in winter. Plant 5–10cm (2–4in) deep.

Perennials for Containers in Sun

ONE OF THE MAIN ADVANTAGES of growing perennials in containers is that they can easily be moved around the garden or patio, just like furniture inside the house. Containers also allow less hardy plants, like some of the sun-lovers below, to be grown outdoors for summer effect, then moved under cover for protection in winter.

Osteospermum 'Silver Sparkler'
OSTEOSPERMUM
☼ ❄   ↕ 60cm (24in) ↔ 45cm (18in)

This vigorous, bushy plant has cream-margined leaves. Dark shoots bear long-stalked white daisy-flowers, darker on the reverse, from summer into autumn. ♛

Agapanthus 'Loch Hope'
AFRICAN LILY
☼ ❄❄❄   ↕ 1.2m (4ft) ↔ 60cm (24in)

This bold, clump-forming lily is hardy outside in all but the coldest areas. Deep blue trumpet-flowers are carried in loose heads from late summer into autumn. ♛

Canna 'Assaut'
INDIAN SHOT
☼ ❄   ↕ 1.5m (5ft) ↔ 50cm (20in)

A striking perennial with bold, purple-brown leaves and stout, erect, leafy stems that bear heads of gladiolus-like, orange-scarlet flowers in summer and autumn.

OTHER PERENNIALS FOR CONTAINERS IN SUN

Agapanthus praecox subsp. *orientalis*
Agave americana 'Variegata'
Argyranthemum 'Vancouver'
Begonia sutherlandii, see p.46
Bidens ferulifolia
Francoa sonchifolia, see p.33
Hedychium gardnerianum, see p.47
Lotus berthelotii
Rehmannia elata
Salvia gesneriiflora

Argyranthemum 'Jamaica Primrose'
ARGYRANTHEMUM
☼ ❄   ↕ ↔ 1m (3ft)

A bushy evergreen with slender stems and fine-cut, grey-green leaves. Long-stalked, primrose-yellow daisies are borne over a long period from spring into autumn. ♛

Eucomis bicolor
PINEAPPLE FLOWER
☼ ❄❄❄   ↕ 45cm (18in) ↔ 30cm (12in)

The dense, beautiful but curious heads of pale green, purple-edged flowers have pineapple-like crowns, and rise over strap-shaped, fleshy leaves in late summer. ♛

Verbena 'Peaches and Cream'
VERBENA
☼ ❄   ↕ 45cm (18in) ↔ 50cm (20in)

In summer, the mound of toothed, rough-hairy, dark green leaves is covered by domed heads of pale orange-pink flowers, which age to apricot- then creamy yellow.

Perennials for Containers in Shade

S HADY PATIOS, BACKYARDS, and similar sunless situations, particularly when paved or close to the house, are not always the easiest places to accommodate plants unless they are grown in containers. Foliage perennials are especially useful in shade, and while many also bear attractive flowers, they are striking as specimens, or grouped, in containers.

OTHER PERENNIALS FOR
CONTAINERS IN SHADE

Bergenia cordifolia 'Purpurea', see p.120
Dryopteris erythrosora, see p.148
Hakonechloa macra 'Aureola', see p.130
Helleborus argutifolius, see p.120
Heuchera 'Pewter Moon'
Hosta 'Zounds', see p.66
Lilium longiflorum
Saxifraga 'Mount Nachi'
Tolmiea menziesii 'Taff's Gold',
   see p.131

Aspidistra elatior
ASPIDISTRA, CAST IRON PLANT
☀ ☀ ❄❄   ↕ ↔ 60cm (24in)

Thriving in shade, this old favourite for parlours always looks in good health with its broad, strap-shaped, beautifully veined and glossy, evergreen foliage.

Hosta 'Sum and Substance'
PLANTAIN LILY
☀ ☀ ❄❄❄❄   ↕ 75cm (30in) ↔ 90cm (36in)

One of the best hostas for brightening a shady corner, with its bold clump of heart-shaped, yellow-green to yellow leaves. It bears pale lilac flowers in summer.

Matteucia struthiopteris
SHUTTLECOCK FERN
☀ ❄❄❄   ↕ 1.2m (4ft) ↔ 50cm (20in)

The bold, elegant shuttlecock of laddered fronds surrounds a central cluster of dark brown, spore-bearing fronds from late summer on. It needs moist compost.

Corydalis flexuosa
'China Blue'
☀ ❄❄❄   ↕ 25cm (10in) ↔ 20cm (8in)

Worth growing just for its attractive, ferny, bright green winter foliage, which dies down in early summer as the racemes of tubular, striking blue flowers fade.

Liriope muscari
LILYTURF
☀ ☀ ❄❄❄   ↕ 30cm (12in) ↔ 45cm (18in)

Dense tufts of evergreen, strap-shaped, dark green leaves are joined in autumn by stiff, crowded spikes of violet-mauve flowers. Good for ground cover too.

Rodgersia pinnata 'Superba'
RODGERSIA
☀ ☀ ☀ ❄❄❄   ↕ 1.2m (4ft) ↔ 75cm (30in)

This vigorous clump-former has the dual attractions of bold, fingered, veiny leaves, bronze-purple when young, and conical, rich pink flower plumes in summer.

71

Climbing Perennials

MOST CLIMBING PERENNIALS cultivated in the garden are woody-stemmed and have a permanent presence above ground. There are, however, a surprising number of herbaceous perennials that have twining or scrambling stems ideal for clothing walls, fences, and trellis, or for training over shrubs and trees or similar supports. As well as flowers and foliage, some also offer decorative fruits and seed heads, or richly tinted autumn leaves.

SPECIFIC USES

OTHER CLIMBING PERENNIALS

Aconitum episcopale
Aconitum hemsleyanum
Calystegia hederacea 'Flore Pleno'
Clematis × *eriostemon*
Dicentra macrocapnos
Lathyrus latifolius 'Blushing Bride'
Lathyrus rotundifolius
Tropaeolum ciliatum
Tropaeolum tuberosum
Tropaeolum tuberosum var.
  lineamaculatum 'Ken Aslet'

Clematis × *durandii*
CLEMATIS
☼ ❄❄   ↕ 2m (6ft) ↔ 1m (3ft)

Perfect for ground cover or training over a small bush, the slender stems bear single summer flowers with creamy stamens and wide-spaced, indigo-blue tepals. ♈

Lathyrus grandiflorus
EVERLASTING PEA
☼ ☼ ❄❄❄   ↕↔ 1.5m (5ft)

An old cottage-garden favourite, providing dense cover with its rampant, slender stems. Long-stalked clusters of pink, red, and purple flowers open in summer.

Humulus lupulus 'Aureus'
GOLDEN HOP
☼ ☼ ❄❄❄❄   ↕↔ 6m (20ft)

The twining stems of this powerful, fast-growing climber blanket its support with golden yellow leaves. Bunches of greenish yellow seed heads appear in autumn. ♈

Lathyrus latifolius 'Albus'
PERENNIAL PEA
☼ ☼ ❄❄❄❄   ↕↔ 2m (6ft)

Easy and reliable, this strong-growing scrambler is ideal for a wall or hedge, or for covering a steep bank. In summer and autumn, it produces white pea-flowers. ♈

Tropaeolum speciosum
FLAME CREEPER
☼ ☼ ❄❄❄ᴾᴴ   ↕↔ 3m (10ft)

Spectacular when in flower in summer and autumn, the long-spurred, flame-red blooms are followed by blue fruits with red collars. It requires cool, moist soil. ♈

Perennials with Leaves Suitable for Cutting

I N THE HOME, AS IN THE GARDEN, foliage is as important and decorative as flowers. Many perennials can provide a regular and reliable supply of attractive leaves for cutting whenever required. Useful for adding a green, grey, or golden foil to flower arrangements, cut leaves will also make an effective display by themselves.

Paeonia lactiflora 'Edulis Superba'
PEONY
☼ ☼ ✳✳✳ ↕ ↔ 90cm (36in)

Most herbaceous peonies have attractive, rich green foliage with contrasting red or purplish stalks. This one also has double pink flowers that are excellent for cutting.

OTHER PERENNIALS WITH LEAVES SUITABLE FOR CUTTING

Arum italicum 'Marmoratum', see p.141
Astilbe × arendsii 'Fanal'
Bergenia cordifolia 'Purpurea', see p.120
Galax urceolata
Hakonechloa macra 'Aureola', see p.130
Helleborus argutifolius, see p.120
Hosta 'Shade Master'
Hosta 'Zounds', see p.66
Phormium tenax, see p.123
Polystichum munitum, see p.148
Rodgersia pinnata, see p.67

Hosta 'Hadspen Blue'
PLANTAIN LILY
☼ ☼ ✳✳✳ ↕ 25cm (10in) ↔ 60cm (24in)

Hostas are invaluable for cut foliage, and those with blue-grey leaves are especially useful. This exceptional example has handsome bold, heart-shaped leaves.

Hosta 'Green Fountain'
PLANTAIN LILY
☼ ☼ ✳✳✳ ↕ 45cm (18in) ↔ 1m (3ft)

This hosta's arching, lance-shaped, wavy-margined, glossy leaves form a bold clump, and are ideal for picking. Arching stems bear pale mauve flowers in summer.

Iris pallida 'Argentea Variegata'
IRIS
☼ ☼ ✳✳✳ ↕ 80cm (32in) ↔ 60cm (24in)

One of the most spectacular variegated perennials, with sword-shaped, boldly margined leaves lasting long into autumn. Fragrant flowers open in early summer.

Polygonatum odoratum 'Variegatum'
SOLOMON'S SEAL
☼ ☼ ✳✳✳ ↕ 60cm (24in) ↔ 30cm (12in)

In time, this charming perennial forms a clump of arching reddish shoots, with rich green, cream-margined leaves. In spring, it bears clusters of pendent bell-flowers.

Perennials for Cut Flowers

THE AVAILABILITY OF CUT FLOWERS for home decoration is one of the most enjoyable bonuses of growing perennials. Cutting, preferably from well-established plants, should be selective, leaving most of the clumps virtually intact, while providing enough flowers for an arrangement. Although some perennials, such as asters, have long been popular among florists, many more bear flowers suitable for cutting. Once cut, stand the flowers in a container of water overnight before use.

Astilbe 'Professor van der Wielen'
ASTILBE
☼ ◐ ❋❋❋　　‡ 1.2m (4ft) ↔ 1m (3ft)

One of the boldest and most satisfying astilbes for cool, moist soil. In summer, tall, arching plumes of tiny white flowers rise over mounds of much-divided leaves.

Catananche caerulea
BLUE CUPIDONE
☼ ❋❋❋　　‡ 80cm (32in) ↔ 30cm (12in)

The slender clusters of erect, wiry stems are tipped in summer with papery, pearly white buds, opening to blue cornflowers. The flowers are also attractive when dried.

Aquilegia McKana Group
COLUMBINE
☼ ◐ ❋❋❋❋‡ 75cm (30in) ↔ 60cm (24in)

This striking but short-lived perennial produces its large, long-spurred flowers in shades of blue, yellow, and red from late spring through to midsummer.

> **OTHER SPRING-FLOWERING PERENNIALS FOR CUT FLOWERS**
>
> *Bergenia* 'Beethoven', see p.32
> *Convallaria majalis*
> *Doronicum* × *excelsum* 'Harpur Crewe'
> *Galanthus* 'Atkinsii', see p.88
> *Narcissus* 'Actaea'
> *Narcissus* 'Mount Hood', see p.91
> *Polygonatum* × *hybridum*
> *Primula vulgaris*
> *Tulipa* 'Purissima'
> *Viola odorata*

Aster × *frikartii* 'Wunder von Stäfa'
ASTER
☼ ❋❋❋　　‡ 70cm (28in) ↔ 40cm (16in)

A reliable plant for a late summer or early autumn border, with a multitude of long-lasting blue, orange-centred daisies. Its stems may flop if not given support. ♛

Gaillardia 'Kobold'
BLANKET FLOWER
☼ ❋❋❋　　‡ 30cm (12in) ↔ 45cm (18in)

Also known as 'Goblin', this downy, bushy plant is relatively short-lived, but displays large, brilliant red, yellow-tipped daisy-flowers during summer and early autumn.

Iris unguicularis 'Mary Barnard'
IRIS
☼ ✳✳✳ ↕ 30cm (12in) ↔ 60cm (24in)

The fragrant, solitary flowers of this sun-loving iris appear from late winter to early spring, and are best picked when in bud. Its evergreen leaves form a grassy clump.

Leucanthemum × *superbum* 'Cobham Gold'
☼ ☀ ✳✳✳✳ ↕ 60cm (24in) ↔ 20cm (8in)

This lovely selection is one of the shasta daisies, which are all excellent for cutting. It forms robust clumps, with double white flowers during summer and early autumn.

Lilium African Queen Group
TRUMPET LILY
☼ ☀ ✳✳✳ ↕ 1.5m (5ft) ↔ 30cm (12in)

Most lilies are good for cutting, and this is no exception. Its tall stems bear narrow, crowded leaves, and terminal umbels of fragrant, nodding flowers in summer.

OTHER SUMMER-FLOWERING
PERENNIALS FOR CUT FLOWERS

Achillea 'Coronation Gold', see p.108
Agapanthus 'Blue Giant', see p.90
Alstroemeria ligtu hybrids
Crocosmia masoniorum, see p.110
Echinacea purpurea
Galtonia candicans
Gypsophila paniculata 'Bristol Fairy', see p.99
Paeonia lactiflora 'Sarah Bernhardt', see p.113

Schizostylis coccinea 'Viscountess Byng'
KAFFIR LILY
☼ ✳✳✳ ↕ 60cm (24in) ↔ 30cm (12in)

A very useful autumn-flowering perennial, forming a clump, or in time a patch, of narrow, iris-like leaves, and bearing loose spikes of star-shaped, pale pink flowers.

Solidago 'Laurin'
GOLDEN ROD
☼ ✳✳✳ ↕ 75cm (30in) ↔ 45cm (18in)

This compact version of an old-fashioned, cottage-garden stalwart bears branched, spreading heads of deep yellow flowers on clumps of leafy stems in late summer.

Liatris spicata 'Kobold'
GAYFEATHER
☼ ✳✳✳ ↕ 50cm (20in) ↔ 45cm (18in)

A striking and reliable perennial for moist but well-drained soils. It forms a clump of slender leaves, with erect, dense purple flower spikes in late summer and autumn.

Paeonia officinalis
COMMON PEONY
☼ ✳✳✳ ↕ ↔ 70cm (28in)

This bold, clump-forming peony produces handsome, divided, deep green foliage. The large, single, garnet-red blooms, with golden yellow stamens, appear in summer.

Perennials with Decorative Winter Seed Heads

SPECIFIC **U**SES

MOST GARDENERS NOW RECOGNIZE that taking too tidy an approach to the garden at the end of the growing season can rob them of some striking winter effects. Any perennial that has a dried superstructure of seed heads can provide attractive winter interest, and their architectural beauty will be further enhanced by a covering of snow or hoar frost.

Miscanthus sinensis 'Kleine Fontäne'
MISCANTHUS
☼ ✲✲✲   ↕ 1.5m (5ft) ↔ 1.2m (4ft)

In autumn, handsome clumps of tall, erect stems, with narrow leaves, bear finger-like spikelets, which turn fluffy and from buff to white in winter. Ideal for small gardens.

Achillea filipendulina
ACHILLEA
☼ ✲✲✲   ↕ 1.2m (4ft) ↔ 45cm (18in)

The flattened seed heads of this clump-forming, stiff-stemmed perennial provide a ready platform for snow or hoar frost. Its yellow flowers are produced in summer.

Echinops ritro
GLOBE THISTLE
☼ ◐ ✲✲✲   ↕ 60cm (24in) ↔ 45cm (18in)

When covered in frost, the globular, spiky seed heads of this easy-to-grow perennial look like decorative baubles. The flowers emerge bright blue in late spring. ♆

OTHER PERENNIALS WITH DECORATIVE WINTER SEED HEADS

Actaea simplex
Astilbe chinensis 'Superba'
Eupatorium purpureum
  'Atropurpureum', see p.24
Filipendula rubra 'Venusta'
Iris sibirica
Miscanthus sinensis 'Ferner Osten'
Sedum spectabile, see p.108
Thalictrum lucidum

Chasmanthium latifolium
SPANGLE GRASS
☼ ◐ ✲✲✲   ↕ 1m (3ft) ↔ 60cm (24in)

This gorgeous grass forms loose clumps of leafy stems, which bear lax or drooping clusters of flattened, green or pink-tinted spikelets, turning pale brown in winter.

Gypsophila paniculata
'Compacta Plena'
☼ ✲✲✲   ↕ 30cm (12in) ↔ 60cm (24in)

A compact, dwarf form of the well-known baby's breath (*G. paniculata*). Small, double, soft pink to white flowers create a spangled effect in seed when covered in frost.

Monarda 'Beauty of Cobham'
BERGAMOT
☼ ◐ ✲✲✲   ↕ 90cm (36in) ↔ 45cm (18in)

Flowering during late summer and early autumn, this lovely plant bears crowded heads of pink flowers, with purple bracts that turn a warm brown in winter. ♆

Nassella tenuissima
FEATHER GRASS
☼ ❆❆❆　　　↕↔60cm (24in)

A densely tufted grass with ever-moving,
erect then arching stems. These bear long,
feathery heads of green-white spikelets,
which turn a warm buff colour in winter.

Phlomis tuberosa
PHLOMIS
☼ ❆❆❆　　↕1.5m (5ft) ↔90cm (36in)

Throughout winter, the striking clumps of
tall, leafless stems carry dense brown seed
heads. Two-lipped, rose-lilac flowers with
reddish calyces are produced in summer.

Phlox paniculata 'Lichtspel'
BORDER PHLOX
☼ ❆❆❆　　↕1.2m (4ft) ↔60cm (24in)

During summer, the clumps of erect, leafy
stems carry panicles of lilac-rose flowers.
The stems and remaining flowerheads
fade to a warm pale brown during winter.

Phormium tenax Purpureum Group
NEW ZEALAND FLAX
☼ ☼ ❆❆　　↕2–2.8m (6–8ft) ↔2m (6ft)

All the phormiums have decorative seed
capsules in winter, but this group is more
reliable than most. The high-branching
stems lift the capsules like trophies. ♈

Veronicastrum virginicum
CULVER'S ROOT
☼ ☼ ❆❆❆　　↕2m (6ft) ↔45cm (18in)

Tapered spikes of blue-purple flowers top
dense clumps of erect stems, with whorled
leaves, in summer and autumn. In winter,
the spikes lengthen and turn brown.

Perennials Attractive to Bees, Butterflies, and Other Insects

COLOURFUL BUTTERFLIES are always welcome visitors to our gardens, but many other less decorative insects in fact have more important roles to play. These include bees, which are essential as garden pollinators, and also hoverflies, whose larvae feed on aphids and act as a form of natural pest control. They will all be attracted by the following perennials.

OTHER PERENNIALS ATTRACTIVE TO BEES AND BUTTERFLIES

Achillea 'Moonshine'
Allium 'Globemaster', see p.88
Asclepias incarnata
Aster amellus 'Veilchenkönigin', see p.100
Centranthus ruber, see p.92
Eryngium × *tripartitum*, see p.37
Linaria purpurea 'Canon Went'
Monarda 'Squaw', see p.111
Nepeta sibirica 'Souvenir d'André Chaudron'

Allium hollandicum 'Purple Sensation'
ORNAMENTAL ONION
☼ ✻✻✻   ↕90cm (36in) ↔ 10cm (4in)

All the alliums are attractive to insects but this one is particularly impressive. The tall stems carry spangled globes of starry, deep violet flowers during summer.

Leuzea centauroides
LEUZEA
☼ ✻✻✻   ↕1.2m (4ft) ↔ 60cm (24in)

This bold clump-former has handsome, silver-grey foliage. During summer, erect, branching stems bear striking, rose-pink flowerheads with scaly, silvery bracts.

Calamintha nepeta 'White Cloud'
LESSER CALAMINT
☼ ☀ ✻✻✻   ↕45cm (18in) ↔ 75cm (30in)

Bees especially love this small-flowered perennial. Throughout summer, the low mound of crowded, aromatic leaves is peppered with tiny, pure white blooms.

Cephalaria gigantea
GIANT SCABIOUS
☼ ☀ ✻✻✻   ↕2.5m (8ft) ↔ 90cm (36in)

A special favourite with bees, this giant scabious produces clumps of deeply lobed leaves, and tall, branched stems carrying primrose-yellow flowerheads in summer.

Doronicum pardalianches
LEOPARD'S BANE
☼ ✻✻✻   ↕90cm (36in) ↔ 1.2m (4ft)

In time, this creeping perennial will form a substantial patch of heart-shaped, softly-hairy leaves. Yellow daisy-heads are borne over a long period in spring and summer.

Salvia pratensis Haematodes Group
MEADOW CLARY
☼ ☼ ✳✳✳ ‡ 90cm (36in) ↔ 30cm (12in)

Short-lived but free-seeding, this meadow clary produces large, branching heads of blue-violet flowers in summer, above rosettes of aromatic, large green leaves. ♆

Echinops ritro 'Veitch's Blue'
GLOBE THISTLE
☼ ☼ ✳✳✳ ‡ 1.2m (4ft) ↔ 75cm (30in)

During summer, the spherical, spiky blue flowerheads make this a favourite with both children and bees. Its spine-toothed, deep-cut leaves are white-downy beneath.

Lavandula stoechas
FRENCH LAVENDER
☼ ✳✳✳ ‡ ↔ 60cm (24in)

Bushy, with a dense, compact habit, this aromatic evergreen has narrow, grey green leaves, and long-stalked spikes of purple flowers in late spring and summer. ♆

Sedum 'Herbstfreude'
ICE PLANT
☼ ✳✳✳ ‡ ↔ 60cm (24in)

Often known as *S.* 'Autumn Joy', this will lure butterflies and bees with its deep pink autumn flowers, maturing copper-red. Its fleshy leaves are grey-bloomy. ♆

Inula hookeri
INULA
☼ ✳✳✳ ‡ ↔ 90cm (36in)

One of the best plants for attracting bees to the garden. The bold clumps of downy, leafy stems produce golden daisy-heads from woolly buds in summer and autumn.

Melittis melissophyllum
BASTARD BALM
☼ ☼ ✳✳✳ ‡ ↔ 30cm (12in)

This softly-downy balm has four-angled stems and honey-scented leaves. Loved by bees, the purple-lipped, white to pink flowers open in spring and early summer.

Solidago 'Goldenmosa'
GOLDEN ROD
☼ ✳✳✳ ‡ 1m (3ft) ↔ 60cm (24in)

A compact, bushy perennial with erect, leafy stems, and conical heads of bright yellow flowerheads from late summer into autumn. Ideal for smaller gardens. ♆

Perennials Tolerant of Air Pollution

SPECIFIC USES

AIR POLLUTION FROM ANY SOURCE can have a detrimental effect on plants, and severe or prolonged exposure may ultimately cause plant deaths. Fortunately, such cases are the exception rather than the rule, and the following perennials can generally be relied on to tolerate all but the most extreme conditions found in industrial areas or roadside sites.

Leucanthemum × *superbum* 'T.E. Killin'
SHASTA DAISY

☼ ❄❄❄   ↕ ↔ 60cm (24in)

The large, double white flowerheads of this reliable, summer-blooming shasta daisy have yellow anemone centres. They are excellent for cutting.

Geranium pratense 'Plenum Caeruleum'

☼ ◐ ❄❄❄   ↕ 90cm (36in) ↔ 60cm (24in)

All forms of this well-known cranesbill are reliable. This strong-growing selection produces attractive, small, loosely double, lavender-blue flowers during summer.

Achillea ptarmica The Pearl Group
SNEEZEWORT

☼ ❄❄❄   ↕ 75cm (30in) ↔ 60cm (24in)

This well-proven, tough perennial forms clumps of aromatic, narrow, toothy leaves. The dense heads of button-like white flowers are produced in summer.

Lupinus 'My Castle'
LUPIN

☼ ❄❄❄   ↕ 90cm (36in) ↔ 75cm (30in)

In summer, the bold clump of erect stems and finger-like leaves is topped by long spires of deep rose-pink pea-flowers. It needs protection where slugs abound.

Aster novae-angliae 'Andenken an Alma Pötschke'

☼ ◐ ❄❄❄   ↕ 1.2m (4ft) ↔ 60cm (24in)

Often known simply as 'Alma Pötschke', this clump-forming michaelmas daisy lights up the early autumn days with its brilliant salmon-pink daisy-flowers.

Geum 'Lady Stratheden'
GEUM

☼ ◐ ❄❄❄   ↕ ↔ 60cm (24in)

An old favourite, and a contrast to scarlet *G.* 'Mrs. Bradshaw', with loose sprays of semi-double, rich yellow summer flowers, and deeply divided, fresh green leaves. ♧

OTHER FLOWERING PERENNIALS TOLERANT OF AIR POLLUTION

Anaphalis margaritacea var. *yedoensis*
Anemone × *hybrida* 'September Charm', see p.102
Dicentra 'Spring Morning'
Geranium × *magnificum*
Liatris spicata
Lupinus 'The Chatelaine'
Lychnis chalcedonica
Sidalcea candida
Solidago 'Fireworks'

OTHER FOLIAGE PERENNIALS
TOLERANT OF AIR POLLUTION

Acanthus mollis Latifolius Group
Artemisia ludoviciana 'Silver Queen',
   see p.86
Bergenia cordifolia 'Purpurea', see p.120
Crambe cordifolia, see p.28
Cynara cardunculus, see p.136
Macleaya cordata 'Flamingo'
Myrrhis odorata, see p.55
Symphytum × uplandicum 'Axminster Gold'
Telekia speciosa, see p.129

Solidago 'Golden Wings'
GOLDEN ROD
☼ ✳✳✳   ↕ 1.8m (6ft) ↔ 90cm (36in)

During late summer and autumn, the
erect, leafy stems of this robust perennial
are crowned with spreading, branched
heads of golden yellow flower clusters.

Lupinus 'Noble Maiden'
LUPIN
☼ ✳✳✳   ↕ 90cm (36in) ↔ 75cm (30in)

A lovely lupin, with tapered racemes of
creamy white pea-flowers in summer,
rising above the clump of divided foliage.
Like most lupins, it is attractive to slugs.

Pentaglottis sempervirens
GREEN ALKANET
◐ ☼ ✳✳✳✳   ↕ 90cm (36in) ↔ 60cm (24in)

The robust clump of overwintering, hairy
leaves is joined in spring by erect, leafy
stems bearing rich blue, bird's-eye flowers.
Excellent for hedge bottoms or woodland.

Malva moschata
MUSK MALLOW
☼ ✳✳✳   ↕ 90cm (36in) ↔ 60cm (24in)

Attractive and easily grown, this perennial
forms clumps of finely divided, aromatic
leaves and bears racemes of pink mallow
flowers from midsummer onwards.

Potentilla 'Gibson's Scarlet'
POTENTILLA
☼ ✳✳✳   ↕ 45cm (18in) ↔ 60cm (24in)

Popular for borders and striking in flower,
this potentilla produces its bright scarlet
blooms in summer above clumps of long-
stalked, deeply divided leaves.   ♈

Veronica spicata 'Rotfuchs'
VERONICA
☼ ✳✳✳   ↕ ↔ 30cm (12in)

Erect, tapering spikes of eye-catching,
deep pink flowers rise above the low
clump of willow-like leaves in summer.
Its German name means 'Red Fox'.

Perennials Tolerant of Coastal Exposure

EXPOSURE TO STRONG WINDS, SALT SPRAY, AND SUN are the three main features of life by the seaside. As the soil here is also often sandy or shingly and free-draining, plants must be both robust and adaptable to survive. A surprising number of perennials can cope successfully with these conditions and are ideal for a coastal garden.

Euphorbia nicaeensis
SPURGE
☼ ✻✻✻　　　↕ 80cm (32in) ↔ 45cm (18in)

This superb evergreen plant is valued for its reddish green stems and narrow, blue-bloomy leaves. Green-yellow flowerheads appear in late spring and summer.

Allium giganteum
GIANT ONION
☼ ✻✻✻　　　↕ 1.5m (5ft) ↔ 15cm (6in)

Round heads of starry, lilac-pink flowers top the tall stems of this striking plant in summer. Its two strap-shaped, gray-green basal leaves wither before flowering. ♈

Cichorium intybus 'Roseum'
CHICORY
☼ ✻✻✻　　　↕ 1.2m (4ft) ↔ 60cm (24in)

A tap-rooted perennial producing a clump of jaggedly lobed and toothed leaves. Spikes of dandelion-like pink flowerheads are carried on branched stems in summer.

Geranium sanguineum 'Max Frei'
BLOODY CRANESBILL
☼ ✻✻✻　　　↕ 20cm (8in) ↔ 30cm (12in)

The neat, rounded hummocks of deeply cut, evergreen leaves are often richly red-tinted in autumn. A mass of deep magenta flowers emerges throughout summer.

Centaurea hypoleuca 'John Coutts'
KNAPWEED
☼ ✻✻✻　　　↕ 60cm (24in) ↔ 45cm (18in)

In summer, erect stems bear long-lasting, fragrant, deep rose-pink cornflower-heads above bold clumps of deeply lobed, wavy-edged leaves, grey-white beneath.

Erigeron 'Charity'
FLEABANE
☼☼ ✻✻✻✻　　　↕ 60cm (24in) ↔ 45cm (18in)

Leafy clumps of stems produce cheerful, lilac-pink, yellow-centered daisy-heads, singly or in clusters, during summer. The flowers are a favourite with bees.

Glaucium flavum
YELLOW HORNED POPPY
☼ ✻✻✻　　　↕ 60cm (24in) ↔ 45cm (18in)

Usually found on sand or shingle in the wild, this poppy bears bloomy blue-green leaves and stems, and yellow flowers in summer followed by narrow, curved fruits.

Kniphofia 'Atlanta'
RED HOT POKER

☼ ☀ ❄❄❄   ↕ 1.2m (4ft) ↔ 75cm (30in)

A magnificent evergreen forming bold
clumps of strap-shaped, gray-green leaves.
Stout-stemmed orange-red pokers open to
yellow flowers in late spring and summer.

OTHER PERENNIALS TOLERANT OF COASTAL EXPOSURE

Anthemis punctata subsp. *cupaniana*
Centranthus ruber, see p.92
Crambe cordifolia, see p.28
Dierama pulcherrimum, see p.28
Erigeron glaucus
Helichrysum italicum, see p.127
Nipponanthemum nipponicum
Oenothera stricta 'Sulphurea', see p.35
Othonna cheirifolia
Yucca filamentosa

Papaver orientale 'Cedric Morris'
ORIENTAL POPPY

☼ ❄❄❄   ↕ ↔ 90cm (36in)

An exquisite form of a cottage-garden staple
forming bold clumps of hairy grey leaves.
Its large, frilly-margined, soft pink blooms
open from late spring to summer.   ♈

Platycodon grandiflorus
BALLOON FLOWER

☼ ☀ ❄❄❄   ↕ 60cm (24in) ↔ 30cm (12in)

The large, purple-blue bell-flowers open
from balloon-like, inflated buds during
late summer. Blue-green leaves clothe the
clumps of erect, branching stems.

Pennisetum alopecuroides 'Hameln'
FOUNTAIN GRASS

☼ ❄❄   ↕ 1m (3ft) ↔ 1.4m (4½ft)

Borne in summer, the bottlebrush-like,
greenish white heads of spikelets, ageing
to grey- then golden brown, arch on long
stems over the elegant mounds of leaves.

Senecio cineraria 'Silver Dust'
SENECIO

☼ ❄❄❄   ↕ ↔ 30cm (12in)

Silver-grey felt covers the deeply divided
leaves and stems of this striking, woody-
based evergreen. Loose heads of mustard-
yellow flowers are borne in summer.   ♈

Perennials Tolerant of Exposure Inland

OTHER PERENNIALS TOLERANT OF EXPOSURE INLAND

Achillea ptarmica 'Boule de Neige', see p.54
Alchemilla mollis, see p.90
Astilbe chinensis var. *pumila*
Cynoglossum nervosum
Geranium himalayense 'Gravetye'
Primula denticulata
Pulmonaria saccharata 'Mrs. Moon'
Sinacalia tangutica, see p.124
Veronica gentianoides

EXPOSURE TO PERSISTENT or strong winds, particularly in cold areas, can severely damage or stunt the growth of garden plants. There is a surprisingly large variety of hardy perennials, however, that will grow, if not thrive, in such conditions, especially if they are given some form of shelter or protection from the worst of the elements.

SPECIFIC USES

Alchemilla conjuncta
LADY'S MANTLE
☼ ☼ ✳✳✳ ↕10cm (4in) ↔50cm (20in)

A tough, creeping perennial, providing excellent ground cover with its carpet of attractively fingered leaves, silvery-silky beneath. Green flowers open in summer.

Astrantia 'Hadspen Blood'
MASTERWORT
☼ ☼ ✳✳✳ ↕45cm (18in) ↔60cm (24in)

Attractive enough with its clumps of long-stalked, deeply lobed and toothed leaves, this masterwort has the added bonus of loose heads of dark red flowers in summer.

Brunnera macrophylla
BRUNNERA
☼ ✳✳✳ ↕45cm (18in) ↔60cm (24in)

In spring, this tough, reliable perennial produces branched heads of bright blue, forget-me-not flowers above bold clumps of heart-shaped, softly-hairy leaves. 🏆

Anaphalis margaritacea
PEARLY EVERLASTING
☼ ✳✳✳ ↕↔60cm (24in)

The erect clumps of grey-woolly stems bear narrow leaves, white-woolly beneath, and dense clusters of papery, 'everlasting' flowerheads from summer to autumn.

Bergenia × *schmidtii*
ELEPHANT'S EAR
☼ ☼ ✳✳✳ ↕30cm (12in) ↔60cm (24in)

One of the most dependable perennials, reliably bearing large clusters of rose-pink flowers from late winter to spring, above mounds of leathery, evergreen leaves. 🏆

Centaurea montana 'Alba'
PERENNIAL CORNFLOWER
☼ ✳✳✳ ↕45cm (18in) ↔60cm (24in)

This handsome form of the popular, blue-flowered perennial bears bold, pure white cornflowers above clumps of grey-green, leafy stems from late spring into summer.

Euphorbia polychroma
SPURGE
☼ ◐ ❋❋❋ ↕ 40cm (16in) ↔ 30cm (12in)

An invaluable and utterly reliable plant,
forming a rounded clump of leafy stems
which bear long-lasting, greenish yellow
flowerheads from spring into summer. ♔

Leucanthemum × superbum 'Wirral
Pride'
☼ ◐ ❋❋❋ ↕ 75cm (30in) ↔ 60cm (24in)

In summer, the dark green-leaved stems
of this bold, clump-forming perennial bear
solitary, large, double white daisy-heads
with yellowish anemone centres.

Polemonium 'Lambrook Mauve'
JACOB'S LADDER
☼ ◐ ❋❋❋ ↕ ↔ 45cm (18in)

Erect, branching stems bear loose clusters
of lilac-blue bell-flowers among the
rounded clumps of deeply divided leaves
during late spring and early summer. ♔

Primula 'Wanda'
PRIMROSE
☼ ◐ ❋❋❋ ↕ 15cm (6in) ↔ 20cm (8in)

This long-established and reliable garden
primrose never fails to produce its dark
claret-red flowers, above clumps of toothy
leaves, for a long period in spring. ♔

Rhodiola rosea
ROSEROOT
☼ ❋❋❋ ↕ ↔ 20cm (8in)

Dense heads of tiny yellow flowers top
the low clump of fleshy, leafy, blue-green
bloomy stems in summer. It is ideal for a
rock garden, dry wall, or as edging.

Thermopsis rhombifolia
THERMOPSIS
☼ ◐ ❋❋❋ ↕ ↔ 90cm (36in)

In early summer, spires of lupin-like
yellow flowers rise above leaves divided
into threes. This creeping perennial forms
extensive patches, and can be invasive.

Low-allergen Perennials

F OR PEOPLE WHO SUFFER FROM ASTHMA, hayfever, or other allergies aggravated by air-borne pollen, gardening and gardens often have to be avoided at certain times of the year, especially during summer. Brushing or touching the foliage or flowers of certain plants can also cause or exacerbate some skin allergies. The following insect-pollinated perennials, however, can usually be relied upon to be non-allergenic, and will allow everyone to enjoy the garden all year round.

Campanula trachelium 'Bernice'
NETTLE-LEAVED BELLFLOWER
☼ ☀ ❆❆❆ ‡75cm (30in) ↔ 30cm (12in)

A beautiful perennial, forming clumps of erect stems with sharply toothed leaves, and axillary, double, violet-blue bell-flowers in summer. It may need support.

Ajuga reptans 'Catlin's Giant'
BUGLE
☼ ☀ ❆❆❆ ‡15cm (6in) ↔ indefinite

Excellent for ground cover, this bugle has large, brown-green, evergreen leaves that age to green. Dark blue flower spikes are borne in late spring and summer. ♈

Astilbe × *arendsii* 'Irrlicht'
ASTILBE
☼ ☀ ❆❆❆ ‡↔50cm (20in)

In late spring and early summer, striking, erect plumes of tiny white flowers top this astilbe's clumps of much-divided, dark green leaves. It enjoys a moist soil.

Aquilegia chrysantha 'Yellow Queen'
COLUMBINE
☼ ☀ ❆❆❆ ‡90cm (36in) ↔ 60cm (24in)

The branched stems of this vigorous, erect perennial bear attractive, divided, ferny leaves, and slender-spurred, golden yellow flowers during late spring and summer.

Bergenia 'Bressingham White'
ELEPHANT'S EAR
☼ ☀ ❆❆❆❆ ‡45cm (18in) ↔ 60cm (24in)

During spring, fleshy, upright stems freely bear loose clusters of bell-shaped, pure white flowers above the robust clumps of large, leathery, evergreen leaves. ♈

Digitalis 'Glory of Roundway'
FOXGLOVE
☼ ☀ ❆❆❆ ‡90cm (36in) ↔ 30cm (12in)

This choice hybrid of *D. purpurea* and *D. lutea* has branched, narrow-leaved stems, and long racemes of funnel-shaped, pale yellow, pink-tinted flowers in summer.

Geranium psilostemon
ARMENIAN CRANESBILL
☼ ☼ ❄❄❄ ↕ 1.2m (4ft) ↔ 90cm (36in)

Fantastic in flower, this striking cranesbill
sends up a mound of dense, leafy stems,
which are covered throughout summer with
bright magenta, black-eyed blooms. ♛

Hosta 'Blue Blush'
PLANTAIN LILY
☼ ☼ ❄❄❄ ↕ 20cm (8in) ↔ 40cm (16in)

One of the most striking hostas, forming
clumps of lance-shaped, strongly veined,
blue-green leaves. It bears bell-shaped,
lavender-blue flowers in summer.

Paeonia lactiflora 'Duchesse de
Nemours'
☼ ☼ ❄❄❄ ↕ ↔ 80cm (32in)

The large, fragrant, double white flowers
of this strong-growing peony have yellow-
based inner petals. Flushed green in bud,
the blooms open in early summer. ♛

Penstemon 'Andenken an
Friedrich Hahn'
☼ ☼ ❄❄❄ ↕ 75cm (30in) ↔ 60cm (24in)

Also known as *P.* 'Garnet', this is probably
the most reliable perennial penstemon. Its
deep red flowers are produced on strong,
leafy stems from midsummer onwards. ♛

Sidalcea 'Oberon'
CHECKERBLOOM
☼ ❄❄❄ ↕ 1.2m (4ft) ↔ 45cm (18in)

During summer, the clumps of erect, leafy
stems bear loose racemes of clear rose-
pink mallow-flowers. The stem leaves are
deeply lobed, the basal ones less so.

Veronica spicata subsp. *incana*
SPIKED SPEEDWELL
☼ ❄❄❄ ↕ 60cm (24in) ↔ 45cm (18in)

The dense spikes of purple-blue flowers,
borne throughout summer, are in striking
contrast to the densely silver-hairy stems
and mat of silvery foliage beneath. ♛

**OTHER LOW-ALLERGEN
PERENNIALS**

Allium 'Globemaster', see p.88
Aruncus dioicus, see p.24
Astilbe x *arendsii* 'Snowdrift'
Dicentra spectabilis
Epimedium x *versicolor* 'Sulphureum'
Hemerocallis 'Golden Chimes'
Hosta 'Honeybells', see p.116
Iris sibirica
Polemonium 'Lambrook Mauve',
  see p.85

Viola cornuta
HORNED VIOLET
☼ ☼ ❄❄❄ ↕ 15cm (6in) ↔ 40cm (16in)

An excellent and reliable small perennial
with a low-spreading, slightly bushy habit
and lightly scented, lilac-blue to violet
flowers in late spring and summer. ♛

Slug-proof Perennials

SLUGS AND SNAILS UNDOUBTEDLY have a voracious appetite when they discover a tasty plant, but what they devour in one garden they will often only nibble at in another. Some plants, such as many hostas, are always a gourmet meal for slugs and snails and are readily consumed. Others, especially those with hard-textured, hairy, or poisonous leaves, are often relatively ignored. Here is a selection of the most reliably slug- and snail-proof perennials for the garden.

Bergenia 'Silberlicht'
ELEPHANT'S EAR
☼ ☼ ❋❋❋ ↕ 40cm (12in) ↔ 30cm (12in)

Fleshy, shining, evergreen leaves form a basal mound above which, in spring, rise erect, fleshy stems bearing loose clusters of white flowers that age to pink.

Corydalis lutea
YELLOW CORYDALIS
☼ ☼ ❋❋❋ ↕ 35cm (14in) ↔ 30cm (12in)

The mound of ferny, evergreen leaves is used by snails as a refuge but rarely eaten. Slender racemes of tubular yellow flowers are borne from late spring to early autumn.

Allium 'Globemaster'
ORNAMENTAL ONION
☼ ❋❋❋ ↕ 80cm (32in) ↔ 30cm (12in)

Magnificent for group plantings, this bulb has arching, strap-shaped leaves, and huge spangled heads of deep violet flowers in summer. Loved by butterflies and bees. ♈

OTHER SLUG-PROOF PERENNIALS

Aconitum carmichaelii 'Arendsii',
 see p.102
Artemisia ludoviciana
Arum italicum 'Marmoratum', see p.141
Campanula persicifolia
Colchicum 'Waterlily', see p.102
Epimedium pinnatum subsp. *colchicum*,
 see p.46
Helleborus foetidus
Lobelia siphilitica
Sedum telephium 'Matrona', see p.139

Aster ericoides 'Esther'
MICHAELMAS DAISY
☼ ❋❋❋ ↕ 70cm (28in) ↔ 30cm (12in)

Bushy clumps of leafy, slender-branched stems are topped by broad heads of small pink, yellow-eyed daisies in late summer and autumn. Useful for its late flowering.

Galanthus 'Atkinsii'
SNOWDROP
☼ ❋❋❋ ↕ 20cm (8in) ↔ 8cm (3in)

Ideal for naturalizing, this strong-growing bulb has narrow, fleshy, blue-green leaves. In late winter, erect stems bear pendent white flowers with green markings. ♈

Geranium macrorrhizum
CRANESBILL
☼ ☀ ✳✳✳✳   ↕ 50cm (20in) ↔ 60cm (24in)

An adaptable and reliable, semi-evergreen carpeter, with lobed, aromatic leaves often colouring well in autumn. Clusters of pink to purple flowers appear in early summer.

Helleborus x *nigercors*
HELLEBORE
☼ ✳✳✳   ↕ 30cm (12in) ↔ 90cm (36in)

Welcome clusters of saucer-shaped, white or pink-tinted flowers open from winter to spring above the basal clump of divided, coarse-toothed, evergreen leaves. ♈

Hosta 'Halcyon'
PLANTAIN LILY
☼ ☀ ✳✳✳   ↕↔ 70cm (28in)

One of the best slug-proof hostas, forming bold clumps of attractive, heart-shaped, bluish grey leaves. It produces pendent, blue-grey bell-flowers during summer. ♈

Iris chrysographes
IRIS
☼ ✳✳✳   ↕↔ 50cm (20in)

One of my favourite species, this iris forms erect clumps of sword-shaped, grey-green leaves, with stems of fragrant, velvety, dark purple flowers borne in summer. ♈

Pulmonaria angustifolia subsp. *azurea*
PULMONARIA
☼ ☀ ✳✳✳   ↕ 25cm (10in) ↔ 45cm (18in)

A nice change from spotted varieties, with its low clump of rough-hairy green leaves. In spring, it bears nodding clusters of rich gentian-blue, tubular flowers, red in bud.

Rudbeckia hirta
BLACK-EYED SUSAN
☼ ☀ ✳✳✳   ↕ 80cm (30in) ↔ 90cm (36in)

If kept moist in summer, this cheery plant will bear a succession of dark-eyed, rich yellow daisies, good for cutting, from mid-summer to autumn.

Sedum
spectabile 'Iceberg'
ICE PLANT
☼ ✳✳✳   ↕↔ 45cm (18in)

Reliable and easy to grow, with mounds of grey-green leaves and fleshy stems topped by flattened heads of white flowers from summer to autumn. Loved by butterflies.

Rabbit-proof Perennials

IT IS PROBABLY TRUE to say that rabbits are the most serious source of plant damage and loss in the garden, especially in country areas or those close to large, open spaces. Rabbits can eat their way through a bed or border faster than any slug or snail, and although various methods are recommended for their control, it does no harm to include some perennials in the garden that rabbits usually find unpalatable or uninteresting.

Bergenia stracheyi
ELEPHANT'S EAR
☼ ❋❋❋ ↕ 20cm (8in) ↔ 30cm (12in)

The low mound of leathery, evergreen leaves is crowned in early spring by dense clusters of fragrant pink bell-flowers. It is excellent for ground cover or path edging.

Aster ericoides 'Golden Spray'
ASTER
☼ ❋❋❋ ↕ 90cm (36in) ↔ 30cm (12in)

From late summer into autumn, branched heads of small white, pink-tinted daisies, with rich yellow centres, are produced on a bushy clump of erect, leafy stems. ♛

Euphorbia griffithii 'Fireglow'
SPURGE
☼☼ ❋❋❋ ↕ 75cm (30in) ↔ 90cm (36in)

A vigorous, creeping perennial, eventually forming large patches of leafy stems that colour richly in autumn. Terminal clusters of fiery orange flowers open in summer.

Agapanthus 'Blue Giant'
AFRICAN LILY
☼ ❋❋❋ ↕ 90cm (36in) ↔ 60cm (24in)

In late summer and early autumn, stout stems bearing large, loose heads of rich blue flowers rise above the bold clump of long, strap-shaped green leaves.

Alchemilla mollis
LADY'S MANTLE
☼☼ ❋❋❋ ↕↔ 35cm (14in)

This adaptable, reliable plant has mounds of downy, scalloped and lobed, grey-green leaves, topped by yellowish green flower clusters in summer. Will seed around. ♛

Astilbe 'Straussenfeder'
ASTILBE
☼☼ ❋❋❋ ↕ 90cm (36in) ↔ 60cm (24in)

Known also as 'Ostrich Plume', which neatly describes its arching sprays of pink flowers in summer and autumn. Young leaves are attractively bronze-tinted. ♛

Helleborus hybridus
LENTEN ROSE
☼ ❋❋❋ ↕↔ 45cm (18in)

A beautiful and sought-after group of hybrids, bearing semi-evergreen leaves and large, nodding, saucer-shaped flowers in a range of colours from late winter to spring.

Lamium maculatum 'Beacon Silver'
DEAD NETTLE
☼ ☀ ❅❅❅ ↕ 20cm (8in) ↔ 1m (3ft)

Extensive carpets of toothed, silvery, green-margined leaves provide excellent, semi-evergreen ground cover. Clusters of pale pink flowers are borne in summer.

OTHER RABBIT-PROOF PERENNIALS

Aconitum 'Blue Sceptre'
Anemone x *hybrida* 'Königin Charlotte', see p.56
Aquilegia vulgaris 'William Guiness'
Aster novi-belgii 'Marie Ballard'
Convallaria majalis 'Fortin's Giant'
Crocosmia 'Lucifer'
Kniphofia triangularis, see p.111
Nepeta nervosa
Pulmonaria saccharata
Sedum telephium 'Matrona', see p.139

Paeonia officinalis 'Rubra Plena'
PEONY
☼ ☀ ❅❅❅ ↕ 75cm (30in) ↔ 90cm (36in)

The reliable, old-fashioned, double red peony of cottage gardens. It forms clumps of glossy green leaves, and bears crimson blooms with ruffled petals in summer. ♛

Narcissus 'Mount Hood'
DAFFODIL
☼ ☀ ❅❅❅❅ ↕ 45cm (18in) ↔ 50cm (20in)

A classic large-flowered trumpet daffodil, producing gorgeous white flowers with cream-coloured trumpets in spring. It is superb when planted in groups. ♛

Trollius x *cultorum* 'Earliest of All'
GLOBEFLOWER
☼ ☀ ❅❅❅❅ ↕ 50cm (20in) ↔ 40cm (16in)

Not the first, but still an early perennial, forming loose clumps of deep-cut leaves. Branched stems bear globular, clear yellow flowers in spring. Prefers heavy soils.

Veratrum album
FALSE HELLEBORE
☼ ☀ ❅❅❅ ↕ 2m (6ft) ↔ 60cm (24in)

Worth growing for its large, handsomely pleated leaves alone, this bold perennial is impressive in groups. The tall plumes of white flowers in summer are a bonus.

Deer-proof Perennials

AFTER RABBITS AND HARES, the most destructive garden visitors are deer, although, like rabbits, they are mainly a problem for gardeners in rural and wooded areas. It can be disheartening to find favourite plants repeatedly demolished by browsing deer, but providing deterrents or erecting fences is often impractical and expensive. One effective alternative, however, is to grow at least some perennials that deer are known to find uninteresting or, better still, unpalatable.

Aconitum lycoctonum subsp. *vulparia*
WOLFSBANE
☼ ☼ ❄❄❄ ↕ 1.5m (5ft) ↔ 90cm (36in)

This handsome perennial has finely cut, glossy green leaves and produces straw-yellow flowers in summer. Its roots were once used in parts of Europe as wolf bait.

Artemisia ludoviciana 'Silver Queen'
ARTEMISIA
☼ ❄❄❄ ↕↔ 75cm (30in)

A clump-forming but creeping perennial, worth growing for its lance-shaped, silver-white leaves, and white-woolly flower-heads borne from summer onwards. ♔

Astilbe 'Deutschland'
ASTILBE
☼ ☼ ❄❄❄ ↕ 50cm (20in) ↔ 30cm (12in)

In summer, erect panicles of white flowers top the bright, glossy green mound of deeply divided leaves. Good for cutting, it needs some moisture in summer to excel.

OTHER DEER-PROOF PERENNIALS

Aconitum napellus 'Carneum'
Allium schoenoprasum 'Forescate',
    see p.54
Asplenium scolopendrium, see p.148
Aster novi-belgii 'Royal Velvet'
Bergenia 'Ballawley', see p.141
Epimedium perralderianum, see p.40
Geranium sanguineum
Helleborus hybridus, see p.90
Iris foetidissima
Kniphofia uvaria
Lamium maculatum 'White Nancy'
Paeonia lactiflora 'Bowl of Beauty'
Rudbeckia fulgida var. *sullivantii*
    'Goldsturm', see p.23
Sisyrinchium striatum
Tellima grandiflora, see p.121
Trollius × cultorum 'Earliest of All',
    see p.91

Centranthus ruber
RED VALERIAN
☼ ❄❄❄ ↕ 90cm (36in) ↔ 60cm (24in)

Often found on old walls, this woody-based perennial has bold clumps of leafy, grey-green stems, and fragrant, pink, red, or white flowers. It thrives in alkaline soil.

Digitalis purpurea Excelsior Group
FOXGLOVE
☼ ❄❄❄ ↕ 2m (6ft) ↔ 60cm (24in)

A bold and colourful, short-lived perennial or biennial, with a rosette of hairy leaves, and a tall spire of funnel-shaped flowers in pastel shades in early summer.

Narcissus 'Spellbinder'
DAFFODIL
☼ ☀ ✳✳✳✳   ↕ ↔ 50cm (20in)

A strong-growing daffodil, especially impressive when planted in bold drifts. The spring flowers are sulphur-yellow, with coronas fading to white with age. ♔

Geranium macrorrhizum 'Bevan's Variety'
☼ ☀ ✳✳✳✳ ↕ 50cm (20in) ↔ 60cm (24in)

An excellent, all-round, semi-evergreen plant, especially useful as ground cover. It flowers in early summer, and has aromatic leaves that often colour well in autumn.

Papaver orientale 'Beauty of Livermere'
☼ ✳✳✳✳   ↕ ↔ 90cm (36in)

From late spring into summer, erect, hairy stems bear crimson-scarlet flowers, with basal black blotches, above a bold clump of deeply cut, hairy leaves.

Iris orientalis
IRIS
☼ ✳✳✳✳   ↕ ↔ 90cm (36in)

This robust perennial forms erect clumps or patches of strap-shaped leaves. In early summer, stiff stems carry a succession of white, yellow-stained flowers. ♔

Lysimachia clethroides
LOOSESTRIFE
☼ ☀ ✳✳✳✳ ↕ 90cm (36in) ↔ 60cm (24in)

A vigorous perennial once established, forming a clump of erect, narrowly leafy stems. Its characteristic swan-neck spikes of white flowers are borne in summer. ♔

x *Solidaster luteus* 'Lemore'
HYBRID GOLDEN ROD
☼ ✳✳✳✳   ↕ ↔ 80cm (32in)

The dense clumps of erect stems, clothed in narrow leaves, sport sparsely branched heads of pale lemon-yellow flowers from summer to autumn. Good for cutting. ♔

93

FLORAL EFFECT

FLOWERS ARE THE GREATEST ATTRIBUTE of many perennials, and can be relied upon to bring colour and fragrance to any garden or home. With blooms in all shades and shapes, in some cases produced over several months, there is scope for imaginative combinations, and for flowers all year round.

△ SUMMER BLOOMS *Mixed colours and flower forms are the strength of this scree planting, which flanks an informal path.*

Anemone × hybrida
'September Charm'
for autumn flowers

Whatever their other attractions, most gardeners grow perennials for their often abundant and reliably borne flowers. In all but the coldest areas, where snow or ice lie heavy on the garden during winter, there is hardly a day in the year when a perennial of some kind is not flowering. From spring to summer, and on into autumn, perennials can provide gardens with an unbroken, colourful and often fragrant display. Even in winter, there is a small but reliable fraternity of perennials that flowers despite the often poor light and intimidating cold.

FLOWER COLOUR

With flowers ranging from white and subtle pastel shades to strident reds and golden yellows, perennials will bring a truly formidable range of colours to the garden. These colours can be used to create varied effects, depending on whether you choose to mix them in a natural arrangement, or match them as part of a more structured theme. The strong colour contrasts often seen in the wild, where perennials such as golden rod (*Solidago*) and blue michaelmas daisies (*Aster*) grow together, can also be used to inspire plantings in the garden – or even recreated using the same or similar plants. Alternatively, a selection of plants with similarly toned blooms, whether hot, cool, or pale in colour, can be grown together to evoke a particular mood. For a more formal design, themed borders using only one flower colour are also an option.

FORM AND STRUCTURE

Flowerheads make an important, if temporary, contribution to the form and structure of a garden landscape. Varying from the statuesque to the fragile, the spheres, plumes, sprays, tall spikes, or flattened flowerheads of perennials can be combined for eye-catching contrast and effect.

△ HOT COLOURS *A fiery display of* Hemerocallis *'Stafford' and* Lilium *'Enchantment' brings warmth to a border.*

◁ STRONG CONTRAST *Striking effects can be achieved by using a few contrasting colours, here mainly blue and yellow.*

▷ INFORMAL BEAUTY *Pale oriental poppies, foxgloves, and* Dictamnus *make a delightful study in height and colour.*

Perennials with Spring Flowers

NO GARDEN PERENNIALS are more eagerly awaited than those that flower in spring. This is especially true in cold climates, where there is often little colour in the garden to relieve the long, bleak winters. With the increasing warmth and daylight of spring, the garden is rejuvenated as a wealth of perennials, including many bulbs, burst into flower.

Hylomecon japonica
HYLOMECON
☼ ☼ ❄❄❄   ↕ ↔ 30cm (12in)

This charming poppy relative is excellent in woodland, especially as a ground cover. It has deeply divided, toothed leaves and bears its simple flowers into early summer.

Bergenia 'Sunningdale'
ELEPHANT'S EAR
☼ ☼ ❄❄❄   ↕ 45cm (18in) ↔ 60cm (24in)

The evergreen, rounded, leathery leaves turn a warm copper-red in winter. Spring brings loose clusters of bell-shaped, lilac-magenta flowers on fleshy red stems.

Chionodoxa luciliae
SNOW GLORY
☼ ❄❄❄   ↕ 15cm (6in) ↔ 10cm (4in)

One of the loveliest and most reliable of early spring bulbs, with loose clusters of starry, sky-blue, white-eyed flowers. It is impressive planted in groups or drifts. 🏆

OTHER EVERGREEN PERENNIALS WITH SPRING FLOWERS

Aurinia saxatilis
Bergenia × *schmidtii*, see p.84
Epimedium pinnatum subsp. *colchicum*, see p.52
Erysimum 'Bowles' Mauve'
Euphorbia characias subsp. *wulfenii* 'Lambrook Gold'
Helleborus argutifolius, see p.120
Helleborus foetidus
Iberis sempervirens

Boykinia jamesii
BOYKINIA
☼ ❄❄❄❄ PH   ↕ ↔ 15cm (6in)

A choice perennial, bearing loose sprays of frilled, pinkish red, green-centred bell-flowers above its hummocks of rounded or kidney-shaped, glandular-hairy leaves.

Doronicum 'Frühlingspracht'
DORONICUM
☼ ☼ ❄❄❄   ↕ 40cm (16in) ↔ 90cm (36in)

Its German name, 'Spring Beauty', aptly describes this colourful perennial, with its double, golden yellow flowerheads above clumps of heart-shaped, scalloped leaves.

Lathyrus vernus 'Alboroseus'
SPRING VETCHLING
☼ ☼ ❄❄❄   ↕ 40cm (16in) ↔ 45cm (18in)

The crowded, erect stems of this reliable clump-former bear deeply divided leaves and loose, one-sided racemes of pink and white pea-flowers. Excellent with bulbs. 🏆

Primula denticulata var. *alba*
DRUMSTICK PRIMULA
☼ ☼ ❊❊❊   ↕ ↔ 45cm (18in)

This is the white form of a popular and easily grown perennial. Its rounded heads of yellow-eyed flowers are carried on stout stems above lush, leafy rosettes.

Pulmonaria 'Mawson's Blue'
PULMONARIA
☼ ☼ ❊❊❊❊   ↕ 35cm (14in) ↔ 45cm (18in)

Low clumps of softly-hairy leaves and clusters of dark blue flowers appear from late winter to spring. A pretty alternative to pulmonarias with spotted leaves.

Leucojum vernum var. *carpathicum*
SPRING SNOWFLAKE
☼ ☼ ❊❊❊   ↕ 25cm (10in) ↔ 15cm (6in)

Charming for group plantings, this bulb forms tufts of strap-shaped, fleshy leaves. Erect, fleshy stems bear nodding white bell-flowers with yellow-tipped segments.

Narcissus 'King Alfred'
DAFFODIL
☼ ☼ ❊❊❊❊   ↕ 45cm (18in) ↔ 30cm (12in)

Spectacular in large groups or drifts, this long-established daffodil is very popular for naturalizing. The large, golden yellow trumpet-flowers open on strong stems.

Narcissus 'Thalia'
DAFFODIL
☼ ☼ ❊❊❊❊   ↕ 35cm (14in) ↔ 15cm (6in)

One of a group of hybrids of *N. triandrus*, this beautiful daffodil has upright stems, each carrying a pair of nodding, milk-white flowers with yellow-tinged throats.

OTHER HERBACEOUS PERENNIALS WITH SPRING FLOWERS

Adonis vernalis, see p.104
Bergenia ciliata
Brunnera macrophylla, see p.84
Cardamine heptaphylla
Euphorbia polychroma, see p.85
Hacquetia epipactis, see p.43
Helleborus hybridus, see p.90
Pachyphragma macrophyllum
Trollius × cultorum 'Earliest of All', see p.91

FLORAL EFFECT

Perennials with Flowers from Early to Midsummer

AFTER THE INITIAL RUSH OF FLOWERS during spring, the scene is set for the countless perennials that flower from early to midsummer or, in some cases, beyond. They include many of our most popular and reliable garden plants, as well as others perhaps less well known though equally desirable, and provide us with the first blooms for summer borders.

Buphthalmum salicifolium
BUPHTHALMUM
☼ ☀ ❋❋❋ ↕ 60cm (24in) ↔ 45cm (18in)

Yellow daisy-flowers, excellent for cutting, are borne continuously during summer. The clumps of erect stems are clothed in narrow, willow-like, dark geen leaves.

Aconitum 'Ivorine'
MONKSHOOD
☼ ☀ ❋❋❋ ↕ ↔ 90cm (36in)

A vigorous, bushy perennial with deeply lobed, jaggedly cut leaves. In late spring and early summer, branching stems carry dense racemes of hooded ivory flowers.

Baptisia australis
FALSE INDIGO
☼ ❋❋❋ ↕ 1.5m (5ft) ↔ 90cm (36in)

The long racemes of blue, white-marked pea-flowers in early summer are followed by inflated seed pods. Stems and three-parted leaves are a bloomy blue-green. ♈

SMALL PERENNIALS WITH EARLY/ MIDSUMMER BLOOMS

Amsonia orientalis
Anthericum liliago, see p.36
Centaurea hypoleuca 'John Coutts', see p.82
Digitalis grandiflora
Geranium endressii
Hemerocallis 'Golden Chimes'
Incarvillea delavayi, see p.124
Paradisea liliastrum
Polemonium carneum

Delphinium 'Fanfare'
DELPHINIUM
☼ ❋❋❋ ↕ 2.2m (7ft) ↔ 45cm (18in)

Tall and beautiful, this impressive plant has deeply cut, lobed leaves, and dense, branched racemes of semi-double, white-eyed, silver-mauve summer flowers. ♈

Geranium 'Johnson's Blue'
CRANESBILL
☼ ☀ ❄❄❄   ↕ 45cm (18in) ↔ 60cm (24in)

One of the best garden cranesbills, this forms a clump of long-stalked, deep-cut leaves and freely bears lavender-blue summer flowers with paler eyes. ♔

Gypsophila paniculata 'Bristol Fairy'
☼ ❄❄❄   ↕ ↔ 1.1m (3½ft)

A favourite with florists, this popular perennial produces a loose mound of slender, branching stems and clouds of small, double white summer flowers. ♔

Hemerocallis middendorffii
DAYLILY
☼ ❄❄❄   ↕ 90cm (36in) ↔ 45cm (18in)

In early summer, the star-shaped, fragrant, orange-yellow flowers open from reddish brown buds over a bold clump of arching, semi-evergreen, strap-shaped leaves.

Iris 'Blue Eyed Brunette'
BEARDED IRIS
☼ ☀ ❄❄❄   ↕ 90cm (36in) ↔ 60cm (24in)

The typical fans of sword-shaped, grey-green leaves are topped, in early summer, by striking, large, reddish brown flowers with lilac splashes and golden beards. ♔

MEDIUM TO TALL PERENNIALS WITH EARLY/MIDSUMMER BLOOMS

Actaea racemosa
Aruncus dioicus, see p.24
Crambe cordifolia, see p.28
Euphorbia griffithii 'Fireglow', see p.90
Geranium psilostemon, see p.87
Iris sibirica
Macleaya microcarpa 'Kelway's Coral Plume'
Papaver orientale 'Cedric Morris', see p.83

Malva alcea var. *fastigiata*
MALLOW
☼ ❄❄❄   ↕ 80cm (32in) ↔ 60cm (24in)

The continuous display of large, five-petalled, deep pink mallow-flowers often lasts into autumn. Finely divided leaves clothe the narrow clumps of erect stems.

Scabiosa caucasica 'Clive Greaves'
SCABIOUS
☼ ❄❄❄   ↕ ↔ 60cm (24in)

This long-established favourite is always reliable in its flowering. The flattened, lavender-blue flowerheads, excellent for cutting, are borne over a long period. ♔

Stachys macrantha
STACHYS
☼ ❄❄❄   ↕ 60cm (24in) ↔ 30cm (12in)

From early summer onwards, the already attractive rosettes of wrinkly, scalloped, heart-shaped leaves are joined by spikes of long-tubed, pink-purple flowers.

FLORAL EFFECT

Perennials with Flowers from Mid- to Late Summer

Many of the perennials that flower in the middle of summer do so over a long period, taking advantage of the available warmth and sunlight. The following selection includes some plants that begin flowering in early summer, and others that continue blooming into early autumn, earning their place in the garden by extending the period of interest.

Aster amellus 'Veilchenkönigin'
ASTER
☼ ❋❋❋   ‡ 50cm (20in) ↔ 45cm (18in)

An excellent late summer perennial with clumps of erect, leafy stems topped by broad, flattened heads of yellow-centred, violet-purple daisy-flowers. ♛

Coreopsis grandiflora 'Badengold'
TICKSEED
☼ ☼ ❋❋❋   ‡ 90cm (36in) ↔ 45cm (18in)

This bright, cheerful-looking perennial has finely divided leaves and clumps of erect stems bearing orange-centred, deep yellow daisies throughout summer.

Digitalis × mertonensis
FOXGLOVE
☼ ☼ ❋❋❋   ‡ 90cm (36in) ↔ 30cm (12in)

"Crushed strawberry" exactly describes the colour of the tubular summer flowers of this robust, clump-forming plant. Its veiny leaves are also attractive. ♛

Inula ensifolia
INULA
☼ ☼ ❋❋❋   ‡ 60cm (24in) ↔ 30cm (12in)

A thoroughly reliable plant with narrow leaves and dense, bushy clumps of erect stems. These carry golden yellow daisy-heads continuously over a long period.

Kniphofia 'Samuel's Sensation'
TORCH LILY
☼ ☼ ❋❋❋   ‡ 1.5m (5ft) ↔ 75cm (30in)

From late summer to early autumn, the bold clumps of long, strap-shaped leaves are dwarfed by stiff-stemmed heads of bright scarlet flowers, ageing to yellow. ♛

OTHER PERENNIALS WITH FLOWERS IN MIDSUMMER

Campanula latifolia var. *macrantha*
Centranthus ruber, see p.92
Crocosmia 'Lucifer'
Galega 'His Majesty'
Hemerocallis 'Stafford'
Macleaya cordata
Prunella grandiflora
Stachys macrantha
Veronica austriaca subsp. *teucrium*
  'Crater Lake Blue'

Lavatera × *clementii* 'Rosea'
MALLOW

☼ ❋❋　　　　　↕ ↔ 2m (6ft)

Easily one of the most popular and
reliable mallows, forming a large, woody-
based, semi-evergreen bush, covered with
deep pink flowers during summer. ♉

OTHER PERENNIALS WITH
FLOWERS IN LATE SUMMER

Anemone × *hybrida* 'Königin Charlotte',
　see p.56
Aster cordifolius 'Sweet Lavender'
Crocosmia 'Severn Sunrise'
Gentiana asclepiadea, see p.113
Helenium 'Septemberfuchs', see p.110

Nepeta sibirica
NEPETA

☼ ☼ ❋❋❋　↕ 90cm (36in) ↔ 45cm (18in)

Aromatic, toothy leaves clothe the erect
clumps of four-angled stems. The long,
interrupted spikes of large, deep violet to
lilac-blue flowers are loved by bees.

Salvia × *sylvestris*
'Mainacht'

☼ ❋❋❋　　　↕ 60cm (24in) ↔ 30cm (12in)

Its German name, 'May Night', aptly
describes the velvety, dark indigo-blue
flowers, with purple bracts, borne in long
spikes on leafy, four-angled stems. ♉

Monarda 'Prärienacht'
BERGAMOT

☼ ☼ ❋❋❋　↕ 90cm (36in) ↔ 60cm (24in)

The dense clumps of downy, four-angled
stems bear crowded heads of purple-lilac
flowers with red-tinted green bracts. All
parts are aromatic when bruised.

Physostegia virginiana 'Vivid'
OBEDIENT PLANT

☼ ☼ ❋❋❋　↕ 60m (24in) ↔ 30cm (12in)

During summer, spikes of bright purple-
pink flowers, excellent for cutting, top
the dense clumps of four-angled, smooth,
erect stems, clothed in narrow leaves. ♉

Verbena bonariensis
VERBENA

☼ ❋❋　　　　　↕ 2m (6ft) ↔ 45cm (18in)

Bees, butterflies, and hoverflies are all
attracted to the delicate clusters of tiny,
lilac-purple flowers that crown the tall,
branching stems. It will seed freely. ♉

FLORAL EFFECT

101

Perennials with Autumn Flowers

FOR MANY GARDENERS, especially in cool-temperate zones, autumn is dominated by the brilliant tints of dying leaves and the equally colourful effect of seed heads, berries, and other fruits. Comparatively few perennials choose to flower at this time, but those that do are all the more valued, as their late displays enliven the garden before the onset of winter.

FLORAL EFFECT

Cyclamen hederifolium
DWARF CYCLAMEN
☀ ❋❋❋   ↕ 10cm (4in) ↔ 15cm (6in)

Neatly lobed, beautifully marbled leaves follow the exquisite, slender-stalked, pink or white flowers. Useful for ground cover under trees or for group plantings. ♛

Aconitum carmichaelii 'Arendsii'
MONKSHOOD
☀ ☼ ❋❋❋   ↕ 1.2m (4ft) ↔ 60cm (24in)

A bold, clump-forming perennial valued for its stems of dense, deeply cut, dark green leaves and panicles of helmeted, purple-blue, dark-eyed flowers.

Actaea matsumurae 'Elstead'
BUGBANE
☀ ❋❋❋   ↕ 1.2m (4ft) ↔ 60cm (24in)

The tall, arching stems of this graceful perennial bear long, cylindrical racemes of tiny white flowers above deeply divided, dark green to purple-tinted leaves. ♛

Leucanthemella serotina
MOON DAISY
☀ ☼ ❋❋❋   ↕ 2m (6ft) ↔ 90cm (36in)

Late and lovely, this bold daisy has clumps of tall, leafy stems and sprays of big white blooms that face and follow the sun. Once known as *Chrysanthemum uliginosum*. ♛

Anemone × *hybrida* 'September Charm'
JAPANESE ANEMONE
☀ ☼ ❋❋❋   ↕ 75cm (30in) ↔ 60cm (24in)

All the so-called Japanese anemones are reliable and useful. This one forms clumps of dark shoots with three-lobed leaflets and a long succession of clear pink flowers. ♛

Colchicum 'Waterlily'
AUTUMN CROCUS
☀ ❋❋❋   ↕ 12cm (5in) ↔ 10cm (4in)

This is one of the most spectacular dwarf bulbs, especially in large drifts. Its double, slender-tubed, pinkish lilac blooms may need support. Leaves emerge in spring. ♛

Nerine bowdenii 'Mark Fenwick'
NERINE
☀ ❋❋❋   ↕ 45cm (18in) ↔ 30cm (12in)

Spectacular in autumn, this bulb's smooth stems flaunt loose umbels of lily-like pink flowers. The narrow, strap-shaped leaves follow later. It is superb in group plantings.

Schizostylis coccinea 'Major'
KAFFIR LILY

☼ ❄❄ ↕ 60cm (24in) ↔ 30cm (12in)

This member of the *Gladiolus* family bears narrow, flattened, sword-shaped leaves and bold spikes of large, satiny red flowers. Plant it in groups for a striking effect. ♟

OTHER PERENNIALS WITH AUTUMN FLOWERS

Aster cordifolius 'Sweet Lavender'
Colchicum speciosum 'Album'
Eupatorium purpureum
  'Atropurpureum', see p.24
Kniphofia triangularis, see p.111
Leucojum autumnale
Sedum spectabile 'Carmen'
Sinacalia tangutica, see p.124
Tricyrtis hirta f. *alba*
Verbena bonariensis, see p.101

Strobilanthes atropurpurea
STROBILANTHES

☼ ☼ ❄❄❄ ↕ 1.2m (4ft) ↔ 90cm (36in)

Not commonly grown but an excellent perennial, freely bearing curved, hooded, indigo-blue or purple flowers on densely branched, bushy, and leafy stems.

Sedum 'Vera Jameson'
STONECROP

☼ ❄❄❄ ↕ 25cm (10in) ↔ 45cm (18in)

A true gem among the autumn-flowering sedums, this has low hummocks of pink-purple, bloomy leaves and crowded heads of star-shaped, rose-pink flowers. ♟

Tricyrtis formosana
TOAD LILY

☼ ☀ ❄❄❄ ↕ 80cm (32in) ↔ 45cm (18in)

The curious white, red-purple-spotted flowers of this erect, clump-forming plant deserve a close look to fully appreciate their beauty. The foliage is handsome too. ♟

Vernonia crinita
VERNONIA

☼ ☼ ❄❄❄ ↕ 2m (6ft) ↔ 90cm (3ft)

From late summer to autumn, flattened clusters of reddish purple flowerheads top the erect, strong-growing, narrow-leaved stems of this stately vernonia.

Perennials with Winter Flowers

IN COOL-TEMPERATE CLIMATES, where winter brings most growth to a standstill, the appearance of any plant in flower is always a surprise. However, certain perennials, including many bulbs, bloom in winter despite the hostile conditions. Those suggested here will provide interest at a time when other herbaceous plants have died down or lost their leaves.

Eranthis hyemalis
WINTER ACONITE
☼ ☀ ✳✳✳   ↕ 8cm (3in) ↔ 5cm (2in)

Plant this aconite in quantity to encourage large drifts. Its cup-shaped, bright yellow flowers are a cheery sight above the ruffs of toothed leaves in winter and spring. ♛

OTHER PERENNIALS WITH WINTER FLOWERS

Adonis amurensis
Bergenia × *schmidtii*, see p.84
Eranthis hyemalis 'Guinea Gold'
Galanthus nivalis 'Flore Pleno'
Helleborus argutifolius, see p.120
Helleborus × *sternii* Blackthorn Group
Narcissus 'Rijnveld's Early Sensation'
Petasites fragrans
Pulmonaria rubra 'Redstart'
Viola odorata

Adonis vernalis
ADONIS
☼ ✳✳✳   ↕ 38cm (15in) ↔ 45cm (18in)

In late winter and spring, cupped, golden yellow flowers top the clumps of deeply divided, ferny, bright green leaves. It will flower earlier in containers or if sheltered.

Crocus tommasinianus
CROCUS
☼ ☀ ✳✳✳   ↕ 10cm (4in) ↔ 7.5cm (3in)

Easily naturalized, this popular bulb bears slender-tubed, scented, pale silvery lilac to reddish purple flowers from winter to early spring, above narrow leaves. ♛

Arisarum vulgare
MONK'S COWL
☼ ☀ ✳✳✳   ↕ 15cm (6in) ↔ 13cm (5in)

This curious *Arum* relative bears broadly arrow-shaped green leaves, followed by hooded, brown- or purple-striped flowers, each with a protruding "nose".

Cyclamen coum f. *albissimum*
HARDY CYCLAMEN
☼ ☀ ✳✳✳   ↕ 10cm (4in) ↔ 15cm (6in)

The low hummocks of kidney-shaped, fleshy green or attractively marbled leaves are accompanied in winter by small white flowers with carmine-red mouths.

Galanthus nivalis 'Sandersii'
SNOWDROP
☼ ✳✳✳   ↕ ↔ 10cm (4in)

A charming and unusual variation of the familiar snowdrop, in which the flower ovaries and the tips of the inner segments are bright yellow. It is slow to increase.

Iris unguicularis 'Walter Butt'
IRIS
☼ ❄❄❄❄   ↕ 30cm (12in) ↔ 40cm (16in)

Over many weeks, this beautiful winter-flowerer produces a succession of large, fragrant, pale lavender-blue flowers from clumps of narrow, evergreen leaves.

Galanthus reginae-olgae subsp. *vernalis*
SNOWDROP
☼ ❄❄❄   ↕ ↔ 10cm (4in)

Borne in late winter and spring, the faintly scented, nodding white flowers have inner segments tipped green. It differs from the common snowdrop in its darker leaves.

Lathraea clandestina
BLUE TOOTHWORT
☼ ☼ ❄❄❄❄   ↕ 5cm (2in) ↔ 30cm (12in)

This parasitic plant can grow on the roots of trees such as alder, willow, and poplar. Two-lipped mauve flowers emerge from the white, scaly clumps during late winter.

Helleborus foetidus Wester Flisk Group
STINKING HELLEBORE
☼ ☼ ❄❄❄❄   ↕ 80cm (32in) ↔ 45cm (18in)

The stems, finger-like leaves, and flower-stalks of this outstanding, evergreen plant are suffused with red. The pendent, pale green bell-flowers have purple mouths.

Helleborus niger 'Potter's Wheel'
CHRISTMAS ROSE
☼ ❄❄❄❄   ↕ 30cm (12in) ↔ 45cm (18in)

A reliable selection of a favourite cottage-garden perennial, producing bowl-shaped white flowers, with green eyes, above low clumps of leathery, overwintering foliage.

Narcissus 'Bowles' Early Sulphur'
DAFFODIL
☼ ☼ ❄❄❄❄   ↕ 20cm (8in) ↔ 13cm (5in)

Bearing mid-yellow flowers in late winter, this seedling of *N. asturiensis* is one of the earliest-flowering small daffodils. It forms clumps of narrow, strap-shaped leaves.

Perennials with a Long Flowering Season

GIVEN THAT MOST GARDEN PERENNIALS, especially during spring, flower for a relatively limited period, it is natural that those with a more extended flowering season should be eagerly sought after by gardeners. These perennials usually bloom throughout summer or from summer into autumn, and will bring an element of continuity to the garden.

Geranium × riversleaianum
'Russell Prichard'
☼ ☀ ❄❄❄ ↕ 30cm (12in) ↔ 1m (3ft)

Ideal for ground cover, this low-grower has trailing stems clothed in neatly lobed, sharp-toothed, grey-green leaves. Deep magenta flowers appear in summer. ♕

Astrantia major 'Shaggy'
MASTERWORT
☼ ☀ ❄❄❄ ↕ 90cm (36in) ↔ 45cm (18in)

Clusters of tiny flowers, surrounded by large, jagged, green-tipped white bracts, open on branching stems in summer. The deeply cut leaves form bold clumps. ♕

Dicentra 'Stuart Boothman'
DICENTRA
☀ ❄❄❄ ↕ 30cm (12in) ↔ 40cm (16in)

A creeping perennial forming clumps of divided, fern-like, blue-grey leaves. Sprays of locket-shaped, pendent, deep pink flowers emerge from spring to summer. ♕

OTHER PERENNIALS WITH A LONG FLOWERING SEASON

Acanthus spinosus
Anthemis 'Susanna Mitchell'
Aster × frikartii 'Mönch', see p.22
Diascia 'Coral Belle'
Geranium wallichianum 'Buxton's Variety'
Lavatera × clementii 'Rosea', see p.101
Oenothera speciosa 'Rosea', see p.27
Scabiosa 'Butterfly Blue '
Viola cornuta Alba Group, see p.33

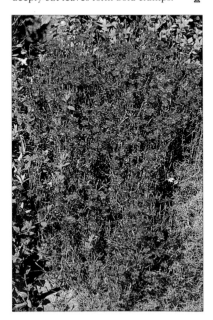

Dianthus deltoides
MAIDEN PINK
☼ ❄❄❄ ↕ 20cm (8in) ↔ 30cm (12in)

This reliable pink bears dark-eyed, white, pink, or red flowers throughout summer, above mats of slender, narrow-leaved stems. Thrives on well-drained soil. ♕

Epilobium glabellum of gardens
EPILOBIUM
☼ ☀ ❄❄❄ ↕↔ 20cm (8in)

During summer, the clumps of arching stems, densely clothed in semi-evergreen leaves, bear creamy white or pink-tinted flowers. Prefers a site in cool, damp shade.

Geum 'Red Wings'
GEUM
☼ ☀ ❄❄❄ ↕ 60cm (24in) ↔ 40cm (16in)

Flowering freely throughout summer, this perennial produces semi-double, brilliant scarlet flowers on branched stems, above clumps of softly-hairy, fresh green foliage.

Scabiosa caucasica 'Miss Willmott'
SCABIOUS

☼ ❄❄❄   ↕ 90cm (36in) ↔ 60cm (24in)

Large, solitary white flowerheads, with creamy white centres, adorn the clumps of erect stems in summer. The grey-green stem leaves are deeply divided. 🏆

Oenothera macrocarpa
OZARK

☼ ❄❄❄   ↕ 15cm (6in) ↔ 50cm (20in)

Better known as *O. missouriensis*, this vigorous plant has prostrate stems, willowy leaves, and a succession of golden yellow flowers from late spring into autumn. 🏆

Tradescantia Andersoniana Group 'Isis'
TRADESCANTIA

☼ ☼ ❄❄❄❄   ↕ ↔ 50cm (20in)

Dense clumps of erect stems, clothed in long-tapering, strap-shaped leaves, carry clusters of large, three-petalled, dark blue flowers from summer to autumn. 🏆

Phygelius × *rectus* 'African Queen'
CAPE FIGWORT

☼ ❄❄   ↕ 1m (3ft) ↔ 1.4m (4½ft)

A free-flowering plant with loose clumps of four-angled, woody-based stems. The pendent, tubular, pale red flowers, borne in summer, have yellow mouths. 🏆

Salvia microphylla
SAGE

☼ ☼ ❄❄   ↕ ↔ 1.2m (4ft)

The softly-hairy, evergreen leaves of this woody-based perennial or subshrub smell of blackcurrants when bruised. Its bright red flowers open from summer to autumn.

Viola 'Bowles' Black'
VIOLA

☼ ☼ ❄❄❄   ↕ 10cm (4in) ↔ 20cm (8in)

A charming pansy relative with evergreen tufts of leafy stems. It bears a succession of velvety black flowers, with golden eyes, from spring to autumn. Seeds freely.

FLORAL EFFECT

Perennials with Flowers in Flattened Heads or Sprays

THERE ARE MANY WAYS of creating interest in a border other than using plants of differing heights or varying foliage. One is to plant perennials that branch horizontally, or have flattened flowerheads or flowers borne along the same plane. These will provide a sharp contrast to plants that have an upright or rounded habit, or bear tall spikes of flowers.

FLORAL EFFECT

Achillea 'Coronation Gold'
ACHILLEA
☼ ✳✳✳ ↕ 90cm (36in) ↔ 45cm (18in)

The flattened heads of tiny yellow flowers in summer and autumn are excellent for cutting and drying. Deeply divided, silver-grey leaves form an evergreen clump. ♔

Chaerophyllum hirsutum 'Roseum'
CHAEROPHYLLUM
☼ ☼ ✳✳✳✳ ↕ 60cm (24in) ↔ 50cm (20in)

One of the loveliest of its family, it bears flattened, lilac-pink flowerheads in early summer, above clumps of hairy stems covered in ferny, deeply divided leaves.

Sedum spectabile
ICE PLANT
☼ ✳✳✳ ↕ ↔ 45cm (18in)

This staple of cottage gardens is adored by butterflies and bees. During late summer, flattened heads of pink flowers cover the low mound of fleshy, greyish leaves. ♔

Selinum wallichianum
SELINUM
☼ ☼ ✳✳✳ ↕ 1.2m (4ft) ↔ 60cm (24in)

A lovely member of the carrot family, with erect stems and divided, ferny leaves. In summer and autumn, tiny white flowers, with black anthers, are borne in flat heads.

Aster lateriflorus 'Horizontalis'
ASTER
☼ ☼ ✳✳✳ ↕ 60cm (24in) ↔ 40cm (16in)

This dense, bushy aster has a distinctive horizontal-branching habit, small leaves, and tiny pink-mauve flowers in autumn, when the leaves turn coppery purple. ♔

Sambucus ebulus
DANE'S ELDER
☼ ☼ ✳✳✳ ↕ 90cm (36in) ↔ indefinite

Bold, deeply divided leaves clothe this vigorous, suckering elder's erect stems. Its large, sweet-scented white flowerheads in summer are followed by black berries.

OTHER PERENNIALS WITH FLAT HEADS OR SPRAYS OF FLOWERS

Achillea filipendulina 'Gold Plate'
Aster amellus 'King George'
Aster amellus 'Sonia'
Chaerophyllum hirsutum
Heracleum maximum
Ligularia dentata
Sambucus adnata
Sedum 'Herbstfreude', see p.79
Solidago 'Crown of Rays'
Solidago 'Summer Sunshine'

Perennials with Flowers in Spikes

PERENNIALS WITH TALL, SPIKE-LIKE HEADS of flowers can create bold and dramatic effects, bringing structure and height to garden displays as they rise above other plants in stiff, tight spires or elegant, tapering racemes. In most flower spikes, the blooms open from the base upwards but some, like those of *Liatris spicata*, open from the top first.

Ligularia 'The Rocket'
LIGULARIA
☼ ☀ ✳✳✳   ↕ 1.8m (6ft) ↔ 1m (3ft)

Tall, black-stemmed spires of tiny yellow flowers rise impressively in summer above the piles of long-stalked, heart-shaped, toothy leaves. Best in moist soil. ♉

Delphinium 'Butterball'
DELPHINIUM
☼ ✳✳✳   ↕ 1.5m (5ft) ↔ 75cm (30in)

In early summer, and sometimes again later, this gorgeous delphinium's sturdy, erect stems bear dense, tapered racemes of semi-double, creamy white flowers.

Epilobium angustifolium var. *album*
ROSE BAY, WILLOW HERB
☼ ☀ ✳✳✳   ↕ 1.5m (5ft) ↔ 1m (3ft)

The erect stems of this vigorous perennial are clothed in narrow, willow-like leaves, and sport long spires of white flowers with green sepals in summer. Will seed freely.

OTHER PERENNIALS WITH FLOWERS IN SPIKES

Actaea racemosa
Asphodeline lutea, see p.28
Eremurus × *isabellinus* Shelford hybrids
Heuchera cylindrica
Liatris spicata
Lysimachia ephemerum, see p.137
Lythrum virgatum 'The Rocket'
Verbascum chaixii
Veronicastrum virginicum f. *album*,
    see p.35

Digitalis parviflora
RUSTY FOXGLOVE
☼ ✳✳✳   ↕ 1.2m (4ft) ↔ 45cm (18in)

Quite different to the common foxglove (*D. purpurea*), the stiff, architectural spikes of golden brown, red-veined flowers rise above low, leafy rosettes during summer.

Kniphofia 'Erecta'
TORCH LILY
☼ ☀ ✳✳✳   ↕ 90cm (36in) ↔ 60cm (24in)

A robust, clump-forming plant with stiff stems and strap-shaped leaves. The dense pokers of coral-red flowers become erect after opening in late summer and autumn.

Verbascum chaixii 'Album'
NETTLE-LEAVED MULLEIN
☼ ✳✳✳   ↕ 90cm (36in) ↔ 45cm (18in)

Striking and reliable, this mullein bears erect, often branched stems crowded with white, mauve-centred flowers in summer, over semi-evergreen, hairy leaf-rosettes. ♉

Perennials with Hot, Fiery-coloured Flowers

OTHER PERENNIALS WITH
ORANGE FLOWERS

Crocosmia × crocosmiiflora 'Jackanapes'
Euphorbia griffithii 'Fireglow', see p.90
Fritillaria imperialis
Kniphofia 'Prince Igor', see p.29
Kniphofia rooperi
Lilium 'Enchantment'
Lilium superbum
Pilosella aurantiaca
Potentilla 'William Rollison'
Primula bulleyana

FIERY-COLOURED FLOWERS may not appeal to gardeners with delicate tastes, but for many others, they inject life and passion into the garden. Reflecting the intensity and warmth of the sun, a single fiery-flowered perennial can brighten an otherwise bland border, while combining a few of them in a mixed planting will create a riot of colour.

FLORAL EFFECT

Asclepias tuberosa
BUTTERFLY WEED
☼ ❄❄❄   ↕ 90cm (3ft) ↔ 60cm (24in)

It may be a weed in its homeland, but in the garden the glowing orange flowers that crown the erect stems in late summer are a joy. Beware of the caustic, milky sap.

Dahlia 'Bishop of Llandaff'
DAHLIA
☼ ❄   ↕ 1.1m (3½ft) ↔ 45cm (18in)

In late summer, the semi-double, glowing red blooms of this popular perennial are strikingly off-set by its dusky-red stems and leaves. Protect the tubers in winter. ⚱

Geum coccineum
GEUM
☼ ☀ ❄❄❄   ↕ 50cm (20in) ↔ 30cm (12in)

Slender, branching stems carry orange-red flowers, with golden stamens, above a loose clump of deeply divided, hairy green leaves during spring and summer.

Crocosmia masoniorum
MONTBRETIA
☼ ☀ ❄❄❄   ↕ 1.2m (4ft) ↔ 60cm (24in)

A classic perennial, with bold clumps of sword-shaped, pleated leaves, and arching spikes of trumpet-shaped, rich orange-red flowers in summer. Good for cutting. ⚱

Gaillardia 'Dazzler'
BLANKET FLOWER
☼ ❄❄❄   ↕ 75cm (30in) ↔ 45cm (18in)

This bushy, often short-lived perennial has big, daisy flowerheads in summer and early autumn. The orange-red blooms are yellow-tipped with maroon centres. ⚱

Helenium 'Septemberfuchs'
HELENIUM
☼ ❄❄❄   ↕ 1.5m (5ft) ↔ 60cm (24in)

In late summer and autumn, stout clumps of erect, leafy stems carry a multitude of bright orange-brown, yellow-suffused daisy-flowers with brown hearts.

Lychnis chalcedonica 'Flore Pleno'
DOUBLE MALTESE CROSS
☼ ✳✳✳ ↕ 1.2m (4ft) ↔ 45cm (18in)

The single-flowered plant is attractive, but this is even better. In summer, erect, hairy, leafy stems bear dense clusters of double scarlet flowers. May need support.

Potentilla 'Monsieur Rouillard'
POTENTILLA
☼ ✳✳✳ ↕ 45cm (18in) ↔ 60cm (24in)

This potentilla has a loose clump of erect or spreading stems with deeply divided leaves. Its double, deep blood-red flowers, with yellow markings, open in summer.

Hemerocallis fulva 'Flore Pleno'
DAYLILY
☼ ☼ ✳✳✳ ↕ 75cm (30in) ↔ 1.2m (4ft)

In summer, erect stems bearing trumpet-shaped, double, orange-brown flowers, with dark red centres, rise above the bold clump of strap-shaped, arching leaves.

Primula 'Inverewe'
CANDELABRA PRIMULA
☼ ☼ ✳✳✳ ↕ ↔ 75cm (30in)

A strong-growing, semi-evergreen primula for damp sites, with a rosette of toothed leaves. Mealy-white stems carry whorls of striking, bright red flowers in summer.

Kniphofia triangularis
RED HOT POKER
☼ ✳✳✳ ↕ 75cm (30in) ↔ 45cm (18in)

A late-flowering and reliable red hot poker, producing clumps of narrow, grassy leaves, and numerous spikes of reddish orange flowers during autumn.

Monarda 'Squaw'
BERGAMOT
☼ ✳✳✳ ↕ 90cm (36in) ↔ 45cm (18in)

In summer and autumn, the hairy stems, forming bold clumps, bear dense clusters of bright red flowers, loved by bees. The leaves are aromatic when bruised.

OTHER PERENNIALS WITH RED FLOWERS

Chrysanthemum 'George Griffiths'
Crocosmia 'Lucifer', see p.122
Geum 'Red Wings', see p.106
Hemerocallis 'Stafford'
Heuchera 'Red Spangles'
Lobelia 'Will Scarlet'
Papaver orientale 'Beauty of
    Livermere', see p.93
Potentilla 'Flamenco'
Potentilla 'Gibson's Scarlet', see p.81

FLORAL EFFECT

111

Perennials with Cool-coloured Flowers

PINK, BLUE, AND PALE YELLOW are all colours that are cool to the eye, and bring a delicate subtlety to plantings in the garden. White too, plays a similar role, and when used with care and discretion, these cool-coloured flowers can have a soothing, almost therapeutic effect, particularly if they bloom during the heat of summer.

Centaurea pulcherrima
CENTAUREA
☼ ❋❋❋   ↕ 40cm (16in) ↔ 60cm (24in)

Slender stems rise from clumps of deeply lobed or entire, woolly-backed leaves to bear lovely rose-pink, pale-centred corn-flowers from late spring to early summer.

OTHER PERENNIALS WITH EARLY, COOL-COLOURED FLOWERS

Aquilegia 'Hensol Harebell'
Corydalis flexuosa 'China Blue', see p.71
Dicentra spectabilis 'Alba', see p.114
Epimedium x *versicolor* 'Sulphureum'
Omphalodes cappadocica 'Cherry Ingram'
  Paeonia mlokosewitschii, see p.157
  Polemonium caeruleum
Pulmonaria 'Mawson's Blue', see p.97
Veratrum album, see p.91

Agapanthus 'Snowy Owl'
AFRICAN LILY
☼ ☼ ❋❋❋   ↕ 1.2m (4ft) ↔ 60cm (24in)

In late summer, sturdy stems carry large, loosely rounded umbels of bell-shaped, pure white flowers above the bold clumps of narrow, strap-shaped green leaves.

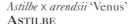

Astilbe x *arendsii* 'Venus'
ASTILBE
☼ ☼ ❋❋❋   ↕ 90cm (36in) ↔ 45cm (18in)

Large, frothy, conical plumes of tiny pink flowers rise above robust clumps of much-divided, bright green, handsome leaves in early summer. It prefers a moist soil.

Anchusa azurea 'Loddon Royalist'
ALKANET
☼ ❋❋❋   ↕ 90cm (36in) ↔ 60cm (24in)

The branched heads of attractive, deep blue flowers, with white bird's-eyes, top tall, sturdy clumps of erect, rough-hairy and leafy stems during early summer. ♔

Campanula persicifolia 'Telham Beauty'
☼ ☼ ❋❋❋   ↕ 90cm (36in) ↔ 30cm (12in)

A lovely form of a popular, cottage-garden perennial, the tall, slender stems bearing racemes of large, light blue bell-flowers in summer. Both easy to grow and reliable.

Chrysanthemum 'Clara Curtis'
CHRYSANTHEMUM
☼ ❋❋❋   ↕ 75cm (30in) ↔ 60cm (24in)

Fine-cut leaves cover the bushy, woody-based clump of stems. The scented, long-lasting, clear pink daisy-heads are borne freely from late summer into autumn.

Iris winogradowii
IRIS
☼ ❄❄❄ ↕7.5cm (3in) ↔10cm (4in)

In early spring, primrose-yellow flowers, with green-flecked falls, rise above tufts of four-sided, slender leaves. Excellent for containers, troughs, or a rock garden. ♈

Penstemon heterophyllus
'Blue Gem'
☼ ◑ ❄❄❄ ↕ ↔40cm (16in)

Striking in flower, this evergreen or semi-evergreen, woody-based perennial bears slender, glossy leaves, and dense, erect racemes of tubular blue summer flowers.

Delphinium 'Blue Bees'
DELPHINIUM
☼ ❄❄❄ ↕1m (3ft) ↔45cm (18in)

The upright, branching, wiry stems bear deeply cut leaves, and racemes of long-spurred, clear blue, white-eyed flowers in early summer and again in late summer.

Monarda 'Croftway Pink'
BERGAMOT
☼ ◑ ❄❄❄ ↕90cm (36in) ↔60cm (24in)

Popular with bees, this aromatic perennial has erect stems clothed in paired leaves. In summer, it freely bears clusters of clear rose-pink flowers with dark bracts. ♈

OTHER PERENNIALS WITH LATE, COOL-COLOURED FLOWERS

Agapanthus 'Midnight Blue', see p.26
Geranium × *oxonianum* 'A.T. Johnson'
Liatris spicata 'Floristan Weiss'
Oenothera stricta 'Sulphurea', see p.35
Phlox paniculata 'Fujiyama', see p.115
Phygelius × *rectus* 'Moonraker'
Platycodon grandiflorus f. *albus*
Salvia uliginosa
Schizostylis coccinea 'Viscountess Byng', see p.75

Gentiana asclepiadea
WILLOW GENTIAN
☼ ◑ ❄❄❄ ↕90cm (36in) ↔60cm (12in)

Pairs of willow-like leaves clothe the bold clumps of arching stems. Pale or deep blue flowers emerge from the upper leaf axils from late summer to autumn. ♈

Paeonia lactiflora 'Sarah Bernhardt'
PEONY
☼ ◑ ❄❄❄ ↕ ↔90cm (36in)

This robust perennial produces clumps of erect, leafy stems, which bear very large, fragrant, fully double, rose-pink blooms in early summer. Excellent for cutting. ♈

Sidalcea 'Elsie Heugh'
CHECKERBLOOM
☼ ❄❄❄ ↕90cm (36in) ↔45cm (18in)

A reliable plant with erect or spreading stems that bear deeply lobed stem leaves, and tall racemes of long-lasting, satiny, purple-pink mallow-flowers in summer. ♈

Perennials with Pale-coloured Flowers

PALE-COLOURED FLOWERS can provide one of the most effective means of illuminating a dark corner or shaded border in the garden. Shining out against a backdrop of dark foliage, they attract and reflect any available light, and can even draw attention to borders and beds at the end of the day when darkness is falling.

Dictamnus albus
BURNING BUSH
☼-☼ ✳✳✳ ↕ 90cm (36in) ↔ 60cm (24in)

A slow-growing plant forming clumps of deeply divided, aromatic foliage, and in early summer bold, erect racemes of white flowers with conspicuous stamens. ♔

Coreopsis verticillata 'Moonbeam'
TICKSEED
☼-☼ ✳✳✳ ↕ 50cm (20in) ↔ 45cm (18in)

In summer, a profusion of lemon-yellow flowerheads covers this low, bushy plant. Its slender, branched stems bear finely cut leaves. Ideal for the front of a border.

OTHER PERENNIALS WITH PALE-COLOURED FLOWERS

Cephalaria gigantea, see p.78
Iris 'Cliffs of Dover'
Kniphofia 'Maid of Orleans'
Leucanthemum × *superbum* 'Wirral Pride', see p.85
Persicaria bistorta 'Superba'
Polemonium carneum
Potentilla recta var. *sulphurea*
Ranunculus bulbosus 'F.M. Burton'
Salvia govaniana

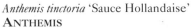

Anthemis tinctoria 'Sauce Hollandaise'
ANTHEMIS
☼ ✳✳✳ ↕↔ 60cm (24in)

Long-stalked, yellow-centred, pale cream daisy-heads are borne freely over many weeks during summer, above clumps of finely divided, dark green leaves.

Campanula persicifolia 'Chettle Charm'
PEACH-LEAVED BELLFLOWER
☼-☼ ✳✳✳ ↕ 90cm (36in) ↔ 30cm (12in)

One of the loveliest varieties of a popular perennial, with tall, slender stems, narrow leaves, and loose sprays of pale summer bell-flowers, tinged blue at the edges. ♔

Dicentra spectabilis 'Alba'
BLEEDING HEART
☼ ✳✳✳ ↕ 60cm (24in) ↔ 45cm (18in)

This beautiful and elegant perennial has ferny, pale green foliage, and produces long stems hung with locket-shaped white flowers from late spring to summer. ♔

Gaura lindheimeri
GAURA
☼-☼ ✳✳✳ ↕ 1.2m (4ft) ↔ 90cm (36in)

Branched, willowy stems of slender leaves give this gaura a bushy, loose habit. Pink buds open to elegant sprays of white star-flowers in late summer and autumn. ♔

Phlox paniculata 'Fujiyama'
BORDER PHLOX
☼ ☼ ❄❄❄ ↕ 90cm (36in) ↔ 60cm (24in)

Impressive, large heads of snow-white flowers crown the stout clumps of upright, leafy stems in late summer. This is one of the best perennials for white flowers. ♔

Phygelius aequalis 'Yellow Trumpet'
PHYGELIUS
☼ ❄❄ ↕ 1m (3ft) ↔ 1.2m (4ft)

This strong-grower has clumps of four angled, woody-based, leafy stems bearing loose racemes of drooping, tubular, pale yellow flowers in summer and autumn. ♔

Gillenia trifoliata
INDIAN PHYSIC
☼ ☼ ❄❄❄ ↕ 1m (3ft) ↔ 60cm (24in)

Wiry, reddish stems bear divided, bronze-green leaves, and sprays of small white flowers in spring and summer. Decorative red calyces remain after the petals fall. ♔

Kirengeshoma palmata
KIRENGESHOMA
☼ ❄❄❄ ↕ 1.2m (4ft) ↔ 75cm (30in)

A handsome perennial with dark stems and large, boldly toothed or lobed leaves. Sprays of waxy, pale yellow flowers are borne in autumn. It enjoys moist soil. ♔

Kniphofia 'Little Maid'
TORCH LILY
☼ ☼ ❄❄❄ 60cm (24in) ↔ 45cm (18in)

In autumn, erect stems rise from clumps of grassy leaves to bear long, dense spikes of tubular, buff-tinted yellow flowers, pale green in bud, and fading to ivory.

Trollius × *cultorum* 'Alabaster'
GLOBEFLOWER
☼ ☼ ❄❄❄ ↕ 60cm (24in) ↔ 40cm (16in)

Beautiful, rounded, pale primrose-yellow flowers rise on long stems above clumps of long-stalked, lobed, glossy leaves from late spring to summer. It likes moist soil.

Perennials with Fragrant Flowers

IT IS OFTEN SURPRISING to find that a beautiful flower does not have a scent to match. However, most highly fragrant perennials have relatively small flowers, and those with large, scented blooms are frequently white or pale coloured. Many fragrant flowers are at their best at the end of the day, when night-flying pollinators visit the garden.

Iris graminea
PLUM TART IRIS
☼ ☀ ❄❄❄   ↕ 40cm (16in) ↔ 30cm (12in)

During late spring and early summer, the small, violet-purple flowers of this clump-forming, grassy-leaved iris emit a distinct, fruity fragrance, like hot plums. ▽

PERENNIALS WITH FRAGRANT WINTER AND SPRING FLOWERS

Convallaria majalis
Crocus laevigatus
Erysimum cheiri 'Bloody Warrior'
Galanthus 'Brenda Troyle'
Galanthus 'S. Arnott'
Hyacinthoides non-scripta
Iris unguicularis
Narcissus jonquilla
Narcissus 'Rugulosus'
Petasites fragrans
Viola odorata

Dianthus 'Doris'
MODERN PINK
☼ ❄❄❄   ↕↔ 40cm (16in)

Double, pale pink, dark-centred flowers top the blue-grey, bloomy, narrow-leaved stems of this much-loved and reliable pink in summer and early autumn. ▽

Hemerocallis 'Marion Vaughn'
DAYLILY
☼ ☀ ❄❄❄   ↕ 85cm (34in) ↔ 75cm (30in)

During summer, clusters of very fragrant, lemon-yellow trumpet-flowers are borne freely on erect stems above bold clumps of semi-evergreen, strap-shaped leaves. ▽

Erysimum cheiri 'Harpur Crewe'
WALLFLOWER
☼ ❄❄❄   ↕ 30cm (12in) ↔ 60cm (24in)

The scent of wallflowers is one of the joys of spring. Although short-lived, they are available in many flower colours. This one bears cheerful, double yellow blooms.

Hosta 'Honeybells'
PLANTAIN LILY
☼ ☀ ❄❄❄   ↕ 75cm (30in) ↔ 1.2m (4ft)

A vigorous clump-former with attractive, heart-shaped, veined, and wavy-margined leaves. Fragrant white or lavender-blue-streaked flowers open in late summer. ▽

Lilium regale
REGAL LILY
☼ ❄❄❄   ↕ 1.5m (5ft) ↔ 40cm (16in)

One of the most famous of fragrant lilies, this is a must for sunny gardens. Robust stems flaunt bold clusters of white, pink-striped trumpet-flowers in summer. ▽

Narcissus poeticus var. *recurvus*
OLD PHEASANT'S EYE
☼ ◐ ❄❄❄ ↕ 35cm (14in) ↔ 30cm (12in)

Beautiful, crisp white flowers with pale
yellow, red-rimmed cups rise above the
narrow, strap-shaped leaves in late spring.
In time, it forms clumps or patches. ♈

Nicotiana sylvestris
ORNAMENTAL TOBACCO PLANT
☼ ◐ ❄ ↕ 1.5m (5ft) ↔ 60cm (24in)

The bold, leafy stems carry large heads of
long-tubed, fragrant white flowers during
summer. Perennial in warm sites, it is best
treated as biennial in colder areas. ♈

Phlox maculata 'Alpha'
MEADOW PHLOX
☼ ◐ ❄❄❄ ↕ 90cm (36in) ↔ 60cm (24in)

More elegant than the popular border
variety, this phlox produces erect clumps
of leafy stems, which bear large heads of
fragrant pink flowers during summer. ♈

Primula auricula var. *albocincta*
AURICULA
☼ ◐ ❄❄❄ ↕ ↔ 20cm (8in)

Gorgeous for a rock garden or container,
with clumps of evergreen, greyish, white-
edged leaves topped by umbels of yellow,
white-eyed, scented flowers in spring.

Tulbaghia violacea
TULBAGHIA
☼ ❄❄ ↕ 50cm (20in) ↔ 25cm (10in)

Erect stems carry loose umbels of fragrant
lilac flowers in summer and early autumn
over clumps of narrow, grey-green leaves.
It will thrive in a warm, sunny site.

Verbena corymbosa 'Gravetye'
VERBENA
☼ ❄❄ ↕ 90cm (3ft) ↔ 60cm (24in)

Beautiful when in flower, this perennial
produces dense heads of pinkish purple,
white-eyed flowers throughout summer,
which give off a sweet perfume.

FOLIAGE EFFECT

WHILE MOST FLOWERS bloom for a relatively brief period, foliage can provide a continuous source of drama and atmosphere in the garden. Perennials that have contrasting leaf shapes, textures, and colours will enliven beds and borders, and can also make a striking display as specimen plants.

Hosta 'Big Daddy' for bold foliage

△ DELICATE CONTRAST *A feathery-leaved* Dicentra *complements the silver-splashed, rounded foliage of a* Lamium.

Foliage provides a constant focus in the garden, acting as both a foil for flowers and a firm basis for design. Perennials in this section offer a huge range of leaf shapes, colours, and arrangements which, used thoughtfully or with flair, can be combined for spectacular effects. Large-leaved perennials, such as ornamental rhubarbs (*Rheum*), can make impressive specimen plants, or add structure and impact to beds and borders. Foliage perennials will also prove their worth in containers, providing a satisfying, long-lasting display that can be moved around the garden. Richly tinted foliage is often associated with autumn, but it is worth remembering that many perennials offer leaves that are attractively variegated or coloured for much of the year. Excellent for brightening a dull border, they are also useful for shady sites where other plants may struggle to flower without sufficient sun. In winter, when most other perennials lie below ground, those with evergreen or overwintering leaves, such as bergenias and hardy ferns, can also be used to bring interest and life to the garden landscape.

FOLIAGE CHARACTERISTICS

Leaf arrangement, shape, and colour are all important elements to consider when combining foliage perennials for eye-catching contrasts and effects.

ARRANGEMENT *of leaves is a characteristic feature of every plant. Exploit this to bring structure and texture to the garden.*

SHAPE AND SIZE *can be contrasted for extra interest. Leaves with jagged, feathery, or spiny margins will all create different effects.*

COLOUR *in foliage can be used to create a calm, dark backdrop, or to bring brightness and warmth to shady sites in the garden.*

◁ COLOUR CONTAINER *Yellow-striped* Hakonechloa *and blue-leaved* Acaena *contrast here with upright* Imperata.

▷ DRAMATIC LEAVES *Perennials with bold foliage make good specimen plants or can be used to great effect in a border.*

Perennials with Evergreen or Overwintering Foliage

IN WINTER, when most herbaceous perennials have died down to below ground level and no longer provide a focus in the garden, it is important to have at least a scattering of plants with evergreen leaves or foliage that overwinters in an attractive state. Even when flowerless, these plants will bring continual colour and interest to any garden.

Asarum europaeum
ASARABACCA
☼ ☀ ❄❄❄   ↕ 8cm (3in) ↔ 30cm (12in)

One of the best perennials for ground cover, and attractive all year round. In late spring, the dense carpet of kidney-shaped, glossy leaves hides curious little flowers.

Helleborus argutifolius
CORSICAN HELLEBORE
☼ ☼ ❄❄❄   ↕ ↔ 90cm (36in)

This handsome plant can be admired all year. Pale green, overwintering stems bear beautifully veined, prickle-toothed leaves, and apple-green flowers in late winter. ♈

Kniphofia caulescens
RED HOT POKER
☼ ☼ ❄❄❄   ↕ 1.2m (4ft) ↔ 90cm (36in)

An impressive kniphofia, producing large clumps of fine-toothed, blue-green leaves, topped in late summer by imposing, coral-red flower spikes, fading to yellow. ♈

Bergenia cordifolia 'Purpurea'
ELEPHANT'S EAR
☼ ☼ ❄❄❄   ↕ 60cm (24in) ↔ 75cm (30in)

The leathery, rounded, deep green leaves form a low patch, becoming purple- or red-tinted in winter. In winter and early spring, it has magenta-purple flowers. ♈

Iris foetidissima 'Variegata'
GLADWYN
☼ ☼ ❄❄❄   ↕ ↔ 60cm (24in)

A superb, variegated form of gladwyn, its evergreen, strap-shaped, shiny leaves are boldly margined white. Orange seedheads follow the purple summer flowers. ♈

Phormium cookianum subsp. *hookeri* 'Tricolor'
☼ ❄❄   ↕ ↔ 2m (6ft)

One of the most colourful evergreen perennials, developing a large mound of arching, leathery, glossy green leaves with creamy yellow and red margins. ♈

120

Polypodium interjectum 'Cornubiense'
POLYPODY
☼ ☼ ❄❄❄ ↕↔40cm (16in)

The much-divided, rich green fronds of
this strong-growing, creeping fern provide
excellent ground cover. It is also suitable
for a rock garden, wall, or container.

Pulmonaria saccharata 'Leopard'
PULMONARIA
☼ ☼ ❄❄❄ ↕30cm (12in) ↔60cm (24in)

One of the best overwintering, silvery-
spotted pulmonarias, it makes particularly
effective ground cover. Violet-red flowers
are produced from winter to late spring.

Tellima grandiflora
FRINGE CUPS
☼ ❄❄❄ ↕80cm (32in) ↔30cm (12in)

The clump of long-stalked, heart-shaped,
hairy and scalloped leaves will overwinter
in all but severe conditions. Loose spikes
of greenish white flowers appear in spring.

**OTHER EVERGREEN OR OVER-
WINTERING PERENNIALS**

Acanthus mollis 'Hollard's Gold'
Astelia chathamica
Bergenia 'Bressingham Ruby'
Epimedium pinnatum subsp. *colchicum*,
  see p.52
Helleborus foetidus Wester Flisk Group,
  see p.105
Iris japonica
Liriope muscari 'Variegata'
Phlomis russeliana
Phormium tenax, see p.123
Polystichum munitum, see p.148
Polystichum setiferum Divisilobum
  Group
Reineckia carnea
Santolina chamaecyparissus
Shibataea kumasasa
Yucca filamentosa

Vinca minor 'Argenteovariegata'
PERIWINKLE
☼ ☼ ❄❄❄ ↕15cm (6in) ↔indefinite

All periwinkles are useful as ground cover,
but this also has leaves with attractive,
creamy white margins. Pale violet-blue
flowers open in spring and autumn. ♔

FOLIAGE EFFECT

Perennials with Strap- or Sword-shaped Leaves

ᴘERENNIALS WITH CLUMPS of long, narrow leaves are irresistible and always striking. Regardless of whether the leaves stand stiff and upright, or bend and arch in a more graceful manner, they are valuable for contrasting with more conventional, broad-leaved perennials in beds or borders, and can also be used as dramatic specimen plants.

FOLIAGE EFFECT

Arundo donax 'Macrophylla'
ARUNDO
☼ ❄❄❄   ↕ 5m (15ft) ↔ 2m (6ft)

This giant, evergreen grass produces long, arching, glaucous leaves, and bamboo-like stems flaunting feathery plumes in summer. It prefers a warm, sheltered site.

Eryngium agavifolium
ERYNGIUM
☼ ❄❄   ↕ 1.2m (4ft) ↔ 60cm (24in)

The sharply toothed, glossy, evergreen leaves form a striking, erect clump, above which sturdy stems carry cylindrical heads of tiny, greenish white flowers in summer.

Iris pseudacorus 'Variegata'
YELLOW FLAG
☼ ◐ ❄❄❄   ↕ ↔ 1.2m (4ft)

A vigorous iris for wet sites, forming a large patch of tall green leaves with bold white or creamy yellow bands. In summer, yellow flowers are borne on erect stems. ♈

EVERGREEN PERENNIALS WITH STRAP- OR SWORD-SHAPED LEAVES

Beschorneria yuccoides
Crocosmia paniculata
Dianella tasmanica
Eryngium eburneum, see p.28
Eryngium pandanifolium
Iris confusa
Iris foetidissima
Watsonia pillansii
Yucca filamentosa
Yucca recurvifolia

Crocosmia 'Lucifer'
MONTBRETIA
☼ ◐ ❄❄   ↕ 1.2m (4ft) ↔ 45cm (18in)

A bright and cheerful perennial, forming a clump of robust, sword-shaped leaves. Its arching, branched spikes of brilliant red, late-summer flowers are good for cutting. ♈

Hemerocallis 'Gentle Shepherd'
DAYLILY
☼ ◐ ❄❄❄   ↕ 65cm (26in) ↔ 1.2m (4ft)

During summer, the bold clump of semi-evergreen, narrow, arching green leaves is topped by wide-spreading, ivory-white flowers with green throats.

Iris sibirica 'Perry's Blue'
IRIS
☼ ◐ ❄❄❄   ↕ 1.2m (4ft) ↔ 1m (3ft)

Erect clumps of narrow, grass-like leaves are joined in early summer by blue-violet flowers on upright, soldier-like stems. Its winter seed capsules are also decorative.

Sisyrinchium striatum 'Aunt May'
SISYRINCHIUM

☼ ❋❋❋ ↕ 50cm (20in) ↔ 30cm (12in)

This iris-like perennial has striking fans of sword-shaped, grey-green leaves, boldly striped creamy yellow. In summer, it bears straw-yellow flowers in stiff spikes.

Kniphofia 'Wrexham Buttercup'
TORCH LILY

☼ ❋❋❋ ↕ 1.2m (4ft) ↔ 60cm (24in)

The long, arching, narrow green leaves of this perennial form a dense clump. Its poker-like heads of rich yellow flowers are carried on strong stems in summer.

Persicaria macrophylla
PERSICARIA

☼ ◐ ❋❋❋ ↕↔ 30cm (12in)

A semi-evergreen perennial with lance-shaped, conspicuously veined leaves, and dense spikes of pink to red flowers borne through summer into autumn.

Phormium tenax
NEW ZEALAND FLAX

☼ ❋❋ ↕ 4m (12ft) ↔ 2m (6ft)

Few perennials are as eye-catching as this flax, with its sword-shaped, glaucous-grey, evergreen leaves, and statuesque panicles of waxy, dark red flowers in summer. ♈

Yucca flaccida
YUCCA

☼ ❋❋❋ ↕ 55cm (22in) ↔ 1.5m (5ft)

Reliable and evergreen, this yucca forms a bold rosette of narrow, dark blue-green leaves with wispy marginal fibres. Large heads of ivory flowers emerge in summer.

HERBACEOUS PERENNIALS WITH STRAP- OR SWORD-SHAPED LEAVES

Agapanthus 'Blue Giant', see p.90
Asphodelus albus
Bletilla striata
Crinum x *powellii*, see p.46
Crocosmia masoniorum, see p.110
Gladiolus communis subsp. *byzantinus*, see p.39
Hemerocallis fulva
Iris 'Shelford Giant'
Kniphofia 'Royal Standard'
Moraea spathulata
Nerine bowdenii

FOLIAGE EFFECT

123

Perennials with Deep-cut or Jagged Leaves

THE NUMBER OF PERENNIALS with bold, entire leaves has led to an increase in demand for plants that have deeply cut, divided, or jaggedly cut foliage to use with them as a contrast. Fortunately, their number and variety are great, and many of them also have the added advantage of attractive flowers.

Rodgersia henrici
RODGERSIA
☼ ☀ ✳✳✳   ↕ ↔ 1m (3ft)

All rodgersias sport handsome foliage, but this one is particularly desirable. It has large, horse-chestnut-like leaves, and pink or white flower plumes in summer.

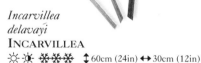

Astilbe 'Bronce Elegans'
ASTILBE
☼ ☀ ✳✳✳   ↕ 30cm (12in) ↔ 25cm (10in)

One of the smallest and daintiest astilbes, forming hummocks of ferny, glossy, dark green leaves, and neat little plumes of pinkish red flowers in late summer. 🏆

Incarvillea delavayi
INCARVILLEA
☼ ☀ ✳✳✳   ↕ 60cm (24in) ↔ 30cm (12in)

Already attractive with its clump of bold, deeply divided, dark green leaves, this plant really catches the eye in summer when its rose-pink trumpet-flowers open.

Sinacalia tangutica
CHINESE RAGWORT
☼ ☀ ✳✳✳   ↕ 1.2m (4ft) ↔ indefinite

The creeping rootstock produces stout, dark stems clothed in jaggedly cut leaves. In autumn, substantial, conical heads of yellow flowers emerge. It can be invasive.

Actaea simplex Atropurpurea Group
BUGBANE
☼ ✳✳✳   ↕ 1.2m (4ft) ↔ 60cm (24in)

The loose clumps of large, much-divided, dark green to purplish leaves are topped during autumn by long, cylindrical, dark-stemmed racemes of tiny white flowers.

Ligularia przewalskii
LIGULARIA
☼ ☀ ✳✳✳   ↕ 2m (6ft) ↔ 1m (3ft)

Easily recognized, this robust perennial develops large clumps of rounded, sharply divided, deep-cut leaves. Dark-stemmed spires of yellow flowers open in summer. 🏆

OTHER PERENNIALS WITH
DEEP-CUT OR JAGGED LEAVES

Acanthus spinosus
Aconitum japonicum
Astrantia major 'Shaggy', see p.106
Geranium palmatum, see p.129
Kirengeshoma palmata, see p.115
Ligularia japonica
Rheum palmatum var. *tanguticum*, see p.129
Rodgersia pinnata, see p.67
Rodgersia podophylla, see p.139

Perennials with Feathery Foliage

SOME PERENNIALS HAVE LEAVES so finely divided that they create a striking feathery or ferny effect. This provides the perfect foil for more dramatic foliage, or for hot-coloured flowers that stand out against the delicate leaves. Many will also make excellent specimen plants in a prominent site in the garden, or featured in containers.

Meum athamanticum
BALDMONEY, SPIGNEL
☼ ❋❋❋　　　↕ 45cm (18in) ↔ 30cm (12in)

Like fennel, this is a member of the carrot family, with similarly feathery, deeply divided, aromatic leaves. Dense heads of tiny white flowers are borne in summer.

Adiantum pedatum
MAIDENHAIR FERN
☼ ❋❋❋　　　↕ ↔ 40cm (16in)

Given time and a sheltered, moist site, this lovely, hardy fern will develop a large clump of slender, glossy black stalks with delicate, much-divided fronds. ♈

Corydalis cheilanthifolia
CORYDALIS
☼ ☼ ❋❋❋　　↕ 30cm (12in) ↔ 25cm (10in)

Each finely divided, orange-tinted leaf is like a green feather. Slender racemes of deep yellow flowers are borne in spring and summer. It will seed around if happy.

OTHER PERENNIALS WITH FEATHERY FOLIAGE

Achillea millefolium 'Cerise Queen'
Adiantum venustum
　Adonis vernalis, see p.104
　　Argyranthemum gracile 'Chelsea Girl'
　　Artemisia alba 'Canescens'
　　　Ferula communis
　　　　Paesia scaberula
Polystichum setiferum
　　Plumosodivisilobum Group
Selinum wallichianum, see p.108

Aruncus aethusifolius
ARUNCUS
☼ ☼ ❋❋❋　　↕ 25cm (10in) ↔ 40cm (16in)

A charming plant with small hummocks of finely divided, crisp green leaves, which turn orange or yellow in autumn. Small white flower plumes appear in summer. ♈

Foeniculum vulgare 'Purpureum'
PURPLE FENNEL
☼ ❋❋❋　　　↕ 1.8m (6ft) ↔ 45cm (18in)

This aromatic fennel has finely divided, plumed leaves, which are bronze-purple when young, ageing to blue-green. Flat heads of yellow flowers open in summer.

Onychium japonicum
CARROT FERN
☼ ☼ ❋❋❋　　↕ 50cm (20in) ↔ 30cm (12in)

An elegant fern, producing a dense clump of finely divided, bright green fronds on slender, wiry stalks. Some variants are less hardy and are best cultivated under glass.

125

Perennials with Spiny Leaves

THE JAGGED EFFECT of spiny or prickly leaved plants has a definite appeal for some gardeners. Often architectural in habit, as well as ornamental, these distinctive plants can bring structure to borders or make bold specimens. Many are particularly useful for dry sites, as their spiny leaves are specially adapted to minimize water loss.

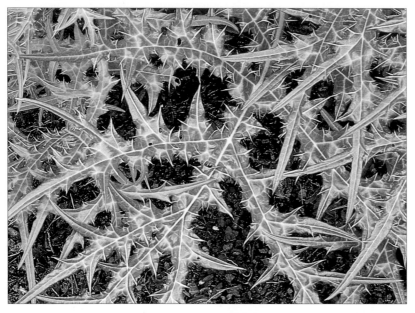

Acanthus spinosus Spinosissimus Group

☼ ☼ ❄❄❄   ↕ 1.2m (4ft) ↔ 60cm (24in)

The large, deeply divided, green or grey-green leaves have white midribs and spiny margins. Tall racemes of purple-bracted white flowers open in spring and summer.

Aciphylla aurea
GOLDEN SPANIARD
☼ ❄❄❄   ↕ ↔ 1m (3ft)

This slow-growing, evergreen plant forms an imposing rosette of stiff, spine-tipped, deeply divided, grey-green leaves with bold, golden yellow midribs and margins.

Eryngium maritimum
SEA HOLLY
☼ ❄❄❄   ↕ ↔ 30cm (12in)

Found in maritime sands or gravels in the wild, this sea holly has formidably spiny, deeply lobed, leathery, bloomy, blue-grey leaves. Pale blue flowers open in summer.

Eryngium variifolium
ERYNGO
☼ ❄❄❄   ↕ 35cm (14in) ↔ 25cm (10in)

A beautiful evergreen, forming a rosette of rounded, silver-veined leaves. In summer, erect, branched stems bear small, grey-blue flowerheads with spiny white collars.

OTHER PERENNIALS WITH SPINY LEAVES

Berkheya macrocephala
Echinops sphaerocephalus
Eryngium pandanifolium
Eryngium proteiflorum
Erythrina crista-galli, see p.46
Fascicularia bicolor, see p.47
Festuca punctoria
Onopordum acanthium
Puya alpestris, see p.47
Yucca gloriosa, see p.37

Puya chilensis
PUYA
☼ ❄❄❄   ↕ 4m (12ft) ↔ 2m (6ft)

After several years, a tall, stout stem with a head of waxy, yellow-green flowers rises from the massive rosette of rapier-like, spine-toothed, leathery, evergreen leaves.

FOLIAGE EFFECT

126

Perennials with Aromatic Leaves

SCENTS CAN MAKE an important and evocative contribution to a garden, and are most commonly associated with the fragrance of flowers. The leaves of most perennials, however, also give off at least a faint aroma, and some even have foliage with a very distinctive or strong scent. In a number of cases, this is released by simply brushing against the plant.

Nepeta 'Six Hills Giant'
CATMINT
☼ ☀ ❄❄❄ ‡ 90cm (36in) ↔ 60cm (24in)

This dense, bushy, clump-forming plant bears aromatic, light grey-green leaves, and leafy spikes of lavender-blue summer flowers. Loved, but also damaged, by cats.

Helichrysum italicum
CURRY PLANT
☼ ❄❄ ‡ 60cm (24in) ↔ 90cm (36in)

Aromatic, evergreen, narrow, felted, silver-grey leaves clothe the woolly stems of this woody-based perennial or subshrub. Deep yellow flowerheads open in summer. ♈

Agastache foeniculum 'Alabaster'
ANISE HYSSOP
☼ ❄❄❄ ‡ 90cm (36in) ↔ 30cm (12in)

Downy, anise-scented leaves, paler green beneath, clothe the erect stems. Spikes of two-lipped white flowers, loved by bees, are borne from midsummer to autumn.

OTHER PERENNIALS WITH AROMATIC LEAVES

Acorus calamus
Foeniculum vulgare 'Purpureum', see p.125
Helichrysum italicum subsp. *serotinum*
Ipheion uniflorum 'Wisley Blue'
  Melittis melissophyllum, see p.79
  Mentha × *gracilis* 'Variegata'
Mentha × *piperita* f. *citrata*
  Mentha suaveolens 'Variegata'
  Myrrhis odorata, see p.55
Origanum vulgare
Salvia elegans 'Scarlet Pineapple'

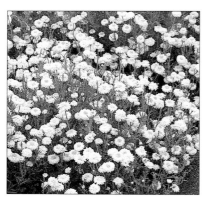

Chamaemelum nobile 'Flore Pleno'
CHAMOMILE
☼ ❄❄❄ ‡ 30cm (12in) ↔ 45cm (18in)

This small, creeping, aromatic perennial produces dense mats of finely divided, hairy leaves. Long-stalked, double white flowerheads are borne freely in summer.

Melissa officinalis
LEMON BALM
☼ ☀ ❄❄❄ ‡ 1m (3ft) ↔ 60cm (24in)

When rubbed, the leaves of this bushy perennial release a sharp lemon aroma. In summer, its four-angled stems bear spikes of pale yellow flowers that fade to white.

Salvia officinalis 'Icterina'
SAGE
☼ ❄❄❄ ‡ ↔ 30cm (12in)

A variegated form of the popular kitchen-garden herb, forming a low, woody-based mound of attractive, aromatic, evergreen, woolly, green and yellow leaves. ♈

FOLIAGE EFFECT

Perennials with Bold Leaves

OTHER HERBACEOUS PERENNIALS WITH BOLD LEAVES

Darmera peltata, see p.66
Gunnera manicata
Hedychium gardnerianum, see p.47
Hosta sieboldiana
Inula magnifica
Ligularia dentata 'Desdemona'
Petasites japonicus var. *giganteus*
Rodgersia aesculifolia, see p.25
Silphium terebinthinaceum
Veratrum album, see p.91

PERENNIALS WITH BIG, BOLD LEAVES, like those of hostas and ornamental rhubarbs, provide gardens with some of the most memorable show-stoppers. In sites where space is no object, they are eye-catching planted in groups or drifts, but they can be just as successful, and possibly even more dramatic, as single specimens in smaller gardens.

Aralia cachemirica
ARALIA
☼ ☀ ✳✳✳   ↕ 3m (10ft) ↔ 2m (6ft)

Given a good site, this aralia forms a huge, suckering clump of large, arching, divided leaves. Black berries follow tall, branched heads of tiny flowers in early summer.

Dicksonia antarctica
AUSTRALIAN TREE FERN
☼ ☀ ✳✳   ↕ 6m (20ft) ↔ 4m (12ft)

This majestic, evergreen fern has a single rhizome forming a false, erect trunk, which is clothed in a thick mass of roots and crowned with a huge ruff of fronds. ♈

Astilboides tabularis
ASTILBOIDES
☼ ✳✳✳   ↕ 1.5m (5ft) ↔ 1.2m (4ft)

In summer, slender plumes of tiny, creamy white flowers rise above the big clumps of long-stalked, rounded, sharply lobed, and softly-downy leaves. It enjoys moist soils.

OTHER EVERGREEN PERENNIALS WITH BOLD LEAVES

Beschorneria yuccoides
Geranium maderense
Helleborus argutifolius, see p.120
Indocalamus tessellatus
Ligularia japonica
Phormium cookianum subsp. *hookeri* 'Tricolor', see p.120
Phormium tenax, see p.123
Woodwardia unigemmata
Yucca gloriosa, see p.37

Filipendula purpurea
FILIPENDULA
☼ ☀ ✳✳✳   ↕ 1.2m (4ft) ↔ 60cm (24in)

Large, deeply lobed and toothed leaves cover the bold clumps of erect, crimson-purple stems. In summer, tall, branched plumes of carmine-red flowers appear. ♈

FOLIAGE EFFECT

128

Geranium palmatum
CRANESBILL
☀ ☼ ❄❄❄   ↕ ↔ 1m (3ft)

Branched heads of purplish pink flowers
top the large rosettes of long-stalked,
sharp-toothed, deeply lobed, evergreen
leaves in summer. ♛

Hosta 'Big Daddy'
PLANTAIN LILY
☀ ☼ ❄❄❄   ↕ 60cm (24in) ↔ 1m (3ft)

Aptly named, this hosta has mounded
clumps of large, rounded to heart-shaped,
veined and puckered, blue-grey, bloomy
leaves, and greyish white summer flowers.

Rheum palmatum var. *tanguticum*
ORNAMENTAL RHUBARB
☀ ☼ ❄❄❄   ↕ 2.5m (8ft) ↔ 1.8m (6ft)

The striking, huge, toothed and jaggedly
lobed leaves are red-suffused when young.
In summer, branched heads of white, red,
or pink flowers emerge. Superb by water.

Telekia speciosa
TELEKIA
☀ ❄❄❄   ↕ 2m (6ft) ↔ 1.2m (4ft)

This strapping plant forms a large patch of
branching stems, which bear heart-shaped
leaves, and yellow, later brown-centred,
daisy heads in late summer and autumn.

Rheum 'Ace of Hearts'
ORNAMENTAL RHUBARB
☀ ☼ ❄❄❄   ↕ 1.2m (4ft) ↔ 90cm (36in)

The heart-shaped leaves, in impressive
mounds, are red-veined above and purple-
red beneath. Branching stems carry sprays
of pale pinkish white flowers in summer.

Symplocarpus foetidus
SKUNK CABBAGE
☀ ☼ ❄❄❄   ↕ ↔ 60cm (24in)

Curious, hooded, purplish red flowers in
spring are followed by the clump of large,
rather leathery leaves. An excellent bog
plant, it needs plenty of moisture.

Veratrum viride
INDIAN POKE
☀ ☼ ❄❄❄   ↕ 2m (6ft) ↔ 60cm (24in)

The clumps of pleated, rich green leaves,
which appear in spring, are more striking
than the tall, branched spikes of star-shaped,
yellowish green summer flowers. ♛

FOLIAGE EFFECT

129

Perennials with Yellow- or Gold-variegated Foliage

VARIEGATED PERENNIALS and ornamental grasses that have leaves blotched or spotted yellow or gold are often prized for their ability to bring warmth and light to borders dominated by dark green foliage. Many of these perennials also make impressive specimen plants, either grown in containers or in small beds.

Convallaria majalis 'Hardwick Hall'
LILY-OF-THE-VALLEY
☀ ❄❄❄ ↕ 23cm (9in) ↔ 30cm (12in)

A choice form of a much-loved perennial, slowly developing patches of erect stems. The pairs of attractively veined, bright green leaves have narrow, paler margins.

Aquilegia vulgaris Vervaeneana Group
GRANNY'S BONNET
☀ ☀ ❄❄❄ ↕ 90cm (36in) ↔ 45cm (18in)

The prettily divided leaves are streaked and mottled yellow in this curious form of an old cottage-garden favourite. Spring or summer flowers are white, pink, or purple.

Hakonechloa macra 'Aureola'
ORNAMENTAL GRASS
☀ ☀ ❄❄❄ ↕ 35cm (14in) ↔ 40cm (16in)

One of the most pleasing of all grasses, with low mounds of yellow, green-striped leaves. In autumn, it bears airy panicles of spikelets and the leaves flush red. ▽

OTHER YELLOW- OR GOLD-VARIEGATED PERENNIALS

Hosta 'Great Expectations'
Hosta sieboldii f. *kabitan*
Hosta montana 'Aureomarginata', see p.153
Hosta ventricosa var. *aureomaculata*
Lamium maculatum 'Golden Anniversary'
Mentha x *gracilis* 'Variegata'
Phormium 'Yellow Wave'
Polygonatum odoratum 'Variegatum'
Saxifraga 'Aureopunctata'

Carex oshimensis 'Evergold'
SEDGE
☀ ☀ ❄❄❄❄ ↕ 30cm (12in) ↔ 35cm (14in)

This bright little evergreen plant forms a dense, low clump of arching, grass-like, dark green leaves, each with a broad, creamy yellow central stripe. ▽

Cortaderia selloana 'Aureolineata'
PAMPAS GRASS
☀ ❄❄❄ ↕ 2.2m (7ft) ↔ 1.5m (5ft)

A variegated form of a familiar, evergreen grass, producing huge mounds of arching, saw-toothed, yellow-margined leaves. Tall flower plumes in summer are a bonus. ▽

Hosta 'Gold Standard'
PLANTAIN LILY
☀ ❄❄❄ ↕ 65cm (26in) ↔ 1m (3ft)

This singularly attractive perennial forms clumps of heart-shaped, greenish yellow leaves fading to green margins. Tall stems bear lavender-blue flowers in summer.

Miscanthus sinensis 'Zebrinus'
ZEBRA GRASS
☼ ❄❄❄   ↕ ↔ 1.2m (4ft)

This old favourite is especially popular for specimen planting. The bold clumps of slender, cane-like stems bear long, narrow green leaves banded white or pale yellow.

Trifolium pratense 'Susan Smith'
CLOVER
☼ ❄❄❄   ↕ 15cm (6in) ↔ 45cm (18in)

The characteristic clover leaves of this mat-forming perennial have green leaflets that are curiously but attractively netted with golden yellow veins.

Hosta ventricosa 'Aureomarginata'
PLANTAIN LILY
☼ ❄❄❄   ↕ 50cm (20in) ↔ 1m (3ft)

Big, bold clumps of heart-shaped, deep-veined green leaves have irregular yellow margins ageing creamy white. In summer, tall stems bear deep purple flowers. ♛

Symphytum 'Goldsmith'
COMFREY
☼ ☼ ❄❄❄   ↕ ↔ 30cm (12in)

Superb ground cover, this creeping plant forms large patches of hairy leaves with irregular gold or cream margins. Blue and white, pink-tinted flowers occur in spring.

Yucca flaccida 'Golden Sword'
YUCCA
☼ ❄❄❄   ↕ 1.5m (5ft) ↔ 1m (3ft)

A bold, clump-forming evergreen, bearing stiff, sword-like, blue-green leaves with central yellow bands. Panicles of white bell-flowers emerge in late summer. ♛

OTHER YELLOW-STRIPED GRASSES

Alopecurus pratensis 'Aureovariegatus'
Glyceria maxima var. *variegata*
× *Hibanobambusa tranquillans*
  'Shiroshima'
Miscanthus sinensis 'Goldfeder'
Miscanthus sinensis 'Variegatus'
Molinia caerulea 'Variegata'
Phragmites australis 'Variegatus'
Pleioblastus auricomus
Spartina pectinata 'Aureomarginata'

Iris pallida 'Variegata'
IRIS
☼ ❄❄❄   ↕ 1.2m (4ft) ↔ 60cm (24in)

An effective variegated perennial, with stout clumps of sword-shaped, grey-green or green leaves striped light yellow. In late spring, it bears scented blue flowers. ♛

Tolmiea menziesii 'Taff's Gold'
PICK-A-BACK PLANT
☼ ☼ ❄❄❄   ↕ 50cm (20in) ↔ 60cm (24in)

Loose clumps of semi-evergreen, prettily lobed, hairy leaves are pale green, spotted and blotched cream and pale yellow. The tiny flowers are of little consequence.

Perennials with White- or Cream-variegated Foliage

I̤T IS A CURIOUS FACT that there are far more perennials with white- or cream-variegated foliage than with yellow or gold variegation. Patterned with stripes, spots, blotches, marbling, or marginal lines, these leaves provide a useful contrast for plants with green or purple foliage, and can brighten up dark corners or dull combinations in the garden.

FOLIAGE EFFECT

Armoracia rusticana 'Variegata'
HORSERADISH
☀ ❄❄❄   ↕ 1m (3ft) ↔ 45cm (18in)

This variegated form of the well-known horseradish has clumps of large, coarse, wholly or partially white leaves. Branched stems of white flowers appear in summer.

Convallaria majalis 'Albostriata'
LILY-OF-THE-VALLEY
☀ ❄❄❄   ↕ 23cm (9in) ↔ 30cm (12in)

A beautiful variety of a favourite garden perennial, with leaves longitudinally striped creamy white. Sprays of nodding, fragrant white bell-flowers open in spring.

Hemerocallis fulva 'Kwanso Variegata'
DAYLILY
☀ ❄❄❄   ↕ 75cm (30in) ↔ 1.2m (4ft)

Long, strap-shaped, arching leaves with white margins form a bold clump. During summer, double, orange-brown flowers rise above the foliage on strong stems.

Brunnera macrophylla 'Dawson's White'
BRUNNERA
☀ ❄❄❄   ↕ 45cm (18in) ↔ 60cm (24in)

In spring, the low mounds of softly-hairy, heart-shaped leaves, irregularly margined in creamy white, are crowned by sprays of bright blue, forget-me-not flowers.

Euphorbia characias subsp. *wulfenii* 'Burrow Silver'
☀ ❄❄   ↕ ↔ 1.2m (4ft)

Bushy and woody-based, this evergreen has dense, grey-green leaves with creamy margins. Rounded heads of bright yellow-green flowers open in spring and summer.

Hosta 'Shade Fanfare'
PLANTAIN LILY
☀ ❄❄❄   ↕ 45cm (18in) ↔ 60cm (24in)

Excellent for ground cover, the clumps of bold, heart-shaped leaves have irregular cream margins fading to white. Lavender-blue flowers are borne in summer. ♛

Phlox paniculata 'Harlequin'
PERENNIAL PHLOX

☼ ❄❄❄❄ ⬍ 1.2m (4ft) ↔ 1m (3ft)

Robust clumps of erect stems bear leaves boldly margined in creamy white, and are topped by panicles of fragrant, red-purple flowers in summer.

Symphytum × *uplandicum* 'Variegatum'
COMFREY

☼ ◐ ❄❄❄❄ ⬍ 90cm (36in) ↔ 60cm (24in)

A tough, deep-rooted perennial, producing a spectacular clump of white-margined leaves. In summer, striking variegated stems bear blue and pink flowers. 🏆

OTHER PERENNIALS WITH WHITE- OR CREAM-VARIEGATED FOLIAGE

Astrantia major 'Sunningdale Variegated'
Brunnera macrophylla 'Hadspen Cream'
Iris pallida 'Argentea Variegata', see p.73
Lysimachia punctata 'Alexander'
Mentha suaveolens 'Variegata'
Polemonium caeruleum 'Brise d'Anjou'
Polygonatum × *hybridum* 'Striatum'
Scrophularia auriculata 'Variegata'

Physostegia virginiana 'Variegata'
PHYSOSTEGIA

☼ ◐ ❄❄❄❄ ⬍ ↔ 45cm (18in)

Both the willow-like leaves and the erect stems of this easily grown perennial are grey-green, variegated white. Magenta-pink flower spikes emerge in late summer.

Myosotis scorpioides 'Maytime'
WATER FORGET-ME-NOT

☼ ❄❄❄❄ ⬍ ↔ 30cm (12in)

Strikingly variegated, this waterside plant forms patches of bold, white-margined leaves. Its sprays of bright blue flowers are produced in early summer.

Pulmonaria 'Roy Davidson'
LUNGWORT

☼ ◐ ❄❄❄❄ ⬍ 30cm (12in) ↔ 60cm (24in)

Clumps of semi-evergreen, roughly-hairy, white-spotted leaves provide good ground cover, with clusters of tubular, blue and red flowers in spring. It will seed around.

Vinca major 'Variegata'
LARGE PERIWINKLE

☼ ◐ ❄❄❄❄ ⬍ 45cm (18in) ↔ 2m (6ft)

This fast-growing, scrambling evergreen forms blankets of striking, paired, creamy white-margined leaves. Pale blue flowers are borne from late winter into spring. 🏆

FOLIAGE EFFECT

133

Perennials with Yellow or Gold Foliage

A SURPRISING NUMBER of garden perennials have produced sports with yellow- or gold-suffused leaves. In some plants, the best foliage effect is achieved in spring; in others the colour is retained through summer. All have an important role in the garden, especially in semi-shaded or dimly lit corners, or as a contrast to greens and purples.

FOLIAGE EFFECT

Hosta 'Midas Touch'
PLANTAIN LILY
☼ ☼ ✲✲✲   ↕ 50cm (20in) ↔ 65cm (26in)

There are many golden leaved hostas available, but this is one of the best. It has big, bold, handsomely corrugated foliage and bears lavender-blue summer flowers.

Aquilegia 'Mellow Yellow'
GRANNY'S BONNET
☼ ✲✲✲   ↕ 60cm (24in) ↔ 45cm (18in)

An attractive form of a plant common to cottage gardens, with golden leaves in spring, paling to yellow-green in summer, when white to pale blue flowers appear.

Carex elata 'Aurea'
BOWLES' GOLDEN SEDGE
☼ ☼ ✲✲✲   ↕ 70cm (28in) ↔ 90cm (36in)

Probably the best golden-leaved perennial for waterside sites, this clump-forming sedge has arching, grassy, bright golden leaves. Superb by streams or pools. ♔

Lamium maculatum 'Cannon's Gold'
DEAD NETTLE
☼ ✲✲✲   ↕ 20cm (8in) ↔ 1m (3ft)

The coarsely toothed, semi-evergreen leaves of this plant form a soft yellow carpet in spring and summer. Its mauve-pink flowers emerge in early summer.

Campanula garganica 'Dickson's Gold'
BELLFLOWER
☼ ☼ ✲✲✲   ↕ 5cm (2in) ↔ 30cm (12in)

This cheerful perennial forms a hummock of neat little toothy, kidney-shaped leaves. These turn golden in summer at the same time as small blue flowers are borne.

Centaurea montana 'Gold Bullion'
PERENNIAL CORNFLOWER
☼ ✲✲✲   ↕ 45cm (18in) ↔ 60cm (24in)

A beautiful, golden-leaved version of an old garden favourite. The pronounced leaf colour in spring and early summer is a perfect foil for the large blue cornflowers.

Lysimachia nummularia 'Aurea'
GOLDEN CREEPING JENNY
☼ ☼ ✲✲✲   ↕ 5cm (2in) ↔ indefinite

One of the brightest and most reliable gold-leaved plants, its evergreen carpet of creeping stems turns greenish yellow in shade. Yellow flowers open in summer. ♔

Melissa officinalis 'All Gold'
LEMON BALM
☼ ✲✲✲   ↕↔ 60cm (24in)

This bushy perennial produces a dense clump of lemon-scented, yellow-suffused stems and leaves. It is especially effective during spring and early summer.

Stachys byzantina 'Primrose Heron'
LAMB'S EARS
☼ ✲✲✲   ↕ 45cm (18in) ↔ 60cm (24in)

A vigorous evergreen perennial, forming a close carpet of velvety, hairy grey stems, and 'lamb's ear' leaves, which are suffused yellow in spring and early summer.

Tanacetum vulgare 'Isla Gold'
GOLDEN TANSY
☼ ✲✲✲   ↕↔ 90cm (36in)

The golden form of a fine garden stalwart, with bold clumps of erect stems clothed in finely divided, aromatic, yellowy leaves. It bears yellow flowerheads in summer.

Tradescantia Andersoniana Group 'Blue and Gold'
☼ ◑ ✲✲✲   ↕↔ 45cm (18in)

During summer, rich blue, three-petalled flowers on erect, fleshy stems contrast well with this clump-forming perennial's long, strap-shaped, gold-suffused leaves.

Valeriana phu 'Aurea'
GOLDEN VALERIAN
☼ ◑ ✲✲✲   ↕ 1.5m (5ft) ↔ 60cm (24in)

The prime attraction of this tall, branching perennial is its gold spring foliage, which gradually fades to green in summer. Its small white flowers open in late summer.

OTHER PERENNIALS WITH GOLD FOLIAGE

Acanthus mollis 'Hollard's Gold'
Acorus gramineus 'Ogon'
Carex elata 'Knightshayes'
Deschampsia flexuosa 'Tatra Gold'
Dicentra spectabilis 'Gold Heart'
Filipendula ulmaria 'Aurea'
Gaura lindheimeri 'Corrie's Gold'
Helleborus foetidus 'Gold Bullion'
Hosta 'Sum and Substance', see p.71
Hosta 'Zounds', see p.66
Lamium maculatum 'Aureum'
Luzula sylvatica 'Aurea'
Milium effusum 'Aureum', see p.33
Persicaria amplexicaulis 'Cottesbrooke Gold'
Symphytum ibericum 'Gold in Spring'
Thymus × citriodorus 'Archer's Gold'
Veronica prostrata 'Trehane'

FOLIAGE EFFECT

135

Perennials with Silver or Blue-grey Foliage

PERENNIALS WITH SILVER or blue-grey foliage (often the entire plant is similarly coloured) are particularly valuable in the garden for separating strong-coloured plants, such as those with red, purple, or even green leaves. They can also provide a lovely foil for pastel-coloured flowers, especially those in pink, lavender-purple, pale blue, and yellow. While there is a vast choice of perennials for use in grey or silver borders, they can also make a striking display as specimen plants or grouped together with other contrasting foliage perennials in containers. Most plants with silver leaves prefer a warm, sunny situation.

Cynara cardunculus
CARDOON

☼ ✹✹✹ ↕ 1.5m (5ft) ↔ 1.2m (4ft)

The deeply divided, spiny, silvery grey leaves of this statuesque plant form big, bold clumps. During summer, stout blue flowerheads open on branched stems. ♔

Anaphalis triplinervis 'Sommerschnee'
PEARLY EVERLASTING

☼ ✹✹✹ ↕ 80cm (32in) ↔ 60cm (24in)

A German selection of a reliable perennial. The clumps of grey stems bear leaves that are white-woolly beneath, and dense white flower clusters in late summer. ♔

Cerastium tomentosum
SNOW-IN-SUMMER

☼ ✹✹✹ ↕ 8cm (3in) ↔ 1.5m (5ft)

One of the best grey ground-cover plants for walls and sunny banks. White flowers pepper the carpet of evergreen, downy leaves from late spring into summer.

Artemisia ludoviciana var. albula
ARTEMISIA

☼ ✹✹✹ ↕ 1.2m (4ft) ↔ 60cm (24in)

The erect clumps of slender, woolly stems bear willow-like, sharp-toothed, aromatic, white-woolly leaves, and dense white flower clusters in summer and autumn.

Crambe maritima
SEA KALE

☼ ✹✹✹ ↕ 75cm (30in) ↔ 60cm (24in)

This distinctive, bold, mound-forming plant has large, deep-lobed, twisted, blue-green, bloomy leaves, and branched heads of small white flowers in early summer. ♔

Dicentra 'Langtrees'
DICENTRA

☼ ✹✹✹ ↕ 30cm (12in) ↔ 45cm (18in)

A charming plant, with mounds of ferny, silvery blue leaves, topped in late spring and early summer by nodding clusters of white flowers. Forms patches in time. ♔

Galanthus elwesii Glaucous Forms
SNOWDROP
☼ ◑ ✳✳✳   ↕15cm (6in) ↔8cm (3in)

Eventually forming large colonies, this vigorous, bold snowdrop has broad, blue-green leaves, and nodding white flowers with green-marked inner segments.

EVERGREEN PERENNIALS WITH SILVER OR BLUE-GREY FOLIAGE
Acaena saccaticupula 'Blue Haze'
Artemisia 'Powis Castle', see p.26
Astelia chathamica
Celmisia spectabilis
Euphorbia nicaeensis, see p.82
Festuca glauca 'Elijah Blue'
Heuchera 'Pewter Moon'
Kniphofia caulescens, see p.120
Stachys byzantina 'Big Ears'
Tanacetum argenteum

Hosta 'Blue Moon'
PLANTAIN LILY
◑ ✳✳✳   ↕10cm (4in) ↔30cm (12in)

Slow-growing, but worth waiting for, with its attractive clump of bloomy, blue-green, heart-shaped leaves, and dense racemes of mauve-grey flowers borne in summer.

HERBACEOUS PERENNIALS WITH SILVER OR BLUE-GREY FOLIAGE
Aquilegia vulgaris 'Nivea'
Cynara Scolymus Group
Hosta 'Hadspen Blue', see p.73
Iris pallida
Lychnis flos-jovis
Macleaya cordata
Rudbeckia maxima
Sanguisorba obtusa
Thalictrum flavum subsp. *glaucum*, see p.35

Helictotrichon sempervirens
BLUE OAT GRASS
☼ ✳✳✳   ↕1.5m (5ft) ↔60cm (24in)

A striking, evergreen grass, forming a bold clump of stiff, narrow, grey-blue leaves. A sheaf of erect stems bears panicles of tiny spikelets above the leaves in summer. ♈

Lysimachia ephemerum
LOOSESTRIFE
☼ ◑ ✳✳✳✳   ↕1m (3ft) ↔30cm (12in)

The erect stems of this fine perennial are densely clothed in willowy, bloomy, sea-green leaves and sport slender spires of small white flowers in summer.

Verbascum olympicum
MULLEIN
☼ ✳✳✳   ↕2m (6ft) ↔60cm (24in)

This stately, silvery, white-woolly biennial or perennial has a rosette of overwintering leaves, and tall, branched stems that bear dense spikes of yellow flowers in summer.

Perennials with Purple, Red, or Bronze Foliage

WHEN USED SELECTIVELY in garden plantings, perennials with unusual deep purple, bronze, or red foliage can provide a striking contrast among plants with lighter green, grey, or even yellow leaves. In some perennials, like *Actaea simplex* 'Brunette', the colour is long-lasting or even permanent, while in others it is mainly a spring display created by newly emerging foliage and stems. Sometimes the rich leaf colour is also attractively overlaid by a lovely pale bloom, as is the case in several sedums.

FOLIAGE EFFECT

Artemisia lactiflora Guizhou Group
CHINESE MUGWORT
☼ ❄❄❄   ↕ 1.5m (5ft) ↔ 1m (3ft)

A vigorous perennial, producing clumps of branching, dark purple-flushed stems and deeply cut leaves. Sprays of tiny white flowers open from summer into autumn.

EVERGREEN PERENNIALS WITH
PURPLE, RED, OR BRONZE LEAVES

Ajuga reptans 'Atropurpurea'
Euphorbia amygdaloides 'Purpurea'
Phormium 'Maori Chief'
Phormium tenax Purpureum Group,
    see p.77
Salvia officinalis 'Purpurascens'
Sedum spathulifolium 'Purpureum'
Sempervivum 'Othello'
Uncinia rubra
Veronica umbrosa 'Georgia Blue'

Heuchera 'Rachel'
CORAL FLOWER
☼ ◑ ❄❄❄   ↕ 60cm (24in) ↔ 45cm (18in)

This striking plant forms a low clump of large, crinkled and lobed, shiny, bronze-purple leaves, bright purple beneath. Tiny off-white summer flowers open in sprays.

Actaea simplex 'Brunette'
BUGBANE
☼ ❄❄❄   ↕ 1.2m (4ft) ↔ 60cm (24in)

This superb perennial has clumps of large, divided, purplish brown leaves. Arching stems bear tall racemes of purplish white flowers above the foliage in autumn. ♔

Euphorbia dulcis 'Chameleon'
SPURGE
☼ ◑ ❄❄❄❄   ↕ ↔ 30cm (12in)

The branching, purplish stems bear small red-purple leaves, which colour richly in autumn. Clouds of purple-tinted flowers are borne in summer. It will seed around.

Imperata cylindrica 'Rubra'
IMPERATA
☼ ◑ ❄❄❄   ↕ 40cm (16in) ↔ 30cm (12in)

An attractive grass with erect, leafy shoots and long green leaves that soon turn deep blood-red from the tips down. In summer, it bears sprays of silver-white spikelets.

Ranunculus ficaria 'Brazen Hussy'
LESSER CELANDINE
☼ ☀ ❄❄❄   ↕ 5cm (2in) ↔ 15cm (6in)

The small rosettes or patches of long-stalked, heart-shaped, glossy, chocolate-brown leaves are an ideal backing for the shining, golden yellow flowers in spring.

Sedum telephium 'Matrona'
ICE PLANT
☼ ❄❄❄   ↕ 60cm (24in) ↔ 30cm (12in)

From late summer into autumn, flattened heads of starry pink flowers rise on stout, fleshy, purple-red stems above the robust clumps of fleshy, bloomy purple leaves. ♖

Ophiopogon planiscapus 'Nigrescens'
LILYTURF
☼ ☀ ❄❄❄   ↕ 20cm (8in) ↔ 30cm (12in)

Ideal for ground cover, the low, evergreen tufts of narrow, leathery, blackish purple leaves form patches in time. It has slender purple-white flower sprays in summer. ♖

Rodgersia podophylla
RODGERSIA
☼ ☀ ❄❄❄   ↕ 1.5m (5ft) ↔ 1.8m (6ft)

Bronze-red when young, the large clumps of long-stalked, deeply divided and lobed leaves colour red again in autumn. White flower plumes are borne in summer. ♖

HERBACEOUS PERENNIALS WITH PURPLE, RED, OR BRONZE LEAVES

Anthriscus sylvestris 'Ravenswing'
Clematis recta 'Purpurea'
Foeniculum vulgare 'Purpureum',
  see p.125
Heuchera micrantha var. *diversifolia*
  'Palace Purple'
Lysimachia ciliata 'Firecracker'
Penstemon digitalis 'Husker Red'
Sedum telephium subsp. *maximum*
  'Atropurpureum'

Phormium 'Dazzler'
NEW ZEALAND FLAX
☼ ❄❄❄   ↕ 1m (3ft) ↔ 1.2m (4ft)

This flax has stout clumps of evergreen, arching, strap-shaped, leathery leaves, impressively striped red, orange, and pink on a bronze-purple background.

Sedum 'Sunset Cloud'
ICE PLANT
☼ ❄❄❄   ↕ 25cm (10in) ↔ 45cm (18in)

One of the best of the low-growing purple sedums, it has fleshy, trailing or lax stems, bloomy foliage, and flattened pink flower-heads in late summer and autumn.

Perennials with Richly Tinted Autumn Foliage

ALL TOO OFTEN when we think of autumn colour in the garden we look to woody, deciduous plants, like maples or sumachs, ignoring the merits of the many herbaceous perennials, like those below, which also produce a burst of bright colour before winter arrives.

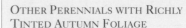

OTHER PERENNIALS WITH RICHLY TINTED AUTUMN FOLIAGE

Amsonia hubrichtii
Aruncus aethusifolius, see p.125
Ceratostigma plumbaginoides, see p.50
Darmera peltata, see p.66
Euphorbia griffithii 'Fireglow', see p.90
Geranium macrorrhizum, see p.89
Hosta fortunei
Imperata cylindrica 'Rubra', see p.138
Miscanthus sinensis 'Malepartus', see p.146
Osmunda regalis, see p.67

Geranium wlassovianum
CRANESBILL
☼ ☼ ❊❊❊ ↕ ↔ 60cm (24in)

The clumps of long-stalked, deeply lobed, softly-downy and velvety leaves emerge pinkish bronze in spring, then turn a rich red, with purple-bronze tints, in autumn.

Calamagrostis x *acutiflora* 'Karl Foerster'
☼ ☼ ❊❊❊ ↕ 1.8m (6ft) ↔ 60cm (24in)

This striking, clump-forming ornamental grass has stiffly erect stems and arching leaves. The pinky bronze spikelets turn a warm buff or pale brown in autumn.

Schizachyrium scoparium
LITTLE BLUESTEM
☼ ❊❊❊ ↕ 1m (3ft) ↔ 30cm (12in)

The dense tufts of arching, greyish green leaves and upright stems turn purple to orange-red in autumn. Narrow heads of whiskery spikelets are borne in summer.

Darmera peltata 'Nana'
UMBRELLA PLANT
☼ ☼ ❊❊❊❊ ↕ 35cm (14in) ↔ 60cm (24in)

A dwarf form of the umbrella plant, with long-stalked, rounded leaves that turn red or orange-copper in autumn. Leafless stems bear clusters of pink spring flowers.

Pennisetum setaceum 'Rubrum'
FOUNTAIN GRASS
☼ ❊❊ ↕ 1m (3ft) ↔ 60cm (24in)

Spectacular and strong-growing, this grass forms a clump of erect, rich purple stems and leaves. The arching or pendent pink, slender spikes fade to pink-buff or white.

Sedum aizoon
STONECROP
☼ ❊❊❊ ↕ ↔ 45cm (18in)

In autumn, the clumps of erect, reddish stems and fleshy, coarsely toothed leaves turn red or orange-red. Flattened heads of yellow star-flowers open in summer.

Perennials with Decorative Winter Foliage

IF PERENNIALS WITH RICHLY TINTED FOLIAGE in autumn are useful in the garden, then those with decorative foliage in winter are invaluable. When many plants have either died down or lost their leaves, these perennials will brighten up borders and beds with their yellow- or white-variegated, red-suffused, silver-hairy, or beautifully marbled leaves.

Epimedium x *rubrum*
EPIMEDIUM
☼ ☀ ❄❄❄ ↕ ↔ 30cm (12in)

Red-flushed when young, the clumps of much-divided leaves become red-tinted in autumn, and remain throughout winter. Spring flowers are crimson and yellow. ♔

OTHER PERENNIALS WITH DECORATIVE WINTER FOLIAGE

Asplenium scolopendrium Crispum Group, see p.149
Euphorbia characias subsp. *wulfenii* 'Purple and Gold'
Galax urceolata
Helleborus argutifolius 'Pacific Frost'
Phormium 'Sundowner'
Pulmonaria saccharata 'Leopard', see p.121
Tellima grandiflora Rubra Group

Arum italicum 'Marmoratum'
ARUM
☼ ❄❄❄ ↕ 30cm (12in) ↔ 25cm (10in)

One of the most reliable and eye-catching winter foliage plants, with arrow-shaped, pale-veined, shiny leaves. Greenish white flowers are borne in early spring. ♔

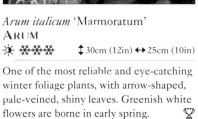

Celmisia semicordata
NEW ZEALAND DAISY ☼ ☀
❄❄❄PH ↕ 50cm (20in) ↔ 30cm (12in)

Grey-green above and silvery beneath, the sword-shaped, silky-hairy leaves form a bold rosette or clump. Grey-downy stems bear large daisy heads in summer.

Bergenia 'Ballawley'
ELEPHANT'S EAR
☼ ☀ ❄❄❄ ↕ 60cm (24in) ↔ 45cm (18in)

The low clumps of leathery, glossy green leaves turn rich bronze-purple or purplish red in winter. In spring, upright red stems carry clusters of crimson bell-flowers. ♔

Cyclamen coum Pewter Group
HARDY CYCLAMEN
☼ ❄❄❄ ↕ 8cm (3in) ↔ 10cm (4in)

A beautiful selection of a popular, winter-flowering cyclamen, with kidney-shaped, silvered, often dark-green-centred leaves. Reddish pink flowers add to its charm. ♔

Sasa veitchii
SASA
☼ ☼ ☀ ❄❄❄ ↕ 1.5m (5ft) ↔ indefinite

This vigorous, creeping bamboo has bold, evergreen leaves that wither at the edges in autumn, giving them decorative white margins for winter. It needs lots of space.

141

SPECIALIST PLANTS

CERTAIN PERENNIALS are now some of the most enthusiastically collected garden plants. Valued for their foliage, flowers, or form, their increasing availability is making it easier than ever to establish a specialist collection.

Polystichum munitum
for moisture
or shade

△ HELLEBORES *Excellent for ground cover;* Helleborus hybridus *seedlings are some of the most desirable perennials.*

Imagine a garden filled with 100 different hardy geraniums, or 50 assorted peonies, or even a multitude of hardy ferns. In fact, there are many such gardens, and they are on the increase as the fashion for collecting members of a single genus or family continues to catch gardeners' imaginations. Although collecting has appealed to plantsmen and women in Europe for the last 400 years at least, and for many centuries more in China and Japan, enthusiasm for specialist perennials has recently greatly increased.

The perennials in this section are among the most sought after plants. Some, such as snowdrops and geraniums, have long been popular, with numerous varieties already available, and many more introduced each year. Others, like ornamental grasses, which have the combined attraction of elegant habit, foliage, and seed heads, and hellebores and epimediums, have been "discovered" more recently, but are now avidly collected.

MIX AND MATCH

While the search for as many varieties of a particular perennial as possible can be a mixture of fun and adventure, the entire garden does not have to be filled with just one plant and its variations. If you are selective, choosing only the best varieties or those that appeal to you, it is possible to combine a collection of specialist perennials with other garden plants to provide varied, year-round appeal.

ESTABLISHING A COLLECTION

So many different perennials are available that it is easy to establish a collection to suit the size and situation of your garden. Sedums or saxifrages, for example, can be grown in a small urban backyard using troughs or containers, and if your chosen plants are large shrubs or bush roses, ground-cover plants such as hardy geraniums can be grown beneath them. With the right conditions, several collections can be established together: hardy ferns, snowdrops, pulmonarias, and epimediums will all thrive in each other's company.

△ PEONIES *Famed for their foliage and flowers, classics like* Paeonia 'Smouthii' *will make a striking show in the garden.*

◁ GERANIUMS *Justifiably popular and very easy to grow, geraniums are perfect for ground cover, or for borders and beds.*

▷ MIXED GRASSES *When planted for contrasting effect, as here, ornamental grasses can make a spectacular collection.*

Small Grasses and Sedges

L ONG NEGLECTED, perennial grasses and sedges are now being rediscovered and increasingly cultivated for their ornamental value. Ideal for smaller gardens, those suggested below will make a striking addition to a border, or as specimen plants, especially in containers.

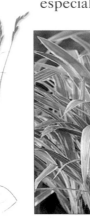

Chionochloa conspicua
PLUMED TUSSOCK GRASS
☼ ❄❄❄   ↕1.2m (4ft) ↔1m (3ft)

Graceful, branched heads of creamy white spikelets, maturing pale silver-brown, rise on tall shoots in summer above the clump of evergreen, reddish brown-tinted leaves.

Carex muskingumensis
PALM SEDGE
☼ ❄❄❄   ↕60cm (24in) ↔45cm (18in)

With its loosely tufted habit, erect, leafy shoots, and horizontally spreading leaves, this sedge resembles a miniature cabbage palm (*Cordyline australis*) or a bamboo.

Carex siderosticha 'Variegata'
SEDGE
☼◑ ❄❄❄❄   ↕30cm (12in) ↔40cm (16in)

One of the most ornamental sedges, with a creeping habit useful for ground cover. Its arching, strap-shaped, white-margined leaves form a low, dense hummock.

Carex phyllocephala 'Sparkler'
TENJIKE SEDGE
☼◑ ❄❄   ↕↔45cm (18in)

A strikingly variegated sedge with erect stems topped by dense crowns of narrow, spreading, grass-like leaves with cream margins. Prefers moist soil in a warm site.

OTHER SMALL GRASSES

Bouteloua gracilis
Festuca glauca 'Golden Toupee'
Imperata cylindrica 'Rubra', see p.138
Miscanthus sinensis 'Sioux'
Nassella tenuissima, see p.77

Chionochloa rubra
RED TUSSOCK GRASS
☼ ❄❄❄   ↕↔60–90cm (24–36in)

From mountains and bogs, this tough, rugged perennial is grown for its dense mound of quill-like, copper-red leaves. Prefers moist soil. Excellent in a container.

Deschampsia cespitosa 'Goldschleier'
TUFTED HAIR GRASS
☀ ☀ ❄❄❄❄^{PH}   ↕ ↔ 1m (3ft)

During summer, slender shoots bearing showers of tiny green spikelets, maturing to bright silvery yellow, rise above the bold clumps of narrow, evergreen leaves.

Elymus magellanicus
ELYMUS
☀ ❄❄❄   ↕ 60cm (24in) ↔ 30cm (12in)

Both the tufts of long, slender leaves, and the shoots that carry narrow flower-spikes in summer, are an intense, almost electric blue. Excellent as a specimen plant.

Festuca glauca 'Blaufuchs'
BLUE FESCUE
☀ ❄❄❄   ↕ 30cm (12in) ↔ 25cm (10in)

Good for contrast, this is one of the best small, blue-leaved grasses. Its name, 'Blue Fox', aptly describes the dense tufts of narrow, bright blue leaves and stiff shoots.

Hordeum jubatum
FOXTAIL BARLEY   ☀ ❄❄

↕ 45–75cm (18–30in) ↔ 30–45cm (12–18in)

A short-lived perennial commonly grown as an annual. It is best from seed, planted in drifts to best enjoy its long-whiskered salmon-pink flower spikes in summer.

Pennisetum orientale
FOUNTAIN GRASS
☀ ❄❄❄   ↕ 60cm (24in) ↔ 75cm (30in)

A superb specimen plant with a dense, neat mound of narrow leaves, and arching shoots bearing spikes of soft, long-bristled, pink-tinted spikelets in summer.   ♔

Stipa barbata
FEATHER GRASS
☀ ❄❄❄   ↕ 75cm (30in) ↔ 15cm (6in)

The small clump of narrow leaves gives rise in summer to slender, arching plumes of long-whiskered spikes. Best on a well-drained or stony soil, with dwarf shrubs.

Stipa pulcherrima
FEATHER GRASS
☀ ❄❄❄❄   ↕ 75cm (30in) ↔ 45–60cm (18–24in)

Named for its exquisite, slender, feathery, arching plumes in summer. They are greenish at first, then age to fluffy white, when the seeds depart in the wind.

Large Ornamental Grasses

GROWN AS SPECIMENS IN A LAWN, or in a bed underplanted with smaller perennials, these bold grasses can create a grand spectacle, especially in late summer or autumn when in flower. They are all easy to cultivate and can be planted singly or in groups for a more immediate effect.

Miscanthus sinensis 'Cabaret'
MISCANTHUS
☼ ❄❄❄   ↕ 1.8m (6ft) ↔ 1.2m (4ft)

Conspicuous white stripes line the leaves of this attractive, clump-forming grass. In autumn, it bears feathery flowerheads that rise above the foliage.

Miscanthus sinensis 'Malepartus'
MISCANTHUS
☼ ❄❄❄   ↕ 2.1m (7ft) ↔ 1.5m (5ft)

An impressive grass forming a dense clump of erect stems with arching leaves that sometimes turn golden orange in autumn. Silvery flower plumes appear in autumn.

Calamagrostis brachytricha
REED GRASS
☼ ☼ ❄❄❄   ↕ 1.2m (4ft) ↔ 1m (3ft)

Dense clumps of erect shoots bear narrow heads of purplish spikelets in late summer or autumn. Excellent for winter effect, the spikelets later turn a warm brown.

Cortaderia richardii
TOE TOE
☼ ❄❄❄   ↕ 3m (10ft) ↔ 2m (6ft)

During summer, tall shoots extend from the mound of arching, evergreen leaves to flaunt graceful, drooping, creamy white, shaggy plumes, persisting into winter. ♔

Cortaderia selloana 'Sunningdale Silver'
☼ ❄❄❄   ↕ 3m (10ft) ↔ 2.5m (8ft)

A big, bold, evergreen, pampas grass with sturdy stems bearing large, silvery white plumes that last well into winter. This is a popular and well-proven variety. ♔

Miscanthus sinensis 'Morning Light'
MISCANTHUS
☼ ❄❄❄   ↕ ↔ 1.2m (4ft)

Considered to be the best all-round miscanthus due to its neat habit. It has a fountain-like clump of white-edged leaves and reddish flower plumes in autumn.

Panicum virgatum 'Warrior'
BLUE SWITCH GRASS
☼ ❄❄❄　　　↕ 1.5m (5ft) ↔ 45cm (18in)

A tough, clump-forming grass with crowded, erect, leafy stems crowned from midsummer with loose plumes. In autumn, the whole plant turns golden yellow.

Pennisetum macrourum
PENNISETUM
☼ ❄❄　　　↕ 1.8m (6ft) ↔ 1.2m (4ft)

This evergreen, clump-forming grass bears long, poker-like flower spikes in late summer and early autumn. They age from pale green to pale brown then purple.

Molinia caerulea susbp. *arundinacea* 'Windspiel'
☼ ❄❄❄　　　↕ 2.1m (7ft) ↔ 40cm (16in)

The rounded clump of arching leaves is topped from late summer by slender, upright stems carrying large, glistening plumes that tremble in the wind.

Panicum virgatum 'Heavy Metal'
BLUE SWITCH GRASS
☼ ❄❄❄　　　↕ 1.5m (5ft) ↔ 45cm (18in)

A glaucous blue grass forming a tight clump of stiffly erect, leafy stems that never flop after rain. They are topped from mid-summer with airy heads of pinkish flowers.

OTHER LARGE GRASSES

Arundo donax 'Macrophylla', see p.122
Cortaderia selloana 'Rendatleri', see p.28
Miscanthus sacchariflorus
Miscanthus sinensis 'Silberfeder'
Miscanthus sinensis 'Zebrinus', see p.131

Stipa gigantea
GIANT OAT, GOLDEN OAT
☼ ❄❄❄　　　↕ 2–2.4m (6–7ft) ↔ 1m (3ft)

One of the loveliest large grasses with clumps of evergreen leaves topped in summer by showers of golden, long-whiskered flowers that pale with age. ♛

SPECIALIST PLANTS

147

Ferns for Moisture or Shade

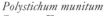

Of ALL NON-FLOWERING PERENNIALS, ferns are easily the most garden-worthy, offering an exciting variety of shapes and heights for use as specimen plants or in bold groupings. Most of the following ferns are of medium to large size, and will thrive given humus-rich soil, moisture, and shade.

Asplenium scolopendrium
HART'S TONGUE FERN
☼ ☼ ✳✳✳   ↕↔ 60cm (24in)

This bold fern is easily recognized by its long, leathery, strap-shaped, evergreen fronds, marked beneath with stripes of brown spores. Fond of alkaline soil.

OTHER FERNS FOR MOISTURE OR SHADE

Dryopteris affinis 'Cristata'
Dryopteris dilatata
Dryopteris filix-mas
Dryopteris goldieana
Matteuccia struthiopteris, see p.71
Osmunda cinnamomea
Osmunda regalis, see p.67
Polystichum braunii

Athyrium filix-femina
LADY FERN
☼ ✳✳✳   ↕ 1.2m (4ft) ↔ 60cm (24in)

Finely divided, herbaceous, light green fronds form a graceful shuttlecock, with a green or red-brown central stalk. It is especially good for waterside sites.

Dryopteris erythrosora
JAPANESE RED SHIELD FERN
☼ ☼ ✳✳✳   ↕↔ 60cm (24in)

One of the most colourful of hardy ferns, its coppery red young fronds in spring and summer contrast with the shiny, dark green, overwintering, mature fronds.

Dryopteris wallichiana
WALLICH'S WOOD FERN
☼ ✳✳✳   ↕ 90cm (36in) ↔ 75cm (30in)

The erect fronds of this lovely fern form a big, semi-evergreen shuttlecock and have dark-scaly stalks. Its fronds grow taller if rich soil and shelter are provided.

Polystichum munitum
SWORD FERN
☼ ☼ ✳✳✳   ↕ 90cm (36in) ↔ 1.2m (4ft)

Once it is established, this luxuriant fern can transform an otherwise dull corner or border. Its laddered, evergreen fronds will form a large, handsome clump.

Polystichum polyblepharum
JAPANESE TASSEL FERN
☼ ☼ ✳✳✳   ↕ 60cm (24in) ↔ 90cm (36in)

The distinctive shuttlecock of prickle-toothed, much-divided fronds is covered at first with golden hairs. It is particularly effective when planted with other ferns.

Polystichum setiferum
SOFT SHIELD FERN
☼ ☼ ✳✳✳   ↕ 1.2m (4ft) ↔ 90cm (36in)

This graceful and beautiful fern develops a large, loose shuttlecock of evergreen, finely divided, dark green fronds. It will thrive on a shady bank or ditch.

Ferns for Walls and Crevices

FERNS THAT PREFER growing in the crevices of rocks and cliffs in the wild are mostly small to very small in size. They can be established in similar situations in the garden, in damp stone walls where space between the stones allows, or they may be used as charming container or trough plants.

Asplenium adiantum-nigrum
BLACK SPLEENWORT
☼ ☀ ❄❄❄ ↕ 15cm (6in) ↔ 20cm (8in)

A tough little evergreen fern with wiry black stalks and triangular, much-divided, leathery, shiny green fronds. It thrives in alkaline soils.

Asplenium ceterach
RUSTY-BACK FERN
☼ ☀ ❄❄❄ ↕ 12.5cm (5in) ↔ 25cm (10in)

This is quite unlike any other hardy fern in its tuffet of scaly-backed, deeply lobed, strap-shaped, evergreen fronds, which curl in times of drought, recovering after rain.

OTHER FERNS FOR WALLS AND CREVICES

Adiantum capillus-veneris
Asplenium viride
Cheilanthes tomentosa
Cystopteris fragilis
Pellaea atropurpurea
Polypodium cambricum
Polypodium interjectum 'Cornubiense', see p.121

Asplenium ruta-muraria
WALL RUE
☼ ☀ ❄❄❄ ↕ 10cm (4in) ↔ 12.5cm (5in)

Often found with *A. trichomanes* in the wild, this wall rue forms dense colonies of small, much-divided, leathery, evergreen fronds. It is fond of alkaline conditions.

Asplenium scolopendrium Crispum Group
HART'S TONGUE FERN
☼ ☀ ❄❄❄ ↕ 50cm (20in) ↔ 60cm (24in)

The strap-shaped, wavy-margined, shiny fronds of this curiously attractive, evergreen fern gradually form a bold clump. Also ideal for the front of a shady border.

Asplenium trichomanes
MAIDENHAIR SPLEENWORT
☼ ☼ ☀ ❄❄❄ ↕ 15cm (6in) ↔ 20cm (8in)

Delicate-looking but tough, this little fern produces an evergreen rosette of slender, black-stalked fronds with neatly paired divisions. It prefers alkaline conditions. ♔

Polypodium cambricum
Pulcherrimum Group
☼ ☼ ❄❄❄ ↕ 45cm (18in) ↔ 60cm (24in)

The decorative, regularly and deeply divided, triangular to lance-shaped fronds have crested tips, and emerge in summer, staying fresh and green until late winter.

Woodsia polystichoides
HOLLY FERN WOODSIA
☼ ❄❄❄ ↕ 20cm (8in) ↔ 25cm (10in)

One of the prettiest ferns for walls or rock crevices, producing small clumps of lance-shaped, deeply divided, pale green fronds. It may be damaged by late spring frosts. ♔

149

Tall, Vigorous Bamboos

THE VIGOUR, LUSH INFORMALITY, and glossy, ever-moving, evergreen foliage of these tall-growing bamboos make them ideal for screening, especially on moist, well-drained soils in sheltered sites. Superb for large gardens or woodland, where their thicket-forming habit is no problem.

Semiarundinaria fastuosa
NARIHIRA BAMBOO
☀ ☀ ✳✳✳ ↕ 5m (15ft) ↔ 4m (12ft)

This stately, erect bamboo has purple-brown-striped canes, with dense sprays of foliage. Clump-forming in cool climates, it spreads extensively in warmer areas. ♔

OTHER TALL, VIGOROUS BAMBOOS

Phyllostachys aurea
Phyllostachys aureosulcata
Phyllostachys aureosulcata 'Spectabilis'
Phyllostachys edulis
Phyllostachys nigra 'Boryana'
Phyllostachys vivax 'Aureocaulis'
Pleioblastus simonii
Semiarundinaria yashadake
Yushania maculata

Chimonobambusa quadrangularis
SQUARE-STEMMED BAMBOO
☀ ✳✳ ↕ 5m (16ft) ↔ indefinite

The older canes of this very fast-growing bamboo are peculiarly four-angled, and mature from green to brown. They carry large sprays of arching, shiny green leaves.

Pseudosasa japonica
METAKE
☀ ☀ ✳✳✳✳ ↕ 6m (20ft) ↔ indefinite

A handsome bamboo, commonly grown for screening. The heavy mass of striking green foliage forces the dense stands of green canes to arch at the tips in maturity. ♔

Phyllostachys viridiglaucescens
PHYLLOSTACHYS
☀ ☀ ✳✳✳ ↕ 5m (16ft) ↔ indefinite

Like all *Phyllostachys* species, it bears pairs of branches from the cane joints. Large stands of green canes arch widely under the weight of its lush, glossy foliage. ♔

Chimonobambusa tumidissinoda
QIONGZU CANE
☀ ✳✳✳ ↕ 5m (15ft) ↔ indefinite

Recently introduced from China, this bamboo with swollen cane joints is famous as a source of walking sticks. The sprays of narrow leaves ideally need shade.

Yushania anceps
ANCEPS BAMBOO
☀ ☀ ✳✳✳ ↕ 4m (12ft) ↔ indefinite

The most popular bamboo for screening, forming a dense thicket of slender, glossy canes, with arching to pendent branches thickly clothed in fresh green foliage. ♔

Clump-forming Bamboos

THERE ARE FEW MORE ELEGANT and impressive evergreen perennials than those bamboos that slowly increase to form single clumps of canes. They are best displayed as specimens in a sheltered lawn, bed, or woodland glade, and are lovely by water as long as they are not planted in wet soil.

OTHER CLUMP-FORMING BAMBOOS
Chusquea culeou 'Tenuis'
Fargesia denudata
Fargesia robusta
Himalayacalamus falconeri 'Damarapa'
Thamnocalamus crassinodus 'Kew Beauty'
Thamnocalamus spathiflorus

Chusquea culeou
FOXTAIL BAMBOO
☼ ☀ ✲✲✲✲ ↕ 6m (20ft) ↔ 2.5m (8ft)

The densely packed, yellowish or green canes form an impressive, vase-shaped clump, and look like fox-tails with their branch clusters crowded at each joint. ♈

Fargesia nitida
FOUNTAIN BAMBOO
☼ ☀ ✲✲✲✲ ↕ 5m (15ft) ↔ 3m (10ft)

This aptly named bamboo has a bold, dense clump of slender, arching, purplish canes, which mature to yellow-green and bear showers of narrow leaves. ♈

Fargesia murielae
UMBRELLA BAMBOO
☼ ✲✲✲✲ ↕ 4m (12ft) ↔ 3m (10ft)

A popular specimen plant, forming a vase-shaped clump of arching, bloomy white canes, ageing through green to yellowish green, with plumes of slender leaves. ♈

Semiarundinaria yamadorii
SEMIARUNDINARIA
☼ ☀ ✲✲✲✲ ↕ 3m (10ft) ↔ 2m (6ft)

Well-furnished with a mass of handsome, dense green foliage, this is a bamboo of real character and value. Its tall, narrow green canes form a dense, upright clump.

Thamnocalamus tessellatus
ZULU BAMBOO
☼ ☀ ✲✲✲✲ ↕ 4m (12ft) ↔ 2m (6ft)

Conspicuous, papery white sheaths clothe the tall canes of this dense, clump-forming bamboo, giving them a banded effect. It was once used to make Zulu shields.

Geraniums for Collectors

HARDY GERANIUMS, or cranesbills as they are known, are among the most popular of all perennials. This is partly because of their many uses in the garden, and partly due to their great variety of habit, foliage, and flowers. No garden should be without at least a few of the following.

OTHER GERANIUMS FOR COLLECTORS

Geranium 'Brookside', see p.33
Geranium clarkei 'Kashmir Pink'
Geranium maculatum f. *albiflorum*
Geranium palmatum, see p.129
Geranium × *riversleaianum* 'Russell Prichard', see p.106
Geranium sinense
Geranium wlassovianum, see p.140

Geranium 'Salome'
CRANESBILL
☼ ◐ ❄❄❄   ↕ 30cm (12in) ↔ 2m (6ft)

The faintly marbled leaves of this low-grower are suffused yellow when young. Dusky violet-pink flowers, with dark veins and eyes, appear from summer to autumn.

Geranium himalayense 'Plenum'
CRANESBILL
☼ ◐ ❄❄❄   ↕ 25cm (10in) ↔ 60cm (24in)

Also known as 'Birch Double', this pretty cranesbill is ideal for the front of a border. It has neatly divided leaves, and loosely double, old-fashioned blooms in summer.

Geranium 'Nimbus'
CRANESBILL
☼ ◐ ❄❄❄   ↕ 40cm (16in) ↔ 60cm (24in)

This low-grower spreads by underground, creeping stems to form a mound of prettily divided leaves, which are yellowish when young. It has purple-pink summer flowers.

Geranium sylvaticum 'Amy Doncaster'
WOOD CRANESBILL
☼ ◐ ❄❄❄   ↕ 70cm (28in) ↔ 50cm (18in)

In summer, this lovely form of the wood cranesbill bears white-eyed, deep purple-blue flowers. It commemorates the plantswoman who first selected it in her garden.

Geranium kishtvariense
CRANESBILL
☼ ◐ ❄❄❄   ↕ 30cm (12in) ↔ 60cm (24in)

Creeping, underground stems form a low patch of wrinkled, deeply lobed leaves. Brilliant pinkish purple, finely lined flowers appear in summer and autumn.

Geranium phaeum 'Lily Lovell'
MOURNING WIDOW
☼ ◐ ❄❄❄   ↕ 80cm (32in) ↔ 45cm (18in)

A charming form of the mourning widow cranesbill, with attractively lobed, light green leaves, and showers of rich mauve, white-eyed flowers during summer.

Geranium wallichianum
CRANESBILL
☼ ◐ ❄❄❄   ↕ 30cm (12in) ↔ 90cm (36in)

The attractively lined, lilac-purple flowers of this carpeting cranesbill are borne over a long period from summer into autumn. Its marbled leaves are shallowly lobed.

Hostas for Collectors

THE ALREADY BEWILDERING NUMBER of hostas increases each year, with new variations in leaf shape, size, texture, and colour, and the bonus of attractive flowers. The favourites selected here are ideal for planting singly, or in groups or drifts. They are also handsome container plants for paved areas.

*Hosta
lancifolia*
PLANTAIN LILY
☼ ☀ ❄❄❄ ↕ 45cm (18in) ↔ 75cm (30in)

Long grown in gardens, this reliable hosta forms a loose clump of narrow, glossy, dark green leaves, good for ground cover. It has racemes of purple flowers in summer. ⚘

Hosta 'Buckshaw Blue'
PLANTAIN LILY
☼ ☀ ❄❄❄ ↕ 35cm (14in) ↔ 60cm (24in)

The heart-shaped, slightly "dished" leaves are boldly veined and beautifully bloomy, forming a striking clump. Nodding flowers open in short-stalked racemes in summer.

Hosta gracillima
PLANTAIN LILY
☼ ☀ ❄❄❄ ↕ 5cm (2in) ↔ 18cm (7in)

Charming for containers, rock gardens, or walls, this tiny hosta's spreading, narrow leaves have wavy margins. It bears slender spires of pinkish violet flowers in autumn.

> ### OTHER HOSTAS FOR COLLECTORS
>
> *Hosta* 'Aphrodite'
> *Hosta* 'Great Expectations'
> *Hosta* 'Northern Halo'
> *Hosta* 'Patriot'
> *Hosta* 'Sagae'
> *Hosta* 'Snowden'
> *Hosta* 'Sum and Substance', see p.XX
> *Hosta* 'Summer Fragrance'
> *Hosta* 'Zounds', see p.60

Hosta montana 'Aureomarginata'
PLANTAIN LILY
☼ ☀ ❄❄❄ ↕ 70cm (28in) ↔ 90cm (36in)

Slow to establish but worth the wait, this is a superb specimen plant for containers or borders. It has long-stalked, large, shiny leaves, irregularly margined in bright gold.

Hosta 'Golden Tiara'
PLANTAIN LILY
☼ ☀ ❄❄❄ ↕ 30cm (12in) ↔ 50cm (20in)

One of the best small hostas, it forms a compact clump of heart-shaped, yellowy-margined leaves. It has tall racemes of lavender-purple flowers in summer. ⚘

Hosta hypoleuca
PLANTAIN LILY
☼ ☀ ❄❄❄ ↕ 45cm (18in) ↔ 90cm (36in)

This attractive species has large, pale green leaves, with a grey bloom above and striking, mealy-white undersides. It bears pale mauve to white flowers in summer.

Hosta tokudama
PLANTAIN LILY
☼ ☀ ❄❄❄ ↕ 35cm (14in) ↔ 90cm (36in)

Beautiful but slow-growing, this hosta has pale mauve to white flowers in summer, and forms a compact clump of rounded to heart-shaped, corrugated, glaucous leaves.

Snowdrops for Collectors

I F YOU ARE THRILLED BY THE SIGHT of a drift of common snowdrops in the late winter garden or in woodland, then prepare for a pleasant surprise. There are dozens of lesser known varieties of snowdrop, each with its own particular charm and characteristics, and most are very easy to cultivate.

Galanthus nivalis Scharlockii Group
SNOWDROP
☀ ❄❄❄   ↕↔10cm (4in)

This curious form of the common snow-drop has nodding, green-tipped flowers, with spathes split into two segments that stand above the blooms like rabbit's ears.

Galanthus 'Augustus'
SNOWDROP
☀ ❄❄❄   ↕15cm (6in) ↔8cm (3in)

This robust snowdrop has relatively wide, silver-channelled leaves, and distinctly rounded, large flowers with green-tipped inner segments. It forms colonies in time.

OTHER SNOWDROPS FOR
COLLECTORS

Galanthus 'Benhall Beauty'
Galanthus elwesii 'Comet'
Galanthus 'Merlin'
Galanthus nivalis subsp.
   imperati 'Ginns'
Galanthus nivalis 'Lady Elphinstone'
Galanthus nivalis 'Sandersii', see p.104
Galanthus 'S. Arnott'

Galanthus 'Magnet'
SNOWDROP
☀ ❄❄❄   ↕20cm (8in) ↔6cm (3in)

The distinguished, scented flowers sway in the slightest breeze on their unusually long, slender stalks. This is one of the best and most reliable snowdrops.   ♔

Galanthus 'Ophelia'
SNOWDROP
☀ ❄❄❄   ↕15cm (6in) ↔20cm (8in)

A must for every collection, this very early snowdrop has fully double blooms on slender stalks. The outer segments have pinched tips, sometimes marked green.

Galanthus 'John Gray'
SNOWDROP
☀ ❄❄❄   ↕15cm (6in) ↔8cm (3in)

Exquisite and early flowering, this is one of the most collectable snowdrops. It has pendent flowers on long, slender stalks, with inner segments marked green.

Galanthus 'Mighty Atom'
SNOWDROP
☀ ❄❄❄   ↕12cm (5in) ↔8cm (3in)

An outstanding, easily grown snowdrop, bearing attractive, slender-stalked flowers with inner segments that are distinctively stained green at their tips.

Galanthus reginae-olgae
SNOWDROP
☀ ❄❄   ↕10cm (4in) ↔8cm (3in)

The earliest-flowering snowdrop, usually blooming in autumn before its green, silver-channelled leaves emerge. It is slow to increase, growing best in a sunny site.

Hellebores for Collectors

HELLEBORES ARE AMONG some of the most fashionable and collectable perennials for partially shaded sites in the garden. The range of species is not great, but despite this, an ever-increasing number of named hybrids and selected seedlings are being made available.

Helleborus × sternii 'Boughton Beauty'
HELLEBORE
☼ ☼ ❄ ❄ ❄   ↕ ↔ 50cm (20in)

In late winter, green-tinted pink flowers rise above the hummock of evergreen, beautifully veined and marbled, greyish leaves. Needs protection in cold areas.

Helleborus atrorubens
HELLEBORE
☼ ☼ ❄ ❄ ❄   ↕ 30cm (12in) ↔ 45cm (18in)

A choice species, with circular, deeply divided, long-stalked leaves, often purple-tinted when young. Its starry, late winter flowers vary from deep purple to green.

Helleborus multifidus subsp. *hercegovinus*
HELLEBORE
☼ ☼ ❄ ❄ ❄   ↕ 30cm (12in) ↔ 45cm (18in)

Best known for the lacy effect of its finely dissected leaves, this hellebore also bears attractive, yellowish or pale green flowers in late winter or early spring.

Helleborus torquatus Party Dress Group
HELLEBORE
☼ ☼ ❄ ❄ ❄   ↕ 40cm (16in) ↔ 30cm (12in)

A delightful, if unusual, group of small hellebores, which produces multi-petalled flowers in a variety of colours from winter to early spring, before the leaves emerge.

Helleborus odorus
HELLEBORE
☼ ☼ ❄ ❄ ❄   ↕ ↔ 50cm (20in)

This showy, easy-to-grow species is free-flowering, with masses of scented, green to yellow-green flowers in late winter or early spring. A bold, clump-forming plant.

> **OTHER HELLEBORES FOR COLLECTORS**
>
> *Helleborus dumetorum*
> *Helleborus × ericsmithii*, see p.33
> *Helleborus hybridus* Ballard's Group
> *Helleborus × nigercors* 'Alabaster'
> *Helleborus niger* 'Potter's Wheel',
>   see p.105
> *Helleborus purpurascens*
> *Helleborus torquatus*

Helleborus lividus
HELLEBORE
☼ ☼ ❄ ❄   ↕ 45cm (18in) ↔ 30cm (12in)

Silver-veined, evergreen leaves, tinted pink beneath, are accompanied by apple-green, pink-flushed flowers in winter. Best grown in an alpine house in cold areas. ♔

Helleborus vesicarius
HELLEBORE
☼ ❄ ❄ ❄   ↕ 45cm (18in) ↔ 30cm (12in)

This curious but desirable hellebore bears small, cupped, green and purple blooms in late winter and early spring, followed by inflated pods. It is dormant in summer.

Epimediums for Collectors

THE INTRODUCTION OF many new species from China has elevated epimediums to among the most collectable of perennials. As woodland plants with attractive evergreen or deciduous foliage, they form excellent ground cover, and are also effective for underplanting beneath deciduous shrubs.

Epimedium acuminatum
EPIMEDIUM

☀ ❋❋❋   ↕ 45cm (18in) ↔ 75cm (30in)

A magnificent, clump-forming evergreen with large, lance- or arrow-shaped leaflets, and long-spurred, pale purple, or purple and white flowers in spring and summer.

Epimedium davidii
EPIMEDIUM

☀ ❋❋❋   ↕ 30cm (12in) ↔ 45cm (18in)

The dark, shining stems of this choice species bear evergreen, divided leaves, and racemes of nodding, long-spurred yellow flowers from spring into summer.

OTHER EPIMEDIUMS TO COLLECT

Epimedium franchetii
Epimedium grandiflorum 'Lilafee'
Epimedium grandiflorum f. *violaceum*
Epimedium grandiflorum
  'White Queen'
Epimedium ogisui
Epimedium pinnatum subsp. *colchicum*,
  see p.52
Epimedium x *versicolor* 'Sulphureum'

Epimedium grandiflorum
'Rose Queen'

☀ ❋❋❋   ↕ 30cm (12in) ↔ 45cm (18in)

The heart-shaped, prickle-toothed leaflets form a low mound and are prettily tinted when young. Showers of long-spurred, deep rose-pink flowers open in spring. ♔

Epimedium leptorrhizum
EPIMEDIUM

☀ ❋❋❋   ↕ 25cm (10in) ↔ 45cm (18in)

In time, this creeping evergreen develops patches of stems with attractively veined, prickle-toothed leaflets. Its long-spurred flowers open in spring and early summer.

Epimedium x perralchicum
'Frohnleiten'

☀ ❋❋❋❋   ↕ 40cm (16in) ↔ 60cm (24in)

Worth growing for its foliage alone, as the prickle-toothed, glossy, dark green leaves are beautifully bronze-tinted when young. Pendent spring flowers are bright yellow.

Epimedium stellulatum 'Wudang Star'
EPIMEDIUM

☀ ❋❋❋   ↕ 40cm (16in) ↔ 30cm (12in)

Multitudes of small, starry white flowers, with bold yellow beaks, are borne on wiry stems in spring above the heart-shaped, prickle-toothed, shiny, evergreen leaflets.

Epimedium x versicolor 'Versicolor'
EPIMEDIUM

☀ ❋❋❋   ↕↔ 30cm (12in)

This is a real charmer with its low clump of evergreen foliage, attractively tinted when young. The loose sprays of yellow, pink-suffused flowers open in spring.

Peonies for Collectors

WILD HERBACEOUS PEONIES, bearing their simple, usually single blooms of fragile petals and golden stamens, never fail to bring a touch of quality to the garden. Although their flowering period is relatively brief, they frequently have decorative foliage that extends their value in the garden.

Paeonia 'Smouthii'
PEONY
☼ ☼ ❋❋❋   ↕ ↔ 70cm (28in)

A little-known but reliable hybrid which forms clumps of finely divided leaves. It produces fragrant, cup-shaped, bright red blooms in late spring and early summer.

Paeonia cambessedesii
MAJORCAN PEONY
☼ ❋❋❋   ↕ 55cm (22in) ↔ 60cm (24in)

Very distinctive, this peony has purple- and red-flushed stems with shiny, metallic grey-green leaves which are red or purple beneath. Spring flowers are rose-pink. ♎

Paeonia mascula subsp. *arietina*
PEONY
☼ ☼ ❋❋❋   ↕ 75cm (30in) ↔ 60cm (24in)

This stout clump-former has handsome, deeply divided, greyish green leaves, and bears bowl-shaped, reddish pink flowers with creamy yellow stamens during spring.

OTHER PEONIES TO COLLECT

Paeonia delavayi
Paeonia lactiflora 'White Wings'
Paeonia lactiflora 'Whitleyi Major'
Paeonia obovata
Paeonia obovata var. *alba*
Paeonia peregrina 'Otto Froebel'
Paeonia tenuifolia 'Rosea'
Paeonia veitchii var. *woodwardii*
Paeonia 'Yao Huang'

Paeonia tenuifolia
PEONY
☼ ❋❋❋   ↕ ↔ 45cm (18in)

Quite unlike any other species, this forms bold clumps of beautiful, finely dissected leaves. The cupped, deep red flowers are borne in late spring and early summer.

Paeonia emodi
HIMALAYAN PEONY
☼ ☼ ❋❋❋   ↕ ↔ 80cm (32in)

In late spring, slightly nodding, cupped, fragrant white flowers are carried by the handsome clump of branched stems with deeply divided leaves. Enjoys semi-shade.

Paeonia mlokosewitschii
CAUCASIAN PEONY
☼ ☼ ❋❋❋   ↕ ↔ 70cm (28in)

This well-known peony has stout clumps of downy, grey-green leaves. Its lemon-yellow, late-spring and summer blooms are followed by brilliant red seed capsules. ♎

Paeonia wittmanniana
PEONY
☼ ☼ ❋❋❋   ↕ ↔ 90cm (36in)

An outstanding species, with bold clumps of glossy, dark green leaves. Bowl-shaped, pale yellow flowers, borne from late spring to summer, are followed by red seed pods.

CLIMBERS

THE MOST COMMON climbers are woody-stemmed perennials or shrubs with scrambling or otherwise long, slender stems. Self-clinging by adhesive tendril tips or aerial roots, or in need of artificial support from wire or a trellis, they may be trained into trees and shrubs, and to cover walls or other structures.

△ IVY-CLAD SHED *This bold-leaved ivy (Hedera colchica 'Dentata Variegata') is perfect for covering an unsightly wall.*

△ *Abutilon megapotamicum*

All plants recommended in this section are either true climbers, or shrubs suitable for training against walls. They offer a large variety of effects, from colourful or prolific flowers to decorative or unusual fruits. Many have attractive leaves, and some deciduous climbers are also noted for their autumn tints. Once established, both wall shrubs and climbers can support further plants, creating, when planned, a continuous, multi-season feature. All the climbers recommended on the following pages are deciduous unless specified as evergreen.

CLIMBING TO THE SUN

Numerous climbers grown for their flowering qualities thrive best in a sunny site; most honeysuckles for instance, and climbing roses. Two popular favourites, clematis and wisteria, prefer to have their heads in the sun and their roots shaded (place a large stone or tile over their roots). When grown against a wall, climbers benefit from the reflected heat, which helps ripen growth and initiate flower bud formation.

WOODLAND SHADE

The cooler conditions of sunless walls, often combined with moist but well-drained soils, are a perfect home for many natural woodland climbers. Ivies are a good example, especially coloured-leaved varieties, which flourish on shady or partially shaded walls, as do those lovely South American woodlanders, *Lapageria* and *Berberidopsis*.

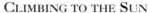

△ SUPPORT IN DISGUISE *Evergreen, spring-flowering ceanothus and twining honeysuckle beautifully decorate this pole.*

◁ PRETTY WINDOW *Wisteria, rose, and two clematis varieties combine to provide a delightful frame for this window.*

▷ SUMMER SENSATION *A luxuriant early summer growth of clematis, purple vine, and golden hop clothes this wall.*

Climbers for Warm, Sunny Walls and Fences

SUNNY WALLS AND FENCES are excellent for climbers. When carefully selected and matched, several can be trained to grow into one another to give continuous effect. The surface, especially of a brick or stone wall, absorbs heat, and this helps promote growth, and encourages flowering. All the climbers featured here require support from wires or netting.

Lonicera × *americana*
HONEYSUCKLE
☼ ❄❄❄   ↕ ↔ 7m (22ft)

This free-flowering scramber has clusters of fragrant, pink-tubed, creamy yellow flowers from summer into early autumn. Its leaves are purplish when young.

Actinidia kolomikta
ACTINIDIA
☼ ❄❄❄   ↕ ↔ 4.5m (13ft)

This striking climber is slow to establish, but it is worth the wait. It has bold, heart-shaped leaves, often splashed cream and pink, and white flowers in summer. ♈

Passiflora caerulea
BLUE PASSION FLOWER
☼ ❄❄   ↕ ↔ 10m (30ft)

Fast-growing with fingered leaves, this climber bears beautiful, unusual flowers from summer into autumn. They may be followed by attractive seed pods. ♈

Clematis 'Bill MacKenzie'
CLEMATIS
☼ ❄❄❄   ↕ ↔ 7m (22ft)

Vigorous and scrambling, this clematis has beautiful, lantern-like, nodding flowers in late summer and autumn. These are followed by pretty, silky seed heads. ♈

Clematis 'Jackmanii'
CLEMATIS
☼ ❄❄❄   ↕ ↔ 3m (10ft)

A long-established garden favourite, this climbs by twining leaf stalks. Masses of large, velvety, dark purple flowers, turning violet with age, appear in summer. ♈

Rosa Dublin Bay ('Macdub')
CLIMBING ROSE
☼ ❄❄❄   ↕ ↔ 2.2m (7ft)

'Dublin Bay' is a climbing floribunda rose of dense growth, with glossy, dark green leaves and clusters of double, fragrant flowers from summer to early autumn. ♈

Vitis vinifera 'Purpurea'
CLARET VINE
☼ ✳✳✳ ↕↔7m (22ft)

A vigorous form of the grape vine, with young leaves that mature to wine-purple. These colour richly in autumn, when small bunches of blue-black grapes ripen. ♔

SELF-CLINGING CLIMBERS FOR SUNNY WALLS AND FENCES

Campsis radicans
Cissus striata
Decumaria barbara
Decumaria sinensis, see p.172
Ficus pumila
Parthenocissus tricuspidata 'Lowii'
Trachelospermum asiaticum, see p.175
Trachelospermum jasminoides, see p.171
Trachelospermum jasminoides
    'Variegatum'

Rosa 'Madame Grégoire Staechelin'
CLIMBING ROSE
☼ ✳✳✳ ↕↔3m (10ft)

One of the most beautiful climbing roses, this is vigorous, with shining green leaves and abundant clusters of rounded, slightly fragrant flowers in summer. ♔

OTHER CLIMBERS FOR SUN

Araujia sericifera
Campsis × *tagliabuana* 'Madame Galen'
Clematis armandii, see p.170
Dregea sinensis
Jasminum officinale f. *affine*
Lonicera periclymenum 'Graham
    Thomas', see p.169
Mandevilla laxa
Mutisia ilicifolia
Rosa banksiae 'Lutea'
Sollya heterophylla
Trachelospermum asiaticum
Wisteria sinensis, see p.173

Rosa 'Maigold'
CLIMBING ROSE
☼ ✳✳✳ ↕↔4m (12ft)

This vigorous climber has thorny stems and lush foliage. Fragrant bronze-yellow blooms, reddish in bud, appear in early summer, and less profusely in autumn. ♔

Solanum laxum 'Album'
SOLANUM
☼ ✳✳ ↕↔6m (20ft)

Semi-evergreen and slender-stemmed, this climber will grow vigorously through any support. Loose clusters of star-flowers occur from summer into autumn. ♔

Wisteria floribunda 'Alba'
WHITE JAPANESE WISTERIA
☼ ✳✳✳ ↕↔9m (28ft)

The handsome leaves of this powerful climber are divided. Long spikes of white pea-flowers emerge in early summer. Thrives in neutral to slightly acid soils. ♔

CLIMBERS

Climbers for Sunless Walls and Fences

THE COOLER CONDITIONS normally found in places that do not receive the sun's glare directly suit a good number of climbers, many of which grow naturally in woodland, or similarly shaded places in the wild. Most need to be tied to a wire or trellis support, and even the self-clinging ones, such as ivy, benefit from this for a year or two after planting.

C L I M B E R S

Berberidopsis corallina
CORAL PLANT
☼ ☀ ✳✳✳**PH**⟱   ↕ ↔ 4.5m (14ft)

Coral Plant's long, rambling stems, with heart-shaped evergreen leaves, need tying to a support. Pendent, globular flowers are carried from summer into autumn.

Clematis x *jouiniana* 'Praecox'
CLEMATIS
☼ ☀ ✳✳✳✳   ↕ ↔ 3m (10ft)

Vigorous and sprawling, this dense-growing climber should be trained to a support. Its coarse foliage backs masses of small, fragrant, tubular flowers in late summer.⟱

Clematis montana f. *grandiflora*
CLEMATIS
☼ ☀ ✳✳✳   ↕ ↔ 10m (30ft)

In time, this vigorous climber will produce blankets of leafy growth, bronze-purple when the leaves are young. Large white spring flowers are borne in abundance. ⟱

Clematis 'Nelly Moser'
CLEMATIS
☼ ✳✳✳   ↕ ↔ 3.5m (11ft)

Large, single, pale mauve flowers, with a carmine stripe on each petal, cover this popular twining clematis in early summer. Their colour fades in strong sunlight. ⟱

Hedera colchica 'Dentata Variegata'
PERSIAN IVY
☼ ☀ ✳✳✳   ↕ ↔ 5m (15ft)

A spectacular evergreen with broad-based, leathery leaves, each irregularly margined creamy white. Shoots have aerial roots that cling to the surface of a support. ⟱

OTHER DECIDUOUS CLIMBERS FOR SUNLESS WALLS

Akebia trifoliata
Aristolochia macrophylla
Hydrangea anomala subsp. *petiolaris*, see p.175
Parthenocissus henryana, see p.175
Parthenocissus tricuspidata 'Lowii'
Parthenocissus tricuspidata 'Robusta'
Schizophragma hydrangeoides
Schizophragma hydrangeoides 'Moonlight'
Schizophragma hydrangeoides 'Roseum'

Hedera colchica 'Sulphur Heart'
PERSIAN IVY
☼ ☀ ✳✳✳   ↕ ↔ 5m (15ft)

This dramatic ivy, with its boldly gold-splashed leaves, is similar to *H. colchica* 'Dentata Variegata' *(above)*. They are most effective when grown together. ⟱

Hedera helix 'Eva'
IVY
☼ ☀ ❄❄❄   ↕ ↔ 1.2m (4ft)

The evergreen leaves of this very popular, variegated common ivy cultivar are green and grey-green with broad, creamy white margins. It is self-clinging.

Lapageria rosea
CHILEAN BELLFLOWER
☼ ☀ ❄❄❄ PH ⚘   ↕ ↔ 5m (15ft)

Strongly twining stems support leathery evergreen leaves and, from summer into late autumn, beautiful, pendulous, tubular flowers with fleshy petals. ♈

Lonicera japonica 'Halliana'
JAPANESE HONEYSUCKLE
☼ ☀ ☀ ❄❄❄   ↕ ↔ 10m (30ft)

Evergreen or semi-evergreen, this prolific, twining climber produces loose clusters of fragrant flowers, emerging white and aging to yellow, from summer into autumn. ♈

Hedera helix 'Green Ripple'
IVY
☼ ☀ ❄❄❄   ↕ ↔ 1.2m (4ft)

This is a distinct cultivar of common ivy in which the bright evergreen leaves, with pale veins, are deeply lobed and pointed. Self-clinging, it is ideal for low walls.

Humulus lupulus 'Aureus'
GOLDEN HOP
☼ ☀ ❄❄❄   ↕ ↔ 6m (20ft)

A strong-growing herbaceous climber, this has hairy, twining stems and boldly lobed yellow-green leaves. Clusters of green fruits (hops) are produced in autumn. ♈

OTHER EVERGREEN CLIMBERS FOR SUNLESS WALLS

Hedera pastuchovii 'Ann Ala'
Holboellia latifolia
Lardizabala biternata
Pileostegia viburnoides, see p.171

Schizophragma integrifolium
SCHIZOPHRAGMA
☼ ☀ ❄❄❄   ↕ ↔ 12m (40ft)

In time, this slow-growing, self-clinging climber will reach great heights. Flattened heads of creamy white flowers appear in summer, among pointed green leaves. ♈

C L I M B E R S

Shrubs for Warm, Sunny Walls and Fences

SUNNY WALLS AND FENCES are a bonus to the gardener as they offer both the warmth and shelter necessary for less hardy plants. They are also ideal for shrubs with trailing or fragile stems that need some support. Most will greatly increase their average height when grown against a wall. Careful pruning and training onto wires or a trellis may be necessary.

M B E R S

Abutilon megapotamicum
ABUTILON

☼ ❄❄❄   ↕ ↔ 3m (10ft)

This free-growing shrub is of virtually pendulous habit with slender stems and, from late spring to autumn, flowers that resemble colourful Chinese lanterns. ♧

Callistemon pallidus
BOTTLEBRUSH

☼ ❄❄❄ PH   ↕ ↔ 3m (10ft)

In flower, bottlebrushes are among the most exotic of evergreen shrubs. This is certainly no exception, with its brushes of creamy yellow flowers, borne in summer.

Ceanothus arboreus 'Trewithen Blue'
CATALINA CEANOTHUS

☼ ❄❄❄   ↕ ↔ 6m (20ft)

This strong-growing evergreen shrub is ideal for covering a large surface. It flowers for many weeks in late winter and spring. Prefers well-drained, lime-free soils. ♧

Buddleja crispa
BUDDLEJA

☼ ❄❄   ↕ ↔ 2.5m (8ft)

The oval leaves of this choice shrub are all covered in a woolly pelt of soft, greyish white down. Its small, fragrant flowers are carried in dense clusters in summer.

> **OTHER DECIDUOUS SHRUBS FOR WARM, SUNNY WALLS AND FENCES**
>
> *Abeliophyllum distichum*
> *Buddleja officinalis*
> *Caesalpinia gilliesii*
> *Callistemon citrinus* 'Splendens', see p.196
> *Chimonanthus praecox* 'Grandiflorus', see p.236
> *Clianthus puniceus*
> *Colquhounia coccinea*
> *Edgeworthia chrysantha*
> *Indigofera heterantha*, see p.194
> *Lagerstroemia indica*
> *Lavatera maritima*
> *Prunus mume* 'Beni-shidore'
> *Punica granatum* 'Rubrum Flore Pleno'
> *Ribes speciosum*
> *Viburnum macrocephalum*
> *Vitex agnus-castus* var. *latifolia*
> *Xanthoceras sorbifolium*, see p.195

Cytisus battandieri
MOROCCAN BROOM

☼ ❄❄   ↕ ↔ 4m (12ft)

Moroccan Broom is worth growing for its leaves alone, each divided into three parts, and covered in soft, silky silvery hairs. Its summer flowers are pineapple-scented. ♧

Acca sellowiana
PINEAPPLE GUAVA
☼ ❄❄   ↕ ↔ 3m (10ft)

The summer flowers of this interesting evergreen shrub have fleshy, edible petals and crimson stamens. Edible, egg-shaped fruits are produced after a hot summer.

Robinia hispida
ROSE ACACIA
☼ ❄❄❄   ↕ ↔ 2.5m (8ft)

Large rose-pink pea-flowers are borne in drooping clusters from late spring into summer. The leaves, with numerous lush green leaflets, are held on fragile stems. ♛

Fremontodendron 'California Glory'
FREMONTODENDRON
☼ ❄❄   ↕ ↔ 8m (25ft)

This fast-growing evergreen has beautiful yellow flowers from spring into autumn. Prune regularly if it is on a small fence or wall, ensuring the roots are not too wet. ♛

Rosa × odorata 'Mutabilis'
CHINA ROSE
☼ ❄❄   ↕ ↔ 3m (10ft)

This vigorous China rose is popular for its dark purple shoots, coppery young leaves, and lovely fragrant summer flowers. It will grow taller than usual against a wall. ♛

> **OTHER EVERGREEN SHRUBS FOR WARM, SUNNY WALLS AND FENCES**
>
> *Abelia floribunda*
> *Carpenteria californica*, see p.228
> *Ceanothus* 'Concha'
> *Viburnum awabuki*

Desmodium elegans var. *spicatum*
DESMODIUM
☼ ❄❄   ↕ ↔ 2–3m (6–10ft)

From late summer into autumn, long racemes of pink flowers project from soft, downy leaves. Except in cold areas, old growth is best pruned back every spring.

Itea ilicifolia
ITEA
☼ ❄❄❄   ↕ ↔ 5m (15ft)

On warm evenings from late summer into autumn, long greenish catkins give off a honey-like aroma. The dark green, glossy, holly-like leaves are evergreen. ♛

Solanum crispum 'Glasnevin'
SOLANUM
☼ ❄❄   ↕ ↔ 6m (20ft)

Vigorous and scrambling, this shrub is evergreen in warmer areas. Loose clusters of star-shaped flowers appear over a long period in summer. Needs support. ♛

165

Shrubs for Sunless Walls and Fences

SOME GARDENERS may perceive a wall or fence that does not receive direct sunlight as a curse, and consider it unsightly. It need not be a problem, however, as long as it receives some light. Many shrubs (and climbers) will thrive, and some even prefer the normally cooler conditions of such a site, while others   flower freely in or out of the sun.

Forsythia suspensa
WEEPING FORSYTHIA
☼ ☼ ☀ ✳✳✳   ↕ ↔ 3m (10ft)

A vigorous, rambling shrub, this requires regular pruning and training to prevent it from becoming overpowering. Star-shaped flowers wreathe the branches in spring. ♔

Azara microphylla
AZARA
☼ ☀ ✳✳   ↕ ↔ 6m (20ft)

This elegant evergreen will grow to small tree size if allowed. Arching branchlets are clothed with leaves and, in late winter or spring, tiny vanilla-scented flowers. ♔

Chaenomeles × superba 'Rowallane'
ORNAMENTAL QUINCE
☼ ☼ ☀ ✳✳✳   ↕ ↔ 1.5m (5ft)

Superb in spring, when the previous year's branches are hidden beneath brilliant red flower clusters. Like 'Moerloosei', best pruned and trained close to the wall. ♔

Garrya elliptica (male form)
SILK-TASSEL BUSH
☼ ☼ ☀ ✳✳✳   ↕ ↔ 5m (15ft)

From midwinter through to early spring the branches are draped with long tassels, which tremble in the slightest breeze. This shrub has leathery evergreen leaves.

Chaenomeles speciosa 'Moerloosei'
ORNAMENTAL QUINCE
☼ ☼ ☀ ✳✳✳   ↕ ↔ 2.5m (8ft)

A reliable, adaptable, and vigorous shrub, this carries large flower clusters in spring and early summer, followed by aromatic fruits. Prune, and train on wires. ♔

Euonymus fortunei 'Silver Queen'
SILVER QUEEN EUONYMUS
☼ ☼ ☀ ✳✳✳   ↕ ↔ 2.5m (8ft)

A handsome evergreen shrub, low and bushy in a bed, but rising higher against a wall if trained. Glossy dark green leaves have broad, irregular creamy margins.

Illicium anisatum
CHINESE ANISE
☼ ☀ ✳✳   ↕ ↔ 2.5m (8ft)

The aromatic leaves of this slow-growing evergreen are joined by loose clusters of yellow, star-shaped flowers in spring. The wood also has a strong, agreeable aroma.

Jasminum humile
HIMALAYAN JASMINE
☼ ☼ ☀ ❄❄❄   ↕↔2m (6ft)

The numerous greenish stems of this
bushy evergreen are clothed in attractive,
much-divided leaves. It sports clusters of
yellow flowers from spring into autumn.

**OTHER EVERGREEN SHRUBS FOR
SUNLESS WALLS AND FENCES**

Azara serrata
Camellia 'Inspiration'
Crinodendron hookerianum, see p.200
Euonymus fortunei 'Emerald Gaiety',
   see p.184
Garrya × issaquahensis
   'Glasnevin Wine'
Jasminum humile 'Revolutum'
Pyracantha 'Orange Glow', see p.239

Kerria japonica 'Pleniflora'
BATCHELOR'S BUTTONS
☼ ☼ ☀ ❄❄❄   ↕↔3m (10ft)

Popular and easy to grow, this vigorous
shrub has long green shoots that require
support, along with sharply toothed
leaves, and rich yellow spring flowers. ♔

Pyracantha rogersiana
FIRETHORN
☼ ☼ ☀ ❄❄❄   ↕↔3m (10ft)

The spiny branches of this strong-growing
evergreen are clothed in narrrow, glossy
leaves. Flower clusters in early summer
are replaced by orange-red berries. ♔

**OTHER DECIDUOUS SHRUBS FOR
SUNLESS WALLS AND FENCES**

Chaenomeles speciosa 'Geisha Girl'
Chaenomeles speciosa 'Nivalis'
Chaenomeles speciosa 'Snow'
Chaenomeles × superba
   'Crimson and Gold'
Chaenomeles × superba 'Pink Lady'
Cotoneaster horizontalis
Edgeworthia chrysantha
Lonicera × purpusii 'Winter Beauty',
   see p.237

Jasminum nudiflorum
WINTER JASMINE
☼ ☼ ☀ ❄❄❄   ↕↔3m (10ft)

This is a most popular and reliable winter-
flowering shrub, with long shoots bearing
yellow flowers through winter into spring.
Prune after flowering to keep neat. ♔

Piptanthus nepalensis
EVERGREEN LABURNUM
☼ ☼ ☀ ❄❄   ↕↔3m (10ft)

This strong-growing shrub has lush semi-
evergreen or evergreen foliage. Its clusters
of bright yellow pea-flowers are produced
from spring into summer.

Ribes laurifolium (male form)
RIBES
☼ ☼ ❄❄   ↕↔2m (6ft)

A curious, slow-growing evergreen currant
which needs training to gain height. Its
bold leaves are joined by drooping flower
clusters from late winter into early spring.

Climbers to Train into Trees and Shrubs

I F YOU LACK WALLS OR FENCES, encourage climbers to grow into trees or large shrubs, where they can create spectacular effects when in flower or leaf. It is important to match each climber to its supporting plant: grow strong climbers into large trees and weaker ones into small trees or shrubs.

Careful pruning may be necessary to control growth.

Clematis rehderiana
CLEMATIS

☼ ❋❋❋   ↕ ↔ 7m (22ft)

As well as a dense growth of divided leaves, loose clusters of primrose-yellow, cowslip-scented flowers cover this twining climber from late summer into autumn. ♔

OTHER FOLIAGE CLIMBERS FOR TRAINING INTO TREES

Ampelopsis aconitifolia
Aristolochia macrophylla
Hedera colchica 'Dentata Variegata', see p.162
Humulus lupulus 'Aureus', see p.163
Vitis vinifera 'Purpurea', see p.161

Akebia quinata
CHOCOLATE VINE

☼ ☼ ❋❋   ↕ ↔ 10m (30ft)

The clusters of vanilla-scented, brownish purple flowers in spring are followed by sausage-shaped fruits. This vigorous semi-evergreen climbs by twining.

Clematis 'Madame Julia Correvon'
CLEMATIS

☼ ❋❋❋   ↕ ↔ 3.5m (11ft)

This twining climber with slender stems, freely produces magnificent, four-petalled wine-red flowers with cream-coloured stamens, from summer to early autumn. ♔

Celastrus orbiculatus Hermaphrodite Group

☼ ☼ ❋❋❋   ↕ ↔ 20m (70ft)

The leaves of this strong-growing climber turn yellow in autumn, when capsules of orange seeds first appear; the seeds continue into winter. ♔

Clematis montana var. *rubens*
CLEMATIS

☼ ❋❋❋   ↕ ↔ 10m (30ft)

Dense curtains of growth, covered with masses of pink flowers in late spring and early summer, are formed by this twining climber. Many good selections exist.

Hedera colchica
PERSIAN IVY

☼ ☼ ☀ ❋❋❋   ↕ ↔ 10m (30ft)

Persian Ivy is a strong-growing, evergreen, self-clinging climber, which also makes a splendid ground cover. Its shining, dark green leaves are pointed and leathery. ♔

Rosa 'Albertine'
CLIMBING ROSE
☼ ✳✳✳   ↕↔5m (15ft)

An old and popular vigorous rambling
rose, 'Albertine' has thorny reddish stems
and richly fragrant, double salmon-pink
flowers, freely borne in summer. ♔

Vitis coignetiae
JAPANESE VINE
☼ ✳✳✳   ↕↔20m (70ft)

This vigorous vine climbs by means of
twining tendrils, and is chiefly grown for
its handsome, heart-shaped leaves, which
turn crimson and scarlet in autumn. ♔

Lonicera periclymenum
'Graham Thomas'
☼ ✳✳✳   ↕↔7m (22ft)

Vigorous and dense-growing, this twining
climber has oval leaves and, in summer,
loose clusters of freely borne, fragrant
flowers that are white, ageing to yellow. ♔

Rosa filipes 'Kiftsgate'
CLIMBING ROSE
☼ ✳✳✳   ↕↔10m (30ft)

Rampant if unpruned, this rose has fresh,
glossy green foliage and branched heads of
fragrant, yellow-centred white flowers in
summer, followed by small red hips. ♔

OTHER FLOWERING CLIMBERS FOR TRAINING INTO TREES
Clematis 'Jackmanii', see p.160
Clematis 'Perle d'Azur'
Clematis viticella 'Purpurea Plena Elegans'
Hydrangea anomala subsp. *petiolaris*, see p.175
Jasminum officinale
Rosa 'Rambling Rector'
Schisandra rubriflora
Wisteria sinensis, see p.173

Fallopia baldschuanica
RUSSIAN VINE
☼ ✳✳✳   ↕↔12m (40ft)

Well known, popular, and rampant, this
twining climber has string-like tassels of
white or pink-tinged flowers in summer
and early autumn. Dislikes dry soils. ♔

Tropaeolum speciosum
FLAME NASTURTIUM
☼ ✳✳✳   ↕↔3m (10ft)

Brilliant, long-spurred flowers adorn this
climber, with fleshy, twining stems and
long-stalked leaves, from summer into
autumn. Bright blue fruits follow. ♔

Wisteria floribunda 'Multijuga'
WISTERIA
☼ ✳✳✳   ↕↔10m (30ft)

In early summer, this vigorous, twining
climber produces fragrant lilac, darker-
flushed pea-flowers in handsome, pendent
tassels up to 1.2m (4ft) long. ♔

Evergreen Climbers

IVIES APART, the number of evergreen climbers suitable for gardens in cool, temperate regions is relatively few, when compared with the abundance of deciduous climbers. This makes them all the more valuable, especially in winter, when their persistent foliage provides a welcome touch of colour, and they can be used to hide unsightly structures, as well as providing useful shelter for wildlife. Most evergreen climbers need support; but self-clinging plants are specified here.

Hedera helix 'Buttercup'
GOLDEN IVY
☼ ☼ ✳✳✳✳   ↕ ↔ 6m (20ft)

The three-lobed leaves of this self-clinging climber form a dense cover. They become a rich yellow in summer, though excessive sun can scorch them.

Clematis cirrhosa
CLEMATIS
☼ ✳✳✳   ↕ ↔ 3m (10ft)

Slender, twining stems and small, fern-like leaves form a dense curtain. Loose clusters of nodding, bell-shaped, creamy flowers open from late winter into early spring.

Clematis armandii
CLEMATIS
☼ ✳✳✳   ↕ ↔ 5m (15ft)

The leaflets of this vigorous climber are dark, glossy green. Fragrant white or pink-flushed flowers are borne in bold clusters in early spring. Best in a sheltered position.

Clematis x *cartmanii* 'Avalanche'
CLEMATIS
☼ ☼ ✳✳   ↕ ↔ 3–5m (10–15ft)

This vigorous clematis bears finely cut, ferny leaves and an abundance of large white flowers in spring. It needs a firm support and careful training.

Hedera canariensis 'Gloire de Marengo'
CANARY ISLAND IVY
☼ ☼ ✳✳   ↕ ↔ 5m (15ft)

A long-established and well-proven ivy suitable for a warm, sheltered wall. The large, lobed leaves are cream-variegated, making a striking contrast with green forms.

Hedera helix 'Cavendishii'
ENGLISH IVY
☼ ☼ ✳✳✳   ↕ ↔ 8m (24ft)

Superb and reliable, the self-clinging stems are crowded with neatly lobed leaves margined creamy yellow. Also good in containers or as ground cover. ♈

Hedera helix 'Maple Leaf'
ENGLISH IVY
☼ ☀ ❄❄❄   ↕↔2m (6ft)

An unusual form with deeply lobed and
toothed leaves. It gives a dense cover and
will grow as ground cover, combining well
with small-leaved, variegated ivies.

OTHER EVERGREEN CLIMBERS

Cissus striata
Clematis cirrhosa var. *balearica*
Clematis fasciculiflora
Hedera canariensis 'Marginomaculata'
Hedera colchica 'Sulphur Heart', see p.162

Holboellia latifolia
HOLBOELLIA
☼ ☀ ❄❄❄   ↕↔7m (22ft)

The evergreen, many fingered leaves of
this vigorous twiner create a dense cover
punctuated by bell-shaped, fragrant,
violet-tinged white flowers in spring.

Hydrangea seemannii
CLIMBING HYDRANGEA
☼ ☀ ❄❄   ↕↔10m (30ft)

A vigorous, self-clinging climber making
a dense, dark green cover. Shallowly
domed, lace-cap heads of white then
greenish white flowers appear in summer.

Pileostegia viburnoides
PILEOSTEGIA
☼ ☀ ❄❄   ↕↔6m (20ft)

This slow-growing hydrangea relative is
self-clinging, climbing by aerial roots. Its
branched heads of tiny creamy flowers
open in late summer and early autumn. ♛

Trachelospermum jasminoides
STAR, OR CONFEDERATE, JASMINE
☼ ❄❄   ↕↔6m (20ft)

Best started on supporting wires, this self-
clinging climber has dark green leaves that
may turn red in winter. Clusters of creamy
white summer flowers are fragrant.   ♛

171

Climbers with Fragrant Flowers

Mention fragrant climbers, and most people instantly picture honeysuckle scrambling over a hedge or framing a cottage door. No one would deny its attraction, but there are many other climbers whose flowers produce fragrances which, once experienced, are not forgotten.

Clematis flammula
CLEMATIS
☼ ✻✻✻   ↕ ↔ 5m (15ft)

The herbaceous stems of this vigorous climber are clothed with deeply divided green leaves and, in late summer and early autumn, almond-scented white flowers.

Clematis montana 'Mayleen'
CLEMATIS
☼ ✻✻✻   ↕ ↔ 8–10m (25–30ft)

An extremely vigorous climber suitable for growing into a tree. The bronze-coloured young foliage is an ideal backing for the masses of pink, late spring flowers.

Clematis terniflora
CLEMATIS
☼ ✻✻✻   ↕ ↔ 5m (15ft)

This vigorous climber forms a dense tangle of growth if not pruned. Small, starry white flowers appear on the current year's growth after a hot summer in autumn.

Decumaria sinensis
DECUMARIA
☼ ✻✻   ↕ ↔ 4m (12ft)

This self-clinging evergreen climber has aerial roots, fairly narrow, pointed leaves, and heads of tiny, greenish white, honey-scented flowers, borne freely in spring.

Holboellia latifolia
HOLBOELLIA
☼ ◑ ✻✻✻   ↕ ↔ 7m (22ft)

A vigorous evergreen, twining climber with leaves held limply when young. Flowers appear in spring, sometimes followed by sausage-shaped purple fruits.

OTHER CLIMBERS WITH
FRAGRANT FLOWERS

Clematis montana 'Fragrant Spring'
Clematis montana var. *wilsonii*
Clematis rehderiana, see p.168
Dregea sinensis
Jasminum × *stephanense*
Lonicera caprifolium
Mandevilla laxa
Trachelospermum jasminoides, see p.171

Rosa 'Wedding Day'
CLIMBING ROSE
☀ ✳✳✳   ↕↔8m (25ft)

The yellow buds of this climbing rose,
with glossy green leaves and thorny stems,
open in summer to richly scented, creamy
white flowers. Blooms age to pale pink.

Lonicera periclymenum 'Serotina'
LATE DUTCH HONEYSUCKLE
☀ ☀ ✳✳✳   ↕↔5m (15ft)

Vigorous and twining, with young purple
shoots, this climber produces long-tubed,
fragrant purple flowers, fading to yellow
within, in summer. Bears red berries. 🏆

Wisteria brachybotrys 'Shiro-kapitan'
JAPANESE WISTERIA
☀ ☀ ✳✳✳   ↕↔10m (30ft)

One of the loveliest wisterias, bearing
drooping clusters of large, fragrant white
flowers in late spring and early summer.
Previously known as *W. venusta*.

Jasminum officinale
'Argenteovariegatum'
☀ ✳✳✳   ↕↔5m (15ft)

Strong-growing and semi-evergreen, this
climber has twining stems, much-divided
cream-margined leaves, and richly fragrant,
pink-budded, white summer flowers. 🏆

Lonicera periclymenum 'Sweet Sue'
HONEYSUCKLE
☀ ☀ ✳✳✳   ↕↔2–3m (6–10ft)

An attractive, twining climber suited to a
raised bank. During summer it is covered
with clusters of sweet-scented white
flowers; red berries follow in autumn.

Wisteria sinensis
CHINESE WISTERIA
☀ ✳✳✳   ↕↔20m (70ft)

Pruning is required if this twining climber
is grown against a wall. Its leaves are fresh
green, and the crowded tassels of fragrant
summer flowers, lilac and pale violet. 🏆

Climbing Annuals and Biennials

MOST OF THE CLIMBERS commonly grown from seed, and treated as annuals in cool gardens, are actually perennial in the wild, or when cultivated in warmer climates. When they are planted in containers, many of these can be overwintered under glass, and some may survive for several years outside in a warm, sheltered spot, especially where winters are mild.

Rhodochiton atrosanguineus
PURPLE-BELL VINE
☼ ❄   ↕ ↔ 5m (15ft)

Borne from spring to autumn, the curious, pendulous blooms of this strong-growing climber each have a rose-pink, bell-like calyx and a maroon-black tubular flower. ♈

Cobaea scandens
CUP AND SAUCER VINE
☼ ❄   ↕ ↔ 6m (20ft)

Climbing by tendrils, this vigorous, leafy perennial has curious yellow-green, cup-shaped flowers that turn purple with age. Each rests on a saucer-like green calyx. ♈

Ipomoea 'Heavenly Blue'
MORNING GLORY
☼ ❄   ↕ ↔ 3m (10ft)

Sporting lovely, large sky-blue flowers from summer into autumn, this vigorous annual or perennial has twining stems and long-pointed, heart-shaped leaves.

OTHER CLIMBING ANNUALS

Ipomoea alba
Lablab purpureus
Maurandya barclayana
Phaseolus coccineus
Tropaeolum peregrinum

Eccremocarpus scaber
CHILEAN GLORY FLOWER
☼ ❄   ↕ ↔ 3m (10ft)

This vigorous evergreen, scrambling sub-shrub climbs by means of tendrils. It has ferny leaves and spikes of orange, red, or yellow tubular flowers in summer. ♈

SWEET PEAS

Lathyrus odoratus 'Annabelle'
Lathyrus odoratus 'Anniversary'
Lathyrus odoratus 'Painted Lady'
Lathyrus odoratus 'White Supreme'
Lathyrus odoratus 'World's Children'

Thunbergia alata
BLACK-EYED SUSAN
☼ ❄   ↕ ↔ 3m (10ft)

A succession of striking, dark-eyed, orange-yellow flowers covers this vigorous, twining annual through summer and into autumn. It bears abundant, heart-shaped leaves.

Self-clinging Climbers

FEW SELF-CLINGING CLIMBERS, apart from the ubiquitous ivies, are hardy enough for cool, temperate gardens, especially when compared with the large number that climb by other means. Hardy, self-clinging species, therefore, have a value of their own, not only for clothing walls and fences, but also for growing up the stems or trunks of suitable trees. This selection includes climbers that cling by means of aerial roots and those that have tendrils tipped with sucker pads.

Parthenocissus henryana
PARTHENOCISSUS
☼ ☼ ☼ ✷✷✷　　　$\updownarrow$ ↔ 6m (20ft)

This free-growing ornamental vine clings by adhesive tendrils tips. Leaves, divided into five, silver-veined, velvety green or bronze leaflets, colour richly in autumn. ♉

Hedera helix 'Oro di Bogliasco'
IVY
☼ ☼ ☼ ✷✷✷　　　$\updownarrow$ ↔ 3m (10ft)

Striking and easy to recognize, this ivy has dark, glossy evergreen leaves with a gold central splash. Green-leaved reversions should be removed as soon as they appear.

Hydrangea anomala subsp. *petiolaris*
CLIMBING HYDRANGEA
☼ ☼ ☼ ✷✷✷　　　$\updownarrow$ ↔ 10m (30ft)

The stems of this robust shrub, which will climb by means of aerial roots, have rich brown peeling bark. Its white flowers, in lace-cap flowerheads, open in summer. ♉

OTHER SELF-CLINGING CLIMBERS

Campsis radicans
Decumaria barbara
Decumaria sinensis, see p.172
Euonymus fortunei 'Coloratus'
Ficus pumila
Hedera canariensis 'Gloire de Marengo', see p.170
Hedera colchica, see p.168
Hedera colchica 'Sulphur Heart', see p.162
Hedera helix 'Cavendishii', see p.170
Hedera helix 'Pedata'
Hedera nepalensis
Hydrangea anomala subsp. *anomala*
Hydrangea seemannii, see p.171
Hydrangea serratifolia
Parthenocissus tricuspidata 'Lowii'
Pileostegia viburnoides, see p.171
Schizophragma hydrangeoides
Schizophragma integrifolium

Parthenocissus tricuspidata 'Veitchii'
BOSTON IVY
☼ ☼ ☼ ✷✷✷　　　$\updownarrow$ ↔ 15m (50ft)

Commonly, but incorrectly, referred to as Virginia Creeper, this vigorous vine soon clothes walls with its ivy-like green leaves. These colour brilliantly in autumn.

Trachelospermum asiaticum
☼ ✷✷　　　$\updownarrow$ ↔ 6m (20ft)

Self-clinging in a wind-free situation, the slender stems of this climber twine round any support. Clusters of fragrant, creamy white flowers in summer age to yellow. ♉

SHRUBS

ORNAMENTAL SHRUBS in the garden are the bridge between trees and perennials, forming the middle layer in mixed borders or beds. Their flexibility is legendary. Many shrubs are so distinctive in habit or impressive in flower or leaf that they make excellent single specimens in a lawn or border, where they can freely develop to their fullest potential.

△ *Aucuba japonica* 'Crotonifolia'

△ INSECT PARADISE *The nectar-filled flowers of the Butterfly Bush* (Buddleja davidii) *attract bees and other insects too.*

THE BEAUTY OF SHRUBS

- Flowering and fruiting shrubs attract wildlife, birds, and insects.
- Offer numerous forms and shapes.
- Provide flowers for every season of the year, including winter.
- Evergreens are attractive in winter.
- Ideal specimens for lawns or beds.
- Excellent in mixed plantings with perennials, climbers, and/or conifers.
- Useful for massed spring effect.
- Provide good ground cover.

The range of shrubs stretches from small carpeting plants, right through to the larger stalwarts. Between is a host of shrubs whose habits make a substantial contribution to garden design. Horizontally extending branches such as *Viburnum plicatum* 'Mariesii', arching or weeping growth such as the brooms *(Cytisus)*, and those of upright habit such as *Viburnum sargentii* 'Onondaga' can all play a part in creating pleasing and useful architectural effects.

SOME TOUGH, SOME TENDER

Most shrubs in this section are winter hardy, but some prefer to be planted in warmer sites. In cold areas, grow tender shrubs in pots and bring them under cover for the winter. Some shrubs flourish during summer, but are cut back by winter frost. These plants are known as subshrubs, and any dead growth should be removed when re-growth commences in spring.

STABILITY OR DIVERSITY

Evergreens bring an important sense of stability and continuity to the garden, most notably when deciduous or herbaceous plants are leafless or below ground. Shrubs in this section are deciduous unless described as evergreen. Numerous deciduous shrubs are worth growing for their foliage alone, especially those having bold or otherwise dramatic leaves, perhaps variegated or coloured. Some produce brilliant autumn tints, of which just one can make a real impact in the garden.

△ GROUND COVER *The Partridge-berry* (Gaultheria procumbens) *is an effective and attractive lime-free ground cover.*

◁ SPRING PAGEANT *Rhododendrons and evergreen azaleas grow together in the wild, and combine well in the garden.*

▷ LATE SUMMER MAGIC *This mop-headed form of* Hydrangea macrophylla *provides a reliable show late in the season.*

Large Shrubs for Specimen Planting

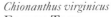

Most Gardens have at least one situation suitable for planting something particularly special – maybe in a lawn, a courtyard, or as a border feature. A tree is frequently chosen for this role, but a refreshing alternative is to consider one of the following ultimately large and impressive shrubs instead. All have character and presence as well as flowers.

Abelia triflora
ABELIA
☼ ❄❄ ↕ 4–5m (13–15ft) ↔ 3m (10ft)

A strong-growing shrub that spreads with age, bearing clusters of small and fragrant, rosy white flowers in early summer. Its corrugated grey stems are of winter interest.

Aesculus parviflora
BOTTLEBRUSH BUCKEYE
☼ ☼ ❄❄❄ ↕ 3m (10ft) ↔ 5m (15ft)

A bold thicket or mound of leaves, bronze-red when young, and turning yellow in autumn, will form in time. Long, tapering flower spikes are produced in summer. ♚

Azara serrata
AZARA
☼ ❄❄ ↕↔ 3–4m (10–13ft)

A dense, rounded bush with bright green, serrated, evergreen foliage, joined in late spring to midsummer by fluffy yellow flowers along the upper sides of the shoots.

Buddleja colvilei 'Kewensis'
BUDDLEJA
☼ ☼ ❄❄❄ ↕↔ 6m (20ft)

A strong-growing shrub often grown against a wall in cold areas. It has bold foliage and clusters of dark pink or red, bell-shaped flowers in early summer.

Chionanthus virginicus
FRINGE TREE
☼ ❄❄❄ ↕ 3m (10ft) ↔ 4m (12ft)

This large, bushy shrub bears bold, deep green leaves that turn yellow in autumn. Sprays of fragrant white flowers drape the branches in summer. Dislikes dry soils.

Clerodendrum trichotomum
GLORY TREE
☼ ❄❄❄ ↕ 3m (10ft) ↔ 4m (12ft)

The leaves of this spreading shrub are aromatic. Pink or greenish buds open into clusters of fragrant white flowers from late summer. Turquoise-blue berries follow.

Clethra barbinervis
JAPANESE CLETHRA
☼ ❄❄❄ ↕ 3m (10ft)

This shrub has large, boldly veined leaves and clusters of white, bell-shaped, fragrant flowers from late summer. Its red and yellow autumn colours are a bonus. ♚

Magnolia liliiflora 'Nigra'
MAGNOLIA
☼ ☼ ❄❄❄❄ PH ↨ 3m (10ft) ↔ 3m (10ft)

One of the most satisfactory and reliable magnolias, this forms a compact mound of glossy leaves. Flowers appear from spring into summer, and in early autumn. ♔

Pieris formosa var. *forrestii* 'Wakehurst'
PIERIS
☼ ❄❄❄ PH ↨ 3m (10ft) ↔ 3m (10ft)

The young, new leaves of this handsome, mounded evergreen emerge brilliant red in spring. These follow drooping sprays of white lily-of-the-valley flowers. ♔

Heptacodium miconioides
SEVEN SON FLOWER OF ZHEJIANG
☼ ☼ ❄❄❄ ↨ 3–5m (10–15ft)

A strong-growing shrub with attractive, peeling bark and bold foliage. Large heads of fragrant white flowers appear from late summer to autumn, followed by red calyces.

OTHER LARGE SHRUBS FOR SPECIMEN PLANTING

Aesculus californica
Camellia x *williamsii* 'Brigadoon'
Elaeagnus 'Quicksilver', see p.294
Genista aetnensis
Hydrangea paniculata 'Pink Diamond'
Hydrangea macrophylla 'Mariesii'
Mahonia x *media* 'Lionel Fortescue'
Malus toringo subsp. *sargentii*
Photinia x *fraseri* 'Red Robin'
Syringa x *josiflexa* 'Bellicent'

Ligustrum sinense
CHINESE PRIVET
☼ ☼ ❄❄❄ ↨ 5m (15ft) ↔ 5m (15ft)

Upright at first, this strong-growing semi-evergreen spreads with age. Its arching, leafy branches terminate in large heads of tiny, sweet-scented white summer flowers.

Vitex agnus-castus var. *latifolia*
CHASTE TREE
☼ ❄❄ ↨ ↔ 3–4m (10–15ft)

This vigorous shrub bears attractive, aromatic leaves and large spikes of fragrant blue flowers in autumn. Prune hard in late winter to encourage strong shoots.

Medium-sized Shrubs

Sᴏᴍᴇ ᴏꜰ ᴛʜᴇ ʟᴏᴠᴇʟɪᴇꜱᴛ and most desirable of all shrubs are found in the medium size range of 1.5–2.5m (5–8ft) in height. Where space is no object, many of these can be planted to glorious effect in groups, or even drifts. In smaller gardens where space is limited, any of the shrubs featured here makes an impressive single specimen in the lawn. They may also be used in combination with smaller shrubs or ground cover to create informal groups in beds or borders.

Hydrangea macrophylla 'Lilacina'
LACE-CAP HYDRANGEA
☼ ✳✳✳ ↕ 1.5m (5ft) ↔ 2m (6ft)

This shrub is particularly lovely when in flower in late summer. Its lace-cap flowerheads are carried above mounds of slender, pointed leaves. Dislikes dry soils. ♔

Clerodendrum bungei
CLERODENDRUM
☼ ✳✳✳ ↕ 2m (6ft) ↔ indefinite

From late summer into autumn, fragrant, deep pink flowerheads nestle among the aromatic, heart-shaped leaves. A suckering shrub, this has erect purple shoots. ♔

Exochorda 'The Bride'
EXOCHORDA
☼ ✳✳✳ ↕ 1.5m (5ft) ↔ 2.5m (8ft)

Wider than it is tall, this mounded shrub is covered by pure white blossoms in spring and early summer. Its arching or weeping branches are densely leafy. ♔

OTHER DECIDUOUS MEDIUM-SIZED SHRUBS
Buddleja lindleyana
Cytisus scoparius 'Cornish Cream'
Deutzia 'Strawberry Fields'
Lavatera x *clementii* 'Barnsley', see p.197
Neillia thibetica, see p.191
Paeonia delavayi var. *ludlowii*, see p.217
Philadelphus 'Belle Etoile'
Spiraea x *vanhouttei*, see p.203
Syringa x *persica*, see p.195
Weigela 'Mont Blanc'

Deutzia x *elegantissima* 'Rosealind'
DEUTZIA
☼ ✳✳✳ ↕ 1.5m (5ft) ↔ 1.5m (5ft)

This is among the best flowering shrubs for smaller gardens. Its mound of arching, leafy branches are wreathed in clusters of pink flower in summer. ♔

Hydrangea aspera
HYDRANGEA
☼ ✳✳✳ ↕ 2.5m (8ft) ↔ 2.5m (8ft)

The large, downy leaves of this impressive shrub are an excellent foil for the lace-cap flowerheads with marginal florets in late summer and autumn. Dislikes dry soils.

Lavatera x *clementii* 'Rosea'
TREE MALLOW
☼ ✳✳✳ ↕ 2m (6ft) ↔ 2m (6ft)

Tree Mallow is one of the most continuous and free-flowering of all garden shrubs, with its pink blooms opening throughout summer. The lobed leaves are downy. ♔

Syringa pubescens subsp. *microphylla*
'Superba'
☼ ❋❋❋ ↕ 2m (6ft) ↔ 2m (6ft)

Slender-stemmed and spreading, with
pointed leaves, this lilac produces fragrant
pink flowerheads, darker in bud, from late
spring right through to early autumn. ♔

Viburnum plicatum 'Pink Beauty'
VIBURNUM
☼ ◐ ❋❋❋ ↕ 2m (6ft) ↔ 1.5m (5ft)

Elegant, spreading, layered branches carry
neat, pleated leaves and, in early summer,
lace-cap flowerheads that are white when
they emerge, and mature to pink. ♔

OTHER EVERGREEN
MEDIUM-SIZED SHRUBS

Berberis linearifolia 'Orange King'
Daphne bholua
Escallonia 'Apple Blossom', see p.206
Jasminum humile 'Revolutum'

Philadelphus coronarius 'Variegatus'
MOCK ORANGE
☼ ❋❋❋ ↕ 2.5m (8ft) ↔ 2.5m (8ft)

Striking, white-margined leaves are the
main attraction of this dense, bushy shrub.
Its richly fragrant flower clusters, in late
spring and early summer, are a bonus. ♔

Paeonia delavayi
TREE PEONY
☼ ◐ ❋❋❋ ↕ 2m (6ft) ↔ 1.5m (5ft)

Cup-shaped, dark crimson flowers, each
with a leafy bract beneath it, are borne on
long stalks in early summer, above bold,
deeply cut, bright green leaves. ♔

Pieris japonica
PIERIS
☼ ◐ ❋❋❋❋ PH ↕ 2m (6ft) ↔ 2m (6ft)

This compact evergreen shrub has narrow,
leathery leaves, which are bronze when
young. Drooping tassels of white flowers
appear in late winter and early spring.

Viburnum sargentii
'Onondaga'
☼ ◐ ❋❋❋ ↕ 2.5m (8ft) ↔ 1.5m (5ft)

The maple-like foliage of this vigorous
shrub are bronze when young, and colour
richly in autumn. Its beautiful spring lace-
cap flowers are white, but pink in bud. ♔

SHRUBS

Small Shrubs

T̄HE VARIETY OF ATTRACTIVE small shrubs available to gardeners is exciting, if potentially bewildering. In large gardens, many of these can be planted in groups of three to five or more, but where space is more limited, any of the following will make an attractive and satisfying feature as a single plant, either alone or used as a centrepiece in a mixed border. They include some of the best small shrubs, and most are sun-loving.

Cytisus x *praecox* 'Warminster'
WARMINSTER BROOM
☼ ❉❉❉   ↕ 1.2m (4ft) ↔ 1.5m (5ft)

This is one of the most reliable of all small flowering shrubs. In late spring, its slender green branches are wreathed with small, scented, creamy yellow pea-flowers. ♛

Caryopteris x *clandonensis* 'Arthur Simmonds'
☼ ❉❉❉   ↕ 75cm (30in) ↔ 75cm (30in)

Numerous clusters of small lavender-blue flowers adorn this bushy, mound-forming shrub in late summer and early autumn. It has slender stems and grey-green leaves.

Cistus x *aguilarii* 'Maculatus'
SUN ROSE
☼ ❉❉   ↕ 1.2m (4ft) ↔ 1.2m (4ft)

Magnificent white flowers, each with dark red blotches and a yellow eye, appear in summer. Wavy-edged leaves, clammy to the touch, cover this bushy evergreen. ♛

OTHER SMALL DECIDUOUS SHRUBS
Acer palmatum 'Garnet', see p.224
Berberis sieboldii
Berberis thunbergii 'Aurea', see p.220
Caryopteris x *clandonensis* 'First Choice'
Cytisus 'Boskoop Ruby'
Daphne x *burkwoodii* 'Somerset'
Daphne mezereum
Hydrangea involucrata 'Hortensis'
Prunus glandulosa 'Alba Plena'
Salix reticulata, see p.211
Spiraea japonica 'Goldflame', see p.221

Ceratostigma willmottianum
HARDY PLUMBAGO
☼ ❉❉   ↕ 1m (3ft) ↔ 1m (3ft)

This loosely domed shrub carries cobalt-blue flowers from late summer through to autumn, when its neat, pointed leaves turn red. Dies down in severe winters. ♛

Cistus x *hybridus*
SUN ROSE
☼ ❉❉❉   ↕ 75cm (30in) ↔ 1.2m (4ft)

A broad mound of wrinkled, wavy-edged leaves is obscured in summer by masses of white, yellow-eyed flowers, pink when in bud. Among the hardiest sun roses.

Deutzia gracilis
DEUTZIA
☼ ❉❉❉   ↕ 1m (3ft) ↔ 1m (3ft)

The bright green leaves of this elegant shrub form a most attractive backdrop for its white flower clusters that last from late spring to early summer.

Fuchsia 'Mrs Popple'
FUCHSIA

☼ ❄❄   ↕ 1.2m (4ft) ↔ 1.2m (4ft)

One of the hardiest fuchsias, this vigorous shrub has glossy foliage, and a continuous supply of flowers that resemble Chinese lanterns from summer into autumn. ▽

Philadelphus 'Manteau d'Hermine'
MOCK ORANGE

☼ ❄❄❄   ↕ 75cm (30in) ↔ 1.5m (5ft)

When the clusters of long-lasting, fragrant, double, creamy white flowers are borne in summer, they cover this broad, low shrub of compact, bushy habit. ▽

Potentilla fruticosa 'Abbotswood'
SHRUBBY POTENTILLA

☼ ❄❄❄   ↕ 75cm (30in) ↔ 1.2m (4ft)

In summer and early autumn, this low-domed bush is plastered with small white flowers, resembling miniature roses. Its deeply divided leaves are grey-green. ▽

Rhododendron yakushimanum
RHODODENDRON

☼ ☼ ❄❄❄❄ PH ↕ 1m (3ft) ↔ 1.5m (5ft)

One of the most popular and reliable small rhododendrons, it forms a tight evergreen dome. Its trusses of pink flowers, in late spring and early summer, turn to white.

Hebe recurva
HEBE

☼ ❄❄   ↕ 60cm (24in) ↔ 1.2m (4ft)

This low, dome-shaped evergreen hebe produces narrow blue-grey leaves, and an abundance of white flowers, carried on small, slender spikes in summer.

OTHER SMALL EVERGREEN SHRUBS

Artemisia arborescens
Aucuba japonica 'Rozannie', see p.214
Choisya 'Aztec Pearl', see p.212
Daphne tangutica Retusa Group
Erica terminalis
Halimium 'Susan'
Hedera helix 'Poetica Arborea'
Phlomis italica, see p.199
Pieris japonica 'Little Heath', see p.213
Prostanthera cuneata, see p.230
Sarcococca confusa

Phygelius x *rectus* 'Moonraker'
PHYGELIUS

☼ ❄❄   ↕ 1.5m (5ft) ↔ 1.5m (5ft)

Long, upright spires of pendulous, tubular, creamy yellow flowers are held by this striking evergreen or semi-evergreen from summer into autumn. Of suckering habit.

Salix hastata 'Wehrhahnii'
WILLOW

☼ ❄❄❄   ↕ 1m (3ft) ↔ 1.5m (5ft)

This handsome, shrubby little willow is well worth growing for the dumpy silvery catkins that emerge in spring, before its leaves unfurl. Dislikes dry soils. ▽

S H R U B S

Shrubs for Ground Cover

THE NUMBER OF SHRUBS that make good ground cover is enormous. Some have far-reaching, trailing, or creeping stems that lie close to the soil surface, while others produce short ascending or arching branches that give a low, mounded effect. Yet more are of a suckering nature. To achieve good results as quickly as possible, ground cover shrubs should be planted in groups of three or five, or even more, depending on the area to be covered. Remove weeds before planting.

Euonymus fortunei 'Emerald 'n' Gold'
EVERGREEN EUONYMUS
☼ ☼ ☀ ❄❄❄ ‡ 60cm (24in) ↔ 1.2m (4ft)

This adaptable, bright-foliaged evergreen forms dense hummocks of green shoots and gold-margined leaves, usually pink-tinted in winter. Climbs if supported. ♔

Cornus canadensis
CREEPING DOGWOOD
☼ ☀ ❄❄❄❄ ‡ 13cm (5in) ↔ 30cm (12in)

In late spring and early summer, the starry, white-bracted flowerheads of this carpeting perennial are borne above ruffs of oval leaves. Red berries follow. ♔

OTHER EVERGREEN SHRUBS FOR GROUND COVER
Arctostaphylos uva-ursi 'Vancouver Jade'
Ceanothus gloriosus
Ceanothus griseus 'Yankee Point'
Ceanothus thyrsiflorus var. *repens*
Cistus salviifolius 'Avalanche'
Cotoneaster cochleatus
Daboecia cantabrica
Gaultheria procumbens
Rubus tricolor
Ulex gallii 'Mizen Head'

Cotoneaster dammeri
COTONEASTER
☼ ☀ ❄❄❄ ‡ 8cm (3in) ↔ 2m (6ft)

This is one of the best evergreen ground-covering shrubs. Its densely leafy, trailing stems are studded with white flowers in summer and red berries in winter. ♔

Euonymus fortunei 'Emerald Gaiety'
EVERGREEN EUONYMUS
☼ ☀ ☀ ❄❄❄ ‡ 1m (3ft) ↔ 1.5m (5ft)

Tough, adaptable, and easy to grow, this shrub forms a dense, low cover of rounded leaves, margined white and marbled grey. Leaves are often pink-tinted in winter. ♔

× *Halimiocistus sahucii*
SUN ROSE
☼ ❄❄❄ ‡ 30cm (12in) ↔ 1.2m (4ft)

Crowded with narrow, dark green leaves, this dense, low, bushy evergreen is covered with small, rose-like, yellow-eyed, white flowers in late spring and early summer. ♔

Hedera helix 'Glacier'
IVY

☼ ☼ ☀ ❆❆❆   ↕ 10cm (4in) ↔ 3m (10ft)

One of the best variegated ivies suitable
for ground cover, this will climb if given
support. The evergreen silver-grey leaves
each have an irregular white margin. ⚱

Hedera helix 'Ivalace'
IVY

☼ ☼ ☀ ❆❆❆   ↕ 10cm (4in) ↔ 1.5m (5ft)

Dense hummocks or patches of glossy
dark green are formed by this good-looking
ground cover. Leaves are shallowly lobed
and crinkled. Will climb with support. ⚱

Hypericum calycinum
ROSE OF SHARON

☼ ☼ ❆❆❆   ↕ 30cm (12in) ↔ 1.5m (5ft)

The creeping roots of this evergreen form
a close green carpet of leafy shoots, topped
by golden yellow flowers, with red-tipped
stamens, from summer into autumn.

Leptospermum rupestre
LEPTOSPERMUM

☼ ❆❆❆   ↕ 8cm (3in) ↔ 2m (6ft)

This evergreen shrub will create a packed
carpet of tiny, deep green leaves, studded
in summer with small white flowers. Its
leaves turn bronze in the winter cold. ⚱

**OTHER DECIDUOUS SHRUBS
FOR GROUND COVER**

Cotoneaster adpressus
Prunus pumila var. *depressa*
Salix nakamurana var. *yezoalpina*
Salix uva-ursi

Viburnum davidii
VIBURNUM

☼ ☼ ❆❆❆   ↕ 1m (3ft) ↔ 1.5m (5ft)

Broad mounds of boldly veined evergreen
leaves need space. The white flowers are
small, and pollinated female plants bear
striking blue berries from autumn. ⚱

Vinca minor
LESSER PERIWINKLE

☼ ☀ ❆❆❆   ↕ 10cm (4in) ↔ 1.5m (5ft)

Long, slender, prostrate stems and paired,
glossy green leaves provide reliable ground
cover. Charming blue, purple, or white
flowers open from spring into summer.

Small Shrub Roses for Limited Space

NUMEROUS SHRUB ROSES are medium to large in size, and require considerable space in which to develop to their full potential. Fortunately, certain roses are of lesser stature and therefore suitable for planting where space is limited. Some of the following may need support to prevent their slender stems from flopping to the ground when in flower.

Rosa gallica var. *officinalis*
APOTHECARY'S ROSE
☼ ❋❋❋   ↕ 1m (3ft) ↔ 1m (3ft)

Lush foliage and an abundant supply of scented, semi-double, deep pink flowers cover this spreading, low-branching species rose in summer. Hips are attractive. ♔

Rosa x *centifolia* 'Cristata'
CRESTED MOSS ROSE
☼ ❋❋❋   ↕ 1.5m (5ft) ↔ 1.2m (4ft)

Distinct green, mossy buds open to reveal richly scented pink blooms on nodding stalks in summer. The rather lax stems of this prickly bush may need support. ♔

Rosa gallica 'Versicolor'
ROSA MUNDI, GALLICA ROSE
☼ ❋❋❋   ↕ 1m (3ft) ↔ 1m (3ft)

This well-known rose began as a mutation of *R. gallica* var. *officinalis*, and differs in its flowers, which are pale pink with crimson stripes. Prune to maintain its size. ♔

Rosa 'Buff Beauty'
HYBRID MUSK ROSE
☼ ❋❋❋   ↕ 1.2m (4ft) ↔ 1.2m (4ft)

A popular and reliable rose with shining green foliage that is coppery brown when young. Deliciously scented, fully double flowers are freely borne in summer. ♔

Rosa x *centifolia* 'Muscosa'
COMMON MOSS ROSE
☼ ❋❋❋   ↕ 1.5m (5ft) ↔ 1.2m (4ft)

Coarse foliage provides a good backdrop for the richly scented pink flowers opening from mossy buds in summer. This loose-stemmed bush may need support.

OTHER SMALL SHRUB ROSES
Rosa carolina
Rosa 'Cécile Brünner'
Rosa Chianti ('Auswine')
Rosa x *damascena* var. *versicolor*
Rosa 'De Rescht'
Rosa x *harrisonii* 'Lutea Maxima'
Rosa 'Madame Knorr'
Rosa 'Marchesa Boccella'
Rosa 'Perle d'Or'
Rosa pimpinellifolia 'Dunwich Rose'
Rosa 'White Pet'

SHRUBS

Low-growing Roses for Ground Cover

I N SUNNY SITUATIONS, low-spreading roses or those with trailing stems provide a useful and charming ground cover. They are particularly suited to steep banks, wall tops, or beneath plantings of other roses, especially those whose stems become unsightly with age. In recent years, a host of new, free-flowering cultivars has become available. Where space permits, you can achieve impressive displays with generous plantings, but in small gardens a single plant can give as much pleasure.

Rosa Grouse ('Korimro')
GROUND COVER ROSE
☼ ✳✳✳　　　‡45cm (18in) ↔ 3m (10ft)

In summer, this free-growing rose, with its long, trailing stems and shining, evergreen foliage, produces a succession of small, fragrant, pale pink　　blooms.　♀

Rosa x *jacksonii*
'Max Graf'
☼ ✳✳✳　　　‡45cm (18in) ↔ 3m (10ft)

Large, single flowers have an apple scent, and are carried in summer. The shining, bright green foliage of this dense rose is carried on long, trailing stems.

Rosa 'Nozomi'
GROUND COVER ROSE
☼ ✳✳✳　　　‡45cm (18in) ↔ 1.2m (4ft)

This charming creeping rose has arching stems clothed with small, neat, dark green leaves, and bears single blush-pink and white flowers in summer.　♀

OTHER GROUND COVER ROSES

Rosa Bonica ('Meidomonac')
Rosa Berkshire ('Korpinka')
Rosa Lancashire ('Korstesgli')
Rosa 'Macrantha'
Rosa Magic Carpet ('Jaclover')
Rosa Oxfordshire ('Korfullwind')
Rosa 'Paulii'
Rosa Pheasant ('Kordapt')
Rosa Rosy Cushion ('Interall'), see p.241
Rosa White Flower Carpet ('Noaschnee')
Rosa Wiltshire ('Kormuse')

Rosa Partridge ('Korweirim')
GROUND COVER ROSE
☼ ✳✳✳　　　‡45cm (18in) ↔ 3m (10ft)

The pure white flowers of this rose, borne in abundance throughout summer, are small and fragrant. It is similar in growth to *R.* Grouse, to which it is related.

MINIATURE ROSES

Rosa Anna Ford ('Harpiccola')
Rosa Baby Love ('Scrivlov')
Rosa Chelsea Pensioner ('Mattche')
Rosa Cider Cup ('Diclulu')
Rosa Gentle Touch ('Dicladida')
Rosa Little Bo-peep ('Poullen')
Rosa Pretty Polly ('Meitonje')
Rosa Robin Redbreast ('Interrob')
Rosa Sweet Magic ('Dicmagic')
Rosa Tear Drop ('Dicomo')
Rosa White Cloud ('Korstacha')

Rosa 'Seagull'
CLIMBING ROSE
☼ ✳✳✳　　　‡60cm (24in) ↔ 4m (12ft)

'Seagull' is a strong-growing climbing rose, good for ground cover where space allows. Large, branched clusters of fragrant, semi-double white flowers open in summer.　♀

S H R U B S

187

Large Shrub Roses for Specimen Planting

M OST SHRUB ROSES in the wild occur as single, scattered specimens, with space to expand and show their flowers to advantage. In gardens where space permits, shrub roses should be grown in the same way, either singly, or in groups as highlights in mixed borders. Grow spreading kinds alone on the lawn, where their display can be admired from all sides.

Rosa 'Madame Isaac Pereire'
BOURBON ROSE
☼ ✸✸✸   ↕ 2.2m (7ft) ↔ 2m (6ft)

This lovely bourbon rose has a vigorous, prickly, arching growth. Richly fragrant flowers, deep rose with magenta shading, appear from summer into autumn. ♈

OTHER SHRUB ROSES WITH FRUITS
Rosa davidii
Rosa fedtschenkoana
Rosa 'Hillieri'
Rosa macrophylla
Rosa macrophylla 'Master Hugh'
Rosa moyesii
Rosa roxburghii
Rosa 'Scabrosa'
Rosa setipoda
Rosa sweginzowii
Rosa wintonensis

Rosa 'Complicata'
GALLICA ROSE
☼ ✸✸✸   ↕ 2.2m (7ft) ↔ 2.5m (8ft)

A bold, reliable gallica rose with vigorous, thorny, arching branches. Lightly scented, single, white-centred pink flowers occur in summer. May also be trained into trees. ♈

Rosa Alexander ('Harlex')
HYBRID TEA ROSE
☼ ✸✸✸   ↕ 1.7m (5½ft) ↔ 75cm (30in)

This strong-growing hybrid tea rose with erect stems makes an excellent informal hedge. Lightly fragrant, double red flowers are carried from summer into autumn. ♈

Rosa Iceberg ('Korbin')
FLORIBUNDA ROSE
☼ ✸✸✸   ↕ 1.5m (5ft) ↔ 1.2m (4ft)

Iceberg is a popular, reliable floribunda rose with strong, upright growth, glossy foliage, and clusters of fully double, lightly scented flowers in summer and autumn. ♈

Rosa 'Marguerite Hilling'
SHRUB ROSE
☼ ✸✸✸   ↕ 2.2m (7ft) ↔ 2.2m (7ft)

This is a vigorous shrub with dense, leafy growth. In summer, and to a lesser degree autumn, it is crowded with large, fragrant, deep pink flowers with pale centres. ♈

Rosa 'Geranium'
SPECIES ROSE
☼ ✻✻✻   ↕ 3m (10ft) ↔ 2.2m (7ft)

This tall, vigorous species rose is upright.
Its branches arch widely and sport small,
saucer-shaped summer flowers that are
followed by flagon-shaped red hips. ▽

Rosa 'Roseraie de l'Haÿ'
RUGOSA ROSE
☼ ✻✻✻   ↕ 2.2m (7ft) ↔ 2m (6ft)

A strong-growing rugosa rose of dense
habit, this has attractive green foliage and
richly scented, velvety, deep crimson
flowers from summer into autumn. ▽

Rosa 'Tour de Malakoff'
PROVENCE ROSE
☼ ✻✻✻   ↕ 2m (6ft) ↔ 1m (3ft)

Provence rose of vigorous, open growth,
and bearing fragrant, loose rosette flowers
in summer. The magenta blooms fade to a
greyish purple. May require support.

Rosa 'Nevada'
SHRUB ROSE
☼ ✻✻✻   ↕ 2.2m (7ft) ↔ 2.2m (7ft)

This vigorous, leafy shrub rose produces
an abundance of scented, creamy white
flowers in summer – fewer in autumn.
The flowers turn pink in hot weather. ▽

Rosa soulieana
SPECIES ROSE
☼ ✻✻✻   ↕ 3m (10ft) ↔ 3m (10ft)

The distinct stems of this rose are prickly,
and its foliage is bluish green. Numerous
scented summer flowers are yellow in bud
and open white. May need support. ▽

OTHER LARGE SHRUB ROSES
FOR SPECIMEN PLANTING

Rosa 'Alba Semiplena'
Rosa 'Blanche Double de Coubert'
Rosa 'Dupontii'
Rosa rubiginosa, see p.239
Rosa 'Fritz Nobis'
Rosa 'Frühlingsgold'
Rosa glauca, see p.223
Rosa 'Madame Hardy'
Rosa 'Nymphenburg'
Rosa 'White Grootendorst'

Rosa
'Pink Grootendorst'
☼ ✻✻✻   ↕ 2m (6ft) ↔ 1.5m (5ft)

A rugosa hybrid of bushy, upright growth,
this has prickly stems and wrinkled leaves.
Dense clusters of rosette flowers occur
from summer, continuing into autumn. ▽

Rosa xanthina 'Canary Bird'
SPECIES ROSE
☼ ✻✻✻   ↕ 2.2m (7ft) ↔ 2.2m (7ft)

The arching branches of this vigorous
species rose carry small, fern-like foliage.
Musk-scented yellow flowers appear in
spring, fewer in autumn. ▽

SHRUBS

Shrubs for Heavy Clay Soils

I F YOU HAVE A CLASSIC clay soil; one that is heavy and sticky when wet, shrinking and cracking when it is dry, then it is a good idea to try to improve it by careful drainage and by adding liberal and frequent amounts of coarse grit, together with rough, especially fibrous, organic matter. Avoid working clay soil when it is wet. Despite the doom and gloom that is commonly associated with heavy clay, however, a large and diverse selection of shrubs can thrive in such soils.

Cytisus 'Killiney Red'
BROOM
☼ ❄❄❄❄ ⁿPH   ↕ 1m (3ft) ↔ 1.2m (4ft)

One of many brooms tolerant of clay soils, 'Killiney Red' is a dwarf, compact variety. Slender green shoots carry many flowers in late spring and early summer.

Berberis darwinii
DARWIN'S BARBERRY
☼ ❄❄❄   ↕ 3m (10ft) ↔ 4m (12ft)

This large, mounded evergreen shrub is densely covered with small, dark green leaves. Clusters of orange-yellow flowers in spring are followed by black berries. ♈

OTHER DECIDUOUS SHRUBS FOR HEAVY CLAY SOILS

Colutea × *media* 'Copper Beauty'
Cotinus coggygria 'Royal Purple',
  see p.224
Cytisus × *praecox* 'Allgold', see p.196
Deutzia × *elegantissima* 'Rosealind',
  see p.180
Kerria japonica 'Pleniflora', see p.167
Magnolia 'Susan'
Prunus glandulosa 'Alba Plena'
Rhododendron occidentale, see p.202
Ribes sanguineum 'White Icicle'
Sambucus nigra 'Guincho Purple',
  see p.225
Spiraea × *vanhouttei*, see p.203
Syringa vulgaris 'Charles Joly'
Viburnum sargentii 'Onondaga'
  see p.181
Weigela coraeensis

Chaenomeles × *superba* 'Nicoline'
ORNAMENTAL QUINCE
☼ ☼ ❄❄❄   ↕ 1m (3ft) ↔ 1.5m (5ft)

The branches of this tough, reliable shrub are studded in spring with a profusion of large scarlet flowers. These are followed by small yellow, apple-like fruits. ♈

Escallonia 'Langleyensis'
ESCALLONIA
☼ ❄❄❄   ↕ 2m (6ft) ↔ 2m (6ft)

Evergreen and wind-tolerant, this tried and tested shrub has arching stems, small, glossy leaves on weeping branches, and tiny bunches of pink summer flowers. ♈

Hydrangea arborescens 'Grandiflora'
HYDRANGEA
☼ ☼ ❄❄❄   ↕ 1.5m (5ft) ↔ 2m (6ft)

Large heads of white flowers appear from summer through to early autumn. Broad, oval leaves clothe this tough and reliable, mounded shrub. Dislikes dry soils. ♈

S H R U B S

Magnolia stellata 'Waterlily'
STAR MAGNOLIA
☼ ❊❊❊　　　↕ 3m (10ft) ↔ 4m (12ft)

Eventually broader than it is high, this charming shrub is slow-growing. Fragrant, multi-petalled blooms cover the branches in spring. Leaves are yellow in autumn. ♈

Neillia thibetica
NEILLIA
☼ ❊❊❊　　　↕ 2.5m (8ft) ↔ 2.5m (8ft)

The flowers of this strong-growing shrub are held in lax, tail-like spikes, on arching branches amid its jagged, pointed leaves, from late spring into early summer. ♈

Philadelphus 'Virginal'
MOCK ORANGE
☼ ❊❊❊　　　↕ 3m (10ft) ↔ 2.5m (8ft)

A strong-growing shrub, this is deservedly one of the most popular, due to its great abundance of large, richly fragrant, double or semi-double white summer flowers.

Potentilla fruticosa 'Elizabeth'
SHRUBBY POTENTILLA
☼ ❊❊❊　　　↕ 75cm (30in) ↔ 1.5m (5ft)

A broad, low mound of densely crowded branches and small, deeply divided leaves, this is covered, from late spring through to autumn, with bright yellow flowers.

Rhododendron 'Mrs G.W. Leak'
RHODODENDRON
☼ ◑ ❊❊❊　　　↕ 4m (12ft) ↔ 4m (12ft)

This large evergreen shrub is particularly striking in late spring, when it is covered with bold trusses of pink, funnel-shaped flowers, splashed brown and crimson.

**OTHER EVERGREEN SHRUBS
FOR HEAVY CLAY SOILS**

Aucuba japonica 'Crotonifolia',
　see p.218
Berberis sargentiana
Choisya ternata, see p.228
Escallonia rubra 'Crimson Spire'
Osmanthus × *burkwoodii*, see p.229
Pyracantha 'Orange Glow', see p.239
Skimmia × *confusa* 'Kew Green',
　see p.205
Viburnum davidii, see p.185

Spiraea japonica 'Anthony Waterer'
SPIRAEA
☼ ❊❊❊　　　↕ 1.2m (4ft) ↔ 1.2m (4ft)

Erect and compact, this is an extremely popular flowering shrub. It produces dark green, jaggedly toothed leaves, and flat crimson-pink flowerheads in summer.

Spiraea nipponica 'Snowmound'
SPIRAEA
☼ ❊❊❊　　　↕ 2m (6ft) ↔ 2m (6ft)

Tufts of white flowers are carried all along the upper sides of densely leafy, arching stems, making this a spectacular shrub at its peak in early summer. ♈

S
H
R
U
B
S

Shrubs for Lime-free Soils

THE SHRUBS PREFERRING, if not demanding, lime-free or acid soils are relatively few in number, but encompass some of the loveliest, most popular shrubs. Rhododendrons, camellias, and heathers are well-known lime-haters, but many other shrubs have similar requirements. Although they thrive in naturally acid soils, many of these plants will grow reasonably well in specially prepared beds, or in containers filled with lime-free compost.

Daboecia cantabrica 'Bicolor'
ST DABEOC'S HEATH
☼ ✸✸✸✸ PH   ↕45cm (18in) ↔60cm (24in)

This low, bushy evergreen shrub is dense and wiry, with nodding white, purple, or purple-striped flowers, held in loose spikes, from late spring into autumn. ♔

Camellia x *williamsii* 'Donation'
CAMELLIA
☼ ✸✸✸✸ PH   ↕3m (10ft) ↔2m (6ft)

One of the best camellias for general cultivation, this free-growing, upright evergreen carries an abundance of large flowers from late winter into spring. ♔

Desfontainea spinosa
DESFONTAINEA
☼ ✸✸✸ PH   ↕2m (6ft) ↔1.5m (5ft)

Tubular red flowers are borne in the leaf axils of this slow-growing evergreen, from midsummer to autumn. The leaves are small, and holly-like. Dislikes dry soils. ♔

Calluna vulgaris 'Annemarie'
HEATHER, LING
☼ ✸✸✸✸ PH   ↕45cm (18in) ↔45cm (18in)

Reliable and free-flowering, this heather forms a compact bush. Long spires of double, light pink flowers rise above dark evergreen foliage in autumn. ♔

Camellia japonica 'Adolphe Audusson'
JAPANESE CAMELLIA
☼ ✸✸✸ PH   ↕3m (10ft) ↔2.5m (8ft)

This reliable camellia is a dense, bushy evergreen with glossy, dark green leaves. Large, deep red, gold-stamened flowers appear from late winter into spring. ♔

Clethra delavayi
CLETHRA
☼ ✸✸✸ PH   ↕4m (12ft) ↔3m (10ft)

Dense, horizontal spikes of fragrant white flowers, pink when in bud, give this shrub a most distinguished appearance when they open in summer. Dislikes dry soil.

Enkianthus cernuus var. *rubens*
ENKIANTHUS
☼ ✸✸✸✸ PH   ↕2.5m (8ft) ↔2m (6ft)

In late spring, bunches of fringed, bell-shaped, deep red flowers hang beneath its neat rosettes of leaves. The leaves colour richly in autumn. Dislikes dry soils. ♔

Erica cinerea 'C.D. Eason'
BELL HEATHER
☼ ❄❄❄❄ PH ↕ 30cm (12in) ↔ 60cm (24in)

From summer to autumn, this dense, low-growing evergreen is covered by crowded spikes of carmine pink, pitcher-shaped flowers. It has needle-like leaves. ♔

Pieris 'Forest Flame'
PIERIS
☼ ❄❄❄❄ PH ↕ 4m (12ft) ↔ 2m (6ft)

The leaves of this erect evergreen emerge crimson, and then pale to pink and cream before turning glossy green. Its sprays of white flowers appear in spring. ♔

Rhododendron 'May Day'
RHODODENDRON
☼ ☼ ❄❄❄❄ PH ↕ 1.5m (5ft) ↔ 1.5m (5ft)

Excellent for all but the very coldest areas, this flat-topped or domed evergreen bears dark green leaves, and is covered in spring with trusses of red trumpet-flowers. ♔

Kalmia latifolia
CALICO BUSH
☼ ☼ ❄❄❄❄ PH ↕ 3m (10ft) ↔ 3m (10ft)

Free-flowering and impressive, this shrub, clad in cheerful glossy evergreen leaves, bears clusters of small pink flowers, darker when in bud, in early summer. ♔

> **OTHER DECIDUOUS SHRUBS FOR LIME-FREE SOIL**
>
> *Clethra alnifolia* 'Humming Bird'
> *Enkianthus campanulatus*
> *Enkianthus perulatus*
> *Fothergilla gardenii*, see p.227
> *Menziesia ciliicalyx*
> *Rhododendron* 'Homebush', see p.213
> *Rhododendron* 'Hotspur'
> *Rhododendron schlippenbachii*
> *Vaccinium corymbosum*, see p.203
> *Zenobia pulverulenta*

> **OTHER EVERGREEN SHRUBS FOR LIME-FREE SOIL**
>
> *Calluna vulgaris* 'Kinlochruel'
> *Camellia* 'Spring Festival'
> *Camellia* × *williamsii* 'Saint Ewe'
> *Crinodendron hookerianum*, see p.200
> *Erica australis* 'Riverslea'
> *Grevillea juniperina* f. *sulphurea*
> *Kalmia latifolia* 'Ostbo Red'
> *Leptospermum scoparium* 'Red Damask'
> *Rhododendron* 'Peter John Mezitt'
> *Rhododendron yakushimanum*, see p.183

Rhododendron 'Hinomayo'
EVERGREEN AZALEA
☼ ☼ ❄❄❄❄ PH ↕ 1.5m (5ft) ↔ 1.5m (5ft)

This dense, twiggy evergreen is crowded with small leaves, and plastered in spring by little funnel-shaped pink flowers. It will not tolerate dry soils. ♔

Rhododendron 'Narcissiflorum'
GHENT AZALEA
☼ ❄❄❄❄ PH ↕ 2m (6ft) ↔ 2m (6ft)

A vigorous shrub that produces masses of pale yellow, darker-flushed flowers with a sweet scent in spring and early summer. Leaves often colour bronze in autumn. ♔

S H R U B S

193

Shrubs for Alkaline Soils

FAR FROM BEING PROBLEMATIC, alkaline soils are suitable for a huge variety of shrubs, many of which actually thrive in the high pH, and the warmer, free-draining conditions that prevail there. A number of these plants are also drought-tolerant, although this does not mean moisture is not essential. Such soils need to be given organic matter as well, in the form of a mulch. Sufficient water and enough organic matter improves the ability of most garden shrubs to grow well, and keeps leaves a healthy green.

Indigofera heterantha
INDIGOFERA
☼ ❄❄❄   ↕ 1.5m (5ft) ↔ 1.7m (5½ft)

This multi-stemmed shrub has arching branches clothed in fern-like leaves. Small, rich mauve-pink pea-flowers are produced all through summer into autumn. ♛

Buddleja davidii 'Dartmoor'
BUTTERFLY BUSH
☼ ❄❄❄   ↕ 2.5m (8ft) ↔ 2.5m (8ft)

In late summer and autumn, distinctive flowerheads, popular with butterflies and bees, cover this vigorous shrub. Its arching branches carry long, pointed leaves. ♛

Kolkwitzia amabilis 'Pink Cloud'
BEAUTY BUSH
☼ ❄❄❄   ↕ 3m (10ft) ↔ 3m (10ft)

A vigorous shrub of mounded habit, this has small, oval leaves, and masses of bell flowers in spring and early summer. Pale, bristly seed clusters follow. ♛

Deutzia longifolia 'Veitchii'
DEUTZIA
☼ ❄❄❄   ↕ 2.2m (7ft) ↔ 1.7m (5½ft)

One of the most reliable of all deutzias, this has arching branches, narrow leaves, and large clusters of star-shaped summer flowers that are rich, lilac-stained pink. ♛

Hibiscus syriacus 'Red Heart'
HIBISCUS
☼ ❄❄❄   ↕ 2.2m (7ft) ↔ 2.2m (7ft)

The branches of this slow-growing shrub spread with age. Boldly lobed leaves unfurl late in the season. Large flowers are carried from late summer into autumn. ♛

OTHER EVERGREEN SHRUBS
FOR ALKALINE SOIL

Berberis darwinii, see p.190
Choisya 'Aztec Pearl', see p.212
Escallonia 'Iveyi'
Itea ilicifolia, see p.165
Jasminum humile, see p.167
Mahonia × media 'Buckland', see p.237
Olearia macrodonta, see p.214
Osmanthus × burkwoodii, see p.229
Sarcococca hookeriana var. *digyna*,
    see p.237

Osmanthus delavayi
OSMANTHUS
☼ ☀ ❋❋❋　　↕ 2.2m (7ft) ↔ 2.2m (7ft)

Mounded, evergreen shrub, with slender, arching stems packed with small, dark green leaves. In spring, clusters of small, sweet-smelling, tubular flowers appear. ♈

Santolina pinnata subsp.
neapolitana 'Sulphurea'
☼ ❋❋❋　　↕ 70cm (28in) ↔ 1m (3ft)

Long-stalked, button-shaped clusters of tiny flowers top narrow, feathery leaves in midsummer. This is a low, dome-shaped evergreen shrub of dense habit.

Weigela 'Looymansii Aurea'
WEIGELA
☀ ❋❋❋　　↕ 1.5m (5ft) ↔ 1.1m (3½ft)

This shrub is principally grown for its golden foliage, which later becomes yellowish green. Funnel-shaped flowers open in late spring and early summer.

Philadelphus 'Boule d'Argent'
MOCK ORANGE
☼ ❋❋❋　　↕ 1.5m (5ft) ↔ 1.5m (5ft)

One of several mock oranges suitable for small gardens, this has a bushy habit and arching branches. Striking clusters of lightly fragrant flowers appear in summer.

Spiraea canescens
SPIRAEA
☼ ❋❋❋　　↕ 2.2m (7ft) ↔ 1.7m (5½ft)

The arching stems of this graceful shrub are covered, for much of their length, with clusters of tiny white summer flowers, set above small grey-green leaves.

Xanthoceras sorbifolium
XANTHOCERAS
☼ ❋❋❋　　↕ 3m (10ft) ↔ 2.2m (7ft)

An uncommon, unusual shrub of upright growth, with much-divided leaves and erect flower spikes from late spring. It may produce large fruits after a hot summer. ♈

Prunus tenella
DWARF RUSSIAN ALMOND
☼ ❋❋❋　　↕ 70cm (28in) ↔ 1.2m (4ft)

This low, bushy shrub has many slender stems, narrow, glossy green leaves, and bright pink flowers crowding the branches in spring. 'Fire Hill' is a superb selection.

Syringa x *persica*
PERSIAN LILAC
☼ ❋❋❋　　↕ 2.2m (7ft) ↔ 2.2m (7ft)

A reliable and justifiably popular lilac, this forms a large bush in time. Slender branches bear spectacular conical heads of fragrant flowers in late spring. ♈

OTHER DECIDUOUS SHRUBS FOR ALKALINE SOILS

Abelia triflora
Buddleja alternifolia 'Argentea'
Chaenomeles speciosa 'Moerloosii',
　see p.166
Cotinus coggygria 'Notcutt's Variety'
Dipelta floribunda
Forsythia x *intermedia* 'Lynwood',
　see p.204
Hydrangea paniculata 'Pink Diamond'
Rubus 'Benenden', see p.235

S H R U B S

Shrubs for Sandy Soils

NUMEROUS SHRUBS favour sandy soils because they are usually warm and free-draining. In times of drought, however, sandy soils can turn to dust, and plants growing in them may require a great deal of irrigation. Such soils can, of course, be improved by changing their structure with the addition of peat substitutes, or liberal and regular amounts of moisture-retentive organic matter, but it is still a good idea to plant shrubs tolerant of drought and rapid drainage.

Cytisus × *praecox* 'Allgold'
BROOM
☼ ✳✳✳   ↕ 2m (6ft) ↔ 2m (6ft)

The slender, arching shoots of this shrub form a compact mound. Its grey-green branchlets are crowded with small, long-lasting yellow pea-flowers in spring. ♗

Callistemon citrinus 'Splendens'
BOTTLEBRUSH
☼ ✳✳✳   ↕ 2m (6ft) ↔ 2m (6ft)

Brilliant red, tightly packed, brush-like spikes adorn this evergreen in summer. It has many arching stems, and branches of narrow, leathery, glossy green leaves. ♗

OTHER SHRUBS FOR SANDY SOIL
Brachyglottis 'Sunshine', see p.204
Cistus populifolius subsp. *major*
Cytisus nigricans
Genista tenera 'Golden Shower'
Halimodendron halodendron
Hippocrepis emerus
Indigofera ambylantha
Lupinus arboreus, see p.207
Potentilla fruticosa 'Elizabeth' see p.191
Robinia hispida 'Macrophylla'
Santolina chamaecyparissus, see p.223

Ballota acetabulosa
BALLOTA
☼ ✳✳✳   ↕ 60cm (24in) ↔ 75cm (30in)

This grey-green, woolly plant has erect stems with rounded leaves, and bears tiny, two-lipped pink flowers in summer. Prune back hard, if damaged in cold winters.

Brachyglottis monroi
SHRUBBY SENECIO
☼ ✳✳✳   ↕ 1m (3ft) ↔ 1.5m (5ft)

Low-domed and compact, this evergreen shrub is crowded with small, wavy-edged, dark green, white-backed leaves. It carries yellow daisy-flowers in summer. ♗

Cistus × *purpureus*
SUN ROSE
☼ ✳✳✳   ↕ 1m (3ft) ↔ 1m (3ft)

In early summer, this rounded, bushy evergreen carries single, rose-like flowers. Narrow grey-green leaves are a perfect foil for its deep purplish pink blooms. ♗

Lotus hirsutus
HAIRY CANARY CLOVER
☼ ✳✳✳   ↕ 60cm (24in) ↔ 60cm (24in)

This small, mounded shrub is entirely covered with silvery grey down. Clusters of little white pea-flowers in summer are followed by attractive reddish pods. ♗

Grevillea 'Canberra Gem'
GREVILLEA
☼ ✳✳✳ PH   ↕ 2m (6ft) ↔ 2m (6ft)

One of the hardiest grevilleas, 'Canberra Gem' forms an evergreen mound of green, needle-like leaves. Loose flower clusters are borne from late winter into spring. ♈

Hibiscus syriacus 'Woodbridge'
HIBISCUS
☼ ✳✳✳   ↕ 2.5m (8ft) ↔ 3m (10ft)

Slow-growing and late-leafing, this shrub is upright at first, spreading as it matures. Beautiful, saucer-shaped pink flowers are produced in late summer and autumn. ♈

Lespedeza thunbergii
LESPEDEZA
☼ ✳✳✳   ↕ 1.5m (5ft) ↔ 2.5m (8ft)

This is one of the best autumn-flowering shrubs. Its long, arching stems become weighed down with large sprays of purple pea-flowers. May require support. ♈

Lavatera × *clementii* 'Barnsley'
TREE MALLOW
☼ ✳✳✳   ↕ 2m (6ft) ↔ 2m (6ft)

All through summer, this semi-evergreen carries a succession of lovely, pale blush-pink, almost white, red-eyed flowers. Its lobed leaves are sage-green and downy.

Potentilla fruticosa 'Manchu'
SHRUBBY POTENTILLA
☼ ✳✳✳   ↕ 45cm (18in) ↔ 60cm (24in)

Twiggy branches, clothed with silver-grey leaves, form a low mound. The bush is densely packed with small, single white flowers from late spring into early autumn.

Romneya coulteri
CALIFORNIA POPPY
☼ ✳✳✳   ↕ 2m (6ft) ↔ 2m (6ft)

This strong-growing plant, with blue-grey stems and deeply cut foliage, produces large, fragrant white poppy-flowers in late summer. These have golden stamens. ♈

S H R U B S

Shrubs for Dry, Sunny Sites

COUNTLESS SHRUBS thrive in situations that are sunny and relatively dry; if your winters are mild, then the choice is both immense and exciting. Where winter temperatures are not as favourable, make use of any shelter available, be it a backing wall or protection provided by more hardy plants nearby. Many of the shrubs thriving in dry, sunny situations hail from regions such as the Mediterranean, where sun, heat, and stony, well-drained soils often go hand in hand.

S H R U B S

Euphorbia characias subsp. *wulfenii*
SHRUBBY EUPHORBIA
☼ ❋❋❋   ↕ 1m (3ft) ↔ 1m (3ft)

This evergreen produces erect, biennial stems, with grey-green leaves in one year, followed the next spring by large heads of little yellow-green, cup-shaped flowers.

Cistus x *cyprius*
SUN ROSE
☼ ❋❋❋   ↕ 2m (6ft) ↔ 1.5m (5ft)

Large white flowers, with yellow stamens and red blotches, open in early summer. Both the shoots and leaves of this vigorous evergreen are sticky to the touch.   ♈

OTHER SHRUBS FOR DRY SUN

Abutilon x *suntense* 'Violetta'
Carpenteria californica, see p.228
Caryopteris incana
Colquhounia coccinea
Fremontodendron 'California Glory', see p.165
Grevillea 'Canberra Gem', see p.197
Grevillea juniperina f. *sulphurea*
Xanthoceras sorbifolium, see p.195
Zauschneria californica subsp. *cana* 'Dublin', see p.37

Erythrina crista-galli
CORAL TREE
☼ ❋   ↕ 2m (6ft) ↔ 2m (6ft)

Eye-catching spikes of waxy coral-red flowers open in late summer. The prickly shoots bear leaves, each composed of three leaflets. Dies right back in cold winters.

Euryops pectinatus
EURYOPS
☼ ❋   ↕ 1m (3ft) ↔ 1m (3ft)

An evergreen mound of deeply cut grey-green leaves is topped with long-stalked, bright yellow, daisy-like flowers, from late winter through to early summer.   ♈

Grindelia chiloensis
GRINDELIA
☼ ❋❋   ↕ 75cm (30in) ↔ 60cm (24in)

Reminiscent of a golden cornflower, this evergreen bears long-stalked, bright yellow daisy-flowers from late winter into early summer. It is sticky to the touch.

Hibiscus syriacus 'Oiseau Blue'
HIBISCUS
☼ ❋❋❋   ↕ 2.5m (8ft) ↔ 2m (6ft)

Erect at first, this slow-growing and late-leafing shrub spreads with age, and carries a wealth of large lilac-blue flowers in late summer and autumn. ♆

Phlomis fruticosa
JERUSALEM SAGE
☼ ❋❋   ↕ 1m (3ft) ↔ 1m (3ft)

This low, mound-forming evergreen shrub is worth growing for its downy, aromatic grey-green leaves alone; golden flowers during summer are an added bonus. ♆

Phlomis italica
PHLOMIS
☼ ❋❋   ↕ 1m (3ft) ↔ 60cm (24in)

The stems and leaves of this low, upright evergreen are covered with grey-green, woolly hairs. Whorls of two-lipped summer flowers are a lovely shade of lilac-pink.

Fabiana imbricata f. *violacea*
FABIANA
☼ ❋❋   ↕ 2.5m (8ft) ↔ 2m (6ft)

The stems of this upright to vase-shaped evergreen are clothed with tiny, heath-like leaves, and crowded in early summer with pale violet flowers. Avoid shallow chalk. ♆

Olearia × *scilloniensis*
'Darrien-Smith'
☼ ❋❋   ↕ 1.5m (5ft) ↔ 1.5m (5ft)

During late spring, the stems and narrow, wavy-edged leaves of this dense evergreen are almost completely obscured by masses of white, daisy-like flowers. ♆

Sophora davidii
SOPHORA
☼ ❋❋❋   ↕ 1.5m (5ft) ↔ 2m (6ft)

Loose-stemmed when young, this shrub becomes dense and spiny with age. Bluish white pea-flowers are produced among its small, deeply divided leaves in summer.

S H R U B S

199

Shrubs Tolerant of Shade

OU MAY BE SURPRISED at the range of shrubs suitable for growing in shade. Many are woodlanders in the wild, preferring to grow where they are not directly exposed to the sun's rays. This does not mean they can survive without any light – all green-leaved plants need light to photosynthesize. Some, however, are more tolerant of lower light levels than others, and it is these that are most successful when planted in the shade of deciduous trees, or that cast by buildings.

S H R U B S

Euonymus fortunei 'Sunshine'
EVERGREEN EUONYMUS
☼ ☀ ❄❄❄   ↕ 60cm (24in) ↔ 1.5m (5ft)

A low-growing, dense evergreen shrub crowded with leathery, gold-margined leaves, looking bright gold from afar. Ideal as ground cover or as a specimen shrub.

Euonymus fortunei   var. *vegetus*
EVERGREEN EUONYMUS
☼ ☀ ❄❄❄   ↕ 30cm (12in) ↔ 2m (6ft)

The presence of both creeping and erect stems enable this tough, bushy evergreen to form extensive patches. Its green leaves and pinkish seed capsules are numerous.

Crinodendron hookerianum
LANTERN TREE
☼ ☀ ❄❄❄^{PH}▽   ↕ 3m (10ft) ↔ 2m (6ft)

From late spring through to early summer, the branches of this handsome evergreen are strung with beautiful red flowers that resemble lanterns. Dislikes dry soils. ⟡

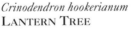

OTHER DECIDUOUS SHRUBS
TOLERANT OF SHADE

Cornus canadensis, see p.184
Euonymus obovatus
Hydrangea macrophylla
  'Générale Vicontessa de Vibraye'
Hypericum androsaemum
Kerria japonica
Rhodotypos scandens, see p.203
Rubus odoratus
Rubus spectabilis 'Olympic Double'
Symphoricarpos x *chenaultii* 'Hancock'

Daphne laureola subsp. *philippi*
SPURGE LAUREL
☼ ☀ ☀ ❄❄❄   ↕ 30cm (12in) ↔ 60cm (2ft)

A dwarf variety of a woodland evergreen, this is just as effective when grown in full sun. Crowded light green flower clusters emerge in late winter and early spring.

Hydrangea macrophylla 'Veitchii'
LACE-CAP HYDRANGEA
☼ ☀ ❄❄   ↕ 1.5m (5ft) ↔ 2.5m (8ft)

Broader than it is high, this bold-foliaged bush carries heads of tiny flowers, each surrounded by a ring of larger florets, from mid- to late summer. Dislikes dry soils. ⟡

200

Hydrangea serrata 'Bluebird'
LACE-CAP HYDRANGEA

☼ ☀ ❄❄   ↕ 1.2m (4ft) ↔ 1.5m (5ft)

The pointed leaves of this dense, bushy shrub often colour well in autumn. Violet-blue, lace-cap flowers in summer have pale marginal florets. Dislikes dry soils. ♔

Pachysandra terminalis
JAPANESE SPURGE

☼ ☀ ❄❄❄   ↕ 10cm (4in) ↔ 20cm (8in)

This evergreen, suckering shrublet likes moist soils, and makes a superb ground cover for shade. Its dark green leaves back little white flower spikes in spring. ♔

Skimmia japonica 'Wakehurst White'
SKIMMIA

☼ ☀ ❄❄❄   ↕ 75cm (30in) ↔ 75cm (30in)

If you plant a male variety of this dense, low evergreen nearby to effect pollination, this spring-flowering skimmia cultivar will produce an abundance of white berries.

Lonicera pileata
SHRUBBY HONEYSUCKLE

☼ ☀ ❄❄❄   ↕ 60cm (24in) ↔ 2m (6ft)

Its low and wide-spreading habit makes this an excellent evergreen ground cover. Tiny, inconspicuous late spring flowers are occasionally followed by violet berries.

Prunus laurocerasus 'Otto Luyken'
CHERRY LAUREL

☼ ☀ ❄❄❄   ↕ 75cm (30in) ↔ 1.2m (4ft)

The branches of this low evergreen shrub are clothed with narrow, glossy, leathery leaves. Erect spikes of white flowers in late spring are followed by black fruits. ♔

OTHER EVERGREEN SHRUBS TOLERANT OF SHADE

Aucuba japonica 'Rozannie', see p.214
Buxus sempervirens 'Latifolia Maculata'
Daphne pontica
x *Fatshedera lizei*, see p.212
Fatsia japonica, see p.216
Osmanthus heterophyllus
Rubus tricolor
Ruscus hypoglossum
Sarcococca confusa
Viburnum davidii, see p.185

Mahonia nervosa
CASCADES MAHONIA

☼ ☀ ❄❄❄❄^PH   ↕ 60cm (24in) ↔ 1m (3ft)

This evergreen, suckering shrub produces short, erect stems with handsome leaves that turn red or purplish in winter. Spikes of yellow flowers appear in early summer.

Vinca major 'Variegata'
VARIEGATED LARGE PERIWINKLE

☼ ☀ ❄❄❄   ↕ 30cm (12in) ↔ 1.5m (5ft)

Striking, variegated leaves are margined creamy white, and form a superb ground cover that is rampant if unchecked. Blue flowers last from spring to autumn. ♔

SHRUBS

Shrubs Tolerant of Damp Sites and Watersides

Pᴇʀᴍᴀɴᴇɴᴛʟʏ ᴍᴏɪꜱᴛ ꜱᴏɪʟꜱ, or sites that occasionally flood, are not ideal planting spots. This makes shrubs tolerant of wet conditions valuable to gardeners faced with damp or boggy areas. Where practical and desirable, you can improve such soils by draining, but if you decide to leave them alone, the following plants will generally thrive.

Aronia arbutifolia
Rᴇᴅ Cʜᴏᴋᴇʙᴇʀʀʏ

☼ ◐ ✻✻✻   ↕ 3m (10ft) ↔ 2m (6ft)

This vigorous shrub forms clumps of erect stems that eventually arch widely. Small white spring flowers are followed by red berries. Its leaves turn red in autumn.

Lindera benzoin
Sᴘɪᴄᴇ Bᴜꜱʜ

☼ ✻✻✻✻ᴾᴴ   ↕ 3m (10ft) ↔ 3m (10ft)

The bright green foliage of this free-growing shrub is aromatic and turns clear yellow in autumn. Clusters of small, greenish yellow flowers appear in spring.

Myrica gale
Sᴡᴇᴇᴛ Gᴀʟᴇ, Bᴏɢ Mʏʀᴛʟᴇ

☼ ✻✻✻✻ᴾᴴ   ↕ 1m (3ft) ↔ 1m (3ft)

Catkins crowd this small, aromatic shrub in spring, before its blue-green leaves unfurl. Fruiting spikes, seen here, follow. Tolerant of extremely boggy conditions.

Physocarpus opulifolius 'Dart's Gold'
Nɪɴᴇ-ʙᴀʀᴋ

☼ ✻✻✻   ↕ 2m (6ft) ↔ 2m (6ft)

Golden yellow leaves, carried from spring and all through summer, eclipse the late spring flowers of this tough and adaptable shrub. The bark on older stems peels. ♛

Clethra alnifolia
Sᴡᴇᴇᴛ Pᴇᴘᴘᴇʀ Bᴜꜱʜ

☼ ◐ ✻✻✻✻ᴾᴴ   ↕ 2m (6ft) ↔ 1.5m (5ft)

Spikes of small, sweetly scented white flowers are produced in late summer. The toothed leaves of this upright, frequently suckering shrub give yellow autumn tints.

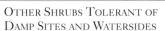

Oᴛʜᴇʀ Sʜʀᴜʙꜱ Tᴏʟᴇʀᴀɴᴛ ᴏꜰ Dᴀᴍᴘ Sɪᴛᴇꜱ ᴀɴᴅ Wᴀᴛᴇʀꜱɪᴅᴇꜱ

Amelanchier canadensis
Aronia melanocarpa
Calycanthus floridus
Cephalanthus occidentalis
Clethra alnifolia 'Ruby Spice'
Cornus alba 'Aurea', see p.220
Cornus alba 'Elegantissima'
Cornus stolonifera 'Flaviramea', see p.238
Hamamelis vernalis
Myrica cerifera
Neillia thibetica, see p.191
Photinia villosa, see p.303
Physocarpus opulifolius 'Diabolo'
Sorbaria tomentosa var. *angustifolia*
Viburnum lantanoides
Viburnum opulus 'Xanthocarpum'
Viburnum sieboldii

Rhododendron occidentale
Aᴢᴀʟᴇᴀ

☼ ✻✻✻✻ᴾᴴ   ↕ 2m (6ft) ↔ 2m (6ft)

Bold clusters of fragrant, funnel-shaped flowers appear in early summer, and vary from white to pink or pale yellow. Glossy green leaves colour richly in autumn. ♛

S H R U B S

Rhodotypos scandens
RHODOTYPOS

☼ ☼ ✲✲✲   ↕ 2m (6ft) ↔ 2m (6ft)

Pure white flowers, borne from late spring through summer, are followed by small, shining black fruits. This vigorous shrub has toothed, conspicuously veined leaves.

SHRUBBY WILLOWS TOLERANT OF DAMP OR WATERSIDES

Salix acutifolia
Salix elaeagnos
Salix exigua, see p.223
Salix gracilistyla 'Melanostachys'
Salix hookeriana
Salix irrorata
Salix koriyanagi
Salix purpurea 'Nana'
Salix triandra
Salix udensis 'Sekka'

Spiraea x *vanhouttei*
BRIDAL WREATH

☼ ✲✲✲   ↕ 1.5m (5ft) ↔ 1.5m (5ft)

The arching stems of this strong-growing shrub form a dense mound. Clusters of white flowers are carried all along the upper sides of its branches in summer.

Salix daphnoides
VIOLET WILLOW

☼ ✲✲✲   ↕ 6m (20ft) ↔ 6m (20ft)

This vigorous shrub is grown for its pale violet winter shoots. Male forms such as 'Aglaia' have attractive catkins in spring, silver at first, then turning to yellow.

Vaccinium corymbosum
SWAMP BLUEBERRY

☼ ☼ ✲✲✲✲[PH]   ↕ 1.5m (5ft) ↔ 1.5m (5ft)

Clusters of small flowers in late spring are white or pale pink in colour, and followed by edible black berries. In autumn, the leaves of this bushy shrub turn crimson.

Viburnum opulus
GUELDER ROSE

☼ ☼ ✲✲✲   ↕ 4m (12ft) ↔ 4m (12ft)

White, lace-cap flowerheads opening in summer give way to clusters of glistening red berries. The leaves of this vigorous shrub are orange, purple, or red in autumn.

Shrubs Tolerant of Air Pollution

OTHER EVERGREEN SHRUBS TOLERANT OF AIR POLLUTION

Aucuba japonica 'Rozannie', see p.214
Camellia japonica 'Adolphe Audusson', see p.192
Cotoneaster sternianus, see p.232
Elaeagnus × *ebbingei* 'Gilt Edge', see p.219
Euonymus fortunei 'Emerald Gaiety', see p.184
Sarcococca hookeriana var. *digyna*, see p.237

THE DAYS WHEN INDUSTRIAL POLLUTION was commonplace in most, if not all, manufacturing towns and cities are thankfully now ended. Other forms of pollution, however, remain a problem, particularly from vehicle exhausts, hence the value of shrubs showing some degree of tolerance. The following are among the most successful.

Brachyglottis 'Sunshine'
SHRUBBY SENECIO
☀ ✳✳✳   ↕ 1m (3ft) ↔ 1.5m (5ft)

Of all flowering shrubs, this is one of the most reliable and popular, with its striking grey-green foliage, silvery when young, and bright yellow summer flowers. ♈

Forsythia × *intermedia* 'Lynwood'
FORSYTHIA, GOLDEN BELL
☀ ☀ ✳✳✳   ↕ 3m (10ft) ↔ 2.5m (8ft)

Spectacular in flower, and thus deservedly popular; the branches of this robust shrub are wreathed with masses of rich yellow bell-shaped, star-like flowers in spring. ♈

Buddleja davidii 'Royal Red'
BUTTERFLY BUSH
☀ ✳✳✳   ↕ 4m (12ft) ↔ 4m (12ft)

The arching branches of this vigorous shrub produce silvery leaves that become green in summer, when its fragrant flower spikes, lasting into autumn, appear. ♈

Hypericum 'Hidcote'
SHRUBBY HYPERICUM
☀ ☀ ✳✳✳   ↕ 1.2m (4ft) ↔ 1.5m (5ft)

From summer into autumn, this vigorous evergreen or semi-evergreen shrub carries a long succession of large, golden yellow flowers amid neat, dark green foliage. ♈

Mahonia aquifolium 'Smaragd'
OREGON GRAPE
☀ ☀ ✳✳✳   ↕ 75cm (30in) ↔ 1.5m (5ft)

This low-growing, spreading evergreen bears glossy green, spine-toothed leaves, bronze when young. Bright yellow flower clusters are produced in spring.

SHRUBS

Skimmia x *confusa* 'Kew Green'
SKIMMIA

☼ ☀ ☀ ✳✳✳ ↕ 75cm (30in) ↔ 1.2m (4ft)

Deep green, aromatic leaves are topped in spring by dense, conical heads of fragrant, creamy white flowers. An excellent and adaptable, mounded evergreen shrub. ♗

Olearia x *haastii*
DAISY BUSH

☼ ✳✳✳ ↕ 2m (6ft) ↔ 2m (6ft)

Crowded heads of fragrant white, daisy-like flowers cover this tough, reliable, compact evergreen in summer. Its small, oval leaves have white-felted undersides.

OTHER DECIDUOUS SHRUBS TOLERANT OF AIR POLLUTION

Amelanchier lamarckii, see p.264
Buddleja 'Pink Delight'
Colutea x *media* 'Copper Beauty'
Lonicera involucrata var. *ledebourii*
Sambucus nigra 'Guincho Purple',
  see p.225
Sorbaria tomentosa var. *angustifolia*
Spartium junceum, see p.207
Viburnum opulus 'Notcutt's Variety'
Weigela coraeensis

Rhododendron 'Susan'
RHODODENDRON

☼ ✳✳✳✳ PH ▼ ↕ 3m (10ft) ↔ 3m (10ft)

Compact, bushy, and quite vigorous, this evergreen bears rounded flower trusses in spring. The flowers, with dark margins and purple spots, fade to near-white. ♗

Syringa vulgaris 'Madame Lemoine'
LILAC

☼ ✳✳✳ ↕ 4m (12ft) ↔ 3m (10ft)

Spectacular, crowded heads of fragrant white flowers are produced in late spring and early summer. Upright when young, it spreads with age. ♗

Philadelphus 'Beauclerk'
MOCK ORANGE

☼ ✳✳✳ ↕ 2.5m (8ft) ↔ 2m (6ft)

This lovely shrub is well worth growing for its abundance of large, broad-petalled white flowers, carried from early to mid-summer. The blooms are fragrant. ♗

Ribes sanguineum 'Pulborough Scarlet'
FLOWERING CURRANT

☼ ✳✳✳ ↕ 2.5m (8m) ↔ 2m (6ft)

Fairly upright when young, and spreading as it matures, this vigorous shrub's aromatic leaves are preceded, or accompanied, by pendent red flower clusters in spring. ♗

Tamarix tetrandra
TAMARISK

☼ ✳✳✳ ↕ 4m (12ft) ↔ 4m (12ft)

The dark shoots of this loose-stemmed shrub all are clothed with scale-like green leaves. In late spring and early summer, crowded plumes of tiny flowers appear. ♗

SHRUBS

Shrubs Tolerant of Coastal Exposure

CONTRARY TO POPULAR BELIEF, a great number of shrubs can be grown in gardens near the sea. Some are more than happy to take the full blast of coastal winds and even salt spray. Others, however, while tolerant to a degree, prefer some shelter to thrive. Those listed here are among the most reliable for seaside gardens.

Escallonia 'Apple Blossom'
ESCALLONIA
☼ ✳✳✳   ↕ 2m (6ft) ↔ 2m (6ft)

Shining, dark green foliage clothes this dense evergreen shrub. Clusters of pink and white flowers, the colour of apple blossom, adorn it in summer. ♈

Atriplex halimus
TREE PURSLANE
☼ ✳✳✳   ↕ 2m (6ft) ↔ 2m (6ft)

This bushy evergreen shrub, with its attractive, silvery grey foliage, is partially deciduous in cold areas. It is excellent as a specimen, or as an informal hedge.

OTHER DECIDUOUS SHRUBS TOLERANT OF COASTAL EXPOSURE

Colutea × *media* 'Copper Beauty'
Cytisus 'Killiney Red', see p.190
Elaeagnus angustifolia
Elaeagnus 'Quicksilver', see p.294
Halimodendron halodendron
Hydrangea macrophylla 'Ayesha'
Lycium barbarum
Rosa rugosa, see p.209
Tamarix ramosissima 'Rubra'
Tamarix tetrandra, see p.205

Bupleurum fruticosum
SHRUBBY HARE'S-EAR
☼ ✳✳   ↕ 2m (6ft) ↔ 2m (6ft)

A bushy evergreen shrub, this is mainly grown for its shining, dark bluish green leaves, though it does carry tiny yellowish flowerheads from summer into autumn.

Buddleja globosa
ORANGE BALL TREE
☼ ✳✳✳   ↕ 3m (10ft) ↔ 3m (10ft)

When in flower in summer, the tiny, tight, globular orange-yellow heads make this shrub stand out. Robust, with bold leaves, it is semi-evergreen in mild areas. ♈

Colutea arborescens
BLADDER SENNA
☼ ✳✳✳   ↕ 2.5m (8ft) ↔ 2.5m (8ft)

A vigorous shrub of open habit, this has small, much-divided leaves. The clusters of yellow pea-flowers in summer are replaced by inflated seed capsules.

Fuchsia magellanica
FUCHSIA, LADY'S EARDROPS
☼ ✳✳✳   ↕ 2m (6ft) ↔ 2m (6ft)

Dense, leafy mounds make this ideal as a specimen plant or an informal hedge. Its lantern-like flowers hang freely from the shoots from midsummer into autumn.

Hebe x *franciscana* 'Blue Gem'
HEBE

☼ ❋❋　　　↕ 60cm (24in) ↔ 1.2m (4ft)

This evergreen shrub is a familiar sight on promenades in coastal towns. Short violet flower spikes are carried from summer through to early winter.

Hydrangea macrophylla
'Lanarth White'

☼ ☼ ❋❋❋　　↕ 1.5m (5ft) ↔ 2m (6ft)

In summer, long-lasting, domed heads of dark blue, fertile flowers and starry white, sterile florets cover this reliable, compact, mounded shrub. Light green leaves. ♔

Olearia nummulariifolia
DAISY BUSH

☼ ❋❋❋　　　↕ 2m (6ft) ↔ 2m (6ft)

Stiff shoots crowded with tiny, leathery evergreen leaves characterize this rounded shrub. Small, fragrant flowers open near the ends of the branches in summer.

Spartium junceum
SPANISH BROOM

☼ ❋❋❋　　↕ 2.5m (8ft) ↔ 2.5m (8ft)

Spanish Broom is a vigorous shrub with smooth, dark green, almost leafless shoots, and sprays of fragrant yellow pea-flowers, lasting from early summer into autumn. ♔

OTHER EVERGREEN SHRUBS
TOLERANT OF COASTAL EXPOSURE

Brachyglottis 'Sunshine', see p.204
Elaeagnus macrophylla
Escallonia 'Iveyi'
Olearia macrodonta 'Major'

Lupinus arboreus
TREE LUPIN

☼ ❋❋❋　　　↕ 1m (3ft) ↔ 1m (3ft)

This vigorous, mounded semi-evergreen, with the fingered leaves typical of lupins, bears numerous tapered spikes of fragrant yellow flowers in early summer.

Tamarix ramosissima
TAMARISK

☼ ❋❋❋　　　↕ 4m (12ft) ↔ 4m (12ft)

Openly branched and vigorous, this shrub has feathery blue-green foliage on long branches, and plumes of tiny pink flowers from late summer into early autumn.

S H R U B S

Shrubs for Screening or Hedges

S HRUBS SUITABLE FOR HEDGING can be pruned or clipped annually for a formal effect, or allowed to develop a more natural appearance. Those of stronger growth and ultimately large habit are useful for screening, to hide intrusive views, filter noise, or lessen the effect of wind. Sizes given refer to the average ultimate size of a single plant without pruning.

OTHER SHRUBS FOR
SMALL HEDGES

Berberis thunbergii 'Red Pillar'
Buxus sempervirens 'Suffruticosa',
  see p.240
Hebe × *franciscana* 'Blue Gem',
  see p.113
Ilex cornuta 'Burfordii'
Ilex crenata 'Convexa'
Lavandula angustifolia 'Hidcote',
  see p.204
Myrtus communis subsp. *tarentina*

Berberis × *stenophylla*
BERBERIS
☼ ✻✻✻   ↕ 2.5m (8ft) ↔ 2.5m (8ft)

Popular as an informal hedge, this tough, adaptable evergreen has slender, arching stems, narrow, dark green leaves, and tiny, golden yellow flowers in spring. ♈

Cotoneaster lacteus
COTONEASTER
☼ ✻✻✻   ↕ 4m (12ft) ↔ 3m (10ft)

One of the best evergreens for a formal hedge or an informal screen, this bears veined leaves, white summer flowers, and red berries from autumn into winter. ♈

OTHER EVERGREEN SHRUBS
FOR SCREENING OR HEDGES

Berberis darwinii, see p.190
Elaeagnus macrophylla
Escallonia rubra 'Crimson Spire'
Escallonia rubra var. *macrantha*
Euonymus japonicus
Ilex aquifolium
Olearia macrodonta, see p.214
Pittosporum colensoi
Pittosporum crassifolium
Viburnum tinus

Buxus sempervirens 'Handsworthensis'
HANDSWORTH BOX
☼ ☼ ✻✻✻   ↕ 3m (10ft) ↔ 3m (10ft)

This evergreen is upright, densely leafy, and strong-growing, making it reliable as a formal hedge or screen. Its leathery deep green leaves are rounded or oblong.

Cotoneaster simonsii
COTONEASTER
☼ ✻✻✻   ↕ 2.5m (8ft) ↔ 2m (6ft)

Shiny deciduous or semi-evergreen leaves cover this vigorous shrub, ideal as a formal hedge. White flowers open in summer, and red berries ripen from autumn. ♈

Elaeagnus x *ebbingei*
ELAEAGNUS
☼ ❄❄❄　　　↕4m (12ft) ↔ 4m (12ft)

Small, fragrant, silvery white flowers crowd the branches in autumn, among shining green leaves. This vigorous evergreen is suitable for formal and informal screens.

Griselinia littoralis
BROADLEAF
☼ ❄❄　　　↕6m (20ft) ↔ 5m (15ft)

This vigorous evergreen shrub, with bright green leaves, is excellent grown alone, or mixed, as it is here, with *Prunus cerasifera* 'Nigra'. Well-suited to seaside gardens. ♈

Prunus laurocerasus 'Rotundifolia'
CHERRY LAUREL
☼ ◐ ● ❄❄❄　↕3m (10ft) ↔ 2m (6ft)

Cherry Laurel is the most commonly used laurel for formal hedging, with its striking, glossy green evergreen leaves, and upright growth. Can also be grown informally.

Ilex aquifolium 'Argentea Marginata'
SILVER-MARGINED HOLLY
☼ ❄❄❄　　　↕8m (25ft) ↔ 4m (12ft)

One of the best formal hedges or screens, this shrub or tree has cream-margined, prickly toothed, evergreen leaves, and red fruits when pollinated by a male holly. ♈

Prunus lusitanica
PORTUGAL LAUREL
☼ ◐ ❄❄❄　　↕6m (20ft) ↔ 6m (20ft)

Particularly impressive in spring, when it produces white flower tassels, this bushy evergreen shrub carries shining, slender, pointed green leaves on red stalks. ♈

Fuchsia 'Riccartonii'
FUCHSIA, LADY'S EARDROPS
☼ ❄❄　　　↕2m (6ft) ↔ 2m (6ft)

Superb as an informal hedge, particularly in coastal areas, this vigorous shrub soon forms a dense bush, and is strung with lantern-like flowers from late summer. ♈

OTHER DECIDUOUS SHRUBS FOR SCREENING OR HEDGES

Berberis thunbergii f. *atropurpurea*
Carpinus betulus
Chaenomeles speciosa
Crataegus monogyna
Fagus sylvatica, see p.281
Hydrangea macrophylla 'Joseph Banks'
Prunus spinosa
Rhamnus frangula 'Aspleniifolia'
Symphoricarpos x *doorenbosii* 'White Hedge'

Rosa rugosa
RAMANAS ROSE
☼ ❄❄❄　　　↕1.5m (5ft) ↔ 1.5m (5ft)

This species rose is popular as an informal hedge, with its large, wrinkled leaves and purplish red flowers opening from summer into autumn, followed by tomato-red hips.

209

Shrubs for Rock Gardens, Raised Beds, and Screes

NUMEROUS SHRUBS NEAT IN HABIT, and attractive in flower, foliage, and fruit are prevented by their small size from being used in a mixed border, unless it is well away from the domination of larger, stronger-growing neighbours. Such shrubs are ideal for planting in rock gardens or raised beds where their special, smaller charms can better be appreciated.

Genista lydia
GENISTA
☼ ❋❋❋ ↕ 55cm (22in) ↔ 75cm (30in)

This shrub is a superb sight in late spring and early summer, when it is covered with clusters of tiny pea-flowers. Ideal for a dry wall top, where its stems can tumble. ♈

OTHER ROCK GARDEN SHRUBS

Anthyllis hermanniae 'Minor'
Berberis x *stenophylla*
　'Corallina Compacta'
Convolvulus cneorum, see p.222
Crassula sarcocaulis
Daphne sericea Collina Group
Hypericum olympicum 'Citrinum'
Ozothamnus selago
Penstemon pinifolius
Sorbus poteriifolia
Teucrium polium

Acer palmatum 'Corallinum'
JAPANESE MAPLE
☼ ☼ ❋❋❋ ↕ 75cm (30in) ↔ 45cm (18in)

A striking, slow-growing, compact shrub, capable of twice the above size in moist, rich, well-drained soils. Grown mainly for its brilliant coral-pink growths in spring.

Daphne tangutica Retusa Group
DAPHNE
☼ ☼ ❋❋❋ ↕ 70cm (28in) ↔ 70cm (28in)

A domed shrub with leathery evergreen leaves, this bears fragrant flowers, purple when in bud, in clusters from late spring, followed by bright red berries.

Berberis empetrifolia
BERBERIS
☼ ❋❋❋❋PH ↕ 30cm (12in) ↔ 45cm (18in)

The stems of this dwarf evergreen are wiry and prickly, and its branches clothed with small, narrow, spine-tipped leaves. Tiny golden flowers appear in late spring.

Euryops acraeus
EURYOPS
☼ ❋❋❋ ↕ 30cm (12in) ↔ 30cm (12in)

Distinctive shrub, forming a small mound of narrow silvery leaves, above which late spring flowers rise on thin, downy stalks. Thrives in sun and well-drained soils. ♈

Hebe cupressoides 'Boughton Dome'
HEBE
☼ ❋❋ ↕ 30cm (12in) ↔ 45cm (18in)

This attractive evergreen mound of tiny, dark grey-green leaves resembles a dwarf juniper and produces clusters of white summer flowers. Needs good drainage.

Helianthemum 'Fire Dragon'
ROCK ROSE
☼ ❄❄❄   ↕ 28cm (11in) ↔ 55cm (22in)

This evergreen carpet-forming shrub has narrow grey-green leaves and is plastered with brilliant orange-scarlet flowers from late spring, continuing into summer. ♈

Penstemon serrulatus
PENSTEMON
☼ ❄❄❄   ↕ 60cm (24in) ↔ 30cm (12in)

A loose semi-evergreen shrub, this forms clumps of dark green foliage, and erect stems that bear branched heads of tubular blue to purple flowers in summer.

Punica granatum var. *nana*
DWARF POMEGRANATE
☼ ❄❄❄   ↕ 60cm (24in) ↔ 60cm (24in)

The glossy leaves of this charming little pomegranate turn gold in autumn. Funnel-shaped flowers appear in early autumn. Appreciates warmth and good drainage.

Linum arboreum
TREE FLAX
☼ ❄❄❄   ↕ 28cm (11in) ↔ 30cm (12in)

Clusters of bright yellow flowers appear throughout summer, whenever the sun shines. This low, dome-shaped evergreen needs warmth and good drainage. ♈

Parahebe catarractae
PARAHEBE
☼ ❄❄   ↕ 30cm (12in) ↔ 30cm (12in)

This choice, reliable plant forms loose mounds of evergreen leaves and, in late summer and early autumn, sprays of small flowers with crimson and white centres. ♈

OTHER CARPETING SHRUBS

Chamaecytisus purpureus 'Atropurpureus'
Cistus salviifolius 'Avalanche'
Genista sagittalis
Helianthemum apenninum
Hypericum empetrifolium subsp. *oliganthum*

Salix reticulata
RETICULATE WILLOW
☼ ❄❄❄   ↕ 4cm (1½in) ↔ 30cm (12in)

Carpets of prostrate stems are clothed in oval leaves that are pale beneath and net-veined above. Male plants have pretty spring catkins. Best in moist soils. ♈

Shrubs for Containers

JUST ABOUT ANY SHRUB can be planted in a container, although some are more suitable than others. Generally, large and vigorous shrubs are best avoided unless you prune them regularly. Pots and tubs are particularly useful on patios, terraces, and in courtyards; or for growing tender shrubs, to move to shelter in cold weather. For those who garden on a particular soil type and who wish to grow a plant unsuited to it, containers provide a practical solution to this problem.

Felicia amelloides 'Santa Anita'
FELICIA
☼ ❄   ↕ 30cm (12in) ↔ 30cm (12in)

Long-stalked, yellow-eyed, blue daisy-like flowers rise above a bushy mound of oval evergreen leaves, from late spring through to autumn. ⊻

OTHER TENDER SHRUBS FOR CONTAINERS

Abutilon 'Canary Bird'
Brugmansia x *candida* 'Knightii'
Cestrum nocturnum
Nerium oleander

Choisya 'Aztec Pearl'
CHOISYA
☼ ☼ ❄❄❄   ↕ 1.2m (4ft) ↔ 1.2m (4ft)

The fingered leaves of this free-growing evergreen are aromatic. Its fragrant white flower clusters, pink in bud, occur in late spring, and again in late summer. ⊻

Aloysia triphylla
LEMON VERBENA
☼ ❄❄   ↕ 2m (6ft) ↔ 2m (6ft)

Mainly grown for its deliciously lemon-scented leaves, this slender-stemmed bush produces flimsy flower spikes in summer. Prune in late winter to control size. ⊻

Cestrum elegans
CESTRUM
☼ ❄   ↕ 3m (10ft) ↔ 2m (6ft)

The arching stems and leafy branches of this vigorous evergreen shrub bow beneath its freely produced clusters of tubular red flowers from spring through summer. ⊻

x *Fatshedera lizei*
FATSHEDERA
☼ ☼ ❄❄   ↕ 2m (6ft) ↔ 2m (6ft)

This handsome evergreen shrub forms a loose mound of boldly lobed, shining, dark green leaves. Loose heads of small cream flowers are carried in autumn. ⊻

Fuchsia 'Celia Smedley'
FUCHSIA
☼ ❄❄   ↕ 1.5m (5ft) ↔ 1m (3ft)

Vigorous and upright, this is one of the more hardy fuchsias. Pendulous, pinkish white and red flowers, with greenish white tubes, open throughout summer. ⊻

Fuchsia 'Thalia'
FUCHSIA

☼ ❄   ↕ 1m (3ft) ↔ 1m (3ft)

Deservedly popular, this erect shrub bears
drooping clusters of long, slender flowers,
carried in summer above dark reddish
green, velvety leaves. ♔

Lantana camara
LANTANA

☼ ❄   ↕ 1.5m (5ft) ↔ 1.5m (5ft)

This prickly-stemmed, summer-flowering
evergreen is rampant in hot climates, but
easily controlled by tip-pruning. Several
colours, changing with age, are available.

Mimulus aurantiacus
SHRUBBY MIMULUS

☼ ❄   ↕ 60cm (24in) ↔ 1m (3ft)

A succession of two-lipped orange-yellow
flowers are borne from late spring through
to autumn. The narrow evergreen leaves
of this low bush are sticky to the touch. ♔

**OTHER HARDY SHRUBS
FOR CONTAINERS**

Camellia japonica 'Adolphe Audusson',
  see p.192
Camellia 'Spring Festival'
Camellia × *williamsii* 'Debbie'
Hydrangea macrophylla 'Pia'
Mahonia aquifolium 'Apollo'
Prunus laurocerasus 'Otto Luyken',
  see p.201
Rhododendron 'Hydon Dawn'
Rhododendron 'Vuyk's Scarlet'
Skimmia × *confusa* 'Kew Green',
  see p.205

Pieris japonica 'Little Heath'
PIERIS

☼ ☼ ❄❄❄❄   ↕ 1.2m (4ft) ↔ 1m (3ft)

A choice, compact evergreen, this pieris is
grown mainly for its small, slender, white-
margined leaves, which are red when they
emerge in spring. Slow-growing. ♔

Prostanthera rotundifolia
ROUND-LEAVED MINT BUSH

☼ ❄   ↕ 1.5m (5ft) ↔ 1.5m (5ft)

When they are bruised, the tiny leaves of
this dense, rounded evergreen are sweetly
aromatic. Masses of bell-shaped flowers
open from spring into early summer. ♔

Rhododendron 'Homebush'
KNAPHILL AZALEA

☼ ☼ ❄❄❄   ↕ 2m (6ft) ↔ 1.5m (5ft)

This charming, relatively compact shrub
is popular on account of its tight, rounded
heads of trumpet-shaped flowers that are
produced in late spring. ♔

SHRUBS

Evergreen Shrubs

WHERE WINTER TEMPERATURES are not low enough to severely inhibit their growth, shrubs having evergreen foliage provide some of the most worthwhile ornamental subjects for the garden. They come in an impressive range of shapes, sizes, textures, and colours, adding variety as well as permanence to the mixed bed or border. Most have flowers and perhaps fruit as a bonus. Some evergreen shrubs are so distinguished that they are ideal as courtyard or lawn specimens, while others with a low spreading habit make effective ground cover in sun or shade. Less hardy evergreens are usually more successful when grown in the shelter of other shrubs or a wall.

Elaeagnus pungens 'Maculata'
ELAEAGNUS
☼ ❄❄❄   ↕ 2.5m (8ft) ↔ 3m (10ft)

Robust and dense with brown, scaly branchlets, this shrub has gold-splashed green leaves. Clusters of tiny, scented, creamy white flowers occur in autumn.

Aucuba japonica   'Rozannie'
JAPANESE LAUREL
☼ ☀ ❄❄❄   ↕ 75cm (30in) ↔ 75cm (30in)

The tiny female flowers of this compact dwarf shrub appear in spring, and produce red fruits when pollinated. This cultivar is excellent in a bed or in a container. ♔

Olearia macrodonta
NEW ZEALAND HOLLY
☼ ☀ ❄❄   ↕ 3.5m (11ft) ↔ 3.5m (11ft)

This sturdy shrub has attractive, pale brown, ultimately shaggy, bark and holly-like leaves. Fragrant, daisy-like white flowerheads appear in early summer. ♔

Buxus sempervirens 'Vardar Valley'
BOX
☼ ☀ ❄❄❄   ↕ 75cm (30in) ↔ 1.2m (4ft)

This valuable cultivar of the Common Box has a low, wide-spreading habit. With its glossy, densely packed leathery leaves, it is superb for ground cover in most soils.

Daphne odora 'Aureomarginata'
WINTER DAPHNE
☼ ❄❄   ↕ 1.1m (3½ft) ↔ 1.2m (4ft)

For a warm, sheltered corner, this is a most reliable evergreen. Sweetly scented flowers are borne from winter into spring, and its leaves have narrow yellow margins. ♔

OTHER EVERGREEN SHRUBS

Berberis 'Goldilocks', see p.239
Camellia japonica 'Hagoromo'
Choisya ternata, see p.228
Cleyera japonica 'Fortunei'
Danae racemosa
Elaeagnus macrophylla
Fatsia japonica, see p.216
Mahonia × media 'Buckland', see p.237
Rhododendron bureavii
Skimmia × confusa 'Kew Green',
  see p.205

SHRUBS

Ozothamnus rosmarinifolius
OZOTHAMNUS
☼ ❄❄ ↕ 2m (6ft) ↔ 1.5m (5ft)

The erect stems of this vigorous shrub are crowded with thread-like leaves. Its tiny, scented flowers occur in early summer. Needs a warm, well-drained site.

Prunus lusitanica subsp. *azorica*
PORTUGAL LAUREL
☼ ☼ ❄❄❄ ↕ 6m (20ft) ↔ 6m (20ft)

This vigorous form of the Portugal Laurel is densely branched with light green leaves, red at first. Shining, dark purple fruits follow fragrant summer flowers. ♔

Pittosporum tenuifolium
'Irene Paterson'
☼ ❄❄ ↕ 2.5m (8ft) ↔ 1.1m (3½ft)

A broadly columnar shrub, this has thin black stems and small, wavy, waxy leaves, marbled white when mature, pink-tinted in winter. Excellent for containers. ♔

EVERGREEN GROUND COVER SHRUBS

Ardisia japonica
Arctostaphylos uva-ursi 'Vancouver Jade'
Ceanothus gloriosus
Ceanothus thyrsiflorus var. *repens*
Gaultheria shallon
Hypericum calycinum, see p.185
Mahonia nervosa, see p.201
Rubus tricolor
Sarcococca hookeriana var. *humilis*
Viburnum davidii, see p.185

Vaccinium glaucoalbum
VACCINIUM
☼ ❄❄❄ ᴾᴴ ↕ 60cm (24in) ↔ 75cm (30in)

Handsome and compact, this low-growing shrub has leathery green leaves. Drooping clusters of pink-tinted white spring flowers are followed by blue-black berries. ♔

Prunus laurocerasus 'Zabeliana'
CHERRY LAUREL
☼ ☼ ❄❄❄ ↕ 80cm (32in) ↔ 2.2m (7ft)

A tough, wide-spreading form of the Cherry Laurel, with narrow, glossy leaves. Flower spikes in late spring are followed by red, ripening to shiny black, fruits.

Rhododendron 'Dora Amateis'
RHODODENDRON
☼ ☼ ❄❄❄ ᴾᴴ ↕ 60cm (2ft) ↔ 60cm (2ft)

This free-flowering dwarf rhododendron of compact habit has glossy foliage, and terminal trusses of funnel-shaped, pink-tinged white flowers in late spring. ♔

Viburnum 'Pragense'
VIBURNUM
☼ ❄❄❄ ↕ 2.5m (8ft) ↔ 2.5m (8ft)

The narrow green leaves of this vigorous shrub are boldly veined on top. Creamy white flowers, pink-tinged in bud, are produced in domed heads in spring. ♔

S H R U B S

Shrubs with Bold Leaves

EXPERIENCED GARDENERS sensibly choose plants as much for their foliage effect as for their attractive flowers. This is particularly important with large plants such as shrubs that occupy a greater area than the average perennial. Where a shrub has both flowers and leaves worthy of attention, then give serious consideration to its inclusion; these dual-purpose plants certainly earn their place in the garden. The following is but a small selection; there are many more.

Hydrangea aspera 'Macrophylla'
HYDRANGEA
☀ ❄❄❄ ↕ ↔ 2.5m (8ft)

The large, rugged leaves of this bold shrub are roughly hairy. From late summer, the branches are capped with broad, domed, blue and white, lace-cap flowerheads.

Aralia elata 'Aureovariegata'
ANGELICA TREE
☀ ❄❄❄ ↕ ↔ 5m (15ft)

This broad bush has stout branches with large, handsome yellow-margined leaves. Large white flowerheads appear in autumn. Remove green suckers if they appear.

Decaisnea fargesii
DECAISNEA
☀ ☀ ❄❄❄ ↕ ↔ 3–6m (10–20ft)

A lanky stemmed shrub that suckers to form colonies. The large, ash-like leaves turn yellow in autumn. Plant in groups to encourage blue autumn seed pods to form.

Hydrangea quercifolia
OAK-LEAVED HYDRANGEA
☀ ❄❄❄ ↕ 1.5m (5ft) ↔ 2.5m (8ft)

Boldly lobed leaves, that colour richly in autumn, cover this bushy shrub and form a broad mound. Dense white flowerheads occur from summer into autumn. ♛

Eriobotrya japonica
LOQUAT
☀ ❄❄ ↕ 4m (12ft) ↔ 4m (12ft)

Leathery, prominently veined, dark green leaves distinguish this evergreen shrub or small tree. Fragrant white autumn flowers are followed by orange-yellow fruits. ♛

Fatsia japonica
FATSIA
☀ ☀ ❄❄❄ ↕ 3m (10ft) ↔ 3m (10ft)

This domed evergreen bears handsome, long-stalked, deeply lobed, shining green leaves. Branched clusters of white flowers in autumn precede black berries. ♛

OTHER SHRUBS WITH BOLD LEAVES

Hydrangea sargentiana
Magnolia delavayi
Mahonia lomariifolia
Prunus laurocerasus 'Latifolia'
Sambucus canadensis 'Maxima'

Nandina domestica
SACRED BAMBOO
☼ ☼ ❄❄   ↕ ↔ 2m (6ft)

A clump-forming, erect evergreen with
ruffs of large, much-divided leaves, purplish
when young. White flowers appear in
midsummer, followed by red berries.

Paeonia delavayi var. *ludlowii*
TREE PEONY
☼ ☼ ❄❄❄   ↕ 2.5m (8ft) ↔ 2.5m (8ft)

Loose-stemmed, with boldly cut, bright
green leaves, this shrub has yellow flowers
in late spring and early summer. *P. delavayi*,
with deep red flowers, is similar in leaf. ♀

Rhus glabra
SMOOTH SUMACH
☼ ❄❄❄   ↕ 2.5m (8ft) ↔ 2.5m (8ft)

Smooth shoots support regularly divided,
deep blue-green leaves that colour richly
in autumn. Summer flowers are followed
by red-brown fruits on female plants. ♀

Salix fargesii
FARGE'S WILLOW
☼ ☼ ❄❄❄   ↕ ↔ 3m (10ft)

Noted for its spreading or vase-shaped
habit, polished mahogany red young
shoots, and its handsome, saw-toothed,
glossy leaves. A fine specimen shrub.

217

Variegated-leaved Shrubs

VARIEGATION COMES in a number of forms. Generally a green leaf has a white or yellow margin; occasionally a white or yellow leaf has a green margin. There are, however, a host of shrubs with green, grey, or purple leaves, that are spotted, blotched, or streaked a lighter shade. Two-colour variegation may be joined by paler or darker shades of the dominant colours. The bolder the variegation, the more dramatic the effect when planted with foliage of one colour.

Buxus sempervirens 'Elegantissima'
VARIEGATED BOX
☼ ❄❄❄   ↕ 1.7m (5½ft) ↔ 1.1m (3½ft)

Neat and slow-growing, this is easily the best variegated form of the Common Box. The bush is dome-shaped, with small evergreen, white-margined leaves. 🏆

Cornus alba 'Variegata'
SILVER VARIEGATED DOGWOOD
☼ ❄❄❄   ↕ 2.2m (7ft) ↔ 2.2m (7ft)

A reliable, variegated dogwood that bears white-margined grey-green leaves on reddish shoots. Prune hard in late winter for brighter stems and larger leaves.

Buddleja davidii 'Harlequin'
BUTTERFLY BUSH
☼ ❄❄❄   ↕ 2.5m (8ft) ↔ 2.5m (8ft)

A vigorous and attractive shrub, this has arching stems and creamy white-margined leaves. Large, dense spikes of red-purple flowers occur from summer into autumn.

OTHER DECIDUOUS VARIEGATED SHRUBS

Berberis thunbergii 'Rose Glow'
Daphne × *burkwoodii* 'Carol Mackie'
Fuchsia magellanica 'Sharpitor'
Hypericum × *moserianum* 'Tricolor'
Ligustrum sinense 'Variegatum'
Lonicera nitida 'Silver Beauty'
Philadelphus coronarius 'Variegatus'
Sambucus nigra 'Pulverulenta'
Stachyurus 'Magpie'
Weigela 'Praecox Variegata'

Aucuba japonica 'Crotonifolia'
SPOTTED LAUREL
☼ ☀ ❄❄❄   ↕ 2m (6ft) ↔ 1.7m (5½ft)

The jade green shoots of this spectacular, dense, bushy shrub develop into shiny, leathery green leaves, blotched yellow. This laurel is a most reliable evergreen. 🏆

Cornus mas 'Variegata'
VARIEGATED CORNELIAN CHERRY
☼ ☀ ❄❄❄   ↕ 4m (12ft) ↔ 4m (12ft)

This dense, bushy shrub has leaves with bold white margins. Small clusters of tiny yellow flowers stud the twigs in late winter, before the leaves unfurl. 🏆

Cotoneaster atropurpureus 'Variegatus'
VARIEGATED COTONEASTER
☼ ❋❋❋ ↕ 45cm (18in) ↔ 1.2m (4ft)

Also known as *C. horizontalis* 'Variegatus', the low, wide-spreading stems are densely clothed with tiny, cream-margined leaves. These are tinted red in autumn. ♔

Ilex aquifolium 'Ferox Argentea'
SILVER HEDGEHOG HOLLY
☼ ☀ ❋❋❋ ↕ 4m (12ft) ↔ 1.5m (5ft)

An attractive, bushy evergreen holly, with small, prickly leaves that have creamy white margins. This is a male form, useful as a pollinator for berrying hollies. ♔

Rhamnus alaternus 'Argenteovariegata'
VARIEGATED BUCKTHORN
☼ ❋❋❋ ↕ 2.5m (8ft) ↔ 1.7m (5½ft)

A handsome, bushy evergreen, this has small, glossy grey-green leaves, margined creamy white. Discreet yellow flowers will produce red berries in a hot summer. ♔

Viburnum tinus 'Variegatum'
VARIEGATED LAURUSTINUS
☼ ☀ ❋❋ ↕ 2.5m (8ft) ↔ 2m (6ft)

The leaves of this mounded or conical evergreen are boldly and irregularly margined. Red-budded, fragrant white flowers occur from autumn through winter.

Elaeagnus × *ebbingei* 'Gilt Edge'
ELAEAGNUS
☼ ❋❋❋ ↕ 2.5m (8ft) ↔ 2.5m (8ft)

This robust evergreen shrub has brown, scaly stems and shining green leaves, with golden yellow margins. Its small sweetly fragrant flowers open in autumn. ♔

OTHER EVERGREEN VARIEGATED SHRUBS

Camellia × *williamsii* 'Golden Spangles'
Euonymus fortunei 'Silver Queen', see p.222
Euonymus japonicus 'Chollipo'
Euonymus japonicus 'Ovatus Aureus'
Pieris japonica 'Little Heath', see p.213
Pittosporum 'Garnettii'
Prunus laurocerasus 'Castlewellan', see p.233
Vinca minor 'Illumination'

Osmanthus heterophyllus 'Variegatus'
VARIEGATED FALSE HOLLY
☼ ☀ ❋❋❋ ↕ 2.2m (7ft) ↔ 1.2m (4ft)

This evergreen bush of relatively slow growth has small, white-margined, holly-like leaves. Clusters of little, sweetly scented white flowers occur in autumn. ♔

Weigela 'Florida Variegata'
VARIEGATED WEIGELA
☼ ❋❋❋ ↕ 1.5m (5ft) ↔ 1.5m (5ft)

One of the most popular and easily grown variegated shrubs, with distinctly edged leaves that provide a perfect foil for pink flowers in late spring and early summer. ♔

SHRUBS

Shrubs with Golden or Yellow Leaves

THERE IS NOTHING like a bright splash of yellow or gold foliage to bring a most welcome touch of warmth to the garden, especially in the depths of winter. An abundance of shrubs, both evergreen and deciduous, have leaves in varying shades of yellow. Careful use of these can create striking contrasts with green- or purple-leaved plants.

Berberis thunbergii 'Aurea'
BARBERRY
☼ ❊❊❊   ↕ 75cm (30in) ↔ 75cm (30in)

The low, dense, compact mound of small, rounded leaves is vivid yellow at first, and becomes yellow-green later. It is liable to scorch in full sun, except in cool summers.

Calluna vulgaris 'Gold Haze'
HEATHER, LING
☼ ❊❊❊   ↕ 50cm (20in) ↔ 45cm (18in)

One of many similar heathers available from nurseries, 'Gold Haze' has packed foliage of a golden hue, brighter in winter. White flowers appear in late summer. ♉

Choisya ternata 'Sundance'
MEXICAN ORANGE-BLOSSOM
☼ ☼ ❊❊   ↕ 1.5m (5ft) ↔ 2m (6ft)

The bright yellow, aromatic leaves of this evergreen, mounded shrub fade with age. Fragrant white flowers are produced in late spring. Dislikes cold winds. ♉

Cornus alba 'Aurea'
GOLDEN-LEAVED DOGWOOD
☼ ☼ ❊❊❊   ↕ 3m (10ft) ↔ 3m (10ft)

This vigorous dogwood forms a sizeable mound of dark red branches, clothed, all through summer and into autumn, with broad, lovely soft yellow leaves. ♉

Erica arborea 'Albert's Gold'
TREE HEATH
☼ ❊❊❊   ↕ 2m (6ft) ↔ 2m (6ft)

The twiggy branches are densely crowded with tiny leaves, giving plumes of golden yellow throughout the year. Masses of honey-scented white flowers in spring. ♉

Fuchsia 'Genii'
FUCHSIA
☼ ☼ ❊❊❊   ↕ 1.4m (4½ft) ↔ 75cm (30in)

This small, colourful, upright shrub has red shoots and bright lime-yellow foliage. It carries small, pendulous violet and red flowers from summer into autumn. ♉

Ligustrum 'Vicaryi'
VICARY GIBBS GOLDEN PRIVET
☼ ◐ ✳✳✳   ↕ 3m (10ft) ↔ 3m (10ft)

This is a vigorous semi-evergreen shrub of
dense, bushy habit. The sweetly scented
white flowers and bright yellow leaves are
carried throughout the summer.

OTHER DECIDUOUS SHRUBS WITH GOLDEN OR YELLOW LEAVES

Acer palmatum 'Aureum', see p.292
Caryopteris x *clandonensis*
  'Worcester Gold'
Ceratostigma willmottianum 'Desert Skies'
Cornus mas 'Aurea'
Fuchsia 'Golden Marinka'
Physocarpus opulifolius 'Dart's Gold',
  see p.202
Ptelea trifoliata 'Aurea', see p.293
Ribes alpinum 'Aureum'
Rubus cockburnianus 'Goldenvale'
Rubus parviflorus 'Sunshine Spreader'
Sambucus nigra 'Aurea', see p.241
Sambucus racemosa 'Plumosa Aurea'
Spiraea japonica 'Candlelight'
Syringa vulgaris 'Aureua'
Viburnum lantana 'Aureum'
Weigela 'Looymansii Aurea', see p.195

Sambucus racemosa 'Sutherland Gold'
☼ ✳✳✳   ↕ 3m (10ft) ↔ 3m (10ft)

The large, deeply divided yellow leaves of
this vigorous golden elder do not readily
scorch. Clusters of yellow flowers, borne in
spring, are followed by red berries.   ♔

Lonicera nitida 'Baggesen's Gold'
BAGGESEN'S GOLD LONICERA
☼ ✳✳✳   ↕ 5m (15ft) ↔ 5m (15ft)

Attractive, tiny yellow leaves crowd the
slender, arching shoots of this dense, bushy
evergreen. Capable of greater height when
trained against   a wall.   ♔

Philadelphus coronarius 'Aureus'
GOLDEN MOCK ORANGE
☼ ✳✳✳   ↕ 2.5m (8ft) ↔ 1.5m (5ft)

The yellow spring leaves of this shrub fade
to greenish in late summer, and can scorch
in full sun. Creamy white flowers in late
spring and early summer, are fragrant.   ♔

Ribes sanguineum 'Brocklebankii'
GOLDEN FLOWERING CURRANT
☼ ✳✳✳   ↕ 1m (3ft) ↔ 1.2m (4ft)

Although clusters of pink flowers decorate
this bushy shrub in spring, the aromatic
golden yellow leaves, liable to scorch in
full sun, are its main attraction.

OTHER EVERGREEN SHRUBS WITH GOLDEN OR YELLOW LEAVES

Aucuba japonica 'Sulphurea Marginata'
Calluna vulgaris 'Beoley Gold'
Erica erigena 'Golden Lady'
Erica vagans 'Valerie Proudley'
Escallonia laevis 'Gold Brian'
Escallonia laevis 'Gold Ellen'
Euonymus japonicus 'Ovatus Aureus'
Ilex x *attenuata* 'Sunny Foster'
Ilex crenata 'Golden Gem'
Ligustrum ovalifolium 'Aureum'

Spiraea japonica 'Goldflame'
SPIRAEA
☼ ✳✳✳   ↕ 75cm (30in) ↔ 1m (3ft)

Leaves on a low, dense mound of twiggy
branches emerge orange-red, then turn to
golden yellow, and finally to green. Small
summer flowerheads are rose-pink.

Viburnum opulus 'Aureum'
GOLDEN GUELDER ROSE
☼ ✳✳✳   ↕ 2.5m (8ft) ↔ 2m (6ft)

Bright yellow, maple-like leaves are red-
bronze when young. Its white flowerheads
appear in summer, followed by red berries
in autumn. Leaves scorch in hot sun.

S H R U B S

Shrubs with Silver or Blue-grey Leaves

THE SILVERY FLASH of blue-grey leaves when the sunlight catches them shifting in a breeze is a pleasing sight in any garden. Silver-foliaged shrubs can also be grown for their softening effect near leaves of a darker or brighter hue. The silvery colour may be due to a silky or woolly coating of hairs, silvery scales, or a white, powdery bloom.

Convolvulus cneorum
CONVOLVULUS
☼ ❊❊   ↕ 75cm (30in) ↔ 1m (3ft)

Silky, silvery leaves and stems make this one of the loveliest dwarf evergreen shrubs. White, yellow-throated flowers cover it from late spring to late summer.

Berberis dictyophylla
BARBERRY
☼ ❊❊❊   ↕ 2m (6ft) ↔ 2m (6ft)

This graceful shrub has striking stems and leaves with a whitish bloom. Light yellow summer flowers give way to berries that, with the leaves, turn scarlet in autumn.

Calluna vulgaris 'Silver Queen'
HEATHER, LING
☼ ❊❊❊❊ᴾᴴ   ↕ 40cm (16in) ↔ 45cm (18in)

Although it produces mauve-pink flower spikes in late summer and early autumn, this dwarf evergreen is popular mainly for its silver-grey, downy foliage.

Hebe pimeleoides 'Quicksilver'
HEBE
☼ ❊❊❊   ↕ 25cm (10in) ↔ 60cm (24in)

The dark, wiry stems and branches of this low, spreading evergreen shrub bear small silver-blue leaves, and short spikes of pale lilac flowers in summer.

OTHER EVERGREEN SHRUBS WITH SILVER OR BLUE-GREY LEAVES

Acacia baileyana
Artemisia arborescens
Artemisia 'Powis Castle'
Ballota pseudodictamnus
Brachyglottis 'Sunshine', see p.204
Cassinia leptophylla
Cistus 'Grayswood Pink'
Dendromecon rigida
Elaeagnus macrophylla
Euryops acraeus, see p.210
Olearia × *mollis*
Rhododendron campanulatum
  subsp. *aeruginosum*
Rhododendron cinnabarinum
  Concatenans Group
Teucrium fruticans
Yucca glauca
Yucca gloriosa

Cistus × *argenteus*
'Peggy Sammons'
SUN ROSE
☼ ❊❊   ↕ 1m (3ft) ↔ 1m (3ft)

The pale pink flowers of this lovely, bushy evergreen are freely produced in summer, and resemble small, single roses. Grey-green leaves and stems are downy.

OTHER DECIDUOUS SHRUBS WITH SILVER OR BLUE-GREY LEAVES

Buddleja alternifolia 'Argentea'
Buddleja nivea
Elaeagnus 'Quicksilver', see p.294
Hippophae rhamnoides, see p.284
Lotus hirsutus, see p.196
Romneya coulteri, see p.197
Rosa fedtschenkoana
Rubus thibetanus, see p.239
Salix elaeagnos
Salix lanata

Helichrysum italicum
CURRY PLANT
☼ ❈❈ ↕ 60cm (24in) ↔ 1m (3ft)

Thread-like leaves crowd the erect stems
of this low, aromatic evergreen subshrub.
Its leaves and stems are silvery grey and
downy, and summer flowers are yellow. ♈

Leptospermum lanigerum
LEPTOSPERMUM
☼ ❈❈❈PH ↕ 3m (10ft) ↔ 2m (6ft)

The reddish shoots of this evergreen bush
are clothed in narrow grey or silvery grey
leaves. Its small white flowers are freely
produced in early summer.

Perovskia 'Blue Spire'
RUSSIAN SAGE
☼ ❈❈❈ ↕ 1.2m (4ft) ↔ 1.2m (4ft)

Spires of small violet-blue flowers open in
late summer and autumn, from grey-white
upright stems. These are all clothed with
deeply cut grey-green leaves. ♈

Rosa glauca
SPECIES ROSE
☼ ❈❈❈ ↕ 2m (6ft) ↔ 2m (6ft)

The leaves of this rose, on reddish violet
stems, are glaucous purple in sun, mauve-
tinted grey-green in shade. Early summer
flowers and autumn fruits are a bonus. ♈

Salix exigua
COYOTE WILLOW
☼ ❈❈❈ ↕ 4m (12ft) ↔ 1.5m (5ft)

This tall, upright shrub has long flexuous
stems, each clothed with beautiful leaves,
narrow, silvery and silky, ever-shifting and
shimmering in the slightest breeze.

Santolina chamaecyparissus
COTTON LAVENDER
☼ ❈❈❈ ↕ 75cm (30in) ↔ 1m (3ft)

Narrow, aromatic, woolly whitish leaves
crowd this evergreen shrub, forming a low,
dense dome. Long-stalked, button-like
yellow flowerheads occur in summer. ♈

S H R U B S

Shrubs with Purple, Red, or Bronze Leaves

Purple or reddish foliage in spring or summer can be extremely useful in the garden, providing that it is not overdone. These relatively sombre colours are particularly effective when contrasted with silver or grey foliage; even more dramatic effects can be achieved when they are placed alongside plants with yellow or gold foliage.

S H R U B S

Berberis thunbergii 'Red Chief'
BARBERRY
☼ ✳✳✳ ↕ 1.2m (4ft) ↔ 1.2m (4ft)

'Red Chief' is a vigorous, upright or vase-shaped shrub, spreading as it matures. It has bright red, arching shoots and narrow, glossy-topped, red-purple leaves.

Acer palmatum 'Garnet'
JAPANESE MAPLE
☼ ✳✳✳ ↕ 4m (12ft) ↔ 4m (12ft)

This strong-growing shrub, with an open, spreading habit, has slender, dark shoots clothed in large, deep garnet-red leaves with finely cut lobes. Dislikes dry soils.

Corylus maxima 'Purpurea'
PURPLE-LEAVED FILBERT
☼ ✳✳✳ ↕ 6m (20ft) ↔ 6m (20ft)

Vase-shaped at first, spreading later, this popular form of the filbert is planted for its large, deep purple leaves. Purplish catkins drape branches in late winter.

Acer palmatum 'Red Pygmy'
JAPANESE MAPLE
☼ ✳✳✳ ↕ 1.5m (5ft) ↔ 1.2m (4ft)

The dark purple leaves of this densely branched, slow-growing shrub turn green with age. Leaves on mature plants differ from the juvenile leaves shown here.

Berberis thunbergii 'Atropurpurea Nana'
BARBERRY
☼ ✳✳✳ ↕ 60cm (24in) ↔ 60cm (24in)

This dwarf, dome-shaped shrub of dense, twiggy habit has small, rounded, reddish purple leaves and is particularly suitable for growing on the rock garden.

Cotinus coggygria 'Royal Purple'
SMOKE TREE
☼ ✳✳✳ ↕ 4m (12ft)

One of the most popular shrubs for foliage, this will form a dense mound of rounded, deep red-purple leaves. Plumes of tiny, smoky pink flowers appear in summer.

Hebe 'Amy'
HEBE
☼ ❄   ↕ 1m (3ft) ↔ 1m (3ft)

The glossy, dark coppery purple leaves of this small, rounded evergreen shrub turn green in time. Rich violet-purple flowers are borne in short spikes in summer.

OTHER EVERGREEN SHRUBS WITH PURPLE, RED, OR BRONZE LEAVES

Daphne x *houtteana*
Leucothoe 'Scarletta'
Nandina domestica 'Nana Purpurea'
Osmanthus heterophyllus 'Purpureus'

Pittosporum tenuifolium 'Tom Thumb'
PITTOSPORUM
☼ ❄❄❄   ↕ 60cm (24in) ↔ 60cm (24in)

The dark shoots of this dome-shaped dwarf evergreen shrub are crowded with shining, crinkly-edged leaves of a deep reddish purple. These emerge green. ♔

Prunus x *cistena*
PURPLE-LEAVED SAND CHERRY
☼ ❄❄❄   ↕ 1.5m (5ft) ↔ 1.5m (5ft)

The Purple-leaf Sand Cherry is a small, erect shrub with glossy leaves, red at first, maturing to deep reddish purple. Small blush-white flowers appear in spring. ♔

Prunus spinosa 'Purpurea'
PURPLE-LEAVED SLOE
☼ ❄❄❄   ↕ 4m (12ft) ↔ 4m (12ft)

This is a dense, bushy shrub or small tree, with spiny branches and bright red leaves, that change to a deep reddish purple. Small, pale pink flowers open in spring.

OTHER DECIDUOUS SHRUBS WITH PURPLE, RED, OR BRONZE LEAVES

Acer palmatum 'Bloodgood'
Itea virginica 'Henry's Garnet'
Physocarpus opulifolius 'Diabolo'
Weigela florida 'Foliis Purpureis'

Prunus cerasifera 'Hessei'
PURPLE-LEAVED PLUM
☼ ❄❄❄   ↕ 4m (12ft) ↔ 4m (12ft)

In spring, snow-white blossom precedes the leaves, which emerge green and then turn bronze-purple with cream or pink variegation. Bushy form of the cherry plum.

Sambucus nigra 'Guincho Purple'
PURPLE-LEAVED ELDER
☼ ❄❄❄   ↕ 4m (12ft) ↔ 4m (12ft)

The deeply divided leaves of this vigorous shrub are green at first, maturing to dark purple, then red in autumn. Its pink-budded summer flowers open white. ♔

S H R U B S

225

Shrubs with Colourful Leaf Tints in Autumn

GIVEN FAVOURABLE CONDITIONS, most deciduous shrubs will produce colourful tints before their leaves are shed in autumn; those here have been chosen for their quality and reliability. The impact of a group of shrubs in autumn colour is spectacular, but even a single well-selected and sited shrub can provide eye-catching effects in a small garden.

Cotinus 'Flame'
SMOKE BUSH
☼ ✻✻✻   ↕ 4m (12ft) ↔ 4m (12ft)

Strong-growing and bushy, this shrub has plumes of purplish pink summer flowers. Its bold leaves turn fiery orange and red in autumn. The sap may cause a rash. ♖

OTHER SHRUBS WITH COLOURFUL LEAF TINTS IN AUTUMN

Acer palmatum 'Osakazuki', see p.296
Acer palmatum 'Seiryû'
Aronia x *prunifolia* 'Brilliant'
Berberis sieboldii
Cornus alba
Enkianthus perulatus
Fothergilla major
Rhododendron 'Corneille'
Vaccinium corymbosum, see p.203
Viburnum opulus 'Notcutt's Variety'

Berberis thunbergii
JAPANESE BARBERRY
☼ ✻✻✻   ↕ 1.4m (5ft) ↔ 1.4m (5ft)

Arching, thorny branches are clothed with small leaves, orange and red in autumn. Tiny yellow flowers are produced in spring and scarlet berries follow in autumn. ♖

Acer palmatum var. *heptalobum*
JAPANESE MAPLE
☼ ☼ ✻✻✻   ↕ 6m (20ft) ↔ 6m (20ft)

Most Japanese maples are worth growing for their impressive autumn tints. The large, seven-lobed green leaves of this one turn red or orange-red. Dislikes dry soils.

Callicarpa japonica
BEAUTY BERRY
☼ ✻✻✻   ↕ 1.4m (4½ft) ↔ 1.4m (4½ft)

The leaves of this bushy shrub turn mauve or rose-madder in autumn. When planted in groups, small violet berries are usually produced at the same time.

Disanthus cercidifolius
DISANTHUS
☼ ✻✻✻✻ᴾᴴ   ↕ 3m (10ft) ↔ 3m (10ft)

This spreading shrub is grown principally for its rounded blue-green leaves. During autumn, they turn a rich wine-purple, then crimson and orange. Dislikes dry soils. ♖

Ribes odoratum
BUFFALO CURRANT
☼ ☀ ❄❄❄   ↕ 2m (6ft) ↔ 1.5m (5ft)

This open-habited shrub has upright stems loosely clothed with lobed and rounded leaves that turn red and purple in autumn. Golden spring flowers are clove-scented.

Euonymus alatus
WINGED SPINDLE
☼ ❄❄❄   ↕ 2m (6ft) ↔ 3m (10ft)

Compact, and with curious corky, winged branches, this is a spectacular autumn shrub. The leaves turn every shade from pink through to brilliant crimson. ♧

Fothergilla gardenii
FOTHERGILLA
☼ ☀ ❄❄❄❄ PH   ↕ 1m (3ft) ↔ 1m (3ft)

Although the small white flowerheads in spring are pretty enough, autumn leaves in brilliant orange, red, and purple are surely this fothergilla's most impressive feature.

Hamamelis vernalis 'Sandra'
OZARK WITCH HAZEL
☼ ☀ ❄❄❄❄ PH   ↕ 3m (10ft) ↔ 3m (10ft)

Young purple leaves mature green, then become yellow, orange, red, and purple in autumn. Tiny, crowded, spidery, scented yellow flowers follow in late winter. ♧

EVERGREEN SHRUBS WITH COLOURFUL WINTER LEAF TINTS

Calluna vulgaris 'Boskoop'
Leucothoe 'Scarletta'
Mahonia nervosa, see p.133
Nandina domestica 'Fire Power'

SHRUBS

227

Shrubs with Fragrant Flowers

W̲HEN PRESENTED with a lovely flower, most people will instinctively take a sniff, assuming that a pleasing scent accompanies a beautiful blossom. Sadly, this is not always the case. Numerous shrubs do have fragrant flowers though, and these include some whose fragrance is far more noticeable or appealing than the appearance of the flower itself.

Coronilla valentina subsp. *glauca*
CORONILLA

☼ ✻✻ ↕ 1.4m (4½ft) ↔ 1.4m (4½ft)

The leaves of this bushy evergreen are blue-green and fleshy. Clusters of small yellow pea-flowers are borne continuously from winter into early summer. 🏆

Acacia dealbata
MIMOSA, SILVER WATTLE

☼ ✻✻✻[PH]▾ ↕ 6m (20ft) ↔ 6m (20ft)

Popular with florists, this fast-growing evergreen has feathery blue-green leaves and plumes of bright yellow flower-heads from winter into spring. 🏆

Carpenteria californica
CARPENTERIA

☼ ✻✻ ↕ 2m (6ft) ↔ 2m (6ft)

The evergreen leaves of this bushy shrub are leathery and dark green, and the bark is papery and peeling. Its summer flowers are white with yellow centres. 🏆

Daphne x *burkwoodii* 'Somerset'
DAPHNE

☼ ✻✻✻ ↕ 1.2m (4ft) ↔ 1.2m (4ft)

This narrow-leaved, bushy shrub is one of the best daphnes for general cultivation. In late spring, it is plastered with clusters of small, starry pink and white flowers.

Buddleja 'West Hill'
BUTTERFLY BUSH

☼ ✻✻✻ ↕ 3m (10ft) ↔ 3m (10ft)

This vigorous shrub, with softly hairy, pointed, grey-green leaves, bears tapered plumes of tubular, orange-eyed, lilac-blue flowers from summer into autumn.

Choisya ternata
MEXICAN ORANGE-BLOSSOM

☼ ◐ ✻✻ ↕ 2m (6ft) ↔ 2m (6ft)

This good-looking evergreen forms a dense mound of glossy, aromatic leaves. White flowers are freely borne in late spring and again, less abundantly, in autumn. 🏆

OTHER HARDY SHRUBS WITH FRAGRANT FLOWERS

Abelia triflora
Berberis julianae
Buddleja crispa, see p.164
Ceanothus x *delileanus*
   'Gloire de Versailles'
Clethra alnifolia 'Paniculata'
Colletia hystrix 'Rosea'
Daphne mezereum
Dipelta floribunda
Elaeagnus 'Quicksilver', see p.294
Genista tenera 'Golden Shower'
Osmanthus delavayi, see p.195
Philadelphus 'Belle Etoile'
Rhododendron 'Exquisitum'
Ribes odoratum, see p.227
Sarcococca confusa
Skimmia japonica 'Fragrans'
Syringa villosa

SHRUBS

Erica arborea var. *alpina*
TREE HEATH
☼ ❄❄❄ PH   ↕ 2m (6ft) ↔ 2m (6ft)

Bright green, needle-like evergreen leaves crowd this dense, compact, upright shrub. Plumes carrying masses of tiny, honey-scented flowers are produced in spring. ♛

Osmanthus x *burkwoodii*
OSMANTHUS
☼ ❄❄❄   ↕ 3m (10ft) ↔ 3m (10ft)

This strong-growing, compact evergreen shrub is densely packed with small, dark green, leathery leaves, and carries masses of small white flowers in spring. ♛

OTHER SEMI-HARDY SHRUBS WITH FRAGRANT FLOWERS

Azara petiolaris
Buddleja asiatica
Buddleja auriculata
Buddleja officinalis
Cytisus 'Porlock'
Daphne bholua 'Jacqueline Postill', see p.236
Edgeworthia chrysantha
Elaeagnus macrophylla
Erica x *veitchii* 'Exeter'
Euphorbia mellifera
Hoheria lyallii
Itea ilicifolia, see p.165
Lomatia myricoides
Myrtus communis
Olearia solandri
Pittosporum tobira
Rhododendron 'Lady Alice Fitzwilliam'

Rhododendron luteum
COMMON YELLOW AZALEA
☼ ❄❄❄ PH   ↕ 2.5m (8ft) ↔ 2.5m (8ft)

Rounded trusses of funnel-shaped flowers in spring are a lovely yellow colour. Rich green leaves turn to shades of crimson, purple, and orange in autumn. ♛

Syringa vulgaris 'Madame Antoine Buchner'
☼ ❄❄❄   ↕ 4m (12ft) ↔ 4m (12ft)

Upright at first, this bushy shrub spreads later. Pink-mauve flowers, in magnificent crowded heads, are purple-red in bud and open in late spring and early summer.

Viburnum x *carlcephalum*
VIBURNUM
☼ ❄❄❄   ↕ 3m (10ft) ↔ 3m (10ft)

This vigorous, bushy shrub bears white flowers, pink in bud, in rounded and crowded heads in spring. Its dark green leaves often colour richly in autumn. ♛

SHRUBS

Shrubs with Aromatic Leaves

GARDENERS ARE NORMALLY aware of fragrance in flowers, but the aroma of foliage is all too often neglected. The leaves of many shrubs are aromatic, but for most the scent is subtle, and only detectable when leaves are bruised. Some, such as the gummy leaves of cistus, are more obvious when it is hot and sunny.

SHRUBS

Rosmarinus officinalis 'Roseus'
ROSEMARY
☼ ❋❋   ↕ 1.5m (5ft) ↔ 1.5m (5ft)

Of dense habit when pruned, this is a pink-flowered version of a popular evergreen. Narrow leaves crowd its stems, as do the flowers in late spring and early summer.

Cistus ladanifer
GUM CISTUS
☼ ❋❋   ↕ 1.2m (4ft) ↔ 1.2m (4ft)

The narrow, willow-like, dark green leaves of this evergreen shrub are coated, like the branches, in a sticky, aromatic gum. Large white flowers open in summer. ♔

Elsholtzia stauntonii
MINT BUSH
☼ ❋❋❋   ↕ 1.5m (5ft) ↔ 1.5m (5ft)

This bushy subshrub has sharply toothed leaves that smell of mint when bruised. Dense spikes of mauve flowers are carried in late summer and early autumn.

Salvia microphylla 'Kew Red'
SAGE
☼ ❋❋   ↕ 1.2m (4ft) ↔ 1m (3ft)

The slender, upright stems of this bushy shrub are clothed with apple-green leaves. Spikes of brilliant scarlet flowers are borne from summer into early autumn.

OTHER EVERGREEN SHRUBS WITH AROMATIC LEAVES

Choisya ternata, see p.228
Drimys lanceolata
Escallonia laevis
Gaultheria procumbens, see p.176
Helichrysum italicum, see p.223
Illicium anisatum, see p.166
Lavandula angustifolia 'Imperial Gem'
Myrtus communis
Rhododendron cinnabarinum
Santolina chamaecyparissus, see p.223

OTHER DECIDUOUS SHRUBS WITH AROMATIC LEAVES

Aloysia triphylla, see p.212
Artemisia abrotanum
Comptonia peregrina
Myrica gale, see p.202

Prostanthera cuneata
PROSTANTHERA
☼ ❋❋❋   ↕ 1m (3ft) ↔ 1.4m (4½ft)

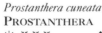

The branches of this shrub are crowded with tiny, glossy, dark green leaves that smell of wintergreen. It produces masses of white flowers in spring. ♔

Shrubs with Ornamental Fruit

MOST SHRUBS with ornamental fruit, especially the many berrying kinds, bring a welcome touch of colour to the garden, and provide birds and small rodents with a useful source of food. Many fruit freely, but some need to be planted in groups to effect pollination, while others, such as holly and pernettya require only a single male in a group of females.

Ilex × meserveae 'Blue Princess'
BLUE HOLLY
☼ ☼ ✻✻✻   ↕ 3m (10ft) ↔ 1.2m (4ft)

This is a dense, upright evergreen with spiny, purple-tinged leaves. Red berries are freely borne when its spring flowers are pollinated by those of a male form.

Callicarpa bodinieri var. *giraldii*
CALLICARPA
☼ ✻✻✻   ↕ 2.2m (7ft) ↔ 2m (6ft)

The shoots are clustered with small, bright mauve or pale violet berries in autumn, when the leaves are mauve-tinted. Plant several together for good pollination.

Euonymus hamiltonianus 'Red Elf'
SPINDLE
☼ ☼ ✻✻✻   ↕ ↔ 3m (10ft)

Upright at first, this strong-growing shrub spreads with age. It is mainly grown for the clusters of deep pink capsules that split to reveal orange seeds in autumn.

OTHER SHRUBS WITH ORNAMENTAL FRUIT

Berberis 'Rubrostilla'
Cotoneaster salicifolius 'Rothschildianus'
Decaisnea fargesii, see p.216
Euonymus europaeus 'Red Cascade'
Viburnum opulus 'Xanthocarpum'

Cotoneaster frigidus 'Fructu Luteo'
TREE COTONEASTER
☼ ☼ ✻✻✻   ↕ 6m (20ft) ↔ 6m (20ft)

This large, strong-growing shrub or small, multi-stemmed tree has bold foliage, white flowers in summer, and bunches of long-lasting yellow berries in autumn.

Gaultheria mucronata 'Wintertime'
PERNETTYA
☼ ✻✻✻✻ PH   ↕ 1m (3ft) ↔ 1.2m (4ft)

Include a male plant in a group for good pollination, and this suckering evergreen will bear white berries from autumn into winter. Forms dense clumps in time.

Viburnum wrightii var. *hessei*
VIBURNUM
☼ ☼ ✻✻✻   ↕ 1m (3ft) ↔ 1m (3ft)

Heads of small white flowers are produced in early summer, and form bunches of red berries in autumn. The broad, veined leaves often colour richly in autumn.

SHRUBS

231

Shrubs that Provide Berries for Birds

MANY WOULD SAY A GARDEN is incomplete without the presence of birds, be they resident or just regular visitors. Songbirds are particularly desirable. In spring and summer, there is plenty of food to attract them, but in autumn and winter it can be scarce, so it is best to entice the birds by planting some shrubs that produce reliable crops of berries.

Cotoneaster frigidus 'Cornubia'
COTONEASTER
☼ ☼ ❊❊❊   ↕ 6m (20ft) ↔ 6m (20ft)

This strong-growing semi-evergreen shrub has clusters of tiny white flowers in early summer, and ample bunches of large red berries from autumn into early winter. ♈

Ilex aquifolium 'J.C. van Tol'
VAN TOL'S HOLLY
☼ ☼ ❊❊❊   ↕ 6m (20ft) ↔ 4m (12ft)

This extremely popular holly carries few-spined leaves, and red berries that crowd the purple shoots in winter. It will fruit even when no male plant is present. ♈

OTHER LARGE SHRUBS THAT PROVIDE BERRIES FOR BIRDS
Amelanchier x *grandiflora* 'Ballerina'
Aralia spinosa
Aronia arbutifolia 'Erecta'
Berberis jamesiana
Cornus mas, see p.236
Cotoneaster bullatus
Cotoneaster frigidus, see p.272
Elaeagnus multiflora
Ligustrum sinense, see p.179
Prunus laurocerasus
Rubus spectabilis
Sambucus canadensis 'Maxima'
Sambucus racemosa
Viburnum opulus, see p.203

Cotoneaster sternianus
COTONEASTER
☼ ☼ ❊❊❊   ↕ 3m (10ft) ↔ 3m (10ft)

The branches of this evergreen or semi-evergreen shrub are clothed with small grey-green leaves, and covered in autumn with clusters of orange-red berries. ♈

Crataegus schraderiana
HAWTHORN
☼ ☼ ❊❊❊   ↕ 5m (15ft) ↔ 5m (15ft)

A mass of white flowers covers this large shrub or small tree, in late spring or early summer. These blooms are followed by drooping clusters of dark purple-red haws.

Leycesteria formosa
HIMALAYAN HONEYSUCKLE
☼ ☼ ❊❊❊   ↕ 2m (6ft) ↔ 1.5m (5ft)

An upright shrub (or subshrub in colder climates), this carries drooping clusters of white flowers with claret-coloured bracts in summer. Reddish purple berries follow. ♈

SHRUBS

Lonicera xylosteum
FLY HONEYSUCKLE
☼ ☼ ✻✻✻   ↕ 3m (10ft) ↔ 3m (10ft)

Strong-growing and bushy, this shrub has
spreading or arching branches, and bears
creamy white flowers in spring or early
summer, followed by red berries.

Mahonia aquifolium
OREGON GRAPE
☼ ☼ ☼ ✻✻✻   ↕ 1m (3ft) ↔ 1.5m (5ft)

The glossy green leaves of this dense, low
evergreen shrub are prickly. Its bloomy
blue-black berries are preceded in spring
by crowded yellow flower clusters.

Sambucus nigra
ELDERBERRY
☼ ☼ ✻✻✻   ↕ 6m (20ft) ↔ 6m (20ft)

This, the typical wild elderberry, produces
flattened heads of fragrant, creamy white
flowers in early summer, followed by its
heavy bunches of tiny black berries.

Prunus laurocerasus 'Castlewellan'
VARIEGATED CHERRY LAUREL
☼ ☼ ✻✻✻   ↕ 5m (15ft) ↔ 5m (15ft)

Dense and compact, this bright-foliaged
evergreen has green- and cream-marbled
leaves. White flower spikes in late spring
are followed by shining black fruits.

**OTHER SMALL SHRUBS THAT
PROVIDE BERRIES FOR BIRDS**

Berberis 'Rubrostilla'
Berberis wilsoniae
Coriaria terminalis
Cotoneaster horizontalis
Prunus laurocerasus 'Otto Luyken',
see p.210
Daphne mezereum
Daphne tangutica
Gaultheria mucronata 'Pink Pearl'
Gaultheria shallon
Hedera helix 'Arborescens', see p.234
Mahonia nervosa, see p.201
Rubus illecebrosus
Sarcococca confusa
Sorbus reducta
Vaccinium corymbosum, see p.203
Vaccinium parvifolium
Vaccinium vitis-idaea Koralle Group

Viburnum opulus 'Compactum'
GUELDER ROSE
☼ ☼ ✻✻✻   ↕ 1.5m (5ft) ↔ 1.5m (5ft)

The maple-like leaves of this dense shrub
colour richly in autumn, when its bunches
of bright red berries appear. Lace-cap
heads of white flowers open in spring. ⚜

Shrubs Attractive to Butterflies

FLOWERING SHRUBS that appeal to butterflies offer a bonus that few gardeners would wish to ignore. Many are also sweetly scented. The nectar of their flowers is attractive to butterflies, as well as to a host of other insect beneficiaries, including hoverflies and bees. All these industrious creatures help to make the garden a more interesting and lively place.

Buddleja davidii 'Peace'
BUTTERFLY BUSH
☼ ❄❄❄   ↕4m (12ft) ↔4m (12ft)

Buddlejas come in many colours, and are among the most popular plants with bees and butterflies. 'Peace' has fragrant white flower spikes from summer into autumn.

Escallonia 'Donard Seedling'
ESCALLONIA
☼ ❄❄❄   ↕3m (10ft) ↔3m (10ft)

A long-time favourite, this reliable shrub has arching stems, each densely clothed in glossy evergreen leaves. Masses of pale pink buds open white or blush in summer.

Hedera helix 'Arborescens'
TREE IVY
☼ ☼ ☀ ❄❄❄   ↕1.4m (4½ft) ↔2m (6ft)

This ivy forms a dense evergreen mound of glossy leaves. Heads of brownish green flowers in autumn are a veritable honey pot for late-flying insects.

Calluna vulgaris 'Anthony Davis'
HEATHER, LING
☼ ❄❄❄❄ᴾᴴ   ↕45cm (18in) ↔50cm (20in)

This fine, bushy heather is crowded with grey-green evergreen foliage. Long sprays of white flowers are produced from late summer into early autumn. ♗

Hebe albicans
HEBE
☼ ❄❄❄   ↕60cm (24in) ↔1m (3ft)

In summer, spikes crowded with white flowers grow from the upper leaf axils of this dwarf, mounded, compact hebe. Its evergreen leaves are blue-green. ♗

Lavandula angustifolia 'Hidcote'
LAVENDER
☼ ❄❄❄   ↕60cm (24in) ↔75cm (30in)

Long-stalked spikes with small, fragrant violet flowers rise above the narrow grey-green leaves of this aromatic evergreen in summer. A deservedly popular plant. ♗

Pyracantha 'Watereri'
FIRETHORN

☼ ☀ ✳✳✳   ↕ 2.5m (8ft) ↔ 2.5m (8ft)

The spreading branches of this vigorous
evergreen bear narrow, glossy, dark green
leaves. White flower clusters occur in early
summer, and red berries in winter.

Rubus 'Benenden'
RUBUS

☼ ✳✳✳   ↕ 3m (10ft) ↔ 3m (10ft)

The strong, upright stems of this shrub are
arching, and eventually wide-spreading.
Lovely flowers, like small white roses, are
borne in late spring and early summer. ♛

Syringa × *hyacinthiflora* 'Esther Staley'
LILAC

☼ ✳✳✳   ↕ 4m (12ft) ↔ 3m (10ft)

Upright at first, and spreading later, this
is a strong-growing, bushy shrub. Striking,
dense heads of fragrant lilac-pink flowers
appear from spring into early summer. ♛

**OTHER SMALL SHRUBS
ATTRACTIVE TO BUTTERFLIES**

Aster albescens
Cotoneaster conspicuus 'Decorus'
Lavandula stoechas
Salvia lavandulifolia

**OTHER LARGE SHRUBS
ATTRACTIVE TO BUTTERFLIES**

Buddleja 'West Hill', see p.228
Buddleja 'Pink Delight'
Clerodendrum bungei, see p.180
Cotoneaster lacteus, see p.208
Cotoneaster sternianus, see p.232
Escallonia 'Edinensis'
Escallonia 'Langleyensis', see p.190
Ligustrum sinense, see p.179
Spiraea veitchii
Viburnum betulifolium

S H R U B S

Ligustrum quihoui
PRIVET

☼ ☀ ✳✳✳   ↕ 2.5m (8ft) ↔ 2.5m (8ft)

A most elegant privet, this has slender,
arching branches, glossy evergreen leaves,
and branched, conical heads of tiny white
flowers from late summer into autumn. ♛

Salvia officinalis
COMMON SAGE

☼ ✳✳✳   ↕ 60cm (24in) ↔ 1m (3ft)

Sage is a popular culinary herb. It forms a
mound of semi-evergreen, aromatic grey-
green leaves, and produces spikes of two-
lipped purple-blue flowers in summer.

Thymus vulgaris
COMMON THYME

☼ ✳✳   ↕ 30cm (12in) ↔ 25cm (10in)

Most often used in the herb garden, this
dwarf subshrub has narrow, aromatic grey-
green leaves, and slender spikes of pale
purplish pink flowers all through summer.

Winter-flowering Shrubs

FLOWERING SHRUBS are at no time more welcome and more valued than during the winter months. This is partly due to their being few in number and, having fewer rivals, they command our full attention, particularly when planted where their flowers are easily seen against a darker background such as a wall or an evergreen hedge. If the blooms have an attractive fragrance as well, this makes them all the more desirable, especially to the blind or partially sighted.

Daphne bholua 'Jacqueline Postill'
DAPHNE

☼ ☼ ✳✳   ↕ 2m (6ft) ↔ 1.5m (5ft)

Best in a sheltered position, this vigorous, upright evergreen bears clusters of richly fragrant flowers that bloom over a long period. Dislikes dry soils. ♔

Erica carnea 'Springwood White'
WINTER HEATH

☼ ☼ ✳✳✳   ↕ 15cm (6in) ↔ 45cm (18in)

This reliable, scented evergreen shrublet forms a good, low ground cover with its dense, needle-like foliage. Spikes of small white bell-flowers continue into spring. ♔

Chimonanthus praecox 'Grandiflorus'
WINTERSWEET

☼ ✳✳✳   ↕ 2.5m (8ft) ↔ 3m (10ft)

This large, slow-growing, spreading shrub is justly famous for its deliciously fragrant, small, cup-shaped flowers. These are pale yellow with a purple heart. ♔

Cornus mas
CORNELIAN CHERRY

☼ ☼ ✳✳✳   ↕ 5m (15ft) ↔ 5m (15ft)

The twigs of this broad, rounded shrub or small tree are studded with little clusters of tiny yellow flowers. These twigs are also useful for cutting to display inside.

OTHER WINTER-FLOWERING
SHRUBS

Abeliophyllum distichum
Camellia sasanqua 'Narumigata'
Daphne odora 'Aureomarginata',
  see p.214
Erica carnea 'Myretoun Ruby'
Erica × *darleyensis* 'Kramer's Rote'
Erica × *darleyensis* 'Silberschmelze'
Garrya elliptica 'James Roof'
Hamamelis × *intermedia* 'Pallida'
Rhododendron dauricum 'Midwinter'

Hamamelis × *intermedia* 'Jelena'
WITCH HAZEL

☼ ☼ ✳✳✳✳ᴾᴴ   ↕ 4m (12ft) ↔ 4m (12ft)

In autumn, the large, softly hairy leaves turn orange-red and scarlet, and in winter, spidery orange flowers densely crowd the bare twigs. Dislikes dry soils. ♔

SHRUBS

Sycopsis sinensis
SYCOPSIS

☼ ☀ ✻✻✻   ↕ 5m (15ft) ↔ 4m (12ft)

This uncommon, erect evergreen shrub carries glossy, dark green, pointed leaves, and produces compact clusters of tiny flowers. Grows best in a sheltered site.

Mahonia × *media* 'Buckland'
MAHONIA

☼ ☀ ✻✻✻   ↕ 3m (10ft) ↔ 3m (10ft)

Erect at first, this big and bold evergreen spreads with age. Long, cylindrical spikes of tiny, fragrant yellow flowers are borne above divided, prickle-toothed leaves. ♛

Viburnum × *bodnantense* 'Dawn'
WINTER-FLOWERING VIBURNUM

☼ ☀ ✻✻✻   ↕ 3m (10ft) ↔ 2.5m (8ft)

From autumn all through to spring, the leafless twigs of this popular and reliable shrub are studded with clusters of strongly fragrant pink flowers, darker in bud. ♛

Lonicera × *purpusii* 'Winter Beauty'
WINTER HONEYSUCKLE

☼ ☀ ✻✻✻   ↕ 2m (6ft) ↔ 4m (12ft)

Vigorous, and with a spreading habit, this honeysuckle is mainly grown for its small, sweetly fragrant white flowers. These are carried over a very long period. ♛

Sarcococca hookeriana var. *digyna*
CHRISTMAS BOX, SWEET BOX

☼ ☀ ☀ ✻✻✻   ↕ 1.2m (4ft) ↔ 1m (3ft)

This suckering evergreen in time forms dense clumps of upright shoots. Clusters of tiny, sweetly scented white flowers are carried in the axils of its narrow leaves. ♛

Viburnum tinus 'Eve Price'
LAURUSTINUS

☼ ☀ ✻✻✻   ↕ 2.5m (8ft) ↔ 2.5m (8ft)

Heads of reddish buds open into many white flowers with a subtle fragrance from autumn onwards. Neat and rounded, this shrub has glossy, dark evergreen leaves. ♛

SHRUBS

Shrubs with Ornamental Twigs in Winter

O RNAMENTAL FEATURES that enliven a garden in winter are to be welcomed. In addition to the indisputable attraction of winter flowers and evergreen foliage, the stems and twigs of many plants offer surprisingly decorative colours and forms. The dramatic effect of some, such as dogwood and willow, can be improved by hard pruning.

SHRUBS

Cornus stolonifera 'Flaviramea'
GOLDEN-TWIGGED DOGWOOD

☼ ☀ ❄❄❄ ↕ 2m (6ft) ↔ 3m (10ft)

The greenish yellow winter shoots of this vigorous suckering and layering shrub are brighter if regularly pruned, and in full sun. Leaves turn yellow in autumn. ♔

Cornus alba 'Sibirica'
WESTONBIRT DOGWOOD

☼ ☀ ❄❄❄ ↕ 2m (6ft) ↔ 2m (6ft)

This dogwood is the best in cultivation for coloured stems. It produces red winter shoots, and large summer leaves when pruned. These give rich autumn tints. ♔

SHRUBS WITH ORNAMENTAL BARK FOR WINTER EFFECT
Abelia triflora
Clethra barbinervis
Deutzia × *wilsonii*
Dipelta floribunda
Euonymus alatus, see p.227
Euonymus phellomanus
Heptacodium miconioides
Prunus tomentosa
Rhododendron barbatum
Stephanandra tanakae

Cornus sanguinea 'Winter Beauty'
DOGWOOD

☼ ☀ ❄❄❄ ↕ 1.5m (5ft) ↔ 2m (6ft)

With regular pruning, this shrub produces winter stems that are a fiery orange-yellow at the base, shading to pink and red at the tips. Leaves turn golden yellow in autumn.

Corylus avellana 'Contorta'
CORKSCREW HAZEL

☼ ☀ ❄❄❄ ↕ 5m (15ft) ↔ 5m (15ft)

Charming lamb's tail catkins enliven the coiled and twisted shoots of this strong-growing shrub in late winter. Prune suckers out from stock as soon as they appear. ♔

OTHER COLOURED-STEMMED SHRUBS FOR WINTER EFFECT
Cornus alba 'Kesselringii'
Kerria japonica 'Pleniflora', see p.167
Leycesteria formosa, see p.232
Rosa sericea f. *pteracantha*
Rubus biflorus
Rubus thibetanus, see p.239
Salix alba subsp. *vitellina*
Salix alba subsp. *vitellina* 'Britzensis'
Salix fargesii, see p.217
Salix irrorata

Shrubs with Spines or Thorny Branches

FOR MANY GARDENERS, shrubs whose stems or branches are spiny or thorny have a positive security value as they can deter prowlers and other uninvited guests. Others find they are at best a nuisance, and at worst a danger. Whatever your attitude to plants that happen to be hostile to the touch, they undeniably include some very fine ornamental shrubs.

Rubus thibetanus
WHITE-STEMMED BRAMBLE
☼ ☀ ❄❄❄ ↕ 2.5m (8ft) ↔ 3m (10ft)

Clumps of thorny, bloomy-white, purple-barked winter stems become clothed with prettily divided, fern-like, silvery-hairy leaves. Small summer flowers are pink. ♔

OTHER SHRUBS WITH SPINES OR THORNY BRANCHES
Berberis pruinosa
Colletia hystrix
Colletia paradoxa
Paliurus spina-christi
Poncirus trifoliata
Pyracantha 'Mohave'
Rosa roxburghii
Rubus cockburnianus
Rubus ulmifolius 'Bellidiflorus'
Ulex europaeus 'Flore Pleno'

Berberis 'Goldilocks'
BARBERRY
☼ ☀ ❄❄❄ ↕ 4m (12ft) ↔ 4m (12ft)

The stems and arching branches of this bushy evergreen are viciously spiny. It has shiny, dark green, prickle-toothed leaves, and golden yellow flowers in spring.

Pyracantha 'Orange Glow'
FIRETHORN
☼ ☀ ❄❄❄ ↕ 4m (12ft) ↔ 4m (12ft)

This vigorous evergreen shrub has spiny branches, glossy green oblong leaves, clusters of white flowers in summer, and orange berries in autumn and winter. ♔

Rosa rubiginosa
SWEET BRIAR, EGLANTINE
☼ ❄❄❄ ↕ 2.5m (8ft) ↔ 2.5m (8ft)

The arching, thorny stems of this vigorous shrub are clothed in apple-scented leaves. It produces single pink flowers in summer, and small red hips in autumn.

Zanthoxylum piperitum
JAPAN PEPPER
☼ ☀ ❄❄❄ ↕ 2.5m (8ft) ↔ 2.5m (8ft)

The erect, ascending, spiny stems of this bushy shrub bear aromatic, glossy green leaves that become yellow in autumn. Red fruits in autumn contain peppery seeds.

Rabbit-proof Shrubs

SHRUBS THAT RABBITS IGNORE are surely all worthy of consideration, particularly by gardeners in rural areas. It may be the taste of the leaves and shoots, or their texture, that is unpalatable to rabbits, but whatever it is, such plants are extremely valuable where these furry creatures are a problem. It may be assumed that most other forms of the shrubs featured here, as well as their immediate relatives, are also rabbit-proof.

Hypericum kouytchense
SHRUBBY HYPERICUM
☼ ❄❄❄   ↕ 75cm (30in) ↔ 1.2m (4ft)

From summer into autumn, the arching stems of this mounded semi-evergreen carry numerous yellow flowers. These are followed by bronze-red seed capsules. ♉

Aucuba japonica
DOG LAUREL
☼ ◐ ☀ ❄❄❄   ↕ 2.5m (8ft) ↔ 2m (6ft)

Long, pointed, glossy, dark green leaves cover this dense evergreen. Female plants produce red berries when pollinated by a male. Several forms exist, some variegated.

Fuchsia 'Tom Thumb'
FUCHSIA
☼ ❄❄   ↕ 50cm (20in) ↔ 50cm (20in)

Dwarf and upright, this neat fuchsia has small, glossy green leaves, and showers of charming, pendent red and purple flowers, through summer and into early autumn. ♉

Kalmia angustifolia 'Rubra'
SHEEP LAUREL
☼ ❄❄❄❄ᴾᴴ   ↕ 45cm (18in) ↔ 1m (3ft)

Sheep Laurel forms a low, bushy mound of narrow evergreen leaves. It produces clusters of small, deep red flowers in early summer. Dislikes dry soils.

Buxus sempervirens 'Suffruticosa'
EDGING BOX
☼ ❄❄❄   ↕ 75cm (30in) ↔ 75cm (30in)

All forms of box are unpalatable to rabbits. This dense and compact cultivar has long been used as a low, evergreen edging to beds and borders, as well as in parterres. ♉

Gaultheria mucronata 'Mulberry Wine'
PERNETTYA
☼ ❄❄❄❄ᴾᴴ   ↕ 1m (3ft) ↔ 1m (3ft)

This low evergreen with pointed, leathery leaves on wiry branches, spreads in time. When pollinated by a male, large berries are borne from autumn through winter. ♉

Rhododendron 'Strawberry Ice'
EXBURY AZALEA
☼ ❄❄❄❄ᴾᴴ   ↕ 2.5m (8ft) ↔ 2.5m (8ft)

Showy clusters of yellow-throated, pale pink trumpet-flowers are carried in spring. The leaves of this bushy azalea may colour attractively before they fall in autumn. ♉

Sambucus nigra   'Aurea'
GOLDEN ELDER
☼ ✳✳✳   ↕4m (12ft) ↔4m (12ft)

This large, bushy shrub has golden yellow leaves, and bears flattened heads of tiny, fragrant white flowers in summer. Shining black berries follow in autumn.   ♈

Rosa Rosy Cushion ('Interall')
SHRUB ROSE
☼ ✳✳✳   ↕1m (3ft) ↔1.2m (4ft)

Glossy green foliage offsets clusters of scented pink flowers, with white centres, throughout summer. A strong-growing rose, this is low, dense, and spreading. ♈

DEER-PROOF SHRUBS
Berberis × *stenophylla*, see p.208
Buddleja 'Lochinch'
Hypericum forrestii
Mahonia × *media* 'Buckland', see p.237
Rhododendron 'Exquisitum'
Romneya coulteri, see p.197
Spiraea nipponica 'Snowmound', see p.191
Viburnum sargentii 'Onondaga', see p.181
Weigela 'Victoria'

Skimmia japonica
SKIMMIA
☼ ◐ ✳✳✳   ↕1.2m (4ft) ↔1.2m (4ft)

This bushy mound of aromatic evergreen leaves is dotted with white flower clusters in spring and, if both sexes are present, female plants then produce red berries.

Rosmarinus officinalis
ROSEMARY
☼ ✳✳   ↕1.5m (5ft) ↔1.5m (5ft)

Rosemary is a popular, aromatic evergreen bush. Small, purplish blue flowers clothe the branches all through summer, along with its narrow grey-green leaves.

Ruscus aculeatus
BUTCHER'S BROOM
◐ ◑ ✳✳✳   ↕75cm (30in) ↔1m (3ft)

Tough and adaptable, this evergreen shrub forms clumps of erect stems, crowded with spine-tipped leaves. When pollinated, the female plants produce long-lasting fruits.

OTHER RABBIT-PROOF SHRUBS
Ceanothus thyrsiflorus var. *repens*
Cornus sanguinea 'Winter Beauty', see p.238
Cotoneaster horizontalis
Daphne tangutica
Prunus laurocerasus 'Otto Luyken', see p.201
Spiraea japonica 'Anthony Waterer', see p.191
Vinca major 'Variegata', see p.201
Vinca minor, see p.185

SHRUBS

CONIFERS

ALL CONIFERS ARE EITHER trees or shrubs but, as is usual, I have chosen to treat them separately. They comprise a distinct and primitive group of woody plants and add an individual element to the garden. All but a few are evergreen. The deciduous kinds, specified in the descriptions, offer the interesting feature of autumn colour.

△ *Tsuga heterophylla*

△ DOMED SPECIMEN Chamaecyparis pisifera *'Filifera Aurea' makes an ideal golden yellow specimen for a larger lawn.*

Conifers are extremely versatile, due to their great variety in size, form, colour, and texture. You can use them for countless effects and situations. Many are of such noble proportions and elegance of form that they can make magnificent specimens for important positions.

DECORATIVE FOLIAGE
Conifer foliage tends to be either small and scale-like, as in cypress and *Thuja*, or long and needle-like, as in pine, spruce, and cedar. Junipers have needle-like or scale-like leaves and, in some cases, both. Yew, for example, has narrow, strap-shaped leaves, and many conifer cultivars have lovely mossy or soft, feathery juvenile foliage. Add to this all the shades of blue,

green, and yellow, as well as the interesting variegations, and it is obvious why conifers occupy such a special place among garden plants. Deciduous conifers such as larch, *Metasequoia*, and *Ginkgo* brighten the autumn with a final flash of gold or yellow before their leaves fall.

TOO BIG, TOO SOON
As with broad-leaved trees, consider the vigour, ultimate height and shape, and intended purpose of your chosen conifer. Some species used as hedging, for instance, grow rapidly and require regular pruning to achieve the best results. Do not plant fast-growing hedges if you cannot maintain them – there are numerous small- to medium-sized conifers for limited space.

THE BEAUTY OF CONIFERS

- Large conifers are linchpins, giving a feeling of permanence to a garden.
- Offer a wonderfully wide selection of shapes, colours, and textures.
- Contribute evergreen foliage effects, especially valuable in winter.
- Deciduous foliage changes seasonally.
- Dwarf and slow-growing conifers are ideal for rock gardens, patios, screes.
- Provide shelter in the garden when used as screens, hedges, windbreaks.

△ WINTER APPEAL *The rich reddish brown bark of deciduous* Metasequoia glyptostroboides *is impressive.*

◁ CONIFERS AND HEATHERS *This is an excellent example of the use of conifers with late winter-flowering ericas.*

▷ COLOUR AND TEXTURE *Just a few well-chosen conifers combine to create a colourful and extremely effective feature.*

Large Conifers

Some of the most spectacular large trees in the world are conifers. Given the evergreen nature of all but a small minority, they bring a sense of permanence and continuity to the large garden or estate. Most conifers are comparatively long-lived. They generally thrive best on deep, moist, but well-drained soils, although they are remarkably adaptable to most sites. A handful are tolerant of wet sites, but few will survive in completely waterlogged conditions.

CONIFERS

Abies nordmanniana
CAUCASIAN FIR
☼ ☀ ❄❄❄   ↕ 25m (80ft) ↔ 9m (28ft)

The spreading branches of this columnar to conical fir are packed with slender green leaves. Erect, greenish brown cones appear in summer on the upper branches. ♆

Araucaria araucana
CHILE PINE, MONKEY PUZZLE
☼ ❄❄❄   ↕ 18m (60ft) ↔ 12m (40ft)

When young, this tree is conical, and has whorled branches to ground level. Finally, it is mop-headed with a tall stem. Broad, sharp leaves densely clothe the branches.

Cedrus libani
CEDAR OF LEBANON
☼ ❄❄❄   ↕ 24m (78ft) ↔ 15m (50ft)

This conifer is a familiar sight in parks. Conical when young, it later assumes the typical flat-topped and tiered cedar-habit. Sharp leaves are green to blue-green. ♆

OTHER LARGE COLUMNAR OR NARROW, CONICAL CONIFERS

Abies grandis
Abies magnifica
Calocedrus decurrens
Cedrus atlantica 'Fastigiata'
Chamaecyparis lawsoniana 'Alumii'
Chamaecyparis lawsoniana 'Intertexta'
Chamaecyparis lawsoniana 'Wisselii',
   see p.248
x *Cupressocyparis leylandii*
   'Naylor's Blue'
Cupressus sempervirens
Metasequoia glyptostroboides, see p.252
Picea abies 'Cupressina'
Pinus strobus 'Fastigiata'
Taxodium distichum, see p. 253
Taxodium distichum var. *imbricatum*
   'Nutans', see p.251
Thuja plicata 'Atrovirens'

Cryptomeria japonica
JAPANESE RED CEDAR
☼ ☀ ❄❄❄   ↕ 20m (70ft) ↔ 7m (22ft)

The narrow leaves of this columnar to conical tree are arranged spirally on the shoots. Fibrous bark is reddish brown, and its small green cones mature to brown. ♆

Ginkgo biloba
MAIDENHAIR TREE
☼ ☀ ❄❄❄   ↕ 20m (70ft) ↔ 7m (22ft)

This distinctive deciduous conifer has an ancient pedigree. Conical when young, with rising branches, it later spreads. Fan-shaped leaves turn yellow in autumn. ♆

Picea abies
NORWAY SPRUCE
☼ ☼ ❄❄❄   ↕ 25m (80ft) ↔ 7m (22ft)

Norway Spruce, the traditional Christmas
tree, is conical at first, but broadens and
spreads with age. Its layered branches are
closely packed with dark green needles.

OTHER LARGE CONIFERS OF ULTIMATELY SPREADING HABIT

Cedrus atlantica f. *glauca*, see p.263
Cupressus macrocarpa, see p.254
Larix decidua
Larix × *marschlinsii*
Larix kaempferi
Larix kaempferi 'Blue Rabbit'
Larix × *pendula* 'Pendulina'
Picea sitchensis
Pinus ayacahuite
Pinus muricata, see p.255
Pinus nigra, see p.257
Pinus ponderosa
Pinus radiata, see p.257
Pinus × *schwerinii*
Pinus sylvestris
Pinus wallichiana
Pseudotsuga menziesii
Tsuga heterophylla, see p.253

Pinus jeffreyi
JEFFREY PINE
☼ ❄❄❄   ↕ 20m (70ft) ↔ 9m (28ft)

This robust, distinguished pine is conical
or rounded at first, then broad-columnar
later. Its fissured bark is dark grey-brown,
and its long needles are blue-green. ☑

Sequoia sempervirens
REDWOOD, COAST REDWOOD
☼ ☼ ❄❄❄   ↕ 30m (100ft) ↔ 8m (25ft)

Conical when it is young, this distinctive
conifer becomes columnar later. It has rich
red, fibrous, spongy bark, and its branches
are clothed with lush, yew-like foliage. ☑

Sequoiadendron giganteum
WELLINGTONIA, BIG TREE
☼ ❄❄❄   ↕ 30m (100ft) ↔ 11m (35ft)

Renowned worldwide for its longevity, this
species will form a tall column of down-
curved branches, clothed with blue-green
foliage. Bark is reddish brown. ☑

Wide-spreading and Vase-shaped Conifers

CONIFERS WITH ASCENDING or wide-spreading branches, ultimately wider than they are high, are numerous. They make excellent single specimens where a severe or formal line, such as the straight edge of a long border, needs to be broken or softened. Alternatively, consider them as a feature in a lawn, where their full spread can be admired.

Cupressus macrocarpa 'Gold Spread'
MONTEREY CYPRESS
☼ ✳✳✳   ↕ 1m (3ft) ↔ 2.5m (8ft)

This ornamental form of the Monterey Cypress is low and compact. Horizontal or slightly ascending branches are densely crowded with bright yellow foliage.

Juniperus × *pfitzeriana* 'Blue and Gold'
JUNIPER
☼ ✳✳✳   ↕ 1.5m (5ft) ↔ 1.5m (5ft)

The stems crowding the base of this fine juniper are packed with intense blue-grey foliage, scattered with sprays of creamy yellow. Whole shoots can be creamy yellow.

Juniperus × *pfitzeriana*
'Pfitzeriana Glauca'
☼ ✳✳✳   ↕ 2m (6ft) ↔ 4m (12ft)

'Pfitzeriana Glauca' is a strong-growing juniper of dense habit, whose ascending and spreading stems are densely crowded with prickly blue-grey foliage.

Juniperus chinensis
'Expansa Variegata'
☼ ✳✳✳   ↕ 75cm (30in) ↔ 2m (6ft)

Low and wide-spreading, this is a vigorous juniper with virtually horizontal branches, crowded by prickly, bluish green foliage, interspersed with creamy white sprays.

Juniperus × *pfitzeriana*
'Pfitzeriana Aurea'
☼ ✳✳✳   ↕ 2m (6ft) ↔ 4m (12ft)

The terminal shoots and closely packed foliage of this strong-growing juniper are suffused golden yellow in summer, and become yellowish green in winter.

Juniperus chinensis 'Plumosa Aurea'
JUNIPER
☼ ✳✳✳   ↕ 1.5m (5ft) ↔ 2m (6ft)

The many stems of this compact juniper are crowded with plume-like sprays, each crammed with yellow, scale-like foliage that turns bronze-gold in winter.

Juniperus virginiana 'Grey Owl'
JUNIPER

☀ ❄❄❄   ↕ 2.5m (8ft) ↔ 4m (12ft)

A handsome and strong-growing juniper,
its ascending branches are densely clothed
with soft, silvery grey foliage. A most
effective, and ultimately large, shrub. ♔

Juniperus squamata 'Blue Carpet'
JUNIPER

☀ ❄❄❄   ↕ 30cm (12in) ↔ 2m (6ft)

The wide-spreading stems of this vigorous
juniper form a large, low carpet of prickly
glaucous-blue foliage. It is one of the most
effective plants of its kind. ♔

Juniperus sabina 'Tamariscifolia'
JUNIPER

☀ ❄❄❄   ↕ 1m (3ft) ↔ 2m (6ft)

This effective and low-growing form of
the Savin juniper produces close-packed
layers of spreading branches, each densely
clothed in bright green, prickly leaves.

Taxus baccata 'Dovastonii Aurea'
YEW

☀ ☀ ❄❄❄   ↕ 5m (15ft) ↔ 6m (20ft)

This elegant shrub or small tree has tiers
of horizontal branches and long, sweeping
branchlets. Leaves on golden shoots have
bright yellow margins. Non-fruiting. ♔

CONIFERS

Columnar or Narrowly Conical Conifers

SLENDER OR NARROW CROWNS are great assets in conifers, allowing them to be planted in restricted spaces. Their generally compact nature means that they very rarely, if ever, need to be pruned, and their strong, vertical lines make them ideal for breaking or lifting otherwise low plantings, as well as providing a striking focal point.

Austrocedrus chilensis
CHILEAN CEDAR
☼ ✳✳✳   ↕ 12m (40ft) ↔ 3m (10ft)

The short, ascending branches of this uncommon, dense conifer are clothed in feathery sprays of green or blue-green, scale-like foliage. Small terminal cones.

OTHER COLUMNAR CONIFERS

Calocedrus decurrens
Cupressus sempervirens
  'Swane's Gold', see p.262
Juniperus chinensis 'Aurea'
Juniperus virginiana 'Glauca'
Sequoiadendron giganteum 'Glaucum'
Taxus baccata 'Standishii'
Thuja occidentalis 'Holmstrup'
Thuja occidentalis 'Malonyana'
Thuja occidentalis 'Spiralis'
Thuja plicata 'Collyer's Gold', see p.262

OTHER COLUMNAR CYPRESSES

Chamaecyparis lawsoniana
  'Alumii Magnificent'
C. lawsoniana 'Columnaris'
C. lawsoniana 'Elwoods' Pillar'
C. lawsoniana 'Fraseri'
C. lawsoniana 'Grayswood Pillar'
C. lawsoniana 'Green Pillar', see p.256
C. lawsoniana 'Hillieri'
C. lawsoniana 'Kilmacurragh'
C. lawsoniana 'Pottenii'
C. lawsoniana 'Winston Churchill'

Chamaecyparis lawsoniana 'Wisselii'
LAWSON CYPRESS
☼ ✳✳✳   ↕ 15m (50ft) ↔ 3m (10ft)

A distinctive form of Lawson cypress, this has erect, close-packed branches and blue-green foliage in three-dimensional sprays. Tiny cones in spring are brick-red. ♈

Cupressus sempervirens Stricta Group
ITALIAN CYPRESS
☼ ✳✳   ↕ 15m (50ft) ↔ 3m (10ft)

The grey-green, scale-like leaves that form this characteristic narrow column are held in erect sprays. Fairly large, shiny grey-brown cones ripen in their second year. ♈

Juniperus chinensis 'Keteleeri'
CHINESE JUNIPER
☼ ✳✳✳   ↕ 15m (50ft) ↔ 5m (15ft)

This columnar to narrowly conical tree of dense, compact habit has closely packed sprays of grey-green, scale-like foliage. Excellent and reliable for formal planting.

CONIFERS

Juniperus communis 'Hibernica'
IRISH JUNIPER
☼ ✱✱✱   ↕4m (12ft) ↔50cm (20in)

This popular, much-planted juniper forms
a slender column composed of crowded,
needle-like leaves. Each of these has a
silver line on its inside face. ♔

Pinus omorika
SERBIAN SPRUCE
☼ ☼ ✱✱✱   ↕18m (60ft) ↔5m (15ft)

The downswept branches of this spire-like
spruce arch at their tips, and are crowded
with narrow, dark green leaves. Clusters of
long purple cones mature to brown. ♔

Taxus baccata 'Fastigiata Robusta'
YEW
☼ ☼ ✱✱✱   ↕10m (30ft) ↔1.5m (5ft)

In habit, this yew is erect, columnar, and
eventually cigar-shaped, with ascending,
close-packed branches. Narrow, dark green
leaves are arranged all round the shoots.

Juniperus scopulorum 'Skyrocket'
JUNIPER
☼ ✱✱✱   ↕8m (25ft) ↔75cm (30in)

One of the narrowest of all conifers, this
is a tall, slender, columnar juniper with a
compact habit. Crowded sprays of blue-
grey, scale-like foliage pack the branches.

Pinus sylvestris Fastigiata Group
SCOTS PINE
☼ ✱✱✱   ↕6m (20ft) ↔1m (3ft)

This is a columnar form of the Scots pine.
The bark is reddish brown and its erect,
close-packed branches are clothed with
blue-green needles. Dislikes exposed sites.

Thuja occidentalis 'Smaragd'
AMERICAN ARBOR-VITAE
☼ ☼ ✱✱✱   ↕2.5m (8ft) ↔75cm (30in)

The branches of this dense, narrowly
conical conifer are clothed with flattened
sprays of rich green foliage, which has a
pleasant "fruity" scent when bruised. ♔

CONIFERS

249

Medium-sized Conifers

A WIDE SELECTION of conifers exists in the height range of 6–15m (20–50ft), including many wild species that have both botanical interest and ornamental merit. Even more abundant are the numerous cultivars of conifers such as the Lawson Cypress, Hinoki Cypress, and the various Thuja species. Any of these is worth considering in all but very small gardens. Most are winter hardy, but those that are less so will grow happily in milder areas or in a sheltered site.

Cupressus cashmeriana
KASHMIR CYPRESS
☼ ☼ ❄❄❄   ↕ 12m (40ft) ↔ 5.5m (18ft)

This beautiful conical tree, which spreads with age, is perfect for a sheltered site. Its blue-green foliage is carried in elegant, drooping sprays. Dislikes dry soils. ♔

Abies koreana
KOREAN FIR
☼ ☼ ❄❄❄   ↕ 10m (30ft) ↔ 5m (15ft)

The ascending or spreading branches of this broad, conical tree are densely clothed with dark green, silvery-backed needles. Even small plants bear violet-blue cones.

Chamaecyparis obtusa
'Tetragona Aurea'
☼ ❄❄❄   ↕ 10m (30ft) ↔ 5m (15ft)

Easily recognized and popular, this Hinoki cypress is bushy when young, becoming loosely conical. Moss-like sprays of yellow foliage clothe its angular branches. ♔

OTHER MEDIUM-SIZED CONIFERS

Athrotaxis laxifolia
Chamaecyparis lawsoniana 'Columnaris'
Chamaecyparis nootkatensis 'Pendula'
Cupressus arizonica 'Pyramidalis'
Juniperus chinensis 'Aurea'
Pinus parviflora
Pinus sylvestris Aurea Group, see p.262
Pseudolarix amabilis
Sciadopitys verticillata
Thuja occidentalis 'Spiralis'
Tsuga mertensiana

Chamaecyparis obtusa 'Crippsii'
HINOKI CYPRESS
☼ ❄❄❄   ↕ 10m (30ft) ↔ 5m (15ft)

This popular, colourful, loosely conical conifer has bright golden, aromatic foliage borne in large, flattened sprays. Rounded cones are brown. Dislikes dry soils. ♔

Cunninghamia lanceolata
CHINA FIR
☼ ☼ ❄❄❄❄   ↕ 13m (43ft) ↔ 5m (15ft)

The branches of this columnar conifer are all lined with two rows of narrow, glossy green leaves, silvery beneath, and sharp. Does not like exposed sites, or dry soils.

Fitzroya cupressoides
ALERCE
☼ ❄❄❄   ↕ 10m (30ft) ↔ 5m (15ft)

Columnar when young, this bushy, juniper-like tree becomes more lax in habit later. It has peeling, reddish brown bark and sprays of white-banded, scale-like leaves.

Taxodium distichum var. *imbricatum*
'Nutans'
☀ ❋❋❋ ↕ 15m (50ft) ↔ 5m (15ft)

Pond Cypress is a deciduous, columnar
tree. Its ascending branches are crowded
above with slender sprays of bright green
foliage. Ideal in deep or moist soils. ♖

Pinus aristata
BRISTLECONE PINE
☀ ❋❋❋ ↕ 8m (25ft) ↔ 5m (15ft)

Suitable for any but the smallest gardens,
this slow-growing, dense, bushy pine has
branches crowded with dark blue-green,
white-flecked needles. Cones are whiskery.

Picea breweriana
BREWER SPRUCE
☀ ☀ ❋❋❋ ↕ 12m (40ft) ↔ 6m (20ft)

This is one of the most distinctive of the
spruces. Its spreading branches support
long, pendulous branchlets, clothed with
narrow leaves. Cylindrical brown cones. ♖

Podocarpus salignus
PODOCARPUS
☀ ❋❋ ↕ 10m (30ft) ↔ 6m (20ft)

A most attractive columnar tree (broadly
conical later), this podocarpus has stringy,
reddish brown bark and narrow, shiny,
willow-like leaves. Dislikes dry soils. ♖

Tsuga canadensis
EASTERN HEMLOCK
☀ ☀ ❋❋❋ ↕ 15m (50ft) ↔ 10m (30ft)

This multi-stemmed tree has pendent or
arching sprays of small, dark green, silver-
backed leaves. Cones are freely borne and
ripen to brown. Dislikes dry soils.

C O N I F E R S

251

Conifers for Heavy Clay Soil

A LARGE NUMBER OF CONIFERS will grow in heavy clay soil, providing it is not always waterlogged. They encompass an extremely wide selection of sizes and shapes, and have foliage of great variety, both in colour and texture. These are hardy, easy to grow, and evergreen unless specified deciduous.

Cryptomeria japonica
'Elegans Compacta'

☼ ❆❆❆   ↕ 3m (10ft) ↔ 2m (6ft)

This is a dense, billowy, bushy form of the Japanese Red Cedar. The fresh green foliage is soft to touch, and turns a rich reddish bronze colour in winter. ♗

Pinus heldreichii
BOSNIAN PINE

☼ ❆❆❆   ↕ 18m (60ft) ↔ 9m (28ft)

A handsome tree of dense, conical habit, this pine broadens as it ages. Its special features include rich green needles, white hairy buds, and cobalt-blue cones. ♗

Pinus peuce
MACEDONIAN PINE

☼ ❆❆❆   ↕ 18m (60ft) ↔ 6m (20ft)

Worth growing where space is available, this impressive pine has densely crowded grey-green needles and pendent, curved and cylindrical, resin-flecked cones.

OTHER EVERGREEN CONIFERS FOR HEAVY CLAY SOIL

Abies koreana, see p.150
Chamaecyparis lawsoniana
  'Triomf van Boskoop'
Picea likiangensis
Picea purpurea
Pinus aristata, see p.251
Pinus coulteri
Pinus ponderosa
Saxegothaea conspicua
Thuja plicata, see p.257

Metasequoia glyptostroboides
DAWN REDWOOD

☼ ☼ ❆❆❆   ↕ 20m (70ft) ↔ 5m (15ft)

The feathery leaves of this magnificent deciduous conifer turn tawny pink in autumn. An ancient and vigorous tree, it is narrowly conical to columnar. ♗

Pinus mugo 'Mops'
MOUNTAIN PINE

☼ ❆❆❆   ↕ 1m (3ft) ↔ 1.2m (4ft)

This dwarf mountain pine in time forms a compact mound of dark green needles. Ideal for a large rock garden, or a big pot, but it is slow-growing. ♗

Pinus strobus
WEYMOUTH PINE

☼ ❆❆❆   ↕ 20m (70ft) ↔ 9m (28ft)

A well-known conical pine, this broadens with age. Open branches bear slender grey-green needles and pendulous cones. Will not tolerate air pollution.

Pinus thunbergii
JAPANESE BLACK PINE
☼ ❄❄❄   ↕13m (43ft) ↔8m (25ft)

Its dark green needles and hairy silvery buds distinguish this easy-to-grow pine. Conical when young, and broadening with age, this makes an excellent coastal tree.

Taxodium distichum
SWAMP CYPRESS
☼ ❄❄❄   ↕20m (70ft) ↔9m (28ft)

This attractive deciduous, conical conifer is excellent for a damp site. It has fibrous, reddish brown bark and feathery green leaves that turn gold in autumn. ♛

Thuja koraiensis
KOREAN ARBOR-VITAE
☼ ❄❄❄   ↕7m (22ft) ↔3m (10ft)

Loose and slow-growing, this columnar conifer has broad sprays of bright green, scaly foliage, silver-white beneath. When bruised, the foliage smells of almonds.

OTHER DECIDUOUS CONIFERS
FOR HEAVY CLAY SOILS

Ginkgo biloba, see p.244
Larix decidua
Taxodium distichum var. *imbricatum*
  'Nutans', see p.251

Taxus baccata Aurea Group
GOLDEN YEW
☼ ◐ ❄❄❄   ↕5m (15ft) ↔3m (10ft)

The leaves of this striking golden form of the Common Yew become green in their second year. Trim it annually to obtain a neat, conical habit, as seen here.

Tsuga heterophylla
WESTERN HEMLOCK
☼ ◐ ❄❄❄❄↓ᴾᴴ   ↕20m (70ft) ↔10m (30ft)

Slender branches, crowded with green, silver-backed needles and drooping at the tips, form graceful layers. This fast-growing conical conifer has small cones. ♛

Conifers for Dry, Sunny Sites

Many conifers are native to warm, dry regions of the world, and a good number of these are readily available for planting in gardens where warm, dry summers are a regular feature. Some are vigorous, and soon create shade; others are slow-growing. All are evergreen, and best planted when small to give them the best chance of establishing.

Pinus cembroides
MEXICAN PINYON
☼ ❄❄❄   ↕ 6m (20ft) ↔ 5m (15ft)

This unusual and attractive, slow-growing pine is bushy and conical when young, becoming rounded with age. Stout, stiff grey-green needles crowd its branches.

OTHER PINES FOR DRY, SUNNY SITES

Pinus aristata, see p.251
Pinus armandii
Pinus brutia var. *eldarica*
Pinus bungeana
Pinus contorta
Pinus coulteri
Pinus edulis
Pinus pinaster
Pinus sylvestris
Pinus yunnanensis

Cedrus deodara
DEODAR
☼ ❄❄❄   ↕ 25m (80ft) ↔ 12m (40ft)

A handsome, vigorous conifer, this has long, drooping branches when young, and ultimately assumes a typical flat-topped cedar shape, with layered branches. ▽

Juniperus drupacea
SYRIAN JUNIPER
☼ ❄❄❄   ↕ 12m (40ft) ↔ 1.5m (5ft)

Distinctive and very easily recognized, this juniper of close columnar habit is superb as a specimen in the lawn or in a border. It has bright green, needle-like leaves.

Cupressus macrocarpa
MONTEREY CYPRESS
☼ ❄❄❄   ↕ 20m (70ft) ↔ 22m (76ft)

This popular, fast-growing conifer, with its sprays of feathery green foliage, is often grown in coastal areas as a screen. When young it is columnar, but spreads with age.

Juniperus rigida
TEMPLE JUNIPER
☼ ❄❄❄   ↕ 8m (25ft) ↔ 5m (15ft)

Loosely branched, and often sprawling, this tree or large bush has drooping sprays of needle-like green leaves that become bronze in winter, and peeling bark.

Pinus halepensis
ALEPPO PINE
☼ ❄❄❄   ↕ 14m (46ft) ↔ 6m (20ft)

Excellent for growing in sandy soils, this pine rounds with age. Needles on juvenile trees are blue-green; bright green on older trees. Egg-shaped cones are glossy orange.

C O N I F E R S

Pinus muricata
BISHOP PINE
☼ ❄❄❄❄▽ PH ‡ 18m (60ft) ↔ 9m (28ft)

This tough and adaptable, fast-growing
pine is columnar at first, broadening and
often becoming flat-topped later. It is very
good on poor, or lime-free, sandy soils. ♔

Pinus pinea
STONE PINE, UMBRELLA PINE
☼ ❄❄❄ ‡ 12m (40ft) ↔ 10m (30ft)

Conical when young, Stone Pine gradually
develops its characteristic head of packed,
radiating branches. Mature trees have dark
green foliage, juveniles have blue-green. ♔

Pinus virginiana
SCRUB PINE, VIRGINIA PINE
☼ ❄❄❄❄ PH ‡ 14m (46ft) ↔ 9m (28ft)

Loose and often untidy, this is a pine with
densely crowded grey to yellow-grey
needles on pinkish white shoots. It bears
small, prickly orange-brown winter cones.

Taxus cuspidata
JAPANESE YEW
☼ ☼ ☀ ❄❄❄ ‡ 5m (15ft) ↔ 5m (15ft)

This multi-branched shrub opens out and
spreads with age. Yellowish green leaves,
sometimes red-brown in winter, clothe its
branches. Female plants bear red fruits.

Torreya californica
CALIFORNIAN NUTMEG
☼ ❄❄ ‡ 18m (60ft) ↔ 8m (25ft)

An impressive, upright conifer, this has
whorled branches and long, narrow, spine-
tipped leaves. If pollinated, female trees
produce pendent, olive-like fruits.

> ### OTHER CONIFERS FOR DRY, SUNNY SITES
>
> *Abies bracteata*
> *Abies concolor*
> *Abies pinsapo*
> *Abies pinsapo* 'Glauca'
> *Abies vejarii*
> *Cupressus arizonica*
> *Cupressus arizonica* 'Pyramidalis'
> *Cupressus duclouxiana*
> *Cupressus lusitanica*
> *Cupressus sempervirens*
> *Juniperus chinensis*
> *Juniperus deppeana* 'Silver Spire'
> *Juniperus formosana*
> *Juniperus oxycedrus*
> *Juniperus virginiana*
> *Picea likiangensis*
> *Picea purpurea*
> *Tsuga heterophylla*, see p.253

CONIFERS

Conifers for Hedges, Windbreaks, or Screening

OTHER CONIFERS FOR HEDGES
AND SCREENING

Chamaecyparis lawsoniana 'Blue Jacket'
Chamaecyparis lawsoniana 'Fraseri'
Chamaecyparis lawsoniana
   'Golden Wonder'
Chamaecyparis lawsoniana
   'Pembury Blue', see p.263
x *Cupressocyparis leylandii* 'Gold Rider'
Thuja occidentalis 'Europa Gold'
Thuja plicata 'Atrovirens'
Tsuga heterophylla, see p.253

CONIFERS ARE SUPERB subjects for hedging and screens as most are evergreen, and provide an attractive permanent effect once established. The filtering effect on winds, and subsequent benefit to plants they are sheltering, has also long been recognized. Most conifers used for formal hedges or screening are ultimately big and need regular trimming.

Chamaecyparis lawsoniana 'Green Hedger'

☼ ✳✳✳   ↕ 15m (50ft) ↔ 6m (20ft)

Well clothed down to its base with sprays of rich green foliage, this is one of the best cypresses for screening. It is conical as a single specimen. Dislikes dry soils. ♔

Chamaecyparis lawsoniana 'Green Pillar'

☼ ✳✳✳   ↕ 15m (50ft) ↔ 3m (10ft)

Good for screens or hedges, this columnar cypress is moderately sized, and requires little clipping. Its vertical sprays of green foliage are gold-tinged in early spring.

x Cupressocyparis leylandii LEYLAND CYPRESS

☼ ✳✳✳   ↕ 24m (78ft) ↔ 5.5m (18ft)

One of the fastest growing of all conifers – too fast for many gardens – this is ideal as a temporary screen or tall hedge. Its foliage is dark green or grey-green.

x Cupressocyparis leylandii 'Castlewellan'

☼ ✳✳✳   ↕ 25m (80ft) ↔ 5.5m (18ft)

'Castlewellan' is commonly planted as a hedge or screen. It grows rapidly but can be cut back hard. Densely packed bronze-yellow foliage is golden on young plants.

Picea asperata CHINESE SPRUCE

☼ ✳✳✳   ↕ 15m (50ft) ↔ 10m (30ft)

The yellow-brown shoots of this tough, conical spruce are all crowded with blue-grey, needle-like foliage. Adaptable to most soils, it makes a useful windbreak.

CONIFERS

Pinus nigra
AUSTRIAN PINE

☼ ❄❄❄   ↕ 25m (80ft) ↔ 20m (70ft)

This tough, rugged, ultimately large tree is excellent as a windbreak for exposed sites. It has a domed crown and spreading branches. Dislikes dry soils. ♛

Taxus baccata
YEW

☼ ☼ ☀ ❄❄❄   ↕ 12m (40ft) ↔ 10m (30ft)

Yew, with its narrow, blackish green leaves, is popular for hedging. Regular clipping will encourage a dense habit, which is particularly effective in topiary. ♛

Taxus × media 'Hicksii'
HICK'S YEW

☼ ☼ ☀ ❄❄❄   ↕ 6m (20ft) ↔ 2m (6ft)

Tough, adaptable, and slow-growing, this yew is very good for screening or hedging. Columnar when young, it matures to vase-shaped. Bears red fruit if pollinated. ♛

OTHER CONIFERS FOR WINDBREAKS

Cupressus macrocarpa, see p.254
Larix decidua
Larix kaempferi
Picea sitchensis
Pinus cembra
Pinus contorta
Pinus contorta var. *latifolia*
Pinus heldreichii, see p.252
Pinus sylvestris
Pinus thunbergii, see p.253
Sequoiadendron giganteum, see p.245

Pinus radiata
MONTEREY PINE

☼ ❄❄❄❄ PH   ↕ 25m (80ft) ↔ 20m (70ft)

An impressive, large pine for shelter on exposed sites, except in cold inland areas, this has bold bunches of green needles, and attractive male cones in spring. ♛

CONIFERS FOR SMALL HEDGES

Chamaecyparis lawsoniana 'Globosa'
Chamaecyparis thyoides 'Ericoides'
Cryptomeria japonica 'Elegans Nana'
Platycladus orientalis 'Rosedalis'
Thuja occidentalis 'Sunkist'

Thuja plicata
WESTERN RED CEDAR

☼ ☼ ❄❄❄   ↕ 25m (80ft) ↔ 8m (25ft)

This handsome, conical conifer makes a first-rate hedge or screen, with its close-packed sprays of glossy, scale-like foliage that smells of pineapple when bruised.

C O N I F E R S

257

Slow-growing or Dwarf Conifers

SLOW-GROWING CONIFERS, or those with a naturally dwarf habit, are ideal for small gardens, rock gardens, raised beds, or containers. Most are mutations of a normal-sized tree and are propagated by grafting onto seedling stock. Few other hardy, woody plants offer such a range of shape, form, and colour, all year round.

Chamaecyparis lawsoniana 'Gnome'
DWARF CYPRESS
☼ ❄❄❄   ↕30cm (12in) ↔ 30cm (12in)

Dense, slow-growing form of the Lawson Cypress, this has flat sprays of scale-like foliage. Occasional tufts of coarse growth should be cut away to maintain shape.

Abies balsamea 'Nana'
DWARF FIR
☼ ❄❄❄   ↕50cm (20in) ↔ 75cm (30in)

This low-domed form of the Balsam Fir is dense and compact. The short, spreading, glossy green leaves have two greyish bands beneath, and crowd the branchlets.

Abies nordmanniana
'Golden Spreader'
☼ ❄❄❄   ↕45cm (18in) ↔ 1.2m (4ft)

This form of the Caucasian Fir is low-spreading and flat-topped. The crowded leaves are yellow above, yellowish-white beneath, and golden yellow in winter. ♔

OTHER DWARF CONIFERS OF ROUNDED OR DOMED HABIT

Picea abies 'Gregoryana'
Pinus mugo 'Ophir'
Pinus strobus 'Minima'
Pinus sylvestris 'Beuvronensis'
Pinus wallichiana 'Umbraculifera'
Platycladus orientalis 'Meldensis'
Thuja occidentalis 'Sunkist'
Thuja occidentalis 'Tiny Tim'
Thujopsis dolabrata 'Nana'
Tsuga canadensis 'Jeddeloh'

Abies concolor 'Compacta'
DWARF FIR
☼ ❄❄❄   ↕1.1m (3½ft) ↔ 1.3m (4½ft)

Ideal for larger rock gardens, this is a handsome, compact form of the Colorado Fir. Its habit is irregular, with branches of narrow, spreading, greyish blue leaves. ♔

Cedrus libani 'Sargentii'
DWARF CEDAR
☼ ❄❄❄   ↕75cm (30in) ↔ 2.5m (8ft)

This splendid, low-domed form of the Cedar of Lebanon has long, weeping branches, with needle-like blue-green leaves. Train the main stem to give height.

Chamaecyparis obtusa 'Nana Aurea'
DWARF CYPRESS
☼ ❄❄❄   ↕1.3m (4½ft) ↔ 65cm (26in)

An excellent golden dwarf conifer for general cultivation, this slow-growing, conical form of the Hinoki Cypress has fan-shaped sprays of scale-like foliage. ♔

CONIFERS

Juniperus squamata 'Blue Star'
DWARF JUNIPER

☼ ❄❄❄   ↕ 45cm (18in) ↔ 50cm (20in)

The branches of this slow-growing juniper of squat habit are densely crowded with needle-like, silvery blue leaves. A most satisfactory blue-grey dwarf conifer. ♈

Picea pungens 'Montgomery'
DWARF SPRUCE

☼ ❄❄❄   ↕ 1.1m (3½ft) ↔ 1.1m (3½ft)

This reliable, dome-shaped form of the Colorado Spruce is ideal for larger rock gardens or as a specimen. Sharp, pointed greyish needles crowd its branches.

Pinus heldreichii 'Schmidtii'
DWARF PINE

☼ ❄❄❄   ↕ 1m (3ft) ↔ 75cm (30in)

A slow-growing form of the Bosnian Pine that forms a globular or conical bush, this is compact in habit. Its short branches are crowded with needle-like green leaves. ♈

OTHER DWARF CONIFERS OF COLUMNAR OR CONICAL HABIT

Abies lasiocarpa 'Compacta'
Chamaecyparis lawsoniana 'Ellwood's Gold'
× *Cupressocyparis leylandii* 'Hyde Hall'
Juniperus communis 'Compressa'
Juniperus communis 'Sentinel'
Picea glauca 'Alberta Blue'
Picea glauca var. *albertiana* 'Laurin'
Pinus parviflora 'Negishi'
Thuja plicata 'Rogersii'

Picea glauca var. *albertiana* 'Conica'
DWARF SPRUCE

☼ ❄❄❄   ↕ 1.3m (4½ft) ↔ 60cm (24in)

This popular form of the Alberta White Spruce develops a tight, conical habit if stray side shoots are removed. Needle-like green leaves crowd the branchlets.

OTHER SLOW OR DWARF CONIFERS

Chamaecyparis obtusa 'Caespitosa'
Chamaecyparis obtusa 'Rigid Dwarf'
Cryptomeria japonica 'Vilmoriniana'
Picea glauca var. *albertiana* 'Alberta Globe'
Platycladus orientalis 'Elegantissima'

Thuja plicata 'Stoneham Gold'
DWARF RED CEDAR

☼ ❄❄❄   ↕ 1.7m (5½ft) ↔ 75cm (30in)

A choice form of the Western Red Cedar, developing a conical habit. The aromatic, scale-like leaves are borne in flat sprays and become darker as they mature. ♈

C O N I F E R S

Conifers for Ground Cover

A RANGE OF MUTATIONS from taller growing conifers is available, in addition to the many conifers, including several junipers, of naturally creeping or trailing habit. These are grafted or, in some cases, grown from cuttings, and spread low over the ground to form a dense, carpet-like cover. Found in several colours, their foliage may also vary in arrangement and shape. Where space permits, plant several together to create a striking tapestry effect.

Picea abies 'Reflexa'
NORWAY SPRUCE
☼ ❄❄❄   ↕ 45cm (18in) ↔ 5m (15ft)

The branches of this unusual, irregular, low-growing form of the Norway Spruce are long, prostrate, and crowded in green needle-like leaves that form a dense mat.

Juniperus communis 'Green Carpet'
JUNIPER
☼ ❄❄❄   ↕ 12cm (5in) ↔ 1.2m (4ft)

This prostrate juniper makes an excellent ground cover, and blends well with others of its kind. Its branches are crowded with prickly, needle-like, bright green leaves. ♈

Juniperus procumbens 'Nana'
CREEPING JUNIPER
☼ ❄❄❄   ↕ 30cm (12in) ↔ 2m (6ft)

Slightly raised mats or carpets, are formed by the tightly packed, prostrate branches of this dwarf juniper. Bristly blue-green leaves crowd its shoots. ♈

OTHER CONIFERS FOR GROUND COVER

Juniperus horizontalis 'Blue Chip'
Juniperus horizontalis 'Jade River'
Juniperus horizontalis
   'Turquoise Spreader'
Picea abies 'Repens'
Picea pungens 'Procumbens'
Taxus baccata 'Cavendishii'
Taxus baccata 'Repandens'
Taxus baccata
   'Summergold'

Juniperus horizontalis 'Plumosa'
CREEPING JUNIPER
☼ ❄❄❄   ↕ 15cm (6in) ↔ 2m (6ft)

Seen here next to *J. horizontalis* 'Glauca', with which it combines well, this reliable ground cover has sprays of grey-green foliage, turning bronze-purple in winter. ♈

Microbiota decussata
MICROBIOTA
☼ ☀ ❄❄❄   ↕ 30cm (12in) ↔ 2m (6ft)

The arching, spray-like branches of this low-growing, wide-spreading conifer are densely clothed with bright green, scale-like leaves, turning bronze in winter. ♈

Taxus baccata
'Repens Aurea'
☼ ☀ ❄❄❄   ↕ 45cm (18in) ↔ 2m (6ft)

Short, overlapping branchlets, crowded with yellow-margined leaves, dark green in shade, fill the long branches of this low-spreading form of the Common Yew. ♈

Variegated Conifers

THE VARIEGATION IN CONIFERS usually takes the form of white or yellow sprays scattered in otherwise green foliage. Occasionally, however, the additional colour is banded, such as in *Thuja plicata* 'Zebrina' (*see right*), or the overall effect may appear speckled. These variegations may not appeal to all gardeners, but they can provide a pleasing contrast to greens, especially in winter. Such conifers also make interesting single specimens for the lawn.

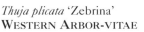

Thuja plicata 'Zebrina'
WESTERN ARBOR-VITAE
☼ ❄❄❄   ↕ 20m (70ft) ↔ 12m (40ft)

A striking conical conifer, this is easily recognised by the dark green sprays of pineapple-scented foliage, boldly banded cream-yellow, and its reddish, fibrous bark.

OTHER VARIEGATED CONIFERS

Chamaecyparis lawsoniana 'Argenteovariegata'
Chamaecyparis lawsoniana 'Ellwood's White'
Chamaecyparis lawsoniana 'Fletcher's White'
Chamaecyparissus nootkatensis 'Aureovariegata'
Juniperus × *pfitzeriana* 'Kuriwao Gold'
Pinus mugo 'Pal Maleter'
Thuja plicata 'Irish Gold'

Calocedrus decurrens 'Aureovariegata'
INCENSE CEDAR
☼ ❄❄❄   ↕ 12m (40ft) ↔ 3m (10ft)

The short, spreading branches of this slow-growing cedar are covered by sprays of aromatic green foliage, interspersed with yellow sprigs.

× *Cupressocyparis leylandii* 'Harlequin'
VARIEGATED LEYLAND CYPRESS
☼ ❄❄❄   ↕ 20m (70ft) ↔ 6m (20ft)

This variegated cultivar is just as easy and vigorous as the species, but its packed, plume-like, grey-green foliage is relieved by scattered, creamy white sprays.

Chamaecyparis nootkatensis 'Variegata'
VARIEGATED NOOTKA CYPRESS
☼ ❄❄❄   ↕ 15m (50ft) ↔ 6m (20ft)

Pendulous sprays of pungent green foliage are coarse to the touch, and interspersed with creamy white sprays. Nootka Cypress is loosely conical and dislikes dry soils.

Juniperus chinensis 'Variegated Kaizuka'
☼ ❄❄❄   ↕ 3m (10ft) ↔ 2m (6ft)

The protruding branches of this distinctly angular, slow-growing juniper are crowded with bright green, almost mossy foliage, marked with patches of creamy white.

Thujopsis dolabrata 'Variegata'
VARIEGATED HIBA
☼ ❄❄❄   ↕ 10m (30ft) ↔ 6m (20ft)

Broad, flattened sprays of aromatic green foliage have silvery marks beneath, and random sprays are splashed creamy white. It is slow-growing, disliking dry soils. ♈

Conifers with Golden or Yellow Foliage

A WIDE VARIETY of conifers with golden or yellow foliage is available for both the large or small garden. In some cases, only the growing tips show yellow; in others, the entire foliage retains this cheerful colour throughout the year, adding a warm glow to the garden during the drab winter months. All those illustrated here are reliable.

OTHER MEDIUM-SIZED TO LARGE CONIFERS WITH GOLDEN FOLIAGE

Cedrus deodara 'Aurea'
Chamaecyparis lawsoniana 'Lanei Aurea'
Chamaecyparis lawsoniana 'Lutea'
Chamaecyparis obtusa 'Crippsii', see p.250
Chamaecyparis obtusa 'Goldilocks'
Juniperus chinensis 'Aurea'
Picea orientalis 'Skylands'
Thuja plicata 'Aurea'
Thuja plicata 'Irish Gold'

Chamaecyparis pisifera 'Filifera Aurea'
SAWARA CYPRESS
☼ ❄❄❄   ↕ 12m (40ft) ↔ 5m (15ft)

This dense, conical or mounded conifer produces numerous long, thread-like branches clothed with tiny, bright yellow leaves. It only slowly increases in size. ♟

Cupressus macrocarpa 'Goldcrest'
MONTEREY CYPRESS
☼ ❄❄   ↕ 10m (30ft) ↔ 3m (10ft)

Still one of the best of its colour, this is a vigorous, columnar or slender, conical tree. It is dense and compact, with crowded, plume-like foliage. Avoid clipping. ♟

Cupressus sempervirens
'Swane's Gold'
☼ ❄❄❄   ↕ 10m (30ft) ↔ 60cm (24in)

For very small gardens, this is probably the best conifer of its shape and colour. It forms a tall, slender column of golden-tinged foliage in dense, crowded sprays. ♟

OTHER SMALL OR SLOW-GROWING CONIFERS WITH GOLDEN FOLIAGE

Cedrus deodara 'Golden Horizon'
Cryptomeria japonica 'Cristata'
Cupressus macrocarpa 'Gold Spread', see p.246
Juniperus communis 'Gold Cone'
Pinus contorta 'Frisian Gold'
Pinus sylvestris 'Moseri', in winter
Thuja occidentalis 'Golden Globe'
Thuja occidentalis 'Trompenburg'
Thuja plicata 'Stoneham Gold', see p.259

Pinus sylvestris Aurea Group
GOLDEN SCOTS PINE
☼ ❄❄❄   ↕ 12m (40ft) ↔ 5m (15ft)

The normally blue-green needles of this slow-growing, broad, columnar tree turn a rich yellow from winter into spring. The colder the winter, the richer the colour. ♟

Thuja plicata 'Collyer's Gold'
WESTERN RED CEDAR
☼ ❄❄❄   ↕ 2m (6ft) ↔ 1m (3ft)

This is a slow-growing conifer of compact, dense, dome-shaped or conical habit. Its crowded sprays of foliage emerge a rich golden yellow colour, and turn light green.

CONIFERS

Conifers with Silver or Blue-grey foliage

WHEN SEEN AGAINST a darker background, blue-grey or silvery conifers have a striking effect in the garden. The Blue Atlas Cedar and the Colorado Spruce, or Blue Spruce, are perhaps the two most well known in general cultivation but, happily, there are many others of similar effect and equal merit, some suitable for small gardens.

Picea glauca 'Coerulea'
WHITE SPRUCE

☼ ✳✳✳　　　↕ 13m (43ft) ↔ 6m (20ft)

This vigorous, conical spruce has branches that are ascending at first, and spread with age. They are crowded with short blue-grey to silver needles. Dislikes dry soils.

Abies concolor 'Candicans'
COLORADO WHITE FIR

☼ ✳✳✳　　　↕ 20m (70ft) ↔ 7m (22ft)

The branches of this handsome conical conifer are clothed with spreading, needle-like leaves, coloured a striking silver-white or blue grey. Dislikes dry soils. ♔

Chamaecyparis lawsoniana
'Pembury Blue'

☼ ✳✳✳　　　↕ 15m (50ft) ↔ 6m (20ft)

An excellent blue-grey cypress, 'Pembury Blue' is a conical tree, bearing numerous sprays of scale-like foliage on its loosely arching branches. Dislikes dry soils. ♔

OTHER CONIFERS WITH SILVER OR BLUE-GREY FOLIAGE
Cedrus deodora 'Karl Fuchs'
Chamaecyparis lawsoniana 'Chilworth Silver'
Chamaecyparis lawsoniana 'Pelt's Blue'
Cupressus arizonica var. *glabra* 'Blue Ice'
Cupressus arizonica 'Pyramidalis'
Picea pungens 'Fat Albert'
Pinus pumila 'Glauca'
Pinus sylvestris 'Bonna'
Pinus wallichiana 'Nana'

Cedrus atlantica f. *glauca*
BLUE ATLAS CEDAR

☼ ✳✳✳　　　↕ 24m (78ft) ↔ 15m (50ft)

This spectacular conifer is recognizable by its fast growth when young, its wide-spreading habit, barrel-shaped cones, and silver-blue needles. Dislikes dry soils. ♔

Juniperus sabina 'Blaue Donau'
SAVIN

☼ ✳✳✳　　　↕ 25cm (10in) ↔ 1.5m (5ft)

Its low, wide-spreading habit makes this a most effective conifer for the rock garden or scree. Branches have ascending tips and are crowded with light blue-grey foliage.

Picea pungens 'Koster'
COLORADO, OR BLUE, SPRUCE

☼ ✳✳✳　　　↕ 13m (43ft) ↔ 5m (15ft)

A striking spruce, this is one of several similar selections. It has scaly grey bark, whorled branches, and prickly, needle-like, silver-blue fading to green leaves. ♔

263

TREES

I BELIEVE THAT ALL PLANTS, no matter how small, are important but, I confess, trees are to me the most inspirational. This is partly due to their size, but more significant is the sense of continuity and permanence that they bring to the garden; to plant a tree, particularly a potentially large or long-lived one, is to express a belief in the future.

△ *Quercus canariensis*

△ CRAB-APPLE CHEER *The cherry-like crab apples of* Malus × robusta *'Red Sentinel' last well into winter.*

THE BEAUTY OF TREES

- Provide a framework or backbone to the garden to tie in other plants.
- Large trees give permanence and continuity to the garden.
- Give shade for plants and people.
- Deciduous trees change seasonally.
- Offer a variety of shapes and sizes.
- Some make excellent specimens.
- Offer protection from the elements, pollution, noise, and prying eyes.
- Give food and/or shelter for wildlife.

Trees are the linchpins in many gardens, holding together diverse design elements. They can offer a seasonal display of flowers, fruit, or foliage, or an attractive habit, as well as provide a useful focal point for one's neighbours. The mountain ash *(Sorbus)*, thorn *(Crataegus)*, and ornamental crab apple *(Malus)* are examples that boast several of these attractive features.

ANNUAL ANTICIPATION
In cooler temperate climates, the number and variety of deciduous trees far exceeds their evergreen counterparts. Evergreen trees do, however, provide an excellent foil, often being used as background trees, screens, or windbreaks, though they should be considered for prime sites where conditions suit. The miracle of renewal – bud flush, flowering, fruiting, and leaf fall – that deciduous trees annually enact, is something we never tire of. All the trees in this section are deciduous unless otherwise stated.

BIG IS NOT ALWAYS BETTER
Trees vary in height and shape, providing plenty of candidates for every type and size of garden. Small trees need not be confined to small gardens, while a single large tree in place of several small ones can provide a welcome focus for all nearby. Whatever your priorities, available space should always be paramount. Large trees need space to develop; it is foolhardy to plant one where space is limited.

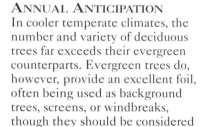

△ GLORIOUS GOLD *Popular and very reliable, golden* Robinia pseudoacacia *'Frisia' brightens dull corners in summer.*

◁ DUAL DELIGHT Amelanchier lamarckii's *lovely snow white spring blossom is matched by its autumn tints.*

▷ NOBLE AUTUMN SPECIMEN *This Tulip Tree* (Liriodendron tulipifera *'Fastigiatum') is ideal for a large lawn.*

Bold Specimens for Large Gardens

TREES THAT ultimately grow to a large size – many native to forests – form an impressive sight in gardens big enough to accommodate them. Where conditions suit, some live to a great age, and may be enjoyed for years to come by future generations.

Catalpa speciosa
WESTERN CATALPA
☼ ❊❊❊   Vigorous growth
↕ 20m (70ft) ↔ 15m (50ft)

The glossy, dark green leaves of this imposing tree are broad at the base, and each has a slender point. Bell-shaped white flowers, spotted lightly inside, are carried in large heads in summer, and followed by slender, pendulous pods.

Fagus sylvatica var. *heterophylla* 'Aspleniifolia'
FERN-LEAVED BEECH
☼ ❊❊❊   Vigorous growth
↕ 25m (80ft) ↔ 25m (80ft)

A tree that combines impressive stature and grace, this beech is often broader than it is tall, and eventually forms a large, dome-shaped crown. The slender, spreading branchlets are clothed in narrow, toothed leaves that turn gold, then brown, in autumn. ♔

Acer saccharinum
SILVER MAPLE
☼ ❊❊❊   Vigorous growth
↕ 25m (80ft) ↔ 15m (50ft)

This handsome, broadly columnar tree spreads with age. Slender branchlets carry jagged leaves with silvery undersides that flash when disturbed by the wind. These turn yellow in autumn. Pendulous selections with more finely cut leaves are available.

Castanea sativa
SWEET, OR SPANISH, CHESTNUT
☼ ☼ ❊❊❊   Vigorous growth
↕ 25m (80ft) ↔ 15m (50ft)

A magnificent tree that develops reddish brown, ridged bark in time. Clusters of slender summer flower spikes precede prickly capsules that contain the familiar edible chestnuts, and the leaves turn yellow in autumn. Best in rich lime-free soils. ♔

Liriodendron tulipifera
TULIP TREE, TULIP POPLAR
☼ ❊❊❊   Vigorous growth
↕ 25m (80ft) ↔ 15m (50ft)

This is one of the noblest ornamental trees, its impressive conical habit spreading with age. Tulip-like flowers appear around mid-summer and its distinctively shaped leaves turn yellow in autumn. Seed-grown trees rarely flower until they are 15–20 years old. ♔

Nothofagus obliqua
ROBLÉ BEECH
☼ ❄❄❄❄ᴾᴴ
Vigorous growth
↕ 20m (70ft) ↔ 18m (60ft)

This elegant relative of the beech tree comes from the southern hemisphere, and it develops a domed crown of slightly drooping branches. The deep green leaves turn red and orange in autumn. Happiest in moist but well-drained soils, in a sheltered site. ♥

Quercus frainetto
HUNGARIAN OAK
☼ ❄❄❄
Vigorous growth
↕ 20m (70ft) ↔ 18m (60ft)

One of the most handsome and distinct of all oaks in leaf, this species has large, glossy green leaves that are boldly and regularly lobed, and borne on stout shoots. Its habit is spreading, and the bark is darkly and deeply fissured. Tolerates most sites and soils.

OTHER BOLD SPECIMEN TREES

Acer cappadocicum
Aesculus hippocastanum 'Baumannii',
     see p.272
          Ailanthus altissima
          Carpinus betulus
          Carya ovata, see p.296
          Corylus colurna, see p.302
          Eucalyptus gunnii, see p.286
          Fraxinus americana
          Juglans nigra
          Magnolia acuminata
          Platanus × hispanica, see p.283
          Platanus orientalis
          Quercus canariensis, see p.279
Quercus cerris
Quercus petraea
          Quercus robur, see p.273
          Tilia 'Petiolaris', see p.289
          Tilia tomentosa

Quercus palustris
PIN OAK
☼ ❄❄❄❄ᴾᴴ
Vigorous growth
↕ 20m (70ft) ↔ 12m (40ft)

Good-looking and dome-shaped, Pin Oak is a superb tree for a large lawn. Spreading branches, the lowest of which are pendent, bear beautiful, sharply lobed leaves. Shining green in summer, they turn spectacular bronze, russet, or red in autumn. ♥

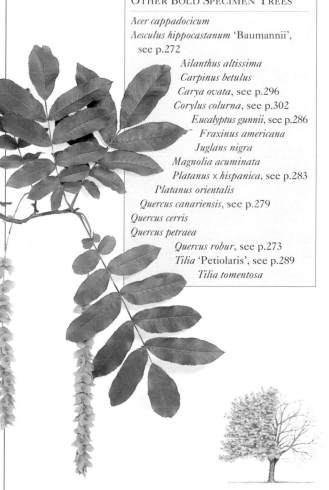

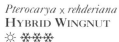

Pterocarya × rehderiana
HYBRID WINGNUT
☼ ❄❄❄
Vigorous growth
↕ 20m (70ft) ↔ 20m (70ft)

In summer, the branchlets of this walnut relative are draped with long catkins that are replaced by even longer strings of green, winged fruits. Its leaves turn a clear yellow in autumn. Thrives in deep soils, or in a moist situation. An imposing tree at all times.

Zelkova carpinifolia
CAUCASIAN ELM
☼ ❄❄❄
Slow growth
↕ 30m (100ft) ↔ 25m (80ft)

This slow-growing tree is one to plant for your grandchildren to enjoy. Mature specimens develop a characteristic dense, broad-topped crown with strongly upswept branches and a short, stout stem. Its green leaves often turn orange-brown in autumn.

Medium-sized Trees

SOME OF THE LOVELIEST trees are found in the medium size range of 6–15m (20–50ft); they are suitable for all but very small gardens. This selection encompasses the full variety of ornamental effects, from spring flowers, through autumn foliage, to attractive winter bark. All these are winter hardy, but others, requiring a sheltered site, are also available.

Magnolia × *loebneri* 'Leonard Messel'
MAGNOLIA   Moderate growth
☼ ✸✸✸   ↕ 10m (30ft) ↔ 6m (20ft)

One of the loveliest of its kind, this magnolia is upright to vase-shaped in habit, becoming conical to rounded in maturity. The leafless branches are flooded during spring with fragrant, multi-petalled, pale lilac-pink flowers, a deeper colour when in bud. ♔

Aesculus × *neglecta* 'Erythroblastos'
SUNRISE HORSE CHESTNUT   Moderate growth
☼ ◐ ✸✸✸   ↕ 10m (30ft) ↔ 6m (20ft)

Grown principally for its spring foliage, this is a choice tree of upright habit, spreading later. The leaves are bright pink when they emerge, changing to yellow and then to green. In autumn the leaves turn orange and yellow. Not suitable for exposed sites. ♔

Magnolia × *kewensis* 'Wada's Memory'
MAGNOLIA   Moderate growth
☼ ✸✸✸   ↕ 10m (30ft) ↔ 7m (22ft)

This tree has a conical or oval crown. The fragrant white flowers that crowd its dense branches in spring are large, lax, and multi-petalled. Its leaves, aromatic when bruised, are dark green above, paler beneath. Spectacular when in full bloom. ♔

Cornus macrophylla
DOGWOOD   Moderate growth
☼ ◐ ✸✸✸   ↕ 12m (40ft) ↔ 10m (30ft)

The branches of this uncommon spreading tree grow in glossy, leafy layers. Flattened clusters of small, creamy white flowers are held above the foliage during summer, and are followed by blue-black berries in autumn. An attractive tree of loosely tiered habit.

> **OTHER MEDIUM-SIZED TREES GROWN FOR FLOWERS**
>
> *Cornus kousa* var. *chinensis*
> *Fraxinus ornus*, see p.277
> *Koelreuteria paniculata*, see p.277
> *Magnolia* × *loebneri* 'Merrill'
> *Oxydendrum arboreum*, see p.275
> *Prunus padus* 'Watereri'
> *Pterostyrax hispida*
> *Pyrus ussuriensis*
> *Sorbus alnifolia*, see p.273
> *Stewartia pseudocamellia*, see p.275

Malus hupehensis
HUPEH CRAB
☼ ✳✳✳   Vigorous growth
↕ 8m (25ft) ↔ 8m (25ft)

The spreading branches of this dense, round-headed tree are
crowded in spring with large, fragrant white flowers, pink in bud.
Small, dark red fruits held on slender stalks follow, and remain
after the leaves have fallen, eventually to be eaten by birds.

Prunus avium 'Plena'
DOUBLE GEAN
☼ ✳✳✳   Vigorous growth
↕ 12m (40ft) ↔ 12m (40ft)

In spring, the rounded to spreading crown of this popular, strong-
growing, flowering cherry is heavily laden with drooping clusters
of clear white, double flowers. The leaves turn an attractive red
and yellow in autumn. Makes an excellent specimen tree.

Prunus jamasakura
HILL CHERRY
☼ ✳✳✳   Moderate growth
↕ 12m (40ft) ↔ 12m (40ft)

This beautiful cherry has a vase-shaped, later spreading, crown.
In spring, the branches are crowded with white or pink blossom.
The leaves are bronze at first, and colour richly in autumn. When
in full bloom, this tree is visible from a considerable distance.

OTHER MEDIUM-SIZED TREES
GROWN FOR FOLIAGE

Acer triflorum, see p.270
Alnus glutinosa 'Imperialis'
Betula maximowicziana
Cladrastis kentukea, see p.278
Parrotia persica, see p.297
Quercus cerris 'Argenteovariegata', see
    p.291
Robinia pseudoacacia 'Frisia', see p.293
Sorbus thibetica 'John Mitchell', see p.294
Tilia mongolica

Styrax japonicus
JAPANESE SNOWBELL
☼ ✳✳✳   Moderate growth
↕ 10m (30ft) ↔ 10m (30ft)

Neat, bright green leaves pack the spreading branches of
this dense-headed tree. The undersides of its branches are
crowded in early summer with drooping white, star-shaped
flowers, each with a yellow beak of stamens.

TREES

269

Small Trees for Limited Space

SELECTING a single tree for a small space is a pleasant but difficult task because there are so many attractive candidates. Plant any of the suggestions here, alone as a specimen, or perhaps in a boundary bed, where it can be enjoyed by neighbours or passers-by.

Aesculus pavia 'Atrosanguinea'
DARK RED BUCKEYE

☼ ❋❋❋   Slow growth   ↕ 5m (15ft) ↔ 4m (12ft)

Because of its slow growth and compact, dome-shaped habit, this tree makes an ideal lawn specimen. The dark green leaves form an excellent backdrop for its red, tubular summer flowers. These are followed by smooth-skinned, pale brown fruits.

Acer palmatum var. *coreanum*
JAPANESE MAPLE

☼ ☼ ❋❋❋   Vigorous growth   ↕ 5m (15ft) ↔ 5m (15ft)

The slender branches of this reliable and easily grown tree are clothed with attractive green leaves that become a spectacular red-orange in autumn. Tiny, reddish purple flower clusters emerge with the leaves in spring. Dislikes dry soils.

Acer triflorum
ROUGH-BARKED MAPLE

☼ ❋❋❋   Slow growth   ↕ 8m (25ft) ↔ 7m (22ft)

The rugged, peeling grey-brown bark of this handsome maple is especially noticeable in winter. Its leaves, comprising three hairy leaflets, give brilliant gold, orange, and red autumn tints. The small, greenish yellow flowers appear in clusters in late spring. ♔

Cornus alternifolia   'Argentea'
VARIEGATED PAGODA DOGWOOD

☼ ❋❋❋   Moderate growth   ↕ 3m (10ft) ↔ 2m (6ft)

In time, distinct layers of slender branches with narrow leaves create a pagoda-effect, making this a perfect specimen tree. You can prune and train it on a single stem or leave it with branches to the base. Its small clusters of white flowers appear in spring. ♔

Cornus florida 'White Cloud'
FLOWERING DOGWOOD
☼ ✳✳✳   Moderate growth
‡5m (15ft) ↔6m (20ft)

This low, bushy tree with a spreading crown needs space to expand. It has two main seasons of interest – the first in spring, when distinctive white flowerheads appear, and the second in autumn, when dark green leaves become suffused red and purple.

Rhus trichocarpa
RHUS
☼ ✳✳✳   Moderate growth
‡7m (22ft) ↔7m (22ft)

In autumn, the large, deeply divided, ash-like green leaves of this spreading tree provide purplish, then orange and red tints, alongside the drooping clusters of bristly yellow fruits. The sap of this tree is poisonous and may cause an allergic reaction.

OTHER SMALL TREES

Acer shirasawanum 'Aureum', see p.292
Amelanchier lamarckii, see p.296
Aralia elata
Crataegus laciniata, see p.276
Fraxinus sieboldiana
Magnolia x *kewensis* 'Wada's Memory', see p.268
Malus x *robusta* 'Red Sentinel', see p.298
Mespilus germanica 'Nottingham'
Prunus 'Kursar'
Sorbus forrestii, see p.299

Eucalyptus pauciflora subsp. *niphophila*
SNOW GUM
☼ ✳✳✳   Moderate growth
‡10m (30ft) ↔8m (25ft)

One of the most popular of all eucalypts, this is worth growing for its evergreen grey-green leaves, and its fluffy clusters of white summer flowers. It is best known, however, for its beautiful bark – green, grey, cream, and silver create a marbled effect. ♔

△ *Sorbus vilmorinii* 'Pearly King'

Eucryphia glutinosa
EUCRYPHIA
☼ ✳✳✳✳ᴾᴴ▾   Moderate growth
‡6m (20ft) ↔5m (15ft)

This much-branched, rather bushy tree has shining, dark green leaflets that turn orange and red in autumn. Clusters of fragrant, rose-like flowers occur from mid- to late summer. It prefers a moist but well-drained soil with its roots shaded from the sun. ♔

Sorbus vilmorinii
CHINESE ROWAN
☼ ✳✳✳   Moderate growth
‡4m (12ft) ↔5m (15ft)

The arching branches of this elegant tree are clothed in neat sprays of fern-like leaves that colour orange or red in autumn. It bears white flowers in late spring, and loose clusters of small pink berries from autumn into early winter. 'Pearly King' is similar. ♔

T R E E S

271

Trees Tolerant of Heavy Clay Soils

C LAY SOILS are frequently among the most fertile in gardens, although their physical characteristics do cause problems. Gardeners can take heart from the following selection of trees, all of which will grow happily in heavy clay, as long as it is not waterlogged.

Alnus incana
GREY ALDER
☼ ✼✼✼   Moderate growth
↕ 18m (60ft) ↔ 10m (30ft)

This is a tough and adaptable tree with a loosely conical habit. Its dark green leaves are strongly veined, and each has a downy grey underside. Drooping yellow catkins drape the branches in late winter or early spring. The Grey Alder dislikes dry soils.

Catalpa bignonioides
INDIAN BEAN TREE
☼ ✼✼✼   Moderate growth
↕ 12m (40ft) ↔ 15m (50ft)

Often broader than it is high, this is a bold, spreading tree. It has light-green, heart-shaped leaves, purple-tinged when young, and bears large, loose heads of bell-flowers with purple and yellow spots in summer. These are followed by long, thin seed pods. ⏛

Aesculus hippocastanum 'Baumannii'
DOUBLE HORSE CHESTNUT
☼ ✼✼✼   Vigorous growth
↕ 30m (100ft) ↔ 15m (50ft)

A large tree with a spreading crown, the Double Horse Chestnut has bold leaves, each divided into broad, finger-like leaflets. It produces erect, conical spires of double white flowers in spring, which have red or yellow markings. Non-fruiting. ⏛

Cotoneaster frigidus
TREE COTONEASTER
☼ ☀ ✼✼✼   Vigorous growth
↕ 10m (30ft) ↔ 10m (30ft)

Although it is most often multi-stemmed with a spreading crown, this cotoneaster can be trained on a single stem. It carries large leaves, and white flowerheads in early summer, to be followed in autumn and early winter by bold bunches of red berries.

+ Laburnocytisus 'Adamii'
ADAM'S LABURNUM
☼ ❄❄❄   Moderate growth
↕ 8m (25ft) ↔ 7m (22ft)

This tree resembles a laburnum in habit and leaf, but the tassels of both yellow and pink flowers that are produced in late spring or early summer, are accompanied by the occasional fuzzy clump of purple-flowered broom.

Quercus robur
ENGLISH OAK
☼ ❄❄❄   Slow growth
↕ 25m (80ft) ↔ 25m (80ft)

A famous tree, and one that is very popular in folk culture, the English Oak fully justifies its position as a symbol of toughness and longevity. Its rugged bark, wavy-lobed green leaves, and long-stalked acorns contribute to its credentials. ♛

Magnolia x
soulangeana ▷

Magnolia x *soulangeana*
MAGNOLIA
☼ ❄❄❄   Moderate growth
↕ 6m (20ft) ↔ 7m (22ft)

Fragrant, goblet-shaped, white, pink, or purple-flushed blooms grace this magnolia from spring through to summer, making it a magnificent tree when in flower. It has a spreading, low-branched crown and bold foliage. There are many excellent cultivars.

> **OTHER TREES TOLERANT OF HEAVY CLAY SOILS**
>
> *Acer pseudoplatanus* 'Brilliantissimum'
> *Betula utilis* 'Jermyns'
> *Carpinus betulus* 'Fastigiata'
> *Crataegus persimilis* 'Prunifolia'
> *Eucalyptus glaucescens*
> *Ilex* × *koehneana* 'Chestnut Leaf', see p.286
> *Malus hupehensis*, see p.269
> *Platanus* × *hispanica*, see p.283
> *Prunus padus* 'Watereri'
> *Quercus palustris*, see p.267
> *Salix pentandra*
> *Sorbus intermedia*
> *Tilia mongolica*

Populus maximowiczii
POPLAR
☼ ❄❄❄   Vigorous growth
↕ 20m (70ft) ↔ 10m (30ft)

This poplar is a tall tree with ascending, then shortly spreading, branches. Its bold, heart-shaped, bright green leaves turn yellow in autumn. The spring catkins produced by female trees ripen to fluffy white in late summer. Dislikes dry soils.

Sorbus alnifolia
SORBUS
☼ ◐ ❄❄❄   Moderate growth
↕ 11m (35ft) ↔ 8m (25ft)

The crown of this tough and adaptable tree is conical or oval, and spreads later. Its bright green leaves become orange and red in autumn. White flower clusters are produced in late spring, and these are followed by bright red fruits in autumn.

T R E E S

273

Trees for Lime-free Soils

FEW TREES WILL ACTUALLY FAIL to grow on alkaline soils, but several perform poorly in such places, preferring soils of an acid, or neutral reaction. The trees shown here grow best in lime-free soils, especially where moisture is available in summer.

Eucryphia × *nymansensis* 'Nymansay'
EUCRYPHIA
☼ ☀ ❄❄❄ PH
Moderate growth
↕ 13m (43ft) ↔ 6m (20ft)

From late summer into early autumn, the shoots of this compact, columnar evergreen tree are crowded with clusters of white, rose-like flowers. Its leaves are typically divided into glossy green leaflets. Enjoys moist, well-drained soils, with its roots shaded. ♛

Cornus nuttallii
PACIFIC DOGWOOD
☼ ☀ ❄❄❄ PH
Vigorous growth
↕ 13m (43ft) ↔ 8m (25ft)

The dark green leaves of this beautiful, free-growing tree become yellow or red in autumn. Tight clusters of tiny spring flowers are surrounded by large white bracts, and followed, in a hot summer, by red fruit clusters. Thrives in moist but well-drained soils.

TREES TOLERANT OF BOTH HIGH ACIDITY AND HIGH ALKALINITY
Betula pendula
Crataegus monogyna
Fagus sylvatica, see p.281
Ilex aquifolium
Populus alba, see p.284
Populus × *canescens*
Quercus cerris
Quercus robur, see p.273
Sorbus × *hybrida*
Sorbus intermedia

Embothrium coccineum Lanceolatum Group
CHILEAN FIRE TREE
☼ ☀ ❄❄
Vigorous growth
↕ 10m (30ft) ↔ 5m (15ft)

Easily one of the most spectacular and eye-catching of all trees when in flower. It is erect in habit when young, broadening later. The long, willow-like leaves are joined in early summer by crowded, firecracker red flowers. Best in moist, free-draining soil.

Magnolia fraseri
FRASER'S MAGNOLIA
☼ ❄❄❄ PH
Moderate growth
↕ 10m (30ft) ↔ 8m (25ft)

Uncommon in general cultivation, this attractive, loose-spreading magnolia is easily distinguished by its enormous green leaves. The large, fragrant flowers are carried from late spring into early summer, and may be followed by cylindrical red fruit clusters.

TREES

Nothofagus nervosa
RAULI
☼ ☀ ✳✳✳✳ PH ▼   Vigorous growth
                              ↕ 20m (70ft) ↔ 12m (40ft)

A straight-stemmed, good-looking tree, with its shoots clothed in
large, conspicuously veined leaves. These emerge bronze, then
become green in summer, and give attractive orange and red
tints in autumn. Rauli is not suitable for exposed sites.

OTHER TREES FOR
LIME-FREE SOILS

Acer japonicum 'Aconitifolium'
Acer rubrum
Eucryphia glutinosa, see p.271
Liquidambar styraciflua
Lyonothamnus floribundus
subsp. *aspleniifolius*
Magnolia 'Heaven Scent'
Nothofagus dombeyi
Nyssa sylvatica
Picrasma quassioides
Quecus rubra

Sassafras albidum
SASSAFRAS
☼ ☀ ✳✳✳✳ PH ▼   Moderate growth
                              ↕ 20m (70ft) ↔ 8m (25ft)

Famous for a medicinal tea brewed from its aromatic root bark,
this handsome tree is clothed with leaves, often lobed, that turn
yellow, orange, or purple in autumn. Its rugged bark and pale
branches are an attraction in winter.

Oxydendrum arboreum
SORREL TREE
☼ ☀ ✳✳✳✳ PH ▼   Moderate growth
                              ↕ 12m (40ft) ↔ 8m (25ft)

This conical, later spreading, tree produces handsome, glossy
green leaves that turn brilliant yellow, red, or purple in autumn.
Tiny, scented flowers appear in late summer and last into
autumn. Thrives in moist, well-drained soils with its roots shaded.

Stewartia pseudocamellia
JAPANESE STEWARTIA
☼ ☀ ✳✳✳✳ PH ▼   Moderate growth
                              ↕ 12m (40ft) ↔ 6m (20ft)

This superb decorative tree has many garden qualities. Spreading
in habit, its reddish brown bark flakes with age to form patches
that are attractive in winter. White flowers open from midsummer,
and the leaves turn a striking orange or red in autumn. ♈

T R E E S

275

Trees for Alkaline Soils

FREE-DRAINING, and warming faster than most other soils in spring, alkaline soils suit a wide range of ornamental trees, some of them very popular and reliable flowering trees. Many hail from regions enjoying warm summers and so appreciate sun and warmth to help ripen their wood and promote flowering.

Albizia julibrissin
PINK SIRIS, SILK TREE
☼ ❄❄
Moderate growth
↕ 10m (30ft) ↔ 10m (30ft)

As a young tree, Pink Siris is more broad than tall, with spreading branches and finely divided, fern-like leaves. Its clusters of fluffy, pink-stamened flowers are produced in late summer and autumn. *A. julibrissin* 'Rosea' is a more hardy selection.

Cercis siliquastrum
JUDAS TREE
☼ ❄❄❄
Moderate growth
↕ 10m (30ft) ↔ 10m (30ft)

Occasionally multi-stemmed, this more often single-stemmed, spreading tree has heart-shaped blue-green leaves. Rosy lilac pea-flowers emerge in spring and are followed by flattened red seed pods. 'Bodnant' is a form with deep purple flowers.

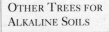

OTHER TREES FOR ALKALINE SOILS

Acer campestre
Acer negundo 'Flamingo', see p.290
Acer platanoides, see p.281
Aesculus hippocastanum 'Baumannii', see p.272
Arbutus x *andrachnoides*, see p.302
Fraxinus sieboldiana
Ligustrum lucidum, see p.286
Malus x *robusta* 'Red Sentinel', see p.298
Morus nigra
Paulownia tomentosa
Prunus 'Shirotae'
Prunus 'Shôgetsu'
Prunus 'Ukon'
Robinia x *margaretta* 'Pink Cascade'
Sophora japonica
Sorbus intermedia
Tilia tomentosa 'Brabant'

△ *Crategus laciniata*

Crataegus laciniata
ORIENTAL THORN
☼ ❄❄❄
Slow growth
↕ 5.5m (18ft) ↔ 5.5m (18ft)

This slow-growing ornamental thorn tree will eventually develop a dense, rounded crown clothed in deeply lobed, dark green leaves. Clusters of pretty white blossoms emerge in late spring, and its large, downy red fruits are produced in autumn.

T R E E S

Fraxinus ornus
MANNA ASH
☼ ❄❄❄   Moderate growth
‡ 15m (50ft) ↔ 13m (43ft)

Typically round-headed, this attractive tree has much-divided, pale green leaves and produces large, branched heads of scented, creamy white flowers from late spring into early summer. Bronze-tinted fruits follow. A reliable tree of compact habit. ♈

Malus floribunda
JAPANESE CRAB
☼ ❄❄❄   Moderate growth
‡ 8m (25ft) ↔ 10m (30ft)

This is one of the most popular and reliable of all the flowering crab apples. Its dense, rounded crown is flooded in spring with pale pink flowers. Masses of pea-sized yellow, red-cheeked fruits are borne in autumn. One of the first crabs to flower. ♈

Koelreuteria paniculata
PRIDE OF INDIA, GOLDEN-RAIN TREE   Moderate growth
☼ ❄❄❄   ‡ 10m (30ft) ↔ 10m (30ft)

The leaves of this domed tree, which is sometimes broader than it is tall, are regularly divided into numerous toothed leaflets, and turn yellow in autumn. Large, branched yellow flowerheads, in late summer, are followed by conspicuous, inflated seed pods. ♈

Prunus × yedoensis
YOSHINO CHERRY
☼ ❄❄❄   Moderate growth
‡ 8m (25ft) ↔ 10m (30ft)

Eventually broad-domed, this cherry has wide-spreading, arching branches. In early spring, these are profusely hung with drooping clusters of almond-scented, white or pale blush blossoms, pink in bud. One of the earliest, most reliable of all flowering cherries. ♈

Laburnum alpinum
SCOTCH LABURNUM
☼ ❄❄❄   Moderate growth
‡ 7m (22ft) ↔ 7m (22ft)

Scotch Laburnum is broad-headed, with a short, stocky stem and lush, deep green, three-parted leaves. Long, pendent chains of bright yellow pea-flowers appear in late spring or early summer and are deliciously fragrant. All parts are poisonous if eaten.

Sorbus aria 'Lutescens'
WHITEBEAM
☼ ❄❄❄   Moderate growth
‡ 11m (35ft) ↔ 8m (25ft)

This is a popular ornamental tree with an erect to oval crown at first, later spreading. Its leaves are creamy white when they first emerge in spring, and become grey-green as they mature. White flowers are produced from late spring into early summer. ♈

TREES

Trees for Dry, Sunny Sites

THOSE WITH gardens in dry, sunny places will be all too familiar with the problems that a summer drought can bring to trees. A fast-draining sandy or gravelly soil can be an added difficulty. Fortunately, some trees tolerate, if not relish, such conditions.

Eucalyptus dalrympleana
MOUNTAIN GUM
☼ ✳✳✳   Vigorous growth
‡ 20m (70ft) ↔ 9m (28ft)

Columnar when young, the handsome Mountain Gum broadens later. Its evergreen leaves are rounded on younger trees, and elongated and drooping later. Leaves are joined by white flower clusters in late summer. Young creamy white bark is attractive. ▽

Celtis australis
SOUTHERN NETTLE TREE
☼ ✳✳✳   Moderate growth
‡ 18m (60ft) ↔ 15m (50ft)

Uncommon, but easy to grow, this ornamental tree has smooth, pale grey bark. It is broadly columnar with a dome-shaped crown, although the branches on older trees are often pendulous. The surfaces of its slender, pointed leaves are rough to the touch.

Cladrastis kentukea
YELLOW-WOOD
☼ ✳✳✳   Moderate growth
‡ 12m (40ft) ↔ 12m (40ft)

This excellent ornamental tree has numerous attractive features: a rounded or dome-shaped crown, ash-like leaves that become clear yellow in autumn, and large, branched, drooping heads of fragrant white pea-flowers that are produced in summer.

Gleditsia triacanthos 'Sunburst'
HONEY LOCUST
☼ ✳✳✳   Moderate growth
‡ 12m (40ft) ↔ 12m (40ft)

The stem and branches of this broad-spreading tree are grey-brown. Its pretty, much-divided, glossy leaves are golden yellow when they emerge, darken to green later, then turn pale yellow in autumn. Honey locusts are tolerant of extreme air pollution. ▽

Maackia amurensis
MAACKIA

Slow growth

☼ ✳✳✳   ↕ 7m (22ft) ↔ 7m (22ft)

This wide-spreading tree with greyish brown bark has ash-like, deep green leaves, silver-blue when young. Dense, stubby spikes of flowers, white, tinged the palest slate-blue, are produced in summer, and held in clusters above the branches.

Sophora japonica 'Violacea'
PAGODA TREE

Vigorous growth

☼ ✳✳✳   ↕ 18m (60ft) ↔ 18m (60ft)

The grey-brown bark of this round-headed tree is prominently ridged. Its ash-like leaves emerge late in the season, and the loose heads of small white, lilac-tinged pea-flowers are borne from late summer into early autumn. Drooping seed pods follow.

Pittosporum crassifolium 'Variegatum'
VARIEGATED KARO

Moderate growth

☼ ✳   ↕ 5m (15ft) ↔ 3m (10ft)

Unless it is trained to a single stem, this evergreen tree, with its dense, bushy crown, will remain shrubby. The leathery leaves are grey-green with a white margin. Small, scented, reddish purple flowers appear in spring. Karo is excellent for mild coastal areas.

OTHER TREES FOR DRY, SUNNY SITES

Arbutus x *andrachnoides*, see p.302
Cercis siliquastrum, see p.276
Fraxinus velutina
Genista aetnensis
Juglans microcarpa
Koelreuteria paniculata, see p.277
Ligustrum lucidum, see p.286
Phillyrea latifolia, see p.284
Quercus suber
Robinia viscosa

Quercus canariensis
ALGERIAN OAK

Moderate growth

☼ ✳✳✳   ↕ 20m (70ft) ↔ 12m (40ft)

The habit of this distinct and handsome oak is broadly columnar when young, and becomes more rounded with age. Its upswept branches are densely covered with large, regularly lobed leaves, which are usually retained into late winter.

Umbellularia californica
CALIFORNIA BAY, HEADACHE TREE

Moderate growth

☼ ✳✳   ↕ 12m (40ft) ↔ 10m (30ft)

A relative of the bay (*Laurus nobilis*), this dense, bushy-headed evergreen tree produces clusters of delicate yellowish flowers in spring. Its bright green, leathery leaves are pungent if crushed and this vapour may cause nausea if inhaled.

TREES

Trees for Watersides

FEW SIGHTS, to me, are more appealing than a weeping willow growing on a river bank. Not many of us are fortunate enough to have a river running through our garden, but there is no reason why a suitable tree should not be planted next to a pool or stretch of water. As long as you maintain a sense of scale, the possibilities are endless.

Pterocarya fraxinifolia
CAUCASIAN WINGNUT
☼ ✺✺✺   Moderate growth
↕ 25m (80ft) ↔ 20m (70ft)

Eventually a large, broad-spreading tree, this has much-divided, ash-like leaves and long, drooping tassels of green flowers. Its green, winged fruits follow. Suckers that appear should always be removed, unless you want to encourage a grove. ⚜

> ### OTHER TREES FOR WATERSIDES
>
> *Alnus firma*
> *Alnus glutinosa* 'Imperialis'
> *Populus alba* 'Richardii'
> *Populus maximowiczii*, see p.273
> *Salix alba* subsp. *vitellina*
> *Salix daphnoides*, see p.203
> *Salix babylonica* var. *pekinensis*
>   'Tortuosa', see p.301

Alnus rubra
RED ALDER
☼ ✺✺✺   Vigorous growth
↕ 15m (50ft) ↔ 10m (30ft)

This is a fast-growing tree of conical habit. In early spring, before the leaves unfurl, its branches are draped with yellowish orange male catkins that can be up to 15cm (6in) long. Its toothed leaves are boldy veined. Older trees have pale grey bark.

△ *Salix × sepulcralis* var. *chrysocoma*

Betula nigra
RIVER BIRCH
☼ ✺✺✺   Moderate growth
↕ 15m (50ft) ↔ 15m (50ft)

The River Birch is distinctive, and quite unlike the more usual white-stemmed kinds. The bark of the stem and main branches is peeling and shaggy, pinkish grey in colour, maturing to dark brown. Its leaves are diamond-shaped and pale beneath.

Salix × sepulcralis var. *chrysocoma*
GOLDEN WEEPING WILLOW
☼ ✺✺✺   Vigorous growth
↕ 20m (70ft) ↔ 25m (80ft)

This is a popular subject for the waterside, but it is too large for the small gardens in which it is often planted. It has long curtains of weeping, golden yellow branches in winter. These are covered with slender, bright green leaves in spring and summer.

Trees for Screening or Windbreaks

I N ADDITION TO CONIFERS, various medium-sized to large, broad-leaved trees make a good line of defence against persistent winds, and can screen unattractive views or unsightly objects. Many also have ornamental features.

Fagus sylvatica
COMMON BEECH
☼ ✳✳✳   Moderate growth   ↕ 35m (120ft) ↔ 15m (50ft)

One of the temperate world's most beautiful trees, this matures to form a dome-shaped crown. Smooth grey bark in winter and pale green leaves in spring, turning shiny mid-green in summer and golden yellow in autumn, make this a tree for all seasons. ♈

Acer platanoides
NORWAY MAPLE
☼ ✳✳✳   Vigorous growth   ↕ 25m (80ft) ↔ 15m (50ft)

One of the most adaptable and reliable of all trees, the Norway Maple develops a rounded crown. Yellow flower clusters emerge in mid-spring, before the leaves appear, followed by green, winged fruits. The leaves turn a rich yellow, red, or orange in autumn. ♈

OTHER TREES FOR SCREENING OR WINDBREAKS

Acer pseudoplatanus
Fraxinus excelsior 'Westhof's Glorie'
Populus nigra 'Italica'
Populus × *canadensis* 'Robusta'
Quercus robur, see p.273
Tilia cordata

△ *Prunus serotina*

Alnus cordata
ITALIAN ALDER
☼ ✳✳✳   Vigorous growth   ↕ 25m (80ft) ↔ 11m (35ft)

This handsome, columnar tree becomes conical later. Bunches of long yellow male catkins drape the branches in late winter or early spring. In summer, its cone-like fruits develop among the large, rounded leaves with shining, dark green upper surfaces. ♈

Prunus serotina
RUM, OR BLACK, CHERRY
☼ ◐ ✳✳✳   Moderate growth   ↕ 15m (50ft) ↔ 13m (43ft)

A free-growing tree with an oval crown of pendulous or arching branches, its deep green, glossy leaves are deciduous, becoming yellow or red in autumn. Small white spring flowers are carried in drooping tassels, and give way to shining black fruits.

Trees Tolerant of Air Pollution

Sites subject to air pollution would not seem to be ideal areas for growing trees. Given adequate soil preparation and after-care, however, a good variety of trees, both large and small, will perform just as they would well as in places enjoying clean air.

Fraxinus angustifolia
NARROW-LEAVED ASH
☼ ❋❋❋   Vigorous growth
↕ 20m (70ft) ↔ 12m (40ft)

More elegant in habit than the Common Ash *(Fraxinus excelsior)*, this large tree has spreading branches that form an attractive oval to rounded crown. Its leaves are regularly divided into narrow, smooth, glossy green leaflets, that become yellow in autumn.

Amelanchier laevis
ALLEGHENY SERVICEBERRY
☼ ☼ ❋❋❋   Moderate growth
↕ 6m (20ft) ↔ 6m (20ft)

Clusters of white flowers flood the branches of this small, often multi-stemmed tree or large shrub in spring. It has a dense, spreading habit, and leaves which are bronze in spring, changing to green in summer, and then red or orange in autumn.

Ilex x *altaclerensis* 'Belgica Aurea'
HIGHCLERE HOLLY
☼ ☼ ❋❋❋   Moderate growth
↕ 8m (25ft) ↔ 3m (10ft)

The bold leaves of this evergreen holly are lance-shaped, with occasional spines. They are a mottled grey-green in colour, and irregularly edged pale or creamy yellow. From autumn onwards, this dense, compact columnar tree also carries red berries. ♼

Crataegus laevigata 'Paul's Scarlet'
PAUL'S SCARLET THORN
☼ ❋❋❋   Moderate growth
↕ 6m (20ft) ↔ 8m (25ft)

This is a popular tree, with a dense, rounded or spreading crown. In late spring and early summer, the branches are covered in numerous clusters of double red flowers. The leaves are glossy dark green. 'Punicea' is similar, with single crimson flowers. ♼

OTHER TREES TOLERANT OF AIR POLLUTION

Acer pseudoplatanus 'Brilliantissimum'
Aesculus x *carnea* 'Briotii'
Ailanthus altissima
Alnus cordata, see p.281
Amelanchier lamarckii, see p.296
Catalpa bignonioides, see p.272
Crataegus persimilis 'Prunifolia'
Magnolia x *soulangeana*, see p.273
Malus baccata var. *mandschurica*, see p.303
Malus x *moerlandsii* 'Profusion'
Phellodendron amurense
Populus x *canadensis* 'Robusta'
Prunus 'Pink Perfection'
Quercus ilex, see p.287
Sorbus aria 'Majestica'
Tilia x *euchlora*
Tilia platyphyllos 'Rubra'

△ *Crataegus laevigata* 'Paul's Scarlet'

Prunus dulcis 'Roseoplena'
DOUBLE ALMOND

☼ ❄❄❄   Moderate growth
‡ 8m (25ft) ↔ 8m (25ft)

In late winter and early spring, the spreading branches of this tree are studded with double, pale pink flowers. These emerge ahead of the dark green, lance-shaped, long and pointed leaves and brighten the dullest of late winter days.

Pyrus calleryana 'Chanticleer'
ORNAMENTAL PEAR

☼ ❄❄❄   Moderate growth
‡ 12m (40ft) ↔ 6m (20ft)

Tough and hardy, this compact, conical tree has rounded, glossy green leaves that turn reddish purple in autumn. The branches are flooded with beautiful white blossoms in spring, at which time the tree is clearly visible from afar.   🏆

Laburnum x *waterei* 'Vossii'
VOSS'S LABURNUM

☼ ❄❄❄   Moderate growth
‡ 7m (22ft) ↔ 7m (22ft)

The crown of this tree, the most commonly planted laburnum, is spreading and crowded with leaves composed of three leaflets. Long, tapering chains of pea-flowers hang from its branches in late spring or early summer. All parts are poisonous if eaten.   🏆

Platanus x *hispanica*
LONDON PLANE

☼ ❄❄❄   Moderate growth
‡ 30m (100ft) ↔ 20m (70ft)

This enormous tree develops a massive piebald stem and a large spreading crown. Broad, maple-like leaves with five big, toothed lobes are carried in summer. From the summer onwards, strings of bristly, spherical fruits hang on single stalks, like baubles.   🏆

Robinia pseudoacacia
BLACK LOCUST, FALSE ACACIA

☼ ❄❄❄   Vigorous growth
‡ 20m (7   0ft) ↔ 12m (40ft)

The shoots of this tough and adaptable tree are prickly, and its leaves ash-like, with oval leaflets. Drooping clusters of white pea-flowers are fragrant, and occur from late spring into early summer. Develops rugged bark in time, and will sucker if hard pruned.   🏆

T R E E S

Trees Tolerant of Coastal Exposure

ONLY THE TOUGHEST TREES will survive the twin problems of strong winds and salt spray in seaside gardens. The following are among the most tolerant, and are well worth considering if only as an outer planting to provide shelter for shrubs and perennials.

Populus alba
WHITE POPLAR, ABELE
☼ ❋❋❋
Vigorous growth
↕ 20m (70ft) ↔ 13m (43ft)

This well-known spreading tree has imposing, grey-fissured bark. The leaves, which vary in shape from rounded and toothed to lobed and maple-like, are dark green above and covered below with a white felt, making a striking contrast when blown by wind.

Hippophae rhamnoides
SEA BUCKTHORN
☼ ❋❋❋
Moderate growth
↕ 6m (20ft) ↔ 6m (20ft)

Due to its bushy habit, careful pruning and training are needed to make a single- or few-stemmed tree. Narrow, silver-grey leaves crowd the thorny branches. Plant both male and female plants to produce brilliant orange berries that last all winter. ♈

Salix alba
WHITE WILLOW
☼ ❋❋❋
Vigorous growth
↕ 20m (70ft) ↔ 13m (43ft)

A handsome willow of conical habit at first, this soon spreads to be as broad as it is tall. Its narrow silvery leaves shimmer in the sun. Suited to damp places, but do not plant near underground drains or water systems, or buildings because of its invasive roots.

> **OTHER TREES TOLERANT OF COASTAL EXPOSURE**
>
> *Alnus rubra*, see p.280
> *Populus* × *canadensis* 'Robusta'
> *Quercus ilex*
> *Tilia cordata*

Phillyrea latifolia
PHILLYREA
☼ ❋❋❋
Slow growth
↕ 8m (25ft) ↔ 8m (25ft)

This little known, but valuable, evergreen tree is rather like a small version of the Holm Oak (*Quercus ilex*). The narrow, glossy, dark green leaves are leathery and toothed. Its tiny cream-yellow flowers are borne in dense clusters from late spring into summer.

Sorbus aucuparia
ROWAN OR MOUNTAIN ASH
☼ ☼ ❋❋❋
Moderate growth
↕ 10m (30ft) ↔ 7m (22ft)

The leaves of this grey-barked tree of spreading habit resemble those of an ash, often turning red or yellow in autumn. Clusters of white spring flowers are followed by drooping bunches of orange-red berries, maturing to bright red. Tough and adaptable.

T R E E S

Trees with Bold Leaves

YOU CAN TRANSFORM your garden by growing a tree with bold foliage. A single specimen with leaves of impressive size is worth planting in its own right, bringing a touch of the tropics to the most mundane planting. Bold foliage can also be effective when contrasted with smaller-leaved subjects. Many bold-foliaged trees have the further bonus of attractive flowers and fruits.

Toona sinensis

TOON, CEDRELA
☼ ❄❄❄
Vigorous growth
↕ 15m (50ft) ↔ 10m (30ft)

This fast-growing tree has large, much-divided leaves that can grow up to 60cm (24in) long. These are bronze-red when young, and turn yellow in autumn. In summer, mature trees carry large, drooping heads of small, fragrant white flowers.

Kalopanax septemlobus
PRICKLY CASTOR OIL TREE
☼ ❄❄❄
Moderate growth
↕ 12m (40ft) ↔ 10m (30ft)

A handsome tree, this has prickly stems and trunk, and maple-like leaves that turn yellow in autumn. Rounded clusters of tiny whitish flowers in late summer are replaced, after a hot summer, by blue-black berries. Thrives in moist, well-drained soils.

OTHER TREES WITH BOLD LEAVES

Aralia elata 'Variegata'
Catalpa bignonioides, see p.272
Juglans ailantifolia
Juglans nigra
Zanthoxylum ailanthoides

Magnolia obovata
JAPANESE BIG-LEAF MAGNOLIA
☼ ❄❄❄❄ PH
Vigorous growth
↕ 20m (70ft) ↔ 10m (30ft)

The large, firm leaves of this magnificent conical tree, broadest in their upper halves, are carried in impressive whorls at the ends of the branches. Strongly fragrant, bowl-shaped flowers are borne in summer, and followed by cylindrical red fruit clusters. ♈

Trachycarpus fortunei
CHUSAN PALM, WINDMILL PALM
☼ ❄❄
Slow growth
↕ 8m (25ft) ↔ 2.5m (8ft)

This is probably the hardiest palm suitable for cool, temperate regions, especially in coastal areas. It is a familiar sight, with its shaggy, fibrous bark, rounded head of fan-shaped, many-fingered leaves, and sprays of fragrant creamy flowers in early summer. ♈

Evergreen Trees

IN TEMPERATE AREAS, evergreen trees (apart from conifers) are greatly outnumbered by deciduous ones. This makes evergreens all the more desirable in the garden, especially in winter when their rich green, coloured, or variegated foliage offers a striking contrast to bare twigs or winter-flowering shrubs. They also provide effective year-round screening.

Ligistrum lucidum
CHINESE TREE PRIVET
☼ ☀ ✽✽✽   Moderate growth
↕ 10–12m (30–40ft) ↔ 10m (30ft)

At all times a handsome tree with its fluted trunk and dense crown of large, glossy dark green foliage. In early autumn, the canopy is smothered with richly scented cream flowerheads. An ideal specimen tree for a large lawn, but avoid exposed sites. ♕

Eucalyptus gunnii
CIDER GUM
☼ ✽✽✽   Vigorous growth
↕ 18–25m (60–80ft) ↔ 9–15m (30–50ft)

The most commonly planted eucalypt in cool-temperate gardens, although it is too vigorous for all but the largest gardens. It has Decorative cream and grey exfoliating bark, leathery, blue, grey, or grey-green leaves, and white fluffy flowerheads in summer. ♕

Ilex x koehneana 'Chestnut Leaf'
HYBRID HOLLY
☼ ☀ ✽✽✽   Moderate growth
↕ 12m (40ft) ↔ 2.5–3.5m (8–12ft)

A bold and noble holly with a compact, well-branched habit, notable for its striking, polished, sweet-chestnut-like leaves, which are leathery and spine-toothed. Abundant red berries appear from autumn to winter when pollinated by a male tree. ♕

Magnolia grandiflora
BULL BAY, SWAMP BAY
☼ ✽✽   Moderate growth
↕ 6–18m (20–60ft) ↔ 4.5–15m (15–50ft)

Easily recognised by its dense, conical or sometimes bushy habit and its large, leathery, polished leaves. Few trees are so long-flowering, the big, bowl-shaped, fragrant, cream flowers from late summer into autumn. Thrives and flowers best in a warm site. ♕

Maytenus boaria
MAITEN
☼ ☼ ❄❄❄   Moderate growth
↕10m (30ft) ↔8m (25ft)

An unusual and elegant tree, this is not unlike a weeping willow in effect. Erect when young, it gradually broadens into a round-headed tree, its branches well-clothed with narrow, glossy green, toothed leaves. Tiny spring flowers are of little ornamental merit.

Pittosporum tenuifolium
KOHUHU
☼ ❄❄   Moderate growth
↕6m (20ft) ↔5m (15ft)

Columnar when young, it is later dome-shaped and compact, with slender branchlets bearing glossy leaves. Small, honey-scented, bell-shaped purple flowers appear in late spring. It is excellent as a screen or single specimen, especially in coastal areas. ♈

OTHER EVERGREEN TREES

Arbutus unedo
Castanopsis cuspidata
Drimys winteri
Eucalyptus coccifera
Eucryphia x *intermedia* 'Rostrevor'
Ilex aquifolium
Ilex pedunculosa
Laurus nobilis
Phillyrea latifolia, see p.284
Prunus lusitanica, see p.209
Trachycarpus fortunei, see p.285

Luma apiculata
LUMA
☼ ☼ ❄❄   Vigorous growth
↕7m (22ft) ↔5m (15ft)

Luma is a splendid all-year-round performer. From midsummer into autumn, the glossy, dark green leaves of this dense-habited tree are interspersed with masses of small white flowers. Golden brown bark peels with age to reveal patches of creamy new bark. ♈

Quercus ilex
HOLM OAK, EVERGREEN OAK
☼ ☼ ❄❄❄   Moderate growth
↕18–24m (60–80ft) ↔18–21m (60–70ft)

A popular, ultimately large tree for screening and as a specimen in large gardens. The rounded canopy is crowded with leathery, glossy dark green leaves, which are variable in shape when young. Clusters of yellow catkins cover the canopy in June. ♈

Rhododendron arboreum
TREE RHODODENDRON
☼ ❄❄❄   Slow growth
↕12m (40ft) ↔3m (10ft)

This magnificent, slow-growing species rhododendron broadens in later life. The leaves are leathery and dark green on top, silver or brownish beneath. Red, pink, or occasionally white, bell-shaped flowers are carried in dense, globular heads in spring.

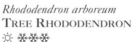

Weeping Trees

NOT EVERY GARDENER likes weeping trees. Some find them too untidy or sad, but a well-sited weeping tree on a lawn, or by water or a border edge, can add both interest and dramatic effect. To attain a good height, such trees generally require further training to a cane or stake for a few years, especially when bought as young, grafted plants.

Fagus sylvatica 'Pendula'
WEEPING BEECH
☼ ✻✻✻   Vigorous growth
↕ 18m (60ft) ↔ 20m (70ft)

A magnificent tree for a large lawn, the Weeping Beech is normally broader than it is high. Its arching or spreading branches are all draped with long, hanging branchlets, and it remains attractive throughout the year. Several other forms are also in cultivation. ♈

Betula pendula 'Youngii'
YOUNG'S WEEPING BIRCH
☼ ☀ ✻✻✻   Vigorous growth
↕ ↔ 8m (25ft)

A popular weeping tree, especially as a lawn feature. It eventually develops a flat-topped or low-domed crown with a curtain of long, slender branches and branchlets clothed with small, glossy green, diamond-shaped leaves, which turn yellow in autumn. ♈

Fraxinus excelsior 'Pendula'
WEEPING ASH
☼ ☀ ✻✻✻   Vigorous growth
↕ 15m (50ft) ↔ 10m (30ft)

Tough and adaptable, this commonly planted, weeping form of the Common Ash has stout, arching branches and pendulous shoots forming a domed crown, broadening with age. As with all weeping trees, train the leader to a tall stake when young. ♈

Cercidiphyllum japonicum f. *pendulum*
WEEPING KATSURA
☼ ☀ ✻✻✻   Vigorous growth
↕ 12m (40ft) ↔ 6m (20ft)

Few hardy trees are more graceful or more pleasing to the eye than the Katsura, especially in autumn when the leaves turn to pale yellow. This gracefully weeping form makes the perfect lawn specimen. It dislikes dry soils. ♈

Ilex aquifolium 'Pendula'
WEEPING HOLLY
☼ ☀ ✻✻✻   Moderate growth
↕ ↔ 4.5–5m (15–18ft)

An excellent evergreen weeping tree for year-round effect. It develops a dome-shaped crown of densely packed, pendulous, purple-barked branches and glossy dark green, prickly leaves. Red berries appear from autumn to winter if a male tree is nearby.

Prunus 'Kiku-shidare-zakura'
CHEAL'S WEEPING CHERRY
☼ ✳✳✳
Moderate growth
↕ 2.5m (8ft) ↔ 3m (10ft)

Normally low-domed, this small, weeping Japanese cherry tree is very popular in gardens where space is at a premium. In spring, the arching and pendent branches are crowded with bright pink, double flowers. It looks particularly effective by a small pool. ♈

Salix caprea 'Kilmarnock'
KILMARNOCK WILLOW
☼ ✳✳✳
Vigorous growth
↕ 2m (6ft) ↔ 1.4m (4½ft)

This dense-crowned form of the Common Sallow or Goat Willow is suitable for even the smallest garden. It has numerous weeping branches, which, in spring, are studded with silver-grey male catkins that turn yellow as they mature.

OTHER WEEPING TREES
Morus alba 'Pendula'
Pyrus salicifolia 'Pendula', see p.294
Sophora japonica 'Pendula'
Salix × *sepulcralis* var. *chrysocoma*, see p.280

Salix caprea
'Kilmarnock' ▷

Prunus pendula 'Pendula Rubra'
WEEPING SPRING CHERRY
☼ ✳✳✳
Moderate growth
↕ 5m (15ft) ↔ 6m (20ft)

The dome-shaped crown of this beautiful, elegant cherry can be trained to a greater height than 5m (15ft) if desired. Masses of small, deep rose pink, single blossoms, carmine in bud, crowd its slender, weeping branches in spring. ♈

Tilia 'Petiolaris'
WEEPING SILVER LIME
☼ ✳✳✳
Vigorous growth
↕ 30m (100ft) ↔ 20m (70ft)

A most notable tree, suitable for large gardens only – a superb specimen for a spacious lawn. The domed crown tops a broad column of weeping branches clothed with dark glossy green, white-backed leaves. Scented flowers appear in late summer. ♈

T R E E S

Trees with Variegated Leaves

BESIDES the novelty appeal they afford, trees with variegated leaves are valuable when used as a contrast against plain green or darker-leaved subjects. This is particularly true of foliage whose variegation consists of a strong white or yellow margin against green.

Acer negundo 'Flamingo'
BOX ELDER
☼ ❋❋❋   Vigorous growth   ↕ ↔ 10m (30ft)

One of the easiest and most decorative of all variegated maples. Its bloomy young shoots and young, pink-suffused leaves age to green with bold white margins. It is best when pruned hard in late winter for bushy effect; the strong shoots give larger foliage. ♈

Gymnocladus dioica 'Variegata'
KENTUCKY COFFEE TREE
☼ ❋❋❋   Slow growth   ↕ 15m (50ft) ↔ 12m (40ft)

Presently a rare tree in cultivation, but well worth searching for. The large, twice-divided leaves are comparatively late in appearing, pink at first, later margined and marbled white, creating a striking effect. A splendid specimen tree for a large lawn or border.

OTHER VARIEGATED TREES

Acer crataegifolium 'Veitchii'
Cornus alternifolia 'Argentea'
Fagus sylvatica 'Purpurea Tricolor'
Fraxinus pennsylvanica 'Variegata'
Zelkova serrata 'Variegata'

Cornus controversa 'Variegata'
WEDDING-CAKE TREE
☼ ❋❋❋   Slow growth   ↕ 10m (30ft) ↔ 10m (30ft)

As a lawn specimen, this beautiful tree is unmatched. Frequently broader than it is high, it develops a tabulated, or tiered, crown of spreading branches, ideally to ground level. These are clothed with slender-pointed leaves, broadly margined creamy white. ♈

Ilex × altaclerensis 'Camelliifolia Variegata'
HIGHCLERE HOLLY
☼ ☼ ❋❋❋❋   Slow growth   ↕ 8m (25ft) ↔ 3m (10ft)

This broadly columnar evergreen is densely packed with short-spreading branches that reach all the way down to the base. Its oblong leaves are glossy dark green colour, and each has a broad yellow margin. Bears red berries when pollinated.

Liriodendron tulipifera 'Aureomarginatum'
VARIEGATED TULIP TREE
☼ ✳✳✳   Vigorous growth
↕ 18m (60ft) ↔ 11m (35ft)

Strong-growing and erect, this tree spreads with age. Its peculiarly shaped leaves are dark green with yellow margins in full sun, and pale to light green in shade. They turn a golden colour in autumn. Established trees produce cup-shaped, greenish white flowers. ♈

Ligustrum lucidum 'Excelsum Superbum'
CHINESE TREE PRIVET
☼ ✳✳✳   Moderate growth
↕ ↔ 10m (30ft)

A striking form of the Chinese Privet Tree with large, glossy evergreen leaves edged with yellow or greenish yellow. It has a dense crown, a compact habit, and fragrant white flowers in autumn. Suitable for a lawn, but avoid cold, exposed sites. ♈

Platanus × *hispanica* 'Suttneri'
LONDON PLANE
☼ ✳✳✳   Vigorous growth
↕ 20m (70ft) ↔ 18m (60ft)

This tree has all the qualities of the London Plane, but differs in its bold and conspicuous, creamy white-variegated foliage. It is most suitable as a specimen tree on a large lawn, especially when grown against a dark background.

Liquidambar styraciflua 'Variegata'
SWEET GUM
☼ ✳✳✳   Moderate growth
↕ 15m (50ft) ↔ 10m (30ft)

Sometimes listed as 'Aurea', this attractive tree develops a conical habit well-clothed with boldly lobed, glossy green leaves blotched and striped yellow; they become pink-tinted then purple-suffused in autumn. Not suited to shallow chalk soils.

Quercus cerris 'Argenteovariegata'
VARIEGATED TURKEY OAK
☼ ✳✳✳   Moderate growth
↕ 10m (30ft) ↔ 12m (40ft)

This broad-spreading oak needs to be given plenty of space to develop and is one of the most effective hardy, variegated trees. Its branches are crowded with bristle-toothed, deeply lobed, dark green, glossy leaves, each with an irregular, creamy white margin.

T R E E S

Trees with Golden or Yellow Leaves

FLOWERING DISPLAYS APART, no trees bring a brighter effect to the garden than those with golden or yellow foliage. A single tree of this kind, especially in a lawn, immediately attracts the attention, as well as providing a bold contrast to a plain or dark background.

Acer shirasawanum 'Aureum'
GOLDEN FULL MOON MAPLE
☼ ☼ ✳✳✳   Slow growth
⬍ 5.5m (18ft) ↔ 5m (15ft)

This beautiful maple is upright to begin with, and spreads later. Its rounded, many-lobed leaves are golden yellow, often with a thin scarlet edge. It is one of the best golden-leaved trees, but may be susceptible to sun-scorch, particularly in hot, dry sites. ♈

Acer cappadocicum 'Aureum'
GOLDEN CAPPADOCIAN MAPLE
☼ ☼ ✳✳✳   Vigorous growth
⬍ ↔ 15–18m (50–60ft)

One of the most satisfactory of large trees with yellow foliage, best planted as a specimen on a large lawn. The sharply five-lobed leaves emerge crimson-purple, soon turning yellow then paling to green-yellow in late summer. Suitable for most soils. ♈

OTHER GOLD OR YELLOW TREES
Alnus incana 'Aurea'
Betula pendula 'Golden Cloud'
Gleditsia triacanthos 'Sunburst', see p.278
Populus alba 'Richardii'
Populus x *canadensis* 'Aurea'
Tilia x *europaea* 'Wratislaviensis'

Acer palmatum 'Aureum'
GOLDEN JAPANESE MAPLE
☼ ✳✳✳   Vigorous growth
⬍ 8m (25ft) ↔ 5m (15ft)

A lovely maple of upright growth initially, later more spreading. The small, neatly five-lobed leaves are an attractive yellow with a touch of scarlet on the margins. New summer growth is even better, and in autumn the leaves turn golden yellow.

Catalpa bignonioides 'Aurea'
GOLDEN INDIAN BEAN TREE
☼ ✳✳✳   Moderate growth
⬍ 10m (30ft) ↔ 10m (30ft)

Eventually, the Golden Indian-bean Tree grows to be domed or round-headed. The large, heart-shaped leaves are bronze-purple when young, and mature to bright yellow. Its bell-shaped white flowers with purple and yellow spots are produced in summer. ♈

Fagus sylvatica 'Zlatia'
GOLDEN BEECH
☼ ☀ ❋❋❋   Moderate growth
↕ 20m (70ft) ↔ 15m (50ft)

Slower growing than the common green-leaved beech, this tree has leaves of a soft yellow at first, becoming green by late summer. In autumn, the foliage ages to the typically golden yellow so familiar to tree lovers.

Laurus nobilis 'Aurea'
GOLDEN SWEET BAY
☼ ❋❋❋   Moderate growth
↕ 12m (40ft) ↔ 5–6m (15–20ft)

A handsome, golden form of the Bay Laurel or Sweet Bay that develops a broad, columnar or conical habit. The closely packed branches are densely clothed with aromatic, evergreen, golden yellow foliage. It is particularly effective in winter. ♔

Ptelea trifoliata 'Aurea'
GOLDEN HOP TREE
☼ ☀ ❋❋❋   Moderate growth
↕ 3m (10ft) ↔ 3m (10ft)

The aromatic, three-parted leaves of this small, round-headed or bushy tree are soft yellow when young, maturing through yellow-green to green. It is less harsh on the eye than most other golden trees. Greenish summer flowers are followed by winged fruits. ♔

Quercus rubra 'Aurea'
GOLDEN RED OAK
☼ ☀ ❋❋❋❋ᴾᴴ   Slow growth
↕ 15m (50ft) ↔ 10m (30ft)

Although it is seldom planted, the Golden Red Oak is a lovely tree, with a spreading crown of large, boldly lobed leaves. These are a clear, soft yellow when they emerge, becoming green later. It prefers a site that is sheltered from cold winds.

Quercus robur 'Concordia'
GOLDEN OAK
☼ ☀ ❋❋❋   Slow growth
↕ ↔ 10m (30ft)

Patience is required with this tree as it is painfully slow to develop. The leaves are such a lovely colour, suffused golden yellow from spring through summer, paling to green eventually. The ultimate specimen tree for a lawn.

Robinia pseudoacacia 'Frisia'
GOLDEN ACACIA
☼ ☀ ❋❋❋   Moderate growth
↕ 15m (50ft) ↔ 8m (25ft)

This is one of the most popular and commonly planted golden-leaved trees. Its much-divided, ash-like leaves are a rich golden colour when young, maturing through yellow to greenish yellow. They then become orange-yellow in autumn. ♔

Trees with Silver or Blue-grey Leaves

COMPARED with the abundance of shrubs, there are very few trees with blue-grey or silver leaves suitable for gardens in cool, temperate climates. Fortunately, the few that are encompass a wide range of sizes. Their presence can contribute much to the garden.

Pyrus salicifolia 'Pendula'
WEEPING WILLOW-LEAVED PEAR
☼ ❄❄❄   Vigorous growth   ↕ 8m (25ft) ↔ 6m (20ft)

This is a popular small tree that will form a domed or mushroom-shaped crown of arching and weeping branches, each clothed in narrow grey, downy leaves. The white flowers produced in spring are followed by small green fruits. Easy and reliable. ♈

Elaeagnus 'Quicksilver'
OLEASTER
☼ ❄❄❄   Moderate growth   ↕ 5m (15ft) ↔ 5m (15ft)

Although it has a bushy habit, this oleaster can be trained on a single stem to form a small tree (as can many large shrubs), with a loose, spreading crown of narrow silver-grey leaves. Fragrant, star-shaped, creamy yellow flowers open in late spring or summer. ♈

OTHER TREES WITH SILVER OR BLUE-GREY LEAVES

Eucalyptus coccifera
Eucalyptus glaucescens
Eucalyptus globulus
Eucalyptus gunnii, see p.286
Populus alba, see p.284
Pyrus nivalis
Salix alba var. *sericea*
Salix exigua, see p.223
Sorbus aria 'Lutescens'
Sorbus wardii

Eucalyptus perriniana
SPINNING GUM
☼ ❄❄   Vigorous growth   ↕ 6m (20ft) ↔ 4m (12ft)

The stems of this small evergreen tree are darkly blotched and they have a white sheen. The leaves on juvenile trees are round, and a shimmering silver-blue, but as the tree matures, its leaves are larger and longer, and their colour more blue-green.

△ *Sorbus thibetica* 'John Mitchell'

Sorbus thibetica 'John Mitchell'
HIMALAYAN WHITEBEAM
☼ ◑ ❄❄❄   Vigorous growth   ↕ 12m (40ft) ↔ 10m (30ft)

This broad, eventually round-headed, tree produces large leaves that are grey-green above when young and white-felted beneath. Leaves of young, vigorous trees can be more than 15cm (6in) long. Clusters of white flowers appear in late spring. ♈

Trees with Purple, Red, or Bronze Leaves

PURPLE- OR BRONZE-LEAVED trees in a garden do not appeal to all gardeners, and there is no doubt that such a strong colour can be an eye-sore in the wrong place. Used with discretion, however, purple foliage can be very effective, especially when contrasted with shades of silver or blue-grey.

Fagus sylvatica Atropurpurea Group
PURPLE BEECH

☼ ✳✳✳   Vigorous growth
↕ 30m (100ft) ↔ 22.5m (75ft)

This striking, round-headed beech is the largest tree of its colour. The oval, wavy-margined leaves are shiny purple, turning a rich coppery colour in autumn. 'Riversii' is also an excellent selection, with rich autumn tints. It is one of the most commonly planted.

Acer platanoides 'Crimson King'
NORWAY MAPLE

☼ ✳✳✳   Vigorous growth
↕ 18m (60ft) ↔ 15m (50ft)

One of the most commonly planted trees of this colour, 'Crimson King' is a large tree with sharply-toothed, deep crimson-purple leaves. Even the clusters of small, deep yellow flowers that occur in spring have a reddish tinge. Displays rich autumn colour. ♉

OTHER TREES WITH PURPLE, RED, OR BRONZE LEAVES

Acer palmatum 'Trompenburg'
Fagus sylvatica 'Purpurea Tricolor'
Malus × moerlandsii 'Liset'
Prunus virginiana 'Schubert'

Cercis canadensis 'Forest Pansy'
REDBUD

☼ ✳✳✳   Moderate growth
↕ 8m (25ft) ↔ 8m (25ft)

This is a small, often multi-stemmed, tree with a broad, rounded crown. It has relatively large, heart-shaped leaves that are a rich reddish purple. The small pink pea-flowers, which are borne in spring, are not always freely produced in temperate climates. ♉

△ *Prunus cerasifera* 'Nigra'

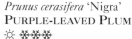

Prunus cerasifera 'Nigra'
PURPLE-LEAVED PLUM

☼ ✳✳✳   Moderate growth
↕ 10m (30ft) ↔ 10m (30ft)

In spring, the branches of this commonly planted, dense-headed tree are flooded with pink flowers. These are followed by its red leaves that turn to blackish purple. 'Pissardii' is very similar, and an equally popular cultivar, with white, pink-budded blooms. ♉

T R E E S

Trees for Autumn Colour

EW SIGHTS warm the heart more than a Japanese maple in autumn, its canopy a blaze of colour. The foliage of many other trees, however, offers equally rich tints, and also more subtle shades of yellow, pink, and purple. These are some of the most reliable.

Amelanchier lamarckii
SNOWY MESPILUS
☀ ☀ ✳✳✳   Moderate growth
‡ 20m (70ft) ↔ 15m (50ft)

A superb tree, Snowy Mespilus has two main seasons of interest: spring, when the bushy crown is a cloud of white blossom, and autumn, when it is ablaze with red and orange foliage. Dislikes dry soils. One of the most reliable trees for autumn colour. ⚱

Acer palmatum 'Osakazuki'
JAPANESE MAPLE
☀ ☀ ✳✳✳   Moderate growth
‡ 6m (20ft) ↔ 6m (20ft)

This beautiful tree is commonly acknowledged to be one of the most impressive and reliable of its kind. It is rounded and bushy, with seven-lobed leaves that turn a brilliant scarlet in autumn. All the Japanese maples dislike exposed sites and dry soils. ⚱

Carya ovata
SHAGBARK HICKORY
☀ ☀ ✳✳✳   Moderate growth
‡ 20m (70ft) ↔ 15m (50ft)

The bold, divided, ash-like leaves of this robust tree with an ultimately spreading crown, turn a rich golden yellow in autumn. Its greyish brown bark peels in vertical plates. This is the most reliable member of a colourful group of hickories. ⚱

Acer rubrum 'Schlesingeri'
RED MAPLE
☀ ✳✳✳   Moderate growth
‡ 15m (50ft) ↔ 12m (40ft)

'Schlesingeri' is an old selection, but still one of the earliest and best of its colour. The three- to five-lobed leaves turn wine-red and have contrasting pale undersurfaces, which are eye-catching even when shed and lying on the ground.

Cercidiphyllum japonicum
KATSURA
☀ ☀ ✳✳✳   Vigorous growth
‡ 18m (60ft) ↔ 15m (50ft)

This is a lovely tree of graceful, spreading habit, with slender branches. Its neatly rounded, paired leaves are bronze when they first unfurl, changing through blue-green in summer to yellow, pink, or purple in autumn. Dislikes dry soils. ⚱

Nyssa sinensis
CHINESE TUPELO
☼ ☀ ✻✻✻

Moderate growth
↕ 12m (40ft) ↔ 10m (30ft)

Erect or conical when young, this lovely tree spreads later. Its long, narrow leaves emerge purplish, turn green, and finish off a brilliant scarlet in autumn; at least equal to the American Tupelo (*N. sylvatica*) in autumn effect. Dislikes dry soils. ♗

Cotinus 'Grace'
SMOKE TREE
☼ ☀ ✻✻✻

Vigorous growth
↕ 5m (15ft) ↔ 5m (15ft)

This can be a small, bushy, round-headed tree, or a large, multi-stemmed shrub. The striking leaves are wine-purple in summer, colouring to a brilliant orange-red later. Large plumes of purplish pink flowers are produced in summer.

OTHER TREES FOR AUTUMN COLOUR

Crataegus persimilis 'Prunifolia'
Fraxinus angustifolia 'Raywood'
Malus tschonoskii
Prunus sargentii, see p.303
Sorbus commixta
 'Embley'

Parrotia persica
PERSIAN IRONWOOD
☼ ☀ ✻✻✻

Moderate growth
↕ 7m (22ft) ↔ 12m (40ft)

The Persian Ironwood will eventually become a broad, spreading tree with piebald bark. It produces small red flower clusters in late winter or early spring, and its glossy green leaves turn yellow, orange, and red-purple in autumn. Dislikes dry soils. ♗

Liquidambar styraciflua 'Lane Roberts'
SWEET GUM
☼ ☀ ✻✻✻

Moderate growth
↕ 20m (70ft) ↔ 11m (35ft)

One of the darkest and most reliable of all the autumn-colouring trees, this handsome specimen of conical, later spreading, habit has shining green maple-like leaves that turn through a range of colours from pale orange to deep red-purple. Dislikes dry soils. ♗

Rhus typhina 'Dissecta'
STAG'S-HORN SUMACH
☼ ✻✻✻

Vigorous growth
↕ 3m (10ft) ↔ 5m (15ft)

Generally wider than it is tall, this low-crowned tree has deeply divided, fern-like leaves that are large and downy. They turn orange-red in autumn, when dense, conical clusters of red fruits are borne. Sensitive skins may react to the sap of this sumach. ♗

TREES

Trees with Autumn-to-winter Fruit

MANY TREES produce attractive fruits in autumn, but few carry them through into winter, when they are of most ornamental value to gardeners, frequently hanging from or clinging to the often leafless branches. Birds, too, appreciate fruits during the winter months.

Malus 'John Downie'
CRAB APPLE
☼ ✳✳✳   Moderate growth
↕ 8m (25ft) ↔ 5m (15ft)

One of the most popular of all ornamental crabs, 'John Downie' is upright at first, and spreads later. White blossom is carried in spring. The slightly elongated, red-flushed orange crab apples that crowd the branches from autumn onwards are edible. ♉

Malus x *zumi* 'Professor Sprenger'
CRAB APPLE
☼ ✳✳✳   Moderate growth
↕ 5.5m (18ft) ↔ 5.5m (18ft)

From autumn onwards, this free-fruiting crab apple, with a dense, dome-shaped crown, bears little, rounded orange-red crab apples. Its pink-budded white flowers open in spring, and the glossy green leaves become yellow in autumn.

Ilex x *altaclerensis* 'Lawsoniana'
HIGHCLERE HOLLY
☼ ☼ ✳✳✳   Moderate growth
↕ 10m (30ft) ↔ 5m (15ft)

This is a dense evergreen holly, with a wide, columnar habit that broadens further with age. It has large, yellow-splashed leaves, and a heavy crop of red berries from autumn onwards. Plant a male form nearby to effect pollination. ♉

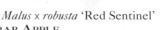

Malus x *robusta* 'Red Sentinel'
CRAB APPLE
☼ ✳✳✳   Moderate growth
↕ 5.5m (18ft) ↔ 5.5m (18ft)

One of the best fruiting crab apples for the smaller garden, this develops a compact, rounded crown. White flowers are borne in spring, and the autumn clusters of glossy-skinned, cherry-like fruits mature to bright red, lasting well into winter. ♉

OTHER TREES WITH AUTUMN-TO-WINTER FRUIT

Arbutus unedo
Crataegus x *lavallei* 'Carrierei'
Crataegus phaenopyrum
Idesia polycarpa (female)
Ilex x *altaclerensis* 'Wilsonii'
Ilex aquifolium 'Bacciflava'
Melia azedarach
Oxydendrum arboreum, see p.275
Pterostyrax hispida
Sorbus hupehensis 'Pink Pagoda'

Photinia davidiana
STRANVAESIA

Moderate growth
☼ ☼ ✳✳✳ ↕ 5m (15ft) ↔ 5m (15ft)

Although it is often grown as a large evergreen shrub, this can be trained on a single stem to form a small tree. White flowers are produced in early summer, and the clusters of bright red berries that appear in autumn last all through the winter months.

Sorbus forrestii
ROWAN

Moderate growth
☼ ☼ ✳✳✳ ↕ 6m (20ft) ↔ 6m (20ft)

Each leaf of this small, rounded tree is composed of numerous leaflets – blue-green in colour. Flattened heads of white flowers are carried in late spring, and the large bunches of small white berries that emerge in the autumn persist all through winter.

Sorbus cashmiriana
KASHMIR ROWAN

Moderate growth
☼ ☼ ✳✳✳ ↕ 8m (25ft) ↔ 8m (25ft)

Erect when young, this openly branched tree has divided leaves that become gold or russet in autumn. Blush-pink flowers open in early summer, and the clusters of marble-sized white berries decorate the branches from autumn onwards. ♈

Sorbus 'Joseph Rock'
ROWAN

Vigorous growth
☼ ☼ ✳✳✳ ↕ 10m (30ft) ↔ 5.5m (18ft)

One of the most popular of all rowans, 'Joseph Rock' has the characteristic vase-shaped crown that spreads with age. Its rich green, regularly divided leaves colour brilliantly in autumn, when the yellow berries, carried in drooping bunches, ripen.

Sorbus commixta
JAPANESE ROWAN

Vigorous growth
☼ ☼ ✳✳✳ ↕ 10m (30ft) ↔ 5.5m (18ft)

This is a handsome rowan with ascending, eventually spreading, branches. It has white flowers in spring, and regularly divided leaves that colour richly in autumn. Large bunches of red berries are borne from autumn onwards. 'Embley' is a superb cultivar.

Sorbus scalaris
ROWAN

Moderate growth
☼ ☼ ✳✳✳ ↕ 10m (30ft) ↔ 10m (30ft)

The glossy green leaves of this wide-spreading tree grow in neat rosettes, and turn red and purple in autumn. Flattened white flowerheads appear in late spring, and its large, densely packed bunches of red berries persist from autumn into winter.

TREES

Ornamental Bark or Shoots in Winter

THE BARK of many trees is attractive or interesting when examined closely, but some trees have coloured or peeling bark that is especially ornamental. Others boast coloured or unusually twisted shoots that have visual appeal, particularly in winter.

Arbutus menziesii
MADRONE
☼ ❋❋❋   Moderate growth
‡ 15m (50ft) ↔ 12m (40ft)

Madrone is a handsome evergreen tree with a spreading crown of dark green leaves. The smooth reddish bark peels away to reveal its pea-green, new bark. White, urn-shaped flowers are produced in early summer; these are followed by orange-red fruits. ⚱

Acer griseum
CHINESE PAPERBARK MAPLE
☼ ☼ ❋❋❋   Moderate growth
‡ 10m (30ft) ↔ 8m (25ft)

Famous for its peeling, papery orange-brown bark, this maple has the characteristic three-parted leaves that turn orange and red in autumn. The branches are ascending at first, spreading later. It is excellent for growing in a border or a large lawn. ⚱

△ *Betula utilis* var. *jacquemontii*

Acer palmatum 'Sango-kaku'
CORAL-BARK MAPLE
☼ ☼ ❋❋❋   Moderate growth
‡ 6m (20ft) ↔ 6m (20ft)

In their first year, the winter shoots of this stunning Japanese maple, borne on ascending branches, are an attractive coral-pink, darkening later. The prettily lobed leaves are orange-yellow in spring, mature to green, and then turn yellow in autumn. ⚱

Betula utilis var. *jacquemontii* 'Doorenbos'
WEST HIMALAYAN BIRCH
☼ ☼ ❋❋❋   Vigorous growth
‡ 15m (50ft) ↔ 8m (25ft)

This strong-growing birch is popular for the white bark of its stem and branches. Its leaves turn yellow in autumn. 'Silver Shadow' and 'Grayswood Ghost' are selections with similarly white bark, as is 'Jermyns', whose catkins drape the branches in spring. ⚱

△ *Prunus serrula*

△ *Eucalyptus
pauciflora* subsp.
niphophila

Prunus serrula
TIBETAN CHERRY

☼ ❋❋❋   Moderate growth
‡ 10m (30ft) ↔ 10m (30ft)

Its mahogany-red, polished and peeling bark makes this one of
the most popular of all cherry trees. Small, inconspicuous white
flowers are produced in spring. Its slender, lance-shaped, pointed
green leaves become yellow in autumn.   ♜

Eucalyptus pauciflora subsp. *niphophila*
SNOW GUM
☼ ❋❋❋   Moderate growth
‡ 10m (30ft) ↔ 8m (25ft)

The leathery grey-green leaves of this evergreen grow on glossy
shoots, bloomy white when young. The bark of its main branches
and stem flakes to form a patchwork of grey, cream, and green.
Fluffy summer flowerheads are white. Plant when small.   ♜

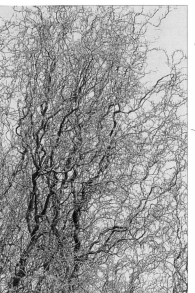

△ *Salix
babylonica* var.
pekinensis 'Tortuosa'

Prunus maackii
MANCHURIAN BIRD CHERRY
☼ ☼ ❋❋❋   Moderate growth
‡ 12m (40ft) ↔ 10m (30ft)

Conical at first, this tree eventually spreads. Its smooth, glossy,
yellowish brown or amber bark peels in bands like that of a birch.
Small white flower spikes are produced in spring, and its leaves
turn yellow in autumn. 'Amber Beauty' also has attractive bark.

Salix babylonica var. *pekinensis* 'Tortuosa'
DRAGON'S CLAW WILLOW
☼ ❋❋❋   Vigorous growth
‡ 15m (50ft) ↔ 10m (30ft)

Erect when young, and spreading later, this willow is easy to
recognize. Its long, twisted branches and shoots are clothed with
narrow, contorted leaves. When the branches are bare in winter,
the dramatic outline of this tree is very striking.   ♜

T R E E S

301

Multi-purpose Trees

WHEN CHOOSING a suitable tree for your garden, it makes sense to consider those offering more than one attraction. This is particularly relevant in small gardens, where space is limited. Fortunately, many trees offer a combination of ornamental features such as attractive flowers, fruit, and foliage, or impressive autumn colour and winter bark.

Cornus 'Porlock'
FLOWERING DOGWOOD
☀ ◐ ✳✳✳ Moderate growth ↕ ↔ 8m (25ft)

Worth growing alone for its star-shaped, creamy white flowerheads, which cover the spreading branches in early summer. These become rose-tinted with age and are replaced in autumn by pendulous, strawberry-like fruits. The leaves persist into winter. ♛

△ *Acer capillipes*

Acer capillipes
SNAKE-BARK MAPLE
☀ ✳✳✳ Moderate growth ↕ 10m (30ft) ↔ 8m (25ft)

Bark and autumn colour are the principal attributes of this most attractive maple with spreading branches, and three-lobed leaves that colour richly. The bark on its stems and main branches is a dark green colour, with silvery or pale green striations. ♛

Corylus colurna
TURKISH HAZEL
☀ ✳✳✳ Moderate growth ↕ 20m (60ft) ↔ 6–10m (20–30ft)

A splendid tree easily recognised by its conical crown – even in old age – and its rugged grey bark in winter. Pendent catkins are borne in late winter, followed by large, heart-shaped leaves, which turn yellow in autumn. ♛

Arbutus x *andrachnoides*
HYBRID STRAWBERRY TREE
☀ ✳✳✳ Moderate growth ↕ 8m (25ft) ↔ 8–10m (25–30ft)

Commonly a multi-stemmed tree, this handsome evergreen is notable for its oxblood red old bark, peeling to pea green new bark. Glossy green, toothed leaves are joined from autumn to spring by drooping clusters of white flowers and red fruits. ♛

Davidia involucrata
DOVE TREE, HANDKERCHIEF TREE
☀ ◐ ✳✳✳ Moderate growth ↕ 15m (50ft) ↔ 10–15m (30–50ft)

A great claimant to the "all-round" tree, this impressive and beautiful tree has rugged bark in winter, rich autumn colour, and striking pendulous, white-bracted flowers in late spring. Its only drawback is that it takes 15 years or so to flower! ♛

△ *Malus baccata* var.
  mandschurica

Malus baccata var. *mandschurica*
MANCHURIAN CRAB
☼ ✻✻✻   Vigorous growth
    ↕ 12m (40ft) ↔ 12m (40ft)

The slender branches of this round-headed tree are flooded with
scented white blossom in spring. Its small, rounded red fruits are
carried from autumn into winter, and the mottled, flaking bark
provides yet another attraction. Reliable and tough.

Prunus sargentii
SARGENT CHERRY
☼ ☀ ✻✻✻   Vigorous growth
    ↕ 10–12m (30–40ft) ↔ 6–10m (20–30ft)

One of the most reliable and strongest-growing of the Japanese
cherries. Abundant, single pink blossoms appear with the
bronze-red young foliage in early spring. In early autumn,
the foliage produces glorious red and orange tints. 🏆

Malus florentina
FLORENTINE CRAB
☼ ☀ ✻✻✻   Moderate growth
    ↕ 10m (30ft) ↔ 5–5.5m (15–18ft)

Dome-shaped at first, then becoming more rounded in habit, this
little-known crab apple has grey and orange-brown, flaking winter
bark. Prettily lobed leaves colour purple or red in autumn, and
showers of small, pink-budded white flowers appear in late spring.

Photinia villosa
PHOTINIA
☼ ☀ ✻✻✻✻✻ᴾᴴ   Moderate growth
    ↕ 5m (15ft) ↔ 5m (15ft)

This small, versatile, wide-spreading tree has dark green leaves
that are bronze-tinted when young, and turn a magnificent fiery
orange-red in autumn. Clusters of white flowers open in spring
and small red fruits are produced from late summer onwards. 🏆

Stewartia monadelpha
STEWARTIA
☼ ✻✻✻✻ᴾᴴ   Moderate growth
    ↕ 10m (30ft) ↔ 8m (25ft)

Upright and conical when it is young, this stewartia spreads with
age. Small white flowers are carried among the green leaves in
summer. The foliage becomes orange and red in autumn, and its
bark peels giving a piebald effect. Dislikes dry soils. 🏆

TREES

Columnar Trees

TREES OF COLUMNAR habit are extremely useful. They are easily accommodated where space is at a premium, such as in small gardens or those that are long and narrow in shape. They are also effective architecturally, for breaking otherwise low or horizontal plantings, as well as for providing a focal point. Most offer other ornamental features.

Acer rubrum 'Columnare'
RED MAPLE
☼ ❄❄❄   Vigorous growth
                        ↕ 15m (50ft) ↔ 5m (15ft)

This cultivar is slender and columnar at first, and its long, upright branches are loosely packed to the stem. These branches broaden later, and are covered in leaves that turn yellow, orange, and red in autumn. *A. rubrum* 'Bowhall' is another excellent cultivar.

Acer saccharum subsp. *nigrum* 'Temple's Upright'
SUGAR MAPLE
☼ ❄❄❄   Slow growth
                        ↕ 12m (40ft) ↔ 5m (15ft)

The ascending branches of this broad, columnar tree are densely clothed with large, five-lobed leaves that turn yellow and orange in autumn. Performs best where summers are warm and winters cold, such as in Europe and North America.

Fagus sylvatica 'Dawyck Purple'
PURPLE DAWYCK BEECH   Vigorous growth
☼ ☀ ❄❄❄   ↕ 20m (70ft) ↔ 5m (15ft)

Described by some as flame-shaped, this deep-purple version of the green-leaved Dawyck Beech is a striking feature in the garden, especially when associated with trees of a lesser size and a more rounded or spreading persuasion. ♔

Hoheria sexstylosa 'Stardust'
RIBBONWOOD   Vigorous growth
☼ ☀ ❄❄❄   ↕ 8m (25ft) ↔ 2–4m (6–12ft)

Few evergreen trees are more suitable for the small garden than this one. As a young tree, it is broadly columnar and compact, broadening into old age. It has small, glossy green, toothy leaves, and masses of star-shaped white flowers from midsummer. ♔

TREES

Liriodendron tulipifera 'Fagistiatum'
TULIP TREE
☼ ☼ ✳✳✳   Moderate growth
↕ 20m (70ft) ↔ 8m (25ft)

The American Tulip Tree is one of the most handsome and distinguished trees for large gardens. This fastigiate form is just as impressive, columnar when young, becoming narrowly conical with age. The curiously shaped leaves turn yellow in autumn. ♈

OTHER COLUMNAR TREES

Carpinus betulus 'Frans Fontaine'
Populus nigra 'Italica'
Populus nigra 'Lombardy Gold'
Sorbus aucuparia 'Hilling's Spire'

△ *Prunus* 'Amanogawa'

Prunus 'Amanogawa'
JAPANESE CHERRY
☼ ✳✳✳   Moderate growth
↕ 10m (30ft) ↔ 4m (12ft)

The branches of this cherry are closely packed at first, but they broaden as it matures. Large, fragrant, semi-double, pale pink flowers crowd its branches in spring. The leaves often give rich autumn tints. One of the most popular of all flowering cherries. ♈

Quercus petraea 'Columna'
SESSILE OAK
☼ ☼ ✳✳✳   Moderate growth
↕ 20m (70ft) ↔ 6m (20ft)

A distinguished form of the European Sessile Oak of columnar to broadly columnar habit, with closely packed, ascending branches and dark green foliage. Like *Q. robur* f. *fastigiata* (*below*), it is well-suited to avenue planting and formal schemes.

Quercus robur f. *fastigiata*
CYPRESS OAK
☼ ✳✳✳   Slow growth
↕ 18m (60ft) ↔ 6m (20ft)

The Cypress Oak is a broad, columnar form of the English Oak. Its ascending branches are thickly clothed with the bright green foliage. *Q. robur* 'Fastigiata Koster' is a very attractive compact selection. Both are long-lived. ♈

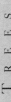

TREES

INDOOR PLANTS

However attractive and comfortably furnished your home, it can be improved by plants. Even small rooms can accommodate at least one, and there is a wealth of choice of colourful flowers and foliage to bring the natural world indoors.

△ AN UNOBTRUSIVE GUEST Isolepis cernua *is small enough to accommodate in the tightest space, so long as light is available.*

◁ INDOOR GARDEN *A conservatory allows you to grow your favourite exotic plants, especially if heat is provided in winter.*

Where do Houseplants Come From?

IF WE WERE TO REPRODUCE at home the environments in which many houseplants grow in the wild, we would have to move out – the conditions in which most of them grow would be very oppressive to us. But knowledge of a plant's native habitat can help you understand and meet at least some of its needs, giving it the best opportunity to flourish in your home. The majority of plants commonly grown indoors come from one of three main climate types: tropical, semi-desert, and Mediterranean.

TROPICAL RAINFOREST
Tropical rainforests are mainly found in south-east Asia, north-east Australia, equatorial Africa, and Central and South America. Here, constant warmth, high humidity,

◁ RAINFOREST CLIMBER *Canopy dwellers such as this* Philodendron erubescens *require medium light and high humidity to thrive – conditions similar to those in their rainforest homes.*

and plentiful rainfall combine to encourage lush, continuous, varied plant growth. Vines and creepers such as *Epipremnum*, *Monstera*, and *Philodendron* climb into the canopy of tall trees, so at home they need plenty of space and the support of a moist moss pole or frame. The trees' often moss-clad branches are home to many epiphytes – non-parasitic plants that prefer to live above the competition on the forest floor. Epiphytes commonly grown as houseplants include many ferns and orchids, and most bromeliads, including *Aechmea*, *Billbergia*, *Tillandsia*, and *Vriesea*. You can grow epiphytes on bark or in hanging baskets made for indoor use. The tropical rainforest's dim, decaying floor, protected from the sun's glare by the canopy, is the natural habitat of many foliage plants like *Aglaonema*, *Anthurium*, *Calathea*, *Dieffenbachia*, and *Syngonium*. In the home, they need a warm humid atmosphere away from direct sun.

ARID OR SEMI-DESERT
Semi-desert habitats are found in parts of southern Africa, the south-west United States, Mexico, and South America. These dry, sunny regions, which can be scorching by day and freezing cold at night, are home to a surprising number of plants, including *Aloe*, *Crassula*, *Euphorbia*, *Haworthia*, *Kalanchoe*, and cacti like *Echinocactus*, *Ferocactus*, *Mammillaria*, *Opuntia*, *Oreocereus*, and *Rebutia*. Many cacti and succulents that enjoy hot, dry conditions are best suited to sunny windowsills or similar spots in the house. However, epiphytic cacti, such as *Rhipsalis* and *Schlumbergera* from Brazil and *Epiphyllum* from Mexico and Central America to the

◁ PUERTO RICAN RAINFOREST *The lush vegetation covers every inch of space as plants compete for light and moisture. The tree hosts an epiphytic bromeliad.*

◁ SEMI-DESERT CLIMATE *Arid regions, like this Arizona canyon, are home to a surprising array of species.* Oreocereus trollii, *left, is a typical dry heat lover.*

NATURAL LIGHT
For the majority of flowering plants, from seasonal plants like *Cyclamen* to exotics such as *Bougainvillea*, good light is the most crucial factor, whatever their origin or heat and humidity requirements. There are also many flowering plants from cool temperate European areas, such as snowdrops and primroses, that are hardy and can be planted in the garden after flowering.

ADAPTABLE SURVIVORS
Remember, plants are extremely adaptable, hence their survival in many challenging habitats. Don't be put off trying to grow them at home; they can tolerate seemingly adverse conditions so long as these are not severe or permanent.

West Indies, are forest dwellers, and therefore cannot tolerate exposure to the hottest summer sun.

TEMPERATE MEDITERRANEAN
In between these two extremes are regions that enjoy a Mediterranean climate of warm, usually dry summers and mild, often wet winters. The Mediterranean basin, South Africa, south-east Australia, parts of the south-west United States, and central Chile are such areas. Many houseplants, including *Boronia*, Cape heaths, *Euryops*, *Myrtus*, *Pelargonium*, *Prostanthera*, *Strelitzia*, and many palms, originate in this type of climate. Indoors, a warm, sunny spot and regular watering are ideal conditions for most of them.

▷ MEDITERRANEAN PALMS *The Canary Island date palm (*Phoenix canariensis)*, right, and the Chilean wine palm (*Jubaea chilensis)*, far right, can both be grown indoors when young.*

Choosing the Right Plants for your Home

THE RIGHT PLANT in the right location will be healthy, full of vitality, and will flourish for years; an unsuitable plant in the wrong place will never perform well, and may even die. So take time to match a houseplant to the conditions in the spot you wish to fill, and consider other factors, such as tolerance of neglect, that may also affect where you place it.

△ BEDROOMS *In your own room, let personal taste dominate – here, bold foliage makes a statement. Temperatures are usually moderate and rarely fluctuate, which is ideal for many plants.*

Foliage begonias for the sitting room

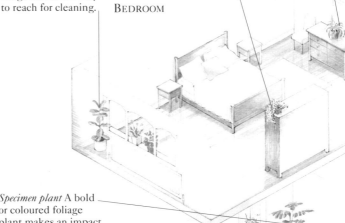

Low-light position Cool, shady spots are ideal for ivies or aspidistras.

Seasonal plant Easy to care for, seasonal plants often provide a splash of colour.

Uncluttered corner Large leaves are easy to reach for cleaning.

BEDROOM

SITTING ROOM

Specimen plant A bold or coloured foliage plant makes an impact in a medium-lit spot.

Medium light This semi-screened window will suit many foliage plants.

Table display Low-growing plants do interrupt the view across the room.

Dry atmosphere Grow bromeliads or any other plants that tolerate dry air above a radiator in winter.

Small feature This bright begonia sets off the pale furnishings.

LIGHT DISTRIBUTION

Low light is tolerated by a limited number of plants

Shady areas are suitable for temporary displays only

Moderate light near the window suits a wide range of plants

Full light Windowsills in full sun offer most light, but this is too strong for many plants

▷ SITTING AND DINING ROOMS *A bold group of plants assembled in the corner of a sitting or dining room creates a wonderful indoor "border". Place them carefully with taller plants at the back, choosing their colours to complement or contrast with the decorative scheme.*

COMMON HAZARDS

Handle poisonous plants with care, and teach children not to eat any plant material or compost. Site poisonous or spiny plants out of reach, and leave walkways clear of hanging baskets or large, floor-standing plants. Attach hanging baskets and brackets securely.

▷ BATHROOMS *A light, warm bathroom, the ideal home for exotic houseplants, is a good place in which to create your own miniature "jungle". Regular showers create humidity, but beware of open windows letting in chilly draughts.*

High humidity Ferns thrive in warm, humid, medium-lit spots like the corner of this bath.

Neglected corner Plants tucked away in corners may be overlooked; yuccas tolerate neglect.

BATHROOM

Exotic specimen This stromanthe, like other exotics, can flourish in a warm bathroom.

LANDING

PROBLEM CORNERS

All plants need some light; few will be happy in dark corners. Use temporary houseplants here, or permanent ones for a few weeks only. Reflect light into the area with mirrors, or paint the surrounding walls white. An aspidistra is one of the few plants that tolerates draughty corners opposite doors.

Clean air Use beneficial plants to help counteract emissions from office equipment.

HOME OFFICE

Draughty hallway The front door brings in cold draughts that may kill plants.

HALL

Heat lover An *Aloe barbadensis* will withstand being near the oven and its leaves can soothe burns.

Mixed herbs for the kitchen

Living colour Use a saintpaulia or other flowering plant to decorate the table.

KITCHEN

Holiday watering Group plants on capillary matting in a cool spot when you are away.

Sunny windowsill This is the ideal location for a selection of herbs.

DESIGNING WITH HOUSEPLANTS

When buying plants, take carpet or paint samples from your room so you can choose a plant that complements or contrasts with the decor. Consider the shape of the plant and its leaves, its overall size, the space you have available, and also how large it will be when mature – many plants on sale are juvenile. If you can't find exactly what you want, remember that a plain green-leaved plant suits any setting.

Windowsill without direct sun Perfect for cuttings. A frequently visited location is also good for a plant "hospital".

◁ KITCHENS *Fluctuating heat and humidity and draughts can be problems here. Position plants in corners, on windowsills, and on surfaces away from work areas. Consider raising cuttings in the kitchen, as you will see them every day.*

Everyday Care

GOOD HUSBANDRY is necessary if you want to grow quality houseplants that are noticed for the right reasons. Having chosen a healthy plant, and found a position that satisfies its needs for light and heat, a regular feeding and watering routine is essential. It may take a little time each day, but the effort will be handsomely rewarded.

SELECTING A HEALTHY SPECIMEN

Buy plants from reputable outlets such as florists or garden centres, rather than from grocery stores or garages where they are often an afterthought. Look around to find a good quality supplier. Avoid buying tender plants, like poinsettias, if they have been displayed on a cold pavement or in a draughty shop.

CHECK FOR PESTS
Look for pests under the leaves and on any flower buds and growing tips.

CHECK FOR STEM ROT
Inspect the centre for any slimy or rotting leaves.

Before you buy, give the plant a quick health check. It should be undamaged, have a good shape, and its leaves should show no signs of wilting. Check for signs of pests or diseases (see left). Flowering plants should have many buds, a few open flowers, and no dead blooms. Bulbs should be plump and undamaged. A plant's roots are also a good indicator of its health – don't be afraid to knock a plant from the pot for a closer look. Ignore any plant with a sparse or poor-looking root system, or one whose pot is congested with roots – a sure sign is if roots are growing through the pot's drainage holes. Ensure the compost is moist, neither bone dry nor waterlogged. Finally, avoid plants with signs of "display fatigue" – tired-looking, lacklustre specimens.

ACCLIMATIZING NEW PLANTS

When you arrive home, unwrap your new plant immediately and water it if necessary. Find a position which suits most of the plant's needs, and allow two or three weeks for it to settle in. Plants may initially shed flowers or leaves in shock, but if you keep providing the correct care, they should recover quickly. Try not to move plants until they are acclimatized.

GIVE NEW PLANTS TIME TO SETTLE IN

LIGHT

Most houseplants thrive in moderate to bright light, and the nearer you can get to satisfying each plant's individual needs, the better it will grow. Note that plants with variegated or coloured leaves usually need higher light levels than green-leaved plants.

Only a few plant groups, like cacti and succulents, can tolerate scorching sun, which can be particularly fierce when it is magnified by the glass of a window. Always provide protection or relief from the hottest summer sun, even for sun-loving plants. Shade-tolerant plants, particularly those with brightly coloured leaves, can be used for temporary display in very dark corners, but remember to move them into a brighter position every two or three weeks to recover. You can also use "grow lamps" or fluorescent tubes to provide light in these conditions and where winter light levels are extremely low.

As plants naturally grow towards the nearest light source, turn their pots regularly to encourage balanced growth. The exceptions are some flowering plants, such as *Schlumbergera*, as turning causes their buds to drop.

SUN-SEEKER
This plant has grown bent over in the direction of a light source.

TEMPERATURE

If the temperature is too low for a plant, its growth slows or stops; too high and its growth is spindly, particularly at low light levels. However, plants will often tolerate lower temperatures (for example in winter) if watering is reduced. Equally, with notable exceptions like cacti and succulents, most plants will tolerate higher temperatures provided humidity is increased and ventilation improved. However, most houseplants prefer a constant temperature; beware of draughts, radiators being switched off at night, or the use of cookers and other household equipment, which can cause heat levels to fluctuate. In addition, when overnight temperatures are low, move plants from windowsills before closing the curtains, as even central heating will not protect plants from the sharp drop in temperature. Otherwise, leave curtains open.

HUMIDITY

As a general rule, the higher the temperature, the higher the humidity plants will need. One easy way of increasing humidity is to mist your plants with an atomizer several times a day. Use tepid soft water; in hard-water areas, use cooled boiled water or fresh rainwater, or you may find chalky deposits on the

MOIST PEBBLE TRAY
Stand pots on a layer of pebbles. Add water to just below the base of the pots, topping up when necessary.

leaves. Do not spray delicate blooms, particularly in bright light, or hairy-leaved plants, and avoid spraying the surrounding furnishings. Alternatively, group plants with similar requirements together, preferably on a pebble tray (see above). Each plant will transpire moisture, increasing humidity. You can also stand a plant inside a larger pot or container, fill the space between the two with moist peat substitute, and water as needed. Enthusiasts might buy a humidifier.

FEEDING

Regular feeding is essential for good results. Use flowering houseplant (or tomato) fertilizer to promote flowering, and foliage houseplant fertilizer (high in nitrogen) for leaf growth. Otherwise, use general fertilizer, which contains balanced nutrients for healthy growth. Where fertilizer for ericaceous plants is recommended, that plant will also benefit from soft water and lime-free compost. Feed only during active growth; unless stated in the individual entry, do not feed a resting plant. Never feed a plant if its compost is dry or waterlogged. Underfeeding makes plants weak and lacklustre; overfeeding causes the roots to scorch and produces symptoms similar to those of overwatering.

FOLIAR FEEDING
Misting with dilute liquid fertilizer boosts flagging plants.

Slow-release fertilizers, in the form of spikes or pills (see below), are added to the compost and are ideal if you are likely to forget to feed your plants; liquid fertilizer or soluble powder types are rapidly absorbed. Special fertilizers are produced for specific plant groups such as African violets, cacti, ericaceous plants, and orchids.

FERTILIZER TYPES

SPIKES	SOLUBLE POWDER	LIQUID	PILLS

WATERING

Water with care – overwatering kills more houseplants than anything else, but give too little water and the roots at the bottom of the pot will desiccate. To judge if a plant needs watering, push your finger into the compost; if soil adheres, it is still moist. Alternatively, squeeze some soil between your fingers to check how moist it is, or use water indicator sticks that change colour when water is needed.

WATER FROM BELOW
Fill the saucer with water; discard any not absorbed.

Always use tepid water. Tap water is fine for most plants, except in hard-water areas, where cooled boiled tap water, or fresh rainwater, should be used. Acid-loving plants like azaleas always need soft water. Plants in small pots, those with hairy leaves, and cyclamen should be watered from below (see left). Otherwise, topwatering (see below), using a watering can with a narrow spout, suits most plants. After watering, drain any excess away; do not allow the pot to stand in a

TOPWATERING
Water the compost, avoiding the leaves.

saucer of water. Plants that have been allowed to dry out should be immersed in water (see below). Remove waterlogged plants from the pot and allow compost to dry before repotting.

REVIVING A PARCHED PLANT
Break up dry soil, then stand the pot in a bowl of tepid water until moist; spray the leaves. Drain, and allow to recover.

CLEANING HOUSEPLANTS

Wipe glossy leaves (right) with a soft, slightly damp cloth or cotton wool. If they are very dusty, use a soft brush first. Do not dust or wipe new leaves, as they are easily damaged. "Leaf shine" can be used occasionally on

smooth leaves but not on young or hairy leaves. Dust hairy leaves with a make-up brush (left). To wash plants, stand them out in light, warm spring or summer rain, or under a tepid, soft-water shower at low pressure. Invert small plants into a bowl of tepid water. Wrap the pot in a plastic bag, or use your fingers, to stop the compost falling out.

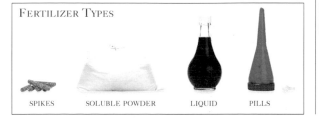

Longer-term Maintenance

ALONGSIDE THE daily routine of house-plant care, other tasks are necessary to ensure that your plants remain in excellent condition. Regular potting on and pruning increases their life span and encourages flowers, foliage, and fruit. Training is essential for climbing plants, providing support and making an eye-catching feature.

WINTER COLOUR

POTTING ON AND REPOTTING

Most plants need potting on (moving to a larger pot) every 2–3 years. Pot on if a plant is too tall for the size of its pot, if roots appear through the drainage holes, if growth is stunted and yellow (even when the plant is fed often), if frequent watering is needed, or if the rootball is congested. Plants such as *Clivia*, and all orchids, should only be potted on if they are "climbing" out of the pot.

Check all plants annually, potting them on in late spring before they begin to grow. New purchases may need immediate potting on. Make sure you are using suitable compost for each plant (see box left).

To remove most plants, soak the rootball by watering heavily, allow the excess to drain, then pull the plant out of its pot. You may need to slide an old kitchen knife between the pot and the compost or even break the pot to do this. An assistant might be useful to hold a large plant while you slide its pot off. If the roots are a solid mass, tease them outwards to encourage them to grow into the new compost. Use a sleeve of paper to remove a prickly plant from its pot.

COMPOST TYPES

HOUSEPLANT
Peat-based compost; loam-based is good for larger plants.

COIR BULB FIBRE
Peat-free mixture that provides good drainage.

CACTUS
Contains slow-release nutrients; use for succulent plants.

CHOOSING A POT

Terracotta pots are porous, so plants in them are unlikely to be overwatered, while plastic pots retain more water, so plants do not need watering as often. Unglazed pots are not waterproof. Heavy clay pots are more stable for tall plants. Stand pots in a saucer to catch drips and avoid damage to furniture. For pots that do not have a hole in the base, use a deeper layer of drainage material, water carefully, and take care that they do not become waterlogged.

THE RIGHT POT

When it is time to pot on, pick a clean pot one or two sizes larger than the old one. Soak new terracotta pots overnight before use. Line the base with broken clay pot fragments, pebbles, or polystyrene pieces to help drainage. Place the plant in the centre of the new pot so the rootball is about 5cm (2in) below the rim. Fill between the pot and the rootball with compost, firming it in as you build up layers. When the compost is just above the rootball, water with tepid water and allow to drain. Stand the plant in moderate light for two weeks before moving into its permanent position. Do not water again until the compost surface begins to dry out. Repot plants in their old pots (see above) to restrict their growth.

REPOTTING
Loosen the compost, replace the top 5cm (2in), fertilize, then replace plant in its pot.

HOW TO POT ON

TIME TO POT ON
Protruding roots indicate this plant needs a new pot.

REMOVE FROM THE POT
Scrape off the top layer of compost from the rootball.

PREPARE THE NEW POT
Add drainage material. Cover with moist compost.

FIRM IN
Place plant in new pot and firm in with compost.

PRUNING

Keep plants under control with light pruning. This is ideally done in spring. Always cut back to an outward-facing bud or pair of buds. Cutting back hard to within a few buds of the base will encourage bushy growth and can regenerate plants that have become old and straggly. Trailing plants like *Tradescantia* or *Plectranthus* respond well to this treatment.

GETTING INTO SHAPE
Pruning improves a plant's shape, thins tangled growth, and controls plant size.

After hard pruning, reduce watering until new growth appears, and then increase as the stems lengthen again. Feeding plants with a general houseplant fertilizer will also help recovery. However, do not prune vigorous plants hard, unless you want to encourage masses of regrowth.

Soft, young growth can be nipped off with a finger and thumb or florists' scissors. This process, known as "pinching out", encourages a bushy growth habit. The material removed is a useful source of cuttings. Harder, mature wood should be cut off with sharp secateurs.

PRUNING TOOLS

SCISSORS   SECATEURS

Remove fading flowerheads immediately, or detach from the flower cluster. There are exceptions, like plants with ornamental fruit, or *Hoya*, which should not be deadheaded because the spurs on which the flowers form bear buds for the next flower cluster.

Finally, encourage well-shaped, healthy specimens by removing any signs of weak, diseased, dying, and dead growth, and any stems spoiling the shape by growing into the centre of the plant, as soon as they appear.

PINCHING OUT
Nip off soft growing tips to promote bushiness and prevent straggly growth.

WHEN YOU ARE ON HOLIDAY

Stand plants on capillary matting or a substitute such as an old towel, and trail one end in a tray of water (left). Alternatively, make a wick from a cotton shoelace or string; dip one end in water and bury the other in the compost. Or simply group plants away from extreme heat or light and ask a friend to water them.

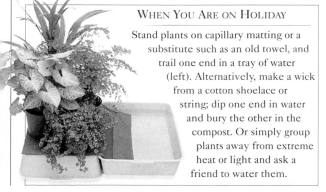

TRAINING

The right method of training a climber will vary according to the plant's growth habit. Natural or coloured canes, used singly or in tripods, are popular supports. Secure the plant's flexible growths to the support with clips, or soft string or raffia (trim the ends neatly). Avoid fixing tightly around the stems. Thin stems of plants like jasmine can be twisted around wire hoops. At the end of the hoop turn the stem back on itself or carry on around. Prune annually and tie in new growth (see right). Plants can also be trained up trellis that is firmed into the compost or attached to a wall. *Cissus* and other plants with tendrils or twining stems will eventually cover the frame and support themselves.

REGULAR TRAINING
Unwind straggling stems, prune, and resecure. Cut out old stems at the base. New growth will develop rapidly.

Moss poles are good supports for climbing or twining plants, especially those with aerial roots and humidity-lovers. Make your own using a tube of chicken wire with crossed bamboo canes at the base. Fill the tube with moss and insert into the pot, surrounding it with compost. Always keep the moss moist. Pin aerial roots to the pole using hairpins or bent wire. As an alternative, wrap a thick layer of sphagnum moss around some narrow plastic piping, and tie it with nylon fishing line. Leave the base of the pipe free of moss so it can be inserted into the compost.

To display air plants, attach them to a piece of dead wood, pack sphagnum moss at the roots, and tie the moss in firmly with nylon line.

GROWING UP A MOSS POLE
Permanently moist moss poles are the best climbing supports.

SUPPORTS FOR TRAINED PLANTS

BAMBOO TRIPOD
Twine tendrils around the canes, tying in the stems.

SINGLE CANE STAKE
Insert cane with care to avoid damaging roots.

SIMPLE WIRE HOOPS
Two hoops are used here; add more if the plant outgrows them.

Propagation

PROPAGATING HOUSEPLANTS is a simple, cheap, and enjoyable way to add to your collection. Spring is the usual time for this, but many plants can be propagated at any time of year. The most popular methods are briefly outlined here; for individual plants, use the method suggested in each entry.

TIP AND SEMI-RIPE CUTTINGS

Tip cuttings are taken from soft shoot tips, while semi-ripe cuttings have a firm base, yielding under pressure. Take cuttings from spring to late summer from non-flowering shoots. Cut with a sharp knife below a leaf joint, 7.5–10cm (3–4in) from the tip of a healthy shoot. Remove bottom leaves, and dip the stem into hormone rooting powder. Make a hole in a pot of cutting compost and insert the stem, lightly firming the compost around it. You can plant several cuttings in one pot. Water well and allow to drain, then label with the date and name and put the pot into a propagator, or use a loosely tied clear poly-thene bag. Do not cover cacti, succulents, or pelargoniums as they will rot. Place in bright light, away from direct sun, at around 18°C (64°F).

CHOOSE A SHOOT
Select a healthy shoot that has not yet flowered. Cut straight across with a sharp knife.

INSERT THE CUTTING
Make a hole using a dibber, a pencil, or your finger, and insert. Firm the compost.

Once there are signs of growth, remove the cuttings from the propagator and allow them to acclimatize for two weeks before moving to the plant's final position.

ROOTING A CUTTING IN WATER

Many plants will root easily in water. Prepare as tip cuttings, removing leaves below water level, and prop the cutting inside the container. Place in bright light, away from sun. If you use a glass jar, change the water regularly. When a good root system has formed, plant up and treat as tip cuttings. Handle fragile roots with care.

STEM CUTTINGS

These are taken from the firm part of the stem, well below the soft growth tip. Using a sharp knife, make one cut just above a leaf joint, and another just under the leaf joint below it. Remove the basal leaves, then follow the procedure for tip cuttings.

LEAF CUTTINGS

This method is often used to increase *Saintpaulia* and *Streptocarpus*. Cut a mature leaf from the centre of the plant, using a sharp knife. Leave 2.5–4cm (1–1½in) of stalk. Insert into the compost at an angle, until the leaf blade just sits on the surface. Treat as tip cuttings.

STEM SECTIONS

Cut mature stem sections, at least 5cm (2in) long, with at least two leaf joints or leaf scars; even if buds are not visible, they will be stimulated into growth. Remove the leaves and press the sections horizontally into the compost until only the top half is exposed. Alternatively, insert them vertically into the compost, burying the end that was nearest to the base of the plant. Then treat as tip cuttings.

DIVISION

This involves teasing the existing plant into sections, each with a growth point, leaves, and a vigorous root system; the divisions are then potted up (see right and below). Many plants form obvious divisions. If not, take the youngest sections from the outer part of the plant. A saw or sharp knife may be needed to divide old, woody plants. Divide in spring or early summer.

UNPOT THE PLANT
Water the plant well, leave it for an hour, then ease it from the pot onto newspaper. Support the crown with your fingers.

DIVIDE THE ROOTBALL
Tease loose compost from the roots and divide the plant carefully at natural breaks.

PLANT UP DIVISIONS
Place divisions in pots and water. Give medium light and a little water until established.

STORAGE ORGANS

Storage organs like rhizomes (right) and tubers can be divided. New growths like bulbils, bulb-lets, cormlets, scales, and tubercles can be detached from the main storage organ.

LAYERING AND AIR LAYERING

Layering (see below) is used for many plants, such as climbers and trailers, that have long, flexible stems that root at the leaf joints. Detach from the parent plant when new roots have formed. Air layering is for more experienced propagators. Make an incision in the plant's stem and tightly enclose it in a polythene sleeve packed with moist sphagnum moss. Keep the moss moist and after about eight weeks, when roots show through the moss, sever the stem below the sleeve, discard the polythene, and pot up the plant.

LAYERING A PHILODENDRON
Peg a mature healthy shoot into a pot of moist compost using a hairpin. Detach from the parent plant when roots have formed.

OFFSETS AND ROSETTES

Offsets are small plants that form around the base of the parent plant; many bromeliads and cacti produce them. Detach the offsets with a sharp knife, retaining as much root as possible, and dust the cuts with fungicide. Transplant them, and protect from direct sunlight until they are established. Some plants produce leaf rosettes that can be detached from the parent in the same way and grown on.

REMOVING AN OFFSET
Look for a well-established offset, clear away the soil around it, and cut it off using a sharp knife.

PLANTLETS

Plantlets are small plants, produced on leaves or fronds, that often root in the compost around the parent plant. Detach or lift them with care and pot into moist compost. Some plantlets, borne on runners, can be put into a separate pot while still attached to the parent plant (right).

PROPAGATING BY RUNNERS
Detach the new plant only when it is well rooted in its new pot.

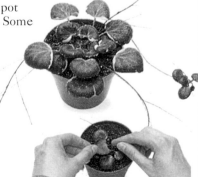

SEED

Sow seed in spring or summer. Use a 9–12cm (3½–5in) pot, filled with firmed seed compost. Water well, or stand the pot in a tray of tepid water to two-thirds its height for about an hour. Allow to drain. Scatter small seeds over the surface and cover thinly with compost or vermiculite, or press larger seeds in gently so they are covered to their own depth in compost, then treat as tip cuttings. If you germinate seeds in an airing cupboard, remove them as soon as growth appears.

HOW TO GROW FROM SEED

SOW THE SEEDS
Scatter a thin layer of seeds and cover finely with compost. Firm larger seeds in gently.

LEAVE TO GERMINATE
Cover pot with a plastic bag or clingfilm. Remove when most of the seeds have germinated.

REMOVE SEEDLINGS
Place seedlings in bright light. Turn regularly. Remove when second set of leaves appears.

PLANT THE SEEDLINGS
Plant in small pots, holding them by the leaves so the stem and roots are not damaged.

SUCCULENT LEAVES

Succulents can be propagated from single leaves. Detach several healthy leaves from a plant, dust the cuts with fungicide, and leave in a bright position for two to three days for protective tissue to form. Insert the cut end of the leaf into a pot filled with one-third cutting compost and two-thirds fine grit. Stand in moderate light, keep the compost slightly moist, and transplant the new plants as they form.

FERN SPORES

Remove a mature frond with brown, dust-like spores on the underside. Place it on a sheet of paper to shed its spores. Scatter the spores over watered peat substitute in a clean pot, cover with plastic, and stand in a saucer of water. Leave in a warm position and refill the saucer as necessary. After several months, small fronds will appear, each of which can be potted up.

Houseplant Problems

HEALTHY HOUSEPLANTS that are well fed, carefully watered, and growing in suitable conditions are less likely to have problems with pests and diseases than those that are weakened through neglect or stress. Check new plants daily for the first few weeks for signs of pests or diseases, isolating them if problems arise. Once established, examine them regularly and deal with problems promptly.

Discoloured yellow leaves

OVERWATERING

Overwatering may be the cause if your plant wilts, the stems and leaves rot, growth is poor, or moss grows on the compost surface. It is certainly a problem for most plants left standing in water. To correct waterlogging, stop watering and take the plant out of the pot. Replace it when the excess moisture has dried out, then water as necessary.

Moss on compost surface

Excess water left in saucer

Rotten leaves

UNDERWATERING

If your plant wilts, has falling leaves, and flowers that fade and drop rapidly, under-watering is probably the cause. It is definitely the case if the compost shrinks from the sides of the pot. To revive a parched plant, soak it thoroughly, breaking up the compost first to allow water to penetrate (see p.15). Then follow the correct watering regime.

Limp, wilted stems and leaves

OVER- AND UNDERFEEDING

Overfeeding can be the cause of excessive soft, weak growth that is vulnerable to sap-sucking pests such as aphids and whitefly. It can also cause root damage, stunted growth, and scorched leaves. To correct these problems, return the plant to a suitable feeding regime. On the other hand, it is possible to starve your plants. Underfeeding makes growth slow or stunted, and leaves pale and lacklustre. Fertilizer may not be absorbed efficiently if plants are potbound. To avoid this, feed plants regularly when they are in active growth, and repot them as soon as they become congested with roots.

Scorched leaves caused by overfeeding

YELLOW LEAVES

Yellow leaves may signal overfeeding, waterlogging, or draughts. If yellow appears between leaf veins, it shows a lack of iron or magnesium; feed the plant (give an acid-loving plant sequestrine). If an acid-loving plant's leaves are pale yellow, you may be watering with hard water or using a compost containing lime.

LIGHT PROBLEMS

Excessive light can make leaves pale yellow, scorched, or even bleached. If so, move the plant to a suitable position with lower light levels, away from direct light or sun. Too little light causes loss of variegation, spindly or arrested growth, leaf drop, and small, pale leaves. Stems may bend towards the light, and flowers may not form. Move to a brighter spot, remove damaged leaves, and cut out or shorten spindly growth.

Brown marks indicate scorching

ROUTINE MAINTENANCE

Inspect your plants as often as possible. Look out for any sign of pests or diseases, and deal with them as soon as possible if they occur. Remove the whole of any damaged leaves; if they remain they may attract fungal diseases. Once any flowers have finished, remove them and their stalks, or the stalks may rot in the centre of the plant.

PLANT MAINTENANCE
Remove dead leaves as they spoil the general appearance of a plant and may also invite disease.

AIR AND VENTILATION

Browning leaf tips and shrivelling leaves and buds are usually caused by a too-dry atmosphere. Raise the humidity by misting or using a pebble tray (see p.313), or move the plant to a more humid location. However, dry, shrivelled leaves can also be caused by overwatering, underwatering, or draughts. In addition, brown leaf tips can be a sign of over-watering, underwatering, too-low temperatures, watering with cold water (always use tepid water), or potbound plants, so make sure you identify the correct cause before treatment.

Suitable ventilation is also important. Draughts can cause leaves to become yellow, shrivel, or drop, and

Shrivelled leaves

Brown leaf tips caused by dry air

leaf tips to become brown. If any of these becomes a problem, move the plant to a more suitable position, avoiding draughts and fluctuating temperatures.

FLOWERING PROBLEMS

If flowers die very quickly, it could be due to over-dry air or temperatures that are too high. Correct these as necessary. If flowers do not appear, it is usually due to insufficient light, or feeding with too much nitrogen. If lack of light is to blame, give high potash fertilizer as well as more light. Moving a plant in bud, or keeping it at an unsuitably low temperature, can cause buds to drop. Prevent this by finding the plant a permanent home at the correct temperature.

ARRESTED GROWTH

If plant growth stops altogether, light levels may be too low, or the plant may be starving or potbound. Nurse your plant by moving it to a brighter position, feeding it regularly with a high nitrogen or general houseplant fertilizer, and repotting if necessary.

COMMON HOUSEPLANT PESTS AND DISEASES

The table below offers advice on identifying and dealing with the most common houseplant pests and diseases. Treatment with chemical sprays is often the most effective remedy for these problems. Some may need several treatments before they are under control,

so don't give up. When you use chemical sprays, always follow the manufacturer's instructions, and use an atomizer kept specially for chemicals. It is best to spray plants outside on a warm, still day, but remember not to leave them standing in hot sun.

PLANT PEST OR DISEASE	APPEARANCE AND SYMPTOMS	CONTROLS	PLANT PEST OR DISEASE	APPEARANCE AND SYMPTOMS	CONTROLS
WHITEFLY	Small white insects, found on leaf under sides; brush the leaf and clouds fly up. They weaken plants by sucking sap and secrete honeydew, causing sooty mould.	Spray the plant with insecticidal soap or use chemicals such as pyrethrum, permethrin, or pirimiphos-methyl. Vary the type of chemicals you use.	**MEALYBUGS**	Grey-white or pink insects, to 4mm (⅛in), covered in white "meal", often found in awkward parts of the plant. They suck sap, secreting honeydew.	Spray the plant with malathion or insecticidal soap.
APHIDS	Small sap-sucking insects, seen on soft growth and buds, that also shed white skins on leaves. They distort tissue, secrete honeydew, and transmit viruses.	Spray with pirimicarb or an environmentally friendly insecticide like derris, soft soap, or pyrethrum.	**DOWNY MILDEW**	Infection causes yellow spots on leaf surfaces, with corresponding grey fuzzy mould below. Mainly a problem on soft-leaved houseplants.	Raise temperature and avoid cool, damp conditions. Remove any infected parts immediately, then spray the plant with a fungicide such as mancozeb.
RED SPIDER MITES	Minute, pale orange mites. They cause mottling, becoming yellowish white, on leaf surfaces. Heavy infestations give the appearance of fine webbing on leaves.	Increase humidity – red spider mites flourish in hot, dry conditions. Spray with insecticidal soap or bifenthrin.	**POWDERY MILDEW**	Powdery mildew appears as grey powder covering the surface of buds, leaves, and flowers. Leaves become distorted, and eventually drop.	Improve ventilation, avoid dryness at the roots, and remove infected parts at once. Spray or dust with a fungicide: sulphur, mancozeb, or carbendazim.
SCALE INSECTS	Flat, yellowish brown, shield-like scale insects are found on stems and leaves, particularly along main veins. They suck sap, secreting honeydew.	Remove insects with a soft, damp cloth. In spring, the mobile young can be seen through a magnifying glass; spray them with malathion or insecticidal soap.	**SOOTY MOULD**	A black fungus that grows on the sticky, sugary secretions left by sap-sucking insects. Sooty mould causes weak growth and spoiled flowers and fruit.	Carefully wipe off the mould using a soft, damp cloth. Control sap-sucking insects like whitefly, scale insects, mealybugs, and aphids, as above.

FLORAL EFFECT

HOUSEPLANTS ARE bought for their flowers more than for any other reason, and the sometimes short-lived appearance of the blooms makes them all the more desirable. Always colourful, flowers invariably draw the eye, so choose them with care – a bowl of bulbs can enliven a plain windowsill, while a single bold flower can transform a dull room.

Ixora 'Jacqueline' for summer flowers

△ WINTER AND SPRING FLOWERS *Daffodils, hyacinths, and primroses, grouped in shallow bowls, provide bright colour and delicious spring fragrance.*

Flowering plants have many points of interest: flower shape, colour, and scent can all turn a houseplant into an eye-catching feature. Bold-coloured flowers bring a cheerful note to a formal room, while those in paler shades can enhance a brighter background or subtly lighten a darker colour scheme. Some flowers offer the bonus of a delicious scent. It is worth thinking carefully before you decide where to place these plants, making sure they are accessible enough for the fragrance to be fully savoured.

Among the most varied attributes of flowering plants are the shapes and sizes of their flowerheads. These range from large, flattened heads of daisy flowers, long, tubular bells, wide trumpets, and tiny stars, to tall spikes, showers, and variously branched clusters.

SEASONAL PERFORMANCE

If you only have room for a few flowering plants, then choose those that bloom continuously or over a long season, or those whose flowers are long-lasting. Remember that you can encourage some plants to flower more than once by careful pruning or deadheading. However, don't forget those hardy house-plants and bulbs that can be planted outside in the garden after they have flowered, where they will give many years more pleasure.

Flowering houseplants are now available all year round, and are often forced to flower outside their natural season. Some are sold solely for one season's flowering display, after which they are thrown away; this may seem wasteful to many keen indoor gardeners. Some, like poinsettias and Cape heaths, can be kept alive to flower again – it is tricky to accomplish, but with patience and care it can be done.

△ BRIGHT COLOUR *This begonia and calceolaria group makes a strong focal point, complemented by the tiny foliage of a compact mind-your-own-business.*

◁ WINDOWSILL COLLECTION *Most flowering houseplants love light, and these popular African violets are no exception.*

▷ STRIKING SPECIMENS *Beautifully shaped and coloured flowers, interesting foliage, and an elegant form make these zantedeschias perfect feature plants.*

Houseplants with Fragrant Flowers

MOST OF US APPRECIATE fragrance in flowers, and there are many fragrant-flowered house-plants. Ideally, they should be sited so that their perfume can be relished at close hand. To enjoy them to the full, place them alone as specimens, rather than mixing different kinds of fragrance in the same room, and remember that their perfume may be overpowering in a small, warm room.

Freesia 'Blue Heaven' ▷
FLORISTS' FREESIA
↕ 40cm (16in) ↔ 25cm (10in)

This South African perennial has flat, pointed leaves, and produces sprays of richly fragrant white flowers, tinted blue-mauve, from late winter to early spring.

☼ Bright, but avoid summer sun ᴇ Warm, but cool in dormancy. Moderate humidity ● Fortnightly as buds form, using flowering houseplant fertilizer ◊ Sparingly, increase when in growth, then reduce ⊞ Cormlets

△ *Boronia megastigma*
BROWN BORONIA
↕ 1m (3ft) or more ↔ 60cm (2ft) or more

An erect, densely twiggy Australian bush clothed in narrow, aromatic leaves and, in spring, nodding, bell-shaped, scented, reddish-brown flowers, yellow within.

☼ Bright, but avoid summer sun ᴇ Moderate to warm. Moderate humidity ● Every three weeks, using fertilizer for ericaceous plants ◊ When dry. Water sparingly in winter ⊞ Semi-ripe cuttings

△ *Exacum affine*
ARABIAN VIOLET
↕ ↔ 20cm (8in)

This pleasing member of the gentian family is compact and bushy, with shiny leaves and blue, pink, or white, scented summer flowers. Treat as annual. ♔

☼ Bright, but avoid summer sun ᴇ Warm. Moderate to high humidity ● Fortnightly ◊ Water when compost surface just dry. Reduce watering in winter ⊞ Seed

OTHER HOUSEPLANTS WITH FRAGRANT FLOWERS

Boronia megastigma 'Heaven Scent'
Brugmansia × *candida*
Cytisus × *spachianus*
Eucharis amazonica
Freesia refracta
Heliotropium 'Chatsworth'
Hoya carnosa
Nerium oleander
Plumeria rubra

◁ *Gardenia augusta* cultivars
GARDENIA
↕ ↔ 1m (3ft)

Few plants have a more exotic fragrance than these. Large, fully double, white to cream flowers show in summer and autumn on a bushy, evergreen shrub. ♔

☼ Bright, but avoid summer sun ᴇ Warm. Moderate to high humidity ● Half-strength fertilizer for flowering ericaceous plants, when watering. Rarely in winter ◊ When dry ⊞ Semi-ripe cuttings

△ *Hyacinthus orientalis* hybrids
HYACINTH
↕ 20cm (8in) ↔ 10cm (4in)

Hyacinths' unrivalled rich fragrance makes them superb for a late winter or spring display. Hybrids are available in various colours; plant out after flowering.

☼ Bright to moderate, with some sun ❄ Cool to moderate. Moderate humidity ◌ Every three weeks ◌ Sparingly, increase as growth appears, keep moist in full growth, and reduce as leaves die ▨ Offsets

△ *Lilium longiflorum*
EASTER LILY
↕ 90cm (3ft) ↔ 50cm (20in)

Large, trumpet-shaped, white summer flowers are richly fragrant. Widely grown for cut flowers, but an ideal winter pot plant if removed to a garden room. 🏆

☼ Bright to moderate. Avoid sun ❄ Moderate to warm. Moderate humidity ◌ Fortnightly as buds appear ◌ Sparingly, keep moist in growth, and reduce as leaves die ▨ Seed, scales, bulbils

△ *Narcissus tazetta* cultivars
TAZETTA NARCISSUS
↕ 50cm (20in) ↔ 15cm (6in)

Many scented cultivars flower from late autumn to spring. Force them for early flowering; afterwards, keep them in a garden room or plant out in a warm spot.

☼ Bright to moderate. Likes some sun ❄ Cool to moderate. Moderate humidity ◌ Fortnightly ◌ Sparingly, increase as growth appears, keep moist in full growth, and reduce as leaves die ▨ Offsets

---

OTHER TEMPORARY HOUSEPLANTS WITH FRAGRANT FLOWERS

Convallaria majalis
Iris reticulata, see p.400
Matthiola incana (Brompton Stock)
Narcissus 'Soleil d'Or'
Nemesia 'Fragrant Cloud'
Viola odorata

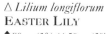

Jasminum polyanthum ▷
PINK JASMINE
↕ 2m (6ft) or more
↔ 1m (3ft) or more

This vigorous, twining shrub, with attractive, dark evergreen leaves, is easily trained to a frame. Richly fragrant, pink-budded white flowers appear from late winter to spring. 🏆

☼ Bright to moderate. Likes some sun ❄ Moderate, avoiding fluctuating temperatures and cool draughts. Moderate humidity ◌ Fortnightly ◌ Keep moist, but avoid waterlogging. In winter, water when dry ▨ Semi-ripe cuttings

◁ *Stephanotis floribunda*
BRIDAL WREATH
↕ 2m (6ft) or more
↔ 30cm (12in) or more

A strong-growing, evergreen, twining shrub best kept small by pruning and training. Waxy, very fragrant white flowers appear from spring to autumn. 🏆

☼ Bright, but avoid summer sun ❄ Warm. Dislikes draughts and fluctuating temperatures. Moderate to high humidity ◌ Fortnightly. Occasionally in winter ◌ When compost surface dry ▨ Tip cuttings, seed

Houseplants with Long-lasting Flowers

PLANTS WHOSE FLOWERS are long-lasting, or whose flowering is continuous or recurrent, are a bonus and well worth considering. They offer good value for money, and are particularly useful if you have room for only one flowering house-plant, or if you wish to add a reliable spot of colour to a drab, colourless location. Such plants perform best with regular deadheading, and in a position which offers cooler temperatures but which also benefits from good light.

◁ *Achimenes* hybrids
HOT WATER PLANT
↕ ↔ 30cm (12in)

Although the individual flowers are short-lived, with regular deadheading these attractive plants will bloom for weeks from summer into autumn. They are available in many colours.

☼ Bright, but avoid summer sun ❚ Warm. Moderate humidity ◖ Fortnightly, using flowering houseplant fertilizer ◌ Water freely in summer, reduce in autumn, keep dry during winter rest, and increase in spring ⬚ Tubercles

---

OTHER CONTINUOUS OR REPEAT-FLOWERING HOUSEPLANTS

Begonia semperflorens cultivars
Brunfelsia pauciflora 'Macrantha'
Catharanthus roseus, see p.374
Cyclamen persicum hybrids, see p.330
Euphorbia milii var. *tulearensis*, see p.386
Fuchsia 'Swingtime'
Hibiscus rosa-sinensis cultivars
Impatiens walleriana hybrids, see p.385
Spathiphyllum wallisii 'Clevelandii', see p.381
Streptocarpus 'Kim', see p.361

◁ *Aechmea fasciata*
URN PLANT
↕ ↔ 50cm (20in)

This splendid bromeliad from Brazil is well worth growing for its beautiful, strap-shaped, silvery-grey leaves alone. The long-lasting, dense head of sugar-pink bracts and mauve-blue flowers is produced in summer. 🏆

☼ Bright, but avoid summer sun ❚ Warm. Low to moderate humidity ◖ Fortnightly, using flowering houseplant fertilizer ◌ When dry. Water sparingly in winter. Keep "urn" topped up in summer ⬚ Offsets

---

△ *Anthurium andraeanum* 'Acropolis'
FLAMINGO FLOWER
↕ ↔ 60cm (2ft)

Breathtaking white spathes complement the polished, heart-shaped green leaves. The exotic flowers are produced through much of the year and seem to last forever.

☼ Bright, but avoid direct sun ❚ Warm, avoiding fluctuation. Moderate to high humidity ◖ Flowering houseplant fertilizer fortnightly ◌ Water when dry. Avoid waterlogging ⬚ Division, offsets

---

△ *Begonia scharffii*
SPECIES BEGONIA
↕ 1.2m (4ft) ↔ 60cm (2ft)

Previously known as *Begonia haageana*, this hairy plant has bronze-green leaves, reddish beneath, and clusters of pinkish-white flowers through winter and spring.

☼ Bright to moderate ❚ Moderate to warm. Moderate humidity ◖ Fortnightly, using flowering houseplant fertilizer. Monthly in winter ◌ Water when dry, unless dormant ⬚ Division, leaf cuttings

Pink-flushed cream flowers

△ *Kalanchoe blossfeldiana* 'Debbie'
KALANCHOE
↕ ↔ 40cm (16in)

A compact, shrub-like houseplant with large, succulent, red-margined green leaves. For many weeks, from winter through to summer, this kalanchoe is topped with dense heads of small, deep coral-pink flowers.

☼ Bright, with some direct sun ▮ Moderate to warm. Low humidity ▲ Feed every three weeks ◊ Water when compost surface dry ▣ Leaf cuttings

△ *Cymbidium* Showgirl
CYMBIDIUM
↕ 45cm (18in) ↔ 60cm (2ft)

Relatively easy to grow, this terrestrial orchid produces long-lasting flowers over a lengthy period in winter and spring. Showgirl is a deservedly popular variety because of its many flower spikes. 🏆

☼ Bright. Needs some winter sun ▮ Moderate to warm. Moderate humidity ▲ Fortnightly, using half-strength flowering houseplant fertilizer. Monthly in winter ◊ Keep moist. Reduce in winter ▣ Division

△ *Impatiens niamniamensis* 'Congo Cockatoo'
BUSY LIZZIE
↕ 60cm (2ft) ↔ 30cm (12in)

Curiously-shaped, red-and-yellow flowers appear at any time of the year on this succulent plant from tropical Africa. A short-lived houseplant with novelty value.

☼ Bright ▮ Warm. Moderate to high humidity ▲ Fortnightly. Occasionally in winter ◊ Water when compost surface dry ▣ Tip cuttings, seed. Roots easily in water

◁ x *Doritaenopsis* Andrew
HYBRID MOTH ORCHID
↕ 60cm (2ft) ↔ 30cm (12in)

A fine orchid, with a basal rosette of fleshy leaves that is topped, throughout most of the year, by a sparsely-branched spike of beautifully-formed, pale pink and rose-pink, long-lived flowers.

☼ Bright, but avoid scorching sun ▮ Moderate to warm, avoiding draughts. High humidity ▲ Fortnightly, using half-strength orchid fertilizer ◊ Keep moist, but avoid waterlogging ▣ Plantlets

OTHER HOUSEPLANTS WITH LONG-LASTING FLOWERS

Anthurium scherzerianum 'Sunshine', see p.332
Aphelandra squarrosa 'Dania', see p.368
Celosia argentea Olympia Series
Cymbidium hybrids, see p.410
Cymbidium mini hybrids
Gerbera jamesonii cultivars
Phalaenopsis hybrids, see p.411

△ *Saintpaulia* 'Bright Eyes'
AFRICAN VIOLET
↕ ↔ 15cm (6in)

African violets are among the most popular of all flowering houseplants. This neat, deep purple variety will produce flowers virtually all year round.

☼ Bright to moderate. Avoid sun ▮ Moderate to warm. Avoid fluctuation. Moderate to high humidity ▲ Fortnightly, using African violet fertilizer. Monthly in winter ◊ When just dry ▣ Division, leaf cuttings

Houseplants with Bold-coloured Flowers

BOLD-COLOURED FLOWERS always attract attention, so they need to be placed with extra care and thought. They should be eye-catching but not distracting, and welcoming but not overwhelming. The bright colours of the plants featured here can be used to transform a sparsely furnished or uninspiring room, or effectively displayed as bold specimen houseplants.

Begonia 'Batik' ▷
WINTER-FLOWERING BEGONIA
↕ 23cm (9in) ↔ 20cm (8in)

Crowded, rose-like, double apricot-pink flowers top the glossy leaves of this neat and compact begonia from late autumn to early spring. Show it off on a windowsill.

☼ Bright to moderate, avoiding summer sun ☷ Moderate to warm. Moderate humidity ⬧ Fortnightly, using flowering houseplant fertilizer. Monthly in winter ⬧ When dry. Stop watering if dormant in winter ▥ Division, tip cuttings

△ *Clivia miniata*
CLIVIA, KAFFIR LILY
↕ ↔ 50cm (20in)

This robust South African perennial is available in several colours; the flowers appear in spring, especially if the plant is potbound. Needs a winter rest. ♔

☼ Bright. Avoid summer sun ☷ Moderate to warm. Moderate humidity ⬧ Fortnightly, using flowering houseplant fertilizer. Occasionally in winter ⬧ When just dry. Water sparingly in winter ▥ Division, seed

---

OTHER HOUSEPLANTS WITH BOLD-COLOURED FLOWERS

Begonia 'Illumination Orange'
Canna 'Lucifer'
Chrysanthemum 'Golden Chalice'
Cyrtanthus elatus
Gerbera Sunburst Series
Nopalxochia ackermannii
Pericallis × *hybrida* 'Spring Glory'
Sinningia 'Waterloo'

Intense magenta bracts

Bougainvillea
'Alexandra' ▷
BOUGAINVILLEA, PAPER FLOWER
↕ ↔ 1m (3ft) or more

Few houseplants evoke the Mediterranean and the tropics better than this thorny scrambler, whose bracts last from summer to autumn. A situation in plenty of light will give best results.

☼ Bright, with some sun ☷ Moderate to warm. Low to moderate humidity ⬧ Fortnightly, using flowering houseplant fertilizer ⬧ When just dry. Water sparingly in winter ▥ Tip cuttings

Calceolaria Herbeohybrida Group ▷
SLIPPER FLOWER
↕ 23cm (9in) ↔ 16cm (6in)

Spring is the time when these curious, blotched, pouched flowers appear, in a range of rich, bright colours. A Victorian favourite, it is best grown on a pebble tray.

☼ Bright, but avoid summer sun ☷ Moderate. Moderate to high humidity ⬧ Fortnightly, using half-strength general houseplant fertilizer ⬧ Keep moist. Do not let the compost dry out ▥ Seed

Euphorbia pulcherrima 'Lilo' ▷
MEXICAN FLAME TREE, POINSETTIA
‡ ↔ 50cm (20in)

These popular shrubs with their flamboyant winter bracts are commonly grown as temporary plants but, with patience, they can be encouraged to flower for a second year or more.

☼ Bright ❄ Warm, avoiding draughts and fluctuation. Moderate to high humidity ◑ Monthly ◊ Water when compost surface just dry. Avoid waterlogging ▨ Tip cuttings

OTHER SHRUBBY HOUSEPLANTS WITH BOLD-COLOURED FLOWERS
Bougainvillea 'Miss Manila'
Bougainvillea 'Scarlett O'Hara'
Euphorbia pulcherrima 'Menorca'
Hibiscus rosa-sinensis 'Scarlet Giant', see p.359
Hydrangea macrophylla 'Hobella'
Nerium oleander 'Mrs George Roeding'

Gerbera 'Freya' ▷
GERBERA, TRANSVAAL DAISY
‡ 65cm (26in) ↔ 35cm (14in)

Big, bold, long-lasting daisy flowers, borne on strong stems, are the trademark of this South African houseplant. It will flower from late spring through to late summer.

☼ Bright, with some sun ❄ Moderate. Low humidity ◑ Fortnightly, using flowering houseplant fertilizer. Occasionally in winter ◊ Water when compost surface dry. Avoid waterlogging ▨ Division, seed

Hippeastrum hybrids ▷
AMARYLLIS
‡ 50cm (20in) ↔ 30cm (12in)

A popular bulbous plant with stunning, trumpet-shaped flowers. It is sold dry in autumn for winter or spring flowering, and with care can be grown for years. Needs summer rest after the leaves die. 🏆

☼ Bright ❄ Moderate to warm. Moderate humidity ◑ Fortnightly during leaf growth, using flowering houseplant fertilizer ◊ Water sparingly as growth starts, keep moist in growth, reduce watering in midsummer, and keep dry when dormant ▨ Bulbils

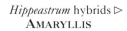

Hibiscus 'Royal Yellow' ▷
ROSE OF CHINA
‡ ↔ 1m (3ft) or more

Sun-loving and a popular choice for windowsills, this plant will flower from spring until autumn in the right place. Numerous cultivars, in many colours and with single or double flowers, are available.

☼ Bright ❄ Warm, avoiding fluctuation. Moderate to high humidity ◑ Fortnightly. Stop feeding at lower temperatures ◊ When compost surface just dry. Water sparingly in winter. Avoid waterlogging ▨ Semi-ripe cuttings

△ *Kalanchoe blossfeldiana* 'Gold Strike'
KALANCHOE
‡ ↔ 40cm (16in)

Golden-yellow flowerheads rise above a mound of fleshy, toothed leaves from winter into spring. Cultivars of this easily grown succulent are sold in many colours.

☼ Bright, with some direct sun ❄ Moderate to warm. Low humidity ◑ Feed every three weeks ◊ Water when compost surface dry ▨ Division, leaf cuttings

Houseplants for Flowers and Foliage

Plants grown specifically for either their flowers or their foliage have a part to play in any decorative scheme in the home, but just as important are those that offer more than one attraction. Many houseplants are worth growing for both foliage and flowers; with beautiful leaves on show when the flowering season is over, they give you the best of both worlds.

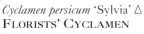

Anthurium andraeanum 'Carre' ▷
FLAMINGO FLOWER
↕ ↔ 60cm (2ft)

Large, long-stalked, heart-shaped, glossy dark green leaves are joined at intervals throughout the year by exotic-looking flowers with shiny red spathes. A striking specimen plant.

☀ Bright, but avoid direct sun 🌡 Warm, avoiding fluctuation. Moderate to high humidity 💧 Fortnightly, using flowering houseplant fertilizer 💧 Water when dry. Avoid waterlogging ✤ Division

Cyclamen persicum 'Sylvia' △
FLORISTS' CYCLAMEN
↕ ↔ 23cm (9in)

Just one of a range of cyclamen offering a stunning combination of beautiful flowers, freely borne in winter, and mounds of striking, silver- and green-zoned foliage.

☀ Bright 🌡 Moderate. Moderate to high humidity 💧 Flowering houseplant fertilizer monthly in winter. Fortnightly in spring 💧 Keep moist in growth, stop when dormant, then water for regrowth ✤ Seed

◁ *Calathea crocata*
CALATHEA
↕ ↔ 30cm (12in)

Handsome for its combination of striking, dusky dark green foliage with purple undersides and erect, long-stalked flowerheads with bright orange bracts. The flowerheads are borne in summer. ♀

☀ Bright to moderate. Avoid direct sun 🌡 Warm, avoiding fluctuation. High humidity 💧 Fortnightly, using foliage houseplant fertilizer. Monthly in winter 💧 Keep moist. Water when dry if cool ✤ Division

△ *Eucomis comosa*
PINEAPPLE LILY
↕ 60cm (2ft) ↔ 30cm (12in)

This is an attractive bulbous plant with a rosette of fleshy, pale green leaves and erect, cylindrical, dense racemes of late summer flowers. It is dormant in winter.

☀ Bright, with some sun 🌡 Cool to moderate. Moderate humidity 💧 Fortnightly, using flowering houseplant fertilizer 💧 When dry, then reduce as leaves die. Keep dry in dormancy ✤ Offsets, seed

Kalanchoe pumila ▷
KALANCHOE

↕ 20cm (8in) ↔ 45cm (18in)

This small, succulent subshrub produces white, bloomy foliage, perfectly matched in spring by pink flowers. An ideal plant for a windowsill or a hanging basket. ♜

☀ Bright, with some sun 🌡 Moderate to warm, but cool in winter. Low humidity 💧 Every three weeks 💧 When compost surface dry. Water sparingly in winter 🪴 Tip or stem cuttings

OTHER HOUSEPLANTS FOR FLOWERS AND FOLIAGE

Aechmea chantinii, see p.366
Aechmea fasciata, see p.324
    Begonia x *credneri*
    Episcia cupreata, see p.398
    Musa velutina
    Pelargonium 'Mrs Henry Cox'
Strelitzia reginae, see p.379
Veltheimia capensis

△ *Senecio grandifolius*
SENECIO

↕ ↔ 1m (3ft) or more

Big, bold leaves on purple-downy stems are crowned in winter by equally large, crowded heads of tiny yellow flowers. Allocate plenty of room for it to grow.

☀ Bright, with some direct sun 🌡 Moderate to warm. Low to moderate humidity 💧 Every three weeks 💧 When compost surface dry. Water sparingly in winter 🪴 Tip cuttings, seed

△ *Ledebouria socialis*
LEDEBOURIA

↕ 13cm (5in) ↔ 8cm (3in)

Sociable is the word for this popular little bulbous plant with purple-backed leaves, which soon fills a pot with its offsets. The flowers are borne in spring and summer.

☀ Bright, but avoid direct sun 🌡 Cool to moderate. Moderate humidity 💧 Monthly 💧 When compost surface dry. Water sparingly during winter 🪴 Division, offsets

Fully open flowerhead of Medinilla magnifica

Medinilla magnifica ▷
ROSE GRAPE

↕ ↔ 90cm (3ft)

A truly magnificent plant, producing big, glossy, boldly-veined leaves, and show-stopping, pendent flowers in spring and summer. Warmth and humidity are vital. ♜

☀ Bright, but avoid direct sun 🌡 Warm, avoiding draughts and fluctuation. High humidity 💧 Monthly 💧 Water when compost surface dry 🪴 Semi-ripe cuttings, air layering

Zantedeschia elliottiana △
GOLDEN ARUM

↕ 60cm (2ft) ↔ 25cm (10in)

An elegant, tuberous perennial with lush, heart-shaped leaves topped in summer by slim, golden-yellow flowers. Hybrids are sold in pink, red, bronze, and orange. ♜

☀ Bright, but avoid summer sun 🌡 Moderate to warm. Moderate to high humidity 💧 Fortnightly 💧 Keep compost moist. Reduce watering during the resting period 🪴 Division, offsets

Houseplants with Winter or Spring Flowers

WINTER NEED NOT deprive you of the pleasure of flowers. Although it can be a dull season in the garden, many different houseplants will bloom at this time, including some of the most spectacular plants for the home, and some trusted favourites. Mass-produced plants forced on to flower need special care if they are to have a long life.

△ *Hyacinthus* 'Pink Pearl'
HYACINTH
↕ 30cm (12in) ↔ 8cm (3in)

Use several in a pot or bowl to display the dense heads of richly fragrant pink flowers. Other hybrids are available. After flowering, plant out in a warm spot.

☼ Bright to moderate. Likes some sun ❄ Cool to moderate. Moderate humidity ◊◊ Every three weeks ◊ Sparingly, increase as growth appears, keep moist in full growth, and reduce as leaves die ▨ Offsets

Cyclamen persicum hybrids ▷
FLORISTS' CYCLAMEN
↕ 30cm (12in) ↔ 25cm (10in)

The gracefully swept back flowers of these hybrids rise above firm, beautifully marbled, silver and green leaves. Hybrids come in many colours and enjoy cool conditions.

☼ Bright ❄ Cool to moderate. Moderate to high humidity ◊◊ Fortnightly in spring, using flowering houseplant fertilizer. Monthly in winter ◊ Keep moist in growth. Keep dry in dormancy ▨ Seed

△ *Erica gracilis*
CAPE HEATH
↕↔ 30cm (12in) or more

A dwarf shrub from South Africa, with tiny, rich cerise flowers. Repot after it has flowered. It will not survive the winter if planted outside in cooler climates.

☼ Bright, but avoid direct sun ❄ Cool. Moderate humidity ◊◊ Fortnightly, using ericaceous houseplant fertilizer ◊ Keep moist, but avoid waterlogging ▨ Semi-ripe cuttings

Euphorbia pulcherrima 'Regina' △
POINSETTIA
↕ 30cm (12in) ↔ 40cm (16in)

Strongly associated with winter, these Mexican plants are always popular. Red-bracted varieties are commonly seen; this compact white form is a welcome change.

☼ Bright ❄ Warm, avoiding draughts and fluctuating temperatures. Moderate to high humidity ◊◊ Monthly ◊ When compost surface just dry. Avoid waterlogging ▨ Tip cuttings

OTHER FORCED BULBS WITH WINTER OR SPRING FLOWERS

Crocus vernus cultivars, see p.377
Galanthus elwesii
Hippeastrum 'Apple Blossom'
Hyacinthus orientalis 'Blue Jacket'
Narcissus papyraceus
Tulipa 'Oranje Nassau'

△ *Justicia rizzinii*
JUSTICIA
↕↔45cm (18in)

Charming and reliable, this small shrub has many small, nodding, red-and-yellow tubular flowers in autumn and winter. Also known as *Jacobinia pauciflora*. ♔

☼ Bright to moderate, avoiding direct sun ▓ Warm, avoiding draughts. Moderate to high humidity ▒ Monthly ◊ Keep moist, but avoid waterlogging ▓ Semi-ripe cuttings, seed

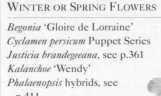

OTHER HOUSEPLANTS WITH WINTER OR SPRING FLOWERS

Begonia 'Gloire de Lorraine'
Cyclamen persicum Puppet Series
Justicia brandegeeana, see p.361
Kalanchoe 'Wendy'
Phalaenopsis hybrids, see
   p.411
Schlumbergera truncata, see p.363
Veltheimia capensis

△ *Lachenalia aloides* 'Nelsonii'
CAPE COWSLIP
↕28cm (11in) ↔5cm (2in)

This bulbous perennial from South Africa makes a pretty late winter and early spring display when several are planted together. Flourishes in a cool room.

☼ Bright, with some sun ▓ Moderate Moderate humidity ▒ Fortnightly in full leaf ◊ Keep dry in dormancy, increase as foliage appears, and after flowering, water when dry ▓ Seed, bulbils

△ *Primula obconica*
POISON PRIMROSE
↕30cm (12in) ↔25cm (10in)

This primula is a winner for a winter or spring display, but note that the roughly hairy leaves can cause a rash on sensitive skins. It is available in a range of colours.

☼ Bright ▓ Cool to moderate. Moderate to high humidity ▒ Fortnightly. Monthly in winter ◊ Water when compost surface just dry. Avoid waterlogging ▓ Seed

△ *Kalanchoe* 'Tessa'
KALANCHOE
↕30cm (12in) ↔60cm (2ft)

Arching, then drooping stems, with succulent, red-margined leaves, carry clusters of pendent, tubular flowers from late winter into spring. One of the best of its kind for indoor cultivation. ♔

☼ Bright, with sun ▓ Moderate to warm, but cool in winter. Low humidity ▒ Every three weeks. Monthly in winter ◊ When compost surface dry. Water sparingly in winter ▓ Tip or stem cuttings

Rhododendron 'Inga' △
INDIAN AZALEA
↕40cm (16in) ↔50cm (20in)

Azalea cultivars, very popular for winter flowers, come in many colours; this one has pale pink-bordered, darker pink flowers. It likes cool conditions, but do not plant outside in cool climates.

☼ Bright to moderate, with some sun ▓ Cool to moderate. Moderate to high humidity ▒ Fortnightly, using ericaceous houseplant fertilizer ◊ Keep moist, but avoid waterlogging ▓ Semi-ripe cuttings

Houseplants with Summer Flowers

SUMMER IS A TIME when the garden is bursting with colour, so it is easy to forget about using flowering plants indoors. Of course, colour can be provided by cut flowers, but these are often short-lived, and there is a wealth of houseplants that flower in summer which, chosen and placed with care, will provide a long-lasting feature in any room. Remember that houseplants should not be exposed to the intense heat of the midday summer sun, although bright indirect light will do no harm.

△ *Begonia* Non-Stop Series
TUBEROUS BEGONIA
‡ ↔ 30cm (12in)

Winter-dormant, tuberous-rooted plants grown for their compact bushy habit, bold leaves, and large double flowers in a range of colours. They are long flowering. ♈

☼ Bright to moderate ‖ Moderate to warm. Moderate humidity ◊ Fortnightly in summer, using flowering houseplant fertilizer ◊ Water when dry. Stop when dormant ▨ Division

Achimenes hybrids ▷
HOT WATER PLANT
‡ ↔ 30cm (12in)

These bushy, sometimes trailing perennials are dormant in winter but produce a mass of leafy stems, with flowers of many colours, from summer into autumn.

☼ Bright, but avoid summer sun ‖ Warm. Moderate humidity ◊ Fortnightly, using flowering houseplant fertilizer ◊ Water freely in summer, reduce in autumn, keep dry in winter, and increase in spring ▨ Tubercles

---

OTHER SUMMER-FLOWERING HOUSEPLANTS IN BOLD COLOURS

Abutilon 'Nabob'
Celosia argentea 'Cristata'
Cyrtanthus elatus
Fuchsia 'Mary'
Hibiscus rosa-sinensis 'Scarlet Giant', see p.359
Pelargonium 'Caligula'
Sinningia 'Waterloo'

◁ *Anthurium scherzerianum* 'Sunshine'
FLAMINGO FLOWER
‡ 60cm (2ft) ↔ 45cm (18in)

One of the most impressive of all flowering evergreens, especially when the brilliant, waxy red spathes appear above the bold leaves in summer. Deserves special attention.

☼ Bright, but avoid direct sun ‖ Warm, avoiding fluctuation. Moderate to high humidity ◊ Fortnightly, using flowering houseplant fertilizer ◊ Water when compost surface dry. Avoid waterlogging ▨ Division

△ *Campanula isophylla*
FALLING STARS
‡ 20cm (8in) ↔ 30cm (12in)

A superb plant for a hanging basket where the leafy, trailing stems of blue or white flowers can be seen. With deadheading, it will continue blooming in autumn. ♈

☼ Bright, but avoid direct sun ‖ Moderate. Moderate humidity ◊ Fortnightly ◊ When compost surface just dry. Reduce watering in winter ▨ Tip cuttings, seed

Ixora 'Jacqueline' ▷
IXORA, JUNGLE FLAME
↕ ↔ 1m (3ft) or more

When the orange-red flower clusters appear, shining above the dark green foliage, this plant is especially beautiful. It is tricky for beginners to grow, as it hates cold air, draughts, and being moved, so once placed, leave it be. Pinch out the tips to encourage bushiness.

☼ Bright, avoiding direct summer sun ❄ Moderate. Moderate to high humidity ◑ Fortnightly, using ericaceous houseplant fertilizer ◊ When compost surface dry. Reduce in winter ✂ Semi-ripe cuttings

△ *Eustoma grandiflorum*
PRAIRIE GENTIAN
↕ 50cm (20in) ↔ 30cm (12in)

Also known as *Lisianthus*, this gentian relative is generally short-lived but gives a rich display of large, erect, satiny, bell-shaped flowers above grey-green foliage.

☼ Bright. Likes some sun ❄ Moderate. Moderate humidity ◑ Fortnightly, using flowering houseplant fertilizer ◊ Water when compost surface dry. Avoid waterlogging ✂ Seed

Saintpaulia 'Mina' ▷
AFRICAN VIOLET
↕ 10cm (4in)
↔ 20cm (8in)

These shocking pink flowers are well worth cultivating. A popular summer houseplant, it will in fact flower almost continuously throughout the year. Saintpaulias can be bought with single or double flowers.

☼ Bright to moderate. No direct sun ❄ Moderate to warm. Moderate to high humidity ◑ Fortnightly, using flowering houseplant fertilizer. Monthly in winter ◊ When just dry ✂ Division, leaf cuttings

OTHER SUMMER-FLOWERING HOUSEPLANTS IN COOL COLOURS

x *Doritaenopsis* Andrew, see p.325
Hedychium coronarium
Pachypodium lamerei, see p.409
Plumbago auriculata
Streptocarpus 'Chorus Line'
Streptocarpus 'Falling Stars'

△ *Gerbera* 'Kozak'
GERBERA, TRANSVAAL DAISY
↕ 65cm (26in) ↔ 35cm (14in)

Large, long-lasting, yellow daisies are carried above a rosette of bold foliage. This tap-rooted plant hates disturbance, so repot with care. Other colours available.

☼ Bright, with some sun ❄ Moderate. Moderate humidity ◑ Fortnightly, using flowering houseplant fertilizer. Occasionally in winter ◊ When compost surface dry. Avoid waterlogging ✂ Division, seed

Streptocarpus 'Paula' ▷
CAPE PRIMROSE
↕ 15cm (6in) ↔ 20cm (8in)

Cape primroses are from the same family as *Saintpaulia*, and are almost as popular. 'Paula' has purple flowers with distinct dark purple veins and yellow throats. 🏆

☼ Bright to moderate. Avoid direct sun ❄ Warm. Moderate to high humidity ◑ Fortnightly, using flowering houseplant fertilizer. Monthly in winter, if not dormant ◊ When dry ✂ Division, leaf cuttings

FOLIAGE EFFECT

ATTRACTIVE FOLIAGE has great long-term value. Plants grown for their decorative leaves will give satisfaction all year round – an excellent reason to cultivate as wide a range as possible. Different houseplants produce leaves in a fascinating variety of shapes, sizes, colours, textures, and even scents.

△ TEXTURE AND FORM *Contrasting growth habits and leaf shapes combine to make this foliage group a pleasing whole.*

giant-sized, deeply-lobed or divided foliage. Plants with strap- or sword-shaped leaves are very versatile as they can fit into narrow or awkward spaces, and their strong vertical or arching shapes provide excellent contrast to plants of mound-forming or spreading habit, or those with broad or rounded leaves. Rough-, hairy-, or smooth-textured and aromatic leaves offer further variety in the home.

Foliage plants are also effective for adding detail above eye-level. Site trailing plants in indoor hanging baskets or in containers on tall pedestals or high shelves.

A SPLASH OF COLOUR

Almost every colour exists in the world of plant foliage. Yellow, silver, red, or purple leaves provide

an attractive foil or background for green-leaved plants. Colourful variegated plants also make superb single specimens. As a rule of thumb, pale or brightly coloured foliage "lifts" dark areas while dark leaves appear best against a pale background. Remember that green, the colour of most foliage, comes in an astonishing range of tones. Dramatic effects can be achieved with the different textures, sizes, growth habits, and shades of colour found on green-leaved plants alone.

Begonia 'Merry Christmas' for silver or grey foliage

Leaves range in size from the selaginella's tiny scale-like foliage to the great leathery blades of a Swiss cheese plant. They also vary enormously in shape, from elegant, frond-like or plumed leaves to

△ SIMPLE STYLE *The small leaves of this delicate-looking pilea are eye-catching and add detail to the trailing stems.*

◁ COLOURFUL VARIETY *A red croton and bright-bordered coleus are set off by varied shapes and tones of green foliage, displayed at different levels.*

▷ DRAMATIC EFFECT *The narrow foliage of this gold-variegated croton makes a bold statement, providing a good focal point for a sitting room or bedroom.*

Houseplants with Small Foliage

SMALL-LEAVED HOUSEPLANTS lend themselves to restricted spaces, particularly where they can be examined in detail, and can be a foil to larger-leaved plants. Those with a trailing habit, in hanging baskets or on high surfaces, will fill narrow gaps, while slow-growing varieties are effective in bottle gardens and terraria. Group plants of contrasting leaf shapes together in a large bowl, trough, or container.

△ *Euonymus japonicus* 'Microphyllus Variegatus'
JAPANESE SPINDLE
‡ 1m (3ft) ↔ 45cm (18in)

This hardy evergreen shrub, with bright, white-margined leaves, can be kept trim by pruning or pinching out. Slow-growing, it is suitable for use with creeping plants.

☼ Bright. Likes some sun ≣ Cool to moderate. Moderate humidity ◊ Every three weeks. Occasionally in winter ◊ When compost surface dry. Water sparingly in winter ▭ Semi-ripe cuttings

Begonia
Brazil (new species) ▷
BEGONIA
‡ 20cm (8in)
↔ 30cm (12in)

Small, rounded, fuzzy-textured, dark green leaves, marked with paler green veins, and with dark red undersides, form the crowded hummock of this intriguing, and as yet unclassified, begonia from Brazil.

☼ Bright to moderate, avoiding summer sun ≣ Moderate to warm. Moderate humidity ◊ Fortnightly in summer, monthly in winter ◊ When dry, unless dormant in winter ▭ Division, tip cuttings

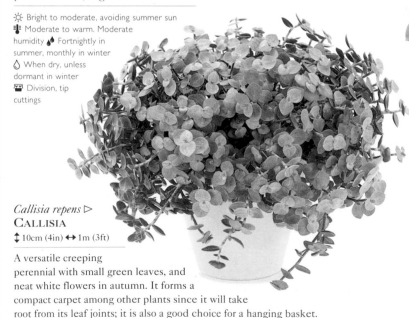

Callisia repens ▷
CALLISIA
‡ 10cm (4in) ↔ 1m (3ft)

A versatile creeping perennial with small green leaves, and neat white flowers in autumn. It forms a compact carpet among other plants since it will take root from its leaf joints; it is also a good choice for a hanging basket.

☼ Bright. Likes some sun ≣ Moderate to warm. Moderate to high humidity ◊ Fortnightly. Occasionally in winter ◊ Water when compost surface dry ▭ Tip cuttings, layering. Roots easily in water

△ *Ficus pumila*
CREEPING FIG
‡ ↔ 80cm (32in) or more

The juvenile form of this evergreen is a useful houseplant, either clipped into a hummock or trained on a frame. Grown against a wall it reaches a good height. ♔

☼ Bright, but avoid summer sun ≣ Moderate to warm. Moderate to high humidity ◊ Fortnightly. Occasionally in winter ◊ When compost surface dry. Reduce at lower temperatures ▭ Tip cuttings

△ *Peperomia rotundifolia*
CREEPING BUTTONS
↕ 15cm (6in) ↔ 30cm (12in)

Best grown in a small hanging basket or in a pot on a high surface where the delicate trailing stems, studded with small, round, fleshy leaves, can be seen to advantage.

☼ Bright to moderate, with some sun ▤ Warm. Moderate to high humidity ◐ Every three weeks. Occasionally in winter ◊ Water when compost surface dry. Avoid waterlogging ▨ Tip cuttings

◁ *Streptocarpus saxorum*
CAPE PRIMROSE
↕ 15cm (6in) ↔ 60cm (2ft)

Fascinatingly different from common Cape primroses, this east African species is prostrate in habit, and branched, with small, thick leaves. It bears charming flowers in spring and summer. ♔

☼ Bright to moderate, avoiding direct sun ▤ Warm. Moderate to high humidity ◐ Fortnightly, using flowering houseplant fertilizer. Monthly in winter, unless dormant ◊ When dry ▨ Tip cuttings

---

OTHER TRAILING HOUSEPLANTS WITH SMALL FOLIAGE

Aptenia cordifolia 'Variegata'
   Ceropegia linearis subsp. *woodii*, see p.390
      Dichondra micrantha
         Ficus pumila 'Minima'
            Hedera helix 'Spetchley'
      Peperomia prostrata
   Senecio rowleyanus, see p.390

△ *Pilea depressa*
PILEA
↕ 10cm (4in) ↔ 30cm (12in)

A creeping evergreen, with trailing stems bearing small, fleshy, bright green leaves. Display as *Peperomia rotundifolia* (above), in a small hanging basket or raised pot.

☼ Bright to moderate, with some sun ▤ Warm. Moderate to high humidity ◐ Every three weeks. Occasionally in winter ◊ Water when compost surface just dry. Avoid waterlogging ▨ Tip cuttings

---

OTHER HOUSEPLANTS WITH SMALL FOLIAGE

Aichryson × *domesticum* 'Variegatum'
Begonia 'Queen Olympus'
Cuphea hyssopifolia, see p.378
Peperomia campylotropa
Punica granatum var. *nana*
Saintpaulia 'Midget Valentine'

Saintpaulia
'Pip Squeek' △
AFRICAN VIOLET
↕ ↔ 10cm (4in)

This neat, compact African violet forms a tuffet of small, dusky green, dark-stalked leaves. Miniature, bell-shaped, pale pink flowers are borne throughout the year.

☼ Bright to moderate, avoiding direct sun ▤ Moderate to warm. Moderate to high humidity ◐ Fortnightly, using African violet fertilizer. Monthly in winter ◊ When just dry ▨ Division, leaf cuttings

---

△ *Tripogandra multiflora*
TRIPOGANDRA
↕ 20cm (8in) ↔ 1m (3ft)

A loose hummock of trailing stems, with small, narrow leaves, is set off by white flowers, freely produced from autumn to spring. Best suited to a hanging basket.

☼ Bright, but avoid direct sun ▤ Moderate. Moderate to high humidity ◐ Fortnightly. Rarely in winter ◊ Keep moist. When compost surface dry in winter ▨ Tip cuttings. Roots easily in water

Houseplants with Large Foliage

HOUSEPLANTS WITH LARGE FOLIAGE always make excellent specimen plants, particularly in larger rooms. Young, small plants can first be displayed as table centre-pieces, and moved as they grow. Large-leaved houseplants make superb focal points, especially when displayed against a plain background to accentuate their striking foliage and bold outlines. They can also be used effectively in a group of different plants, all with similar cultivation requirements but with contrasting shapes and sizes.

△ *Cordyline fruticosa* 'Red Edge'
GOOD LUCK PLANT
↕ 1m (3ft) ↔ 60cm (2ft)

This compact plant with broad green, red-margined leaves is best displayed in a group. Use the bold leaves to contrast with the surrounding furnishings. ♆

☼ Bright, but avoid direct sun ♨ Moderate to warm, avoiding draughts. Moderate to high humidity ♦ Fortnightly. Monthly in winter ♦ Let compost dry before watering, particularly in cool conditions ☷ Division, tip or stem cuttings

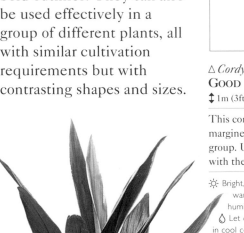

△ *Anthurium crystallinum*
CRYSTAL ANTHURIUM
↕ ↔ 60cm (2ft)

A stunning foliage plant, producing large, velvety, dark green, white-veined leaves that are pink-bronze when young. It needs growing conditions similar to those in its native Colombian rainforest home. ♆

☼ Bright, but avoid direct summer sun. Tolerates some shade ♨ Warm, avoiding draughts. High humidity ♦ Fortnightly in summer. Monthly in winter ♦ Keep moist ☷ Division

---

OTHER HOUSEPLANTS WITH LARGE FOLIAGE

Codiaeum variegatum var. *pictum*, see p.368
Epipremnum aureum, see p.390
Ficus lyrata, see p.395
Philodendron bipinnatifidum, see p.364
Platycerium bifurcatum, see p.407
Spathiphyllum 'Euro Gigant', see p.371
Yucca elephantipes, see p.385

△ *Cordyline fruticosa* 'Lord Robertson'
GOOD LUCK PLANT
↕ 3m (10ft) ↔ 60cm (2ft)

Green and cream leaves gradually turn red-purple with rose margins. Perfect for a richly decorated room, this elegant plant lives up to its aristocratic cultivar name.

☼ Bright, but avoid summer sun ♨ Moderate to warm. Moderate to high humidity ♦ Fortnightly. Monthly in winter ♦ Water only when dry. Reduce in cool conditions ☷ Division, tip or stem cuttings

△ *Dieffenbachia* 'Compacta'
DUMB CANE
↕ 1m (3ft) ↔ 60cm (2ft)

Dumb canes have beautifully mottled leaves, here with elegant cream markings. They have poisonous sap, so wear gloves to handle, and wash hands afterwards.

☼ Bright, but avoid direct sun ♨ Moderate to warm. Moderate to high humidity ♦ Fortnightly. Monthly in winter ♦ Water when compost surface has dried out ☷ Tip cuttings, stem sections

Fatsia japonica ▷
JAPANESE ARALIA
↕ ↔ 2m (6ft)

Ideal for a cooler room, this bold, glossy-leaved aralia can be kept within bounds by pruning, and can be planted outside in most areas if it outgrows its allotted position.

☼ Moderate 🌡 Cool to moderate. Moderate humidity 💧 Fortnightly, using foliage houseplant fertilizer. Once in winter 💧 When dry. Reduce if cool 🌱 Tip cuttings, air layering

△ *Monstera deliciosa*
SWISS CHEESE PLANT
↕ 3m (10ft) or more ↔ 1.2m (4ft) or more

Tropical South American rainforests produce this giant, popular for its vigorous growth and large, beautifully sculpted leaves. An impressive climber, it is best grown up a moss pole or trellis. ⚱

☼ Bright to moderate 🌡 Moderate to warm. Moderate to high humidity 💧 Fortnightly. Twice during winter 💧 Let compost surface dry before watering 🌱 Stem cuttings, air layering

△ *Ficus elastica*
RUBBER PLANT
↕ 3m (10ft) or more ↔ 1m (3ft) or more

The bold form of their leathery, paddle-shaped, glossy dark green leaves make rubber plants highly desirable specimens. Will eventually outgrow an average room.

☼ Bright to moderate 🌡 Moderate to warm. Moderate to high humidity 💧 Foliage houseplant fertilizer fortnightly. Monthly in winter 💧 When dry. Reduce watering if cool 🌱 Tip cuttings, air layering

△ *Grevillea robusta*
SILK OAK
↕ 3m (10ft) or more ↔ 1.5m (5ft) or more

Silk oaks' large leaves are composed of leaflets that create a delicate filigree. In their native Australia they become huge trees. Grow in lime-free compost. ⚱

☼ Bright to shady, avoiding direct sun 🌡 Cool to warm. Moderate humidity 💧 Fortnightly, spring to autumn, using foliage houseplant fertilizer 💧 When dry, using soft water 🌱 Semi-ripe cuttings, seed

△ *Philodendron erubescens* 'Imperial Red'
BLUSHING PHILODENDRON
↕ 3m (10ft) or more ↔ 1m (3ft) or more

The young leaves of this philodendron are deep claret, maturing to dark green, deeply veined and glossy. Bushy when young, it will climb when established.

☼ Bright to moderate 🌡 Warm. Moderate to high humidity 💧 Fortnightly, using foliage houseplant fertilizer. Monthly in winter 💧 Water when compost surface dry 🌱 Tip cuttings

Houseplants with Narrow or Sword-shaped Foliage

NARROW-LEAVED PLANTS can be very effective, especially when contrasted with broad-leaved subjects. Used with flair, many houseplants with sword-shaped foliage can contribute height to a group and break up hard horizontal lines in the display. As specimen plants, tall varieties can provide a strong focal point as well as being useful "fillers" in narrow spaces and awkward corners.

Codiaeum 'Goldfinger' ▷
CROTON
↕ ↔ 1m (3ft) or more

The long, narrow, gold-variegated leaves of this shrub, one of the colourful croton family, bring an exotic flavour to any room. It loves generous amounts of light, heat, and humidity.

☼ Bright, with some sun
❄ Warm, avoiding draughts and fluctuation. Moderate to high humidity ◑ Fortnightly, using foliage houseplant fertilizer. Occasionally in winter ◊ Keep moist. In winter, water when compost surface dry ▥ Tip cuttings

△ *Acorus gramineus* 'Ogon'
JAPANESE SWEET FLAG
↕ 25cm (10in) ↔ 45cm (18in)

Erect when young, this small, clump-forming perennial forms a broad mound of arching, aromatic, green- and gold-striped, narrow leaves. Colour fades in poor light.

☼ Bright to moderate, with some sun
❄ Cool to moderate. Moderate humidity
◑ Every three weeks. Occasionally in winter ◊ Keep moist ▥ Division

Leaves arch with age

Carex conica 'Snowline' ▷
ORNAMENTAL SEDGE
↕ 15cm (6in) ↔ 25cm (10in)

Quite hardy and suitable for an unheated room, this small, densely tufted evergreen is a useful houseplant with narrow, dark green leaves, margined creamy-white and arching outwards.

☼ Bright to shady, with some sun ❄ Cool to moderate. Moderate humidity ◑ Every three weeks. Occasionally in winter ◊ When compost surface dry. Reduce watering in winter ▥ Division

Cordyline australis 'Red Star' △
NEW ZEALAND CABBAGE TREE
↕ 3m (10ft) ↔ 1m (3ft)

When young this plant produces a glorious, leafy rosette, but it soon forms a woody stem with leaves collecting towards the summit. An excellent window plant when young.

☼ Bright to moderate ❄ Moderate to warm. Moderate to high humidity ◑ Fortnightly ◊ Water when compost surface just dry. Reduce watering in winter ▥ Stem sections

Cordyline australis 'Sundance' ▷
NEW ZEALAND CABBAGE TREE
↕ 3m (10ft) ↔ 1m (3ft)

This striking plant from New Zealand has long, narrow, leathery leaves that form a wide arch from the base. Young specimens are ideal for a sunny window position.

☼ Bright to moderate ‖ Moderate to warm. Moderate to high humidity ◓ Fortnightly ◊ Water when compost surface just dry. Reduce watering in winter ▤ Stem sections

△ *Isolepis cernua*
SLENDER CLUB-RUSH
↕ 15cm (6in) ↔ 45cm (18in)

A charming, tufted little rush-like plant with thread-like, arching or drooping leaves and equally slender shoots bearing tiny brown spikes. Useful with small bulbs or ferns.

☼ Bright to shady, with some sun ‖ Cool to moderate. Moderate humidity ◓ Every three weeks. Occasionally in winter ◊ When compost surface dry. Reduce watering in winter ▤ Division

△ *Pandanus veitchii*
SCREW PINE
↕ ↔ 1.2m (4ft) or more

Like a pineapple in habit, except that the white-margined, dark green leaves droop at the tips. A dramatic houseplant, but it has vicious spiny teeth, so place with care.

☼ Bright to moderate, avoiding summer sun ‖ Warm. High humidity ◓ Fortnightly. Occasionally in winter ◊ Keep moist. Reduce watering in winter ▤ Division, stem sections

Magenta-edged evergreen leaves

Dracaena cincta 'Magenta' ▷
DRACAENA
↕ 3m (10ft) ↔ 1.2m (4ft)

Slow-growing and with slender stems, this evergreen will branch with age, displaying its crowded rosettes of long, narrow, arching leaves. Good light gives the best colour.

☼ Bright to moderate, avoiding summer sun ‖ Warm. Moderate to high humidity ◓ Fortnightly. Occasionally in winter ◊ When compost surface dry. Water sparingly in winter ▤ Tip cuttings, stem sections

OTHER HOUSEPLANTS WITH NARROW FOLIAGE

Ananas bracteatus 'Tricolor', see p.358
Billbergia x *windii*, see p.414
Cordyline australis 'Albertii'
Dracaena fragrans 'Janet Craig', see p.388
Nolina recurvata, see p.96
Ophiopogon jaburan 'Vittatus'
Phormium 'Cream Delight'
Phormium 'Crimson Devil'
Tradescantia spathacea
Yucca elephantipes, see p.385

△ *Phormium* 'Sundowner'
NEW ZEALAND FLAX
↕ ↔ 1.5m (5ft)

Bold in habit and in leaf, this has tall, erect, leathery, sword-shaped leaves, with a dull purple centre and broad edges of pink, fading to cream. A fine focal point.

☼ Bright to moderate, with some sun ‖ Cool to moderate. Moderate humidity ◓ Fortnightly. Occasionally in winter ◊ When compost surface dry. Reduce watering in winter ▤ Division

341

Houseplants with Textured Foliage

THE HUGE VARIETY of leaf surfaces that plants present to the touch provide a seemingly unending source of pleasure. Some leaves are rough, with distinctive ridges or wrinkles, while others have a smooth or velvety patina that begs to be stroked. Try using several of these in a feature group. People with sensitive skin should take care with bristly-leaved plants, which can cause skin irritation or a rash.

Begonia 'Beatrice Haddrell' ▷
RHIZOMATOUS BEGONIA
↕ 15cm (6in) ↔ 25cm (10in)

Worth growing just for its sharply angled, almost star-shaped, velvety, dark brownish leaves, which have light green veins and centres and deep red undersides. Sprays of pale pink or white flowers appear from winter into early spring.

☼ Bright to moderate, avoiding summer sun 🌡 Moderate to warm. Moderate humidity 💧 Fortnightly. Monthly in winter 💧 When compost surface dry. Stop watering if winter dormant 🔱 Division

△ *Begonia masoniana*
IRON CROSS BEGONIA
↕ ↔ 50cm (20in)

An old favourite from New Guinea, the iron cross begonia takes its name from the distinctive dark mark in the centre of each bright green, puckered, hairy leaf. A stunning foliage plant. 🏆

☼ Bright to moderate, avoiding summer sun 🌡 Moderate to warm. Moderate humidity 💧 Fortnightly. Monthly in winter 💧 When dry. Stop watering if dormant in winter 🔱 Division, leaf cuttings

OTHER HOUSEPLANTS WITH SMOOTH-TEXTURED FOLIAGE

Anthurium andraeanum
Aspidistra elatior, see p.386
Asplenium nidus, see p.406
Begonia 'Thurstonii'
Codiaeum variegatum var. *pictum,* see p.368
Dracaena fragrans 'Massangeana', see p.375
Ficus elastica, see p.339
Veltheimia capensis

△ *Begonia bowerae*
EYELASH BEGONIA
↕ 25cm (10in) ↔ 18cm (7in)

Easy to grow and very popular, eyelash begonias have crinkly-margined, dark-spotted, whiskery leaves. Grow them on a windowsill where they can be easily seen.

☼ Bright to moderate, avoiding summer sun 🌡 Moderate to warm. Moderate humidity 💧 Fortnightly. Monthly in winter 💧 When compost surface dry. Water sparingly in winter 🔱 Division

◁ *Gynura aurantiaca*
'Purple Passion'
PURPLE VELVET PLANT
↕ 3m (10ft) ↔ 60cm (2ft)

Purple velvet is exactly what the leaves of this scrambling plant from Java look and feel like. To maintain a compact habit, train stems to a support and pinch out the tips. Nip off buds of the evil-smelling flowers when they appear. 🏆

☼ Bright, but avoid summer sun 🌡 Warm. Moderate to high humidity 💧 Fortnightly. Occasionally in winter 💧 Water when compost surface dry. Avoid overwatering 🔱 Tip cuttings

△ *Kalanchoe tomentosa*
PANDA PLANT, PUSSY EARS
↕ 1m (3ft) ↔ 20cm (8in)

Everyone will enjoy stroking the soft, white, felted leaves of this Madagascan shrub; its shoots have the same texture. Avoid wetting leaves when watering. ♈

☼ Bright, with some sun ❄ Moderate to warm, but cool in winter. Low humidity ♠ Every three weeks. Monthly in winter ♦ When dry. Water sparingly in winter ✄ Tip or stem cuttings

△ *Peperomia caperata* 'Luna'
PEPEROMIA
↕ ↔ 20cm (8in)

The corrugated surfaces of these neatly heart-shaped, deep red leaves are not easily forgotten. The foliage is set off by slender spikes of white summer flowers.

☼ Bright to moderate, with some sun ❄ Warm. Moderate to high humidity ♠ Every three weeks. Occasionally in winter ♦ When compost surface dry. Avoid waterlogging ✄ Tip or leaf cuttings

△ *Pilea* 'Silver Tree'
PAN-AMERICAN FRIENDSHIP PLANT
↕ 20cm (8in) ↔ 30cm (12in)

Puckered, quilted, sharply toothed, pointed leaves, strikingly marked with silver on a bronze-green ground, form the low mound of this eye-catching plant.

☼ Bright to moderate, with some sun ❄ Warm. Moderate to high humidity ♠ Every three weeks. Occasionally in winter ♦ Water when compost surface just dry. Avoid waterlogging ✄ Tip cuttings

OTHER HOUSEPLANTS WITH ROUGH-TEXTURED FOLIAGE

Begonia gehrtii
Bertolonia marmorata
Fittonia verschaffeltii var. *argyroneura*
Geogenanthus undatus
Hemigraphis 'Exotica'
Nautilocalyx bullatus
    Pelargonium tomentosum, see p.345
    Peperomia caperata 'Emerald Ripple'
Pilea involucrata
Pilea 'Norfolk'
Saxifraga stolonifera, see p.391

△ *Pelargonium* 'Mabel Grey'
SCENTED-LEAVED PELARGONIUM
↕ 35cm (14in) ↔ 20cm (8in)

Deeply cut and roughly textured, the leaves of this pelargonium are just waiting to be rubbed, which releases their rich lemon aroma. Small mauve flowers are borne in spring and summer. Easy to grow and propagate. ♈

☼ Bright. Likes sun ❄ Moderate to warm, but cool in winter. Low humidity ♠ Fortnightly, using high potash fertilizer ♦ When compost surface dry. Water sparingly in winter ✄ Tip cuttings

◁ *Sinningia* 'Mont Blanc'
GLOXINIA
↕ 30cm (12in)
↔ 45cm (18in)

This warmth-loving plant bears large, fleshy green leaves with a smooth, velvety texture. The foliage is a perfect foil for the big, trumpet-shaped white flowers that are produced in summer. Gloxinias are available in many other colours.

☼ Bright to moderate, avoiding sun ❄ Warm, but moderate when dormant. High humidity ♠ Fortnightly, using flowering houseplant fertilizer ♦ Keep moist, but keep dry when dormant ✄ Division

Houseplants with Aromatic Foliage

JUST AS FRAGRANT flowers are a bonus, so too are aromatic leaves; their scent gives a plant added interest and can freshen stale air. Place these plants where they can be easily touched, as some leaves release their aroma only when rubbed between the fingers. There is a wide range of pelargoniums with aromatic foliage, but the different scents they offer are best not mixed.

△ *Pelargonium* 'Fragrans'
SCENTED-LEAVED GERANIUM
‡ 25cm (10in) ↔ 20cm (8in)

When rubbed, the sage-green, velvety foliage of this small, bushy plant releases a pine fragrance. Small white flowers are produced in clusters in spring and summer. A reliable plant for cultivating on a windowsill.

☼ Bright, with sun ▮ Moderate to warm, but cool in winter. Low humidity ♦ Fortnightly, using high potash fertilizer ◊ When compost surface dry. Water sparingly in winter ▦ Tip cuttings

Myrtus communis ▷
COMMON MYRTLE
‡ ↔ 1m (3ft) or more

Famed since antiquity for its fragrant foliage, this plant also produces scented flowers from summer to autumn, followed by black berries. Traditionally, sprigs of myrtle are included in royal wedding bouquets. Keep small by pruning.

☼ Bright, with sun ▮ Moderate to warm. Low to moderate humidity ♦ Every three weeks ◊ When compost surface dry. Water sparingly in winter ▦ Semi-ripe cuttings

---

OTHER HOUSEPLANTS WITH AROMATIC FOLIAGE

Acorus gramineus 'Ogon', see p.340
Boronia citriodora
Laurus nobilis, see p.402
Plectranthus amboinicus
Plectranthus madagascariensis
Prostanthera ovalifolia
Prostanthera 'Poorinda Ballerina'

Pelargonium crispum
'Variegatum' ▷
SCENTED-LEAVED GERANIUM
‡ 45cm (18in) ↔ 15cm (6in)

A trusted favourite since 1774, with a stiffly upright habit and small, green and cream, crinkly-margined, lemon-scented leaves. Pale mauve flowers are borne in spring and summer. ▽

☼ Bright, with some direct sun ▮ Moderate to warm, but cool in winter. Low humidity ♦ Fortnightly, using high potash fertilizer ◊ When compost surface dry. Water sparingly in winter ▦ Tip cuttings

△ *Pelargonium* 'Graveolens'
ROSE GERANIUM
‡ 60cm (2ft) ↔ 40cm (16in)

Oil of geranium is extracted from the deeply-cut, lemon-scented foliage of this hybrid. It is bushy, but its strong scent makes it an ideal plant for a windowsill.

☼ Bright, with sun ▮ Moderate to warm, but cool in winter. Low humidity ♦ Fortnightly, using high potash fertilizer ◊ When compost surface dry. Water sparingly in winter ▦ Tip cuttings

Branched flower clusters

Attractive, heavily-veined leaves

◁ *Plectranthus oertendahlii*
CANDLE PLANT
↕ 20cm (8in) ↔ 1m (3ft)

A charming plant of trailing habit, with fleshy, rounded and scalloped, pale green aromatic leaves with white veins. White or pale blue flowers are produced intermittently throughout the year. ▽

☼ Bright to moderate, with sun 🌡 Warm, avoiding fluctuation. Low humidity 💧 Fortnightly. Monthly in winter 💧 When dry. Reduce watering in winter Avoid waterlogging ✄ Tip cuttings

△ *Pelargonium* 'Lady Plymouth'
SCENTED-LEAVED GERANIUM
↕ 40cm (16in) ↔ 20cm (8in)

Known in cultivation for 200 years, this pelargonium has deeply cut, bright green leaves, margined with silver, which are eucalyptus-scented when rubbed. ▽

☼ Bright, with sun 🌡 Moderate to warm, but cool in winter. Low humidity 💧 Fortnightly, using high potash fertilizer 💧 When compost surface dry. Water sparingly in winter ✄ Tip cuttings

OTHER PELARGONIUMS WITH AROMATIC FOLIAGE

Pelargonium 'Attar of Roses'
Pelargonium 'Copthorne'
Pelargonium 'Creamy Nutmeg'
Pelargonium 'Lilian Pottinger'
Pelargonium 'Little Gem'
Pelargonium 'Prince of Orange'
Pelargonium 'Village Hill Oak'
Pelargonium 'Welling'

△ *Pelargonium* 'Old Spice'
SCENTED-LEAVED GERANIUM
↕ 30cm (12in) ↔ 15cm (6in)

Attractive pale green leaves impart a pleasant spicy aroma to this erect plant, which also bears clusters of white summer flowers. Fairly bushy when in growth.

☼ Bright, with sun 🌡 Moderate to warm, but cool in winter. Low humidity 💧 Fortnightly, using high potash fertilizer 💧 When compost surface dry. Water sparingly in winter ✄ Tip cuttings

△ *Pelargonium tomentosum*
PEPPERMINT-SCENTED GERANIUM
↕ 90cm (3ft) ↔ 75cm (30in)

White or pale pink flowers, borne from spring to summer, complement the softly grey-woolly, peppermint-scented foliage. This robust plant may need pruning. ▽

☼ Bright, with sun 🌡 Moderate to warm, but cool in winter. Low humidity 💧 Fortnightly, using high potash fertilizer 💧 When compost surface dry. Water sparingly in winter ✄ Tip cuttings

△ *Prostanthera rotundifolia*
MINT BUSH
↕ ↔ 1m (3ft)

Brush against this bush and smell the minty aroma of its tiny leaves. Principally grown for its masses of small purple flowers in spring and early summer. ▽

☼ Bright, with some sun 🌡 Moderate to warm. Low humidity 💧 Fortnightly 💧 Water when compost surface dry. Water sparingly in winter ✄ Stem cuttings

Houseplants with Red, Pink, or Purple Foliage

△ *Hypoestes phyllostachya* 'Splash'
POLKA DOT PLANT
↕↔65cm (26in)

Named for the pale pink splashes on its
thin and otherwise dark green leaves, this
plant's colour is most vivid in good light,
and may revert to green in poor light.

☀ Bright, but avoid summer sun ▓ Warm.
Moderate to high humidity ◔ Fortnightly.
Occasionally in winter ◔ When compost surface
just dry ▧ Tip cuttings. Roots easily in water

P̲URPLE OR SIMILARLY bright-coloured foliage houseplants
can be used to provide a bold, dramatic effect, especially
when set against a pale background or placed in combination
with green, yellow, white, or variegated plants. Good light
levels are usually needed to bring out the rich colours, so
bear each plant's light requirements in mind when placing it.

Begonia rex hybrids ▷
PAINTED-LEAF BEGONIA
↕ 25cm (10in) ↔ 30cm (12in)

The cultivars and hybrids of this
Himalayan begonia, grown principally
for their ornamental foliage, exhibit a
spectacular range of colours including
several in purple and silver shades.

☀ Bright to moderate. Avoid hot sun ▓ Moderate
to warm. Moderate humidity ◔ Fortnightly in
summer. Monthly in winter ◔ When dry. Stop if
dormant in winter ▧ Division, leaf cuttings

**OTHER BEGONIAS WITH
RED, PINK, OR PURPLE
FOLIAGE**

Begonia 'Enech'
Begonia 'Helen Lewis'
Begonia 'Merry Christmas', see p.352
Begonia 'Mini Merry'
Begonia 'Rajah'
Begonia 'Tiny Bright'

△ *Calathea sanderiana*
CALATHEA
↕↔60cm (2ft)

Found wild on Peruvian rainforest floors, this plant forms a bold clump of deep olive-
green leaves, purple beneath and with rose-red parallel stripes, aging to silver, above.
Short conical spikes of violet and white flowers appear among the leaves in summer.

☀ Bright to moderate, avoiding direct sun ▓ Warm, avoiding fluctuation. High humidity ◔ Fortnightly, using
foliage houseplant fertilizer. Monthly in winter ◔ Keep moist. When dry in cool conditions ▧ Division

△ *Leea coccinea* 'Burgundy'
WEST INDIAN HOLLY
↕ 80cm (32in) ↔ 60cm (2ft)

This Burmese shrub, commonly grown in
gardens in the West Indies, produces
handsome sprays of deeply divided, deep
red leaves. A very elegant houseplant.

☀ Bright, but avoid summer sun ▓ Warm, avoiding
fluctuation. Moderate to high humidity ◔ Fortnightly. Occasionally in winter ◔ When dry. Avoid
waterlogging ▧ Semi-ripe cuttings, air layering

Flowers may be pinched out for compact habit

△ *Oxalis purpurata*
OXALIS
↕ ↔ 15cm (6in)

The clover-like, purple-tinted leaves of this southern African plant are rich purple beneath. Cream, white, pink, or purple flowers appear in autumn and winter.

☼ Bright, with some direct sun ≋ Moderate to warm. Moderate humidity ◊ Fortnightly ◊ When compost surface dry. Water sparingly in winter ⊞ Division

△ *Solenostemon* 'Volcano'
COLEUS, FLAME NETTLE
↕ ◂▸ 60cm (2ft)

Coleus leaves come in many different colour combinations, including this green-edged deep red. Pinching out the growing tips will give the plant a compact habit.

☼ Bright ≋ Moderate to warm. Moderate humidity ◊ Weekly. Occasionally in winter ◊ Keep moist, but avoid waterlogging. At lower temperatures, water as compost surface dries ⊞ Tip cuttings. Roots easily in water

△ *Strobilanthes dyerianus*
PERSIAN SHIELD
↕ ↔ 60cm (2ft)

Beautifully veined bronze-green leaves, with silvery-purple markings above and purple undersides, distinguish this plant. Flourishes in high heat and humidity.

☼ Bright, but avoid summer sun ≋ Warm. High humidity ◊ Every three weeks ◊ Water when compost surface dry. Reduce watering in winter ⊞ Tip or stem cuttings

△ *Peperomia obtusifolia* 'Columbiana'
DESERT PRIVET
↕ ↔ 25cm (10in)

The rich purple, fleshy leaves of this peperomia are a striking contrast to the popular, and more typical, green form. This is an excellent plant for a terrarium.

☼ Bright to moderate, with some sun ≋ Warm. Moderate to high humidity ◊ Every three weeks. Occasionally in winter ◊ Water when compost surface dry. Avoid waterlogging ⊞ Tip cuttings

OTHER HOUSEPLANTS WITH RED, PINK, OR PURPLE FOLIAGE

Acalypha wilkesiana 'Musaiça'
Codiaeum 'Flamingo'
Cordyline fruticosa 'Atom'
Cryptanthus 'Pink Starlight'
x *Cryptbergia* 'Rubra'
Gynura aurantiaca 'Purple Passion', see p.342
Hemigraphis alternata
Hypoestes phyllostachya 'Vinrod', see p.398
Iresene herbstii
Mikania dentata
Tradescantia pallida 'Purpurea'

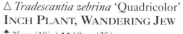

△ *Tradescantia zebrina* 'Quadricolor'
INCH PLANT, WANDERING JEW
↕ 25cm (10in) ↔ 60cm (2ft)

Vigorous, fleshy-stemmed, and easy to grow, this is ideal for a hanging basket or raised surface. The leaves are dark green, striped silver, and flushed pink and red.

☼ Bright, but avoid direct sun ≋ Moderate. Moderate to high humidity ◊ Fortnightly. Rarely in winter ◊ Keep moist. In winter, water when dry ⊞ Tip cuttings. Roots easily in water

FOLIAGE EFFECT

Houseplants with Gold- or Yellow-variegated Foliage

GOLD AND YELLOW are bright, cheerful colours for houseplants, and especially effective displayed against dark, plain backgrounds. Leaves with regular, marginal, or central markings are usually the most distinctive and dramatic, but spotted, blotched, or streaked variegation is also attractive; try combining several different leaf effects. Beware of placing these plants in low light conditions; with very few exceptions, this will cause the gold or yellow to fade.

Aucuba japonica 'Variegata' ▷
SPOTTED LAUREL

↕ 2m (6ft) ↔ 1.5m (5ft)

This tough, evergreen shrub with well-marked yellow variegation is an invaluable pot plant, suitable for cool or low light areas. Maintain a compact size by regular pruning.

☼ Bright to shady, avoiding direct sun ❄ Cool to moderate. Moderate to high humidity ◔ Monthly. Occasionally in winter ◊ When compost surface just dry. Sparingly in winter ✂ Semi-ripe cuttings

Dieffenbachia 'Vesuvius' △
DUMB CANE

↕ ↔ 90cm (3ft)

Boldly spotted, sword-shaped leaves make this tropical South American native a distinctive houseplant. Poisonous when chewed, so keep out of children's reach.

☼ Bright to moderate, avoiding summer sun ❄ Moderate. Moderate to high humidity ◔ Fortnightly, using foliage houseplant fertilizer. Monthly in winter ◊ Water when dry ✂ Tip or stem cuttings

---

OTHER GOLD- OR YELLOW-VARIEGATED HOUSEPLANTS

Abutilon pictum 'Thompsonii'
Calathea lubbersiana
Dracaena fragrans 'Yellow Stripe'
Hedera helix 'Goldchild'
Impatiens 'Fanfare'
Tolmiea menziesii 'Taff's Gold', see p.377

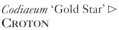

Codiaeum 'Gold Star' ▷
CROTON

↕ ↔ 1m (3ft) or more

Colourful, glossy, leathery foliage makes this plant a striking focal point wherever it is used, but it is worth taking a detailed look too. Needs warmth and bright light.

☼ Bright ❄ Warm. Avoid draughts and fluctuation. Moderate to high humidity ◔ Fortnightly, using foliage houseplant fertilizer. Occasionally in winter ◊ Keep moist. When dry in winter ✂ Tip cuttings

△ *Pelargonium* 'Mrs. Quilter'
ZONAL PELARGONIUM

↕ 40cm (16in) ↔ 15cm (6in)

One of many bright foliage pelargoniums, reliable and easy to grow. Eye-catching, golden-yellow leaves have a distinct bronze zone that deepens in full sun.

☼ Bright, with some sun ❄ Moderate to warm, but cool in winter. Low humidity ◔ Fortnightly, using high potash fertilizer ◊ Water when compost surface dry. Sparingly in winter ✂ Tip cuttings

Yellow-splashed leaflets

Peperomia obtusifolia 'USA' ▷
DESERT PRIVET
↕ ↔ 25cm (10in)

This upright, brightly coloured evergreen plant, with large, fleshy, gold-variegated green leaves, is particularly suitable for a warm and humid spot such as a bathroom shelf. An attractive, versatile houseplant.

☼ Bright to moderate, with some sun 🌡 Warm. Moderate to high humidity 💧 Every three weeks. Occasionally in winter 💧 Water when compost surface just dry. Avoid waterlogging 🪴 Tip cuttings

△ *Sansevieria trifasciata* 'Golden Hahnii'
SANSEVIERIA
↕ 12cm (5in) ↔ 45cm (18in)

Quite unlike the familiar, erect *Sansevieria trifasciata* 'Laurentii' (see p.385), this bears dwarf rosettes of broad, fleshy green leaves with wide stripes of golden yellow. 🏆

☼ Bright to moderate 🌡 Moderate to warm. Low humidity 💧 Fortnightly 💧 When compost surface dry. Water sparingly in winter. Avoid waterlogging 🪴 Division

△ *Schefflera arboricola* 'Yvonette'
SCHEFFLERA
↕ 1.8m (6ft) ↔ 90cm (3ft)

Use this tall schefflera as a specimen plant in a well-lit corner, or let it liven up a group of smaller, evergreen varieties. Prune it if a bushier habit is required.

☼ Bright to moderate 🌡 Warm. Avoid fluctuation. Moderate to high humidity 💧 Fortnightly. Monthly in winter 💧 Water when compost surface dry 🪴 Tip cuttings, air layering

Boat-shaped flower cluster

△ *Pseudopanax lessonii* 'Gold Splash'
PSEUDOPANAX
↕ ↔ 2m (6ft) or more

Normally grown in its juvenile stage, when its long-stalked, five-fingered leaves are splashed with gold, this variegated pseudopanax makes a striking and individual houseplant. As the plant ages, the variegation on the foliage becomes less marked. Prune it to maintain a more compact habit. 🏆

☼ Bright, but avoid direct sun 🌡 Moderate to warm. Moderate humidity 💧 Monthly. Occasionally in winter 💧 When compost surface dry. Reduce watering in winter 🪴 Semi-ripe cuttings

◁ *Tradescantia spathacea* 'Variegata'
BOAT LILY
↕ ↔ 30cm (12in)

The handsome, yellow-striped leaf rosettes of this robust, clump-forming plant have contrasting rich purple leaf undersides. Unusual boat-shaped flower-clusters are produced throughout the year.

☼ Bright to moderate, avoiding direct sun 🌡 Warm. High humidity 💧 Fortnightly. Occasionally in winter 💧 Keep moist. Reduce watering in winter 🪴 Offsets

Houseplants with White- or Cream-variegated Foliage

VARIEGATED LEAVES add character to a plant; house-plants with foliage in cream and white, both neutral and versatile colours, can be used to great decorative effect. Variegation is usually found along leaf margins, but it is worth looking for bold stripes or unusual mottling. To emphasize the cream and white markings, display your plant against a plain dark background.

Acorus gramineus
'Variegatus' ▷
SWEET FLAG
↕ 30cm (12in) ↔ 45cm (18in)

The variegated leaves of this sweet flag, arching with age, have a delicate fragrance when crushed. An excellent plant for a cool room; likes damp compost.

☼ Bright to moderate 🌡 Cool to moderate. Moderate humidity 💧 Every three weeks in summer 💧 Keep moist in summer. In winter, water when compost surface dry ▣ Division

△ *Aglaonema commutatum*
'Pseudobracteatum'
CHINESE EVERGREEN
↕ ↔ 60cm (2ft)

Attractive variegation makes this elegant plant, from the Philippine rainforests, a useful specimen for a table display. It is slow-growing but well worth the wait.

☼ Bright to moderate 🌡 Moderate to warm, avoiding fluctuation. Moderate humidity 💧 Weekly, using foliage houseplant fertilizer. Monthly in winter 💧 When dry ▣ Division, tip cuttings, stem sections

△ *Dracaena fragrans* 'Warneckei'
DRACAENA
↕ 2m (6ft) or more ↔ 60cm (2ft)

Lush and leafy when young, this plant slowly develops a strong stem. Popular with interior designers, it is an efficient remover of pollutants from the air. 🏆

☼ Bright, but avoid summer sun 🌡 Moderate to warm. Moderate to high humidity 💧 Fortnightly. Twice during winter 💧 Water when compost surface dry ▣ Tip cuttings, stem sections

△ *Ficus elastica* 'Tineke'
RUBBER PLANT
↕ 3m (10ft) ↔ 1m (3ft)

This rubber plant has many handsome features: dark grey-green variegation on the large leaves, cream leaf margins, and burgundy leaf stems and midribs.

☼ Bright to moderate 🌡 Cool to warm. Moderate to high humidity 💧 Fortnightly, using foliage house-plant fertilizer. Monthly in winter 💧 Water when compost surface dry ▣ Tip cuttings, air layering

---

OTHER SMALL-LEAVED WHITE- OR CREAM-VARIEGATED HOUSEPLANTS

Aichryson x *domesticum* 'Variegatum'
Ficus benjamina 'Variegata'
Ficus pumila 'White Sonny', see p.363
Glechoma hederacea 'Variegata'
Hedera helix 'White Knight'
Impatiens walleriana 'Variegata'

△ *Hedera helix* 'Eva'
COMMON IVY, ENGLISH IVY
↕ 1.4m (4½ft) ↔ 30cm (12in)

This attractive ivy, with purple shoots and white-margined leaves, will trail or climb; display it in a hanging basket, on a raised shelf, or even in a large terrarium.

☀ Bright to moderate ❆ Cool to moderate. Moderate to high humidity ◌ Fortnightly. Once in mid- and once in late winter ◌ When dry. Water sparingly in winter ✂ Tip cuttings, layering

◁ *Syngonium* 'Arrow'
GOOSEFOOT PLANT
↕ 2m (6ft) ↔ 60cm (2ft)

Compact and pointed green leaves, suffused with creamy variegation, change shape as they mature. Initially bushy, these plants become climbers with age.

☀ Bright to moderate, avoiding direct sun ❆ Warm, avoiding fluctuation. Moderate to high humidity ◌ Fortnightly. Monthly in winter ◌ When dry. Reduce watering in winter ✂ Tip cuttings

---

OTHER LARGE-LEAVED WHITE- OR CREAM-VARIEGATED HOUSEPLANTS

Ananas comosus 'Variegatus', see p.414
× *Fatshedera lizei* 'Variegata'
Fatsia japonica 'Variegata', see p.370
Monstera deliciosa 'Variegata', see p.371
Phormium 'Cream Delight'

△ *Hypoestes phyllostachya* 'Wit'
POLKA DOT PLANT
↕ 30cm (12in) ↔ 23cm (9in)

A striking plant, grown for its marbled leaves. Good light will produce the best foliage. The flowers are insignificant, so pinch out the tips to encourage bushiness.

☀ Bright, but avoid summer sun ❆ Moderate to warm. Moderate to high humidity ◌ Fortnightly. Monthly in winter ◌ When dry. Reduce watering in winter ✂ Tip or stem cuttings. Roots in water

△ *Plectranthus forsteri* 'Marginatus'
CANDLE PLANT, SWEDISH IVY
↕ 30cm (12in) ↔ 90cm (3ft)

Display candle plants in a hanging basket or on an accessible shelf to enjoy their masses of fleshy, aromatic foliage. Pinch out the shoots to promote bushy growth.

☀ Bright, with some direct sun ❆ Moderate to warm. Low to moderate humidity ◌ Fortnightly. Every six weeks in winter ◌ Let compost surface dry before watering ✂ Tip cuttings

△ *Tradescantia fluminensis* 'Variegata'
INCH PLANT, WANDERING JEW
↕ 15cm (6in) ↔ 60cm (2ft)

Show off this delicate, pale green, white-striped foliage by trailing it over the edge of a container. Easy to grow; pinch out the growing tips to encourage branching.

☀ Bright, but avoid direct sun. Variegation fades in shade ❆ Moderate to warm. Moderate to high humidity ◌ Fortnightly. Once in winter ◌ Keep moist. When dry in winter ✂ Tip or stem cuttings

Houseplants with Silver or Grey Foliage

MANY OF THE MOST distinctive houseplants have silver or grey foliage. Some leaves take their colour from bands or stripes, while others gain their silvery appearance from a patina of pale hairs or a dense spotting or marbled effect. All the plants shown here will provide dramatic contrast when grouped with purple- or dark green-leaved varieties.

△ *Begonia* 'Silver'
BEGONIA
↕ 20cm (8in) ↔ 25cm (10in)

Curious but very attractive, this begonia has distinctive, long, pointed leaves, covered with tiny pale hairs that give the upper surfaces a silvery, satin-like sheen.

☼ Bright to moderate, avoiding summer sun ≡ Moderate to warm. Moderate humidity ◊ Fortnightly. Monthly in winter ◊ When dry. Stop if dormant in winter ▦ Division, tip cuttings

Aglaonema 'Silver Queen' ▷
CHINESE EVERGREEN
↕ ↔ 45cm (18in)

One of the most striking and dramatic aglaonemas, bearing large, pointed, long-stalked, almost wholly silver leaves patterned with pale and dark green markings. ♔

☼ Moderate, avoiding summer sun ≡ Moderate to warm. Moderate humidity ◊ Every week, using foliage houseplant fertilizer. Monthly in winter ◊ When dry ▦ Division, tip cuttings, stem sections

OTHER HOUSEPLANTS WITH SILVER OR GREY FOLIAGE

Aechmea fasciata, see p.324
Aglaonema 'Silver King'
Astelia chathamica
Begonia 'Salamander'
Begonia 'Silver Queen'
Begonia venosa, see p.354
Cotyledon orbiculata
Echeveria secunda var. *glauca* 'Gigantea', see p.384

◁ *Begonia* 'Merry Christmas'
PAINTED-LEAF BEGONIA
↕ 25cm (10in) ↔ 30cm (12in)

The large, jaggedly toothed leaves of this *Begonia rex* hybrid are strikingly marked with silver and dark red, and pink-flushed. Pale rose-pink flowers are a bonus in autumn and early winter. ♔

☼ Bright to moderate, avoiding summer sun ≡ Moderate to warm. Moderate humidity ◊ Fortnightly. Monthly in winter ◊ When dry. Stop if dormant in winter ▦ Division, leaf cuttings

△ *Ctenanthe amabilis*
CTENANTHE
↕ ↔ 40cm (16in)

This beautifully variegated foliage plant, from the rainforests of South America, has impressive green and silver zebra marks on its large, paddle-shaped leaves. ♔

☼ Bright to moderate, avoiding direct sun ≡ Warm, avoiding fluctuation. High humidity ◊ Fortnightly, using foliage houseplant fertilizer. Rarely in winter ◊ Water when top half of compost dry ▦ Division

OTHER HOUSEPLANTS WITH FOLIAGE STRIPED, SPLASHED, OR VEINED SILVER OR GREY

Begonia maculata
Calathea makoyana, see p.368
Fittonia verschaffeltii var.
    argyroneura
Peperomia argyreia
Piper crocatum
Pteris cretica 'Albolineata', see p.407
Sonerila margaritacea
Strobilanthes dyerianus, see p.347

Ctenanthe
'Greystar' ▷
CTENANTHE
↕ 1.2m (4ft) ↔ 1m (3ft)

A splendid houseplant with impressive foliage. The silver upper leaf surfaces are set off by contrasting dark green veins and stalks, while the leaf undersides are dark purple.

☼ Bright to moderate, avoiding direct sun ❄ Warm, avoiding fluctuation. High humidity ♦ Fortnightly, using foliage houseplant fertilizer. Occasionally in winter ◊ Water when top half of compost dry ✻ Division

△ *Pteris ensiformis* 'Evergemiensis'
SLENDER BRAKE
↕ ↔ 30cm (12in)

This silver-striped cultivar makes a good contrast to other varieties of fern; it is even more attractive than the green form of this plant, a Victorian favourite.

☼ Bright to moderate, avoiding direct sun ❄ Moderate to warm. Moderate to high humidity ♦ Fortnightly. Monthly in winter ◊ Keep moist, but avoid waterlogging ✻ Division, spores

△ *Peperomia caperata* 'Teresa'
PEPEROMIA
↕ ↔ 20cm (8in)

A charming plant that is perfect for using in a special display, bottle garden, or terrarium. The bronze-purple, puckered, rounded leaves are silvery-sheened above.

☼ Bright to moderate, with some sun ❄ Warm. Moderate to high humidity ♦ Every three weeks. Occasionally in winter ◊ When compost surface dry. Avoid waterlogging ✻ Tip cuttings

△ *Pilea cadierei*
ALUMINIUM PLANT
↕ 30cm (12in) ↔ 21cm (8in)

Eye-catching, silver-splashed green leaves make this perennial from the Vietnamese rainforests a popular houseplant. Pinch out tips to maintain a compact habit. ♆

☼ Bright to moderate, with some sun ❄ Warm. Moderate to high humidity ♦ Every three weeks. Occasionally in winter ◊ Water when compost surface just dry. Avoid waterlogging ✻ Tip cuttings

△ *Soleirolia soleirolii* 'Variegata'
MIND-YOUR-OWN-BUSINESS
↕ 5cm (2in) ↔ 30cm (12in) or more

A useful small plant, with tiny silvered leaves densely crowding the branching stems and, in time, forming a creeping carpet. Good cover under large plants.

☼ Bright to shady, avoiding direct sun ❄ Cool to moderate. Moderate to high humidity ♦ Every three weeks. Rarely in winter ◊ Keep moist, but avoid waterlogging. Sparingly in winter ✻ Division

Houseplants with Unusual Foliage

THE ATTRACTION OF the weird and wonderful is universal. Many of us who collect plants become fascinated by the search for curious varieties, particularly among foliage plants, which offer leaves in a range of different textures, colours, shapes, and sizes. Such plants make good talking points, so display them where they can be easily seen and examined.

Begonia venosa ▷
SHRUB BEGONIA
↕ 90cm (3ft) ↔ 60cm (2ft)

Large, kidney-shaped, fleshy leaves are covered with short white hairs, giving them a frosted appearance. The fragrant white flowers, produced from midsummer onwards, are a bonus.

☀ Bright, but avoid summer sun ≣ Moderate to warm. Low to moderate humidity ♦ Fortnightly. Monthly in winter ◊ Water sparingly. Avoid waterlogging ⬚ Division, tip cuttings

Begonia listada ▷
SHRUB BEGONIA
↕ ↔ 60cm (2ft)

A striking plant with large, dark green leaves, barred with pale green, pointed at both ends and shaped like outstretched wings, one longer than the other. Bears white flowers in autumn and winter.

☀ Bright to moderate. Avoid summer sun ≣ Moderate to warm. Moderate humidity ♦ Fortnightly. Monthly in winter ◊ When compost surface dry. Reduce watering in winter ⬚ Division, tip cuttings

△ *Begonia serratipetala*
SHRUB BEGONIA
↕ ↔ 45cm (18in)

Distinctive for its long-pointed, wavy-margined leaves, bronze-green marked with red veins above, and red beneath, this shrub begonia produces pinky-white flowers from winter to spring.

☀ Bright to moderate, avoiding summer sun ≣ Moderate to warm. Moderate humidity ♦ Fortnightly. Monthly in winter ◊ When compost surface dry. Reduce watering in winter ⬚ Tip cuttings

△ *Codiaeum* 'Red Curl'
CROTON, JOSEPH'S COAT
↕ ↔ 1m (3ft)

Even if you have seen many variations of the croton, this one will amuse you with its long, narrow, corkscrew-like, colourful leaves. It looks well on its own or with green-leaved companions.

☀ Bright, with some sun ≣ Warm, avoiding draughts and fluctuation. Moderate to high humidity ♦ Fortnightly, using foliage houseplant fertilizer. Occasionally in winter ◊ Keep moist. In winter, water when compost surface dry ⬚ Tip cuttings

△ *Cotyledon orbiculata* var. *oblonga*
SILVER CROWN
↕ 60cm (2ft) ↔ 50cm (20in)

This interesting shrubby succulent
plant is dominated, especially when
small, by its rounded, crinkly-edged,
fleshy leaves, covered in a white, waxy
bloom. Good for a sunny windowsill.

☼ Bright, with sun 🌡 Warm, but cool to moderate
in winter. Low humidity 💧 Monthly, using fertilizer
for cacti and succulents 💧 When dry. Water
sparingly in winter 🌱 Tip or leaf cuttings

△ *Crassula perforata*
STRING OF BUTTONS
↕ ↔ 30cm (12in)

A curiosity for a sunny spot. Erect stems
pass through the middle of the paired,
green, succulent leaves. Scented, starry,
white to pink flowers appear in summer.

☼ Bright, with some sun 🌡 Warm, but cool to
moderate in winter. Low humidity 💧 Monthly, using
fertilizer for cacti and succulents 💧 When dry.
Water sparingly in winter 🌱 Tip or leaf cuttings

**OTHER HOUSEPLANTS WITH
UNUSUAL FOLIAGE**

Asplenium bulbiferum
Begonia lubbersii
Cryptanthus zonatus
Cycas revoluta, see p.394
Dionaea muscipula, see p.416
Fascicularia bicolor
Nolina recurvata, see p.394
Passiflora coriacea
Pseudopanax ferox
Tolmiea menziesii, see p.365

△ *Euphorbia trigona* 'Purpurea'
AFRICAN MILK TREE
↕ 1.5m (5ft) ↔ 1m (3ft)

This purple-tinted form of a succulent
spurge is from Namibia. Sitting bolt
upright, it has three-angled stems lined
with leaves that fall at the end of summer.

☼ Bright 🌡 Warm, but cool to moderate in
winter. Low humidity 💧 Monthly, using fertilizer for
cacti and succulents 💧 When compost surface dry.
Water sparingly in winter 🌱 Stem cuttings

△ *Faucaria tigrina*
TIGER JAWS
↕ 10cm (4in) ↔ 20cm (8in)

Most small children will be fascinated
by this plant – the leaves resemble
those of a succulent Venus fly trap, but
with sharp teeth. The yellow flowers in
autumn are a pleasant surprise. 🏆

☼ Bright, with some sun 🌡 Warm, but cool to
moderate in winter. Low humidity 💧 Monthly, using
fertilizer for cacti and succulents 💧 When dry.
Water sparingly in winter 🌱 Stem or leaf cuttings

**OTHER SUCCULENT HOUSE-
PLANTS WITH UNUSUAL FOLIAGE**

Haworthia attenuata f. *clariperla*
Pachyphytum oviferum, see p.409
Sedum pachyphyllum
Senecio rowleyanus, see p.391
Titanopsis calcarea

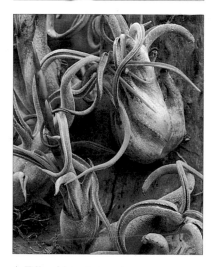

△ *Tillandsia caput-medusae*
AIR PLANT
↕ 40cm (16in) ↔ 24cm (10in)

Curved and twisted, horn-like leaves grow
from a bulbous base that can be attached
to a piece of hanging cork or driftwood.
Blue and red flower spikes show in spring.

☼ Bright, but avoid direct sun 🌡 Warm. Low to
moderate humidity 💧 Every eight weeks 💧 Mist
daily. Mist four times a week in low light and at low
temperatures 🌱 Offsets

LOCATIONS

TEMPERATURE, HUMIDITY, and light determine the environment in any location, and therefore which plants will grow well there. Before choosing a houseplant to suit a particular spot, you should also consider the size of the room, how often it is used, and for what type of activity.

Celosia argentea 'Plumosa' for sunny windowsills

△ SUNNY SITTING ROOM *Glass doors, white walls, and a mirror make the most of all the natural light available, encouraging flowering plants to bloom.*

Remember that indoor "climates" are affected by seasonal changes outside. Increased central heating can make the air very dry in winter, and light levels will generally be greater in summer. You may need to move your plants as the seasons change to keep them healthy.

LIGHT AND HEAT
The number and size of windows in any location will determine the level of natural light. Full light through glass, but not hot summer sun, is appreciated by the majority of plants, particularly those that flower. Poorly-lit corners, where nothing seems to flourish, are more challenging, but can be enlivened by a range of shade-tolerant plants.

Plants that enjoy high heat and humidity, such as tropical species, may not seem to have a place in the home, but many are extremely adaptable and will accept lower temperatures or a drier atmosphere for limited periods. You can also use a pebble tray to raise humidity. Equally adaptable are houseplants that tolerate low light, cool temperatures, or dry air; they will often grow where no others survive.

CHANGING ROOMS
There are few rooms in any home that cannot be improved by a plant. The principal rooms – sitting and dining rooms, bedrooms, studies, bathrooms, and kitchens – can be "decorated" with a great variety of species. Garden rooms and conservatories can support the widest range of plants, depending on their heat and humidity levels, but don't give up on small areas like halls, landings, or washrooms – they can often support at least one plant.

△ OFFICE WINNER *Compact, easy, and tolerant of neglect,* Pilea peperomioides *is a good choice for a busy home office.*

◁ LOW-LIGHT KITCHEN *An impressive Boston fern thrives in this warm kitchen, where light levels are usually low.*

▷ HUMID BATHROOM *Many ferns will appreciate the often damp atmosphere of a warm bathroom, if it is not too bright.*

Houseplants for Sunny Windowsills

A SUNNY WINDOWSILL, its heat magnified by the glass, can be the hottest spot in the house, where only a few plants other than cacti and succulents will survive for long without scorching. However, a host of plants enjoy such a position if they are protected from the excessive heat of midday in summer; draw blinds or curtains or just move them out of the way.

Ananas bracteatus 'Tricolor' ▷
VARIEGATED WILD PINEAPPLE
↕ 70cm (28in) ↔ 50cm (20in)

Striking in foliage and flower, but beware of the viciously spine-toothed leaves. The impressive pineapple flowerhead appears in summer. Needs regular watering. ♔

☼ Bright, with some sun ≋ Warm. Moderate to high humidity ◐ Fortnightly, using flowering houseplant fertilizer ◊ When compost surface just dry ▦ Offsets, rosettes

△ *Celosia argentea* 'Plumosa'
CELOSIA, PLUME FLOWER
↕ ↔ 45cm (18in)

This striking perennial, normally grown as an annual, needs plenty of light. Protect it from midday sun to prolong the richly-coloured, plumed summer flowerhead.

☼ Bright, but avoid hot summer sun ≋ Moderate to warm. Moderate humidity ◐ Fortnightly ◊ Water when compost surface just dry ▦ Seed. Germinates very freely

---

OTHER HOUSEPLANTS FOR SUNNY WINDOWSILLS

Cyrtanthus elatus
Nerium oleander cultivars
Pelargonium 'Graveolens', see p.344
Pentas lanceolata
Plumeria rubra
Punica granatum var. *nana*

Bougainvillea 'Dania' ▷
BOUGAINVILLEA, PAPER FLOWER
↕ ↔ 1m (3ft) or more

Brilliant, bright pink bracts are borne from summer to autumn. This exotic-looking plant can be bought young, trained to a framework, and pruned to control its size, but it will grow larger if given the space.

☼ Bright, with sun ≋ Moderate to warm. Low humidity ◐ Fortnightly, using flowering houseplant fertilizer ◊ When compost surface just dry. Water sparingly in winter ▦ Tip cuttings

Browallia speciosa 'White Troll' ▷
SAPPHIRE FLOWER
↕ ↔ 25cm (10in)

Perennial but usually grown as an annual, the sapphire flower has pointed leaves that are slightly clammy to the touch and produces white summer flowers. Pinch out the tips to encourage a bushy habit.

☼ Bright to moderate, avoiding hot summer sun ≋ Cool to moderate. Moderate humidity ◐ Fortnightly feed ◊ Water when compost surface dry ▦ Seed

△ *Crassula socialis*
CRASSULA
↕ 7cm (3in) ↔ 30cm (12in)

Small, dense rosettes of horny-margined leaves soon form colonies, with heads of miniature, star-shaped white flowers produced in spring. A reliable houseplant.

☼ Bright, with some sun ❄ Warm, but cool to moderate in winter. Low humidity ◗ Monthly, using fertilizer for cacti and succulents ◌ When dry. Water sparingly in winter ▦ Tip or leaf cuttings

OTHER SUCCULENT HOUSE-
PLANTS FOR SUNNY WINDOWSILLS

Anacampseros alstonii
Crassula perfoliata var. *minor*
Euphorbia caput-medusae
Lampranthus purpureus
Portulacaria afra 'Foliis-variegatus'
Pterodiscus speciosus

△ *Huernia thuretii* var. *primulina*
CARRION FLOWER, HUERNIA
↕ ↔ 8cm (3in)

A clump-forming succulent with sharp-angled, grey-green stems, bearing curious, creamy-yellow, red-freckled flowers in summer and autumn. Do not overwater.

☼ Bright, with sun ❄ Warm, but cool to moderate in winter. Low humidity ◗ Monthly, using fertilizer for cacti and succulents ◌ When compost surface dry. Water sparingly in winter ▦ Tip cuttings

△ *Parodia leninghausii*
GOLDEN BALL CACTUS
↕ 60cm (2ft) ↔ 8cm (3in)

Initially ball-shaped or rounded, this cactus later develops into a fat, golden-spined column. Pale yellow flowers are produced from the tips in summer.

☼ Bright, with sun ❄ Warm, but cool to moderate in winter. Low humidity ◗ Monthly, using fertilizer for cacti and succulents ◌ When compost surface dry. Water sparingly in winter ▦ Tip cuttings

△ *Hibiscus rosa-sinensis* 'Scarlet Giant'
CHINESE HIBISCUS,
ROSE OF CHINA
↕ 2m (6ft) or more ↔ 1.5m (5ft) or more

A large plant, but careful pruning controls its size. It loves sun, which encourages free flowering from spring to autumn; the red blooms can be up to 17cm (7in) across.

☼ Bright, with sun ❄ Warm, avoiding fluctuation. Moderate to high humidity ◗ Fortnightly. Stop in cool conditions ◌ When just dry. Water sparingly in winter. Avoid waterlogging ▦ Semi-ripe cuttings

Richly coloured leaves

◁ *Solenostemon* 'Defiance'
COLEUS,
FLAME NETTLE
↕ ↔ 30cm (12in)

Bright green and claret foliage distinguishes this coleus. Many selections are available. Although perennial, these soft-stemmed plants are generally treated as annuals; pinch out tips for bushiness.

☼ Bright, with sun ❄ Warm. Low humidity ◗ Weekly. Occasionally in winter ◌ Keep moist, but avoid waterlogging. In winter, water when just dry ▦ Tip cuttings. Roots easily in water

LOCATIONS

Houseplants for Full Light

A SITUATION IN FULL LIGHT, as long as there is no risk of scorching or overheating, is ideal for many house-plants. The best-lit spots in any house are usually on or near windowsills that receive plenty of daylight; this could even be early morning or late evening sun. However, all the plants featured here will need protection from strong midday sun in summer.

Capsicum annuum 'Carnival Red' ▷
ORNAMENTAL PEPPER
↕ ↔ 60cm (2ft)

A familiar plant, usually treated as an annual, but longer-lasting given cool conditions. In winter, the freely-borne, brilliant orange-red fruits stud the leafy branches.

☼ Bright ﹗ Cool to moderate. Moderate humidity ◗ Fortnightly, alternating general fertilizer with flowering houseplant fertilizer ◍ When just dry ▦ Tip cuttings

△ *Chrysanthemum indicum*
FLORISTS' CHRYSANTHEMUM
↕ ↔ 30cm (12in)

A dwarf form with a compact habit and pale yellow flowers, borne from autumn to winter. A valuable temporary plant and one of many popular chrysanthemums.

☼ Bright, but avoid direct sun ﹗ Cool to moderate. Moderate humidity ◗ Every three weeks ◍ Keep moist, but avoid waterlogging ▦ Tip cuttings

△ *Cordyline fruticosa* 'Kiwi'
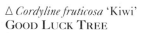
GOOD LUCK TREE
↕ ↔ 2m (6ft)

This suckering plant forms a clump of erect stems clothed in bold foliage that is striped dark green, pale green, and cream, and has subtly pink-tinted margins.

☼ Bright, but avoid summer sun ﹗ Warm. High humidity ◗ Fortnightly. Monthly in winter ◍ When compost surface dry. Reduce watering at lower temperatures ▦ Tip cuttings, stem sections

---

OTHER HOUSEPLANTS FOR FULL LIGHT WITH SOME SUMMER SUN

Capsicum annuum, see p.396
Correa 'Dusky Bells'
Crassula coccinea
Cyrtanthus elatus
Fuchsia 'Ballet Girl'
Gloriosa superba 'Rothschildiana'
Heterocentron elegans
Impatiens walleriana hybrids, see p.385
Kalanchoe 'Wendy'

◁ *Crassula arborescens*
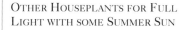
SILVER JADE PLANT
↕ 2m (6ft) ↔ 1.2m (4ft)

Slow-growing but eventually substantial, this succulent shrub bears striking, red-margined, grey-green leaves, and white starry flowers from autumn to winter.

☼ Bright, with some sun ﹗ Warm, but cool to moderate in winter. Low humidity ◗ Monthly, using fertilizer for cacti and succulents ◍ When dry. Water sparingly in winter ▦ Stem or leaf cuttings

Justicia brandegeeana ▷
SHRIMP PLANT

↕ ↔ 90cm (3ft)

Free- and long-flowering, this popular plant has colourful bracts and pendent white flowers, borne throughout the year. It likes some sun. Previously called *Beloperone guttata*. ♔

☼ Bright to moderate, avoiding hottest sun ♨ Warm, avoiding draughts. Moderate to high humidity ♠ Monthly ♦ Keep moist, but avoid waterlogging ⧉ Tip cuttings

△ *Dudleya pulverulenta*
DUDLEYA

↕ ↔ 30cm (12in) or more

Red or yellow starry flowers, produced in spring or early summer, complement this succulent's rosette of fleshy, pointed, silvery grey leaves, borne on a short stem.

☼ Bright, with sun ♨ Warm, but cool to moderate in winter. Low humidity ♠ Monthly, using cactus and succulent fertilizer ♦ When compost surface dry. Water sparingly in winter ⧉ Stem or leaf cuttings

◁ *Smithiantha* 'Orange King'
TEMPLE BELLS

↕ ↔ 30cm (12in)

Beautifully mottled, densely hairy leaves appear in spring after a winter dormancy, topped from summer to autumn by loose heads of pendulous orange flowers.

☼ Bright to moderate. Avoid hot sun ♨ Warm, but moderate in dormancy. High humidity ♠ Fortnightly, using flowering houseplant fertilizer ♦ Keep moist, increasing in growth. Stop in dormancy ⧉ Division

---

OTHER HOUSEPLANTS FOR FULL LIGHT AWAY FROM SUMMER SUN

Achimenes hybrids
Aeschynanthus lobbianus
Aphelandra
  squarrosa 'Dania',
  see p.368
Justicia rizzinii, see p.331
Mandevilla rosea
Pachystachys lutea
Schlumbergera
  truncata, see p.363
Thunbergia alata, see p.393

Hoya carnosa 'Variegata' ▷
WAX PLANT

↕ ↔ 2m (6ft)

Capable of great vigour, this handsome, creamy-variegated form of the twining wax plant can be trained on a frame to keep it neat and manageable. The fragrant, waxy flowers appear in summer.

☼ Bright, but avoid direct sun ♨ Moderate to warm. Moderate to high humidity ♠ Every three weeks, using flowering houseplant fertilizer ♦ Water when compost surface dry. Avoid overwatering ⧉ Tip cuttings

△ *Streptocarpus* 'Kim'
CAPE PRIMROSE

↕ 20cm (8in) ↔ 35cm (14in)

This Cape primrose produces rosettes of downy leaves, and branching sprays of dark purple, white-eyed summer flowers. A classic houseplant for a well-lit spot. ♔

☼ Bright to moderate. Avoid direct sun ♨ Warm. Moderate to high humidity ♠ Flowering houseplant fertilizer fortnightly. Monthly in winter, unless dormant ♦ When dry ⧉ Division, leaf cuttings

Houseplants for Medium Light

MOST ROOMS HAVE an area of medium light, out of direct sunlight but not in shade. It is usually a few metres from a window, or closer if you have sheer curtains or blinds. All the plants here tolerate medium light, but will benefit from a short spell in full light.

Aglaonema 'Marie' ▷
PAINTED DROP TONGUE
↕ 1.2m (4ft) ↔ 60cm (2ft)

Aglaonemas, noted for their subtle leaf patterns, include this bushy form with large, dark green foliage splashed grey-green. A fine specimen houseplant.

☼ Bright to moderate 🌡 Moderate to warm, avoiding fluctuation. Moderate humidity 💧 Foliage houseplant fertilizer weekly. Monthly in winter ◊ When dry 🪴 Division, tip cuttings, stem sections

△ *Begonia* 'Tiger Paws'
EYELASH BEGONIA
↕ 20cm (8in) ↔ 25cm (10in)

An eye-catching houseplant that forms a compact mound of shield-like, lime-green leaves, marked and edged bronze, each with a curious fringe of "eyelash" hairs.

☼ Bright to moderate 🌡 Cool to warm. Moderate humidity 💧 Fortnightly. Monthly in winter ◊ Water when compost surface just dry 🪴 Division, leaf cuttings

△ *Dracaena cincta* 'Bicolor'
DRACAENA
↕ 4m (12ft) ↔ 1m (3ft)

This is one of several variegated forms of *Dracaena cincta*, with cream-edged leaves. Perfect for a semi-shady corner or hallway, or as an architectural feature plant.

☼ Bright to moderate 🌡 Moderate to warm. Moderate to high humidity 💧 Fortnightly. Occasionally during winter ◊ Water when compost surface dry 🪴 Tip cuttings, stem sections

△ *Dracaena fragrans* 'Compacta'
DRACAENA
↕ 2m (6ft) ↔ 1m (3ft)

Masses of dark green leaves top the stems of these robust plants, making them look like shaving brushes. Cut mature plants back hard in spring to promote regrowth.

☼ Bright to moderate. Growth stops in low light 🌡 Moderate to warm. Moderate to high humidity 💧 Fortnightly. Occasionally in winter ◊ When compost surface dry 🪴 Tip cuttings, stem sections

---

OTHER LARGE HOUSEPLANTS FOR MEDIUM LIGHT

Aspidistra elatior 'Milky Way', see p.364
Asplenium nidus, see p.406
Chamaedorea elegans, see p.412
Dracaena marginata, see p.395
Fatsia japonica, see p.339
Monstera deliciosa, see p.339
Nephrolepis exaltata 'Bostoniensis', see p.407
Philodendron 'Medisa', see p.393

△ *Ficus pumila* 'White Sonny'
CREEPING FIG

↕ ↔ 30cm (12in) or more

The tiny leaves of this creeping fig are edged with a bold cream line. In humid conditions, it produces climbing roots and will grow happily up a suitable support.

☼ Bright to moderate 🌡 Moderate to warm. Moderate to high humidity 🌢 Fortnightly, using foliage houseplant fertilizer. Occasionally in winter 🌢 When dry, especially if cool 🌱 Tip cuttings

OTHER SMALL HOUSEPLANTS FOR MEDIUM LIGHT

Adiantum raddianum 'Fritz Luth', see p.380
Aglaonema 'Lilian', see p.374
Cyrtomium falcatum
Hedera helix 'Très Coupé'
Plectranthus verticillatus
Saxifraga stolonifera, see p.391
Schlumbergera × *buckleyi*
Tolmiea menziesii 'Taff's Gold', see p.377

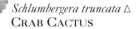

△ *Hedera helix* 'California'
COMMON IVY, ENGLISH IVY

↕ 1m (3ft) ↔ 30cm (12in)

The attractive, mid-green leaves of this ivy vary from triangular to broadly heart-shaped. It is ideal for growing in a hanging basket or for climbing up a support.

☼ Bright to moderate. Poor growth in low light 🌡 Cool to moderate. Moderate to high humidity 🌢 Fortnightly. Twice in winter 🌢 When dry. Water sparingly in winter 🌱 Tip cuttings, layering

Schlumbergera truncata △
CRAB CACTUS

↕ 30cm (12in) ↔ 60cm (2ft)

From late autumn to winter, pendent, deep pink flowers cover this bold cactus, which then has a rest period. Succulent, flattened, segmented stems add interest.

☼ Moderate 🌡 Moderate to warm, but cool when resting. Moderate humidity 🌢 Fortnightly in growth, using high potash fertilizer 🌢 Keep moist in growth. Water sparingly during rest period 🌱 Stem sections

△ *Fittonia verschaffeltii* 'Janita'
NET PLANT, SNAKESKIN PLANT

↕ 15cm (6in) ↔ 30cm (12in) or more

Display this small, dense, creeping net plant on a low surface to appreciate its beautiful pink-netted green leaves. Ideal for terraria or warm, humid bathrooms.

☼ Moderate 🌡 Moderate to warm. High humidity 🌢 Fortnightly. Occasionally in winter 🌢 Water when compost surface just dry. Avoid waterlogging 🌱 Tip cuttings

Philodendron erubescens 'Red Emerald' ▷
BLUSHING PHILODENDRON

↕ 5m (15ft) ↔ 2m (6ft) or more

This stunning form of a vigorous rainforest climber has glossy, emerald-green leaves and dark red main stems and leaf stalks. Best trained up a moss pole.

☼ Bright to shady 🌡 Moderate to warm. Moderate to high humidity 🌢 Fortnightly, using foliage houseplant fertilizer. Monthly in winter 🌢 Water when compost surface dry 🌱 Tip cuttings

Houseplants for Low Light

HOUSEPLANTS THAT THRIVE in low light are a small but resilient group; of course, those featured here will all benefit from a little extra attention to help them look their best. Low-lit areas are typically those furthest from a window or other source of light; however, they do not include dark, dingy corners, where any plant will face a struggle to survive.

LOCATIONS

△ *Fittonia* 'Bianco Verde'
SILVER NET LEAF
‡ 15cm (6in) ↔ 30cm (12in)

Small, variegated leaves and a creeping habit make this fittonia an excellent terrarium plant. It thrives in low light, provided that conditions are suitably warm and moist; group several on a pebble tray to raise humidity.

☼ Moderate to shady, avoiding direct sun ❄ Warm. High humidity 🌢 Fortnightly. Occasionally in winter 🌢 Keep moist, but avoid waterlogging 🌱 Tip cuttings

Aspidistra elatior 'Milky Way' ▷
ASPIDISTRA, CAST IRON PLANT
‡ ↔ 60cm (2ft)

Few plants tolerate poor light levels better than the cast iron plant. It is almost impervious to neglect, but naturally responds well to generous treatment. This spotted form is particularly ornamental; a fine specimen plant.

☼ Moderate to shady. Direct sun will scorch leaves ❄ Moderate to warm. Moderate humidity 🌢 Every three weeks 🌢 When compost surface dry. Dislikes waterlogging 🌱 Division, offsets

Deeply-lobed mature leaf

△ *Duchesnea indica*
MOCK STRAWBERRY
‡ 10cm (4in) ↔ 1.2m (4ft)

A fast-creeping perennial that forms a carpet of runners covered with strawberry-like leaves. Yellow flowers are produced in summer, but to obtain the red fruits, move it to a brighter position.

☼ Moderate to shady ❄ Cool to moderate. Moderate to high humidity 🌢 Every three weeks 🌢 Keep moist. Reduce watering during winter 🌱 Plantlets

◁ *Philodendron bipinnatifidum*
TREE PHILODENDRON
‡ 3m (10ft) ↔ 2m (6ft) or more

One of the most spectacular foliage plants, with its strong stems and large, deeply lobed, long-stalked mature leaves (see inset). Grow this Brazilian shrub on a stout moss pole or frame. ♔

☼ Bright to shady ❄ Warm. Moderate to high humidity 🌢 Fortnightly, using foliage houseplant fertilizer 🌢 Water when compost surface slightly dry 🌱 Division, tip cuttings

Philodendron scandens ▷
HEART LEAF, SWEETHEART PLANT
↕ ↔ 3m (10ft)

Vigorous and, given the space, high climbing, this superb plant has deep glossy green, heart-shaped, slender-pointed leaves that can reach up to 30cm (12in) long. It makes an unusual and impressive sight in a hanging basket, or grow it on a moss pole or frame. ♔

☼ Bright to shady ▐ Moderate to warm. Moderate to high humidity ◖ Fortnightly, using foliage houseplant fertilizer. Monthly in winter ◊ Let the compost surface dry slightly before watering ✂ Tip cuttings

△ *Soleirolia soleirolii*
MIND-YOUR-OWN-BUSINESS
↕ 5cm (2in) ↔ 30cm (12in)

Resembling a moss because of its low, carpeting growth and tiny leaves, this plant makes close ground cover for pots or hanging baskets. Not suitable for terraria.

☼ Bright to shady, avoiding direct sun ▐ Cool to moderate. Moderate to high humidity ◖ Every three weeks. Rarely in winter ◊ Keep moist, but avoid waterlogging. Sparingly in winter ✂ Division

△ *Selaginella martensii*
SELAGINELLA
↕ 15cm (6in) ↔ 30cm (12in)

A curious, tufted fern relative with flattened, frond-like stems, crowded with small, scale-like, glossy green leaves that give the plant a pleasantly soft texture. Makes good cover beneath other plants.

☼ Shady ▐ Warm. High humidity ◖ Every five weeks, using half-strength general houseplant fertilizer ◊ Water when compost surface just dry ✂ Stem cuttings

△ *Schefflera arboricola* 'Luciana'
SCHEFFLERA
↕ 1.8m (6ft) ↔ 90cm (3ft)

Fingered leaves are the hallmark of these evergreen shrubs from Taiwan, which all make excellent houseplants. They branch from the base, so prune to keep small.

☼ Bright to shady ▐ Warm, avoiding fluctuation. Moderate to high humidity ◖ Fortnightly. Monthly in winter ◊ Water when compost surface dry ✂ Tip cuttings, air layering

OTHER HOUSEPLANTS FOR LOW LIGHT

Adiantum raddianum, see p.398
Aucuba japonica 'Crotonifolia'
Chamaedorea elegans, see p.412
Ficus pumila 'White Sonny', see p.363
Hedera canariensis 'Gloire de Marengo'
Howea forsteriana
Spathiphyllum 'Euro Gigant', see p.371
Tolmiea menziesii 'Taff's Gold', see p.377

△ *Tolmiea menziesii*
PIGGYBACK PLANT
↕ 30cm (12in) ↔ 40cm (16in)

This hardy perennial produces young plantlets where the leaf blades join their stalks. Suitable for an unheated room, it looks good in a pot or hanging basket.

☼ Moderate to shady ▐ Cool to moderate. Moderate humidity ◖ Fortnightly. Occasionally in winter ◊ When compost surface dry. Reduce watering in winter ✂ Division, plantlets

Houseplants for Dry Atmospheres

CENTRAL HEATING has both benefits and drawbacks for houseplants. It keeps a room warm, which suits most exotics, but it also causes moisture in the air to evaporate, leaving the room very dry. Regular misting counteracts this, or choose from the range of plants that are tolerant of, if not comfortable in, a dry atmosphere.

LOCATIONS

Adenium obesum ▷
DESERT ROSE
↕ 1.5m (5ft) ↔ 1m (3ft)

A slow-growing succulent bush that develops a swollen base. Red, pink, or white flowers appear from midwinter to spring, usually before the leaves; the early flowers are often a surprise. ♈

☼ Bright, with sun ≣ Warm, but moderate to cool winter rest. Low humidity ♦ Every three weeks, using cactus and succulent or high potash fertilizer ♦ When top 2.5cm (1in) compost dry. Water sparingly in winter ⊞ Tip cuttings

△ *Aloe aristata*
LACE ALOE
↕ 12cm (5in) ↔ 30cm (12in)

Crowded rosettes of spine-tipped leaves are minutely white-toothed and spotted; the orange-red flowers appear in autumn. Easy to grow and very tolerant of neglect.

☼ Bright, with sun ≣ Warm, but moderate to cool in winter. Low humidity ♦ Every three weeks, using fertilizer for cacti and succulents ♦ When top 2.5cm (1in) compost dry. Sparingly in winter ⊞ Offsets

---

OTHER HOUSEPLANTS FOR DRY ATMOSPHERES

Azorina vidalii
Bowiea volubilis
Haemanthus albiflos
Nolina recurvata, see p.394
Pelargonium 'Graveolens', see p.344
Sedum sieboldii 'Mediovariegatum'

Aechmea chantinii ▷
QUEEN OF THE AECHMEAS
↕ 1m (3ft) ↔ 80cm (32in)

As long as the urn-like rosette is topped up, this impressive, red- and yellow-bracted bromeliad tolerates a reasonably dry atmosphere, although it appreciates misting. ♈

☼ Bright, but avoid summer sun ≣ Warm. Low to moderate humidity ♦ Fortnightly ♦ When compost surface dry. Water sparingly in winter. Keep "urn" topped up with water ⊞ Offsets

△ *Astrophytum myriostigma*
BISHOP'S CAP
↕ 23cm (9in) ↔ 25cm (10in)

Spiny when young, and later smooth, this squat, plump-ribbed cactus is covered in minute, white-downy scales. Pale yellow summer flowers grow from the crown. ♈

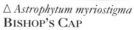

☼ Bright, with sun ≣ Warm, but cool to moderate in winter. Low humidity ♦ Monthly, using fertilizer for cacti and succulents ♦ When compost surface dry. Water sparingly in winter ⊞ Offsets, seed

△ *Euphorbia obesa*
TURKISH TEMPLE
↕ ↔ 15cm (6in)

This plant looks like an *Astrophytum*, but it is in fact a succulent spurge, with typically milky caustic sap. The small yellow flower clusters are produced in summer. ♇

☀ Bright, with sun 🌡 Warm, but cool to moderate in winter. Low humidity 💧 Monthly, using fertilizer for cacti and succulents 💧 When compost surface dry. Water sparingly in winter 🔲 Offsets

Vibrant orange flowerhead

△ *Opuntia microdasys* var. *albispina*
BUNNY EARS
↕ ↔ 60cm (2ft)

A very decorative cactus producing bright yellow flowers in spring and summer. Handle with care; minute white spines stick into skin at the slightest touch.

☀ Bright, with sun 🌡 Warm, but cool to moderate in winter. Low humidity 💧 Monthly, using cactus and succulent fertilizer 💧 When compost surface dry. Sparingly in winter 🔲 Offsets

△ *Tillandsia deiriana*
AIR PLANT
↕ ↔ 30cm (12in)

This vibrantly-coloured air plant is best grown on a piece of driftwood or cork and suspended from a high point that is reachable for misting. It can also be pot grown.

☀ Bright, but avoid direct sun 🌡 Warm. Low humidity 💧 Every eight weeks 💧 Mist daily. Mist four times weekly in low light and cool conditions. Water sparingly 🔲 Offsets

---

OTHER CACTI AND SUCCULENTS FOR DRY ATMOSPHERES

Agave victoriae-reginae
Aloe variegata, see p.386
Kalanchoe daigremontiana
Mammillaria hahniana
Opuntia tunicata
Oreocereus celsianus
Pedilanthus tithymaloides 'Variegatus'

△ *Jatropha podagrica*
JATROPHA
↕ 50cm (20in) or more ↔ 25cm (10in) or more

Swollen stems bear large, tough, long-stalked leaves, whitish beneath. Clusters of red flowers appear at the ends of long stalks in summer. It has caustic sap. ♇

☀ Bright, with sun 🌡 Warm, but cool to moderate in winter. Low humidity 💧 Monthly, using fertilizer for cacti and succulents 💧 When compost surface dry. Water sparingly in winter 🔲 Seed

Grey, curled foliage

◁ *Tillandsia streptophylla*
AIR PLANT
↕ ↔ 45cm (18in)

Striking, curled and arching foliage is joined in late spring or autumn by green bracts and blue and red flowers. Grow in a pot or display on a piece of driftwood.

☀ Bright, but avoid direct sun 🌡 Warm. Low humidity 💧 Every eight weeks 💧 Mist daily. Mist four times weekly in low light and cool conditions. Water sparingly 🔲 Offsets

Houseplants for Warm, Humid Rooms

A WARM, HUMID ENVIRONMENT is perfect for growing many tropical plants, but remember that some need constant moderate to high humidity to flourish, disliking draughts and changes in temperature. Warm bathrooms are a good choice, but beware of open windows letting in unwelcome cold air, and the drying effect of heating. Garden rooms, with controlled temperature and humidity, are ideal, and enable you to nurture exotics or a miniature rainforest.

LOCATIONS

Aphelandra squarrosa 'Dania' ▷
ZEBRA PLANT
↕ ↔ 30cm (12in)

Grow this compact plant for its dark green glossy leaves with their creamy veins and midribs, and its eye-catching flowers with their bright yellow, orange-tipped bracts.

☼ Bright to moderate, avoiding hot sun ≣ Warm, avoiding fluctuation. High humidity ◆ Fortnightly, spring to autumn ◊ Keep moist, but do not over-water. When dry in winter ▦ Tip cuttings

△ *Calathea roseopicta*
PEACOCK PLANT
↕ 24cm (10in) ↔ 15cm (6in)

A distinctive plant bearing beautifully patterned, large foliage, marked deep green; the midrib and leaf margins are a delicate rose-pink. A stunning houseplant. ♈

☼ Moderate ≣ Moderate to warm, avoiding fluctuation. High humidity ◆ Fortnightly. Monthly in winter ◊ Keep moist. At cooler temperatures, water when compost surface just dry ▦ Division

△ *Caladium bicolor* 'Frieda Hemple'
ANGEL'S WINGS
↕ 30cm (12in) ↔ 45cm (18in)

Gloriously coloured, paper-thin leaves emerge in spring and die down in autumn, when the tubers should be lifted and stored for replanting the following spring.

☼ Bright to moderate, avoiding direct sun ≣ Warm, but moderate in dormancy. High humidity ◆ Weekly ◊ Keep moist, reduce in autumn, and keep slightly moist in winter ▦ Division, tubers

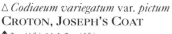

△ *Calathea makoyana*
PEACOCK PLANT
↕ 45cm (18in) ↔ 30cm (12in)

Also known as cathedral windows, this elegant plant has large, oval, mid-green leaves, beautifully traced with darker green and flushed purple beneath. ♈

☼ Moderate ≣ Moderate to warm, avoiding fluctuation. High humidity ◆ Fortnightly. Monthly in winter ◊ Keep moist. At cooler temperatures, water when compost surface just dry ▦ Division

△ *Codiaeum variegatum* var. *pictum*
CROTON, JOSEPH'S COAT
↕ 2m (6ft) ↔ 1.2m (4ft)

This woody-based plant is famous for the colourful variegation along the veins of its glossy leaves. Green and yellow, or red, orange, and purple are predominant.

☼ Bright, but avoid summer sun ≣ Moderate to warm, avoiding fluctuation. High humidity ◆ Fortnightly in summer, using foliage houseplant fertilizer ◊ Keep moist. When dry if cool ▦ Tip cuttings

Maranta leuconeura
var. *kerchoveana* ▷
PRAYER PLANT
↕ ↔ 30cm (12in)

Pale green, satin-sheened leaves, each marked with dark green
"footprints", distinguish this tropical American species and give it its
alternative name, rabbit's foot plant.

☼ Moderate, avoiding direct sun ≣ Moderate
to warm. High humidity ♠ Fortnightly.
Occasionally in winter ◊ Keep moist.
When dry at lower temperatures
⊞ Division, tip cuttings

△ *Cyperus albostriatus*
UMBRELLA PLANT
↕ 60cm (2ft) ↔ 30cm (12in)

Densely tufted and with strap-shaped,
pale green leaves radiating from the ends
of the stems, this plant also produces green
flower clusters from summer to autumn.

☼ Bright to moderate. Avoid summer sun ≣ Cool
to warm. Moderate to high humidity ♠ Fortnightly,
using foliage houseplant fertilizer. Twice in winter
◊ Keep moist. Likes to stand in water ⊞ Division

**OTHER HOUSEPLANTS FOR
WARM, HUMID ROOMS**

Adiantum raddianum 'Gracillimum'
Anthurium crystallinum, see p.338
Calathea crocata, see p.328
Codiaeum 'Petra'
Hypoestes phyllostachya 'Wit', see p.351
Maranta leuconeura var.
 erythroneura, see p.399
Peperomia caperata 'Little
 Fantasy'
Philodendron melanochrysum
Sinningia 'Mont Blanc', see p.343

△ *Fittonia verschaffeltii* var. *pearcei*
'Superba Red'
NET PLANT, SNAKESKIN PLANT
↕ 15cm (6in) ↔ 30cm (12in) or more

A compact plant with dark green leaves
and bright red leaf veins. It makes a neat
display when grouped with several others
in a shallow pot, or is ideal for a terrarium.

☼ Moderate ≣ Moderate to warm. High humidity
♠ Fortnightly. Occasionally in winter ◊ Allow
compost surface to dry slightly before watering.
Dislikes being waterlogged ⊞ Tip cuttings

Stromanthe 'Stripestar' ▷
PEACOCK PLANT
↕ 1.5m (5ft) ↔ 1m (3ft)

Each glossy dark green leaf has
a pale green midrib and
veins, with a dark purple underside
that is prominent as new leaves unfurl.
Not easy to grow but worth the effort.

☼ Bright to moderate, avoiding summer sun
≣ Moderate to warm, avoiding draughts. High
humidity ♠ Fortnightly. Monthly in winter ◊ Keep
moist. When dry at lower temperatures ⊞ Division

Houseplants for Large Rooms

OTHER HOUSEPLANTS FOR LARGE ROOMS

Begonia luxurians
Chamaedorea elegans, see p.412
Cissus rhombifolia 'Ellen Danica', see
  p.376
Ficus elastica 'Robusta', see p.389
Ficus lyrata, see p.395
Musa acuminata 'Dwarf Cavendish'
Sparrmannia africana, see p.387
Yucca elephantipes, see p.385

GENEROUSLY-PROPORTIONED rooms call for dramatic plants to fill the space without dominating it or making it hard for people to move around. Bold-leaved specimens are often a good choice, although large plants with smaller leaves are equally effective when well placed. Some of the suggestions here need careful pruning to restrict their size.

Fatsia japonica 'Variegata' ▷
JAPANESE ARALIA

↕ ↔ 1.5m (5ft) or more

A popular variegated foliage shrub, with large, long-stalked, evergreen leaves, their lobes splashed creamy-white. Tolerates relatively cool conditions, but it needs plenty of elbow room.

☼ Bright to moderate ▮ Cool to moderate. Moderate humidity ◕ Fortnightly, using foliage houseplant fertilizer. Once in winter ◊ When compost surface dry. Reduce watering at low temperatures ▥ Tip cuttings, air layering

△ *Codiaeum* 'Juliet'
CROTON

↕ ↔ 1m (3ft) or more

This handsome evergreen shrub has deeply-lobed, leathery, glossy green leaves, their veins picked out in bright yellow. Plant several in a container, or encourage one to branch out.

☼ Bright, with some sun ▮ Warm, avoiding draughts and fluctuation. Moderate to high humidity ◕ Fortnightly, using foliage houseplant fertilizer. Occasionally in winter ◊ Keep moist. In winter, water when compost surface dry ▥ Tip cuttings

Lime-green variegated foliage

Dracaena fragrans 'Lemon Lime' ▷
DRACAENA

↕ 3m (10ft) or more ↔ 1.2m (4ft) or more

One of the most colourful of a group famed for variegated foliage. The long, tapered leaves are lime green with a wide, cream-edged, dark green central stripe.

☼ Bright to moderate, avoiding summer sun ▮ Warm. Moderate to high humidity ◕ Fortnightly. Occasionally in winter ◊ When dry. Water sparingly in winter ▥ Tip cuttings, stem sections

Ficus bennendijkii 'Alii' ▷
FICUS

↕ 2m (6ft) or more
↔ 75cm (30in) or more

Looking like an evergreen weeping willow, this graceful houseplant has slender stems clothed in long, narrow leaves. Its fairly narrow habit makes it suitable for a variety of spaces.

☼ Bright, but avoid summer sun ▮ Warm. Moderate to high humidity ◕ Fortnightly. Occasionally in winter ◊ When compost surface dry. Reduce watering at lower temperatures ▥ Tip cuttings, air layering

Monstera deliciosa
'Variegata' ▷
SWISS CHEESE PLANT
↕ ↔ 4m (12ft) or more

Grown on a moss pole, this striking climber, with outstanding, deeply-lobed, green and white leaves, will prove a talking point wherever it is placed. If neglected or allowed to dry out, it will become an eyesore. ♛

☼ Bright to moderate ❄ Warm. Moderate to high humidity ◊ Fortnightly. Occasionally in winter ◊ Water when compost surface just dry ✄ Stem cuttings, air layering

*Ravenea
rivularis* ▷
**MAJESTY
PALM**
↕ 3m (10ft) or more
↔ 1.5m (5ft) or more

A beautiful, quite fast-growing palm from Madagascar, with elegant, feather-like leaves. A newcomer to indoor cultivation, it tolerates low light and cool conditions.

☼ Bright to moderate, avoiding summer sun ❄ Moderate to warm. Moderate to high humidity ◊ Fortnightly, using foliage houseplant feed. Monthly in winter ◊ When dry. Avoid waterlogging ✄ Seed

*Murraya
paniculata* ▷
**ORANGE
JESSAMINE**
↕ 3m (10ft)
↔ 1.2m (4ft)

An attractive shrub with dark green, divided, glossy, evergreen leaves, strongly scented if bruised, and clusters of scented, citrus-like flowers from spring to summer.

☼ Bright to moderate, with sun ❄ Moderate to warm. Moderate to high humidity ◊ Fortnightly. Occasionally in winter ◊ When compost surface dry. Water sparingly in winter ✄ Semi-ripe cuttings

△ *Philodendron erubescens* 'Burgundy'
BLUSHING PHILODENDRON
↕ ↔ 3m (10ft) or more

Large, shining, red-flushed, red-veined leaves are borne on dark purple-red stems. Best trained on a moss pole, it is an impressive plant when grown well. ♛

☼ Bright to shady ❄ Warm. Moderate to high humidity ◊ Fortnightly, using foliage houseplant fertilizer. Monthly in winter ◊ Let compost surface dry slightly before watering ✄ Tip cuttings

△ *Spathiphyllum* 'Euro Gigant'
PEACE LILY
↕ ↔ 1m (3ft)

Magnificent at its best, and an excellent specimen. Large, boldly-veined, paddle-like green leaves are joined in spring and summer by tall-stemmed white flowers.

☼ Bright, but avoid direct sun ❄ Moderate to warm. Moderate to high humidity ◊ Fortnightly. Monthly in winter ◊ Water when compost surface dry. Avoid overwatering ✄ Division

LOCATIONS

Houseplants for Sitting and Dining Rooms

IN MOST HOMES the sitting and dining rooms are the largest in the house. They are rooms to feel comfortable in, so all the more reason to include plants. Given their floor spaces, corners, and flat surfaces, they offer great potential for using plants to soften hard lines or edges, complement decor, and promote a relaxing atmosphere.

Chlorophytum comosum 'Variegatum' ▷
SPIDER PLANT
↕ 90cm (3ft) ↔ 60cm (2ft)

Easy and adaptable, this spider plant tolerates poor light and neglect, but thrives in good conditions. It differs from the equally common *Chlorophytum comosum* 'Vittatum' in having white, rather than green, leaf margins. ♔

☼ Bright to moderate, avoiding summer sun
🌡 Moderate to warm. Moderate to high humidity
💧 Fortnightly. Stop at low winter temperatures
💧 Keep moist, but avoid waterlogging. In winter, water when compost surface dry 🪴 Plantlets

△ *Asparagus densiflorus* 'Myersii'
FOXTAIL FERN
↕ ↔ 45cm (18in)

This striking, tuberous-rooted foliage perennial has foxtail-like plumes of tiny, green, needle-like branchlets. Contrast with broad-leaved plants in a group. ♔

☼ Bright to moderate. Avoid hot sun 🌡 Moderate to warm. Moderate humidity 💧 Foliage houseplant fertilizer weekly. Monthly in winter 💧 Keep moist. Water when dry in winter 🪴 Division

> **OTHER FOLIAGE HOUSEPLANTS FOR SITTING AND DINING ROOMS**
>
> *Aspidistra elatior* 'Milky Way', see p.364
> *Dracaena fragrans* 'Massangeana', see p.375
> *Monstera deliciosa*, see p.339
> *Radermachera sinica*

Asparagus falcatus ▷
SICKLETHORN
↕ 3m (10ft) or more ↔ 1m (3ft)

An erect, strong-growing, bright green plant that in the wild clambers into trees by means of tiny spines. Grown indoors, it is more compact and easily controllable.

☼ Bright to moderate. Avoid hot sun 🌡 Moderate to warm. Moderate humidity 💧 Foliage houseplant fertilizer weekly. Monthly in winter 💧 Keep moist. Water when dry in winter 🪴 Division, seed

△ *Corynocarpus laevigatus*
KARAKA
↕ 3m (10ft) or more ↔ 1.5m (5ft) or more

In its native New Zealand the karaka is a woodland tree, but it is slower growing and easily controlled as a houseplant. It has handsome, shining, deep green leaves.

☼ Bright, with some direct sun 🌡 Moderate to warm. Moderate humidity 💧 Monthly. Occasionally in winter 💧 When compost surface dry 🪴 Semi-ripe cuttings, seed

OTHER FLOWERING HOUSEPLANTS
FOR SITTING AND DINING ROOMS

Heliotropium 'Chatsworth'
Impatiens walleriana hybrids, see p.385
Pelargonium 'Sefton'
Primula obconica, see p.331
Sinningia speciosa cultivars

△ *Justicia carnea*
FLAMINGO PLANT
↕ 1.2m (4ft) ↔ 80cm (32in)

This evergreen shrub produces large,
boldly-veined leaves and dense spikes of
two-lipped, pink to rose-pink flowers in
summer or later. Keep bushy by pruning.

☼ Bright to moderate, avoiding direct sun
❆ Warm, avoiding draughts. Moderate to high
humidity ◍ Monthly ◌ Keep moist, but avoid
waterlogging ▨ Semi-ripe cuttings, seed

*Peperomia
caperata*
'Lilian' ▷
PEPEROMIA
↕ 20cm (8in) ↔ 15cm (6in)

The neat tuft of corrugated, deep green
leaves is topped by white flower spikes in
late summer. An ideal plant for growing in
a small space, bottle garden, or terrarium.

☼ Bright to moderate, with some sun ❆ Warm.
Moderate to high humidity ◍ Every three weeks.
Occasionally in winter ◌ When compost surface
dry. Avoid waterlogging ▨ Tip cuttings

△ *Dracaena cincta* 'Tricolor'
DRACAENA
↕ 3m (10ft) ↔ 1.2m (4ft)

A slow-growing shrub or small tree with
slender stems and loose ruffs of long,
narrow, shining green leaves, striped
cream and stained pink along the margins.

☼ Bright to moderate, avoiding direct summer sun
❆ Warm. Moderate to high humidity
◍ Fortnightly. Occasionally in winter ◌ When
compost surface dry. Water sparingly
in winter ▨ Tip or stem cuttings

*Hibiscus rosa-
sinensis* 'Lateritia' ▷
ROSE OF CHINA
↕ 2.5m (8ft) ↔ 1.5m (5ft)

Roses of China are capable of
reaching a large size but can be
pruned in winter to encourage a
more bushy, compact habit. Large,
yellow, deep-throated flowers
appear from spring to autumn.

☼ Bright ❆ Warm, avoiding fluctuation.
Moderate to high humidity ◍ Fortnightly. Stop
feeding at lower temperatures ◌ When
compost surface just dry. Water sparingly in
winter ▨ Tip cuttings

△ *Pericallis* × *hybrida* cultivars
FLORISTS' CINERARIA
↕ 30cm (12in) ↔ 25cm (10in)

Spectacular winter- to spring-flowering
plants, these have a rosette of bold foliage
crowned by usually long-lasting, large,
daisy-like flowers in a variety of colours.

☼ Bright, but avoid direct sun ❆ Cool to
moderate or warm. Moderate to high humidity
◍ Fortnightly ◌ Keep moist, but avoid waterlogging
▨ Seed

Houseplants for Bedrooms

IT WAS ONCE commonly believed that plants in a bedroom or hospital ward, certainly at night, were injurious to health. This misconception may have stemmed from the fact that the leaves of most plants absorb oxygen during the hours of darkness. Nowadays we know that plants in an airy bedroom will provide benefits including increased humidity, a reduction in chemical toxins, and the suppression of airborne microbes. Carefully placed, the houseplants shown here can bring a healthy, relaxing atmosphere to any bedroom.

LOCATIONS

Achimenes hybrids ▷
HOT WATER PLANT
↕ ↔ 30cm (12in)

Blooming profusely from summer into autumn, few houseplants are more free-flowering. Support the floppy stems or grow in a hanging basket or on a pedestal.

☼ Bright. Avoid summer sun ≣ Warm. Moderate humidity ◖ Fortnightly, using flowering houseplant fertilizer ◌ Freely in summer; reduce in autumn; keep dry in winter; increase in spring ▨ Tubercles

Asparagus umbellatus ▷
ASPARAGUS FERN
↕ 1.2m (4ft) ↔ 60cm (2ft)

The asparagus fern makes a cheerful informal houseplant with its clusters of bristle-like, bright green leaves. In its native Canary Islands it is a scrambling perennial, so if pot-grown the stems may need support.

☼ Bright to moderate, avoiding summer sun ≣ Moderate to warm. Moderate humidity ◖ Foliage houseplant fertilizer weekly. Monthly in winter ◌ Keep moist. In winter, water when dry ▨ Division, seed

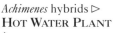

Aglaonema 'Lilian' ▷
CHINESE EVERGREEN
↕ ↔ 60cm (2ft)

This Chinese evergreen produces small, arum-like flowers in summer, but is valued most for its beautifully marked, slender-pointed leaves, borne in a bold clump. Slow-growing but well worth it.

☼ Moderate, avoiding sun ≣ Moderate to warm. Moderate to high humidity ◖ Foliage houseplant fertilizer weekly. Monthly in winter ◌ When dry ▨ Division, tip cuttings

Catharanthus roseus ▷
MADAGASCAR PERIWINKLE
↕ ↔ 30cm (12in)

This easy-to-grow plant forms a low, rounded bush of shiny foliage, and sports large pink, lavender, white, or red periwinkle flowers from late spring to autumn. ♧

☼ Bright, but avoid summer sun ≣ Warm. Moderate humidity ◖ Monthly ◌ Water regularly, keeping permanently moist. Avoid waterlogging ▨ Tip cuttings. Roots easily in water

Pilea microphylla ▷
ARTILLERY PLANT
↕ ↔ 30cm (12in)

This compact pilea forms a small hummock of foliage. It derives its common name from the pollen, which silently and harmlessly "explodes" when ripe. Suitable for a sunless position and best regarded as a temporary plant.

☼ Moderate ≋ Moderate to warm. Moderate to high humidity ♦ Fortnightly. Monthly in winter ◊ Water when compost surface just dry. Avoid waterlogging ▦ Tip cuttings

OTHER FOLIAGE HOUSEPLANTS FOR BEDROOMS

Adiantum raddianum, see p.398
Aspidistra elatior, see p.386
Chlorophytum comosum 'Vittatum', see p.384
Dracaena fragrans 'White Edge'
Nephrolepis exaltata 'Bostoniensis', see p.407

△ *Solenostemon* 'Wizard'
COLEUS, FLAME NETTLE
↕ ↔ 20cm (8in)

Brilliantly coloured leaves are the trademark of coleus; this wide-margined form is excellent for a sunny window or well-lit spot. Pinch out tips for compact growth.

☼ Bright ≋ Warm. Moderate humidity ♦ Weekly. Occasionally in winter ◊ Keep moist, but avoid waterlogging. In winter, water when just dry ▦ Tip cuttings, seed. Roots easily in water

△ *Dracaena fragrans* 'Massangeana'
CORN PALM
↕ 3m (10ft) ↔ 1.2m (4ft)

The stout stems form a miniature tree crowded with glossy green leaves with a greenish-yellow central band. One of the most popular of all dracaenas. ♆

☼ Bright to moderate, avoiding summer sun ≋ Warm. Moderate to high humidity ♦ Fortnightly. Occasionally in winter ◊ When compost surface dry. Water sparingly in winter ▦ Tip cuttings, stem sections

OTHER FLOWERING HOUSEPLANTS FOR BEDROOMS

Begonia tuberosa hybrids
Cyclamen persicum hybrids, see p.330
Impatiens walleriana hybrids, see p.385
Oxalis purpurata, see p.347
Spathiphyllum 'Euro Gigant', see p.371

Dracaena reflexa 'Song of India' ▷
DRACAENA
↕ 3m (10ft) ↔ 1.2m (4ft)

Many-branched and woody-stemmed, this plant eventually grows into a small tree. Its yellow-margined leaves are mostly crowded towards the branch ends.

☼ Bright to moderate, avoiding summer sun ≋ Warm. Moderate to high humidity ♦ Fortnightly. Occasionally in winter ◊ When dry. Water sparingly in winter ▦ Tip cuttings, stem sections

△ *Syngonium podophyllum* 'Pixie'
GOOSEFOOT PLANT
↕ ↔ 30cm (12in)

White-marbled, arrow-shaped leaves, initially clump-forming, divide as this attractive perennial matures and begins to climb. Best grown on a moss pole.

☼ Bright to moderate, avoiding summer sun ≋ Warm, avoiding fluctuation. Moderate to high humidity ♦ Fortnightly. Monthly in winter ◊ When compost surface dry ▦ Tip cuttings

Houseplants for Narrow Spaces

EVERY HOME contains awkward narrow spaces, perhaps with restricted access, which call for small or upright plants rather than large or bushy specimens. They are just the spots to take most climbers, trailers, or compact, well-mannered plants that respond well to occasional pruning. Such situations can be poorly lit, so choose plants that will tolerate a degree of shade.

LOCATIONS

Handsome, glossy leaves

Asparagus setaceus 'Nanus' ▷
ASPARAGUS FERN
↕ ↔ 45cm (18in)

The delicate, feathery, frond-like foliage of this plant is commonly used in button-holes. Unlike the parent species, this compact form will not climb and is ideal for small spaces.

☼ Bright to moderate, avoiding summer sun ❄ Cool to warm. Moderate humidity
💧 Weekly, using foliage houseplant fertilizer. Monthly in winter ○ Keep moist. When compost surface dry at lower temperatures ⚱ Division, seed

OTHER SMALL HOUSE-
PLANTS FOR NARROW SPACES

Achimenes hybrids
Ardisia crispa
Cyperus involucratus 'Nanus'
Ficus pumila 'White Sonny', see p.363
Spathiphyllum 'Petite'

Cissus antarctica ▷
KANGAROO VINE
↕ 3m (10ft) ↔ 60cm (2ft)

This vigorous Australian plant produces attractive, glossy, dark green, leathery leaves with scalloped edges. Provide support, and pinch out the growing tips to control its height and spread.

☼ Bright to moderate, avoiding summer sun
❄ Cool to warm. Moderate to high humidity
💧 Fortnightly. Monthly in winter, at higher temperatures ○ When compost surface dry. Avoid underwatering ⚱ Tip cuttings

△ *Cissus rhombifolia* 'Ellen Danica'
GRAPE IVY
↕ 2m (6ft) ↔ 45cm (18in)

As it climbs by tendrils, train this popular form of grape ivy on a trellis or canes to display its large, glossy, deeply lobed leaves. Young plants are best grown as trailers. Full of character.

☼ Bright to moderate, avoiding summer sun
❄ Cool to warm. Moderate to high humidity
💧 Fortnightly. Monthly in winter, at higher temperatures ○ Allow to dry out before watering. Avoid underwatering ⚱ Tip cuttings

△ *Crocus vernus* cultivars
DUTCH CROCUS
↕ 12cm (5in) ↔ 5cm (2in)

Giving a cheerful late winter or spring display in a cool part of the house, this old favourite, with goblet-shaped flowers in many colours, brightens any narrow space.

☼ Bright ❘ Cool to moderate. Moderate humidity ● Unnecessary ○ Keep moist, but avoid waterlogging ▦ Cormlets. In temperate climates, crocuses can be planted outdoors after flowering

OTHER TALL HOUSEPLANTS OR CLIMBERS FOR NARROW SPACES

Dieffenbachia 'Compacta', see p.338
Dracaena fragrans 'Compacta', see p.362
Ficus bennendijkii 'Alii', see p.370
Hedera helix 'Ivalace'
Schefflera arboricola 'Compacta', see p.389
Yucca elephantipes, see p.385

△ *Euonymus japonicus* 'Aureus'
JAPANESE SPINDLE
↕ 1.5m (5ft) ↔ 60cm (2ft)

Ideal for a cool room or hallway, this delightful, slow-growing, compact plant has gold-splashed, dark green leaves. Can be planted outside if it grows too large.

☼ Bright, with some direct sun ❘ Cool to warm. Moderate humidity ● Monthly, from spring to autumn ○ When compost surface dry. Water sparingly in winter ▦ Tip cuttings

△ × *Fatshedera lizei* 'Pia'
FATSHEDERA
↕ 2m (6ft) ↔ 45cm (18in)

An excellent foliage shrub with glossy, five-lobed, wavy-edged leaves. Grow several together against a pale background to emphasize their leaf shape and form.

☼ Moderate. Tolerates some shade ❘ Cool to warm. Moderate humidity ● Foliage houseplant fertilizer fortnightly. Monthly in winter ○ Water when dry ▦ Tip cuttings, stem sections

△ *Hedera canariensis* 'Montgomery'
CANARY ISLAND IVY
↕ 4m (12ft) ↔ 1m (3ft)

Decorative bronze-purple stems produce large, sharply lobed, mid-green leaves that become a dark glossy green with maturity. May need restrictive pruning with age.

☼ Bright to moderate ❘ Cool to warm. Moderate to high humidity ● Fortnightly. Twice in winter ○ When compost surface dry. Water sparingly in winter ▦ Tip cuttings, layering

△ *Hedera helix* 'Ovata'
COMMON IVY, ENGLISH IVY
↕ 2m (6ft) ↔ 30cm (12in)

This ivy has leathery, unlobed, deep green, triangular leaves, sometimes with wedge-shaped tips. Grow it in a hanging basket or train it up a pole or frame. Sometimes sold as 'Mein Hertz'.

☼ Bright to moderate ❘ Cool to warm. Moderate to high humidity ● Fortnightly. Twice in winter ○ When compost surface dry. Water sparingly in winter ▦ Tip cuttings, layering

△ *Tolmiea menziesii* 'Taff's Gold'
PIGGYBACK PLANT
↕ ↔ 30cm (12in)

Small plantlets occur where each leaf and stalk join, hence the common name of this plant with hairy, gold-mottled green leaves. A good choice for a cool spot.

☼ Bright, but avoid direct sun ❘ Cool to moderate. Moderate humidity ● Fortnightly. Twice in winter, if temperature raised ○ When compost surface dry. Water sparingly in winter ▦ Plantlets

Houseplants for Garden Rooms

GARDEN ROOMS, offering protection from unfavourable weather yet benefiting from unrestricted light, are often the ideal way to provide houseplants with optimum growing conditions, particularly in cool temperate climates. Artificial, consistent heat and humidity levels allow tropical species to grow, but a wide range of plants will thrive even in a cool garden room.

△ *Euryops chrysanthemoides*
EURYOPS
↕ 1m (3ft) ↔ 1.2m (4ft) or more

Worth growing for the cheerful, bright yellow daisy flowers alone. These are borne intermittently throughout the year over a dense, dome-shaped bush of rich green foliage. It can be pruned to maintain the required shape.

☼ Bright, with sun ⟐ Moderate to warm. Moderate humidity ◑ Every three weeks ◌ When compost surface dry. Water sparingly in winter ⊞ Semi-ripe cuttings, seed

Anigozanthos flavidus ▷
KANGAROO PAW
↕ 1.2m (4ft) ↔ 45cm (18in)

Curiously shaped flowers, in either pink or yellow, are produced in clusters in late spring or summer and give this plant its common name. A near-hardy plant that is suitable for a cooler garden room.

☼ Bright to moderate, avoiding summer sun ⟐ Moderate to warm. Moderate humidity ◑ Fortnightly, using fertilizer for ericaceous plants. Occasionally in winter ◌ Keep moist. Reduce watering in winter ⊞ Division, seed

OTHER HOUSEPLANTS FOR GARDEN ROOMS

Coronilla valentina subsp. *glauca*
Eupatorium sordidum
Leonotis ocymifolia
Lithodora rosmarinifolia
Metrosideros kermadecensis 'Variegatus'
Prostanthera rotundifolia, see p.345

Tiny flowers with spreading petals

△ *Argyranthemum* 'Vancouver'
CANARY ISLAND MARGUERITE
↕ ↔ 90cm (3ft)

Abundant, anemone-centred pink flowers, from spring to autumn, give this perennial a long season of interest. Deadheading regularly will encourage more blooms. ♔

☼ Bright, but avoid direct sun ⟐ Cool to moderate. Moderate humidity ◑ Every three weeks ◌ Keep moist, but avoid waterlogging ⊞ Tip cuttings

Cuphea hyssopifolia ▷
FALSE HEATHER
↕ 60cm (2ft) ↔ 80cm (32in)

Bushy and compact, narrow-leaved false heathers are sometimes used as summer bedding plants in cool climates. Masses of small pink, purple, or white flowers are freely produced from summer through to autumn. ♔

☼ Bright, avoiding direct sun ⟐ Cool to moderate. Moderate humidity ◑ Every three weeks. Occasionally in winter ◌ When compost surface dry. Water sparingly in winter ⊞ Tip cuttings

LOCATIONS

△ *Pelargonium* 'Carisbrooke'
REGAL PELARGONIUM
↕ 45cm (18in) ↔ 30cm (12in)

Broad clusters of pale rose-pink flowers, their upper petals blazed with claret, are produced in a flowering season of short duration, from spring to midsummer. ▽

☼ Bright, with sun ▮ Moderate to warm, but cool in winter. Moderate humidity ◍ Fortnightly, using high potash fertilizer ◌ When compost surface just dry. Water sparingly in winter ▦ Tip cuttings

△ *Rehmannia elata*
CHINESE FOXGLOVE
↕ 75cm (30in) or more ↔ 45cm (18in)

Loose-stemmed and downy all over, this perennial member of the foxglove family bears gorgeous, pendulous, pink-purple flowers from summer into autumn. ▽

☼ Bright ▮ Moderate to warm. Moderate humidity ◍ Monthly. Occasionally in winter ◌ When compost surface dry. Water sparingly in winter ▦ Seed

Spectacular creamy-pink flowers

△ *Strelitzia reginae*
BIRD OF PARADISE
↕ 1.5m (5ft) ↔ 1m (3ft)

Instantly recognizable when in flower, this spectacular South African exotic also has a bold clump of handsome paddle-shaped leaves. Plants take several years to flower; the distinctive blooms last several weeks. ▽

☼ Bright, with sun ▮ Moderate to warm. Moderate humidity ◍ Fortnightly. Occasionally in winter ◌ When compost surface dry. Water sparingly in winter ▦ Division, seed

△ *Pittosporum tobira*
JAPANESE MOCK ORANGE
↕ ↔ 2m (6ft) or more

Creamy flower clusters, appearing in late spring and summer, are deliciously scented of orange-blossom. Attractive, glossy evergreen foliage sets off the flowers and can be pruned into shape. ▽

☼ Bright, with some sun ▮ Moderate to warm, but cool in winter. Moderate humidity ◍ Fortnightly. Occasionally in winter ◌ When dry. Water sparingly in winter ▦ Semi-ripe cuttings, seed

OTHER CLIMBING HOUSEPLANTS FOR GARDEN ROOMS

Bomarea caldasii
Jasminum polyanthum, see p.323
Passiflora 'Amethyst', see p.392
Plumbago auriculata
Streptosolen jamesonii

◁ *Zantedeschia* 'Little Suzie'
ARUM LILY
↕ ↔ 60cm (2ft)

Given sufficient moisture during the growing season, this plant will produce a lush clump of foliage, through which the creamy-pink flowers emerge in summer. It is dormant in winter.

☼ Bright, but avoid intense summer sun ▮ Moderate to warm. Moderate humidity ◍ Fortnightly ◌ Keep moist. Reduce watering during resting period ▦ Division, offsets

LOCATIONS

Houseplants for the Home Office

NOWADAYS MANY PEOPLE work from home. Growing plants in a home office (or any workplace) will improve air quality, adding moisture and helping to disperse pollutants including computer emissions; they may even help you think more clearly. Stand plants away from your equipment to prevent watering accidents.

△ *Crassula ovata*
JADE PLANT
↕ ↔ 1m (3ft) or more

One of the easiest houseplants, this slowly forms a small- to medium-sized succulent bush with red-tinted green foliage. White or pink flowers appear in autumn. ♈

☼ Bright, sunny ▮ Warm, but moderate in winter. Low humidity ♦ Monthly, using fertilizer for cacti and succulents ◊ When compost surface dry. Water sparingly in winter ▱ Tip or leaf cuttings

△ *Adiantum raddianum* 'Fritz Luth'
MAIDENHAIR FERN
↕ ↔ 60cm (2ft)

One of the best maidenhair ferns when mature, with beautifully segmented, emerald-green fronds on wiry, shining black stalks. Protect from cold draughts.

☼ Moderate, avoiding direct sun ▮ Moderate to warm. Moderate to high humidity ♦ Fortnightly. Monthly in winter ◊ Keep moist, but avoid waterlogging ▱ Division, spores

△ *Aglaonema* 'Maria Christina'
CHINESE EVERGREEN
↕ ↔ 50cm (20in)

A suckering, clump-forming perennial producing handsome, large, upright green leaves, liberally splashed and striped creamy white and pale green.

☼ Moderate, avoiding summer sun ▮ Moderate to warm. Moderate to high humidity ♦ Weekly, using foliage houseplant fertilizer. Monthly in winter ◊ When dry ▱ Division, tip or stem cuttings

---

OTHER FLOWERING HOUSE-PLANTS FOR THE HOME OFFICE

Anthurium 'Lady Jane'
Gerbera jamesonii
Impatiens walleriana hybrids, see p.385
Kalanchoe blossfeldiana
Pelargonium 'Stellar Apricot'
Schlumbergera x *buckleyi*
Schlumbergera truncata, see p.363

Aechmea fasciata
'Morgana' ▷
URN PLANT
↕ 60cm (2ft) ↔ 75cm (30in)

The big, funnel-shaped rosette of lilac-grey leaves is enhanced in summer by a spectacular, rose-pink, bracted flower-head. A splendid exotic for a pot or hanging basket in the right spot.

☼ Bright, but avoid summer sun ▮ Warm. Moderate to high humidity ♦ Fortnightly ◊ When compost surface dry. Water sparingly in winter. Keep "urn" topped up with water ▱ Offsets

△ *Cryptanthus bivittatus*
EARTH STAR
↕ 10cm (4in) ↔ 25cm (10in)

A curious-looking plant bearing flattened, star-shaped rosettes of sharply-pointed, wavy-margined, green and white-striped leaves; the white may turn pink in sun. ♈

☼ Bright to shady, avoiding direct sun ▮ Warm. High humidity. Mist regularly or stand on pebble tray ♦ Monthly, using flowering houseplant fertilizer. Twice during winter ◊ When top 5cm (2in) of compost dries out ▱ Offsets

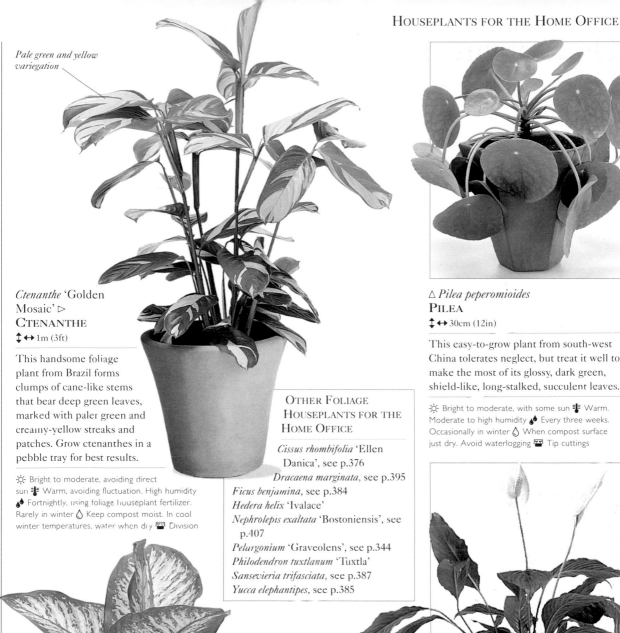

Pale green and yellow variegation

Ctenanthe 'Golden Mosaic' ▷
CTENANTHE
↕ ↔ 1m (3ft)

This handsome foliage plant from Brazil forms clumps of cane-like stems that bear deep green leaves, marked with paler green and creamy-yellow streaks and patches. Grow ctenanthes in a pebble tray for best results.

☼ Bright to moderate, avoiding direct sun ❇ Warm, avoiding fluctuation. High humidity ♠ Fortnightly, using foliage houseplant fertilizer. Rarely in winter ◊ Keep compost moist. In cool winter temperatures, water when dry ▨ Division

△ *Pilea peperomioides*
PILEA
↕ ↔ 30cm (12in)

This easy-to-grow plant from south-west China tolerates neglect, but treat it well to make the most of its glossy, dark green, shield-like, long-stalked, succulent leaves.

☼ Bright to moderate, with some sun ❇ Warm. Moderate to high humidity ♠ Every three weeks. Occasionally in winter ◊ When compost surface just dry. Avoid waterlogging ▨ Tip cuttings

---

OTHER FOLIAGE HOUSEPLANTS FOR THE HOME OFFICE

Cissus rhombifolia 'Ellen Danica', see p.376
Dracaena marginata, see p.395
Ficus benjamina, see p.384
Hedera helix 'Ivalace'
Nephrolepis exaltata 'Bostoniensis', see p.407
Pelargonium 'Graveolens', see p.344
Philodendron tuxtlanum 'Tuxtla'
Sansevieria trifasciata, see p.387
Yucca elephantipes, see p.385

◁ *Dieffenbachia seguine* 'Tropic Snow'
DUMB CANE
↕ ↔ 1m (3ft)

Grow this plant for its bold green foliage marked with pale green and cream variegation; the large leaves give out plenty of water, counteracting dry air. Thrives best on a pebble tray. It is poisonous if chewed, so keep out of the reach of small children. ♉

☼ Bright to moderate. Avoid hot sun ❇ Moderate to warm. Moderate to high humidity ♠ Fortnightly, using foliage houseplant fertilizer. Monthly in winter ◊ When dry ▨ Tip or stem cuttings

△ *Spathiphyllum wallisii* 'Clevelandii'
PEACE LILY
↕ 65cm (26in) ↔ 50cm (20in)

Peace lilies filter toxins from the air and can tolerate low light, so they are useful for an office corner. Display their showy foliage and white flowers to advantage.

☼ Bright to moderate, avoiding direct sun ❇ Moderate to warm. Moderate to high humidity ♠ Fortnightly. Monthly in winter ◊ When compost surface dry. Avoid overwatering ▨ Division

SPECIFIC USES

HOUSEPLANTS ARE without doubt one of the most versatile of all plant groups, with a huge choice for every specific decorative or cultural requirement. Whether you need an architectural form, a selection for a terrarium, or an easy-to-grow houseplant, in the following pages you will find a plant that fits the bill.

△ WINTER ORNAMENT *This collection of solanums and capsicums makes the most of the brightly coloured, decorative fruits, and provides winter colour.*

Homalomena wallisii to improve air quality

There are still many people who are convinced that all houseplants are difficult to grow. Beginners can take heart and try some of the many houseplants that are easy and totally reliable. Some will even tolerate neglect and survive in adverse conditions, although this should never be a reason to forget them. Some flowering plants are hardy and can be planted outside after blooming, giving you two uses for the price of one. All plants produce oxygen as well as absorb impurities from the air, so growing plants indoors is one of the easiest ways of maintaining a healthy home environment.

APPEALING HABITS

The growth habit of some plants, such as climbers and slender-stemmed or trailing plants, is their most interesting and useful feature. Grow trailers in hanging baskets designed for indoor use or in pots placed on raised surfaces such as shelves and cupboards. Such plants can even be used to create a living "curtain" of growth. Equally, many climbers can be trained on to moss poles or frames, providing interest for narrow spaces and awkward corners. Architectural plants that offer impressive forms make fine specimen plants if you have room.

OTHER USES

Many plants from tropical rain-forests demand heat and humidity in order to thrive. Such plants, especially slow-growing or dwarf varieties, can be housed in glazed terraria, glass-panelled tanks, or bell jars, which can become very impressive features. Ornamental fruits or seedheads, like the bright cherry-sized fruits of solanums, are particularly eye-catching in the home, often providing much-needed winter interest. Or why not grow culinary herbs in pots on a sunny kitchen windowsill – a fresh supply is a bonus to any cook.

△ EASY TO GROW *This* Aloe variegata *can withstand neglect, and so can be used where it might be temporarily forgotten.*

◁ HERBS FOR THE KITCHEN *Herbs for cooking can be grown on any warm windowsill or ledge; in the kitchen, they will be close to hand for harvesting.*

▷ ARCHITECTURAL VALUE Nolina recurvata, *with its curved trunk and curious top-knot of leaves, looks most striking when displayed as specimens.*

Houseplants for Beginners

NOTHING ENCOURAGES more than success, which breeds both confidence and the desire to know more. This is certainly true of growing houseplants, and there is a wide range of reliable plants that are particularly suitable for first-time growers. They include plants with a variety of leaf and flower forms, and habits from small to architectural. Most are relatively easy to propagate; when you succeed in caring for these plants, then grow some for your friends.

△ *Chlorophytum comosum* 'Vittatum'
SPIDER PLANT
↕ 90cm (3ft) ↔ 60cm (2ft)

One of the most popular houseplants, with boldly striped leaves and pale, arching stems bearing white starry summer flowers that are replaced by little plantlets. Good in a hanging basket. ♛

☼ Bright to moderate, avoiding summer sun ❄ Moderate to warm. Moderate to high humidity ♦ Fortnightly. Stop feeding at low winter temperatures ◊ Keep moist, but avoid water-logging. Water when dry at low winter temperatures ▭ Plantlets

Echeveria secunda var. *glauca* 'Gigantea' ▷
ECHEVERIA
↕ 8cm (3in) ↔ 15cm (6in)

Grow this striking succulent for its large rosettes of blue-grey fleshy leaves with red-bristled tips. Clusters of red and yellow flowers appear in early summer.

☼ Bright ❄ Warm, but cool in winter. Low humidity ♦ Every three weeks, using cactus or high potash fertilizer ◊ When top 2.5cm (1in) dry. Water sparingly in winter, if shrivelling ▭ Leaf cuttings, offsets

Pendent branches with small leaves

Cyperus involucratus 'Gracilis' ▷
UMBRELLA PLANT
↕ 45cm (18in) ↔ 30cm (12in) or more

A curious, clump-forming sedge with narrow, leafy green bracts crowded at the ends of the erect shoots. The umbrella plant provides a good contrast to ferns or broad-leaved plants.

☼ Bright to shady, avoiding direct sun ❄ Warm. Moderate to high humidity ♦ Fortnightly, using foliage houseplant fertilizer. Occasionally in winter ◊ Likes to be waterlogged. It is impossible to overwater this plant ▭ Division

Ficus benjamina ▷
WEEPING FIG
↕ 2.2m (7ft) ↔ 75cm (30in)

This is an excellent houseplant, well worth growing for its tree-like habit, weeping branches, and small, neatly-pointed leaves. It will occupy plenty of space when mature. ♛

☼ Bright, but avoid summer sun ❄ Moderate to warm, avoiding fluctuation. Moderate to high humidity ♦ Fortnightly. Occasionally in winter ◊ When compost surface dry. Reduce watering at lower temperatures ▭ Tip cuttings

OTHER SUCCULENT HOUSEPLANTS FOR BEGINNERS

Faucaria tigrina, see p.355
Kalanchoe pumila, see p.329
Oscularia caulescens
Pachyphytum oviferum, see p.409
Portulaca socialis
Sedum morganianum, see p.409

△ *Impatiens walleriana* hybrids
BUSY LIZZIE
↕ 30cm (12in) ↔ 35cm (14in)

This very well-known flowering plant has fleshy stems and colourful, slender-spurred blooms throughout summer. The hybrids come in a dazzling array of shades.

☼ Bright ❄ Warm. Moderate to high humidity ♦ Fortnightly. Occasionally in winter ♦ When compost surface dry ⊟ Tip cuttings, seed. Roots easily in water

△ *Saxifraga stolonifera* 'Tricolor'
MOTHER OF THOUSANDS
↕ ↔ 30cm (12in)

Display this plant in a hanging basket or pot on a raised surface where its slender red runners, ending in little plantlets, can hang free. The richly variegated leaves are eye-catching. ♔

☼ Bright, with some direct sun ❄ Cool to moderate, but cooler in winter. Moderate humidity ♦ Fortnightly ♦ When dry. Sparingly in cool conditions ⊟ Division, plantlets

△ *Tradescantia zebrina*
INCH PLANT, WANDERING JEW
↕ ↔ 45cm (18in) or more

Fast-growing and fleshy-stemmed, this popular perennial is a splendid trailing plant for a hanging basket. The leaf surfaces are fascinating in detail. ♔

☼ Bright to moderate ❄ Warm. Moderate to high humidity ♦ Fortnightly. Rarely in winter ♦ Water when compost surface dry ⊟ Division, tip cuttings

△ *Sansevieria trifasciata* 'Laurentii'
MOTHER-IN-LAW'S TONGUE
↕ 1.2m (4ft) ↔ 75cm (30in)

Shown here is the most popular form of this well-known plant. The upright, thick, succulent, dark green, gold-edged leaves are borne from an underground stem. ♔

☼ Bright to moderate ❄ Moderate to warm. Low humidity ♦ Fortnightly ♦ When compost surface dry. Water sparingly in winter. Avoid overwatering ⊟ Division

OTHER HOUSEPLANTS FOR BEGINNERS

Asparagus setaceus
Aspidistra elatior, see p.386
Euphorbia milii var. *tulearensis*, see p.386
Haworthia attenuata, see p.387
Hedera helix 'Eva', see p.351
Plectranthus verticillatus
Schlumbergera truncata, see p.363
Tolmiea menziesii 'Taff's Gold', see p.377

△ *Yucca elephantipes*
SPINELESS YUCCA
↕ 2.5m (8ft) ↔ 2m (6ft)

Presented for sale with its sawn-off stems, this plant looks like an oddity. But it soon grows into a bold exotic specimen, with long, sword-shaped, leathery leaves. ♔

☼ Bright, with some direct sun ❄ Moderate to warm, but cooler in winter. Low humidity ♦ Fortnightly ♦ Keep moist. Water sparingly at lower temperatures ⊟ Stem cuttings

SPECIFIC USES

Houseplants Tolerant of Neglect

SOME PLANTS can survive the toughest conditions – high, low, or fluctuating temperatures and light levels, waterlogging, drought, or starvation. This resilience makes them perfect for students, workaholics, or non-gardeners who want living colour and interest at home. These plants all tolerate neglect, but with care, they'll flourish.

Aloe variegata ▷
PARTRIDGE-BREASTED ALOE
↕ 26cm (10in) ↔ 17cm (7in)

This compact succulent has overlapping, triangular, white-marked leaves. Salmon-pink flowers are borne from late winter to early spring, after a winter rest. 🏆

☼ Bright to moderate ▮ Warm. Moderate to cool winter rest. Low humidity 💧 Every three weeks, using fertilizer for cacti and succulents 💧 When top 5cm (2in) dry. Sparingly in winter ⬚ Offsets

△ *Euphorbia milii* var. *tulearensis*
CROWN OF THORNS
↕ ↔ 1m (3ft)

One of the toughest of all houseplants, and one of the spiniest too, so position it with care. Clusters of showy, pink-bracted flowers appear in spring or summer. 🏆

☼ Bright, with sun ▮ Moderate to warm. Low humidity 💧 Every three weeks, using fertilizer for cacti and succulents 💧 When dry. Reduce in winter. Overwatering causes leaf loss ⬚ Stem cuttings

△ *Asparagus densiflorus* 'Sprengeri'
EMERALD FERN
↕ ↔ 80cm (32in)

The fine, ferny "leaves" of this South African plant are actually flattened stems. A graceful habit and cheerful bright green foliage make this an invaluable plant. 🏆

☼ Bright to moderate, avoiding sun ▮ Moderate to warm. Moderate humidity 💧 Weekly, using foliage houseplant fertilizer. Monthly in winter 💧 Keep moist. Reduce in winter ⬚ Division

△ *Aspidistra elatior*
CAST IRON PLANT
↕ ↔ 60cm (2ft)

A "must" for every home, this almost indestructible Victorian favourite tolerates low light, draughts, and fluctuating temperatures, as its name suggests. 🏆

☼ Moderate to shady. Direct sun scorches leaves ▮ Moderate to warm. Moderate to high humidity 💧 Every three weeks 💧 Water when compost surface dry. Dislikes waterlogging ⬚ Division

△ *Ferocactus latispinus*
FISH-HOOK CACTUS
↕ 25cm (10in) ↔ 38cm (15in)

Spiny and ferocious-looking, this cactus from the Mexican desert can survive heat, cold, and long periods of drought. With care, it may bear violet flowers in summer.

☼ Bright ▮ Warm, but moderate to cool winter rest. Low humidity 💧 Every three weeks, using fertilizer for cacti and succulents 💧 When top 5cm (2in) dry. Sparingly in winter if shrivelling ⬚ Offsets

△ *Haworthia attenuata*
ZEBRA HAWORTHIA
↕ ↔ 13cm (5in)

Neat and compact, this succulent has leaves covered with white pustules, and bears long-lasting, creamy-white flowers in summer. Ideal for a narrow windowsill.

☀ Bright ≡ Warm, with moderate to cool winter rest. Low humidity ♦ Every three weeks, using fertilizer for cacti and succulents ◊ When top 5cm (2in) compost dry. Sparingly in winter ⬚ Offsets

OTHER HOUSEPLANTS
TOLERANT OF NEGLECT

Aloe barbadensis
Asparagus setaceus
Chlorophytum comosum
 'Vittatum', see p.384
Cissus antarctica, see p.376
Crassula arborescens, see
 p.360
Crassula ovata, see p.380
Echeveria 'Black Prince'
Euphorbia obesa, see p.367
Kalanchoe daigremontiana
Kalanchoe pumila, see p.329
Kalanchoe tomentosa, see p.343
Orbea variegata, see p.408
Pachypodium lamerei, see
 p.409
Plectranthus verticillatus
Tolmiea menziesii, see p.365

Sansevieria trifasciata ▷
SNAKE PLANT
↕ 1.2m (4ft) ↔ 75cm (30in)

Grow the snake plant for its elegant, variegated, sword-shaped leaves. Underground rhizomes store water for times of drought. This plant will survive anything but waterlogging or constant repotting; only repot if it is too congested.

☀ Bright to moderate ≡ Moderate to warm. Low humidity ♦ Monthly ◊ When compost surface dry. Water sparingly in winter. Avoid overwatering ⬚ Division, leaf cuttings or sections

Sparrmannia africana ▷
HOUSE LIME
↕ ↔ 2m (6ft) or more

A large, vigorous South African shrub with bold, downy foliage and, in late summer, clusters of white, yellow-stamened flowers. Prune after flowering to encourage more blooms. ▽

☀ Bright, but avoid direct sun ≡ Moderate to warm. Moderate humidity ♦ Fortnightly, using high potash fertilizer ◊ When compost surface dry. Reduce in winter. Avoid waterlogging ⬚ Tip cuttings

Yucca elephantipes
'Variegata' ▷
VARIEGATED
SPINELESS YUCCA
↕ 2.5m (8ft) ↔ 2m (6ft)

This popular and dramatic plant is also robust and ideal as a corner specimen. With age, the narrow, sword-shaped, cream-margined leaves will drop, revealing the yucca's characteristic bare stem.

☀ Bright, with some sun ≡ Moderate to warm, but cool in winter. Low humidity ♦ Fortnightly ◊ Keep moist. Water sparingly at low temperatures ⬚ Stem sections

SPECIFIC USES

Beneficial Houseplants

Recent NASA research into the beneficial effects of plants has shown that they can significantly improve the indoor environment. Houseplants absorb carbon dioxide and breathe out oxygen, adding moisture to the air. They also alleviate "sick building syndrome" by removing airborne pollutants released by building materials, cleaners, and new furnishings. They really do promote a healthy, stress-free environment.

Specific Uses

△ *Chlorophytum comosum*
'Mandaianum'
SPIDER PLANT

↕ ↔ 60cm (2ft) or more

One of the most popular and easily grown houseplants, and an active remover of indoor pollution. Display it where its trailing habit can be seen.

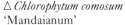 Bright to moderate, avoiding summer sun ☀️ Moderate to warm. Moderate to high humidity ◊ Fortnightly. Stop if cool ◊ Keep moist. When dry if cool ▦ Plantlets

△ *Dieffenbachia seguine* 'Exotica'
DUMB CANE

↕ ↔ 90cm (3ft)

This air-pollutant-removing plant has spectacular, creamy-white variegated leaves. Their large size increases their absorbent capacity. Poisonous if chewed. ▽

☀ Bright to moderate. Avoid hot sun ☀️ Moderate to warm. Moderate to high humidity ◊ Fortnightly, using foliage houseplant fertilizer. Monthly in winter ◊ Water when dry ▦ Tip cuttings, stem sections

△ *Dracaena fragrans* 'Janet Craig'
DRACAENA

↕ 3m (10ft) ↔ 1.2m (4ft)

A striking plant with erect stems and lush, glossy, dark green, strap-shaped leaves. The most effective dracaena for absorbing chemical toxins from the air.

☀ Bright to moderate, avoiding hot sun ☀️ Warm. Moderate to high humidity ◊ Fortnightly. Occasionally in winter ◊ Water when dry. Reduce at lower temperatures ▦ Tip cuttings, stem sections

△ *Ficus benjamina* 'Reginald'
WEEPING FIG

↕ 3m (10ft) or more ↔ 1m (3ft) or more

Very effective at removing airborne chemicals, especially formaldehyde, the most common indoor pollutant. Its glossy green leaves are lime-green when young.

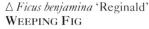 Bright, but avoid summer sun ☀️ Warm, avoiding fluctuation. Moderate to high humidity ◊ Fortnightly. Occasionally in winter ◊ When dry. Reduce watering in cool conditions ▦ Tip cuttings

---

OTHER BENEFICIAL HOUSE-PLANTS FOR FOLIAGE EFFECT

Chamaedorea elegans, see p.412
Chlorophytum comosum 'Vittatum', see p.384
Chrysalidocarpus lutescens, see p.412
Dracaena marginata, see p.395
Epipremnum aureum, see p.390
Nephrolepis exaltata 'Bostoniensis', see p.407
Philodendron scandens subsp. *oxycardium*
Rhapis excelsa, see p.413
Syngonium podophyllum

Homalomena wallisii ▷
QUEEN OF HEARTS
↕ ↔ 90cm (3ft)

The glossy, long-stalked, abruptly pointed foliage is particularly effective at removing ammonia, as well as other pollutants, from the air. A challenging plant to grow well.

☼ Moderate ⧈ Warm, but moderate in dormancy. Dislikes draughts. High humidity ◐ Fortnightly ◊ When compost surface just dry. Water sparingly in winter ▥ Division

---

OTHER BENEFICIAL HOUSE-PLANTS FOR FLORAL EFFECT

Begonia species and hybrids
Chrysanthemum hybrids
Clivia miniata, see p.326
Gerbera jamesonii cultivars
Schlumbergera truncata, see p.363
Tulipa hybrids, see p.401

△ *Ficus elastica* 'Robusta'
RUBBER PLANT
↕ 3m (10ft) or more ↔ 1.8m (6ft)

'Robusta', with its bold, glossy, leathery leaves, is one of the most handsome of the popular evergreen rubber plants. It is very effective at absorbing formaldehyde.

☼ Bright, but avoid summer sun ⧈ Warm. Moderate to high humidity ◐ Fortnightly. Occasionally in winter ◊ When dry. Reduce at lower temperatures ▥ Tip cuttings, air layering

△ *Hedera helix* 'Green Ripple'
COMMON IVY, ENGLISH IVY
↕ 1m (3ft) or more ↔ 30cm (12in) or more

All ivies are efficient at removing air pollutants, but English ivy is particularly good at absorbing the formaldehyde that is found in tobacco smoke and adhesives.

☼ Bright to moderate. Poor growth in low light ⧈ Cool to moderate. Moderate to high humidity ◐ Fortnightly. Occasionally in winter ◊ When dry. Water sparingly in winter ▥ Tip cuttings, layering

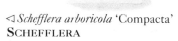

◁ *Schefflera arboricola* 'Compacta'
SCHEFFLERA
↕ 1.8m (6ft) ↔ 90cm (3ft)

Compact in habit and erect-stemmed, this easy-to-grow evergreen produces masses of shining, deep green, fingered leaves. These will absorb chemical pollutants from the air.

☼ Bright to moderate ⧈ Moderate to warm, avoiding fluctuation. Moderate to high humidity ◐ Fortnightly. Monthly in winter ◊ Water when dry ▥ Division, tip cuttings, air layering

△ *Spathiphyllum wallisii*
PEACE LILY
↕ ↔ 60cm (2ft)

An excellent capacity for absorbing acetone, benzene, and formaldehyde, and tolerance of low light, make this plant a winner. White spring and summer flowers.

☼ Bright, but avoid direct sun ⧈ Moderate to warm. Moderate to high humidity ◐ Fortnightly. Monthly in winter ◊ Water when compost dry. Avoid overwatering ▥ Division

SPECIFIC USES

Trailing Houseplants

TRAILING PLANTS with lax stems are excellent subjects for hanging baskets, plinths, or high shelves. Some trail naturally, while others are young specimens of plants that are really climbers. Site trailers carefully so they have plenty of room to grow without being damaged and are easily accessible for watering.

△ *Epipremnum aureum*
DEVIL'S IVY
↕ 2m (6ft) ↔ 1m (3ft)

The young foliage of this handsome rainforest plant is bright green splashed with gold. Treat older plants as climbers. Easily controlled and propagated. ♔

☼ Bright, but avoid direct sun. Variegation fades in shade ◗▮ Moderate to warm. Moderate to high humidity ♦ Fortnightly. Twice in winter ♦ Water when compost surface dry ▦ Tip or stem cuttings

Aporocactus
flagelliformis
f. *flagriformis* △
RAT'S TAIL CACTUS
↕ ↔ 60cm (2ft)

In its native Mexico, this species hangs from trees, rock ledges, and crevices. It is excellent for a hanging basket, but should be sited away from walkways.

☼ Bright, but avoid direct sun ◗▮ Cool to warm. Moderate humidity ♦ Cactus and succulent feed every three weeks, spring to autumn ♦ When dry. Rarely in winter ▦ Division, stem cuttings, seed

OTHER TRAILING HOUSEPLANTS

Campanula isophylla, see p.332
Fuchsia 'Golden Marinka'
Glechoma hederacea 'Variegata'
Lotus maculatus
Oplismenus africanus 'Variegatus'
Rhipsalidopsis gaertneri
Sedum morganianum, see p.409

Ceropegia linearis
subsp. *woodii* △
ROSARY VINE
↕ 90cm (3ft) ↔ 10cm (4in)

This apparently delicate plant is surprisingly tough and can tolerate periods of drought. Pairs of marbled, heart-shaped, succulent leaves hang from the thread-like stems, often accompanied by fascinating slender, mauve-pink vase-shaped flowers. ♔

☼ Bright to moderate ◗▮ Cool to warm. Low humidity ♦ Fortnightly in summer, using high potash or cactus fertilizer ♦ When compost surface dry. Water sparingly in winter ▦ Tubers

△ *Epipremnum* 'Neon'
DEVIL'S IVY
↕ 2m (6ft) ↔ 1m (3ft)

Unusual lime-green leaves distinguish this devil's ivy, shown here when young. Initially a trailing plant, it produces climbing shoots after a year or two.

☼ Bright, but avoid direct sun. Colour fades in shade ◗▮ Moderate to warm. Moderate to high humidity ♦ Fortnightly. Twice in winter ♦ Water when compost surface dry ▦ Tip or stem cuttings

Saxifraga stolonifera ▷
STRAWBERRY GERANIUM
↕ ↔ 30cm (12in)

Numerous plantlets on red runners trail
from a mound of striking leaves marked
with radiating grey-green veins. It is ideal
for a cool room or an unheated porch. 🏆

☼ Bright to moderate 🌡 Cool to warm. Moderate
humidity 💧 Fortnightly. Stop feeding in winter
💧 Water when compost surface starts to dry out
✂ Division, plantlets

△ *Hedera helix* 'Midas Touch'
COMMON IVY, ENGLISH IVY
↕ 1m (3ft) or more ↔ 45cm (18in)

This vigorous ivy is worth growing for its
brightly coloured, green- and yellow-
variegated leaves. One of the most
popular ivies grown as a houseplant 🏆

☼ Bright to moderate 🌡 Cool to moderate.
Moderate to high humidity 💧 Fortnightly. Twice in
winter 💧 Allow to dry before watering. Water
sparingly in winter ✂ Tip cuttings, layering

△ *Hoya lanceolata* subsp. *bella*
MINIATURE WAX PLANT
↕ ↔ 45cm (18in)

When the deliciously fragrant, waxy
flowers appear in summer, leave their
stalks, as buds will form on them for the
next display. Also grown as a climber. 🏆

☼ Bright. Avoid direct sun 🌡 Moderate to warm.
Moderate to high humidity 💧 Every three weeks,
using flowering houseplant fertilizer. Stop in winter
💧 When dry. Rarely in winter ✂ Tip cuttings

△ *Senecio rowleyanus*
STRING OF BEADS
↕ 1m (3ft) ↔ 8cm (3in)

A strange, succulent member of the daisy
family that produces a curtain of trailing
stems with pea-like leaves. Sweetly-
scented white flowers appear in autumn.

☼ Bright to moderate. Avoid summer sun 🌡 Cool
to warm. Low humidity 💧 Every three weeks, using
high potash or cactus fertilizer. Stop in winter
💧 Water when dry. Rarely in winter ✂ Tip cuttings

△ *Tradescantia*
fluminensis 'Albovittata'
INCH PLANT, WANDERING JEW
↕ 1m (3ft) ↔ 15cm (6in)

Pure white flowers, borne in summer, add
interest to this fast-growing plant. Its lax
stems are clothed in fleshy, soft green
leaves, boldly marked with white stripes.

☼ Bright, but avoid summer sun. Variegation fades
in shade 🌡 Moderate to warm. Moderate to high
humidity 💧 Fortnightly. Once in winter 💧 Keep
moist. When dry if cool ✂ Tip or stem cuttings

SPECIFIC USES

391

Climbing Houseplants

MANY CLIMBERS are native to tropical rainforests, where they clamber up tree trunks and branches to reach the light. Large-leaved climbers need plenty of room in which to develop, but more slender varieties are ideal for tight corners or recesses. Climbers should be trained on a moss-clad frame or pole and pruned to size.

Bougainvillea 'Mrs. Butt' ▷
BOUGAINVILLEA, PAPER FLOWER
↕ ↔ 2m (6ft) or more

Deservedly popular in tropical gardens, this plant offers stunning, crimson-shaded magenta, papery bracts. Prune back the previous year's stems hard in midwinter.

☼ Bright, sunny ▮ Cool to warm. Moderate humidity ◕ Fortnightly, using flowering houseplant fertilizer. Stop feeding in winter ◊ Water when dry. Reduce in cool conditions ▥ Tip cuttings

Monstera obliqua ▷
MONSTERA
↕ 3m (10ft) or more ↔ 1.2m (4ft)

Highly perforated leaves give this bold climber an unusual shredded look. It is worth growing for novelty value alone; train up a moss pole or similar support.

☼ Bright to moderate ▮ Moderate to warm. Moderate to high humidity ◕ Fortnightly. Once in late autumn and once in midwinter ◊ Water when just dry ▥ Stem cuttings, air layering

△ *Cissus rhombifolia*
GRAPE IVY
↕ 3m (10ft) ↔ 60cm (2ft)

Boldly-toothed, glossy green leaflets cover this vigorous, tendrilled plant. Trained up canes or trellis, it will create an attractive living screen or room divider. ♟

☼ Bright, but avoid hot sun ▮ Moderate to warm. Moderate to high humidity ◕ Fortnightly, using foliage houseplant fertilizer. Monthly in winter ◊ Allow to dry before watering ▥ Tip cuttings

△ *Epipremnum aureum* 'Marble Queen'
DEVIL'S IVY
↕ 3m (10ft) ↔ 1m (3ft)

An outstanding climber with white-marbled foliage and white leaf stalks. The mass of eye-catching leaves is particularly distinctive when covering a moss pole.

☼ Bright, but avoid direct sun. Variegation fades in shade ▮ Moderate to warm. Moderate to high humidity ◕ Fortnightly. Twice in winter ◊ Water when dry ▥ Tip or stem cuttings

△ *Passiflora* 'Amethyst'
PASSION FLOWER
↕ ↔ 3m (10ft) or more

Vigorous even in cool climates, this plant has exotic flowers. If trained to a frame, prune long shoots to 1.5cm (½in) in spring and re-attach afterwards. Leave old wood.

☼ Bright, with some sun ▮ Moderate to warm. Moderate to high humidity ◕ Flowering houseplant fertilizer fortnightly. Stop in winter ◊ Water when dry. Keep just moist in winter ▥ Stem cuttings

Philodendron 'Medisa' ▷
PHILODENDRON
↕ 3m (10ft) ↔ 1m (3ft)

Red shoots and leaf stalks and
large leaves, golden yellow when
young, make this a very eye-catching
plant. A forest tree-climber in the wild, in
the home it thrives best on a moss pole.

☼ Bright to moderate, avoiding direct sun
🌡 Moderate to warm. Moderate to high humidity
💧 Fortnightly. Monthly in winter 💧 Water when
compost surface just dry 🌱 Tip cuttings

OTHER CLIMBING HOUSEPLANTS

Cissus rhombifolia 'Ellen Danica',
    see p.376
Gelsemium sempervirens
Gloriosa superba 'Rothschildiana'
Hoya carnosa 'Tricolor'
Jasminum polyanthum, see p.323
Piper crocatum
Senecio mikanioides
Stephanotis floribunda 'Alpine'
Syngonium 'Jenny'
Tetrastigma voinierianum

Senecio macroglossus 'Variegatus' ▷
CAPE IVY, WAX VINE
↕ 3m (10ft) ↔ 1m (3ft)

Looking like an ivy with yellow summer
and winter flowers, this daisy relative
climbs by twining stems, which can be
trained up canes or thin stakes.

☼ Bright, with some sun 🌡 Cool to warm.
Moderate humidity 💧 Fortnightly, from spring to
autumn 💧 When compost surface dry. Water
sparingly at low temperatures 🌱 Tip cuttings

△ Syngonium podophyllum 'Imperial White'
GOOSEFOOT PLANT
↕ 2m (6ft) or more ↔ 60cm (2ft)

Grow where the beautifully marked
leaves, which change shape as the plant
matures, can be appreciated. Climbing
stems may be pruned to retain bushiness.

☼ Bright to moderate, avoiding direct sun
🌡 Warm. Moderate to high humidity 💧 Fortnightly,
using foliage houseplant fertilizer. Monthly in winter
💧 When dry. Reduce in winter 🌱 Tip cuttings

△ Thunbergia alata
BLACK-EYED SUSAN
↕ 2m (6ft) ↔ 30cm (12in)

This twining plant produces a display of
rich orange flowers with dark centres from
late spring to autumn, if deadheaded
regularly. Usually grown as an annual.

☼ Bright, with some sun 🌡 Moderate to warm.
Moderate humidity 💧 Fortnightly once established,
using flowering houseplant fertilizer 💧 Allow to dry
out before watering 🌱 Seed

SPECIFIC USES

393

Houseplants for Architectural Effect

NO PLANTS CONTRIBUTE more drama to the visual scheme of a room than those with large or deeply divided leaves or a striking habit. Careful siting is important if a plant's architectural qualities are to become a focal point. As a general rule, the bigger the plant and the space around it, the more effective its scale and form will appear.

Araucaria heterophylla ▷
NORFOLK ISLAND PINE
↕ 2.5m (8ft) or more ↔ 1.2m (4ft) or more

Like so many houseplants, this reaches a large size in its natural environment. Best grown indoors on a single stem, it is then less vigorous but still impressive. 🏆

☼ Bright, but avoid summer sun 🌡 Moderate. Moderate humidity 💧 Fortnightly. Occasionally in winter 💧 When compost surface dry. Water sparingly in winter ▦ Seed

△ *Nolina recurvata*
ELEPHANT'S FOOT, PONY TAIL
↕ 1.8m (6ft) or more ↔ 1m (3ft) or more

An extraordinary-looking plant from Mexico that develops a bulbous base and a great topknot of slender, arching or pendulous leaves. Easy to grow. 🏆

☼ Bright, with sun 🌡 Moderate to warm. Low humidity 💧 Monthly, using fertilizer for cacti and succulents 💧 When compost surface dry. Water sparingly in winter ▦ Tip cuttings, offsets, seed

△ *Cycas revoluta*
SAGO PALM
↕ ↔ 1.5m (5ft)

This primitive evergreen, not a true palm, develops its short trunk very slowly, but the stiff, leathery, deeply divided leaves are spectacular even on a young plant. 🏆

☼ Bright, but avoid direct summer sun 🌡 Warm. Moderate to high humidity 💧 Monthly 💧 Water when compost surface dry ▦ Seed, buds from old or dormant plants

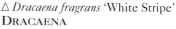

△ *Dracaena fragrans* 'White Stripe'
DRACAENA
↕ 2m (6ft) or more ↔ 1m (3ft)

A striking foliage plant producing stiffly erect stems and generous clusters of long, pointed green leaves, with white-striped margins. This is a bold specimen plant.

☼ Bright to moderate, avoiding summer sun 🌡 Warm. Moderate to high humidity 💧 Fortnightly. Occasionally in winter 💧 When dry. Water sparingly in winter ▦ Tip cuttings, stem sections

OTHER NARROW-LEAVED ARCHITECTURAL HOUSEPLANTS

Cordyline australis
Dracaena draco
Pandanus veitchii, see p.341
Phormium tenax
Sansevieria trifasciata, see p.387
Yucca elephantipes, see p.385

OTHER BROAD-LEAVED ARCHITECTURAL HOUSEPLANTS

Chamaedorea elegans, see p.412
Howea belmoreana, see p.413
Monstera deliciosa, see p.339
Pisonia umbellifera 'Variegata'
Polyscias fruticosa
Radermachera sinica
Rhapis excelsa, see p.413

Dracaena marginata ▷
MADAGASCAR DRAGON TREE
↕ 3m (10ft) ↔ 1.2m (4ft)

Bold tufts of shining, grassy, red-edged green leaves bring a touch of the exotic to any room. This native of Madagascar is one of the most popular dracaenas for indoor cultivation.

Bright to moderate, avoiding summer sun · Warm. Moderate to high humidity · Fortnightly. Occasionally in winter · When dry. Sparingly in winter · Tip cuttings, stem sections

Schefflera arboricola 'Gold Capella' ▷
SCHEFFLERA
↕ 1.8m (6ft) ↔ 1m (3ft)

The umbrella tree is grown as a house-plant for its long-stalked juvenile foliage, which is divided into rich green, gold-splashed leaflets. A dark background or group setting is effective.

Bright to moderate · Warm, avoiding fluctuation. Moderate to high humidity · Fortnightly. Monthly in winter · Water when compost surface dry · Tip cuttings, air layering

△ *Ficus lyrata*
BANJO FIG, FIDDLE-LEAF FIG
↕ 3m (10ft) or more ↔ 1.8m (6ft) or more

Give this plant plenty of elbow room to accommodate its likely spread and show off its spectacular large, waisted leaves. This fig originates in African forests.

Bright. Avoid summer sun · Warm. Moderate to high humidity · Fortnightly. Occasionally in winter · When compost surface dry. Reduce at lower temperatures · Tip cuttings, air layering

Large, feather-shaped fronds

△ *Lytocaryum weddellianum*
DWARF COCONUT PALM
↕ 2m (6ft) ↔ 1.5m (5ft)

One of the most beautiful palms for the home and tolerant of low light. Handle the fragile roots with care when repotting. Formerly sold as *Microcoelum* or *Cocos*.

Moderate to shady · Warm. Moderate to high humidity · Every three weeks · When compost surface dry. Water sparingly in winter. Avoid waterlogging · Seed

△ *Schefflera elegantissima* 'Castor'
FALSE ARALIA, FINGER ARALIA
↕ 2m (6ft) ↔ 90cm (3ft)

This plant produces an elegant, lacy outline. The dark coppery-green leaves have long, narrow leaflets that widen with age. Also known as *Aralia* or *Dizygotheca*.

Bright, avoiding direct sun · Warm, avoiding fluctuation. Moderate humidity · Fortnightly. Monthly at low winter temperatures · Water when dry. Avoid overwatering · Tip cuttings, seed

Houseplants with Ornamental Fruit

HOUSEPLANTS WORTH growing for their fruits alone are in the minority, yet they include some very reliable and colourful varieties. Some of these are seasonal plants, and useful for adding winter interest. They include capsicums, winter cherries, and hardy plants such as *Aucuba* and *Skimmia*. The fruits shown here are mostly inedible, but they are not poisonous unless stated.

Ardisia crenata ▷
CORAL BERRY
‡ 1m (3ft) ↔ 30cm (12in) or more

Chiefly grown for its colourful red berries, freely borne especially in winter, this evergreen has glossy, toothed leaves. Prune in early spring after berries finish.

☼ Bright, but avoid direct sun ▮ Moderate. Moderate to high humidity ◊ Monthly. Occasionally in winter ◊ When compost surface dry. Reduce watering in winter ▦ Semi-ripe cuttings, seed

Capsicum annuum 'Festival Orange' △
ORNAMENTAL PEPPER
‡ ↔ 60cm (2ft)

In winter, this colourful houseplant produces conical, bright orange, long-lasting fruits, strikingly set among the dark green foliage. It will enjoy a position on a sunny windowsill.

☼ Bright, but avoid direct sun ▮ Cool to moderate. Moderate humidity ◊ Fortnightly, alternating general fertilizer with flowering houseplant fertilizer ◊ Water when compost surface just dry ▦ Tip cuttings

---

OTHER HOUSEPLANTS WITH ORNAMENTAL FRUIT

Aechmea fulgens var. *discolor*
Ananas bracteatus 'Tricolor', see p.358
Ardisia crispa
Capsicum annuum 'Masquerade'
  Fuchsia procumbens
  Nertera balfouriana
   Punica granatum var. *nana*

Capsicum annuum ▷
CHRISTMAS PEPPER
‡ 30cm (12in)
↔ 30cm (12in) or more

Commonly available in winter, this well-known houseplant is popular for its usually conical, sometimes rounded, red or yellow, long-lasting fruits. It is usually treated as an annual pot plant.

☼ Bright ▮ Cool to moderate. Moderate humidity ◊ Every week, alternating general fertilizer with flowering houseplant fertilizer ◊ Water when compost surface just dry ▦ Seed

x *Citrofortunella microcarpa* ▷
CALAMONDIN
‡ ↔ 1.2m (4ft)

Miniature oranges, 3–4cm (1¼–1½in) across, make this shrub an attractive houseplant; the fruits are produced at almost any time, even by young plants, but are bitter to the taste.

☼ Bright, but avoid summer sun ▮ Moderate to warm. Moderate to high humidity ◊ Fortnightly, using fertilizer for ericaceous plants. Monthly in winter ◊ Water when compost surface dry ▦ Semi-ripe cuttings

Rhipsalis floccosa ▷
MISTLETOE CACTUS

↕ 45cm (18in) ↔ 24cm (10in)

In spring, mistletoe-like white, sometimes pink-tinted berries are produced on the long, slender stems of this curious weeping cactus. Good for a hanging pot.

☼ Bright 🌡 Moderate to warm, with cool winter rest. Moderate to high humidity 💧 Monthly, using flowering houseplant fertilizer. Occasionally in winter 💧 When dry. Sparingly in winter ✂ Stem sections

△ *Fortunella japonica*
ROUND KUMQUAT

↕ 3m (10ft) or more ↔ 1.5m (5ft) or more

Edible, golden-orange fruits, lasting throughout autumn, are produced by this thorny shrub; fragrant white flowers appear in spring. Closely related to *Citrus*.

☼ Bright, but avoid summer sun 🌡 Moderate to warm. Moderate to high humidity 💧 Fortnightly, using fertilizer for ericaceous plants. Monthly in winter 💧 Keep moist ✂ Semi-ripe cuttings

Long-lasting fruits

Skimmia japonica 'Robert Fortune' ▷
SKIMMIA

↕ 60cm (2ft) ↔ 1m (3ft)

Slow-growing, and usually low-growing when cultivated as a houseplant, this evergreen shrub is a popular choice for its dense clusters of long-lasting, dark red fruits, borne from summer through to winter. 🏆

☼ Moderate to shady 🌡 Cool to moderate. Moderate humidity 💧 Fortnightly 💧 When compost surface just dry. Reduce watering in winter ✂ Semi-ripe cuttings

△ *Nertera granadensis*
BEAD PLANT, CORAL MOSS

↕ 2cm (¾in) ↔ 20cm (8in)

The moss-like, emerald-green cushion or mat of slender, prostrate, interlacing stems is studded with orange berries in autumn. An irresistible plant for a windowsill.

☼ Bright. Avoid summer sun 🌡 Cool to moderate. Moderate to high humidity 💧 Monthly. Occasionally in winter 💧 When compost surface dry. Water sparingly in winter ✂ Division, tip cuttings, seed

OTHER HARDY HOUSEPLANTS WITH ORNAMENTAL FRUIT

Arbutus unedo 'Elfin King'
Aucuba japonica 'Rozannie'
Duchesnea indica, see p.364
Gaultheria procumbens
Pyracantha coccinea 'Red Column'
Vaccinium vitis-idaea Koralle Group

◁ *Solanum pseudocapsicum*
JERUSALEM CHERRY

↕ ↔ 60cm (2ft)

The large, spherical, winter fruits of this plant are orange-red, bright red when ripe, and decorative but poisonous. Generally grown as an annual in the winter season.

☼ Bright, but avoid direct sun 🌡 Cool to moderate. Moderate humidity 💧 Fortnightly, alternating general fertilizer with flowering houseplant fertilizer 💧 Water when just dry ✂ Tip cuttings

SPECIFIC USES

397

Houseplants for Terraria

THESE CLOSED GLASS containers can be home to miniature gardens or jungles. They are draught-free and provide constant humidity and warmth, which allows a good range of interesting and ornamental plants, even "difficult" varieties, to flourish. Reasonably easy to look after, they make a distinctive focal point.

△ *Hypoestes phyllostachya*
POLKA DOT PLANT
↕ 30cm (12in) ↔ 23cm (9in)

Pinch out the slender spikes of small flowers to preserve the effect of the pale-pink-spotted leaves. For a compact habit, also pinch out the growing tips.

☼ Bright, but avoid summer sun ❄ Warm. Moderate to high humidity ♦ Fortnightly. Occasionally in winter ◊ Water when compost surface just dry 🗹 Tip cuttings. Roots easily in water

Adiantum raddianum ▷
DELTA MAIDENHAIR FERN
↕ 60cm (2ft) ↔ 80cm (32in)

A mound of loosely arching, delicately divided fronds, borne on slender, wiry, shining black stalks, is produced by this elegant fern from tropical South America.

☼ Moderate, avoiding direct sun ❄ Moderate to warm. Moderate to high humidity ♦ Fortnightly. Monthly in winter ◊ Keep moist, but avoid waterlogging 🗹 Division, spores

△ *Hypoestes phyllostachya* 'Vinrod'
POLKA DOT PLANT
↕ 30cm (12in) ↔ 23cm (9in)

The rich wine-red leaves, marked with contrasting pink splashes, are a showy alternative to the typical polka dot plant. Keep it compact by pinching out the growing tips and flower spikes.

☼ Bright, but avoid summer sun ❄ Warm. Moderate to high humidity ♦ Fortnightly. Occasionally in winter ◊ Water when compost surface just dry 🗹 Tip cuttings. Roots easily in water

△ *Episcia cupreata*
FLAME VIOLET
↕ 15cm (6in) ↔ 30cm (12in)

A creeping, mat-forming perennial from the Amazon, with attractive leaves, purple beneath and pale-veined above. The red flowers appear throughout summer.

☼ Bright to moderate, avoiding direct sun ❄ Warm. High humidity ♦ Fortnightly. Occasionally in winter ◊ When compost surface just dry. Avoid waterlogging 🗹 Division, tip cuttings

△ *Fittonia verschaffeltii* var. *argyroneura* 'Mini White'
SILVER NET LEAF
↕ 10cm (4in) ↔ 30cm (12in)

This choice creeping and carpeting perennial from the rainforests of Peru has exquisitely silver-veined green leaves. A "must" for any terrarium or bottle garden.

☼ Moderate to shady, avoiding direct sun ❄ Warm. High humidity ♦ Fortnightly. Occasionally in winter ◊ Keep moist, but avoid waterlogging 🗹 Tip cuttings

OTHER FLOWERING HOUSEPLANTS FOR TERRARIA

Episcia 'Cleopatra'
Episcia lilacina
Episcia 'Pink Panther'
Peperomia fraseri
Saintpaulia 'Blue Imp'
Saintpaulia 'Pip Squeek', see p.337
Streptocarpus saxorum, see p.337

△ *Maranta leuconeura* var. *erythroneura*
RED HERRINGBONE PLANT
‡ 25cm (10in) ↔ 30cm (12in) or more

One of the most beautiful and striking foliage plants, from the rainforests of Brazil. Red herringbone plants form mats of large, pale green leaves, with darker zones and red veins.

☼ Moderate, avoiding direct sun ≣ Warm. Moderate to high humidity ◊ Fortnightly. Occasionally in winter ◊ Keep moist, but avoid waterlogging. In winter, water when compost surface just dry ⊞ Division, tip cuttings

△ *Pilea cadierei* 'Minima'
ALUMINIUM PLANT
‡ ↔ 15cm (6in)

A compact form of *P. cadierei* (see p.353), with similar silver and green puckered leaves. It makes a striking specimen in a small terrarium or bell jar; in larger terraria it mixes well with green-leaved companions.

☼ Bright to moderate, with some sun ≣ Warm. Moderate to high humidity ◊ Every three weeks. Occasionally in winter ◊ Water when compost surface just dry. Avoid waterlogging ⊞ Tip cuttings

△ *Pilea involucrata* 'Moon Valley'
FRIENDSHIP PLANT, PILEA
‡ ↔ 30cm (12in)

This trailing or creeping plant must be seen to be believed. The pale green leaves are remarkably puckered and have a network of sunken red veins. Well worth growing in a small terrarium or bell jar.

☼ Bright to moderate, with some sun ≣ Warm. Moderate to high humidity ◊ Every three weeks. Occasionally in winter ◊ Water when compost surface just dry. Avoid waterlogging ⊞ Tip cuttings

△ *Peperomia obtusifolia* 'Greengold'
DESERT PRIVET
‡ ↔ 25cm (10in)

Erect stems and big, fleshy, creamy-yellow leaves variegated with irregular dark and pale green centres make this bushy plant spectacular when well grown.

☼ Bright to moderate, with some sun ≣ Warm. Moderate to high humidity ◊ Every three weeks. Occasionally in winter ◊ When compost surface just dry. Avoid waterlogging ⊞ Tip cuttings

OTHER FOLIAGE HOUSEPLANTS FOR TERRARIA

Bertolonia marmorata
Ficus pumila 'White Sonny', see p.363
Peperomia caperata 'Little Fantasy'
Peperomia marmorata
Pilea involucrata 'Norfolk'
Pilea repens
Selaginella martensii, see p.365
Selaginella uncinata
Sonerila margaritacea 'Hendersonii'

△ *Selaginella kraussiana* 'Aurea'
SPREADING CLUBMOSS
‡ 2.5cm (1in) ↔ indefinite

This easy-to-grow fern relative produces rapidly forking, slender stems, densely crowded with tiny, yellow-green, scale-like leaves. May need reducing in size.

☼ Shady ≣ Warm. High humidity ◊ Every five weeks, using half-strength general houseplant fertilizer ◊ Water when compost surface just dry. Avoid waterlogging ⊞ Stem cuttings

SPECIFIC USES

Dual-purpose Houseplants

A N INCREASING NUMBER of winter-hardy plants are grown indoors; they include foliage plants for rooms with low heat, but more commonly are flowering and bulbous plants for temporary display. So often these "one-off" plants are thrown away after their flowering season is over, when in fact they can be planted in the garden, and left to flower and be enjoyed in future years.

Aster 'Speedy Ruby Red' ▷
MICHAELMAS DAISY
↕ 30cm (12in) ↔ 45cm (18in)

One of several excellent dwarf Michaelmas daisies, with a compact habit and reddish flowers. This plant will give a reliable early autumn display in a cool room, and is easy to divide in spring.

☼ Bright, but avoid direct sun ▮ Moderate. Moderate humidity ◖ Every three weeks ◊ Keep moist, but avoid waterlogging ▱ Division, tip cuttings

△ *Iris reticulata*
MINIATURE IRIS
↕ 15cm (6in) ↔ 8cm (3in)

Planted in early autumn, this bulb bears fragrant flowers in late winter. Charming for a well-lit windowsill; plant out in a bed or rock garden in the autumn. ♈

☼ Bright to moderate, with some sun ▮ Cool to moderate. Moderate humidity ◖ Fortnightly ◊ Water sparingly, increase as growth appears, keep moist, and reduce as leaves die ▱ Division

◁ *Astilbe* 'Deutschland'
ASTILBE
↕ 50cm (20in) ↔ 30cm (12in)

Like many astilbes, this one is commonly forced to flower in early spring. It offers a lovely combination of ferny foliage and splendid, erect, plumed white flowers.

☼ Bright, with some sun ▮ Cool to moderate, with a cool winter rest. Moderate humidity ◖ Fortnightly feed ◊ Keep moist ▱ Division

Dark green ferny foliage

OTHER DUAL-PURPOSE HOUSEPLANTS

Convallaria majalis 'Fortin's Giant'
Erica carnea 'Winter Beauty'
Helleborus niger Blackthorn Group
Passiflora caerulea
Primula Polyanthus Group
Tolmiea menziesii 'Taff's Gold', see p.377

△ *Muscari armeniacum*
GRAPE HYACINTH
↕ 20cm (8in) ↔ 5cm (2in)

In autumn, plant in a pot or pan to enjoy the sight of this cheerful-looking, blue-flowered bulb in spring. Planted outside in sun, it will naturalize in time. ♈

☼ Bright to moderate, with some sun ▮ Cool to moderate. Moderate humidity ◖ Fortnightly ◊ Water sparingly; increase as growth appears; keep moist; reduce as leaves die ▱ Division, offsets

Narcissus hybrids ▷
DAFFODIL
↕ 45cm (18in) ↔ 10cm (4in)

Most, if not all, daffodils make splendid flowering pot plants. Planted in autumn and forced, they can be flowering indoors as early as late winter. Plant them outside the following autumn.

☼ Bright to moderate, with some sun ▮ Cool to moderate. Moderate humidity ◖ Fortnightly ◌ Water sparingly; increase as growth appears; keep moist; reduce as leaves die ▱ Division, offsets

△ *Puschkinia scilloides*
PUSCHKINIA
↕ 15cm (6in) ↔ 5cm (2in)

An excellent subject for a windowsill in a cool room, it should be planted in a pot in autumn for spring flowering. Afterwards, dry off, store, and plant out in autumn.

☼ Bright to moderate, with some sun ▮ Cool to moderate. Moderate humidity ◖ Fortnightly ◌ Water sparingly increase as growth appears, keep moist in full growth, and reduce as leaves die ▱ Division, offsets

△ *Oxalis tetraphylla* 'Iron Cross'
GOOD LUCK PLANT, LUCKY CLOVER
↕ 25cm (10in) ↔ 15cm (6in)

Easily recognizable by its dark purple leaf markings; the flowers appear in summer. It is not fully hardy in cold climates, so plant out in a sunny, well-drained spot.

☼ Bright, with some sun ▮ Moderate to warm, but cool in winter. Moderate humidity ◖ Fortnightly ◌ When compost surface dry. Water sparingly in winter ▱ Division, offsets

Bold flowers available in many colours

◁ *Tulipa* hybrids
TULIP
↕ 60cm (2ft) ↔ 50cm (20in)

An enormous array of tulips is available for indoor use; they enjoy cool rather than heated rooms. After they flower in winter and spring, dry off, store, and plant them outside in the autumn.

☼ Bright to moderate, with some sun ▮ Cool to moderate. Moderate humidity ◖ Fortnightly ◌ Water sparingly, increase as growth appears, keep moist in growth, and reduce as leaves die ▱ Division, offsets

◁ *Primula vulgaris*
PRIMROSE
↕ 15cm (6in)
↔ 20cm (8in)

A neat habit and large, velvety flowers, produced in winter and spring, mark out this familiar perennial. Cultivars and hybrids are sold in many colours. After it has finished flowering, plant outside in a border or bed.

☼ Bright to moderate, avoiding direct sun ▮ Cool to moderate. Moderate humidity ◖ Fortnightly. Monthly in winter ◌ Water when compost surface just dry ▱ Seed

OTHER BULBOUS DUAL-PURPOSE HOUSEPLANTS

Crocus chrysanthus
Cyclamen coum
Galanthus 'Atkinsii'
Hyacinthus orientalis hybrids, see p.323
Scilla siberica

Herbs for the Kitchen

WHERE BETTER TO GROW the herbs you need for cooking than in your kitchen, giving you a constant fresh supply that is immediately to hand? There is a wide range of easy-to-grow herbs suitable for cultivating indoors. Grow them in pots on a window ledge and snip regularly to keep them at a small size. Replace any exhausted plants when necessary.

Allium schoenoprasum ▷
CHIVES
↕ ↔ 15cm (6in) or more

A favourite perennial herb for use in salads, this slender bulbous plant will soon form a clump but should not be allowed to flower. Snip off the decorative flower-heads (see inset) if they appear.

☼ Moderate 🌡 Moderate, but cool in winter. Moderate humidity 💧 Fortnightly 💧 When compost surface dry. Water sparingly in winter 🎴 Division, seed (let flower if seed required)

△ *Mentha spicata* 'Crispa'
CURLY SPEARMINT
↕ ↔ 15cm (6in) or more

Crinkly leaves mark this form of the most popular and commonly cultivated garden mint. It is very vigorous, but can be kept to a manageable size by regular snipping.

☼ Bright, with some direct sun 🌡 Moderate to warm. Moderate humidity 💧 Occasional feed 💧 Keep consistently moist. Water sparingly in winter 🎴 Division

Laurus nobilis ▷
BAY TREE
↕ 60cm (2ft) or more ↔ 30cm (12in) or more

This well-known evergreen grows into a large bush or small tree in the garden, but can easily be kept at a convenient size by regular pinching of the growing tips. 🏆

☼ Bright, with some sun 🌡 Moderate. Moderate humidity 💧 Occasional feed 💧 Water when compost surface dry. Sparingly in winter 🎴 Semi-ripe cuttings

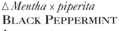

△ *Mentha × piperita*
BLACK PEPPERMINT
↕ ↔ 15cm (6in) or more

Hardy, fast-creeping and clump-forming, with dark stems and fragrant green leaves, this perennial is easily controlled by pinching. Use in teas to aid digestion.

☼ Bright, with some direct sun 🌡 Moderate to warm. Moderate humidity 💧 Occasional feed 💧 Keep moist. Water sparingly in winter 🎴 Division

△ *Ocimum basilicum*
SWEET BASIL
↕ ↔ 15cm (6in) or more

Strongly clove-scented leaves from this annual or short-lived perennial give a spicy flavour to salads and other foods. Pinch out the flowers as they appear.

☼ Bright, with some direct sun 🌡 Warm. Moderate humidity 💧 Fortnightly, using foliage houseplant fertilizer 💧 Water when compost surface dry 🎴 Seed

△ *Origanum vulgare*
OREGANO, WILD MARJORAM
↕ ↔ 15cm (6in) or more

The pungent, peppery-flavoured leaves of this bushy, woody-based perennial are used in bouquet garni. Chew the leaves to gain temporary relief from toothache.

☼ Bright 🌡 Moderate to warm. Moderate humidity 💧 Occasional feed ◊ When compost surface dry. Water sparingly in winter 🗓 Division, semi-ripe cuttings, seed

△ *Petroselinum crispum*
CURLED PARSLEY
↕ ↔ 15cm (6in)

Commonly grown, this bushy biennial herb has congested clusters of emerald-green crispy foliage and is popular as a flavouring or garnish. Treat as annual. ♇

☼ Bright to moderate, avoiding direct sun 🌡 Low to moderate. Moderate humidity 💧 Fortnightly feed ◊ Keep consistently moist. Reduce watering in winter 🗓 Seed

OTHER HERBS FOR THE KITCHEN

Anethum graveolens (dill)
Anthriscus cerefolium (chervil)
Artemisia dracunculus (French tarragon)
Coriandrum sativum (coriander)
Cymbopogon citratus (lemon grass)
Origanum majorana (sweet marjoram)
Rumex scutatus (French sorrel)
Sanguisorba minor (salad burnet)

△ *Rosmarinus officinalis* Prostratus Group
PROSTRATE ROSEMARY
↕ 15cm (6in) ↔ 30cm (12in) or more

A low-growing, spreading form of the popular rosemary, whose aromatic leaves flavour shellfish, pork, and lamb. Blue flowers appear in spring and summer. ♇

☼ Bright 🌡 Moderate to warm. Moderate humidity 💧 Occasional feed ◊ Water when compost surface dry. In winter, water sparingly 🗓 Semi-ripe cuttings, layering

△ *Salvia officinalis*
COMMON SAGE
↕ ↔ 30cm (12in) or more

Pinch out the tips of this evergreen subshrub regularly to maintain a compact habit. Its pungent leaves are used for stuffing poultry and flavouring meat.

☼ Bright 🌡 Moderate to warm. Moderate humidity 💧 Occasional feed ◊ Water when compost surface dry. Water sparingly in winter 🗓 Tip or semi-ripe cuttings, layering, seed

△ *Thymus* x *citriodorus* 'Aureus'
LEMON-SCENTED THYME
↕ 15cm (6in) or more ↔ 20cm (8in)

This pretty, bushy, evergreen shrublet is densely clothed in tiny, gold-dappled, lemon-scented leaves; an excellent herb that is both useful and ornamental. ♇

☼ Bright 🌡 Moderate to warm. Moderate humidity 💧 Feed only if growth poor and leaves yellow ◊ Water when compost surface dry 🗓 Division, tip or semi-ripe cuttings

△ *Thymus vulgaris*
COMMON THYME
↕ 15cm (6in) ↔ 25cm (10in)

Thyme is commonly used in bouquet garni and as a flavouring for soups and stews. A dense evergreen shrublet, of spreading habit, it has tiny green leaves.

☼ Bright 🌡 Moderate to warm. Moderate humidity 💧 Feed only if growth poor and leaves yellow ◊ Water when compost surface dry 🗓 Division, semi-ripe cuttings, seed

403

SPECIALIST PLANTS

COLLECTING MEMBERS of a particular plant family or group is a satisfying and challenging way of growing houseplants. Although members of a family may be botanically related, they often differ greatly in appearance as well as in their individual cultivation requirements.

Succulent *Aeonium* 'Zwartkop' for special interest

△ LONG-LASTING ORCHID *The long life of these large heads of delicately coloured orchid blooms adds to their appeal.*

The popularity of some specialist plant collections may lie in the challenge of growing "difficult" plants. However, as well as those that demand skill and experience, there are houseplant groups that are fairly easy to grow, offering gardeners – especially beginners – the encouragement they need.

SELECTING A PLANT GROUP

There are several factors to bear in mind when choosing a family or group of plants to collect. Beyond personal preference, there are the questions of facilities and space. Not every home can provide the different levels of temperature, light, and humidity required by, say, humidity-loving bromeliads and shade-loving ferns. Some groups require large amounts of space; palms, for example, are not suitable for a small room. It is little wonder that cacti and succulents, with their abundance of dwarf or compact, easy-to-grow species have proved such favourites: they can be comfortably contained on a sunny windowsill or similar position.

Some groups, such as the huge orchid family, offer a wide variety of flower form, colour, or both. For successful orchid cultivation, bear in mind that some are epiphytes, growing on trees and rocks in the wild, while some are terrestrial, rooting in the ground. There is also an extensive range of plants with curious or even abnormal growth habits or foliage, which make an interesting and unusual collection.

◁ FERN COLLECTION *Making the most of a cool, shady wall, this magnificent group of adiantum, asplenium, and nephrolepis displays the variety of leaf textures and growth habits to great effect.*

▷ BRIGHT BROMELIAD *The bold-coloured flowerheads of most bromeliads make them eminently collectable. A warm kitchen provides the perfect opportunity to grow a range of these plants.*

Ferns for Special Interest

A GROUP OF FERNS is one of the most fascinating and satisfying of plant collections because of their great variety, lush foliage, and their acceptance of less than perfect growing conditions. Few plants are more tolerant of low light, and while those of rainforest or tropical origin require warmth and high humidity if they are to thrive, there are many varieties that enjoy cooler conditions or even an unheated room.

Adiantum 'Bicolor' ▷
MAIDENHAIR FERN
↕ ↔ 30cm (12in)

One of many lovely adiantums, with the elegant characteristics of its relatives including beautifully divided emerald-green fronds. A bathroom window is ideal for this plant.

☼ Moderate to shady, avoiding direct sun
🌡 Moderate to warm, avoiding draughts. Moderate to high humidity ◖ Fortnightly. Monthly in winter ◊ Keep moist ⚘ Division, spores

△ *Didymochlaena truncatula*
CLOAK FERN
↕ 1.2m (4ft) ↔ 90cm (3ft)

A large but graceful plant when mature, the cloak fern is prized for its shining green, deeply divided fronds, tinted rosy-pink when young. Develops a short stem.

☼ Moderate to shady, avoiding summer sun
🌡 Moderate to warm. High humidity ◖ Fortnightly. Occasionally in winter ◊ Keep moist, but avoid waterlogging. Reduce in winter ⚘ Division, spores

△ *Asplenium nidus*
BIRD'S NEST FERN
↕ ↔ 90cm (3ft)

Named for its large shuttlecocks or clumps of bold, glossy green fronds, this tropical fern can be very tolerant of home conditions. Excellent for bathrooms.

☼ Moderate. Avoid direct sun 🌡 Warm, avoiding fluctuation and draughts. Moderate to high humidity ◖ Fortnightly, using foliage houseplant fertilizer. Occasionally in winter ◊ Keep moist ⚘ Spores

Blechnum gibbum ▷
DWARF TREE FERN
↕ 75cm (30in) ↔ 60cm (2ft)

This handsome fern from Fiji and New Caledonia develops a fine crown of deeply and regularly divided, leathery fronds. In time, the dwarf tree fern forms a short, densely scaly false stem.

☼ Bright to shady, avoiding direct sun 🌡 Moderate to warm. High humidity ◖ Fortnightly. Occasionally in winter ◊ Water when compost surface dry ⚘ Spores

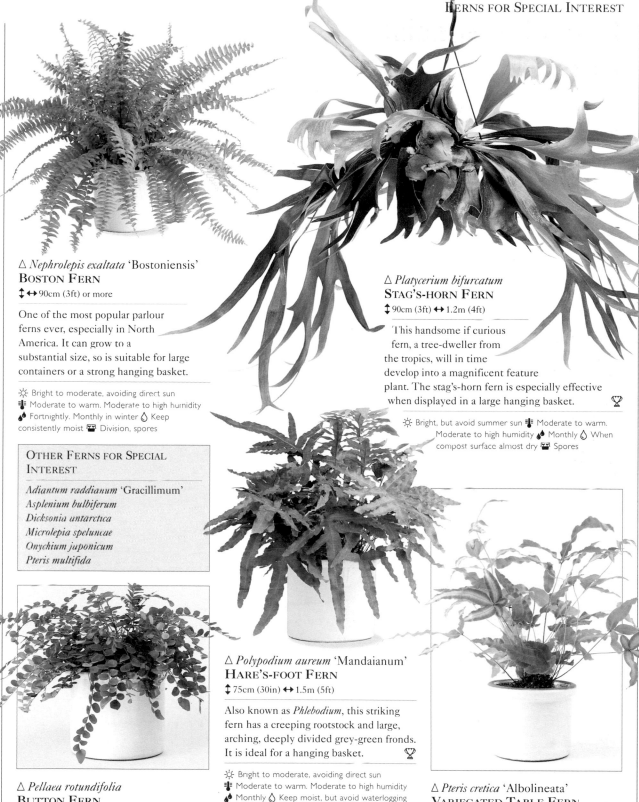

△ *Nephrolepis exaltata* 'Bostoniensis'
BOSTON FERN
↕ ↔ 90cm (3ft) or more

One of the most popular parlour
ferns ever, especially in North
America. It can grow to a
substantial size, so is suitable for large
containers or a strong hanging basket.

☀ Bright to moderate, avoiding direct sun
🌡 Moderate to warm. Moderate to high humidity
💧 Fortnightly. Monthly in winter 💧 Keep
consistently moist 🛋 Division, spores

**OTHER FERNS FOR SPECIAL
INTEREST**

Adiantum raddianum 'Gracillimum'
Asplenium bulbiferum
Dicksonia antarctica
Microlepia speluncae
Onychium japonicum
Pteris multifida

△ *Pellaea rotundifolia*
BUTTON FERN
↕ 20cm (8in) ↔ 30cm (12in)

Tolerant of brighter light than most ferns,
this New Zealand plant forms a loose
hummock of hairy, deeply divided fronds.
It is ideal for growing in a small pot. 🏆

☀ Moderate, avoiding direct sun 🌡 Moderate.
High humidity 💧 Fortnightly. Monthly feed in winter
💧 Keep moist, but avoid waterlogging 🛋 Division,
spores

△ *Polypodium aureum* 'Mandaianum'
HARE'S-FOOT FERN
↕ 75cm (30in) ↔ 1.5m (5ft)

Also known as *Phlebodium*, this striking
fern has a creeping rootstock and large,
arching, deeply divided grey-green fronds.
It is ideal for a hanging basket. 🏆

☀ Bright to moderate, avoiding direct sun
🌡 Moderate to warm. Moderate to high humidity
💧 Monthly 💧 Keep moist, but avoid waterlogging
🛋 Rhizomes, spores

**OTHER FERNS FOR HANGING
BASKETS**

Adiantum diaphanum
Blechnum penna-marina
Davallia canariensis
Davallia mariesii
Goniophlebium biauriculatum

△ *Platycerium bifurcatum*
STAG'S-HORN FERN
↕ 90cm (3ft) ↔ 1.2m (4ft)

This handsome if curious
fern, a tree-dweller from
the tropics, will in time
develop into a magnificent feature
plant. The stag's-horn fern is especially effective
when displayed in a large hanging basket. 🏆

☀ Bright, but avoid summer sun 🌡 Moderate to warm.
Moderate to high humidity 💧 Monthly 💧 When
compost surface almost dry 🛋 Spores

△ *Pteris cretica* 'Albolineata'
VARIEGATED TABLE FERN
↕ 45cm (18in) ↔ 60cm (2ft)

An impressive fern with loose clumps of
erect then arching, deeply divided fronds,
whose narrow-fingered lobes have a bold
stripe along the midrib. Easy to grow. 🏆

☀ Bright, but avoid direct sun 🌡 Warm. Moderate
to high humidity 💧 Fortnightly. Monthly in winter
💧 Keep moist, but avoid waterlogging 🛋 Division,
spores

SPECIALIST PLANTS

407

Cacti and Succulents for Special Interest

RELATIVELY EASY to grow, cacti and succulents introduce many people, especially children, to the world of plants. Most enjoy or will tolerate dry air, although this is no reason to neglect them. Curious growth forms and colourful flowers are among their specialities.

Aeonium 'Zwartkop' ▷
BLACK AEONIUM
↕ ↔ 90cm (3ft)

A dramatic plant that slowly grows into a succulent "tree" with bold rosettes of shining, blackish-purple leaves. Large heads of yellow flowers appear in spring or early summer.

☼ Bright, with direct sun ❄ Warm, but cool to moderate in winter. Low humidity 💧 Monthly, using fertilizer for cacti and succulents ◊ When compost surface dry. Water sparingly in winter 🖤 Leaf cuttings, leaves

△ *Orbea variegata*
STARFISH CACTUS
↕ 10cm (4in) ↔ 30cm (12in)

Easy to grow and tolerant of neglect, this succulent forms clusters of toothed stems. The strong-smelling, star-shaped summer flowers have an exquisite mosaic pattern.

☼ Bright, with sun ❄ Warm, but cool to moderate in winter. Low humidity 💧 Monthly, using fertilizer for cacti and succulents ◊ When compost surface dry. Water sparingly in winter 🖤 Stem sections

△ *Lithops salicola*
LIVING STONE
↕ 5cm (2in) ↔ 23cm (9in)

One of a large group, from semi-desert regions of southern Africa, which mimic the pebbles among which they grow. It flowers from summer to mid-autumn.

☼ Bright, with sun ❄ Warm, but cool to moderate in winter. Low humidity 💧 Monthly, using fertilizer for cacti and succulents ◊ When compost surface dry. Water sparingly in winter 🖤 Offsets

△ *Mammillaria zeilmanniana* 'Ubinkii'
ROSE PINCUSHION
↕ 15cm (6in) ↔ 30cm (12in)

Excellent for beginners because it is free-flowering, even when young. Compact at first, then slowly dividing to form a broad cluster, it bears rose-pink spring flowers.

☼ Bright, with sun ❄ Warm, but cool to moderate in winter. Low humidity 💧 Monthly, using fertilizer for cacti and succulents ◊ When compost surface dry. Water sparingly in winter 🖤 Offsets

△ *Oreocereus trollii*
OLD MAN OF THE ANDES
↕ 90cm (3ft) ↔ 60cm (2ft)

This cactus, multi-branched when mature, forms erect, ribbed stems, clothed in long white hairs and lined with clusters of spines. Bears pink flowers in summer.

☼ Bright, with sun ❄ Warm, but cool to moderate in winter. Low humidity 💧 Monthly, using fertilizer for cacti and succulents ◊ When compost surface dry. Water sparingly in winter 🖤 Offsets

△ *Pachyphytum oviferum*
MOONSTONES
↕ 15cm (6in) ↔ 30cm (12in)

Clusters of smooth, egg-shaped, light green, white-bloomy leaves are flushed lavender-blue. Spikes of orange-red flowers are borne from winter to spring.

☼ Bright, with sun ❄ Warm, but cool to moderate in winter. Low humidity ◊ Monthly, using fertilizer for cacti and succulents ◊ When compost surface dry. Water sparingly in winter ▭ Leaf cuttings

---

OTHER CACTI AND SUCCULENTS FOR SPECIAL INTEREST

Blossfeldia liliputana
Crassula falcata
Echinocactus grusonii
Echinocereus pectinatus
Euphorbia obesa, see p.367
Mammillaria hahniana
Opuntia verschaffeltii
Parodia leninghausii, see p.359
Rebutia spegazziniana
Sedum pachyphyllum

Sedum morganianum ▷
BURRO'S TAIL, DONKEY'S TAIL
↕ 90cm (3ft) ↔ 30cm (12in)

This popular succulent, native to Mexico, has a prostrate habit in the wild but is usually grown in a hanging basket to show off its long, blue-green, leafy stems. ♈

☼ Bright, with sun ❄ Warm, but cool to moderate in winter. Low humidity ◊ Monthly, using fertilizer for cacti and succulents ◊ When compost surface dry. Water sparingly in winter ▭ Stem cuttings

---

Pachypodium lamerei ▷
MADAGASCAR PALM
↕ 2m (6ft) or more
↔ 1.5m (5ft) or more

The spiny stems of this small, tree-like, eventually branching succulent bear long narrow leaves in terminal clusters. White, yellow-throated flowers appear in summer. ♈

☼ Bright, with sun ❄ Warm, but cool to moderate in winter. Low humidity ◊ Monthly, using fertilizer for cacti and succulents ◊ When compost surface dry. Water sparingly in winter ▭ Tip cuttings, seed

Ribbed, spiny stem

△ *Selenicereus grandiflorus*
QUEEN OF THE NIGHT
↕ 3m (10ft) or more ↔ 1m (3ft) or more

A plant to enjoy at night – its 30cm (12in) long, richly fragrant, creamy-white flowers, borne in summer, open only after dark. The long stems need supporting.

☼ Bright, with sun ❄ Warm, but moderate in winter. Low humidity ◊ Monthly, using fertilizer for cacti and succulents ◊ When compost surface dry. Water sparingly in winter ▭ Stem sections

Orchids for Special Interest

ORCHIDS ARE among the most coveted of all the flowering plant families, but contrary to popular belief they are not all the preserve of specialist growers; orchids are now available at many garden centres. Follow the cultivation notes given here, use a specialist orchid compost, and these plants will give endless satisfaction.

Cattleya hybrids ▷
CATTLEYA, CORSAGE ORCHID
↕ 20cm (8in) ↔ 45cm (18in)

Sumptuous and fragrant, these spring blooms are 12cm (5in) across and available in a range of colours. Grow in epiphytic orchid compost in a pot or orchid basket.

☼ Bright to moderate, avoiding direct sun ❄ Moderate to warm. High humidity ◈ Feed with every third watering ◊ When compost surface just moist. Water sparingly in winter ⊞ Division

△ *Miltoniopsis* hybrids
PANSY ORCHID
↕ ↔ 23cm (9in)

These beautiful orchids produce large, fragrant, velvet-textured, pansy-like blooms in autumn. Grow in epiphytic orchid compost in a pot or orchid basket.

☼ Moderate to shady ❄ Moderate. High humidity ◈ Feed with every third watering ◊ When compost surface just dry. Reduce watering at lower temperatures ⊞ Division

Cymbidium hybrids ▷
CYMBIDIUM
↕ 75cm (30in) ↔ 90cm (36in)

Among the most popular and reliable orchids for the home, with long-lasting flowers appearing from winter into spring. Available in a wide range of colours. Grow in any orchid compost.

☼ Bright, with some winter sun ❄ Moderate to warm. Moderate humidity ◈ Fortnightly, using half-strength flowering houseplant fertilizer. Monthly in winter ◊ Keep moist, but avoid waterlogging. Reduce watering in winter ⊞ Division

△ *Paphiopedilum insigne* hybrids
SLIPPER ORCHID
↕ 15cm (6in) ↔ 25cm (10in)

Leathery basal leaves are complemented by leafless shoots, each bearing one or more large flowers with pouched lips from autumn until spring. Grow in a pot, using terrestrial orchid compost.

☼ Bright to moderate, avoiding direct sun ❄ Moderate to warm. High humidity ◈ Feed with every third watering. Occasionally in winter ◊ Keep moist. In winter, water when barely moist ⊞ Division

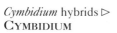

OTHER ORCHIDS FOR SPECIAL INTEREST

x *Brassolaeliocattleya* hybrids
Cattleya mini hybrids
x *Doritaenopsis* hybrids
x *Laeliocattleya* hybrids
Ludisia discolor
Phalaenopsis equestris hybrids

Widely arching, strap-shaped leaves

Phalaenopsis hybrids ▷
MOTH ORCHID
↕ 1m (3ft) ↔ 45cm (18in)

Named the moth orchid after the wing-like shape of its blooms, which are borne in arching sprays throughout the year. Grow in epiphytic orchid compost in a basket or on a piece of bark.

☼ Bright, but avoid scorching sun ‡ Warm, avoiding draughts. High humidity ◊ Fortnightly, using half-strength orchid fertilizer. Monthly in winter ◊ Keep moist, but avoid waterlogging ▧ Division

△ *Pleione bulbocodioides*
PLEIONE
↕ 15cm (6in) ↔ 5cm (2in)

A dwarf, spring-flowering orchid that likes cooler conditions than most, and is suited to a sunless windowsill. Grow in epiphytic orchid compost and allow a winter rest.

☼ Bright to moderate, avoiding direct sun ‡ Cool to moderate. Moderate humidity ◊ Fortnightly when in leaf, using high potash fertilizer ◊ Keep moist after flowering. Keep dry when dormant ▧ Division

△ *Psychopsis papilio*
BUTTERFLY ORCHID
↕ 60cm (2ft) ↔ 30cm (12in)

This epiphytic orchid is a parent of several houseplant hybrids; its racemes of exquisite flowers are borne throughout the year. Grow in a basket or on bark.

☼ Moderate to shady, avoiding direct sun ‡ Warm, avoiding fluctuation. High humidity ◊ Every three weeks ◊ Keep moist, but avoid waterlogging ▧ Division

Ruffled flowers with marbled colour

OTHER ORCHIDS FOR SPECIAL INTEREST

Colmanara hybrids
Cymbidium mini hybrids
Dendrodium nobile (Yamamoto type) hybrids
Dendrobium x *Phalaenopsis* hybrids
x *Odontioda* hybrids
Odontoglossum hybrids
Oncidium hybrids
Paphiopedilum primulinum hybrids

◁ x *Vuylstekeara* Cambria 'Plush'
VUYLSTEKEARA
↕ 23cm (9in) ↔ 45cm (18in)

Ruffled, marbled flowers of many colours appear from spring to autumn on this popular plant, a hybrid of *Cochlioda*, *Miltonia*, and *Odontoglossum*. Grow it in epiphytic orchid compost.

☼ Bright to moderate, avoiding direct sun ‡ Moderate to warm, but cool in winter. High humidity ◊ Monthly. Occasionally in winter ◊ Keep moist. Water sparingly in winter ▧ Division

△ *Phragmipedium* hybrids
SLIPPER ORCHID
↕ ↔ 60cm (2ft)

These terrestrial orchids produce racemes of pouched flowers at intervals throughout the year. Best grown in epiphytic orchid compost in a pot that restricts the roots.

☼ Bright to moderate, avoiding direct sun ‡ Moderate to warm. High humidity ◊ Feed with every third watering. Occasionally in winter ◊ Keep moist. In winter, water when just moist ▧ Division

SPECIALIST PLANTS

411

Palms for Special Interest

Few plants bring a touch of the exotic to the home more readily than palms. Their often large, fan- or feather-shaped evergreen leaves provide any room with a focal point and a sense of visual drama. Palms grow in some of the world's wildest terrains, but many thrive indoors, where they will tolerate less than perfect conditions.

Caryota mitis ▷
Burmese Fish-tail Palm
↕ 3m (10ft) or more ↔ 2m (6ft) or more

This plant is easily recognized by the characteristic fish-tail segments of its large, frond-like, arching leaves. A fairly easy palm to grow indoors, but it needs plenty of room in which to develop. ♈

☼ Bright to moderate, avoiding summer sun ❄ Moderate to warm. High humidity 💧 Fortnightly, using foliage houseplant fertilizer. Monthly in winter 💧 Water when dry. Avoid waterlogging 🌱 Seed

Chrysalidocarpus lutescens ▷
Areca Palm
↕ 2m (6ft) or more ↔ 1.2m (4ft) or more

Naturally clump-forming, this popular palm from Madagascar has numerous erect, slender stems, initially clothed with yellow leaf bases. These later develop into arching, feathery, rich green leaves. ♈

☼ Bright to moderate, avoiding hot sun ❄ Moderate to warm. Moderate to high humidity 💧 Fortnightly, using foliage houseplant fertilizer. Monthly in winter 💧 Water when dry. Avoid waterlogging 🌱 Seed

Chamaedorea elegans ▷
Parlour Palm
↕ ↔ 2m (6ft)

Easily the most popular palm for the home, this plant is fast-growing, elegant, and tolerant of neglect and unfavourable conditions. It is found in Mexican rainforests. ♈

☼ Bright to moderate. Avoid hot sun ❄ Moderate to warm. Moderate to high humidity 💧 Fortnightly, using foliage houseplant fertilizer. Monthly in winter 💧 Water when dry. Avoid waterlogging 🌱 Seed

Cyrtostachys lakka ▷
Sealing-wax Palm
↕ 3m (10ft) or more ↔ 1.5m (5ft) or more

One of the most beautiful and colourful palms, this native of south-east Asia has slender, brilliant scarlet stems supporting erect clusters of feathery leaves.

☼ Bright to moderate, avoiding summer sun ❄ Warm. High humidity 💧 Fortnightly, using foliage houseplant fertilizer. Monthly in winter 💧 When compost surface dry. Avoid waterlogging 🌱 Seed

Howea belmoreana ▷
SENTRY PALM

↕ 3m (10ft) or more

↔ 2m (6ft) or more

A relative of the popular
kentia palm, *Howea
forsteriana*, and just as
tolerant of low light levels
and neglect. With maturity, the
leaves of the sentry palm develop their
large, curved, wide green leaflets. ♕

☼ Bright to moderate, avoiding summer sun
☷ Warm. Moderate to high humidity ♦ Fortnightly,
using foliage houseplant fertilizer. Monthly in winter
◊ Water when dry. Avoid waterlogging ▨ Seed

Phoenix roebelenii ▷
PYGMY DATE PALM

↕ 3m (10ft) ↔ 2m (6ft) or more

With its spreading head of
feathery leaves, on a slender
stem rough with old leaf bases,
this is the perfect miniature
indoor palm tree. Tolerant of
low light levels and neglect, it
will thrive if given care. ♕

☼ Bright to moderate, avoiding
summer sun ☷ Moderate to warm.
Moderate to high humidity ♦ Fortnightly, using foliage houseplant
fertilizer. Monthly in winter ◊ Water
when dry. Avoid waterlogging ▨ Seed

**OTHER PALMS FOR SPECIAL
INTEREST**

Caryota urens
Chamaedorea erumpens
Chamaedorea metallica
Chamaedorea stolonifera
Euterpe edulis
Hedyscepe canterburyana
Howea forsteriana
 Laccospadix australasica
  Lytocaryum weddellianum, see p.395
  Ravenea rivularis, see p.371
  Reinhardtia gracilis

△ *Phoenix canariensis*
CANARY ISLAND DATE PALM

↕ 5m (15ft) or more ↔ 2m (6ft) or more

Large, pinnate leaves give this date palm
architectural interest. It is one of the most
common garden palms in warm regions of
the world, and a superb houseplant. ♕

☼ Bright to moderate. Avoid hot sun ☷ Moderate
to warm. Moderate humidity ♦ Fortnightly, using
foliage houseplant fertilizer. Monthly in winter
◊ Water when dry. Avoid waterlogging ▨ Seed

*Rhapis
excelsa* △
LADY PALM

↕ 3m (10ft) ↔ 1.2m (4ft)

A fine indoor palm with its dense clump
of erect, leafy, bamboo-like stems, the leaf
blades fan-shaped with long, fingered
segments. It is tolerant of neglect. ♕

☼ Bright to moderate. Avoid hot sun ☷ Moderate
to warm. Moderate humidity ♦ Fortnightly, using
foliage houseplant fertilizer. Monthly in winter
◊ Water when dry. Avoid waterlogging ▨ Seed

△ *Washingtonia robusta*
SKYDUSTER

↕ 3m (10ft) or more ↔ 2m (6ft)

Native to north-west Mexico, this fast-
growing palm enjoys good light and is
best suited to the garden room. Develops
a single stem with fan-shaped leaves.

☼ Bright to moderate. Avoid hot sun ☷ Moderate
to warm. Moderate humidity ♦ Fortnightly, using
foliage houseplant fertilizer. Monthly in winter
◊ Water when dry. Avoid waterlogging ▨ Seed

Bromeliads for Special Interest

ALMOST ALL BROMELIADS originate in tropical or sub-tropical America. There is a multitude of species, varying remarkably in shape and colour, although most grown indoors are rosette-forming plants popular for foliage, flowers, or both. They look equally good in pots or hanging baskets.

△ *Billbergia* x *windii*
BILLBERGIA
↕ ↔ 60cm (2ft)

A handsome, clump-forming hybrid with long, arching, strap-shaped green leaves. It bears pendulous heads of green flowers from rose-pink bracts in summer.

☼ Bright, with some sun ≣ Moderate to warm. Moderate to high humidity 🌢 Fortnightly, using flowering houseplant fertilizer 🌢 Water when compost surface just dry 🎴 Offsets

---

OTHER BROMELIADS FOR FOLIAGE INTEREST

Ananas bracteatus 'Tricolor', see p.358
Billbergia Fantasia Group
Cryptanthus 'Pink Starlight'
Neoregelia carolinae 'Tricolor Perfecta'
Vriesea carinata
Vriesea 'Tiffany'

△ *Aechmea morganii*
URN PLANT
↕ 60cm (2ft) ↔ 75cm (30in)

Striking for foliage and flowers, this big, bold bromeliad bears a rosette of glossy, dark green, strap-shaped, loosely arching leaves, and branched spikes of pink bracts and blue summer flowers.

☼ Bright, but avoid summer sun ≣ Warm. Low to moderate humidity 🌢 Fortnightly, using flowering houseplant fertilizer 🌢 Water when compost surface dry. Water sparingly in winter 🎴 Offsets

◁ *Ananas comosus* 'Variegatus'
IVORY PINEAPPLE
↕ 90cm (3ft) ↔ 60cm (2ft)

Creamy-white-margined, dark green leaves, flushed red when young, make this pineapple special; the summer flowers, followed by the fruit, are a bonus. Place with care as the leaves are spiny.

☼ Bright ≣ Warm. Moderate to high humidity 🌢 Fortnightly, using flowering houseplant fertilizer 🌢 Water when compost surface just dry 🎴 Offsets, rosettes

△ *Cryptanthus zonatus* 'Zebrinus'
EARTH STAR, ZEBRA PLANT
↕ 12cm (5in) ↔ 40cm (16in)

A striking, star-shaped rosette plant with leathery, wavy-margined leaves, banded zebra fashion with dark grey-green and silver. Grows among rocks in east Brazil.

☼ Bright to shady, avoiding direct sun ≣ Warm. Moderate to high humidity 🌢 Monthly, using flowering houseplant fertilizer. Rarely in winter 🌢 Water when compost surface dry 🎴 Offsets

△ *Neoregelia carolinae* f. *tricolor*
BLUSHING BROMELIAD
↕ 30cm (12in) ↔ 60cm (2ft)

This spectacular Brazilian rainforest plant has a dense, bold rosette of spine-toothed, shiny green leaves, striped yellowish-white and red. In the summer flowering season, it has a red heart, hence its common name.

☼ Bright, but avoid summer sun ☷ Warm. High humidity ◖ Fortnightly, using flowering houseplant fertilizer ◊ Water when compost surface dry ⬚ Offsets

Tillandsia cyanea ▷
BLUE-FLOWERED TORCH
↕ 30cm (12in)
↔ 20cm (8in)

This striking epiphyte from Ecuador bears tufted rosettes of slender, curved and channelled leaves, topped in late spring or autumn by a paddle-shaped head of rose bracts and violet-blue flowers.

☼ Bright, but avoid direct sun ☷ Warm. Low to moderate humidity ◖ Every two months, using flowering houseplant fertilizer ◊ Water when compost surface dry ⬚ Offsets

△ *Vriesea hieroglyphica*
KING OF BROMELIADS
↕ 90cm (3ft) ↔ 1m (39in)

An impressive plant, with purple-backed leaves that are yellowish-green with darker bands above. Yellow and green flowerheads are borne in summer on erect stems.

☼ Moderate ☷ Warm. Moderate to high humidity ◖ Every three weeks ◊ Water when compost surface dry ⬚ Offsets, seed

OTHER BROMELIADS FOR FLOWER AND BRACT INTEREST

Aechmea chantinii, see p.366
Aechmea fasciata, see p.324
Aechmea Foster's Favorite Group
Billbergia nutans
Billbergia pyramidalis
Guzmania lingulata var. *minor*
Guzmania sanguinea
Tillandsia lindenii

◁ *Tillandsia wagneriana*
AIR PLANT
↕ ↔ 45cm (18in)

Unusual flower spikes with bracts of lavender adorn this epiphyte from the Peruvian Amazon in late spring or autumn, topping a bold, urn-shaped rosette of wavy-margined, crisp green or reddish leaves.

☼ Bright, but avoid direct sun ☷ Warm. Moderate to high humidity ◖ Every two months, using flowering houseplant fertilizer ◊ Water when compost surface dry ⬚ Offsets

△ *Vriesea splendens*
FLAMING SWORD
↕ 90cm (3ft) ↔ 30cm (12in)

Worth growing for its rosettes of pale green leaves banded darker green, purple, or reddish brown. Red-scaled flowerheads on erect stems add summer interest.

☼ Moderate, avoiding direct sun ☷ Moderate to warm. Moderate to high humidity ◖ Every three weeks, using flowering houseplant fertilizer ◊ Water when compost surface just dry ⬚ Offsets

Novelty Houseplants

PLANTS THAT PROVIDE a talking point are welcome in any home. Spectacular flowers or impressive foliage always catch the eye, but so too do plants with an amusing growth habit or with some peculiarity of leaf or flower. Plants not usually grown indoors, or those with a fascinating history, also make good subjects. Novelty plants engage children's imaginations and with luck will inspire a desire to know more about plants.

△ *Dionaea muscipula*
VENUS FLY TRAP
↕ 45cm (18in) ↔ 15cm (6in)

A fascinating, carnivorous, short-lived perennial, of fierce appearance, that you can feed with flies or tiny fragments of raw meat. Prefers rain water to any other.

☼ Bright, with sun ≣ Moderate to warm. High humidity ◊ Feed if desired, but do not overfeed. Plant will also catch own food ◊ Stand pot in a tray and keep waterlogged ▦ Division, leaf cuttings

---

OTHER SUCCULENT NOVELTY HOUSEPLANTS

Conophytum bilobum
Dorstenia foetida
Faucaria tigrina, see p.355
Fenestraria aurantiaca
Haworthia truncata
Kalanchoe daigremontiana
Lithops optica
Orbea variegata, see p.408

Ananas comosus
'Porteanus' △
PINEAPPLE
↕ 1m (3ft) ↔ 50cm (20in)

This plant has a handsome green and yellow rosette with spiny teeth. You can root a pineapple from the severed leafy top of a pineapple fruit, or try growing one from an offset.

☼ Bright, with sun ≣ Warm. Moderate to high humidity ◊ Fortnightly, using flowering houseplant fertilizer ◊ When just dry ▦ Offsets, rosettes

---

Capsicum annuum
'Festival' ▷
ORNAMENTAL PEPPER
↕ ↔ 60cm (2ft)

Extremely ornamental and unusual, this small, bushy evergreen produces an eye-catching variety of different coloured fruits on one plant. It is normally treated as an annual and sold as an ornamental winter plant.

☼ Bright, but avoid direct sun ≣ Cool to moderate. Moderate humidity ◊ Fortnightly, alternating general fertilizer with flowering houseplant fertilizer ◊ When compost surface just dry ▦ Tip cuttings

△ *Epiphyllum laui*
NIGHT-FLOWERING CACTUS
↕ 30cm (12in) ↔ 60cm (2ft) or more

A night-flowering Mexican cactus whose fragrant, exotic-looking white flowers are produced in early summer (they may sometimes also open in daylight).

☼ Bright. Avoid direct sun ≣ Moderate to warm. Moderate to high humidity ◊ Fortnightly, from bud formation until flowering ends ◊ When just dry. Water sparingly in winter ▦ Stem cuttings, seed

Euphorbia pulcherrima
'Silver Star' ▷
POINSETTIA

↕ ↔ 50cm (20in)

Poinsettias seem to
be everywhere
in winter, but
this variety,
with its strange
mixture of leaf and
bract colours, is
uncommon. It
would make an
interesting addition to a group
of red-bracted poinsettias.

☼ Bright ≋ Warm, avoiding draughts and
fluctuating temperatures. Moderate to high
humidity ◊● Monthly ◊ Water when compost
surface just dry. Avoid waterlogging ☷ Tip cuttings

Selaginella lepidophylla ▷
RESURRECTION PLANT

↕ 8cm (3in) ↔ 15cm (6in)

Normally bought as a dried
ball (see inset), this plant will
uncurl into a rosette of rich green
ferny fronds when placed in a dish
of water or pot of damp compost.

☼ Shady ≋ Warm. High humidity ◊● Every five
weeks, using half-strength general houseplant fertilizer
◊ Water when compost surface just dry ☷ Stem cuttings

◁ *Mimosa pudica*
SENSITIVE PLANT

↕ 60cm (2ft) ↔ 40cm (16in)

Usually treated as an annual or
short-lived perennial, this fun plant
has ferny leaves that quickly fold
and droop when touched; be
careful not to overdo it as the plant
takes up to an hour to recover.

☼ Bright to moderate, avoiding direct sun
≋ Warm. High humidity ◊● Monthly
◊ When compost surface just dry. Reduce
watering in winter ☷ Seed

OTHER NOVELTY HOUSEPLANTS

Arachis hypogaea
Darlingtonia californica
Davallia mariesii
Dracunculus vulgaris
Musa coccinea
Pinguicula grandiflora
Sarracenia flava
Tillandsia caput-medusae, see p.355
Tolmiea menziesii, see p.365

Olea europaea ▷
OLIVE

↕ ↔ 3m (10ft) or more

A grey-leaved evergreen tree or bush,
easily kept small by pruning or training in
spring. Older plants produce tiny, fragrant
summer flowers that may bear fruit.

☼ Bright, with sun ≋ Moderate to warm, but cool
in winter. Low humidity ◊● Monthly ◊ When
compost surface dry. Water sparingly in winter
☷ Semi-ripe cuttings, seed

△ *Streptocarpus wendlandii*
CAPE PRIMROSE

↕ 30cm (12in) ↔ 75cm (30in)

Very different to the usual Cape primrose,
this species has a single, enormous, dark
purple-green basal leaf, red-purple
beneath, and blue flowers in summer.

☼ Bright to moderate, avoiding direct sun
≋ Warm. Moderate to high humidity ◊● Fortnightly,
using flowering houseplant fertilizer ◊ When
compost surface just dry ☷ Seed

SPECIALIST PLANTS

417

Index

Plants that are illustrated in the book are indicated by this symbol ▨

A

Abele ▨ 284
Abelia floribunda 165
   A. triflora ▨ 178, 195, 228, 238
Abeliophyllum distichum 164, 236
Abies balsamea 'Nana' ▨ 258
   A. bracteata 255
   A. concolor 255
   A. concolor 'Candicans' ▨ 263
   A. concolor 'Compacta' ▨ 258
   A. grandis 244
   A. koreana ▨ 250, 252
   A. lasiocarpa 'Compacta' 259
   A. magnifica 244
   A. nordmanniana ▨ 244
   A. nordmanniana 'Golden Spreader' ▨ 258
   A. pinsapo 255
   A. pinsapo 'Glauca' 255
   Abies vejarii 255
Abraham-Isaac-Jacob ▨ 41
Abutilon 'Canary Bird' 212
   A. 'Nabob' 332
   A. megapotamicum ▨ 158, ▨ 164
   A. pictum 'Thompsonii' 348
   A. x *suntense* 'Violetta' 198
Acacia baileyana 222
   A. dealbata ▨ 228
Acacia
   False ▨ 283
   Golden ▨ 293
   Rose ▨ 165
Acaena ▨ 118
   A. saccaticupula 'Blue Haze' 50, 137
Acalypha wilkesiana 'Musaica' 347
Acanthus dioscoridis 27, ▨ 32
   A. hirsutus ▨ 26, 36
   A. mollis 'Hollard's Gold' 18, 121, 135
   A. mollis Latifolius Group 28, 40, 81
   A. spinosus 106, 124
   A. spinosus Spinosissimus Group ▨ 126
Acca sellowiana ▨ 165
Acer campestre 276
   A. capillipes ▨ 302
   A. cappadocicum 267
   A. cappadocicum 'Aureum' ▨ 292
   A. crataegifolium 'Veitchii' 290
   A. griseum ▨ 300, 303
   A. japonicum 'Aconitifolium' 275
   A. negundo 'Flamingo' 276, ▨ 290
   A. palmatum 'Aureum' 221, ▨ 292
   A. palmatum 'Bloodgood' 225
   A. palmatum 'Corallinum' ▨ 210
   A. palmatum 'Garnet' 182, ▨ 224
   A. palmatum 'Osakazuki' 226, ▨ 296
   A. palmatum 'Red Pygmy' ▨ 224
   A. palmatum 'Sango-kaku' ▨ 300
   A. palmatum 'Seiryû' 226
   A. palmatum 'Trompenburg' 295
   A. palmatum var. *coreanum* ▨ 270
   A. palmatum var. *heptalobum* ▨ 226
   A. pensylvanicum 'Erythrocladum' 301
   A. platanoides 276, ▨ 281

A. platanoides 'Crimson King' ▨ 295
A. pseudoplatanus 281
A. pseudoplatanus 'Brilliantissimum' 273, 282
A. rubrum 275
A. rubrum 'Columnare' ▨ 304
A. rubrum 'Schlesingeri' ▨ 296
A. saccharinum 266
A. saccharum subsp. *nigrum* 'Temple's Upright' ▨ 304
A. shirasawanum 'Aureum' 271, ▨ 292
A. tegmentosum 301
A. triflorum 269, ▨ 270
Achillea 19
   A. 'Coronation Gold' 75, ▨ 108
   A. filipendulina 29, ▨ 76
   A. filipendulina 'Gold Plate' 108
   A. millefolium 'Cerise Queen' 125
   A. 'Moonshine' 78
   A. ptarmica 'Boule de Neige' ▨ 54, 84
   A. ptarmica The Pearl Group ▨ 80
Achimenes hybrids ▨ 324, ▨ 332, 361, ▨ 374, 376
acid soil, *see* lime-free soil
Aciphylla aurea ▨ 126
Aconite, Winter ▨ 104
Aconitum 'Blue Sceptre' 91
   A. x *cammarum* 'Bicolor' ▨ 24
   A. carmichaelii 'Arendsii' 88, ▨ 102
   A. episcopale 72
   A. hemsleyanum 72
   A. 'Ivorine' ▨ 98
   A. japonicum 124
   A. lycoctonum subsp. *vulparia* ▨ 92
   A. napellus 'Carneum' 92
Acorus calamus 127
   A. gramineus 69
   A. gramineus 'Ogon' 135, ▨ 340, 344
   A. gramineus 'Variegatus' ▨ 350
Actaea matsumarae 'Elstead' ▨ 102
   A. racemosa 99, 109
   A. rubra ▨ 42
   A. simplex 76
   A. simplex 'Brunette' ▨ 138
   A. simplex 'Scimitar' ▨ 24
   A. simplex Atropurpurea Group ▨ 124
Actinidia kolomikta ▨ 160
Adenium obesum ▨ 366
Adiantum 'Bicolor' ▨ 406
   A. capillus-veneris 149
   A. diaphanum 407
   A. pedatum 53, ▨ 125
   A. raddianum 365, 375, ▨ 398
   A. raddianum 'Fritz Luth' 363, ▨ 380
   A. raddianum 'Gracillimum' 369, 407
   A. venustum 125
Adonis amurensis 104
   A. vernalis 97, ▨ 104, 125
Aechmea 308
   A. chantinii 329, ▨ 366, 415
   A. fasciata ▨ 324, 329, 352, 415
   A. fasciata 'Morgana' ▨ 380
   A. Foster's Favourite Group 415
   A. fulgens var. *discolor* 396
   A. morganii 414
Aechmeas, Queen of the ▨ 366
Aegopodium podagraria 'Variegatum' 53
Aeonium 'Zwartkop' ▨ 404, ▨ 408
Aeonium, Black ▨ 408
Aeschynanthus lobbianus 361

Aesculus californica 179
   A. x *carnea* 'Briotii' 282
   A. flava 303
   A. hippocastanum 'Baumannii' 267, ▨ 272, 276
   A. x *neglecta* 'Erythroblastos' ▨ 268
   A. parviflora ▨ 178
   A. pavia 'Atrosanguinea' ▨ 270
Aethionema 'Warley Rose' ▨ 60
African Lily ▨ 70, ▨ 90, ▨ 112
African Milk Tree ▨ 355
African Violet ▨ 325, ▨ 333, ▨ 337
Agapanthus 'Blue Giant' 75, ▨ 90, 123
   A. 'Loch Hope' ▨ 70
   A. 'Midnight Blue' ▨ 26, 113
   A. praecox subsp. *orientalis* 47, 70
   A. 'Snowy Owl' ▨ 112
Agastache 'Firebird' 27
   A. foeniculum ▨ 54
   A. foeniculum 'Alabaster' ▨ 127
Agave americana 'Variegata' 70
   A. victoriae-reginae 367
Aglaonema 308
   A. commutatum 'Pseudobracteatum' ▨ 350
   A. 'Lilian' 363, ▨ 374
   A. 'Maria Christina' ▨ 380
   A. 'Marie' ▨ 362
   A. 'Silver King' 352
   A. 'Silver Queen' ▨ 352
Aichryson x *domesticum* 'Variegatum' 337, 350
Ailanthus altissima 267, 282
air layering, houseplants 317
Air Plant ▨ 355, ▨ 367, ▨ 415
air pollution
   perennials tolerant of 80–1
   shrubs tolerant of 204–5
   trees tolerant of 282–3
Ajuga reptans 'Atropurpurea' 138
   A. reptans 'Catlin's Giant' ▨ 86
   A. reptans 'Jungle Beauty' 18, ▨ 52
   A. reptans 'Multicolor' ▨ 22
Akebia quinata ▨ 168
   A. trifoliata 162
Albizia julibrissin ▨ 276
Alchemilla conjuncta 51, ▨ 84
   A. mollis 40, 84, ▨ 90
Alder
   Grey ▨ 272
   Italian ▨ 281
   Red ▨ 280
Alerce ▨ 250
Alisma plantago-aquatica 69
alkaline (limy) soil 14
   perennials for 32–5
   shrubs for 194–5
   trees for 274, 276–7
Alkanet ▨ 112
   Green ▨ 81
Allegheny Serviceberry ▨ 282
Allium cristophii 27, ▨ 32, 38
   A. flavum 59
   A. giganteum ▨ 82
   A. 'Globemaster' 78, 87, ▨ 88
   A. hollandicum 'Purple Sensation' ▨ 78
   A. insubricum ▨ 62
   A. mairei 63
   A. moly ▨ 44

Acknowledgments

AUTHORS' ACKNOWLEDGMENTS

A number of people have either directly or indirectly influenced the preparation of this book, none more so than my wife, Sue, whose unfailing support, including the typing of my scribbled notes and lists, helped bring it to fruition.

I wish to say a special thank you to my friend Matthew Biggs who was joint author with me of *What Houseplant Where*, most of which has been incorporated into the present book.

Sarah Drew, Jacqueline Postill, Martin Puddle, and James Wickham all made helpful comments based on their considerable collective experience dealing with customers' problems and queries in plant centres.

My thanks also to David Barker, Joyce Cama, Cliff Dad, Dilys Davies, Pat Jackson, Danae Johnston, Chris Mortimer, Bob Mousley, and Ray Wilson of the Hardy Plant Society, who kindly helped with suggestions, as did Jean Fletcher, Hala Humphries, Sabine Liebherr, and George Smith. Beyond these few are the many who have encouraged my interest in perennials over the years. To all of you, my heartfelt thanks.

If we have learned anything in our pursuit of plant knowledge it is that who you know is often the basis of what you know, and this has certainly proved the case in the preparation of this book. Thus the ever-reliable Sarah Drew of the Hillier Plant Centre generously gave us the benefit of her "point of sales" experience, while Jim Gardiner, Curator of the RHS Garden, Wisley, and botanist Adrian Whiteley helped in their different ways. The following also gave us the benefit of their expertise: David Cooke, Royal Botanic Gardens, Kew; Dibleys Nurseries, Ruthin, North Wales; Maggie Garford, African Violet Centre, King's Lynn; John Gibson, Colegraves Seeds, Banbury; Alan Moon, Eric Young Orchid Foundation, Jersey; Stanley Mossop, Boonwood Garden Centre, Cumbria; Dr. Henry Oakeley; and David Rhodes, Rhodes & Rockliffe, Essex.

Five years of travelling the length and breadth of Britain with Channel Four Television's *Garden Club* has taken me to a multitude of gardens large and small, while also introducing me to some helpful and resourceful gardeners. In acknowledging their contribution I should also like to thank the present and former members of the *Garden Club* team, who have helped me in so many ways.

They include John Bennett, Matthew Biggs, Adrian Brennard, Karen Brown, Derek Clarke, Penny Cotter, Mary Foxall, Tony Griggs, Margaret Haworth, Elaine Hinderer, Sylvia Hines, Paddy McMullin, Ken Price, Rebecca Pow, Rebecca Ransome, Jo Redman, Sue Shepherd, Richard Stevens, and Steve Stunt.

Finally, I thank my publishers, especially Mary-Clare Jerram for asking me to compile this book, and Lesley Malkin and Colin Walton, whose enthusiasm and professionalism greatly impressed and encouraged me. I could not have asked for better. My thanks also to Anna Cheifetz, Clare Double and Helen Robson, who must have sweated at times over my schedule but remained calm and focused throughout. Thanks for your patience, guidance, and gentle prodding. I would also like to thank Gill Biggs for her help, and Jessica Biggs for not interrupting.

DORLING KINDERSLEY would like to thank: Lyn Saville and Ian Whitelaw for additional editorial assistance; Gloria Horsfall, and Sue Caffyn for design assistance; Ann Kay and Antonia Johnson for proof reading; Dr. Alan Hemsley for his assistance in finding and identifying plants to photograph; the A–Z team, particularly Ina Stradins, Helen Robson, and Susila Baybars, for their patience with our shared resources, and to Rebecca Davies for all her trips to the post office; Howard Rice for all his additional help; Lesley Malkin and Colin Walton for their support and initial work on this project; Simon Maughan for image scanning; Martin Panter at Arnott and Mason, New Covent Garden, London, for plant supply and assistance with photography facilities; Matthew Ward for all his extra help; Lesley Riley for editorial assistance; Charlotte Oster, Christine Rista, Julia Pashley, and Sarah Duncan for picture research; Mustafa Sami for artwork research and commission

ILLUSTRATION CREDITS

Aspect illustration by Karen Cockrane 15
Tree illustrations by Laura Andrew, Marion Appleton, David Ashby, Bob Bampton, Anne Child, Karen Gavin, Tim Hayward, Janos Marffy, David More, Sue Oldfield, Liz Pepperell, Michelle Ross, Gill Tomlin, Barbara Walker
Illustrations on pages 310–1 by Richard Lee.

PHOTOGRAPHY CREDITS

Key: l=left, r=right, t=top, c=centre, b=bottom
Commissioned photographs: Howard Rice, Colin Walton, and Andrew Henley; main photography in Indoor Plants section by Matthew Ward.
Additional pictures: Peter Anderson 313tl, 315br, 317cl, 317bl, 318br, 390tl, 409tr, 409cr; Deni Bown 345tl, 345bl, 387tc; Jonathan Buckley 331tl; Eric Crichton 410c, 411tc, 411bl; C. Andrew Henley 359bl, 379tc; Neil Fletcher 341br, 379tl; Dave King 314bl, 315cr, 320tr, 321, 335, 357, 383, 402tc, 405; Tom Dobbie 322bl, 323tl, 323b, 324b, 325tr, 332br, 336br, 339t, 339bl, 339bc, 341tr, 342br, 344bl, 346c, 348tl, 349br, 350bc, 362bl, 364t, 365tr, 365c, 368br, 371bc, 373tl, 373br, 376b, 377tl, 380tr, 380br, 381br, 384b, 385tl, 385c, 385b, 386b, 388bl, 390c, 390tr, 391bl, 391tr, 392tl, 392bl, 393tr, 393bc, 395bc, 396bl, 398tl, 399tl, 400tr, 400br, 401tc, 401br, 406bl, 407tl, 407c, 407b, 412bl, 413tl, 413br; John Fielding 379cl; Andrew Lawson 358br; Andrew de Lory 349br; Howard Rice 325tc, 344tr, 361br, 364bl, 385tr, 398bl, 401tl; Bob Rundle 392br; Juliette Wade 329tr; Steven Wooster 331tc, 401tr.
Other Dorling Kindersley photographs by Peter Anderson, Clive Boursnell, Deni Bown, Jonathan Buckley, Andrew Butler, Eric Crichton, Andrew de Lory, Christine Douglas, John Fielding, Neil Fletcher, John Glover, Derek Hall, Jerry Harpur, Sunniva Harte, C. Andrew Henley, Neil Holmes, Jacqui Hurst, Andrew Lawson, Howard Rice, Robert Rundle, Juliette Wade, Colin Walton, Matthew Ward, David Watts, and Steven Wooster.

Dorling Kindersley is grateful to the following for permission to reproduce photographs
Gillian Beckett: 329tl, 372t
Matthew Biggs: 366tl
Bruce Coleman Collection: Jules Cowan 309tl
Dibleys Nurseries, Ruthin, North Wales: 333br

Garden Picture Library: Mark Bolton 147tr; Lynne Brotchie 158bl; Brian Carter 159; Robert Estall 264br; John Glover 15tr, 16bl, 18br, 94tr, 142bl, 176br, 264bl; Neil Holmes 178c; M Lamontagne 265; John Miller 306–7; Jerry Pavia 146br; Howard Rice 334tr; Gary Rogers 15br; JS Sira 172tr, 216tr; Friedrich Strauss 320cr, 382br, 404tr; Ron Sutherland 292bl; Brigitte Thomas 242bl, 243; Michel Viard 404b; Steven Wooster 15bl, 20br, 48bl, 119, 158br, 356bl
John Glover: 244tc, 257tc, 283bl
Derek Gould: 235bl
Harpur Garden Library: 320bl, 334bl
Houses and Interiors: Simon Butcher 310tl; Fotodienst Fehn 382bl
International Interiors: Paul Ryan 311tr, 311bl
Roy Lancaster: 6bl, 6br, 14bl, 28tl, 28bl, 30bl, 36bl, 36tc, 37tr, 42tr, 44tr, 46br, 47bc, 70tl, 77bc, 82tr, 89bc, 104bl, 108tc, 117bc, 124tr, 129tc, 129bc, 133tr, 134cr, 139c, 140bl, 140bc, 141tr, 142tr, 144bl, 144–5, 145br, 146tr, 150bc, 151tl, 155br, 156cl, 156tc, 156cr, 162tr, 165bl, 168bl, 170tc, 170tr, 170bl, 171bl, 172bc, 172bl, 173tr, 173bc, 174tl, 174bl, 175tl, 175tr, 175cr, 179tl, 179cr, 189cr, 183cr, 196bl, 196tc, 197tl, 197tr, 200tr, 201cl, 203bc, 206tl, 208tl, 209tc, 216cl, 216br, 217bc, 221cr, 226tl, 226bc, 226tr, 227tl, 227br, 231br, 232bc, 233tl, 233bl, 234tr, 239tl, 239bl, 242tr, 242br, 244bl, 246tl, 249br, 251tr, 254tl, 255cl, 257tl, 260bl, 260bc, 261tl, 261br, 262tc, 262tr, 264tr, 270bl, 274bl, 286bl, 286br, 288bl, 290tr, 291cr, 292cl, 293tl, 293cl, 293cr, 309br, 328br, 329tc, 340tl, 378br, 378tr
Andrew Lawson: 20bl (designer: Wendy Lauderdale), 147tl, 293tr
Clive Nichols: Chenies Manor Garden, Buckinghamshire: 177; Dartington Hall Garden, Devon: 16br; Longacre, Kent: 16cl
Nature Photographers Ltd: Brinsley Burbage: 257tr
Photos Horticultural: 145cr, 170br, 209cr, 235bc, 247tc, 248tr, 256cr, 257br, 261bc, 263bc, 277bl, 282bl, 283 tr, 305bl; 349tc
Picturesmiths Limited: 146cr, 305tl
Planet Earth Pictures: Robert Jureit 308b
Howard Rice: 19tl, 19tr, 19br, 21, 33bm, 33tr, 45br, 48br, 49, 76tl, 76bl, 76bc, 76br, 77bc, 77tr, 94bl, 94br, 95, 103bc, 118bl, 118tr, 140bl, 143
Harry Smith Collection: 147tc, 171tl, 288br
Harry Smith Collection/Polunin: 280cl, 281br
Matthew Ward: 18cl (container by Malcolm Hillier)
Elizabeth Whiting Associates: Graham Henderson 310br; Spike Powell 356t.

PHOTOGRAPHERS' ACKNOWLEDGMENTS

In England: Alan Shipp, Beth Chatto Gardens, Bressingham Gardens, Broadlands Gardens, Cambridge Alpines, Cambridge Bulbs, Cambridge Garden Plants, Cambridge University Botanic Gardens, David Austin Roses Ltd., Fulbrooke Nursery, Goldbrooke Plants, Hadlow College, Hopleys Plants Ltd., John Morley, Langthorns Plantery, Monksilver Nursery, Paradise Centre, Peter Lewis, Potterton and Martin, Rickard's Hardy Ferns, Mrs. Sally Edwards, West Acre Gardens.
In Australia: Birchfield Herbs (Marcia Voce), Buskers End (Joan Arnold), Elizabeth Town Nursery (John and Corrie Dudley), Essie Huxley, Garden of St. Erth, Island Bulbs (Kevin Fagan, Viv Hale), Lambley Nursery (David Glenn), Moidart Wholesale Nursery (Graham Warwick), Otto Fauser, Penny Dunn, Rosevears Nursery (Rachael Howell) Sally Johansohn, Suz Price, Theresa Watts, Woodbank Nursery (Ken Gallander), Yates.